SOCRATES TO SARTRE

A HISTORY OF PHILOSOPHY

Samuel Enoch Stumpf
Vanderbilt University

REVISED
FIFTH EDITION

McGraw-Hill, Inc.
New York   St. Louis   San Francisco   Auckland   Bogotá
Caracas   Lisbon   London   Madrid   Mexico City   Milan
Montreal   New Delhi   San Juan   Singapore
Sydney   Tokyo   Toronto

SOCRATES TO SARTRE
A History of Philosophy

4567890 DOC DOC 909876

ISBN 0-07-062564-6

This book was set in Times Roman by The Clarinda Company.
The editors were Cynthia Ward and David Dunham;
the production supervisor was Al Rihner.
The cover was designed by Wanda Siedlecka.
R. R. Donnelley & Sons Company was printer and binder.

This book is printed on acid-free paper.

Photo Credits

Part One: Acropolis ruins with Parthenon (Alinari/Art Resource)

Part Two: Cathedral of St. Etienne de Bourges. Begun in the thirteenth century and completed around 1300. (Tudor Publishing Co., New York)

Part Three: Galileo (The Bettmann Archive)

Part Four: René Magritte, *In Praise of Dialectics* (National Gallery, Australia, Felton Bequest)

Library of Congress Cataloging-in-Publication Data

Stumpf, Samuel Enoch, (date).
    Socrates to Sartre: a history of philosophy / Samuel Enoch
  Stumpf. — Rev. 5th ed.
        p.   cm.
    Includes bibliographical references (p.   ) and index.
    ISBN 0-07-062564-6
    1. Philosophy—History.
  B72.S79   1994
  190—dc20   93-48406

ABOUT THE AUTHOR

SAMUEL ENOCH STUMPF holds the Ph.D. from the University of Chicago. He was a Ford Fellow at Harvard University and a Rockefeller Fellow at Oxford University. For fifteen years he was chairman of the philosophy department at Vanderbilt University, served a term as president of Cornell College of Iowa, and returned to Vanderbilt as professor of the philosophy of law in the School of Law and as research professor of medical philosophy in the School of Medicine. He participates in various national organizations and lectures widely in the fields of philosophy, medical ethics, and jurisprudence.

To JEAN

Paul	Mark	Sam
&	&	&
Barbara	Betsy	Jane

CONTENTS

PART TWO
THE MEDIEVAL PERIOD:
The Confluence of Philosophy and Theology

PART THREE
THE MODERN PERIOD:
Philosophy and the Unfolding World of Science

PART FOUR
THE CONTEMPORARY PERIOD:
The Reshaping of the Philosophic Mind

PREFACE

here are many ways to approach the study of philosophy. Neverthe-less, an introduction to philosophy is best achieved through a study of its history. Through this approach, we discover a striking inter-play of ideas as one philosopher after another offers insights about our nature, the nature of human knowledge, and the realities of the world around us. Because philosophers write with a knowledge of what their predecessors have thought, their own work is at once a criticism of earlier thought and a creative contribution at the growing edge of philosophy. Because the history of philosophy is, to such an extent, a history of criticism, I have chosen not to inject my own critical evaluations; rather, I have sought to present each writer's major ideas and thereby focus upon the central problems, conflicts, and contributions of philosophic thought in the West.

This book is addressed to the beginning student of philosophy, to the stu-dent in other disciplines who needs a concise presentation of philosophical ideas, and to interested members of the general reading public. The needs of these groups have prompted me to undertake the task in spite of the obvious pitfalls encountered in condensing the wealth of Western philosophical thought into one short volume.

In this fifth edition of *Socrates to Sartre,* the major new material includes a study of Richard Rorty's attempt to overcome the limitations of contemporary analytic philosophy and of classical theories of knowledge in general, reflecting questions concerning the adequacy of the linguistic turn. I have also added a section on Maurice Merleau-Ponty, whose work expresses developments in contemporary French philosophy, especially through his distinctive theory of the primacy of perception and his philosophical basis of political thought.

Once again, even though the whole book is an elucidation of philosophical ideas, I have added some key concepts to the Glossary. Also, titles have been added to the Bibliography to facilitate further study and to encourage the reader to become acquainted with some original writings and critical commentaries.

As always, I am grateful to my wife, Jean, for the many ways she has been of assistance along the way.

Samuel Enoch Stumpf

SOCRATES
TO
SARTRE

A HISTORY OF PHILOSOPHY

ONE

THE
ANCIENT PERIOD:
THE
SHAPING OF
THE
PHILOSOPHIC
MIND

1

Socrates' Predecessors: Philosophy and the Natural Order

Philosophy began when humans' curiosity and wonder caused them to ask the questions "What are things really like?" and "How can we explain the process of change in things?" What prompted these questions was the gradual recognition that things are not exactly what they seem to be, that "appearance" often differs from "reality." The facts of birth, death, growth, and decay—coming into being and passing away—raised not only the questions about personal destiny but also the larger questions of how things and persons come into existence, can be different at different times, and pass out of existence only to be followed by other things and persons. Many of the answers given to these questions by the earliest philosophers are not as important as the fact that they focused upon just these questions and that they approached them with a fresh and new frame of mind that was in contrast to that of the great poets.

The birthplace of philosophy was the seaport town of Miletus, located across the Aegean Sea from Athens, on the western shores of Ionia in Asia Minor, and for this reason the first philosophers are called either Milesians or Ionians. By the time the Milesian philosophers began their systematic work, roughly around 585 B.C., Miletus had been a crossroads for both seaborne commerce and for cosmopolitan ideas. Its wealth made possible the leisure without which the life of art and philosophy could hardly develop, and the broad-mindedness and inquisitiveness of its people created a congenial atmosphere for the intellectual activity that was to become philosophy. Earlier, Ionia had produced the genius Homer, whose epic poetry projected upon the cosmic scene Mount Olympus, where the gods pursued lives not too different from their human counterparts on earth. This poetic view of the world also related the life of the gods to the life of humans, by describing various ways in which the gods intruded into or interfered with people's affairs. In particular, the Homeric gods would punish people for their lack of moderation and especially for their pride or insubordination, which the Greeks called *hubris*. It is not that Homer's gods are moral and require goodness; they are merely stronger than human beings and exact obedience. Moreover, when Homer suggests that there is a power that he calls "fate," a power to which even the gods are subject, he appears to be reaching for a way of describing a rigorous order in nature to which everyone and everything must be subordinate. But his poetic imagination is dominated so thoroughly by his thinking in human terms that his world is peopled everywhere with human types, and his conception of nature is that of capricious wills at work instead of the reign of physical natural laws. It was Hesiod, writing sometime in the eighth century B.C., who altered this concept of the gods and "fate" by removing from the gods all capriciousness, ascribing to them instead a moral consistency. Although Hesiod retains the notion that the gods control nature, he balances this personal element in the nature of things with an emphasis upon the impersonal operation of the moral law of the universe. The moral order, in Hesiod's view, is still the product of Zeus' commands, but these commands are neither capricious nor calculated, as Homer thought, to gratify the gods, but are rather fashioned for the good of mankind. For Hesiod the universe is a moral order, and from this idea it is a short step to say, without any reference to the gods, that there is an impersonal force controlling the structure of the universe and regulating its process of changes.

It was this short step that the Milesians Thales, Anaximander, and Anaximenes took. Whereas Hesiod still thought in terms of traditional mythology with a peopled universe, philosophy among the Milesians began as an act of independent thought. To ask, as they did, "What are things really like?" and "How can we explain the process of change in things?" indicates a substantial departure from the poetry of Homer and Hesiod and a movement toward what we should call the temperament of science. Although the Milesians can rightly be called primitive scientists, it is a fact of the history of thought that science and philosophy were the same thing in the beginning and only later did various specific disciplines separate themselves from the field of philosophy, medicine being the first to do so. From the very beginning, however, Greek philosophy was an intellectual activity, for it was not a matter only of seeing or believing but of thinking, and philosophy meant thinking about basic questions in a mood of genuine and free inquiry.

WHAT IS PERMANENT IN EXISTENCE?

Thales We do not know as much as we should like about Thales of Miletus, and what we do know is rather anecdotal in nature. He left no writings. All that is available are fragmentary references to him made by later writers who recorded memorable incidents in his career. He was a contemporary of Solon and Croesus, and the years of his life are set between 624 and 546 B.C. During a military campaign against Persia, he apparently solved the difficult logistics problem of enabling the Lydian king's army to cross the wide Halys river by digging a channel that diverted part of the flow, thereby making two narrower rivers over which bridges could be built. While traveling in Egypt, Thales worked out a way of measuring the height of the pyramids, using the simple procedure of measuring a pyramid's shadow at that time of day when one's shadow is equal to one's height. It may have been during these Egyptian travels, too, that he became acquainted with the kinds of knowledge that enabled him to predict the eclipse of the sun on May 28, 585 B.C. In a practical vein, he constructed, while in Miletus, an instrument for measuring the distance of ships sighted at sea, and as an aid to navigation, he urged sailors to use the constellation Little Bear as the surest guide for determining the direction of the north.

It was probably inevitable that anecdotes should be attached to such an extraordinary man as Thales. Plato, in his *Theaetetus*, writes about "the jest which the clever witty Thracian handmaid is said to have made about Thales, when he fell into a well as he was looking up at the stars. She said that he was so eager to know what was going on in heaven that he could not see what was before his feet." Plato adds that "this is a jest which is equally applicable to all philosophers," apparently unaware of another incident in Thales' life that would seem to establish a very keen awareness of what was going on around him. In his *Politics*, Aristotle writes that "there is...the story which is told of Thales of Miletus. It is a story about a scheme for making money, which is fathered on Thales owing to his reputation for wisdom....He was reproached for his poverty, which was supposed to show the uselessness of philosophy; but observing from his knowledge of meteorology (as the story goes) that there was likely to be a heavy crop of olives [during the next summer], and having a small sum at his command, he paid down earnest-money, early in the year, for the hire of all the olive-presses in Miletus and Chios; and he managed, in the absence of any higher offer, to secure them at a low rate. When the season came, and there was a sudden and simultaneous demand for a number of presses, he let out the stock he had collected at any rate he chose to fix; and making a considerable fortune, he succeeded in proving that it is easy for philosophers to become rich if they so desire, though it is not the business which they are really about." But Thales is famous not for his general wisdom or his practical shrewdness, but because he opened up a new area of thought for which he has rightly earned the title of the first philosopher.

Thales' novel inquiry concerned the nature of things. What is everything made of, or what kind of "stuff" goes into the composition of things? What Thales was trying to get at with these questions was some way of accounting for the fact that there are many different kinds of things, such as earth, clouds, and oceans, and that some of these things change from time to time into something else and also that they resemble each other in certain ways. Thales' unique contribution to thought was his notion that in spite of the differences between various things there is, nevertheless, a basic similarity between them all, that *the many* are related to each other by *the One*. He assumed that some single element, some "stuff," a stuff which contained its own principle of action or change, lay at the foundation of all physical reality. To him this One, or this stuff, was *water*.

Although there is no record of how Thales came to the conclusion that water is the cause of all things, Aristotle writes that Thales might have derived it from observation of simple events, "perhaps from seeing that the nutriment of all things is moist, and that heat is generated from the moist and kept alive by it. ... He got his notion from this fact and from the fact that the seeds of all things have a moist nature, and water is the origin of the nature of moist things." Other phenomena such as evaporation or freezing also suggest that water takes on different forms. But the accuracy of Thales' analysis of the composition of things is far less important than the fact that he raised the question concerning the nature of the world. His question had set the stage for a new kind of inquiry, one which could be debated on its merits and could either be confirmed or refuted by further analysis. In spite of his notion that "all things are full of gods," a notion that had apparently no theological significance for him and to which he turned in an attempt to explain the power in things, such as magnetic powers in stones, Thales shifted the basis of thought from a mythological base to one of scientific inquiry. And, again from his primitive starting point, others were to follow him with alternative solutions, but always with his problem before them.

Anaximander   A younger contemporary and a pupil of Thales was Anaximander. He agreed with his teacher that there is some single basic stuff out of which everything comes. Unlike Thales, however, Anaximander said that this basic stuff is neither water nor any other specific or determinate element, arguing that water and all other definite things are only specific variations or offshoots of something which is more primary. It may very well be, he thought, that water or moisture is found in various forms everywhere, but water is only one specific thing among many other elements, and all these specific things require that there be some more elementary stuff to account for their origin. The primary substance out of which all these specific things come, said Anaximander, is an *indefinite* or *boundless* realm. Thus, Anaximander differentiates specific and determinate things from their origin by calling the primary substance the *indeterminate boundless*. Whereas actual things are specific, their source is indeterminate, and whereas things are finite, the original stuff is infinite or boundless.

Besides offering a new idea about the original substance of things, Anaximander advanced the enterprise of philosophy by attempting some explanation for his new idea. Thales had not dealt in any detail with the problem of explaining how the primary stuff became the many different things we see in the world, but Anaximander addressed himself precisely to this question. Although his explanation may seem strange, it represents an advance in knowledge in the sense that it is an attempt to deal with known facts from which hypotheses can be formulated instead of explaining natural phenomena in mythical and nondebatable terms. Still, what Anaximander has to say about the origin of things has the flavor of bold speculation, for in describing the indeterminate boundless as the unoriginated and indestructible primary substance, he speaks of this as also having eternal motion. As a consequence of this motion, the various specific elements come into being as a "separating off" from the original substance, and thus "there was an eternal motion in which the heavens came to be." But first *warm* and *cold* were separated off, and from these two came *moist*; then from these came *earth* and *air*. Anaximander then tried to account for the heavenly bodies and air currents around the earth in what appears to be a mechanical explanation of the orderly movement of the stars. He thought that the earth was cylindrical in shape in contrast to Thales, who thought it was flat as a disk and floated on the water.

Coming to the origin of human life, Anaximander said that all life comes from the sea and that in the course of time, living things came out of the sea to dry land. He suggested that humanity evolved from creatures of a different kind, using as his argument the fact that other creatures are quickly self-supporting, whereas humans alone need prolonged nursing and that, therefore, humanity would not have survived if this had been its original form. Commenting on Anaximander's account of the origin of humanity, Plutarch writes that the Syrians "actually revere the fish as being of similar race and nurturing. In this they philosophize more suitably than Anaximander; for he declares, not that fishes and men came into being in the same parents, but that originally men came into being inside fishes, and that, having been nurtured there—like sharks—and having become adequate to look after themselves, they then came forth and took to the land." Returning again to the vast cosmic scene, Anaximander thought that there were many worlds and many systems of universes existing all at the same time, all of them perishable, there being the constant alternation between their creation and destruction. This cyclical process was for him a rigorous "necessity" as the conflict of opposite forces in nature caused what he called poetically an "injustice" requiring their ultimate destruction. In the only sentence from his writings that has survived, Anaximander gathers up his chief thought by saying, again somewhat poetically, that "From what source things arise, to that they return of necessity when they are destroyed; for they suffer punishment and make reparation to one another for their injustice according to the order of time."

Anaximenes   The third and last of the Milesian philosophers was Anaximenes (about 585–528 B.C.), who was the young "associate" of Anaximander.

As he considered Anaximander's answer to the question concerning the composition of natural things, he was dissatisfied with the notion of the *boundless* as being the source of all things, since it was too vague and intangible. He could understand why Anaximander chose this solution over Thales' notion that water is the cause of all things, because the boundless could help explain the "infinite" background to the wide variety of finite and specific things. Still, the indeterminate boundless had no specific meaning for Anaximenes, and he, therefore, chose to focus upon a definite substance the way Thales had done and, at the same time, tried to incorporate the advance achieved by Anaximander.

To combine Thales' notion of a definite substance with Anaximander's new concept of the boundless in continued motion, Anaximenes designated *air* as the primary substance from which all things come. As the boundless, air is spread everywhere, but unlike the boundless, it is a specific and tangible material substance that can be identified. Moreover, the air's motion is a far more specific process than Anaximander's "separating off," for Anaximenes hit upon the highly respectable concepts of "rarefaction" and "condensation" as the specific forms of motion which lead to describable changes in air. Although air is invisible, we live only as long as we can breathe, and "just as our soul, being air, holds us together, so do breath and air encompass the whole world." But to explain how air is the origin of all things, Anaximenes introduced the important new idea that differences in "quality" are caused by differences in "quantity." The expansion and contraction of air represent quantitative changes, and these changes occurring in a single substance account for the multitude of different things. Expansion, or rarefaction, of air causes warming and, at the extreme, fire, whereas contraction, or condensation, causes cooling and the transformation of air into solids by way of a gradual transition where, as Anaximenes says, "air that is condensed forms winds... if this process goes further, it gives water, still further earth, and the greatest condensation of all is found in stones."

Although these Milesian philosophers appear to have proceeded with scientific concerns and temperaments, they did not form their hypotheses the way modern scientists would, nor did they devise any experiments to test their theories. Their ideas have a dogmatic quality, a mood of positive assertion, rather than the tentativeness of true hypotheses. But it must be remembered that the critical questions concerning the nature and limits of human knowledge had not yet been raised. Nor did the Milesians refer in any way to the problem of the relation between spirit and body. Their reduction of all reality to a material origin certainly raises this question, but it was recognized as a problem only later in the history of thought. Whatever may be the usefulness of their specific ideas about *water*, the *boundless*, and *air* as the primary substance of things, the real significance of the Milesians is, again, that they for the first time raised the question about the ultimate nature of things and made the first halting but direct inquiry into what nature really consists of.

THE MATHEMATICAL BASIS OF ALL THINGS

Pythagoras   Across a span of water from Miletus, located in the Aegean Sea, was the small island of Samos, which was the birthplace of a truly extraordinary and wise man, Pythagoras. From the various scraps of information we have about him and those who were his followers, an incomplete but still fascinating picture of his new philosophic reflections emerges. Apparently dissatisfied with conditions not only on Samos but generally in Ionia during the tyrannical rule of the rich Polycrates, Pythagoras migrated to southern Italy and settled there in the prosperous Greek city of Crotone, where his active philosophic life is usually dated from about 525 to 500 B.C.

We are told by Aristotle that "the Pythagoreans...devoted themselves to mathematics, they were the first to advance this study, and having been brought up in it they thought its principles were the principles of all things...." In contrast to the Milesians, the Pythagoreans said that things *consist of numbers*. Although it is quite strange to say that everything consists of numbers, the strangeness, as well as the difficulty, of this doctrine is greatly overcome when we consider why Pythagoras became interested in numbers and what his conception of numbers was.

Pythagoras became interested in mathematics for what appear to be religious reasons. His originality could be said to consist in his conviction that the study of mathematics is the best purifier of the soul. He is, therefore, referred to as the founder both of a religious sect and at the same time a school of mathematics. What gave rise to the Pythagorean sect was people's yearning for a deeply spiritual religion that could provide the means for purifying the soul and for guaranteeing its immortality. The Homeric gods were not gods in the theological sense, since they were as immoral as human beings and as such could be neither the objects of worship nor the source of any spiritual power to overcome the pervading sense of moral uncleanliness and the anxiety that people had over the shortness of life and the finality of death. The religious movement that had earlier moved into this area of human concern was the religion of Dionysus, which became widespread during the seventh and sixth centuries B.C. The worship of Dionysus satisfied to some extent those yearnings for cleansing and immortality. Organized into small, secret, and mystical societies, the devotees would worship Dionysus under various animal forms. Working themselves into a frenzy of wild dances and song, they would drink the blood of these animals, which they had torn apart in a state of intoxication, and would finally drop in complete exhaustion, convinced that at the height of their frenzy, their bodies had been entered by the spirit of Dionysus, purifying them and conferring his own immortality upon their souls.

The Pythagoreans were clearly concerned with the mystical problems of purification and immortality, and it was for this reason that they turned to science and mathematics, the study of which they considered the best purge for the soul. In scientific and mathematical thought they saw a mode of life that more than any other kind was "pure." Thought and reflection represent a clear contrast to the life of trade and competition for various honors. It was Pythagoras who first distinguished the three different kinds of lives, and by implication the three divisions of the soul, by saying that there are three different kinds of people who go to the Olympian games. The lowest class is made up of those who go there to buy and sell, to make a profit. Next are those who go there to compete, to gain honors. Best of all, he thought, are those who come as spectators, who reflect upon and analyze what is happening. Of these three, the spectator illustrates the thinkers, whose activity as philosophers liberates them from the involvements of daily life and its imperfections. To "look on" is one of the meanings of the Greek word "theory." Theoretical thinking, or pure science and pure mathematics, was considered by the Pythagoreans as a purifier of the soul, particularly as mathematical thought could liberate people from thinking about particular things and lead their thought, instead, to the permanent and ordered world of numbers. The final mystical triumph of the Pythagorean is liberation from "the wheel of birth," from the migration of the soul to animal and other forms in the constant progress of death and birth, for thus the spectator achieves a unity with god and shares his immortality.

To connect this religious concern with the philosophical aspects of the Pythagoreans, mention should be made first of all of their interest in *music*. They considered music highly therapeutic for certain nervous disorders, seeing as they did some relation between the harmonies of music and the harmony of a person's interior life. But their true discovery in the field of music was that the musical intervals between the notes could be expressed in numerical terms. They discovered that the length of the strings of a musical instrument is proportionate to the actual interval of the sounds they produce. They could demonstrate that a string making a sound an octave lower than another string was twice as long as that string, the ratio here being 2:1. All the other intervals could similarly be expressed in numerical ratios, and music became, for the Pythagoreans, a formidable example of the pervasive relevance of numbers in all things, leading Aristotle to say about them that "since they saw that the attributes and the ratios of the musical scales were expressible in numbers; since then all other things seemed in their whole nature to be modeled after numbers, and numbers seemed to be the first things in the whole of nature, and the whole heaven to be a musical scale and a number."

What must have facilitated the development of their doctrine that all things *are* numbers was the Pythagorean practice in counting or their way of writing numbers. Apparently they built numbers out of individual units, using pebbles to count. The number *one* was therefore a single pebble and all other numbers were created by the addition of pebbles, somewhat like our present practice of representing numbers on dice by the use of dots. But the significant point is that the Pythagoreans discovered a relation between arithmetic and geometry. A single pebble, as a point is *one*, but *two* is made up of two pebbles or two points, and these two points make a line. Three points, as in the corners of a triangle, create a plane or area and four points can represent a solid. This suggested to the Pythagoreans a close relationship between number and magnitude, and Pythagoras is credited with discovering that the square of the hypotenuse is equal to the squares of the other two sides of a right-angled triangle. This correlation between numbers and magnitude provided immense consolation to those who were seeking evidence of a principle of structure and order in the universe, and it is understandable that the possibly apocryphal story should have arisen that Hippasus was drowned in the Hellespont for letting out the secret, which anybody could have figured out, that this principle does not hold true in the case of the isosceles right-angled triangle, where the relation between its hypotenuse and its sides cannot be expressed by any numerical ratio, only by an irrational number.

The importance of the relation between number and magnitude was that numbers, for the Pythagoreans, meant certain "figures," such as a triangle, square, rectangle, and so forth. The individual points were "boundary stones" which marked out "fields." Moreover, these "triangular numbers," "square numbers," "rectangular numbers," and "spherical numbers" were differentiated by the Pythagoreans as being "odd" and "even," thereby giving them a new way of treating the phenomenon of the conflict of opposites. In all these forms, numbers were, therefore, far more than abstractions—they were specific kinds of entities. To say, then, as the Pythagoreans did, that all things *are* numbers meant for them that there is a numerical basis for all things which possess shape and size; thus they moved from arithmetic to geometry and then to the structure of reality. All things had numbers, and their odd and even values explained such opposites in things as one and many, square and oblong, straight and curved, rest and motion. Even light and dark are numerical opposites, as are male and female and good and evil.

This way of understanding numbers led the Pythagoreans to formulate their most important philosophical notion, which was, therefore, their most significant contribution to philosophy; namely, the concept of *form*. The Milesians had conceived the idea of a primary *matter* or stuff out of which everything was constituted, but they had no coherent concept of how specific things are differentiated from this single matter. They all spoke of an unlimited stuff, whether it be water, air, or the indeterminate boundless, by which they all meant some primary *matter*. It was the Pythagoreans who now came forth with the conception of *form*. For them, form meant *limit*, and limit is understandable especially in numerical terms. It is no wonder that the two arts in which the Pythagoreans saw the concept of limit best exemplified were music and medicine, for in both of these arts the central fact is harmony, and harmony is achieved by taking into account proportions and limits. In *music* there is a numerical ratio by which different notes must be separated in order to achieve concordant intervals. Harmony is the form that the limiting structure of numerical ratio imposes upon the unlimited possibilities for sounds possessed by the strings of a musical instrument. In *medicine* the Pythagoreans saw the same principle at work, health being the harmony or balance or proper ratio of certain *opposites* such as hot and cold, wet and dry, and the volumetric balance of

Model of the Acropolis *(Royal Ontario Museum)*

various specific elements later known as *biochemicals*. Indeed, the Pythagoreans looked upon the body as they would a musical instrument, saying that health is achieved when the body is "in tune" and that disease is a consequence of undue tensions or the loss of proper tuning of the strings. The concept of number was frequently used, when translated to mean "figure," in connection with health and disease in the literature of early medicine, especially pertaining to the constitution of the human body. The *true* number, or figure, therefore, refers to the proper balance of all the elements and functions of the body. Number, then, represents the application of *limit* (form) to the *unlimited* (matter), and the Pythagoreans referred to music and medicine only as vivid illustrations of their larger concept, namely, that all things *are* numbers.

The brilliance of Pythagoras and his followers is measured to some extent by the enormous influence they had upon later philosophers and particularly upon Plato. There is much in Plato that first came to light in the teachings of Pythagoras, including the importance of the soul and its threefold division and the importance of mathematics as related to the concept of form and the Forms.

ATTEMPTS TO EXPLAIN CHANGE

Heraclitus Whereas earlier philosophers concentrated upon describing what things consist of, Heraclitus shifted attention to a new problem, the problem of *change*. His chief idea was that "all things are in flux," and he expressed this concept of constant change by saying that "you cannot step twice into the same river." The river changes because "fresh waters are ever flowing in upon you." This concept of *flux*, thought Heraclitus, must apply not only to rivers but to all things, including the human soul. Rivers and people exhibit the fascinating fact of becoming different and yet remaining the same. We return to the "same" river although fresh waters have flowed into it, and the adult is still the same person as the child. Things change and thereby take on many different forms, but, nevertheless, they contain something which continues to be the same throughout all the flux of change. Between these many forms and the single continuing element, between the many and the one, there must be, said Heraclitus, some basic *unity*. Developing his novel and influential philosophy around 504–501 B.C., this nobleman from Ephesus described the process of change as a unity in diversity, and he did this with such imaginative skill that although some of his ideas may seem fanciful, much of what he had to say found an important place in the later philosophies of Plato and the Stoics and was deeply admired by Hegel and Nietzsche.

Flux and Fire To describe change as unity in diversity, Heraclitus assumed that there must be *something* which changes, and he argued that this something is *fire*. But he did not simply substitute the element of fire for Thales' water or Anaximenes' air. What led Heraclitus to fasten upon fire as the basic element in things was that fire behaves in such a way as to suggest how the process of change operates. Fire is simultaneously a deficiency and a surplus; it must constantly be fed and it constantly gives off something either in the form of heat, smoke, or ashes. Fire is a process of transformation, then, whereby what is fed into it is transformed into something else. For Heraclitus it was not enough simply to point to some basic element, such as water, as the basic nature of reality, because this would not answer the question of how this basic stuff could change into different forms. When, therefore, Heraclitus fastened upon fire as the basic reality, he not only identified the *something* which changes but thought he had discovered the principle of change itself. To say that everything is in flux meant for Heraclitus that the world *is* an "ever-living Fire" whose constant movement is assured by "measures of it kindling and measures going out." These "measures" meant for Heraclitus a kind of balance between what kindles and what goes out of the fire, and he describes this balance in terms of financial exchange, saying that "all things are an exchange for Fire, and Fire for all things, even as wares for gold and gold for wares." With this explanation of exchange, Heraclitus sought to make the point that nothing is really ever lost in the nature of things. If gold is exchanged for wares, both the gold and the wares still continue to exist although they are now in different hands. Similarly, all things continue to exist although they exchange their form from time to time.

There is a stability in the universe because of the orderly and balanced process of change or flux, the same "measure" coming out as going in, as if reality were a huge fire that inhaled and exhaled equal amounts, preserving all the while an even inventory in the world. This inventory represents the widest array of things, all of them being simply different forms of fire. Flux and change consist of the movements of fire, movements which Heraclitus called the "upward and downward paths." The downward path of fire explains the coming into being of the things we experience so that when fire is condensed it becomes moist and this moisture under conditions of increased pressure becomes water and water, in turn, when "congealed" becomes earth. On the upward path this process is reversed, the earth being transformed into liquid and from this water come the various forms of life. Nothing is ever lost in this process of transformation because, as Heraclitus says, "fire lives the death of earth, and air the death of fire; water lives the death of air, earth that of water." With this description of the constant transformation of things in fire, Heraclitus thought he had explained the rudiments of the unity between the *one* basic stuff and the *many* diverse things in the world. But there was another significant idea that Heraclitus added to his concept of Fire, namely, the idea of *reason* as the universal law.

Reason as the Universal Law   The process of change is not a haphazard movement but the product of God's universal Reason (*logos*). This idea of *Reason* came from Heraclitus' religious conviction that the most real thing of all is the soul, and the soul's most distinctive and important attribute is wisdom or thought. But when Heraclitus speaks about God and the soul, he does not have in mind separate personal entities. For him there is only one basic reality, namely, Fire, and it is this material substance, Fire, which Heraclitus calls the One, or God. Inevitably, Heraclitus was a pantheist, since all things according to him were Fire. The human soul is a part of God, for God is in everything. As wisdom is God's most important attribute, wisdom or thought is also people's chief activity. But inanimate things also contain the principle of reason, since they are also permeated with the fiery element. Because God *is* Reason and since God is the One, permeating all things, Heraclitus believed that God is the universal Reason which holds all things in unity and orders all things to move and change in accordance with thought or principles, and these principles and thought constitute the essence of *law*. God, as Reason, is, therefore, the universal law immanent in all things. All people share this universal law insofar as they possess God or Fire in their own natures and thereby possess the capacity for thought.

Logically, this account of our rational nature would mean that all of our thoughts are God's thoughts, since there is a unity between the One and the many, between God and human beings. We all must share in a common stock of knowledge since we all have a similar relation to God, just as, considering a different aspect of the world, all stones partake in that part of God's Reason which makes them all equally behave according to the "law" of gravity. But people notoriously disagree and often try to make inconsistent kinds of worlds in which to live. Recognizing this fact about human disagreement, Heraclitus said that "those awake have one ordered universe in common, but in sleep every man turns away to one of his own." Just how it is possible for people to "sleep," by which Heraclitus must mean to be thoughtless or even ignorant, if their souls and minds are part of God, is not explained. Still, this concept of a common universe available to all thoughtful people, this participation by all people in God's universal Reason or universal law, was one of the truly significant contributions of Heraclitus to human thought. It was this concept which provided the basis for the Stoics' idea of cosmopolitanism, the idea that all people are equally citizens of the world precisely because they all share in the One, in God's Reason, and contain in themselves some portion of the Fire, sparks of the divine. It was this concept, too, which formed the foundation for the classic theory of natural law, which, with some variations, has had a continuous impact upon Western thought and political practices, as it was preached by the Stoics, was adapted by early and medieval Christian theologians, became a dynamic force in the American Revolution, and is even in modern times a vital theory of the nature of law.

The Conflict of Opposites Although human beings can know the eternal wisdom that directs all things, they do not pay attention to this wisdom and, therefore, "prove to be uncomprehending" of the reasons for the way things happen to them. We are distressed by what appear to us to be meaningless disorders in the world. We are overwhelmed by the presence of good and evil and long for the peace that means the end of strife. But Heraclitus sought to account for strife by saying that it is the very essence of change itself. The conflict of opposites is not a calamity but the permanent condition of all things. If we could visualize the whole process of change, we should know, says Heraclitus, that "war is common and justice is strife and that all things happen by strife and necessity." From this perspective, he says, "what is in opposition is in concert, and from what differs comes the most beautiful harmony." Even death is no longer a calamity, for "after death things await men which they do not expect or imagine." Throughout his treatment of the problem of strife and disorder, Heraclitus emphasizes again and again that the many find their unity in the One, so that what appear to be disjointed events and contradictory forces are in reality intimately harmonized. For this reason he says that "men do not know how what is at variance agrees with itself. It is an attunement of opposite tensions, like that of the bow and the lyre." Fire itself exhibits this tension of opposites and indeed depends upon it. Fire *is* its many tensions of opposites. In the One, the many find their unity so that in the One "the way up and the way down is the same," "good and ill are one," and "it is the same thing in us that is quick and dead, awake and asleep, young and old." This solution of the conflict of opposites rests upon Heraclitus' major assumption that nothing is ever lost but merely changes its form, that the eternal Fire moves with measured pace following the direction of Reason, that change requires opposites

rse things. Still, "to God all things are fair and good and right, but men
....d some things wrong and some right." Heraclitus came to this conclusion
not because he believed that there was a personal God whose judgment it was
that all things are good, but simply because he thought that "it is wise to agree
that all things are one," that the One takes shape and appears in many forms.

Parmenides A younger contemporary of Heraclitus and the founder of
the Eleatic school of philosophy was Parmenides, whose chief philosophical
contribution was a radically novel interpretation of the phenomenon of change.
Parmenides rejected Heraclitus' attempt to explain change as a unity in diversity and at the same time criticized the Milesian philosophers' theories about
the origin of things. Both the Heraclitean and Milesian philosophies assumed
that all things emerge out of something else, that although there is only one
basic stuff in the world, this stuff is the source of a variety of things and that
the process by which the One becomes many is the process of change. Parmenides, on the other hand, rejected the very notion of change, resting his argument on at least two grounds: namely, that if there is a single substance behind all things, the concept of change is absurd logically, and that the
phenomenon of change is basically an illusion.

For Parmenides, the concept of change was logically neither thinkable
nor expressible. He maintained that whatever exists "must *be* absolutely, or
not at all." To exist in an "absolute" way meant for Parmenides that whatever
is, simply *is*. We can never admit, he said, that "anything should come into
being . . . out of not-being." It was this concept of "coming into being" or "becoming" which struck him as absurd, for he maintained that something either
". . . is or it is not." How can you say of anything that it came into being, that
it *changed* from not-being to being? You cannot say about anything that *it* ever
had non-being, for if you can think of an "it," it already exists and, consequently,
there is no process of change because there is no "non-being" from which or
into which a thing or a state of a thing could change. Parmenides said that "it
is the same thing that can be thought that can be"; he expressed this more directly when he wrote, "you will not find thinking without being to which it refers." To think is to think about something and for this reason you cannot think
of anything changing or coming into being. To think of change requires one to
attempt to do the impossible; namely, to think of something in terms of what it
is not. Being, or reality, is what it is and not something else. For this reason it
is impossible to think of change in any clear way since the only thing one can
think about is *being*, or what actually is. It follows, therefore, that *being* is
absolute, that being is not divisible, since all being is alike, and, says Parmenides,
". . . all is full of being. Therefore, it is altogether continuous; for being is close
to being." To make this point with greater force, Parmenides tried to show the
absurdity of the concept of becoming or change by drawing out the implications of saying that something comes to be.

Wherein lies the absurdity of saying that "something comes into being"?
It lies, said Parmenides, in the impossibility of saying consistently or coher-

ently that something can *arise* either out of being or out of non-being. The assumption behind the concept of change, or of becoming, is just this, that something changes from non-being to being or from being to being. But for Parmenides this assumption made no sense for the following reason: If one says that something arises out of being, as Thales and the other Milesians did, there cannot then be any coming-into-being, for, if it arises out of being, it already is. Similarly, if something is said to arise out of non-being, one assumes that non-being is something. But to say that non-being is something is clearly a contradiction since every something has being. The problem of explaining change was, according to Parmenides, equally impossible whether one had in mind explaining the large question of the origin of the total structure of reality or simply some small, particular thing. In either case, the problem is the same, namely, that some form of being must come from being or non-being. But, again, if it comes from being, then it already is, and hence there is no change or becoming, and if it comes from non-being, it is necessary to treat non-being as something in order to avoid the contradiction of saying that something comes from nothing. In either case, if there is any movement, it is from being to being, in which case there is no change, because before the "change" occurs something *is* and after the change it still *is*, in which case there was no change or movement after all.

Speaking of all reality as *It*, Parmenides says that "one path only is left for us to speak of, namely, that *It is*. In this path are very many tokens that what is, is uncreated and indestructible, for it is complete, immovable and without end." There cannot be different shades of being, because either *It* is or *It* is not, and since there is no becoming, being is not divisible. There is as much being in one place as in another, and there is no empty space. From these considerations, Parmenides argued that the *It* or reality is material in nature and is finite. Reality is a spherical, material, motionless, and fully occupied plenum, a continuous mass where there is no reality to emptiness and beyond which there is nothing. Because there is no change, reality is uncreated and is also indestructible and is, therefore, eternal and motionless.

To demonstrate the logical absurdity of the concept of change was not enough to dispel this concept from common sense. Everywhere average people see things in flux, and to them this represents genuine change. But Parmenides rejected the common-sense notion of change by his distinction between appearance and reality. Change, he said, is the confusion of appearance with reality, and, therefore, change is simply an illusion. What lay behind this distinction between appearance and reality was Parmenides' equally important distinction between opinion and truth. Appearance cannot produce more than opinion, whereas reality is the basis of truth. Although common sense would say that things appear to be in flux and, therefore, in a continuous process of change, this opinion based on sensation must, says Parmenides, yield to the activity of reason, which is able to discern the truth about things, and reason tells us that if there is a single substance of which everything consists, then there can be no movement or change. To some extent, the earliest philosopher, Thales, had made a similar point when he said that everything derives from water, as if to say that the appearance of things does not give us the true constitution or stuff of reality. But it was Parmenides who explicitly emphasized these distinctions, which were to become of such decisive importance in Plato's philosophy. Plato took the basic idea of Parmenides regarding the unchangeability of being and, on the basis of this, developed his distinction between the intelligible world and the visible world. Plato also derived from Parmenides' unchangeable being his objective and permanent Idea.

Parmenides was born about 510 B.C. and lived most of his life in Elea, a colony founded by refugee Greeks in the southwest of Italy. He flourished there in more than one capacity, giving the people of Elea laws and establishing a new school of philosophy whose followers became known as Eleatics. At the age of sixty-five, he went to Athens accompanied by his chief pupil Zeno, and there is the tradition that on this visit he conversed with the young Socrates. His rigorous attempt to draw out the logical implications of the assumption that reality consists of a single substance led him to conclude that in spite of what our senses tell us, there can be no motion or change. This severe conclusion inevitably brought forth critical challenges and ridicule, and it was Parmenides' ablest pupil Zeno whose task it became to defend his master's position against his attackers.

Zeno   Born in Elea about 489 B.C., Zeno was over forty years old when his master Parmenides was about sixty-five and when Socrates was a very young man. As a major Eleatic philosopher, Zeno was chiefly concerned with answering Parmenides' critics by showing that their own assumptions led to conclusions even more ridiculous than the ones they were criticizing. The Pythagoreans, for example, rejected the basic assumption Parmenides had accepted; namely, the assumption that reality is One. Instead, they believed in a plurality of things, that there exist a quantity of separate and distinct things and that, therefore, motion and change are real. Their argument seemed to accord more closely with common sense or the testimony of the senses. But the Eleatic approach that Zeno followed required a distinction between appearance and reality. To philosophize, according to Parmenides and Zeno, one must not only look at the world but must also think about it in order to understand it. This emphasis upon the logical relation of ideas to each other is the central characteristic of the Eleatic philosophers, and this is particularly evident in Zeno's arguments.

That the senses give us no clue to reality but only to appearance and, therefore, do not give us reliable knowledge but only opinion was demonstrated by Zeno to his own satisfaction by his reference to the millet seed. If one takes a millet seed, said Zeno, and drops it to the ground, it will not make a sound. But if one takes a half-bushel of millet seeds and lets them fall to the ground, there will be a sound. From this difference, Zeno concluded that our senses have deceived us, for either there is a sound when the single seed falls or there is not a sound when the many seeds fall. To get at the truth of things it is more reliable, then, to go by way of thought than to go by way of sensation.

Zeno's Four Arguments or Paradoxes   In answering the critics of Parmenides, Zeno fashioned his arguments in the form of paradoxes. What he wanted to show was that it is no more possible to demonstrate the reality of motion and change in a world of many things than in the world of the One. Either way, said Zeno, there are insuperable difficulties, but the difficulties connected with proving the reality of motion on the assumption that many things exist are greater than those connected with Parmenides' view. To be sure, casual observers of events think they are observing genuine motion as, for example, when they are spectators at a race or when they see someone shoot an arrow. But, says Zeno, this is all an illusion, for although it *appears* that there is motion, it is not possible to *think* what motion really is or to account for it rationally. To prove the impossibility of motion in a world composed of divisible reality or of multiple units, Zeno formulated the following four arguments:

1. *The racecourse.* Parmenides had said that the One is indivisible and therefore consisted of a single continuous plenum. Against this the Pythagoreans argued for a pluralistic world, saying that the world is divisible into units. If one were to consider, says Zeno, the distance around a racecourse as the Pythagoreans did, one would say that this distance must be divisible into units. According to this example of motion, the runner traverses a series of units of distance from the beginning to the end of the racecourse. But, Zeno asks, just what takes place in this example? Is there really any motion? In order to traverse the racecourse, the runner, according to the Pythagorean hypothesis, would have to traverse an infinite number of points, and would have to do this in a finite number of moments. But the critical question is, how can one traverse an infinite number of points in a finite amount of time? The reason one confronts an infinite number of points is that on the Pythagorean assumption everything is divisible; hence the distance from the beginning to the end of the racecourse is divisible. Thus, the runner cannot reach the end of the course until first reaching the dividing line at the halfway point; but the distance from the beginning to the halfway point can also be divided in half, and the runner must first reach that point, the one-quarter mark, before reaching the halfway point. Likewise, the distance between the beginning and the one-quarter point is divisible, and this process of division must go on to infinitude since there is always a remainder and every such unit is divisible. If, then, the runner cannot reach any point without first reaching its previous midpoint, and if there are an infinite number of points, it is impossible to traverse this infinite number of points in a finite amount of time. For this reason, Zeno concludes that motion does not exist.

2. *Achilles and the tortoise.* In this example, Zeno is not presenting a constructive argument of his own but is simply demonstrating where the Pythagorean premise of plural units leads one. Imagine a race between the swift Achilles and a slow tortoise where Achilles is pursuing the tortoise. Because he is a sport, Achilles gives the tortoise a head start. Zeno argues that Achilles

cannot ever overtake the tortoise because he must always reach the point which the tortoise has passed so that logically the tortoise will always be ahead. The distance between Achilles and the tortoise will always be divisible and, as in the case of the racecourse, no point can be reached before the previous point has been reached, and the effect is that there can be no motion at all, and Achilles, on these assumptions, could never overtake the tortoise. What Zeno thought he had demonstrated here was, again, that although the Pythagoreans claimed the reality of motion, their theory of the plurality of the world made it impossible to think of the idea of motion in a coherent way.

3. *The arrow.* Does an arrow move when the archer shoots it at the target? Here again the Pythagoreans, who had argued for the reality of space and therefore of its divisibility, would have to say that the arrow must occupy a particular position in space. But for an arrow to occupy a position in space equal to its length is precisely what is meant when one says that the arrow is at rest. Since the arrow must always occupy such a position in space equal to its length, the arrow must always be at rest. Moreover, since any quantity, as we saw in the example of the racecourse, is infinitely divisible, the space occupied by the arrow is infinite and as such it must coincide with everything else, in which case everything must be One instead of many. Motion, therefore, is an illusion.

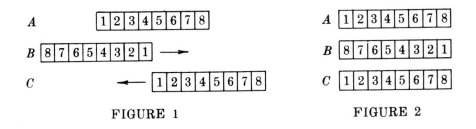

FIGURE 1   FIGURE 2

4. *The relativity of motion.* Imagine three passenger cars of equal length on tracks parallel to each other, each car having eight windows on a side. One car is stationary, and the other two are moving in opposite directions at the same speed.

In Figure 1, car *A* is stationary, and cars *B* and *C* are moving in opposite directions at the same speed until they reach the positions indicated in Figure 2. In order to reach the positions in Figure 2, the front of car *B* would go past four of car *A*'s windows while the front of car *C* would go past all eight of car *B*'s windows. Each window represents a unit of distance, and each such unit is passed in an equal unit of time. Since car *B* went past only four of *A*'s windows while car *C* went past eight of *B*'s windows, and since each window represents the same unit of time, it would have to follow that four units of time are equal to eight units of time or that four units of distance equal eight units of distance, which is absurd. Whatever may be the inner complications of this argument, Zeno's chief point was that motion has no clear definition, that it is a relative concept. In all these arguments, Zeno was simply counterattacking the adversaries of Parmenides, taking seriously their assumption of a pluralistic world, a world where, for example, a line or time is divisible. Instead of proving thereby that motion is real, Zeno thought he had demonstrated that the assumption of a pluralistic world lands one into insoluble absurdities and paradoxes. He, therefore, reiterated the Eleatic thesis that change and motion are illusions and that there is only one being, continuous, material, and motionless. Still, the persistence in common sense of the view that things really do move and that there is indeed change brought forth a new attempt to deal with the problem of the One and the many, and this new attempt is found in the philosophy of Empedocles.

Empedocles For Empedocles the arguments for as well as the arguments against motion and change had some merit. Instead of taking either side, however, he ingeniously combined both points of view in what was the first attempt at synthesizing the major philosophical contributions of his predecessors. He thereby discovered a consistent way of saying that there is change and at the same time affirming that reality is fundamentally changeless. He was an impressive figure in his native Agrigentum, Sicily, where he lived probably from 490 to 430 B.C. His interests and activities ranged from politics and medicine to religion and philosophy. His desire to be remembered as godlike gave rise to the tradition that he ended his life by leaping into the crater of Mt. Etna, hoping thereby to leave no trace of his body so that the people would think that he had gone up to heaven. He wrote his philosophy in the form of poetry, of which only a small portion has survived. From it one discovers not an original or new philosophy but, rather, a new way of putting together what his predecessors had already said.

Empedocles agreed with Parmenides that being is uncreated and indestructible, that it simply *is*, saying that "from what in no wise exists, it is impossible for anything to come into being; and for being to perish completely is incapable of fulfillment and unthinkable; for it will always be there, wherever any one may place it on any occasion." But unlike Parmenides, he did not agree that being consists simply of the One. To accept the notion of the One would require him to deny the reality of motion, but to Empedocles the phenomenon of motion was both too obvious and compelling to deny. He therefore rejected the idea of the One and argued instead that although Parmenides was correct in saying that being is uncreated and indestructible, being is not One but many. It is *the many* which are changeless and eternal. What Empedocles meant was that the objects we see and experience do in fact come into being and are also destroyed, and this change and motion are possible because objects are composed of many material particles. Thus, although objects can change, as Heraclitus had said, the particles of which they are composed do not change but are, as Parmenides had said about being, changeless. It is not the many *objects* that are changeless but the many *particles* of which the objects are composed that have this changeless attribute. But of what did these particles consist?

Empedocles described the particles of which objects are composed as being eternal kinds of material elements. This idea he developed by reinterpreting the philosophies of the Milesians Thales and Anaximenes. Thales had said that the stuff of which everything is composed is water, whereas Anaximenes had designated this stuff as air. Both these philosophers had tried to explain the relation between the One and the many by tracing the many to the One, by saying, for example, as Thales had done, that water becomes the various kinds of objects, as if to say that one kind of matter was transformed into other kinds of matter. Against this view, Empedocles now said that there must be certain forms of matter, such as water and air, to which he then added fire and earth, these four, which are changeless and eternal and are themselves never transformed into something else. This notion that there are four basic kinds of particles is not to be confused with the later theory of Democritus, who argued that all things consist of various arrangements of atoms. What explains the coming into being of objects is therefore not the transformation of any of these basic material elements but simply their mixture, for there is "only a mingling and interchange of what has been mingled." Earth, air, fire, and water, though they are unchangeable particles, do mingle together to form objects and thereby make possible what in common experience we see as change.

Empedocles thought it necessary not only to describe the basis for change in objects through the intermingling of the various types of eternal material particles, but also to designate the specific forces that animate the process of change. The Ionians had assumed that the stuff of nature simply transformed itself into various objects. Only Anaximenes had made any detailed attempt to analyze the process of change with his theory that air becomes different things through the process of condensation and rarefaction.

By contrast, Empedocles assumed that there are in nature positive forces, which he called Love and Hate, or Harmony and Discord. These physical and material forces are what cause the four elements to intermingle and later to separate. The force of Love causes elements to be attracted to each other and to be built up into some particular form or person, and the force of Hate causes the decomposition of things. Expressing this never-ending cycle in his poetic style, Empedocles writes that "this process is clearly to be seen throughout the mass of mortal limbs: sometimes through love all the limbs which the body has as its lot come together into one, in the prime of flourishing life; at another time again, sundered by evil feuds, they wander severally by the breakers of the shore of life. Likewise too with shrub plants and fish in their watery dwelling, and beasts with mountain lairs and diver birds that travel on wings." At the beginning of each cycle of change, the four elements are fully mingled together and are held in Harmony by the governing principle of Love. At the same time, the force of Hate is lurking nearby and when it invades things, the particles fall into Discord and begin to separate until all the air particles, earth particles, and fire and water particles have each been separated into their own four groups, ready again to begin a new cycle as the force of Love returns to attract the elements into harmonious combinations, and this process continues without end.

Anaxagoras A major development in philosophy occurred when Anaxagoras (500–428 B.C.) introduced a novel interpretation of the process by which matter takes on the form of particular things. His major contribution was the concept of *mind* (*nous*), which he distinguished from matter. Anaxagoras agreed with Empedocles that all coming into and going out of being consists merely in the mixture and separation of already existing substances. But he rejected Empedocles' account that the formation of the objects of an experience is the product of the forces of Love and Hate. The process of change called for a more adequate explanation, according to Anaxagoras, than one based on the ambiguous and quasimythical elements of Love and Hate. The world and all its objects appeared to him a well-ordered and intricate structure requiring as a principle of explanation a being with knowledge and power. Such a rational principle is what Anaxagoras proposed in his concept of *mind,* or *nous,* as the principle that provides matter with its order.

According to Anaxagoras, the nature of reality is best understood as consisting of *mind* and *matter*. Before mind has influenced the shape and behavior of matter, matter exists, as a mixture of various kinds of material substances, all uncreated and imperishable. Even when this original mass of matter is divided into actual objects, each part contains all "things" (*spermata*, seeds). Snow, for example, contains the opposites of black and white and is called white only because white predominates in it. In a sense, then, each part contains what is in the whole of reality, each thing having a special "portion" of everything in it.

The process by which this matter was formed into things is, according to Anaxagoras, the process of "separation." This separation was originally achieved (and continues always to occur) through the power of mind. Specifically, mind produced a rotary motion, causing a vortex which spread out so as to encompass more and more of the original mass of matter, forcing a "separation" of various substances. This rotary motion originally caused a separation of matter into two major divisions, a mass which contained the warm, light, rare, and dry, and another mass which contained the cold, dark, dense, and moist. This process of separation is continuous, and there is constant progress in the process of separation. Particular objects are always combinations of substances in which some particular substance predominates. Describing this process in one of the preserved fragments of his last book, Anaxagoras says that "Nous set in order all things that were to be and are now and that will be, and this revolution in which now revolve the stars and the sun and the moon and the air and the aether which are separated off." Continuing, he says, "the revolution itself caused the separating off, and the dense is separated off from the rare, the warm from the cold, the bright from the dark, and the dry from the moist. And there are many portions of many things." Emphasizing the continued mixture of things, he says that "no thing is altogether separated off from anything else except Nous." Forces set in motion in the vortex account for the appearance of the thick and moist at the center and the thin and warm at the circumference, that is, of the earth and the atmosphere. The forces of rotation also caused red-hot masses of stones to be torn away from the earth and to be thrown into the ether, and this is the origin of the stars. The earth, originally mud, was dried by the sun and fertilized by germs contained in the air. Everything, even now, is animated by mind, including life in plants and sense perception in human beings. Mind is everywhere, or as Anaxagoras says, *nous* is "there where everything else is, in the surrounding mass."

Although Anaxagoras considered *nous* the moving or controlling force in the cosmos and in human bodies, his account of the actual role of *nous* was limited. For one thing, the *nous* was not for Anaxagoras the *creator* of matter, since he held that matter is eternal. Moreover, he did not see in *nous the source of any purpose*. His explanation of the origin of particular things in the process of "separation" appears to be a mechanical explanation. Things still appear to be the products of the action of material causes, and mind appears to have no distinctive role apart from starting motion.

Aristotle, who later was so concerned to distinguish the different kinds of causes, expressed a double evaluation of Anaxagoras' views. Comparing Anaxagoras to his predecessors, who were willing "to entrust so great a matter [i.e., the origin of things] to spontaneity and chance," Aristotle wrote that "when [Anaxagoras] said...that reason was present—as in animals, so throughout nature—as the cause of order and of all arrangement, he seemed like a sober man in contrast with the random talk of his predecessors." But, adds Aristotle, Anaxagoras made use of his concept of *nous* only "to a small extent." His criticism was that "Anaxagoras uses reason as a *deus ex machina* for making the world, and when he is at a loss to tell from what cause something necessarily is, then he drags reason in, but in all other cases ascribes events to anything rather than reason." Anaxagoras seemed to provide only an explanation of how matter acquired its rotary motion, leaving the rest of the order of nature to be a product of that motion. Still, what Anaxagoras had to say about reason was of great consequence in the history of philosophy because he thereby introduced a mental principle into the nature of things. He differentiated mind and matter. While he may not have described mind as completely immaterial, he did nevertheless distinguish mind from the matter it had to work with, saying that mind, unlike matter, "is mixed with nothing, but is alone, itself by itself." What made mind different from matter was that it is "the finest of all things and the purest, and it has all knowledge about everything and the greatest power...." Thus, while matter is composite, mind is simple. But Anaxagoras did not distinguish two different worlds, that of mind and that of matter, but saw these two as always interrelated, since mind is "there where everything else is...." Although he had not worked out all the possibilities of his concept of *nous,* this concept was nevertheless destined to have enormous influence in later Greek philosophy.

THE ATOMISTS

Leucippus and Democritus formulated a theory about the nature of things that bears an astonishing resemblance to some twentieth-century scientific views. The atomist philosophy that they elaborated was the final answer to Thales' question before philosophy took a new turn at the hands of Socrates, Plato, and Aristotle. Although it is difficult now to disentangle the individual contribution Leucippus and Democritus each made to this atomistic theory, inasmuch as their writings are lost for the most part, it is known that Leucippus was the founder of the atomist school and that Democritus supplied much of the detailed elaboration of it. Leucippus was a contemporary of Empedocles (490–430 B.C.), whereas Democritus, born in Abdera, Thrace, is reputed to have lived one hundred years, from 460 to 360 B.C. Through his immense learning and painstaking attempt to state with clarity his abstract theory of atomism, Democritus inevitably overshadowed Leucippus, to whom, nevertheless, the credit must be given for the insight that everything is made up of atoms moving in space.

Atoms and the Void   The philosophy of atomism originated, according to Aristotle, as an attempt to overcome the logical consequences of the Eleatic denial of space. Parmenides had denied that there could be many independent things because everywhere there was *being*, in which case the total reality would be One. Specifically, he denied the existence of non-being or the void, because to say that there *is* the void is to say that the void *is something*. It is impossible, he thought, to say that there *is* nothing. Yet, in order to prove that there is motion and change it is necessary to assume that there is empty space in which things can move. But empty space is nothing, yet to say that it *is* meant for Parmenides that space is part of the total *Is*. By arguing that there is only the One, since there could be no areas of non-being between things to give things separate spheres of existing, Parmenides thought he had proved that there could be no motion or change. It was precisely to reject this Eleatic treatment of space or the void that Leucippus formulated his new theory.

Leucippus affirmed the reality of space and thereby prepared the way for a coherent theory of motion and change. What had complicated Parmenides' concept of space was his thought that whatever exists must be *material*, wherefore space, if it existed, must also be material. Leucippus, on the other hand, thought it possible to affirm that space exists without having to say at the same time that it is material. Thus, he described space as something like a receptacle that could be empty in some places and full in others. As a receptacle, space, or the void, could be the place where objects move, and Leucippus apparently saw no reason for denying this characteristic of space. Without this concept of space, it would have been impossible for Leucippus and Democritus to develop that part of their philosophy for which they are best known, namely, that all things consist of atoms.

According to Leucippus and Democritus, the nature of things consists of an infinite number of particles or units called atoms. To these atoms both Leucippus and Democritus ascribed the characteristics that Parmenides had ascribed to the One, namely, indestructibility and, therefore, eternity. Whereas Parmenides had said reality consists of a single One, the atomists now said that there are an infinite number of atoms, each one being completely full, containing no empty spaces, therefore being completely hard and indivisible. These atoms exist in space and differ from each other in shape and size, and because of their small size, they are invisible. Since these atoms are eternal, they did not have to be created. Nature consists, therefore, of two things only: namely, *space,* which is a vacuum, and *atoms*. The atoms move about in space, and their motion leads them to form the objects we experience.

The atomists did not think it was necessary to account for the origin of this motion of the atoms in space. The original motion of these atoms, they thought, was similar to the motion of dust particles as they dart off in all directions in a sunbeam even when there is no wind to impel them. Democritus said that there is no absolute "up" or "down," and since he did not ascribe *weight* to atoms, he thought atoms could move in any and all directions. Things as we know them have their origin in the motion of the atoms. Moving in space, the atoms originally were single individual units, but inevitably they began to collide with each other, and in cases where their shapes were such as to permit them to interlock, they began to form clusters, or what Anaxagoras had called *vortices*. In this the atomists resembled the Pythagoreans, who had said that all things are numbers. Things, like numbers, are made up of combinable units, and things, for the atomists, were simply combinations of various kinds of atoms. Mathematical figures and physical figures were, therefore, thought to be similar.

In the beginning, then, there were atoms in space. Each atom is like the Parmenidean One, but though they are indestructible, they are in constant motion. The stuff about which Thales, Anaximenes, Heraclitus, and Empedocles spoke, namely, water, air, fire, and earth, these the atomists described as different clusters of changeless atoms, the product of the movement of originally single atoms. These four elements were not the primeval "roots" of all other things but were themselves the product of the absolutely original stuff, the atoms.

The atomists had produced a mechanical conception of the nature of things. For them, everything was the product of the collision of atoms moving in space. Their theory had no place in it for the element of *purpose* or *design*, and their materialistic reduction of all reality to atoms left no place, and in their minds no need, for a creator or designer. They saw no need to account either for the origin of the atoms or for the original motion impelling the atoms, since the question of origins could always be asked, even about God. For them, to ascribe eternal existence to the material atoms seemed as satisfactory as any other solution.

So formidable was this atomistic theory that, although it went into a decline after Aristotle and during the Middle Ages, it was revived and provided science with its working model for centuries to come. Sir Isaac Newton

(1642–1727) still thought in atomistic terms when he wrote his famous *Principia*, in which, having deduced the motion of the planets, the comets, the moon, and the sea, he wrote in 1686, "I wish we could devise the rest of the phenomena of Nature by the same kind of reasoning from mechanical principles, for I am induced by many reasons to suspect that they may all depend upon certain forces by which the particles of bodies, by some causes hitherto unknown, are either mutually impelled towards one another and cohere in regular figures, or are repelled and recede from one another." Although Newton assumed God had set things in motion, his physical analysis of nature was restricted to the mechanical principles of matter moving in space. What Leucippus and Democritus had envisioned, therefore, had a long and influential history. Their materialism was soon rejected in the metaphysical theories of Plato and Aristotle, but the theory of bodies in motion as the explanation of nature was revived in the sixteenth century and held sway until the quantum theory and Einstein gave the twentieth century a new conception of matter, denying the attribute of indestructibility to the atoms.

Democritus was concerned with two other philosophical problems besides describing the structure of nature: namely, the problem of knowledge and the problem of human conduct. This portion of his philosophy developed as a reaction to issues raised by Protagoras (490-421 B.C.) concerning the nature of knowledge and by the Sophists, who doubted the possibility of any stable rules for ethics. Although Democritus' views on these subjects derive their force only when seen in relation to the views of Protagoras and the Sophists, with which we shall deal later, it can be said now that Democritus tried to deal with these subjects in a way consistent with his mechanical view of nature.

Being a thorough materialist, Democritus held that *thought* can be explained in the same way that any other phenomenon can, namely, as the movement of atoms. He distinguished between two different kinds of perception, one of the senses and one of the understanding, both of these being physical processes. When the eye sees something, this something is an "effluence" or the shedding of atoms by the object, forming an "image." These atomic images of things enter the eyes (and other organs of sense) and make an impact upon the soul, which is itself made up of atoms. Whereas Protagoras said that our senses are all equally reliable, that everything we sense really is what we sense it to be, Democritus disagreed, saying that "there are two forms of knowledge, the trueborn and the bastard. To the bastard belong all these: sight, hearing, smell, taste, touch. The trueborn is quite apart from these."

What distinguishes these two modes of thought is that whereas "trueborn" knowledge depends only on the object, "bastard" knowledge is affected by the particular conditions of the body of the person involved. This is why two persons can agree that what they have tasted is an apple (trueborn) and still disagree about the taste (bastard knowledge), one saying the apple is sweet and the other saying it is bitter, so that, concludes Democritus, "by the senses we know in truth nothing sure, but only something that changes according to the disposition of the body and of the things that enter into it or resist it." Still,

Democritus had to say that both sensation and thought are the same type of mechanical process.

When Democritus came to the other problem, however, the problem of ethics, he appears to have departed from his mechanical view of things. For one thing, if all reality is mechanically interlocked, there would hardly be any point in giving advice on how to behave, since each person's movements would be determined by the movements of other things, and conduct would not be within a person's control. In spite of this technical contradiction in his philosophy, Democritus developed a very lofty set of rules for human behavior, urging moderation in all things along with the cultivation of culture as the surest way of achieving the most desirable goal of life, namely, cheerfulness.

With the emergence of ethics as its primary concern, philosophy reached one of its major watersheds, closing out the first era where the principal question had been about the natural physical order. Now people would ask more searching questions about how they should behave.

2

Socrates and the Sophists: the Problems of Truth and Goodness

The first philosophers had focused their attention upon nature; the Sophists and Socrates shifted the concerns of philosophy to the study of mankind. Instead of asking the large cosmic questions about the ultimate principle of things, philosophy became preoccupied with questions relating more directly to human behavior. This transition from predominantly scientific concerns to basic ethical questions is explained in part by the failure of the pre-Socratics to arrive at any uniform conception of the cosmos. Inconsistent interpretations of nature had been proposed, and there appeared to be no way of reconciling them. Heraclitus had said that nature consists of a plurality of substances and that everything is in a process of constant change or flux, whereas Parmenides took the opposite view, arguing that reality is a single, static substance, the One, and that motion and change are illusions cast upon our senses by the appearances of things. Had these contradictory cosmologies produced simply an intellectual fatigue by virtue of the sheer difficulty of deciphering the secrets of nature, or an impatience and disinterest in pursuing a philosophic activity that gave no promise of a successful outcome, philosophy might have stopped at this point. As it was, the controversy over the ultimate principle of things had generated a mood of skepticism about the ability of human reason to discover the truth about nature. But this very mood, this skepticism, provided the impulse for a new direction for philosophy, for skepticism itself became the subject of serious concern.

Instead of debating about alternative theories of nature, philosophers now addressed themselves to the problem of human knowledge, asking whether it was possible for the human mind to discover any universal truth. This question had been further aggravated by the disclosure of cultural differences between various races and peoples so that the question about truth became deeply implicated with the problem of goodness. Could there be a universal concept of goodness if people were incapable of knowing any universal truth? The principal parties to this new debate were the Sophists and Socrates.

THE SOPHISTS

The three most outstanding Sophists who emerged in Athens some time during the fifth century B.C. were Protagoras, Gorgias, and Thrasymachus. They were part of a group who had come to Athens either as traveling teachers or, as in the case of Hippias of Elis, as ambassadors, and they called themselves Sophists, or "intellectuals." Coming as they did from different cultures, Protagoras from Abdera in Thrace, Gorgias from Leontini in southern Sicily, and Thrasymachus from Chalcedon, they took a fresh look at Athenian thought and customs and asked searching questions about them. They became the great spokesmen of the Greek enlightenment by forcing the Athenians to consider whether their ideas and customs were founded upon truth or simply upon conventional ways of behaving. Was their distinction between Greeks and barbarians, they asked, as well as that between masters and slaves, based upon evidence or simply upon prejudice? Not only had the Sophists lived in different countries with their different customs, but they had also gathered a wide fund of information based upon the observation of a multitude of cultural facts. Their encyclopedic knowledge of different cultures made them skeptical about the possibility of attaining any absolute truth by which a society might order its life. They forced upon thoughtful Athenians the question whether Hellenic culture was based upon artificial rules or upon nature, whether their religious and moral codes were conventional and, therefore, changeable or *natural* and, therefore, permanent. In a decisive way, the Sophists set the stage for a more deliberate and careful consideration of human nature, how knowledge is acquired, and how humans might order their behavior.

The Sophists were primarily practical men, and the circumstances of Athenian democracy under Pericles were such that their practical skills were quickly put to use. It was their interest and competence in prose and grammar as well as their skill in discourse that made them uniquely pertinent to the current scene. Under Pericles, the aristocracy had been replaced by democracy, and this had the effect of intensifying political life in Athens by drawing the free citizens into political discussion and making them eligible for leadership. But the older aristocratic education had not prepared people for the new conditions of democratic life, for that education had been founded for the most part upon family tradition. There had been no disciplined and theoretical training in the areas of religion, grammar, and the careful interpretation of the poets. The Sophists moved into this cultural vacuum, and their practical interest in teaching filled an urgent need. They became popular lecturers and were the chief source of the new education. What made them particularly sought after was that they professed, above all, to teach the art of *rhetoric*, the art of persuasive speech. The power of persuasion had become a political necessity in the democratic Athens for anyone who hoped to rise to the level of leadership. Because of their extensive knowledge of grammar and their fund of information about various cultures as well as their wide experience derived from their travels and teaching in many places, the Sophists possessed all that was needed to train the emerging new Athenian citizen.

The reputation of the Sophists was at first very favorable. They rendered an immense service by training people to present their ideas clearly and forcefully. Clear speech and the power of persuasion were especially indispensable in a popular assembly where it would be disastrous to permit debate among unskilled speakers who could neither present their own ideas effectively nor discover the errors in their opponents' arguments. But rhetoric became somewhat like a knife in that it could be employed for good or ill use, to cut bread or to kill. Those who possessed the power of persuasion could use that power either to cut through a difficult problem on through psychological resistance to a good idea, on the one hand, or, on the other hand, to put over an idea in which they had a special interest, the intrinsic goodness of which was questionable. The shift from the one use of rhetoric to the other was greatly facilitated by the inherent skepticism of the Sophists. It was their skepticism and relativism that made them suspect. No one would have criticized them for training lawyers, as they did, to be able to argue either side of a case. Surely people deserve to have their defense presented with as much skill as the prosecutor uses against them. As long as the art of persuasion was linked to the pursuit of truth there could be no quarrel with the Sophists. But since they looked upon truth as a relative matter, it was inevitable that they should be charged with teaching the young men how to make a bad case look good or to make the unjust cause appear to be just. Furthermore, they developed the reputation of gathering together young men from good families only to lead them in a critical and destructive analysis of their traditional religious and ethical views. To add further to their ill repute, they departed from the earlier image of the philosopher as a disinterested thinker who did not engage in philosophy for gain. The Sophists, by contrast, charged fees for their teaching and appeared to seek out the rich, who were able to pay these fees. Socrates had studied under the Sophists, but because of his poverty could only afford their "shorter course." This practice of charging fees for their teaching prompted Plato to disparage them as "shopkeepers with spiritual wares."

Protagoras   Among the Sophists who had come to Athens, Protagoras of Abdera was the oldest and, in many ways, the most influential. He is best known for his statement that "man is the measure of all things, of the things that are, that they are, and of the things that are not, that they are not." To say that man is the measure of all things apparently meant to Protagoras that whatever knowledge one could achieve about anything would be limited to one's human capacities. He dismissed any discussion of theology, saying that "About the gods, I am not able to know whether they exist or do not exist, nor what they are like in form; for the factors preventing knowledge are many: the obscurity of the subject, and the shortness of human life." Knowledge, said Protagoras, is limited to our various perceptions and these perceptions will differ with each person. If two persons were to observe the same object, their sensations would be different, because each would occupy a different position in relation to it. Similarly, the same breeze blowing at two people would feel cool to one, while it would be warm to the other. Whether the breeze is or is not cold cannot be answered in a simple way. It is in fact cold for one person and warm for the other. To say that "man is the measure of all things" is, therefore, to say that our knowledge is measured by what we perceive, and if there is something about each of us that makes us perceive things in different ways, there is no standard for testing whether one person's perception is right and another person's wrong. Protagoras thought that the objects we perceive by our various senses must possess all the properties that different people perceive as belonging to them. For this reason, it is impossible to discover what is the "true" nature of anything; a thing has as many characteristics as there are people perceiving it. There is no way to distinguish between "appearance" and "reality"; for the person who says that the breeze is cold it really *is* cold and does not simply appear so just because it feels warm to somebody else. On this theory of knowledge, it would be impossible to build any scientific knowledge, because it rejects the possibility of discovering what nature is really like since there are built-in differences in each observer leading each one to see things differently. Protagoras concluded, therefore, that knowledge is relative to each person.

When he turned to the subject of ethics, Protagoras maintained that moral judgments are relative. He was willing to admit that the idea of law reflects a general desire in each culture for a moral order among all people. But he denied that there was any uniform law of nature pertaining to human behavior that all peoples everywhere could discover. He distinguished between nature and custom or convention and said that laws and moral rules are based, not upon nature, but upon convention. Each society has its own laws and its own moral rules, and there is no way, apart from certain common-sense observations about their relative "soundness," of judging some to be true and others wrong. But Protagoras did not carry this moral relativism to the extreme revolutionary position of saying that because moral judgments are relative, every individual can decide what is moral. Instead, he took the conservative position that the state makes the laws and that these laws should be accepted by everyone because they are as good as any that can be made. Other communities might have different laws, and individuals within a state might think of different laws, but in neither case are these better laws; they are only different. In the interests of a peaceful and orderly society, then, people should respect and uphold the customs, laws, and moral rules their tradition has carefully nurtured. In matters of religion, Protagoras took a similar view, saying that the impossibility of knowing with certainty about the existence and nature of the gods should not prevent anyone from participating in the worship of the gods. The curious outcome of Protagoras' relativism was his conservative conclusion that the young should be educated to accept and support the tradition of their society, not because this tradition is true but because it makes possible a stable society. Still, there could be no question that Protagoras' relativism had seriously dislodged confidence in the possibility of discovering true knowledge and had brought upon his skepticism the heavy criticism of Socrates and Plato.

Gorgias   Gorgias came to Athens from Sicily as ambassador from his native city of Leontini in 427 B.C. He took such a radical view regarding truth that he eventually gave up philosophy and turned instead to the practice and teaching of rhetoric. This radical view differed from Protagoras' in that while Protagoras said that everything is true, that truth is relative to persons and circumstances, Gorgias denied that there is any truth at all. With hair-splitting keenness, employing the mode of reasoning used by the Eleatic philosophers Parmenides and Zeno, Gorgias propounded the extraordinary notions (1) that nothing exists, (2) that if anything exists it is incomprehensible, and (3) that even if it is comprehensible, it cannot be communicated. Taking this third notion, for example, he argued that we communicate with words, but words are only symbols or signs and no symbol can ever be the same as the thing it symbolizes. For this reason, knowledge can never be communicated. By this mode of close reasoning, Gorgias thought he could prove all three of his propositions, or at least that his reasoning was as coherent as any used by those who disagreed with him. He was convinced, consequently, that there could be no reliable knowledge and certainly no truth.

Abandoning philosophy, Gorgias turned to rhetoric and tried to perfect it as the art of persuasion. It is said that he developed, in this connection, the technique of deception, making use of his knowledge of psychology and of the powers of suggestion. Having earlier concluded that there is no truth, he was willing to employ the art of persuasion for whatever practical ends he chose.

Thrasymachus   In the *Republic*, Thrasymachus is portrayed as the Sophist who asserted that injustice is to be preferred to the life of justice. He did not look upon injustice as a defect of character. On the contrary, Thrasymachus considered the unjust person as positively superior in character and intelligence. Indeed, he said that "injustice pays," not only at the meager level of the pickpocket, although there is profit in that too, but especially in the case of those who carry injustice to perfection and make themselves masters of whole cities and nations. Justice, he said, is pursued by simpletons and leads to weakness. Thrasymachus held that people should aggressively pursue their own interests in a virtually unlimited form of self-assertion. He regarded justice as being the interest of the stronger and believed that "might is right." Laws, he said, are made by the ruling party for its own interest. These laws define what is right. In all states alike "right" has the same meaning for "right" is the interest of the party established in power. So, says Thrasymachus, "the sound conclusion is that what is 'right' is the same everywhere: the interest of the stronger party."

Here, then, is the reduction of morality to power, an inevitable logical consequence of the progressive radicalism of the Sophists, which led them to a nihilistic attitude toward truth and ethics. It was Socrates' chief concern to unravel the logical inconsistencies of the Sophists and to rebuild some notion of truth and also establish some firm foundation for moral judgments.

SOCRATES

Many Athenians had mistaken Socrates for a Sophist. The fact is that Socrates was one of the Sophists' keenest critics. That Socrates should have been identified with them was due in part to his relentless analysis of any and every subject, a technique employed also by the Sophists. But between the Sophists and Socrates there was a fundamental difference. The Sophists split hairs to show that equally good arguments could be advanced on either side of any issue. They were skeptics who doubted that there could be any certain or reliable knowledge. Moreover, they concluded that since all knowledge is relative, moral ideas and ideals are also relative. Socrates, on the other hand, had a different motivation for his constant argumentation. He was committed to the pursuit of truth and considered it his mission to seek out the basis for stable and certain knowledge. He was also attempting to discover the foundation for the good life. As he pursued his mission, Socrates devised a method for arriving at truth, linking *knowing* and *doing* to each other in such a way as to argue that to know the good is to do the good, that "knowledge is virtue." Unlike the Sophists, then, Socrates engaged in argumentation, in "dialectic," not for ends destructive of truth or to develop pragmatic skills among lawyers and politicians, but to achieve creative concepts of truth and goodness.

Socrates' Life   Seldom has there been a time and place so rich in genius as the Athens into which Socrates was born in 470 B.C. By this time, Aeschylus had written some of his great dramatic works. Euripides and Sophocles were young boys who were to produce great tragedies that Socrates may very well have attended. Pericles, who was to usher in a great age of democracy and the flowering of art, was still a young man. Socrates could have seen the Parthenon and the statues of Phidias started and completed during his lifetime. By this time, too, Persia had been defeated, and Athens had advanced toward becoming a naval power with control over much of the Aegean Sea. Athens had reached a level of unprecedented power and splendor. But though Socrates grew up in a golden age, his declining years were to see Athens defeated in war and his own life brought to an end in prison where, in 399 B.C., at

Socrates *(New York Public Library Picture Collection)*

the age of seventy-one, he drank the hemlock in compliance with the death sentence meted out by the court that tried him.

Socrates wrote nothing. Most of what we know about him has been preserved by three of his famous younger contemporaries, Aristophanes, Plato, and Xenophon. From these sources Socrates emerges as an intense genius who, along with extraordinary rational rigor, possessed a personal warmth and a fondness for humor. He was a robust man with great powers of physical endurance. In his playful comedy, *The Clouds*, Aristophanes depicts Socrates as a strutting waterfowl, poking fun at his habit of rolling his eyes and referring impishly to his "pupils" and "thinking shop." But from Xenophon comes the portrait of a loyal soldier who has a passion for discussing the requirements of morality and who inevitably attracted the younger men to seek out his advice. Plato confirmed Xenophon's portrait and in addition pictured Socrates as a man with a deep sense of mission and absolute moral purity. In the *Symposium*, Plato relates how Alcibiades, a fair youth, expected to win the amorous affections of Socrates, contriving in various ways to be alone with him, but, says Alcibiades, ". . . nothing of the sort occurred at all: he would merely converse with me in his usual manner, and when he had spent the day with me he would leave me and go his way." In military campaigns, Socrates could go without food longer than anyone else, and while others wrapped themselves up with "prodigious care" against the bitter cold of winter, using "felt and little fleeces" over their shoes, Socrates, says Alcibiades, "walked out in that weather, clad in just such a coat as he was always wont to wear, and he made his way more easily over the ice unshod than the rest of us did in our shoes."

Socrates was capable of intense and sustained concentration. On one occasion during a military campaign, he stood in deep contemplation for a day and night, "till dawn came and the sun rose: then walked away after offering a prayer to the sun." This may have been the occasion on which he experienced what he considered a mandate to pursue the mission of prophetic concern over the moral life of Athenians. He had frequently received messages or warnings from a mysterious "voice," or what he called his *daimon*. Although this "supernatural sign" invaded his thoughts from early childhood, it suggests more than anything else Socrates' sensitivity as a "visionary," particularly his sensitivity to the moral qualities of human actions that make life worth living. He must have been familiar with the natural science of the earlier Ionian philosophers and Anaxagoras, although he does say in the *Apology* that "the simple truth is, O Athenians, that I have nothing to do with physical speculations." For him, such speculations had to give way to the more urgent questions about human nature, about truth, and about goodness. The decisive event that confirmed his mission as a moral philosopher was the reply of the Delphic Oracle. When Chaerophon asked the Oracle whether there was any living person who was wiser than Socrates, the Oracle replied that there was not. Socrates interpreted this reply to mean that he was the wisest because he realized and admitted his own ignorance. In this mood, Socrates set out on his quest for abiding truth and wisdom.

Socrates as a Philosopher   Because Socrates left no writings of his own, there is today some disagreement over what philosophical ideas can be properly attributed to him. Our most extensive sources of his thought are the *Dialogues* of Plato, in which he is, especially in the earlier dialogues, the leading character. But the persistent question is whether Plato is here reporting what Socrates had actually taught or expressing his own ideas through the figure of Socrates. There are those who argue that the Socrates found in Plato's dialogues is the historically correct Socrates. This would mean that Socrates must get all the credit for the novel philosophical activity these dialogues contain, giving Plato credit only for the literary form he devised for preserving, elaborating, and lending precision and color to Socrates' thought. On the other hand, Aristotle distinguished between the philosophical contributions made by Socrates and Plato. To Socrates Aristotle gave the credit for "inductive arguments and universal definitions," and to Plato he ascribed the development of the theory of Forms, the notion that universal Ideas, or Forms, exist independently of the particular things that embody them. The argument, for the most part, is over whether Socrates or Plato developed the theory of Forms. Since Aristotle was himself particularly interested in this subject, having discussed it at length with Plato in the Academy, it seems reasonable to suppose that his distinction between Socrates' and Plato's ideas is accurate. At the same time, some of the early dialogues are clearly accurate representations of Socrates' own thought, as in the case of the *Apology* and the *Euthyphro*. The most plausible solution to the problem, therefore, would be to accept portions of both views, agreeing that the earlier dialogues are portrayals of Socrates' philosophic activity whereas the later dialogues represent Plato's own philosophic development, including his formulation of the metaphysical theory of the Forms. On this basis, Socrates is seen as an original philosopher who developed a new method of intellectual inquiry.

If Socrates was to be successful in overcoming the relativism and skepticism of the Sophists, he had to discover some immovable foundation upon which to build the edifice of knowledge. This foundation Socrates discovered not in the facts of the world outside of humanity but within humans. The interior life, said Socrates, is the seat of a unique activity, the activity of knowing, which leads to the practical activity of doing. To describe this activity, Socrates created the conception of the soul, the *psyche*. For him the soul was not any particular faculty, nor was it any special kind of substance, but was rather the capacity for intelligence and character; it was a person's conscious personality. Socrates further described what he meant by the soul as "that within us in virtue of which we are pronounced wise or foolish, good or bad." By describing it in these terms, Socrates identified the soul with the normal powers of intelligence and character instead of as some ghostly substance. The soul was the structure of personality. However difficult it may have been for Socrates to describe exactly what the soul is, what he was sure of was that the activity of the soul is to *know* and to influence or even direct and govern a person's daily conduct. Although for Socrates the soul was not a *thing*, he could say that one's greatest concern should be the proper care of one's soul so as to "make the soul as good as possible." One takes best care of one's soul when one understands the difference between fact and fancy and builds one's thought upon a knowledge of what human life is really like. Having attained such knowledge, those who have the proper care of their soul in mind will conduct their behavior in accordance with their knowledge of the true moral values. Socrates was primarily concerned with *the good life* and not with mere contemplation.

The immovable point in this conception of the soul was, for Socrates, one's conscious awareness of what some words mean. To know that some things contradict others, that justice cannot mean harming others, represented for Socrates a typical example of the kind of knowledge the soul can attain just by using its powers to know. To act in defiance of this knowledge, to harm someone even when one knows that such behavior is contrary to one's knowledge of justice, is to do violence to one's nature as a human being. Socrates was certain that people could attain sure and reliable knowledge and that only such knowledge could be the proper basis of morality. His first major task was, therefore, to clarify for himself and his followers just how one attains reliable knowledge.

Socrates' Theory of Knowledge: Intellectual Midwifery Socrates was convinced that the surest way to attain reliable knowledge was through the practice of disciplined conversation, acting as an intellectual midwife, a method he called *dialectic*. This was a deceptively simple technique. It would always begin with a discussion of the most obvious aspects of any problem. Socrates believed that through the process of dialogue, where all parties to the conversation were forced to clarify their ideas, the final outcome of the conversation would be a clear statement of what was meant. Although the technique appeared simple, it was not long before anyone upon whom Socrates employed it could feel its intense rigor as well as the discomfort of his irony. In the earliest dialogues in which this method is displayed, as, for example, in the *Euthyphro*, Socrates feigns ignorance about a subject and tries to draw out from the other person his fullest possible knowledge about it. He considered this method of dialectic a kind of intellectual midwifery. His assumption was that by progressively correcting incomplete or inaccurate notions, one could coax the truth out of anyone. His reliance was solely upon the permanent structure of the soul, on one's capacity for knowing and for recognizing lurking contradictions. If the human mind was incapable of knowing something, Socrates would want to demonstrate that, too, believing that no unexamined idea is worth having any more than the unexamined life is worth living. Some dialogues therefore end inconclusively, since Socrates was concerned not with imposing a set of dogmatic ideas upon his listeners but with leading them through an orderly process of thought.

A good example of Socrates' method is found in his dialogue with Euthyphro. The scene is in front of the Hall of King Archon, where Socrates is waiting in the hope of discovering who has brought suit against him for *impi-*

ety, which was a capital offense. He wants to know what that charge means. When young Euthyphro arrives upon the scene, Socrates discovers that he has come to prosecute a suit of his own, charging that his father was guilty of impiety. With devastating irony, Socrates expresses relief at his good fortune in meeting him, for Euthyphro is making the identical charge against his father that has been made against Socrates. Sarcastically, Socrates says to Euthyphro that "not every one could rightly do what you are doing; only a man who is well advanced in wisdom." Only someone who knew exactly what impiety meant would charge anyone with such a serious offense, and to bring such a charge against one's *father* would only corroborate the assumption that the accuser knew what he was talking about. Socrates professes ignorance of the meaning of impiety and asks Euthyphro to explain what it means, since he has charged his father with this offense.

Euthyphro answers Socrates by defining piety as "prosecuting the wrongdoer" and impiety as not prosecuting him. To this Socrates replies that "I did not ask you to tell me one or two of all the many pious actions that there are; I want to know what is the idea of piety which makes all pious actions pious." Since his first definition was unsatisfactory, Euthyphro tries again, this time saying that "what is pleasing to the gods is pious." But Socrates refers to the stories of quarrels among the gods, indicating that the gods disagree among themselves about what is better and worse. The same act, then, can be pleasing to some gods and not pleasing to others, wherefore Euthyphro's second definition is also inadequate. Trying to repair the damage, Euthyphro offers a new definition, saying that "piety is what *all* the gods love, and impiety is what they *all* hate." But, asks Socrates, "do the gods love an act because it is pious, or is it pious because the gods love it?" In short, what is the *essence* of piety? Trying again, Euthyphro says that piety is "that part of justice which has to do with the attention which is due to the gods...." Again, Socrates presses for a clearer definition by asking what kind of attention is due to the gods. By this time, Euthyphro is hopelessly adrift, and Socrates says to him that "it cannot be that you would ever have undertaken to prosecute your aged father for the murder of a laboring man unless you had known exactly what is piety and impiety." And when Socrates presses him once more for a clearer definition, Euthyphro answers, "Another time... Socrates. I am in a hurry now, and it is time for me to be off."

Though the dialogue thus ends inconclusively, as far as the subject of piety is concerned, it is a vivid example of Socrates' method of dialectic and a portrayal of his conception of the philosophical life. More specifically, it illustrates Socrates' unique concern with *definition* as the instrument of clear thought.

Definition   Nowhere is Socrates' approach to knowledge more clearly displayed than in his preoccupation with the process of definition. For him, a definition was a clear and fixed concept. What impressed Socrates was that although particular events or things varied in some respects or passed away, there was something about them that was the same, that never varied and never passed away, and this was their definition, or their essential nature. It was this permanent meaning that Socrates wanted Euthyphro to give him when he asked for that "idea of piety which makes all pious acts pious." In a similar way, Socrates sought the Idea of *Justice* by which acts become just or the Idea of *Beauty* by which particular things are said to be beautiful and the Idea of *Goodness* by which we recognize human acts to be good. No particular thing is perfectly beautiful, but insofar as it is beautiful it is because it partakes of Beauty. Moreover, when a beautiful thing passes away, the Idea of Beauty remains. Socrates was struck by the ability of the mind to think about general ideas and not only about particular things. In some way, the mind, he argued, thinks of two different kinds of objects whenever it thinks about anything. A beautiful flower is at once this particular flower and at the same time a single example or partaker of the general or universal meaning of Beauty. The process of definition was for Socrates the process by which the mind could distinguish or sort out these two objects of thought, namely, the particular (this beautiful flower) and the general or universal (the Idea of Beauty of which this flower partakes so as to make it a beautiful flower). If Socrates asked, "What is a beautiful flower?" or "What is a pious act?" he would not be satisfied with your pointing to this flower or this act. For, although Beauty is in some way connected with something, that thing does not either equal or exhaust the Idea of Beauty. Moreover, although various beautiful things differ from each other, whether they be flowers or persons, they are each called beautiful because in spite of their differences, they share in common that element by which they are called beautiful. Only by the rigorous process of definition does the mind finally grasp the distinction between a particular thing (this beautiful flower) and the general fixed notion (Beauty or beautiful). The process of definition, as Socrates worked it out, was a process for arriving at clear and fixed concepts.

Through his technique of definition, Socrates indicated that true knowledge is more than simply an inspection of facts. Knowledge has to do with the power of the mind to discover in facts the abiding elements that remain after the facts disappear. Beauty remains after the rose fades. To the mind an imperfect triangle suggests *the* Triangle and imperfect circles are seen as approximations to the perfect Circle, the definition of which produces the clear and fixed notion of Circle. Facts can produce a variety of notions, for no two flowers are the same. By the same token, no two persons or no two cultures are the same. If one limited one's knowledge simply to uninterpreted facts, one would conclude that everything is different, that there are no universal likenesses. The Sophists did just this, arguing from the facts they had collected about other cultures that all ideas of justice and goodness are relative. But Socrates would not accept this conclusion. To him the factual differences between people—for example, the differences in their height, strength, and mental ability—did not obscure the equally certain fact that they were all people. By his process of definition, he cut through the obvious factual differences about them to discover what caused all these people to be people in spite of their differences. His clear concept of *Man* provided him with a firm basis for thinking about men. Similarly, though cultures differ, though their actual laws and moral rules differ, still, said Socrates, the Ideas of Law, Justice, and Goodness can be defined as rigorously as the Idea of Man. Instead of leading to intellectual skepticism and moral relativism, Socrates believed that the manifold of facts could yield clear and fixed concepts if one employed the technique of analysis and definition.

Behind the world of facts, then, Socrates believed there was an order in things that the mind could discover. This led him to introduce into philosophy a way of looking at everything in the universe that was more fully developed by Plato and by Aristotle, and this was the *teleological* conception of things, the view that things have a function or purpose. To say that something—for example, a person—has a definable nature is also to say that there is an activity appropriate to his or her nature. If people are rational beings, acting rationally is the behavior appropriate to human nature. From this it is a short step to saying that they *ought* to act rationally. By discovering the essential nature of everything, Socrates believed that he could thereby also discover the intelligible order in everything. In this view, things had not only their own specific natures and functions, but these functions had some additional purpose in the whole scheme of things. There are many kinds of things in the universe, not because of some haphazard mixture, but because each thing does one thing best and all of them acting together make up the orderly universe. Clearly, Socrates could distinguish two levels of knowledge, one based upon the *inspection* of facts and the other based upon the *interpretation* of facts, one based upon particular things and the other based upon general or universal Ideas or conceptions. That universal Ideas, such as Beauty, Straight, Triangle, and Man, were always used in discourse certainly suggested that there was some basis in reality for their use. The big question soon to arise was whether these universal Ideas or words refer to some existing reality in the same way that particular words do. If the word *John* refers to a person existing in a particular place, does the word *Man* also refer to some reality someplace? Whether Socrates dealt with this problem of the metaphysical status of universals depends upon whether we consider Plato or Socrates to be the author of the doctrine of the Forms, of the *theory of Ideas*. Plato certainly taught that these Ideas, whatever they are, are the most real things there are and that they have a separate existence from the particular things we see, which partake of these Ideas. Aristotle rejected this theory of the separate existence of Ideas, arguing that in some way these universal Ideas exist only in the actual things we experience. He indicated, too, that Socrates had not "separated off" these Ideas from things. If Socrates was not the author of the theory of Ideas found in the Platonic dialogues, he was, nevertheless, the one who had fashioned the concept of an intelligible order lying behind the visible world.

Socrates' Moral Thought For Socrates, knowledge and virtue were the same thing. If virtue has to do with "making the soul as good as possible," it is first necessary to know what makes the soul good. Goodness and knowledge are, therefore, closely related. But Socrates said more than simply that goodness and knowledge are related. He identified these two, saying that to know the good is to do the good, that knowledge is virtue. By identifying knowledge and virtue, Socrates meant also to say that vice, or evil, is the absence of knowledge. Just as knowledge is virtue, so, too, vice is ignorance. The outcome of this line of reasoning was Socrates' conviction that no one ever indulged in vice or committed an evil act knowingly. Wrongdoing, he said, is always involuntary, being the product of ignorance.

To equate virtue with knowledge and vice with ignorance may seem to contradict the most elementary experience of most human beings. Our common sense tells us that we frequently indulge in acts that we know to be wrong, so that wrongdoing for us is a deliberate and voluntary act. Socrates would have readily agreed that we commit acts that can be called evil. He denied, however, that people deliberately did evil acts because they knew them to be evil. When people commit evil acts, said Socrates, they always do them thinking that they are good in some way.

When he equated virtue and knowledge, Socrates had in mind a particular conception of virtue. For him, virtue meant fulfilling one's function. As a rational being, a person's function is to behave rationally. At the same time, every human being has the inescapable desire for happiness or the well-being of his or her soul. This inner well-being, this "making the soul as good as possible," can be achieved only by certain appropriate modes of behavior. Because we have a desire for happiness, we choose our acts with the hope that they will bring us happiness. Which acts, or what behavior, will produce happiness? Socrates knew that some forms of behavior *appear* to produce happiness, but in *reality* do not. For this reason, we frequently choose acts that may in themselves be questionable but that we nevertheless think will bring us happiness. Thieves may know that stealing as such is wrong, but they steal in the hope that it will bring them happiness. Similarly, we pursue power, physical pleasure, and property, which are the symbols of success and happiness, confusing these with the true ground of happiness.

The equating of vice with ignorance is not so contrary to common sense after all, for the ignorance Socrates speaks of refers not to the act itself but to its ability to produce happiness. It is ignorance about one's soul, about what it takes to "make the soul as good as possible." Wrongdoing is, therefore, a consequence of an inaccurate estimate of modes of behavior. It is the inaccurate expectation that certain kinds of things or pleasures will produce happiness. Wrongdoing, then, is the product of ignorance simply because it is done with the hope that it will do what it cannot do. Ignorance consists in not knowing that certain behavior cannot produce happiness. It takes a true knowledge of human nature to know what it requires to be happy. It also takes a true knowledge of things and types of behavior to know whether they can fulfill the human requirements for happiness. And it requires knowledge to be able to distinguish between what *appears* to give happiness and what *really* does.

To say, then, that vice is ignorance and is involuntary is to say that no one ever deliberately chooses to damage, disfigure, or destroy his or her human nature. Even when one chooses pain, one does so with the expectation that this pain will lead to virtue, to the fulfillment of human nature, a nature that seeks its own well-being. One always thinks one is acting rightly, but whether one's actions are right depends upon whether they harmonize with true human nature, and this is a matter of true knowledge. Moreover, because Socrates believed that the fundamental structure of human nature is constant, he believed also that certain ways of behaving and, therefore, certain moral values are also constant. This was the basis for his great triumph over the Sophists' skepticism and relativism. Socrates set the direction that moral philosophy would take throughout the history of Western civilization. His thought was modified by Plato, Aristotle, and the Christian theologians, but it remained the dominant intellectual and moral tradition around which other variations developed.

Socrates' Trial and Death   Convinced that the care of the human soul should be one's greatest concern, Socrates spent most of his time examining his own life and the life and thought of other Athenians. While Athens was a secure and powerful democracy under Pericles, Socrates could pursue his calling as a "gadfly" without serious opposition. His relentless quest for the stable and constant moral order underlying people's fitful behavior proved alternately irritating and amusing, giving him the reputation of an intellectual dealing in paradoxes and, worse still, of thinking freely on matters about which many Athenians believed that discussion should be closed. But what Socrates could do without penalty when the economic and military position of Athens was strong he could no longer do in the days of crisis and defeat. His efforts to develop dialectical skill—the skill of raising searching questions about customs in moral, religious, and political behavior—among young men from leading families, had raised suspicions about Socrates earlier, but his actions were not considered a clear and present danger until Athens was at war with Sparta.

A series of events connected with this war eventually led to the trial and sentence of Socrates. One event was the traitorous actions of Alcibiades, whom the Athenians knew was Socrates' pupil. Alcibiades had actually gone to Sparta and had given valuable advice to the Spartans in their war with Athens. Inevitably many Athenians concluded that Socrates must in some way be responsible for what Alcibiades had done. In addition, Socrates found himself in serious disagreement with the Committee of the Senate of Five Hundred, of which he was a member. The issue before them was the case of eight military commanders who were charged with negligence at a naval battle off the islands of Arginusae, a battle that the Athenians won in the end but at the staggering cost of 25 ships and 4,000 men. It was decided that the eight generals involved in this expensive campaign should be brought to trial and that their guilt should be determined not individually but as a group by a single vote. At first the Committee resisted this move, holding it to be a violation of the regular constitutional procedures. But when the prosecutors threatened to add the names of the Committee members to the list of generals, only Socrates stood his ground, and the rest of the Committee capitulated. The generals were then found guilty, and the six of them who were in custody were immediately put to death. These events occurred in 406 B.C.; in 404 B.C., with the fall of Athens, Socrates once again found himself in opposition to a formidable group. Under pressure from the Spartan victor, a Commission of Thirty was set up in order to fashion legislation for the new government of Athens. Instead, this group became a violent oligarchy, arbitrarily executing former stalwarts of Pericles' democratic order and taking property for themselves. Within a year, this oligarchy had been removed by force and a democratic order restored. But unfortunately for Socrates, some of the members of the revolutionary oligarchy had been his close friends, particularly Critias and Charmides. This was another occasion of guilt by association, as in the case of Alcibiades, where Socrates was put in the position of being a teacher of traitors. By this time, irritation had developed into distrust, and in 400/399 B.C., Socrates was brought to trial on the charge, as Diogenes Laertius recorded it, "(1) of not worshipping the gods whom the State worships, but introducing new and unfamiliar religious practices; (2) and, further, of corrupting the young. The prosecutor demands the death penalty."

Socrates could have gone into voluntary exile upon hearing the charges against him. Instead, he remained in Athens and defended himself before a court whose jury numbered about five hundred. His defense, as recorded in Plato's *Apology*, is a brilliant defense of his intellectual activities and a powerful exposure of his accusers' motives and the inadequacy of the grounds for their charges. He made much of his devotion to Athens, including references to his military service and his actions in upholding constitutional procedures in the trial of the generals. His defense is a model of forceful argument, resting wholly upon a recitation of facts and upon the requirements of rational discourse. When he was found guilty, he was given the opportunity to suggest his own sentence. Being convinced not only of his innocence but of the great value his mode of life and teachings had been to Athens, he proposed that Athens should reward him by giving him what he deserved. Comparing himself to someone "who has won victory at the Olympic games with his horse or chariots," Socrates said, "such a man only makes you seem happy, but I make you really happy." Therefore, he said, his reward should be "public maintenance in the prytaneum," an honor bestowed upon eminent Athenians, generals, Olympian winners, and other outstanding men. Affronted by his arrogance, the jury sentenced him to death.

His friends tried to the end to make possible his escape, but Socrates would have none of it. Just as he refused to play on the emotions of the jury by calling attention to his wife and young children, so now he was not impressed by Crito's plea that he should think of his children. How could he undo all he had taught others and unmake his conviction that he must never play fast and loose with the truth? Socrates was convinced that to escape would be to defy and thereby injure Athens and its procedures of law. That would be to strike at the wrong target. The laws were not responsible for his trial and sentence; it was his accusers, Anytus and Meletus, who were at fault. Accordingly, he confirmed his respect for the laws and the procedures by complying with the court's sentence.

Describing Socrates' last moments after he drank the poisonous potion, Plato writes in his *Phaedo* that "Socrates felt himself, and said that when it came to his heart, he should be gone. He was already growing cold...and spoke for the last time. Crito, he said, I owe a cock to Asclepius; do not forget to pay it....Such was the end, Echecrates, of our friend, a man, I think, who was, of all the men of his time, the best, the wisest and the most just."

3

Plato

In Plato, the Greek genius was realized with extraordinary completeness. So powerful was Plato's comprehensive treatment of knowledge that his philosophy became the most influential strand in the history of Western thought. Unlike his predecessors, who focused upon single main problems, Plato brought together all the major concerns of human thought into a coherent organization of knowledge. The earliest philosophers, the Milesians, were concerned chiefly with the constitution of physical nature, not with the foundations of morality. Similarly, the Eleatic philosophers Parmenides and Zeno were interested chiefly in arguing that reality consists of a changeless, single reality, the One. Heraclitus and the Pythagoreans, on the other hand, described reality as always changing, full of flux, and consisting of a vast multitude of different things. Socrates and the Sophists showed less interest in physical nature and, instead, steered philosophy into the arena of morality. Plato's great influence stems from the manner in which he brought all these diverse philosophic concerns into a unified system of thought.

Plato began with the common-sense recognition of the variety of things that pass in parade before our view. To make sense out of these many things, he realized that the mind must discover reasons for the way these physical things behave. This pursuit led him to a world behind the world of things. It was the world of thought and Ideas, the world of science. Physical things, he thought, lead the mind to the science of physics. To understand the science of physics requires, moreover, the intellectual grasp of mathematics, for to understand the behavior of things—not these particular things only, but any and all such things under similar circumstances—the mind must discover the principles and rules that things in their behavior obey. The model for thinking about such rules is the model of mathematics, for mathematics is a way of thinking without being tied to particulars.

Inevitably, mathematics led Plato into the field of metaphysics. If physics is made possible by the mind's emancipation from the world of appearances, by the mind's operation in the world of Ideas "above" or "behind" the world of visible things, one cannot avoid the question whether this world of Ideas *exists* or is *real*. Indeed, Plato was to argue in time that, contrary to common sense, it was this world of Ideas and not the visible world of actual things that is most real, that the Idea *Two*, for example, has a timeless quality, whereas two apples disappear.

At this point, Plato argued that the reason for disagreements among people concerning truth was that they confused these two worlds; only the world of timeless Ideas could produce true knowledge, whereas the world of appearances could produce only opinion. Here Plato followed his great master Socrates in repudiating the skepticism of the Sophists, whose denial that true knowledge can be attained about anything would have made science impossible. Similarly, Plato rejected the moral relativism of the Sophists, arguing that his theory of knowledge formed a reliable bridge from metaphysics to ethics. If, that is, we have knowledge about the true nature of things, of reality, including the true nature of humankind, we have also the basic clue to how humans should behave. Human behavior is at once a personal matter, a matter involving one's compatriots, and, finally, a matter raising the question of one's ultimate destiny. For Plato, these three facets of human concern were to be dealt with through the separate but related disciplines of ethics, politics, and religion. When we consider, then, that Plato rather systematically brought together his theory of knowledge, physics, metaphysics, ethics, politics, and religion, as well as a theory of art, we can all the more appreciate how it was that, along with Aristotle, he shaped the minds of Western civilization, that the moral philosophy and the scientific tradition of Western civilization are essentially the achievements of Plato's thought.

Plato was born in Athens in 428/27 B.C., one year after the death of Pericles and when Socrates was about forty-two years old. Athenian culture was flourishing, and as Plato's family was one of the most distinguished in Athens, his early training must have included the rich ingredients of that culture in the arts, politics, and philosophy. His father traced his lineage to the old kings of Athens and before them to the god Poseidon, while his mother, Perictione, was the sister of Charmides and the cousin of Critias, both of whom were leading personalities in the short-lived oligarchy which followed the fall of Athens in the Peloponnesian War. When his father died, early in Plato's childhood, his mother married Pyrilampes, who had been a close friend of Pericles. Such close ties with eminent public figures had long distinguished Plato's family, especially on his mother's side, where an early relative had been a friend of the great giver of law, Solon, and another distant member of the family was the archon, or the highest magistrate, in 644 B.C.

In such a family atmosphere, it was inevitable that Plato would learn much about public life and develop at an early age a sense of responsibility for public political service. But Plato's attitude toward Athenian democracy was also influenced by what he saw during the last stages of the Peloponnesian War. He saw the inability of this democracy to produce great leaders and saw also the way it treated one of its greatest citizens, Socrates. Plato was present at Socrates' trial and had expressed willingness to guarantee payment of his fine. The collapse of Athens and the execution of his master, Socrates, could well have led Plato to despair of democracy and to begin formulating a new conception of political leadership in which authority and knowledge are appropriately combined. Plato had concluded that as in the case of a ship, where the pilot's authority rests upon knowledge of navigation, so also the ship of state should be piloted by one who has adequate knowledge, a theme which he developed at length in his *Republic*.

Plato was aware of the various modes of philosophy circulating in Athens, but the decisive influence in the formation of his thought was the life and teaching of Socrates. Plato had known Socrates from his early youth, and from his friendship with him had discovered a new meaning for philosophy. Philosophy was for Plato, as for Socrates, not merely a specialized and technical activity but a way of life. Since philosophy would range over all questions both in science and in the realm of human behavior, it would require not only intellectual ability but also certain moral qualities that one associates with the pursuit of truth and of goodness. The purpose of relating all branches of knowledge was, for Plato, to enable people to understand how they fit into the scheme of the universe. Ultimately, by philosophic activity, by the continuous and passionate exercise of the mind, people could relate themselves to the world and also achieve an inner integrity of all their powers and capacities.

Plato did not assume that he had discovered perfect knowledge or absolute truth, any more than Socrates had. What he was certain about was that the surest way of going after knowledge is the dialectic method, the method of dialogue in which a premise or hypothesis is continuously subjected to counterargument. This was Socrates' method, and life. With genuine humility and intellectual receptivity, Socrates pursued an unending quest for just the right way to understand and adjust to those conditions that alone could produce the good life. Though he really never had "pupils," he, nevertheless, became the model for Plato's philosophic life. But whereas Socrates wrote nothing, Plato became a prolific writer. Moreover, while Plato preserved Socrates' dialectic method by casting his writings into dialogue form, he embellished Socrates'

Plato conversing with a student *(The Bettmann Archive)*

moral concern by building around it his metaphysical system, his philosophy of nature and reality.

At the height of his powers, around 387 B.C., after he had written most of his dialogues and when he was about forty years old, Plato founded the Academy at Athens. This was, in a sense, the first university to emerge in the history of Western Europe, and for twenty years, Plato administered its affairs as its director. The chief aim of the Academy was to pursue scientific knowledge through original research. Although Plato was particularly concerned with educating future leaders, he was convinced that their education must consist of rigorous intellectual activity, by which he meant scientific study, including mathematics, astronomy, and harmonics.

The scientific emphasis at the Academy was in sharp contrast to the activities of Plato's contemporary Isocrates, who also engaged in training young men for public life. Isocrates had little use for science, holding that pure research had no practical value or humanistic interest. Instead, he set out to teach techniques of clear and effective expression and persuasion, developing in his students the ability to expound dominant opinions or some particular point of view. But Plato put mathematics into the center of his curriculum, arguing that the best preparation for those who will wield political power is the disinterested pursuit of truth or scientific knowledge. Here the mind is trained to cut through opinion and emotion and, by hard thinking, to confront the facts of reality and to base judgments on knowledge. Plato's emphasis upon rigorous mathematical and scientific study at once repudiated the superficial approach of the Sophists and attracted some of the ablest thinkers to the Academy. A brilliant group of scholars associated with the Academy made significant advances over the mathematical knowledge of the older Pythagoreans, and this activity caused the famous mathematician Eudoxus to bring his own school from Cyzicus to unite with Plato's Academy in Athens.

Plato, it is said, lectured at the Academy without the use of any notes. These lectures were on subjects and ways of treating subjects which were different from what we find in his written *Dialogues*. Plato's lectures were never published because they were never written, although his hearers' notes were circulated. Aristotle entered the Academy in 367 B.C., when he was eighteen years old, and took notes of Plato's lectures. Later, unlike Plato, Aristotle lectured from a written manuscript but never published popular works, which Plato's *Dialogues* were, for the most part, apparently meant to be.

Plato's dialogues number more than twenty—an extensive literary production—and, as mentioned above, most of them were written by the time he had founded the Academy, that is, by the time he was around forty years old. These include, first, a group of early writings, usually called Socratic dialogues because of their preoccupation with ethics, consisting of the *Apology, Crito, Charmides, Laches, Euthyphro, Euthydemus, Cratylus, Protagoras,* and *Gorgias*; the second, or middle, group in which the theory of Ideas and metaphysical doctrines are expounded include the *Meno, Symposium, Phaedo, Republic,* and *Phaedrus*. Later in life, Plato wrote some more technical dialogues dealing with the structure of nature and representing at once the views of one who has had much time to reflect on problems and a mood of deepening religious conviction, these dialogues being the *Theaetetus, Parmenides, Sophist, Statesman, Philebus, Timaeus,* and the *Laws*.

Although the execution of Socrates had deeply disillusioned Plato about politics to the extent of diverting him personally from an active life of public service, Plato nevertheless continued to teach that rigorous knowledge must be the proper training of the ruler. He gained a wide reputation for this view and was invited to Syracuse, a place he traveled to at least three times, to give instruction to a young tyrant, Dionysius II. His efforts did not meet with success since his student's education was started too late and his character was too weak. Plato continued to write in his ripe years, and while still active in the Academy, died in 348/47 B.C. at the age of eighty.

Plato's complete works constitute a full system of philosophy. But Plato did not himself organize his thoughts into such an explicit system, for to him system building seemed artificial. Although his many dialogues do contain the elements of a full system, there is no one work to which we can go to find a schematic arrangement of his thought. Plato wanted to preserve the freedom of his mind so that he could restate his ideas if new insights came to him. He never closed out future discussion of any subject just because he had once written about it. Accordingly, his dialogues reflect his intellectual development and display changes in emphasis and insight. Still, certain clear topics and unique ways of treating them emerge from Plato's works, and to deal with Plato's philosophy we turn now to some of these major topics.

PLATO'S THEORY OF KNOWLEDGE

Plato described how the human mind achieves knowledge, and indicated what knowledge consists of, by means of (1) his allegory of the *Cave*, (2) his metaphor of the *Divided Line*, and (3) his doctrine of the *Forms*.

The Cave Plato asks us to imagine some men living in a large cave where from childhood they have been chained by the leg and by the neck so that they cannot move. Because they cannot even turn their heads, they can only see what is in front of them. Behind them is an elevation that rises abruptly from the level where the prisoners are seated. On this elevation there are other persons walking back and forth carrying artificial objects, including the figures of animals and human beings made out of wood and stone and various other materials. Behind these walking persons is a fire, and farther back still is the entrance to the cave. The chained prisoners can look only forward against the wall at the end of the cave and can see neither each other nor the moving persons nor the fire behind them. All that the prisoners can ever see is the shadows on the wall in front of them, which are projected as persons walk in front of the fire. They never see the objects or the men carrying them, nor are they aware that the shadows are shadows of other things. When they see a shadow and hear a person's voice echo from the wall, they assume that the sound is coming from the shadow, since they are not aware of the existence of anything else. These prisoners, then, recognize as reality only the shadows formed on the wall.

What would happen, asks Plato, if one of these prisoners were released from his chains, were forced to stand up, turn around, and walk with eyes lifted up toward the light of the fire? All of his movements would be exceedingly painful. Suppose he were forced to look at the objects being carried, the shadows of which he had become accustomed to seeing on the wall. Would he not find these actual objects less congenial to his eyes, and less meaningful, than the shadows? And would not his eyes ache if he looked straight at the light from the fire itself? At this point he would undoubtedly try to escape from his liberator and turn back to the things he could see with clarity, being convinced that the shadows were clearer than the objects he was forced to look at in the firelight.

Suppose this prisoner could not turn back, but was instead dragged forcibly up the steep and rough passage to the mouth of the cave and released only after he had been brought out into the sunlight. The impact of the radiance of the sun upon his eyes would be so painful that he would be unable to see any of the things that he was now told were real. It would take some time before his eyes became accustomed to the world outside the cave. He would first of all recognize some shadows and would feel at home with them. If it were the shadow of a man, he would have seen that shape before as it appeared on the wall of the cave. Next, he would see the reflections of men and things in the water, and this would represent a major advance in his knowledge, for what he once knew only as a solid dark blur would now be seen in more precise detail of line and color. A flower makes a shadow which gives very little, if any, indication of what a flower really looks like, but its image as reflected in the water provides the eyes with a clearer vision of each petal and its various colors. In time, he would see the flower itself. As he lifted his eyes skyward, he would find it easier at first to look at the heavenly bodies at night, looking at the moon and the stars instead of at the sun in daytime. Finally, he would look right at the sun in its natural positions in the sky and not at its reflection from or through anything else.

This extraordinary experience would gradually lead this liberated prisoner to conclude that the sun is what makes things visible. It is the sun, too, that accounts for the seasons of the year, and for that reason the sun is the cause of life in the Spring. Now he would understand what he and his fellow prisoners saw on the wall, how shadows and reflections differ from things as they really are in the visible world, and that without the sun there would be no visible world.

How would such a person feel about his previous life in the cave? He would recall what he and his fellow prisoners there took to be wisdom, how they had a practice of honoring and commending each other, giving prizes to the one who had the sharpest eye for the passing shadows and the best memory for the order in which they followed each other so that he could make the best guess as to which shadow would come next. Would the released prisoner still think such prizes were worth having, and would he envy the men who received honors in the cave? Instead of envy he would have only sorrow and pity for them.

If he went back to his former seat in the cave, he would at first have great difficulty, for going suddenly from daylight into the cave would fill his eyes with darkness. He could not, under these circumstances, compete very effectively with the other prisoners in making out the shadows on the wall. While his eye-sight was still dim and unsteady, those who had their permanent residence in the darkness could win every round of competition with him. They would at first find this situation very amusing and would taunt him by saying that his sight was perfectly all right before he went up out of the cave and that now he has returned with his sight ruined. Their conclusion would be that it is not worth trying to go up out of the cave. Indeed, says Plato, "if they could lay hands on the man who was trying to set them free and lead them up, they would kill him."

Most of humanity, this allegory would suggest, dwell in the darkness of the cave. They have oriented their thoughts around the blurred world of shad-ows. It is the function of *education* to lead people out of the cave into the world of light. Education is not simply a matter of putting knowledge into a person's soul that does not possess it, any more than vision is putting sight into blind eyes. Knowledge is like vision in that it requires an organ capable of receiving it. Just as the prisoner had to turn his whole body around in order that his eyes could see the light instead of the darkness, so also it is necessary for the entire soul to turn away from the deceptive world of change and appetite that causes a blindness of the soul. Education, then, is a matter of *conversion,* a complete turning around from the world of appearance to the world of reality. "The con-version of the soul," says Plato, is "not to put the power of sight in the soul's eye, which already has it, but to insure that, instead of looking in the wrong direction, it is turned the way it ought to be." But looking in the right direction does not come easily. Even the "noblest natures" do not always want to look that way, and so Plato says that the rulers must "bring compulsion to bear" upon them to ascend upward from darkness to light. Similarly, when those who have been liberated from the cave achieve the highest knowledge, they must not be allowed to remain in the higher world of contemplation, but must be made to come back down into the cave and take part in the life and labors of the prisoners.

Arguing, as Plato did, that there are these two worlds, the dark world of the cave and bright world of light, was his way of rejecting the skepticism of the Sophists. For Plato knowledge was not only possible, but it was virtually infallible. What made knowledge infallible was that it was based upon what is most *real.* The dramatic contrast between the shadows, reflections, and the actual objects was for Plato the decisive clue to the different degrees to which human beings could be enlightened. Plato saw the counterparts of shadows in all of human life and discourse. Disagreements between people concerning the meaning of justice, for example, were the result of each one's looking at a dif-ferent aspect of the reality of justice. One person might take justice to mean whatever the rulers in fact command the people to do, on the assumption that justice has to do with rules of behavior laid down by the ruler. Just as a shadow bears some relation to the object of which it is the shadow, so this conception of justice has some measure of truth to it, for justice does have some connec-tion with the ruler. But different rulers command different modes of behavior, and there could be no single coherent concept of justice if people's knowledge of justice were derived from the wide variety of examples of it. The Sophists were skeptical about the possibility of true knowledge because they were impressed by the variety and constant change in things, and, they argued, since our knowledge comes from our experience, our knowledge will reflect this variety and will, therefore, be relative to each person. Plato agreed that such knowledge as is based upon our sense experiences would be relative and not absolute, but he would not accept the Sophists' notion that *all* knowledge is relative. "The ignorant," writes Plato, "have no single mark before their eyes at which they must aim in all the conduct of their lives...." If all we could know were the shadows, we could never have reliable knowledge, for these shadows would always change in size and shape depending upon the, to us, unknown motions of the real objects. Plato was convinced that the human mind could discover that "single mark," that "real" object behind all the multitude of shadows, so that the mind could attain true knowledge. There is, he believed, a true Idea of Justice, an Idea that can be blurred by rulers and communities. This line of reasoning lay behind Plato's distinction between the world of sense and the world of thought, between the visible world and the intelligible world. Whereas the allegory of the Cave illustrates these distinctions in dramatic terms, Plato's metaphor of the Divided Line sets forth the stages or levels of knowledge in more systematic form.

The Divided Line   In the process of discovering true knowledge, the mind, says Plato, moves through four stages of development. At each stage, there is a parallel between the kind of object presented to the mind and the kind of thought this object makes possible. These objects and their parallel modes of cognition can be diagramed as follows:

	Objects	y	Modes of Thought	
[The Good] Intelligible World	The Good [Forms]		Knowledge	Knowledge
	Mathematical Objects		Thinking	
[The Sun] Visible World	Things		Belief	Opinion
	Images		Imagining	

x

The vertical line from x to y is a continuous one, suggesting that there is some degree of knowledge at every point. But as the line passes through the lowest forms of reality to the highest, there is a parallel progression from the lowest degree of truth to the highest. The line is divided, first of all, into two unequal parts. The upper and larger part represents the intelligible world and the smaller, lower part the visible world. This unequal division symbolizes the lower degree of reality and truth found in the visible world as compared with the greater reality and truth in the intelligible world. Each of these parts is then subdivided in the same proportion as the whole line, producing four parts, each one representing a clearer and more certain mode of thought than the one below. Recalling the allegory of the Cave, we can think of this line as beginning in the dark and shadowy world at x and moving up to the bright light at y. Going from x to y represents a continuous process of the mind's enlightenment. The objects presented to the mind at each level are not four different kinds of real objects: rather, they represent four different ways of looking at the same object.

Imagining   The most superficial form of mental activity is found at the lowest level of the line. Here the mind confronts images, or the least amount of reality. The word *imagining* could, of course, mean the activity of penetrating beyond the mere appearances of things to their deeper reality. But here Plato means by *imagining* simply the sense experience of appearances wherein these appearances are taken as true reality. An obvious example is a shadow, which can be mistaken for something real. Actually, the shadow *is* something real; it is a real shadow. But what makes imagining the lowest form of knowing is that at this stage the mind does not know that it *is* a shadow or an image that it has confronted. If a person knew that it was a shadow, she would not be in the state of imagining or illusion. The prisoners in the cave were trapped in the deepest ignorance because they were unaware that they were seeing shadows.

Besides shadows, there are other kinds of images which Plato considered deceptive. These are the images fashioned by the artist and the poet. The artist presents images that are at least two steps removed from true reality. Suppose an artist paints a portrait of Socrates. Socrates represents a specific or concrete version of the Ideal Man. Moreover, the portrait represents only the artist's own view of Socrates. The three levels of reality here are, then, (1) the Idea of Man, (2) the embodiment of this Idea in Socrates, and (3) the image of Socrates as represented on canvas. Plato's criticism of art is that it produces images that, in turn, stimulate illusory ideas in the observer. Again, it is when the image is taken as a perfect version of something real that illusion is produced. For the most part, we know that an artist puts on canvas his or her own way of seeing a subject. Still, artistic images do shape thoughts, and if people restrict their understanding of things to these images with all their distortions and exaggerations, they will certainly lack an understanding of things as they really are.

What concerned Plato most were the images fashioned by the art of using words. Poetry and rhetoric were for him the most serious sources of illusion. Words have the power of creating images before the mind, and the poet and rhetorician have great skill in using words to create such images. Plato was particularly critical of the Sophists, whose influence came from this very skill in the use of words. They could make either side of an argument *seem* as good as the other. In a discussion of justice, for example, the Sophist, or any other artist with words, could create the same distortion that we found in the portrait. Justice as understood in Athens could be taken by a pleader and distorted in favor of a special client. This special pleader's version of justice could be a distortion of the Athenian view; also, the Athenian view might very well be a distortion of the Ideal Justice. If we heard only the special pleader's version of justice, we would be at least twice removed from the true Idea of Justice. There is no illusion if the special pleader's distortions of Athenian justice are recognized as such. Moreover, it would be possible for some citizens to recognize that Athenian law itself represented some deviations from the true concept of Justice. Everything depends upon what the mind has access to as its object. The special pleader does present some degree of truth about Justice but in a very distorted form, just as a shadow gives some evidence of some reality. Imagining, however, implies that a person is not aware of observing an image, and, therefore, imagining amounts to illusion and ignorance.

Belief   The next stage after imagining is belief. It may strike one as strange that Plato should use the world *believing* instead of *knowing* to describe the state of mind induced by seeing actual objects. We tend to feel a strong sense of certainty when we observe visible and tangible things. Still, for Plato, seeing constitutes only believing, because visible objects depend upon their context for many of their characteristics. There is, then, a degree of certainty that seeing gives us, but this is not absolute certainty. If the water of the Mediterranean looks blue from the shore but turns out to be clear when taken from the sea, one's certainty about its color or composition is at least open to question. That all bodies have weight because we see them fall may seem a certainty, but this testimony of our vision must also be adjusted to the fact of the weightlessness of bodies in space at certain altitudes. Plato therefore says that believing, even if it is based upon seeing, is still in the stage of opinion. The state of mind produced by visible objects is clearly on a level higher than imagining, because it is based upon a higher form of reality. But although actual things possess greater reality than their shadows, they do not by themselves give us all the knowledge we want to have about them. Again, justice may be seen in a particular context, but to find justice defined in a different way in another culture does raise the question about the true nature of Justice. Whether it be color, weight, or justice, these properties of things and acts are experienced under particular circumstances. For this reason, our knowledge about them is limited to these particular circumstances. But the mind is unsatisfied with this kind of knowledge, knowing that its certainty could very well be shaken if the circumstances were altered. The scientist and the jurist, therefore, do not want to confine their understanding to these particular cases, but look for principles behind the behavior of things.

Thinking   When one moves from believing to thinking, one moves from the visible world to the intelligible world, from the realm of opinion to the realm of knowledge. The state of mind that Plato calls *thinking* is particularly characteristic of the scientist. Scientists deal with visible things but not simply with their vision of them. For them, visible things are symbols of a reality that can be thought but not seen. Plato illustrates this kind of mental activity by referring to the mathematician. Mathematicians engage in the act of "abstraction," of drawing out from the visible thing what that thing symbolizes. When mathematicians see the diagram of a triangle, they think about *triangularity* or triangle-in-itself. They distinguish between the *visible* triangle and the *intelligible* triangle. By using visible symbols, science provides a bridge from the visible to the intelligible world. Science forces one to think, because scientists are always searching for laws or principles. Although scientists may look at a particular object, a triangle or a brain, they go beyond this particular triangle or brain and think about *the* Triangle or *the* Brain. Science requires that we "let go" our senses and rely instead upon our intellects. The mind knows that two and two equal four no matter two of what. It knows also that the angles of an equilateral triangle are all equal, regardless of the size of the triangle. Thinking, therefore, represents the power of the mind to abstract from a visible object that property which is the same in all objects in that class even though each such actual object will have other variable properties: we can, in short, think the Idea "Man" whether we observe small, large, dark, light, young, or old persons.

Thinking is characterized not only by its treatment of visible objects as symbols, but also by reasoning from *hypotheses*. By an hypothesis Plato meant a truth which is taken as self-evident but which depends upon some higher truth: "You know," says Plato, "how students of subjects like geometry and arithmetic begin by postulating odd and even numbers, or the various figures and the three kinds of angle.... These data they take as known, and having adopted them as assumptions, they do not feel called upon to give any account of them to themselves or to anyone else but treat them as self-evident." Using hypotheses, or "starting from these assumptions, they go on until they arrive, by a series of consistent steps, at all the conclusions they set out to investigate." For Plato, then, an hypothesis did not mean what it means to us, namely, a temporary truth. Rather, he meant by it a firm truth but one that is related to a larger context. The special sciences and mathematics treat their subjects as if they were independent truths. All Plato wants to say here is that if we could view all things as they really are, we should discover that all things are related or connected. Thinking or reasoning from hypotheses does give us knowledge of the truth, but it does still bear this limitation, that it isolates some truths from others, thereby leaving the mind still to ask *why* a certain truth is true.

Perfect Intelligence   The mind is never satisfied as long as it must still ask for a fuller explanation of things. But to have perfect knowledge would require that the mind should grasp the relation of everything to everything else, that it should see the unity of the whole of reality. Perfect intelligence represents the mind as completely released from sensible objects. At this level, the mind is dealing directly with the *Forms*. The Forms are those intelligible objects, such as Triangle and "Man," that have been abstracted from the actual objects. The mind is now dealing with these pure Forms without any interference from even the symbolic character of visible objects. Here, also, the mind no longer uses hypotheses, because they represent limited and isolated truths. This highest level of knowledge is approached to the extent that the mind is able to move beyond the restrictions of hypotheses toward the unity of all Forms. It is by the faculty or power of *dialectic* that the mind moves toward its highest goal, for this is the power of seeing at once the relation of all divisions of knowledge to each other. Perfect intelligence therefore means the *synoptic* view of reality and this, for Plato, implies the unity of knowledge.

Plato concludes his discussion of the Divided Line with the summary statement, "now you may take, as corresponding to the four sections, these four states of mind: *intelligence* for the highest, *thinking* for the second, *belief* for the third and for the last *imagining*. These you may arrange as the terms in a proportion, assigning to each a degree of clearness and certainty corresponding to the measure in which their objects possess truth and reality." The highest degree of reality, he argued, was possessed by the *Forms*, as compared with shadows, reflections, and even the visible objects. Just what he meant by the Forms we must now explore in greater detail.

The Platonic Doctrine of Forms or Ideas   Plato's theory of the *Forms* or *Ideas* represents his most significant philosophic contribution. However obscure and unsatisfactory his theory may be to us, it gathers around itself the novel insights that led Plato's philosophy beyond anything that had been thought before him. Basically, the *Forms* or *Ideas* are those changeless, eternal, and nonmaterial essences or patterns of which the actual visible objects we see are only poor copies. There is the Form of *the* Triangle and all the triangles we see are mere copies of that Form. This tentative description of the Forms as nonmaterial realities already indicates what was so novel about this Platonic doctrine: Whereas the pre-Socratic philosophers thought of reality as material stuff of some sort, Plato now designated the nonmaterial Ideas or Forms as the true reality. Similarly, whereas the Sophists thought that all knowledge is relative because the material order, which is all they knew, is constantly shifting and changing, Plato argued that knowledge is absolute because the true object of thought is not the material order but the changeless and eternal order of the Ideas or Forms. Although Socrates anticipated this view by holding that there is an absolute Good, which makes possible our judgments of particular goods, Plato went beyond Socrates' ethical concern by adding to the concept of Good a theory of metaphysics, an explanation of the whole structure of reality and the place of morality in it. Moreover, Plato had fashioned with this theory of Forms a novel explanation of the relation between the One and the many, avoiding Parmenides' conclusion that everything is One and Heraclitus' conclusion that everything is in flux. He was aided by the Pythagorean concept of form as it derived from mathematics. In the end, however, Plato's doctrine of Ideas was something new and became the central concept in all of his philosophy.

The doctrine of Forms represents a serious attempt to explain the nature of existence. We have certain kinds of experiences that raise the question about existence for us. For example, we make judgments about things and behavior, saying about a thing that it is beautiful and about an act that it is good. This suggests that there is somewhere a standard of beauty, which *is* different from the thing we are judging, and that there *is* a standard of good, which is somehow separate from the person or his act that we judge. Moreover, visible things change—they come and go, generate and perish. Their existence is brief. Compared with things, Ideas such as Good and Beautiful seem timeless. They have more *being* than things. Plato concluded, therefore, that the real world is not the visible world but rather the intelligible world. The intelligible world is most real, said Plato, because it consists of the eternal Forms.

There are at least five questions that one might want to ask about the Forms. And although they cannot be answered with precision, the replies to them that are found in his various writings will provide us with Plato's general theory of the Forms.

What Are the Forms? We have already suggested Plato's answer to this question by saying that Forms are eternal patterns of which the objects that we see are only copies. A beautiful person is a copy of Beauty. We can say about a person that she is beautiful because we know the Idea of Beauty and recognize that a person shares more or less in this Idea. In his *Symposium*, Plato suggests that we normally apprehend beauty first of all in a particular object or person. But having discovered beauty in this limited form, we soon "perceive that the beauty of one form is akin to another," and so we move from the beauty of a particular body to the recognition that beauty "in every form is one and the same." The effect of this discovery that all modes of beauty have some similarity is to loosen one's attachment to the beautiful object and to move from the beautiful physical object to the concept of Beauty. When a person discovers this general quality of Beauty, says Plato, "he will abate his violent love of the one, which he will...deem a small thing and will become a lover of all beautiful forms; in the next stage he will consider that the beauty of the mind is more honourable than the beauty of outward form." Then, "drawing towards and contemplating the vast sea of beauty, he will create many fair and noble thoughts and notions in boundless love of wisdom; until on that shore he grows and waxes strong, and at last the vision is revealed to him of a single science, which is the science of beauty everywhere." Plato appears to be saying that beautiful things in their multiplicity point toward a Beauty from which everything else derives its beauty. But this Beauty is not merely a concept: Beauty has objective reality. Beauty is a Form or Idea. Things *become* beautiful: but Beauty always *is*. Accordingly, Beauty has a separate existence from those changing things which move in and out of Beauty.

In the *Republic*, Plato shows that the true philosopher is concerned to know the essential nature of things. When he asks what is justice or beauty, he does not want examples of just and beautiful things. He wants to know what makes these things just and beautiful. The difference between opinion and knowledge is just this, that those who are at the level of opinion can recognize a just act but cannot tell you why it is just. They do not know the essence of Justice, which the particular act shares. Knowledge is not concerned simply with passing facts and appearances, with the realm of *becoming*. Knowledge seeks what truly *is*: its concern is with *Being*. What really is, what has Being, is the essential nature of things: these *essences*, such as Beauty and Goodness, which make it possible for us to judge things as good or beautiful, these are eternal Forms or Ideas.

It would seem that besides the Forms of Beauty and Goodness, there would be many other Forms. Plato speaks of the Ideal Bed of which the beds we see are mere copies. But this raises the question whether there are as many Forms as there are essences or essential natures. Although Plato is not sure that there are Ideas or Forms of dog, water, and other things, he indicates in the *Parmenides* that there are "certainly not" Ideas of mud and dirt. Clearly, if there were Forms behind all classifications of things, there would have to be a duplicate world. These difficulties increase as one tries to specify how many and which Forms there are. Nevertheless, what Plato means by the Forms is clear enough, for he considers them to be the essential archetypes of things, having an eternal existence, apprehended by the mind and not the senses, for it is the mind that beholds "real existence, colorless, formless and intangible, visible only to the intelligence."

Where Do the Forms Exist?   If the Forms are truly real, if they embody Being, it would seem that they must be someplace. But how can the Forms, which are immaterial, have a location? It could hardly be said that they are spatially located. Plato's clearest suggestion on this problem is that the Forms are "separate" from concrete things; they exist "apart from" the things we see. To be "separate" or "apart from" must mean simply that the Forms have an independent existence; they persist even though particular things perish. Forms have no dimension, but the question of their location comes up as a consequence of our language, which implies that Forms, being something, must be someplace in space. It may be that nothing more can be said about their location than the fact that the Forms have an independent existence. But there are two additional ways in which this is emphasized by Plato. For one thing, in connection with his theory of the preexistence of the soul, he says that the human soul was acquainted with the Forms before it was united with the body. Secondly, in the process of creation, the Demiurge or God used the Forms in fashioning particular things, suggesting that the Forms had an existence prior to their embodiment in things. Furthermore, these Forms seem to have originally existed in the "mind of God" or in the supreme principle of rationality, the One. Aristotle says in his *Metaphysics* that "the Forms are the cause of the essence of all other things, and the One is the cause of the Forms." In our treatment of Plato's metaphor of the Divided Line, we showed how Plato traced the journey of the mind from the lowest level of images to the highest level, where the Idea of the Good contained the perfect vision of *reality*.

Just as the sun in the allegory of the Cave was at once the source of light and life, so also, said Plato, the Idea of the Good is "the universal author of all things beautiful and right, parent of light and of the lord of light in this world, and the source of truth and reason in the other." Whether the Forms truly exist in the mind of God is a question, but that the Forms are the agency through which the principle of reason operates in the universe seems to be just what Plato means.

What Is the Relation of Forms to Things? A Form can be related to a thing in three ways, which may be three ways of saying the same thing. First, the Form is the *cause* of the essence of a thing. Next, a thing may be said to *participate* in a Form. And, finally, a thing may be said to imitate or *copy* a Form. In each case, Plato implies that although the Form is separate from the thing, that the Idea of Man is different from Socrates, still, every concrete or actual thing in some way owes its existence to a Form, in some degree participates in the perfect model of the class of which it is a member, and is in some measure an imitation or copy of the Form. Later on, Aristotle was to argue that form and matter are inseparable and that the only real good or beautiful was found in actual things. But Plato would only allow participation and imitation as the explanation of the relation between things and their Forms. He accentuated this view by saying that it was the Forms through which order was brought into the chaos, indicating the separate reality of form and matter. Aristotle's criticism of Plato's view was formidable, since there seems to be no coherent way of accounting for the existence of the Forms apart from actual things. Still, Plato would ask him what makes it possible to form a judgment about the imperfection of something if the mind does not have access to anything more than the imperfect thing.

What Is the Relation of Forms to Each Other? Plato says that "we can have discourse only through the weaving together of Forms." Thinking and discussion proceed for the most part on a level above particular things. We speak in terms of the essences or universals that things illustrate, so we speak of queens, dogs, and carpenters. These are definitions of things and as such are universals or Forms. To be sure, we also refer to specific things in our experiences, such as dark and beautiful and person, but our language reveals our practice of connecting Forms with Forms. There is the Form Animal and such subclasses of Forms as Man and Horse. Forms are, therefore, related to each other as genus and species. In this way Forms tend to interlock even while retaining their own unity. The Form Animal seems to be present also in the Form Horse, so that one Form partakes of the other. There is therefore a hierachy of Forms representing the structure of reality, of which the visible world is only a reflection. The "lower" one comes in this hierarchy of Forms, the closer one comes to visible things and therefore the *less* universal is one's knowledge, as when one speaks of "red apples." Conversely, the higher one goes, or the more abstract the Form, as when one speaks of Apple in general, the broader one's knowledge. The discourse of science is the most abstract, but for that very reason, because it has achieved such independence from particular cases and particular things, it possesses the highest form of knowledge. The botanist who has proceeded in knowledge from *this rose* to Rose and to Flower has achieved the kind of abstraction or independence from particulars of which Plato was here thinking. This does not mean, however, that Plato thought that all Forms could be related to each other: he only meant to say that every significant statement involves the use of some Forms and that knowledge consists of understanding the relations of the appropriate Forms to each other.

How Do We Know the Forms?   Plato indicates at least three different ways in which the mind discovers the Forms. First there is *recollection:* before it was united with the body, the soul was acquainted with the Forms. People now recollect what their souls knew in their prior state of existence. Visible things remind them of the essences previously known. Education is actually a process of reminiscence. Secondly, people arrive at the knowledge of Forms through the activity of *dialectic*, which is the power of abstracting the essence of things and discovering the relations of all divisions of knowledge to each other. And third, there is the power of *desire*, love (*eros*), which leads people step by step, as Plato described in the *Symposium*, from the beautiful object to the beautiful thought and then to the very essence of Beauty itself.

The doctrine of Forms leaves many questions as well as problems. Plato's language gives the impression that there are two distinct worlds, but the relationship of these worlds is not easily conceived. Nor is the relation between Forms and their corresponding objects as clear as one would wish. Still, his argument is highly suggestive, particularly as he seeks to account for our ability to make judgments of value. To say a thing is better or worse implies some standard, which obviously is not there as such in the thing being evaluated. The doctrine of the Forms also makes possible scientific knowledge, for clearly the scientist has "let go" of actual visible particulars and deals with essences or universals, that is, with "laws." The scientist formulates "laws," and these laws tell us something about *all* things, not only the immediate and particular things. Although this whole doctrine of the Forms rests upon Plato's metaphysical views, that ultimate reality is nonmaterial, it goes a long way toward explaining the more simple fact of how it is possible for us to have ordinary conversation. Any discourse between human beings, it would seem, illustrates our independence from particular things. Conversation, Plato would say, is the clue that leads us to the Forms, for conversation involves more than seeing. The eye can see only the particular thing, but the thinking that animates conversation departs from specific things as thought "sees" the universal, the Form. There is, in the end, a stubborn lure in Plato's theory, even though it ends inconclusively.

PLATO'S MORAL PHILOSOPHY

There is a natural progression from Plato's theory of Forms to his philosophy of ethics. If one can be deceived by appearances in the natural physical world, one can be equally deceived by appearances in the moral realm. The kind of knowledge that helps one to distinguish between shadows, reflections, and real objects in the visible world is just the kind of knowledge that we need to discriminate between the shadows and reflections of the genuinely good life. Plato believed that just as there could be no science of physics if our knowledge were limited to visible things, so also there could be no knowledge of a universal Idea of Good if we were limited to the experiences we have of particular cultures. The well-known skepticism of the Sophists illustrated to both Socrates and Plato this connection between knowledge and morality. For the Sophists, believing that all knowledge is relative, denied that people discover any stable and universal moral standards. Their skepticism led the Sophists to some inevitable conclusions regarding morality, namely (1) that moral rules are fashioned deliberately by each community and have relevance and authority only for the people in that place; (2) that moral rules are unnatural, that people obey them only because of the pressure of public opinion, and that if their acts could be done in private, even the "good" among us would not follow the rules of morality; (3) that the essence of justice is power, or that "might is right"; and (4) that in answer to the basic question "what is the good life?" one would have to say that it is the life of pleasure. Against this formidable teaching of the Sophists, Plato brought forth the Socratic notion that "knowledge is virtue" and supplied it with a philosophical elaboration the chief ingredients of which were (1) the concept of the *soul* and (2) the theory of *virtue* as function.

Concept of the Soul   In the *Republic*, Plato describes the soul as having three parts, which he calls *reason, spirit,* and *appetite.* He derived this tripartite conception of the soul from the common experience of internal confusion and conflict that all humans share. When he analyzed the nature of this conflict, he discovered that there are three different kinds of activity going on in a person. First, there is an awareness of a goal or a value, and this is the act of reason. Secondly, there is the drive toward action, the spirit, which is neutral at first but responds to the direction of reason. Last, there is the desire for the things of the body, the appetites. What made him ascribe these activities to the soul was his assumption that the soul is the principle of life and movement. The body by itself is inanimate, and, therefore, when it acts or moves, it must be moved by the principle of life, the soul. That the soul has three parts followed, Plato thought, from the fact that people's internal conflict indicated different springs of action at work. The reason could suggest a goal for behavior only to be overcome by sensual appetite, and the power of the spirit could be pulled in either direction by these sensual desires. Plato illustrated this human condition by his striking figures in the *Phaedrus*, where he portrays the charioteer driving two horses. One horse, says Plato, is good, "needs no touch of the whip, but is guided by word and admonition only." The other is bad, "the mate of insolence and pride... hardly yielding to whip and spur." Though the charioteer has a clear vision of where to go and the good horse is on course, the bad horse "plunges and runs away, giving all manner of trouble to his companion and the charioteer...."

The spectacle of horses moving in opposite directions and the charioteer standing helpless as his commands go unheeded strikes the imagination with particular force because it exhibits so clearly the breakdown of order. The charioteer, by being what he is, namely, the one who holds the reins, has the duty, the right, the function to guide and control the horses. In the same way, the rational part of the soul has the right to rule the spirited and appetitive parts. To be sure, the charioteer cannot get anywhere without the two horses, and for this reason these three are linked together and must work together to achieve their goals. The rational part of the soul has this same sort of relation to its other parts, for the powers of appetite and spirit are indispensable to life itself. Reason works with and upon spirit and appetite, and these two also move and affect the reason. But the relation of reason to spirit and appetite is determined by what reason is: namely, a goal-seeking and measuring faculty. Of course, the passions also engage in goal seeking, for they constantly seek the goal of pleasure. Pleasure is a legitimate goal of life, but the passions, being simply drives toward the things that give pleasure, are incapable of distinguishing between objects that provide higher or longer-lasting pleasure and those that only appear to provide these pleasures.

The peculiar function of the rational part of the soul is to seek the true goal of human life, and it does this by evaluating things according to their true nature. Although the passions or appetites might lead us into a world of fantasy and deceive us into believing that certain kinds of pleasures will bring us happiness, it is the unique role of reason to penetrate the world of fantasy, to discover the true world and thereby direct the passions to objects of love that are capable of producing true pleasure and true happiness. Unhappiness and the general disorder of the human soul are the result of man's confusing appearance with reality. This confusion occurs chiefly when the passions override the reason. This is why Plato argued, as Socrates had before him, that moral evil is the result of *ignorance*. Just as there can be order between the charioteer and the horses only if the charioteer is in control, so also with the human soul—it can achieve order and peace only if the rational part is in control of the spirit and appetites.

Throughout his account of the moral experience of human beings, Plato alternates between an optimistic view of their capacity for virtue and a rather negative opinion about whether they will fulfill their potentiality for virtue. This double attitude rests upon Plato's theory of moral evil. We have already said that evil or vice is caused by ignorance, by false knowledge. False knowledge occurs when the passions influence the reason to think that what appears to bring happiness will do so, although in reality it cannot. When the appetites thus overcome the reason, the unity of the soul is adversely affected. While there is still a unity, this new unity of the soul is inverted, since now the reason is subordinated to the appetites and has thereby lost its rightful place. What makes it possible for this disordered unity to occur, or what makes false knowledge possible? In short, what is the cause of moral evil?

The Cause of Evil: Ignorance or Forgetfulness

The cause of evil is discovered in the very nature of the soul and in the relation of the soul to the body. Before it enters the body, says Plato, the soul has a prior existence. As we have seen, the soul has two main parts, the rational and the irrational. This irrational part in turn is made up of two sections, the spirit and the appetites. Each of the two original parts has a different origin. The rational part of the soul is created by the Demiurge out of the same receptacle as the World Soul, whereas the irrational part is created by the celestial gods, who also form the body. Thus, even before it enters the body, the soul is composed of two different kinds of ingredients. In the soul's prior existence, the rational part has a clear vision of the Forms, of truth, though at the same time, the spirit and appetites already, by their very nature, have a tendency to descend. If one asks why it is that the soul descends into a body, Plato says that it is simply the tendency of the irrational part, the part of the soul that is not perfect, to be unruly and to pull the soul toward the earth. For Plato says that "when perfect and fully winged she [the soul] soars upward...whereas the imperfect soul, losing her wings and drooping in her flight at last settles on the solid ground—there, finding a home, she receives an earthly frame...and this composition of soul and body is called a living and mortal creation." The soul "falls," and that is how it comes to be in a body. But the point is that the soul has an unruly and evil nature in its irrational parts even before it enters the body, so that in one sense the cause of evil is present even in the soul's pre-existent state. It is in "heaven" that the soul alternates between seeing the Forms or the truth and "forgetting" this vision, whereupon its decline sets in. The soul has the inherent possibility of disorder, so that when in fact disorder does occur in the soul, the cause of evil is to be located within the soul itself, being the product of ignorance and forgetfulness of the vision of reality. Evil, in this view, is not a positive thing but is rather a characteristic of the soul wherein the soul is "capable" of forgetfulness, and it is those souls only that do forget the truth that in turn descend, being dragged down by the attraction for earthly things. The soul, then, is perfect by nature, but one aspect of its nature is this possibility to lapse into disorder, for the soul also contains the principle of imperfection as do other parts of creation. Upon its entrance into the body, however, the difficulties of the soul are greatly increased.

Plato believed that the body stimulated the irrational part of the soul to overcome the rulership of reason. The soul's entrance into the body, therefore, is a further cause of disorder or the breakdown of the harmony between the various parts of the soul. For one thing, when the soul leaves the realm of the Forms and enters the body, it moves from the realm of the One to the realm of the many. Now the soul is adrift in the bewildering sea of the multiplicity of things and subject to all sorts of errors because of the deceptive nature of these things. In addition, the body stimulates such activities in the irrational part of the soul as the indiscriminate search for pleasure, exaggerating such appetites as hunger, thirst, and the desire to create offspring, which in turn can become lust. In the body the soul experiences sensation, desire, pleasure, and pain as well as fear and anger. There is love, too, for a wide range of objects varying from the simplest morsel that can satisfy some taste to a love of truth or beauty that is pure and eternal. All this suggests that the body acts as a sluggish encumbrance to the soul, that the spirit and appetites of the soul are peculiarly susceptible to the workings of the body. In this way, then, the body disturbs the harmony of the soul, for the body exposes the soul to stimuli that deflect the reason from true knowledge or that prevent the reason from recalling the truth it once knew.

In the world of people, error is perpetuated whenever a society has the wrong values, causing individuals to accept as their own these wrong values. Every society inevitably acts as a teacher of its members, and for this reason its values will become the values of individuals. Moreover, societies tend to perpetuate the evils and errors committed by earlier generations. Plato underscored this notion by suggesting that in addition to such a social transmission of evil, human souls would reappear via a transmigration, bringing into a new body their earlier errors and judgments of value. It is the body, in the last analysis, that accounts for ignorance, rashness, and lust, for the body disturbs that clear working of the reason, spirit, and appetites by exposing the soul to a cascade of sensations.

Looking back upon Plato's account of the human moral condition, we have seen that he begins with a conception of the soul as existing first of all independently of the body. In this state, the soul enjoys a basic harmony between its rational and irrational parts, a harmony wherein the reason controls the spirit and appetites through its knowledge of the truth. But since the irrational part of the soul has the possibility of imperfection, it expresses this possibility by being attracted through its appetites to the lower regions, dragging with it the spirit and reason. Upon entering the body, the original harmony of the parts of the soul is further disrupted, former knowledge is forgotten, and the inertia of the body obstructs the recovery of this knowledge.

Recovering Lost Morality

For Plato, morality consists in the recovery of one's lost inner harmony. It means reversing the process by which the reason has been overcome by the appetites and the stimuli of the body. The reason must regain its control over the irrational parts of the self. Only knowledge can produce virtue because it is ignorance or false knowledge that has produced evil. People always think that whatever they do will in some way give them pleasure and happiness. No one, says Plato, ever knowingly chooses an act that will be harmful to oneself. One may do "wrong" acts, such as murder or lying, and even admit the wrongness of these and other acts, but one always assumes that some benefit will come from them. This is false knowledge, a kind of ignorance, which people must overcome in order to be moral. To say, then, that "knowledge is virtue" means that false knowledge must be replaced with an accurate appraisal of things or acts and their values.

Before one can go from false to true knowledge, one must somehow become aware that one is in a state of ignorance. It is as if one must be awakened from a "sleep of ignorance." One can be awakened by something that is happening within one or by something external to one or by someone else. Similarly, with regard to knowledge and particularly moral knowledge, human awakening works in these two ways. Assuming, as Plato does, that knowledge is lodged deeply in the mind's memory, this latent knowledge will from time to time come to the surface of consciousness. What the soul once knew is raised to present awareness by the process of *recollection.* Recollection begins first of all when the mind experiences difficulties with the seeming contradictions of sense experience. As one tries to make sense out of the multiplicity of things, one begins to go "beyond" the things themselves to ideas, and this action of the mind is set in motion by one's experience of a problem that needs to be solved. Besides this internal source of awakening, there is Plato's notion of the external agent. In his allegory of the Cave, Plato depicted how men moved from darkness to light, from ignorance to knowledge. But in this allegory he portrays the mood of self-satisfaction among the prisoners; they do not know that they are prisoners, that they are chained by false knowledge and dwell in the darkness of ignorance. Their awakening must come through some external agent. As Plato says, "their release from the chains and the healing of their unwisdom" is brought about by their being "forced suddenly to stand up, turn . . . and walk with eyes lifted to the light." That is, someone must break off the prisoner's chains and turn him around. Then, having been forcibly released, he can be led step by step out of the cave.

Socrates, with the power of his irony and the persistence of his dialectic method, was one of history's most effective awakeners of people from their sleep of ignorance. But besides awakening one, or breaking off his chains, the effective teacher must turn the prisoner around so that he will shift his gaze from shadows to the real world. As we have already noticed, the liberated prisoner will move from shadows to actual objects, to mathematical objects, and finally to a knowledge of the Good. Along this arduous trek, he passes through the realm of opinion, where imagining and belief are the modes of knowing, until he crosses over the divide into the intelligible world, where thinking and true knowing are achieved. As the mind moves progressively from the lower to the higher levels of knowledge, it recalls more of what it once knew and what it must know to achieve inner harmony. One's moral development parallels one's intellectual ascent, for one's growing knowledge intensifies one's love for Truth, Beauty, and Goodness. Inevitably, one's behavior begins to respond to one's expanded knowledge. As the liberated prisoner reflects upon his previous life in the cave, where people won prizes for predicting what shapes the shadows would take upon the wall, he realizes that when he was there he did not even know that these were shadows. Moreover, in light of his new knowledge, those games and prizes seem trivial. Plato was convinced that in real life true knowledge would have the same power to sort out trivial and worthwhile pursuits. Trival pursuits would be incapable of producing a genuine sense of well-being and happiness, whereas worthwhile behavior would lead to such happiness and virtue. Again, virtue means knowledge, a true knowledge of the true consequences of all acts. But to say that knowledge is virtue does not mean that virtue is merely the knowledge of a list of truths. Virtue for Plato has the broader meaning of the fulfillment of a unique function.

Virtue as Fulfillment of Function   Throughout his discussions of morality, Plato viewed the good life as the life of inner harmony, of well-being, of happiness. The key words of morality, namely, *virtue* and *goodness,* had been obscured by the Sophists, who thought that each culture could give these words whatever meanings it wished. For Plato, however, goodness and virtue were intimately connected with the mode of behavior that produced well-being and harmony. For him, harmony could be achieved only if the parts of the soul were doing what the nature of each required that it do. Each part of the soul has a special function and, says Plato, "a thing's function is the work that it alone can do, or can do better than anything else." Here Plato wanted to show that virtue is not a matter of custom or opinion but is rather grounded in the very nature of the soul. It is the very nature of reason to know and to direct the spirit and appetites. Reason has a function, and reason is good only when it is acting as reason should. Clearly, one's reason is not fulfilling its function if it is pushed around by passion. At the same time, spirit has a function, and so do the appetites, and the good life is achieved only when every part is fulfilling its function.

Plato frequently compared the good life to the efficient functioning of things. A knife is good, he said, when it cuts efficiently, that is, when it fulfills its function. We say of physicians that they are good physicians when they fulfill the function of doctoring. Plato then asks, "Has the soul a function that can be performed by nothing else?" Physicians' function is the art of doctoring and musicians, in their own way, engage in an art. Living, said Plato, is likewise an art, and the soul's unique function is the art of living. Comparing the art of music with the art of living, Plato saw a close parallel, for in both cases the art consists of recognizing and obeying the requirements of limit and measure. When musicians tune their instruments, they know that each string should be tightened just so much, no more and no less, for each string has its specific pitch. Musicians' art consists, therefore, in acknowledging the limit beyond which a string should not be tightened and, in playing their instruments, observing the "measure" between intervals. In a similar way, sculptors must be ruled by a vivid awareness of measure and limit, for as they work with their mallet and chisel, they must regulate the force of each stroke by the form they want to accomplish. Their strokes will be heavy as they begin to clear away the larger sections of marble, but as they work around the head of the statue they must have a clear vision of the limits beyond which their chisels must not go, and their strokes must be gentle as they fashion the delicate features of the face.

Similarly, the art of living requires a knowledge of limits and of measure. The soul has various functions, but these functions must operate within the limits set by knowledge or intelligence. Because the soul has various parts, each part will have a special function, and since virtue is the fulfillment of function, there will be as many virtues as there are functions. Corresponding to the three parts of the soul are three virtues, which are achieved when those parts are respectively fulfilling their functions. When, therefore, the appetites are kept within limits and in their measure, avoiding excesses so that they do not usurp the position of the other parts of the soul, this moderation in pleasures and desires leads to the virtue of *temperance*. Also, when the energy of will, which issues from the spirited part of the soul, is kept within limits, avoiding rash or headlong action and becoming instead a trustworthy power in aggressive and defensive behavior, the virtue of *courage* is achieved. Reason, when it remains undisturbed by the onrush of appetites and continues to see the true ideals in spite of the constant changes experienced in daily life, achieves the virtue of *wisdom*. Between these three virtues there are interconnections, for temperance is the rational control of the appetites, and courage is the rational ordering of the spirit. At the same time, each part of the soul has its own function, and when each is in fact fulfilling its special function, a fourth virtue, *justice,* is attained, for justice means giving to each its own due. Justice, then, is the general virtue, which reflects a person's attainment of well-being and inner harmony, which, in turn, is achieved only when every part of the soul is fulfilling its proper function.

By grounding morality in the various functions of the soul, Plato felt that he had overcome the skepticism and relativism of the Sophists. Morality, argued Plato, is not the product of public opinion, nor is right simply a question of might. To be sure, some cultures and some people do in fact believe this to be the case. But Plato would respond by saying that just as the proper function of a hammer is discovered not by opinion but by analyzing the nature and capacities of a hammer, so also the proper behavior for human beings is not prescribed by opinion but is rather required by the very character of the parts of the soul. Although people try to evade the clear limits and measures that the parts of the soul must obey, they cannot avoid the consequences of their acts. Everyone wants to achieve well-being and happiness, and whenever one chooses a mode of behavior, one always assumes that one's act will bring such well-being. But well-being in human nature is the product only of inner harmony, of balance, of a proper order between the parts of the soul. Virtue, therefore, is attained only when each part of the soul is fulfilling its own function. The appetites and the spirit must therefore be subject to the sovereignty of the rational element, which directs one's dynamic capacities and orders the desires and affections according to intelligence.

PLATO'S POLITICAL PHILOSOPHY

In Plato's thought, political theory is closely connected with moral philosophy. Indeed, Plato considered the state as being "man writ large." As justice is the general virtue of the moral person, so also it is justice that characterizes the good society. But Plato does not simply say that there is an interesting or coincidental connection between the just person and the just society. He argues, rather, that there is a structural and natural as well as logical relation between individuals and the state. In the *Republic* Plato argues that the best way to understand the just person is to analyze the nature of the state. "We should begin," he says, "by inquiring what justice means in a state. Then we can go on to look for its counterpart on a smaller scale in the individual." He describes someone who wants to inquire about the just or good person as "a rather short-sighted person told to read an inscription in small letters from some way off. He would think it a godsend if someone pointed out that the same inscription was written up elsewhere on a bigger scale."

The State as Man Writ Large   We have reversed Plato's sequence and have considered the just person first. Although Plato would begin with a study of the state, his whole argument was that the state grows out of the nature of the individual, so that the individual comes logically prior to the state. The state, said Plato, is a natural institution, natural because it reflects the structure of human nature. The origin of the state is a reflection of people's economic needs, for, says Plato, "a state comes into existence because no individual is self-sufficing; we all have many needs." Our many needs require many skills, and no one possesses all the skills needed to produce food, shelter, and clothing, to say nothing of the various arts. There must, therefore, be a division of labor, for "more things will be produced and the work more easily and better done, when every man is set free from all other occupations to do, at the right time, the one thing for which he is naturally fitted." People's needs are not limited to their physical requirements, for their goal is not simply survival but a life higher than an animal's. Still, the healthy state soon becomes affected by a wide range of desires and becomes "swollen up with a whole multitude of callings not ministering to any bare necessity." Now there will be "hunters and fishermen . . . artists in sculpture, painting and music; poets with their attendant train of professional reciters, actors, dancers, producers; and makers of all sorts of household gear, including everything for women's adornment. And we shall want more servants . . . lady's maids, barbers, cooks and confectioners." This desire for more things will soon exhaust the resources of the community and before long, says Plato, "we shall have to cut off a slice of our neighbor's territory . . . and they will want a slice of ours." At this rate, neighbors will inevitably be at war. Wars have their "origin in desires which are the most fruitful source of evils both to individuals and states." With the inevitability of war, it will now be necessary to have "a whole army to go out to battle with any invader, in defence of all this property and of the citizens. . . ." Thus emerge the guardians of the state, who, at first, represent the vigorous and powerful men who will repel the invader and preserve internal order. Now there are two distinct classes of people, those who fill all the crafts—farmers, artisans, and traders—and those who guard the community. From this latter class are then chosen the most highly trained guardians, who will become the rulers of the state and will represent a third and elite class.

The relation between the individual and the state now becomes plain, for the three classes in the state are an extension of the three parts of the soul. The craftsmen or artisans represent as a class the lowest part of the soul, namely, the appetites. The guardians embody the spirited element of the soul. And the highest class, the rulers, represent the rational element. So far, this analysis seems to have logical rigor, for it does not strain the imagination to see the connection (1) between the individual's appetites and the class of workers who satisfy these appetites, (2) between the spirited element in people and the large-scale version of this dynamic force in the military establishment, and (3) between the rational element and the unique function of leadership in the ruler. But Plato was aware that it would not be simple to convince people to accept this system of classes in the state, particularly if they found themselves in a class that might not be the one they would choose if they had the chance.

The assignment of all persons to their respective classes would come only after extensive training, where only those capable of doing so would progress to the higher levels. Although theoretically people would have the opportunity to reach the highest level, they would in fact stop at the level of their natural aptitudes. To make all of them satisfied with their lot, Plato thought it would be necessary to employ a "convenient fiction...a single bold flight of invention." He writes, "I shall try to convince, first the Rulers and the soldiers, and then the whole community, that all that nurture and education which we gave them was only something they seemed to experience as it were in a dream. In reality they were the whole time down inside the earth, being molded...and fashioned...and at last when they were complete, the earth sent them up from her womb into the light of day."

This "noble lie" would also say that the god who fashioned all people "mixed gold in the composition" of those who were to rule and "put silver in the guardians, and iron and brass in the farmers and craftsmen." This would imply that by nature some would be rulers and others craftsmen and that this would provide the basis for a perfectly stratified society. But whereas later societies in Europe assumed that the children born into such a stratified society would stay at the level at which they were born, Plato recognized that children would not always have the same quality as their parents. He said, therefore, that among the injunctions laid by heaven upon the rulers "there is none that needs to be so carefully watched as the mixture of metals in the souls of children. If a child of their own is born with an alloy of iron or brass, they must, without the smallest pity, assign him the station proper to his nature and thrust him out among the farmers and craftsmen." Similarly, if a child with gold or silver is born to craftsmen, "they will promote him according to his value...." Most important of all, Plato thought that everyone should agree on who is to be the ruler and agree also on the reason why the ruler should be obeyed.

The Philosopher-King To Plato it seemed natural that competence should be the qualification for authority. The ruler of the state should be the one who has the peculiar abilities to fulfill that function. Disorder in the state is caused by the same circumstances that produce disorder in the individual, namely, the attempt on the part of the lower elements to usurp the role of the higher faculties. In both the individual and the state the uncontrolled drives of the appetites and spirited action lead to internal anarchy. At both levels, the rational element must be in control. Who should be the captain of a ship—should it be the most "popular" person, or the one who knows the art of navigation? Who should rule the state—should it be someone whose training is in war or commerce? The ruler, said Plato, should be the one who has been fully educated, one who has come to understand the difference between the visible world and the intelligible world, between the realm of opinion and the realm of knowledge, between appearance and reality. The philosopher-king is one whose education, in short, has led him up step by step through the ascending degrees of knowledge of the Divided Line until at last he has a knowledge of the Good, that synoptic vision of the interrelation of all truths to each other.

To reach this point, the philosopher-king will have progressed through many stages of education. By the time he is eighteen years old, he will have had training in literature, music, and elementary mathematics. His literature would be censored, for Plato accused certain poets of outright falsehood and of impious accounts of the behavior of the gods. Music also would be prescribed so that seductive music would be replaced by a more wholesome, martial meter. For the next few years there would be extensive physical and military training, and at age twenty a few would be selected to pursue an advanced course in mathematics. At age thirty, a five-year course in dialectic and moral philosophy would begin. The next fifteen years would be spent gathering practical experience through public service. Finally, at age fifty, the ablest men would reach the highest level of knowledge, the vision of the Good, and would then be ready for the task of governing the state.

The Virtues in the State Whether justice could ever be achieved in a state would depend, Plato thought, upon whether the philosophic element in society could attain dominance. He wrote that "I was forced to say in praise of the correct philosophy that it affords a vantage-point from which we can discern in all cases what is just for communities and for individuals," and he believed that "the human race will not be free of evils until either the stock of those who rightly and truly follow philosophy acquire political authority, or the class who have power in the cities be led by some dispensation of providence to become real philosophers." But justice, as we have already seen, is a general virtue. It means that all parts are fulfilling their special functions and are achieving their respective virtues. Justice in the state will be attained only when and if the three classes fulfill their functions.

As the craftsmen embody the element of the appetites, they will also reflect the virtue of temperance. Temperance is not limited to the craftsmen but applies to all the classes, for it indicates, when it is achieved, the willingness of the lower to be ruled by the higher. Still, temperance applies in a special way to the craftsmen insofar as they are the lowest and must be subordinate to the two higher levels.

The guardians, who defend the state, manifest the virtue of courage. To assure the state that these guardians will always fulfill their function, special training and provision are made for them. Unlike the craftsmen who marry and own property, the guardians will have both property and wives in common. Plato considered these arrangements essential if the guardians were to attain true courage, for courage means knowing what to fear and what not to fear. The only real object of fear for the guardian should be fear of moral evil. He must never fear poverty or privation, and for this reason his mode of life should be isolated from possessions. Although wives will be held in common, this was by no means to suggest any form of promiscuity. On the contrary, Plato believed that men and women were equal in respect to certain things, saying, for example, that "a man and a woman have the same nature if both have a talent for medicine." This being the case, they should both be assigned to the same task whenever they possess the appropriate talent. For this reason, Plato believed that women could be guardians as well as men.

In order to preserve the unity of the members of the class of guardians, the permanent individual family would be abolished, and the whole class would become a single family. Plato's reasoning here was that the guardians must be free not only from the temptation to acquire property, but free also from the temptation to prefer the advantages of one's family to those of the state. Moreover, he thought it rather foolish to take such pains in breeding racing dogs and horses and at the same time rely upon pure chance in producing the guardians and rulers of the state. For this reason, sexual relations would be strictly controlled and would be limited to the special marriage festivals. These festivals would occur at stated times, and the partners, under the illusion that they had been paired by drawing lots, would, instead, be brought together through the careful manipulation of the rulers to ensure the highest eugenic possibilities. Plato does say that "young men who acquit themselves well in war and other duties, should be given, among other rewards and privileges, more liberal opportunities to sleep with a wife," but only for the utilitarian purpose, that "with good excuse, as many as possible of the children may be begotten of such fathers." As soon as children are born to the guardians, they will be taken in charge by officers appointed for that purpose and will be reared in a crèche in the care of nurses living in a special part of the city. Under these circumstances, thought Plato, the guardians would be most likely to fulfill their true function of defending the state without being deflected by other concerns, and would thereby achieve their appropriate virtue of courage.

Justice in the state is therefore just the same as justice in the individual. It is the product of people staying in their place and doing their special task. Justice is the harmony of the virtues of temperance, courage, and wisdom. Since the state is made up of individuals, it will also be necessary for each of these virtues to be attained by each person. For example, even the craftsman must have the virtue of wisdom, not only to keep his appetites in check but also to know that he rightly belongs where he is and must obey the rules. Similarly, as we have seen, the guardians must have sufficient wisdom in order to know what to fear and what not to fear so that they can develop genuine courage. Most important of all, the ruler must come as close as possible to a knowledge of the Good, for the well-being of the state depends upon the ruler's knowledge and character.

The Decline of the Ideal State   If the state is "man writ large," then, said Plato, a state will reflect the kind of people a community has become. What he had in mind was that although human nature is fixed, in that all people possess a tripartite soul, the kind of people they become will depend upon the degree of internal harmony they achieve. The state will therefore reflect these variations in human character. For this reason, Plato argued that "constitutions cannot come out of stocks and stones; they must result from the preponderance of certain characters which draw the rest of the community in their wake. So if there are five forms of government, there must be five kinds of mental constitution among individuals." And these five forms of government are *aristocracy, timocracy, plutocracy, democracy,* and *despotism.*

Plato considered the transition from aristocracy to despotism as a step-by-step decline in the quality of the state corresponding to a gradual deterioration of the moral character of the rulers and the citizens. His ideal state was, of course, aristocracy, in which the rational element embodied in the philosopher-king was supreme and where people's reason controlled their appetites. Plato emphasized that this was only an Ideal, though significant, nevertheless, as a target to aim at. He was deeply disenchanted with politics, particularly because of the way Athens had executed Socrates and had failed to produce consistently good leaders. "As I gazed upon the whirlpool of public life," he said, "[I] saw clearly in regard to all States now existing that without exception their system of government is bad." Still, the norm for a state is *aristocracy,* for in that form is found the proper subordination of all classes.

Even if this Ideal were achieved, however, there would be a possibility for change, since nothing is permanent, and aristocracy would decline first of all into a *timocracy.* This represents a degeneration, for timocracy represents the love of honor, and insofar as ambitious members of the ruling class love their own honor more than the common good, the spirited part of their soul has usurped the role of reason. Although this is only a small break in the structure of the soul, it does begin a process whereby the irrational part assumes a progressively larger role. From love of honor to the desire for wealth is a short step, for it means allowing the appetites to rule.

Even under a timocracy there would be the beginning of a system of private property, and this desire for riches paves the way for a system of government called *plutocracy,* where power resides in the hands of people whose main concern is wealth. And, says Plato, "as the rich rise in social esteem, the virtuous sink." What is serious about plutocracy, according to Plato, is that it breaks the unity of the state into two contending classes, the rich and the poor. Moreover, plutocrats are consumers of goods, and when they have used up their money, they become dangerous because they want more of what they have become accustomed to. The plutocrat is like the person who seeks constant pleasure. But the very nature of pleasure is that it is momentary and must therefore be repeated. There can never be a time of perfect satisfaction; the seeker of pleasure can never be satisfied any more than a leaky pail can be filled. Still, the plutocrat knows how to distinguish three sorts of appetites: (1) the necessary, (2) the unnecessary, and (3) the lawless; and so is torn between many desires. "His better desires will usually keep the upper hand over the worse," and so the plutocrat, says Plato, "presents a more decent appearance than many."

Democracy is a further degeneration, said Plato, for its principles of equality and freedom reflect the degenerate human characters whose whole range of appetites are all pursued with equal freedom. To be sure, Plato's concept of democracy, and his criticism of it, were based upon his firsthand experience with the special form democracy took in the small city-state of Athens. Here democracy was direct in that all citizens had the right to participate in the government. The Athenian Assembly consisted, theoretically at least, of all citizens over eighteen years of age. Thus, Plato did not have in mind modern liberal and representative democracy. What he saw in his day was rather a mode of direct popular government that clearly violated his notion that the rulership of a state should be in the hands of those with the special talent and training for it.

What produced this spirit of equality was the gradual legitimizing of all the appetites under the plutocracy, by the sons of the more restrained father-plutocrats, where the aim of life was to become as rich as possible. And, said Plato, "this insatiable craving would bring about the transition to democracy," for "a society cannot hold wealth in honour and at the same time establish self-control in its citizens." Even the dogs in a democracy exhibit equality and independence by refusing to move out of the way in the streets. It is, however, when the rich and poor find themselves in a contest under plutocracy that the turning point is reached, for "when the poor win, the result is a democracy." Then, "liberty and free speech are rife everywhere; anyone is allowed to do what he likes." Now, "you are not obliged to be in authority...or to submit to authority, if you do not like it...." All this political equality and freedom stem from a soul whose order has been shattered. It is a soul whose appetites are now all equal and free and act as a "mob" of passions. The life of liberty and equality declares that "one appetite is as good as another and all must have their equal rights."

But the continuous indulgence of the appetites leads one inevitably to the point where a single master passion will finally enslave the soul. One cannot yield to every craving without finally having to yield to the strongest and most persistent passion. At this point we say that one is under the tyranny of one's master passion. Likewise, in the state, the passion for money and pleasures leads the masses to plunder the rich. As the rich resist, the masses seek out a strong person who will be their champion. But this person demands and acquires absolute power and makes slaves of the people, and only later do the people realize to what depths of subjugation they have fallen. This is the unjust society, the enlargement of the unjust soul. The natural end of democracy is *despotism.*

PLATO'S VIEW OF THE COSMOS

Although Plato's most consistent and sustained thought centered around moral and political philosophy, he also turned his attention to science. His theory of nature, or physics, is found chiefly in the *Timaeus,* a dialogue he wrote when he was about seventy years old. Plato had not deliberately postponed this subject, nor had he chosen to deal with moral matters instead of promoting the advancement of science. On the contrary the science of his day had reached a blind alley, and there seemed to be no fruitful direction to take in this field. Earlier, according to Plato, Socrates had had "a prodigious desire to know that department of philosophy which is called the investigation of nature; to know the causes of things..." but he was disillusioned by the conflicting answers and theories put forward by Anaximander, Anaximenes, Leucippus and Democritus, and others. Plato shared this same disappointment. Moreover, as his own philosophy took shape, some of his theories about reality cast doubt upon the possibility of a strictly accurate scientific knowledge. Physics, he thought, could never be more than "a likely story." It was particularly his theory of the Forms that rendered science as an exact mode of knowledge impossible. The real world, he said, is the world of Forms, whereas the visible world is full of change and imperfection. Yet, it is about the visible world of things that science seeks to build its theories. How can one formulate accurate, reliable, and permanent knowledge about a subject matter which is itself imperfect and full of change? At the same time, Plato clearly felt that his theory of Forms or Ideas as well as his notions of morality, evil, and truth required that he provide some view of the cosmos in which all these elements of his thought could be brought together in a coherent way. Recognizing, then, that his account of the material world was only "a likely story," or at best probable knowledge, he nevertheless was convinced that what he had to say about the world was as accurate as the subject matter would allow.

Plato's first thought about the world is that, though it is full of change and imperfection, it nevertheless exhibits order and purpose. He rejected the explanation given by Democritus, who had argued that all things came into being through the accidental collision of atoms. When Plato considered, for example, the orbits of the planets, he observed that they were arranged according to a precise series of geometrical intervals, which, when appropriately calculated, produced the basis for the harmonic scale. Plato made much of the Pythagorean use of mathematics in describing the world, though instead of saying, as the Pythagoreans did, that things are numbers, he said that things participate in numbers, that they are capable of a mathematical explanation. This mathematical characteristic of things suggested to Plato that behind things there must be not merely chance and subsequent mechanism but rather thought and purpose.

The cosmos must therefore be the work of *intelligence,* since it is the mind that orders all things. Humanity and the world bear a likeness to each other, for both contain first an intelligible and eternal element, and second a sensible and perishing element. This dualism is expressed in humanity by the union of soul and body. Similarly, the world is a soul in which things as we know them are arranged.

Although Plato said that *mind* orders everything, he did not develop a doctrine of creation. The doctrine of creation holds that things are created *ex nihilo,* out of nothing. But Plato's explanation of the origin of the visible world bypasses this doctrine of creation. Although Plato does say that "that which becomes must necessarily become through the agency of some cause," this agent, which he calls the divine Craftsman or Demiurge, does not bring new things into being but rather confronts and orders what already exists in chaotic form. We have, then, a picture of the Craftsman with the material upon which he will work. Thus, in explaining the generation of things as we know them in the visible world, Plato assumes the existence of all the ingredients of things, namely, that out of which things are made, the Demiurge who is the Craftsman, and the Ideas or Forms or *patterns* after which things are made.

Plato departed from the materialists who thought that all things derived from some original kind of matter, whether in the form of earth, air, fire, or water. Plato did not accept the notion that matter was the basic reality: matter itself, said Plato, must be explained in more refined terms as the composition not of some finer forms of matter but of something other than matter. What we call matter, whether in the form of earth or water, is a reflection of an Idea or Form, and these Forms are expressed through a medium. Things are generated out of what Plato calls the *receptacle,* which he considered the "nurse of all becoming." The receptacle is a "matrix," or a medium that has no structure but that is capable of receiving the imposition of structure by the Demiurge. Another word Plato uses for the *receptacle* is *space,* which, he says, "is everlasting, not admitting destruction; providing a situation for all things that come into being, but itself apprehended without the senses by a sort of bastard reasoning, and hardly an object of belief." There is no explanation of the origin of the receptacle, for in Plato's thought it is underived, as are the Forms and the Demiurge. The receptacle is where things appear and perish.

To an unreflective person, earth and water may appear as solid and permanent modes of matter. But Plato said that they are constantly changing and therefore do not hold still long enough "to be described as 'this' or 'that' or by any phrase that exhibits them as having permanent being." What the senses consider "matter" or "substance" when they apprehend the elements of earth and water are only *qualities,* which appear through the medium of the receptacle "in which all of them are always coming to be, making their appearance and vanishing out of it." Material objects are composed of nonmaterial compounds. Here Plato is again influenced by the Pythagorean perspective when he argues that solid objects of matter are described and defined in geometric terms according to their surfaces. Any surface, he said, can be resolved by triangles, and, in turn, any triangle can be divided into right triangles. These shapes, these triangular surfaces, are irreducible and must therefore be the ingredients of the compound known as matter. The simplest solid, for example, would be a pyramid that consists of four triangular surfaces. Similarly, a cube could be made of six square surfaces, where each square surface is composed of two half squares, that is, two triangles. What we normally call "solid" never contains anything more than "surfaces," so that one can say that "body" or "molecules" are geometric figures. Indeed, the whole universe could be thought of in terms of its geometrical diagram—and could be defined simply as what is happening in space, or as space reflecting various forms. What Plato wanted particularly to establish was the notion that matter is only the appearance of something more basic.

If various kinds of triangles represent the basic constituents of all things, how can one account for the variations in things as well as their stability? What, in short, makes it possible to have the kind of world and universe that we know? Here again Plato was forced to assume that all things must be ordered by mind, that the cosmos is the activity of the World Soul in the receptacle. The world of things is the world of *phenomena,* which is the Greek word for appearances. What is presented to our perception is the multitude of appearances, which, when analyzed, are found to consist of geometric surfaces. These surfaces, again, are primary and irreducible and are found as "raw material" in the receptacle and require some organizing agency to arrange them into triangles and then into phenomena. All this activity is achieved by the World Soul. The World Soul is eternal, though at times Plato appears to say that it is the creation of the Demiurge. Although the World Soul is eternal, the world of appearance is full of change, just as in humans the soul represents the eternal element whereas the body contains the principle of change. The world of matter and body changes because it is composite and always tends to return to its basic constituents, "going into" and "going out of" space. But insofar as the World Soul is eternal, there is, in spite of all the change in the world of our experience, an element of stability and permanence, a structure, a discernible universe.

There is evil in the world, says Plato, because there are obstacles in the way of the Demiurge. The world is not perfectly good even though the Demiurge sought to make it as much like its pattern as possible. Although the Demiurge represents divine reason and the agency that fashioned the order of the universe, "the generation of this cosmos," says Plato, "was a mixed result of the combination of Necessity and Reason." Necessity in this context signifies unwillingness to change and, when applied to the "raw material" of the *receptacle,* it indicates a recalcitrance as though impervious to the ordering of *mind.* In this sense, *necessity* is one of the conditions of evil in the world, for evil is the breakdown of purpose, and purpose is characteristic of mind. Whatever, then, frustrates the working of mind contributes to the absence of order, which is the meaning of evil. This suggests that in human life, too, the circumstance of a recalcitrant body and lower parts of the soul produces evil insofar as mind is not in control. Necessity is expressed in various modes, such as inertia and irreversibility, and reason, even God's reason, must cope with these obstacles while trying to order the world according to a definite purpose.

Finally, there is the question about *time*. According to Plato, time comes to be only after phenomena are produced. Not until there are things as we know them, as imperfect and changing, can there be time. Until then, by definition, whatever is, is eternal. The very meaning of time is change, and therefore in the absence of change there could be no time. Whereas the Forms are time-less, the various copies of them in the receptacle constantly "go in" and "go out," and this going in and out is the process of change, which is the cause of time. Still, time represents the double presence in the cosmos of time and eter-nity; since the cosmos is ordered by mind, it contains the element of eternity, and since the cosmos consists of temporary combinations of surfaces, it con-tains the element of change and time. And since change is not capricious but regular, the very process of change exhibits the presence of eternal mind. This regularity of change, as exhibited, for example, by the regular change or mo-tion of the stars and planets, makes possible the measurement of change and makes it possible to "tell time."

Plato's "likely story" about the cosmos consisted, then, of an account of how the Demiurge fashioned things out of the receptacle, using the Forms as patterns. The World Soul is produced by the Demiurge and is the energizing activity in the receptacle, producing what to us appears to be substance or solid matter though in reality is only qualities caused by the arrangement of geomet-ric surfaces. Evil and time are, in this account, the product of imperfection and change. The world as we know it depends upon an agency and "raw material" that are not found in the physical world as we know it, this agency being mind, and the raw material being explained chiefly in terms of mathematics.

At this point one would wish to engage in a sustained and critical appraisal of Plato's vast system of philosophy. But in a sense, the history of philosophy represents just such a large-scale dialogue, where thinkers arise to agree and disagree with what he taught. So powerful was the mold into which he had cast the enterprise of philosophy that for centuries to come his views dominated the intellectual scene. Indeed, Whitehead once remarked that "the safest gen-eral characterization of the European philosophical tradition is that it consists of a series of footnotes to Plato." Many of these footnotes, it might be added, were written by Plato's prodigious successor, Aristotle, to whom we now turn.

4

Aristotle

ristotle was born in 384 B.C. in the small town of Stagira on the northeast coast of Thrace. His father was the physician to the king of Macedonia. It could be that Aristotle's great interest in biology and science in general was nurtured in his early childhood as it was the custom, according to Galen, for families in the guild of the Asclepiadae to train their sons in the art of dissection. When he was seventeen years old, Aristotle went to Athens to enroll in Plato's Academy, where he spent the next twenty years as a pupil and a member. At the Academy, Aristotle had the reputation of being the "reader" and "the mind of the school." He was profoundly influenced by Plato's thought and personality even though eventually he was to break away from Plato's philosophy in order to formulate his own version of certain philosophical problems. Still, while at the Academy, he wrote many dialogues in a Platonic style, which his contemporaries praised for the "golden stream" of their eloquence. He even reaffirmed, in his *Eudemus,* the very doctrine so central to Plato's thought, the doctrine of the Forms, or Ideas, which he later criticized so severely.

There is no way now to reconstruct with exactness just when Aristotle's thought diverged from Plato's. Plato's own thought, it must be remembered, was in process of change while Aristotle was at the Academy. Indeed, it is usually said that Aristotle studied with Plato during Plato's "later" period, a time when Plato's interests had shifted toward mathematics, method, and natural science. During this time, also, specialists in various sciences, such as medicine, anthropology, and archeology, came to the Academy. This meant that Aristotle was exposed to a vast array of empirical facts, which, because of his temperament, he found useful for research and for his mode of formulating scientific concepts. It may be, therefore, that the intellectual atmosphere of the Academy marked by some of Plato's latest dominant concerns and the availability of collected data in special fields provided Aristotle with a direction in philosophy that was congenial to his scientific disposition.

The direction Aristotle took did eventually cause him to depart from some of Plato's doctrines, though the degree of difference between Plato and Aristotle is still a matter of careful interpretation. But even when they were together at the Academy, certain temperamental differences must have been apparent. Aristotle, for example, was less interested in mathematics than Plato and more interested in empirical data. Moreover, as time went on, Aristotle's gaze seemed to be more firmly fixed upon the concrete processes of nature, so that he considered his abstract scientific notions to have their real habitat in this living nature. By contrast, Plato separated the world of thought from the world of flux and things, ascribing true reality to the Ideas and Forms, which, he thought, had an existence separate from the things in nature. It could be said, therefore, that Aristotle oriented his thought to the dynamic realm of *becoming,* whereas Plato's thought was fixed more upon the static realm of timeless *Being.* Whatever differences there were between these two great minds, the fact is that Aristotle did not break with Plato personally, as he remained at the Academy until Plato's death. Moreover, throughout Aristotle's later major treatises, unmistakable influences of Plato's thought are to be found in spite of Aristotle's unique interpretations and style. But his distinctly "Platonist" period came to an end upon Plato's death, when the direction of the Academy passed into the hands of Plato's nephew Speusippos, whose excessive emphasis upon mathematics was uncongenial to Aristotle, for which reason, among others, Aristotle withdrew from the Academy and left Athens.

It was in 348/47 B.C. that Aristotle left the Academy and accepted the invitation of Hermeias to come to Assos, near Troy. Hermeias had formerly been a student at the Academy and was now the ruler of Assos. Being somewhat of a philosopher-king, he had gathered a small group of thinkers into his court, and here Aristotle was able for the next three years to write, teach, and carry on research. While at Hermeias' court, he married this ruler's niece and adopted daughter, Pythias, who bore him a daughter. Later, when they had returned to Athens, his wife died and Aristotle then entered into a relationship with Herpyllis, which was never legalized but which was a happy, permanent, and affectionate union from which there came a son, Nicomachus, after whom the *Nicomachean Ethics* was named. After his three years in Assos, Aristotle moved to the neighboring island of Lesbos, settling there for the time being in Mitylene,

Aristotle *(Scala/Art Resource)*

where he taught and continued his investigations in biology, studying especially the many forms of marine life. Here he also became known as an advocate of a united Greece, urging that such a union would be more successful than independent city-states in resisting the might of Persia. Then, in 343/42 B.C., Philip of Macedon invited Aristotle to become the tutor of his son Alexander, who was then thirteen years old. As a tutor to a future ruler, Aristotle's interests included politics, and it is possible that it was here that he conceived the idea of collecting and comparing various constitutions, a project he later carried out by collecting digests of the constitutions of 158 Greek city-states. When Alexander ascended the throne after his father Philip's death, Aristotle's duties as tutor had come to an end, and after a brief stay in his hometown of Stagira, he returned to Athens.

Upon his return to Athens in 335/34 B.C., Aristotle embarked upon the most productive period of his life. Under the protection of the Macedonian statesman Antipater, Aristotle founded his own school. His school was known as the Lyceum, named after the groves where Socrates was known to have gone to think and which were the sacred precincts of Apollo Lyceus. Here Aristotle and his pupils walked in the Peripatos, a tree-covered walk, and discussed philosophy, for which reason his school was called *peripatetic*. Besides these peripatetic discussions, there were also lectures, some technical for small audiences and others of a more popular nature for larger audiences. Aristotle is also said to have formed the first great library by collecting hundreds of manuscripts, maps, and specimens, which he used as illustrations during his lectures. Moreover, his school developed certain formal procedures whereby its leadership would alternate among members. Aristotle formulated the rules for these procedures as he also did for the special common meal and symposium once a month when a member was selected to defend a philosophical position against the critical objections of the other members. For twelve or thirteen years Aristotle remained as the head of the Lyceum, not only teaching and lecturing, but above all formulating his main ideas about the classification of the sciences, fashioning a bold new science of logic, and writing his advanced ideas in every major area of philosophy and science, exhibiting an extraordinary command of universal knowledge.

When Alexander died in 323 B.C., a wave of anti-Macedonian feeling arose, making Aristotle's position in Athens very precarious because of his close connections with Macedonia. As Socrates before him, Aristotle was charged with "impiety," but, as he is reported to have said, "lest the Athenians should sin twice against philosophy," he left the Lyceum and fled to Chalcis, where he died in 322 B.C. of a digestive disease of long standing. In his will he expressed sensitive human qualities by providing amply for his relatives, preventing his slaves from being sold and providing that some of his slaves should be emancipated. As with Socrates and Plato, Aristotle's thought was of such decisive power that it was to influence philosophy for centuries to come. From the vast range of his philosophy, we shall consider some aspects of his logic, metaphysics, ethics, politics, and aesthetics.

LOGIC

Aristotle invented formal logic. He also invented the idea of the separate sciences. For him, there was a close connection between logic and science, inasmuch as he considered logic to be the instrument (*organon*) with which to formulate language properly when analyzing what a science involves. Although formal logic is concerned with the forms of human thinking, Aristotle did not limit his interest in logic to the relations of propositions to each other or simply to the consistency of language with itself. His chief interest was with the forms of proof, and for this reason he was particularly concerned with what we can state in precise language about reality, about *what* things exist and *why* they are as they are. Science, as Aristotle understood it, consisted of true statements that accounted for the reasons why things behave as they do and why they *have* to be as they are. In this sense, science consists in the knowledge of the *fact that* and of the *reason why.* It includes both observation *and* a theory that explains what is observed. For example, one can observe steam coming from a kettle on the stove, but this mere observation does not by itself enable us to define "steam" in any systematic or scientific manner. A scientific statement about this observation would reflect a careful sorting out of the essential elements of this observation, setting aside all irrelevant details or "accidents" such as the particular fuel used for the fire and the kind of vessel used for the water, focusing squarely upon the special kind of event this is, the production of steam, and giving reasons for the occurrence of this event by relating heat, water, and steam in such a way that one can know, have proof, why and under what conditions heat and water produce steam. The most important thing about science is therefore the language in which it is formulated. Scientific language must indicate as precisely as possible what constitutes the distinctive subject matter of a science, and it must describe why things act the way they do. Logic, then, is a study of words or language, but not the way a grammarian would study these. Aristotelian logic is the study of the thought for which words are signs; it is an attempt to get at truth by an analysis of the thought that reflects our apprehension or understanding of the nature of things. In short, for Aristotle, logic was the instrument of analysis of human thought as it thinks about reality. To be sure, thought does not always reflect reality accurately, but it is the function of logic always to work toward a more adequate relation between language and reality.

The Categories and the Starting Point of Reasoning   Before one can demonstrate or prove something, one must have a clear starting point for one's reasoning process. For one thing, one must specify the subject matter one is discussing, the specific "kind" of thing one is dealing with. To this one must add the properties and causes that are related to that kind of thing. In this connection, Aristotle developed his doctrine of the *categories,* which explains how we think about things. Whenever we think of a distinct subject matter, we think of a subject and its predicates, or of some *substance* and its accidents. We think the word *man* and also connect the word *man* with such predicates as *tall* and *able.* The word *man* is here a substance, and Aristotle indicates that there are about nine *categories* (meaning predicates) that can be connected with a substance, including *quantity* (e.g., six feet tall), *quality* (e.g., articulate), *relation* (e.g., double), *place* (e.g., at the school), *date* (e.g., last week), *posture* (e.g., standing), *possession* (e.g., clothed), *action* (e.g., serves), and *passivity* (e.g., is served). *Substance* itself can be considered a category, since we, for example, say "he is a man," in which case *man* (a substance) is a *predicate.* These categories represented for Aristotle the classification of concepts that are used in scientific knowledge. They represent the specific ways in which whatever exists does exist or is realized. In our thinking, we arrange things into these categories, classifying such categories into genera, species, and the individual thing. We see the individual as a member of the species and the species as related to the genus. Aristotle did not consider these categories or these classifications as artificial creations of the mind. He thought that they were actually in existence outside the mind and in things. Things, he thought, fall into various classifications by their very nature, and we think of their being members of a species or genus because they *are*. Thinking, as Aristotle saw it, was connected with the way things are, thereby indicating a close relation between logic and metaphysics. Thinking is always about some specific individual thing, a substance. But a thing never simply exists; it exists some*how* and has a reason *why*.

There are always predicates (categories) related to subjects (substances). Some predicates are intrinsic to a thing; such predicates or categories belong to a thing simply because it is what it is. A horse is thought of as having certain predicates *because* it is a horse; it has these predicates in common with all other horses. It also has other predicates, not so intrinsic but rather "accidental," such as color, place, size, and other determinations affecting its relation to other material objects. What Aristotle wants to underscore is that there is a sequence that leads to "science," this sequence being, first of all, the *existence* of things and their processes; secondly, our *thinking* about things and their behavior; and, finally, the transformation of our thought about things into *words*. Language is the instrument for formulating scientific thought. Logic, then, is the analysis of language, of the process of reasoning, of the way language and reasoning are related to reality.

Since scientific language attempts to demonstrate accurately how things behave, such language is concerned both with proof and truth. Proof requires that the process of reasoning rest upon the proper, i.e., valid, relation of terms and propositions to each other. However, Aristotle was concerned not only with consistency, i.e., showing that conclusions validly follow from certain premises. He was also concerned that the premises be true, so that the conclusions would have demonstrative value concerning reality. Aristotle said that "the proper object of unqualified scientific knowledge is something which cannot be other than it is." We have scientific knowledge, he said, "when we think that we know the cause on which the fact depends, as the cause of that fact and no other, and, further, that the fact could not be other than it is." To relate causes and effects involves the multiple acts of observing, judging, and concluding. Observation by itself does not provide us with the definition of things, nor does it give us science as such. What science requires is, first of all, the discovery of a premise, a starting point for reasoning. This premise is a product of *induction*. Our mind, says Aristotle, has a better knowledge of the things close to our senses than of things farther from our senses. For this reason, our minds move from a knowledge of particular things discovered by observation to universal or class ideas, which we do not as such sense. We observe particular people and then form the general idea of Humanity. Having formulated premises by induction, our mind can then employ these premises deductively or demonstratively. Although Aristotle said that "we must get to know the primary premises by induction," he did not develop this aspect of knowledge with its corollaries of hypothesis and experimentation. His emphasis was upon de-

duction and demonstrative reasoning. The basic elements of this form of reasoning were analyzed and systematically organized for the first time by Aristotle through his doctrine of *syllogism.*

The Syllogism   Aristotle defines the syllogism as "discourse in which certain things being stated, something other than what is stated follows of necessity from their being so." This is the principle of implication, and Aristotle was
particularly concerned that scientific discourse should proceed from one valid
step to another with precision. He wanted to discover the rules that would guarantee that conclusions were rightly inferred from their premises. How, then,
could one be sure that a conclusion follows from its premises; or, what makes
it possible for us, assuming that we have two propositions, to derive from these
a third proposition? Aristotle thought he had discovered the answer to these
questions in the basic structure of the syllogism.

The syllogism is a special form of connected language. Scientific demonstrations are possible because certain words stand for certain properties, qualities, or characteristics of things. Such words stand for *essential* properties as
compared with *accidental* properties. To say that people are mortal is to describe one of their essential properties, whereas to say that one has red hair is
to describe something accidental, since to be a human it is not necessary or
essential that one have red, or even any, hair. But it is "essential" to one's
being human that one be mortal, and it is such essential properties of things
that scientific propositions contain. Still, when we ask why it is that people are
mortal, a fact we already know from experience, we are asking for a scientific
or technical "reason why." It is at this point that the specially connected language of the syllogism comes into operation, for the syllogism represents the
linking of propositions about essential properties in such a way that the conclusion necessarily follows. And what makes the conclusion follow is that a
particular term is found in both of the premises, linking these premises together
so that the conclusion necessarily follows. The term that serves this function
of linking propositions is called by Aristotle the *middle,* saying that "I call that
term middle which is itself in another and contains another in itself; in position
also it comes in the middle." Hence, the "reason why" it is true that "all people
are mortal" is that this is a conclusion from two other premises that are linked
together by a middle term, as follows: We say first that "all animals are mortal" and next that "all people are animals" and from this it follows that "all
people are mortals." The middle term here is *animals,* and this term is linked
to the predicate *mortal* and to the subject *all people,* thereby producing the
implication that "all people are mortal."

This syllogism is frequently expressed in the following way:

Major premise: All men are mortal.
Minor premise: Socrates is a man.
Conclusion: Therefore, Socrates is mortal.

Although Aristotle's doctrine of the syllogism is a tool for determining
which relationships between premises and conclusion have consistency, his chief

interest in developing the syllogism was not simply to assure consistent reasoning. His aim was to provide an instrument for scientific demonstration, and for this reason, again, he emphasized the relation between logic and metaphysics, between our way of knowing and what things are and how they behave. That is, he thought that words and propositions are linked together because the things which language mirrors are also linked together. For this reason, Aristotle recognized that it is entirely possible to employ the syllogism consistently without necessarily arriving at science or truth if the premises did not rest upon valid assumptions (i.e., if they did not reflect true reality). Accordingly, Aristotle distinguished between three kinds of reasoning, each of which might use the instrument of the syllogism, but with different results: These are, first, *dialectical* reasoning, which is reasoning from "opinions that are generally accepted"; second, *eristic* or contentious reasoning, which begins with opinions that seem to be generally accepted but are really not; and, third, what Aristotle calls *demonstrative* reasoning, where the premises from which reasoning starts are true and primary.

The value of syllogistic reasoning depended for Aristotle upon the accuracy of the premises. If true scientific knowledge is to be achieved, it is necessary that the premises one uses be more than opinion or even probable truth. Demonstrative reasoning moves backward, as it were, from conclusions to those premises that constitute the necessary beginnings of the conclusion. When we say that "all men are mortal," we in effect move back to those causes and properties in animals that indicate their mortality. We then link men with these properties by including them in the class of animals. Demonstrative reasoning must therefore lay hold of reliable premises, principles, or what Aristotle calls *archai,* i.e., "first things." Demonstrative reasoning is reasoning from true *archai*, that is, accurately defined properties of any thing, class, or distinctive area of subject matter. Valid reasoning therefore presupposes the discovery of true *archai* from which conclusions can be drawn.

How are these first principles, or *archai,* arrived at? Aristotle answers that we learn these *archai* from observation and induction. When we observe certain facts many times, "the universal that is there," he says, "becomes plain." Whenever we observe any particular "that," our memory stores it away; and after observing many similar "thats," there is generated from all these particular "thats" a general term with a general meaning. The mind discovers the universal within the particulars by the process of induction, a process that results in the discovery of additional meanings in the particular "thats" observed.

If one then asks the additional question whether and how we can know that the *archai,* or principles, are true, Aristotle says we know they are true simply because the mind, working with certain facts, recognizes and "sees" their truth. These *archai,* or primary premises, are not in turn demonstrated: If it were necessary to demonstrate every premise, this would involve an infinite regress, since each prior premise would also have to be proved, in which case the enterprise of knowledge could never get started. Aristotle, referring again to the *archai,* or primary premises, says that "not all knowledge is demonstrative: on the contrary, knowledge of the immediate premises is independent of demonstration." Scientific knowledge, he said, rests upon knowledge that is not itself subject to the same proof as scientific conclusions, so that "besides scientific knowledge there is its originative source which enables us to *recognize* the definitions." Here Aristotle used the word *recognize* in contrast to Plato's use of the word *recollect* or *remember* to explain how we know certain truths. To "recognize" a truth is to have a direct intuitive grasp of it, as when we know that two and two equal four. It may be that the occasion for "recognizing" this truth of arithmetic was the act of adding particular things such as bricks or stones. Still, from these specific factual cases the mind "sees" or "recognizes" the truth that certain things belong to a species or genus and that certain relations exist between them, such as two and two equal four. Thus, Aristotle argued that science rests upon primary premises, which are arrived at by intellectual intuition (*nous*). Once these primary premises and definitions of the essential natures of things are in hand, it is then possible to engage in demonstrative reasoning. Insofar as these premises accurately grasp aspects of reality, syllogistic reasoning assures linking of major and minor premises through the agency of the middle term, thereby producing valid conclusions.

METAPHYSICS

In his work entitled *Metaphysics* (a term that indicates the position of this work among his other writings, namely, *beyond,* or coming after, *physics*), Aristotle develops what he called the science of *first philosophy.* Throughout his *Metaphysics,* he is concerned with a type of knowledge that he thought could be most rightly called *wisdom.* This work begins with the statement that "All men by nature desire to know." This innate desire, says Aristotle, is not only a desire to know in order to do or make something. In addition to these pragmatic motives, there is in a person a desire to know certain kinds of things simply for the sake of knowing. An indication of this, says Aristotle, is "the delight we take in our senses; for even apart from their usefulness they are loved for themselves" inasmuch as our seeing "makes us know and brings to light many differences between things."

There are different levels of knowledge. Some people know only what they experience through their senses, as, for example, when they know that fire is hot. But, says Aristotle, we do not regard what we know through the senses as wisdom. To be sure, our most authoritative knowledge of particular things is acquired through our senses. Still, this kind of knowledge tells us only the "that" of anything and not the "why"; it tells us, for example, *that* fire is hot but not *why.* Similarly, in medicine, some men know only *that* medicines heal certain illnesses. This knowledge, based upon specific experiences, is, according to Aristotle, on a lower level than the knowledge of the medical scientist who knows not only "that" a medicine will heal but knows also the reason "why." In the various crafts, the master craftsmen "know in a truer sense and are wiser than the manual workers, because they know the *causes* of the things that are done."

Wisdom is, therefore, more than that kind of knowledge obtained from sensing objects and their qualities. It is even more than knowledge acquired from repeated experiences of the same kinds of things. Wisdom is similar to the knowledge possessed by scientists who begin by looking at something, then repeat these sense experiences, and finally go beyond sense experience by thinking about the *causes* of the objects of their experiences. There are as many sciences as there are definable areas of investigation, and Aristotle deals with many of them, including physics, ethics, politics, and aesthetics. In each case, the respective science is concerned with discovering the causes or reasons or principles underlying the activity of its special subject matter; thus, for example, in physics one asks what causes material bodies to move, in ethics what causes the good life, in politics what causes the good state, and in aesthetics what causes a good poem. Sciences differ not only in their subject matter but also in their relation to each other. Some sciences depend upon others, as when the physicist must rely upon the science of mathematics. In the hierarchy of sciences, Aristotle says that "the science which knows to what end each thing must be done is the most authoritative of the sciences, and more authoritative than any ancillary science." In addition to the specific sciences, then, there is another science, *first philosophy,* or what we now call *metaphysics,* which goes beyond the subject matter of the other sciences and is concerned with "first principles and causes." These "first principles and causes" are the true foundation of *wisdom,* for they give us knowledge not of any particular object or activity, but rather knowledge of true reality.

Metaphysics deals with knowledge at the highest level of abstraction. This knowledge is abstract because it is about what is universal instead of what is particular. Every science has its own level of abstraction inasmuch as it deals with the first principles and causes of its subject matter, as when the physicist talks about the principles of motion in general as distinguished from describing the motion of this planet or that pendulum. Wisdom has to do, then, with the abstract levels of knowledge and not with the levels of visible things, for, as Aristotle says, "sense-perception is common to all, and therefore easy and no mark of Wisdom." True wisdom, first philosophy, or metaphysics is the most abstract and also the most exact of all the sciences because it tries to discover the truly first principles from which even the first principles of the various sciences are derived. True knowledge is therefore found in what is most knowable, and, says Aristotle, "the first principles and the causes are most knowable... and from these, all other things come to be known...." We are led, then, to consider more specifically the subject matter of metaphysics.

The Problem of Metaphysics Defined   The various sciences seek to find the first principles and causes of specific kinds of things, such as material bodies, the human body, the state, a poem, and so on. Unlike these sciences, which ask, "What is such-and-such a thing like and why?" metaphysics asks a far more general question, a question that each science must ultimately take into account, namely, "What does it mean to be anything whatsoever?" What, in short, does it mean *to be?* It was precisely this question that concerned Aristotle in his *Metaphysics,* making metaphysics for him "the science of any existent, as existent." The problem of metaphysics as he saw it was therefore the study of Being and its "principles" and "causes."

Aristotle's metaphysics was to a considerable extent an outgrowth of his views on logic and his interest in biology. From the viewpoint of his logic, "to be" meant for him to be *something* that could be accurately defined and that could therefore become the subject of discourse. From the point of view of his interest in biology, he was disposed to think of "to be" as something implicated in a dynamic process. "To be," as Aristotle saw the matter, always meant to be *something.* Hence, all existence is individual and has a determinate nature. All the categories Aristotle dealt with in his logical works, categories (or predicates) such as *quality, relation, posture, place,* and so on, presuppose some subject to which these predicates can apply. This subject to which all the categories apply Aristotle called *substance (ousia).* To be, then, is to be a particular kind of substance. Also, "to be" means to be a substance as the product of a dynamic process. In this way, metaphysics is concerned with *Being* (i.e., existing substances) and its *causes* (i.e., the processes by which substances come into being).

Substance as the Primary Essence of Things A major clue to what Aristotle means by substance is discovered, he thought, in the way we know a thing. Having in mind again the categories or predicates, Aristotle says that we know a thing better when we know *what it is* than when we know the color, size, or posture it has. The mind separates a thing from all its qualities and focuses upon what a thing really is, upon its *essential nature.* We recognize that all humans are *human* in spite of their different sizes, colors, or ages. *Something* about each concretely different person makes him or her a person in spite of the unique characteristics that make him or her *this particular* person. At this point, Aristotle would readily agree that these special characteristics (categories, predicates) also exist, have some kind of being. But the being of these characteristics is not the central object of metaphysical inquiry. The central concern of metaphysics is the study of substance, the essential nature of a thing. In this view, substance means "that which is not asserted of a subject but of which everything else is asserted." Substance, that is, is what we know as basic about something, *after* which we can say other things about *it.* Whenever we define something, we get at its essence *before* we can say anything about it, as when we speak of a large table or a healthy person. Here table and person are understood in their "essence," in what makes them a table or a person, before they are understood as large or healthy. To be sure, we can know only specific and determinate things, actual individual tables or persons. At the same time, the essence, or substance, of a table or a person has its existence peculiarly separate from its categories or its qualities. This does not mean that a substance is ever in fact found existing separately from its qualities. Still, if we can know the essence of a thing, "tableness" let us say, as "separable" from these particular qualities, round, small, and brown, there must be some universal essence that is found wherever one sees a table; and this essence or substance must be independent of its particular qualities inasmuch as the essence is the same even though in the case of each actual table the qualities are different. What Aristotle seems to be saying is that a thing is more than the sum of its particular qualities. There is something "beneath" (*sub stance*) all the qualities; thus, any specific thing is a combination of qualities, on the one hand, and a substratum to which the qualities apply, on the other. With these distinctions in mind, Aristotle was led, as was Plato before him, to consider just how this essence, or universal, was related to the particular thing. What, in short, makes a substance a substance; is it *matter* as a substratum or is it *form?*

Matter and Form Although Aristotle distinguished between *matter* and *form,* he nevertheless said that we never find matter without form or form without matter in nature. Everything that exists is some concrete individual thing, and every *thing* is a unity of matter and form. Substance, therefore, is a composite of form and matter.

Plato, it will be recalled, argued that Ideas or Forms, such as Man or Table, had a separate existence. Similarly, he treated *space* as the material substratum, or the stuff out of which individual things were made. For Plato, then, this primary stuff of space was molded by the eternally existing Forms into individual shapes. This was Plato's way of explaining how there could be many individual things that all have one and the same, that is, universal, nature or essence while still being individual. This universal, Plato said, is the Form, which exists eternally and is separate from any particular thing and is found in each thing only because the thing (this table) *participates* in the Form (tableness, or Ideal Table).

Aristotle rejected Plato's explanation of the universal Forms, rejecting specifically the notion that the Forms existed separately from individual things. Of course, Aristotle did agree that there are universals, that universals such as Man and Table are more than merely subjective notions. Indeed, Aristotle recognized that without the theory of universals, there could be no scientific knowledge, for then there would be no way of saying something about all members of a particular class. What makes scientific knowledge effective is that it discovers classes of objects (for example, a certain form of human disease), so that whenever an individual falls into this class, other facts can be assumed also to be relevant. These classes, then, are not merely mental fictions but do in fact have objective reality. But, said Aristotle, their reality is to be found not anywhere else than in the individual things themselves. What purpose, he asked, could be served by assuming that the universal Forms existed separately? If anything, this would complicate matters, inasmuch as everything, that is, not only individual things but also their relationships, would have to be reduplicated in the world of Forms. Moreover, Aristotle was not convinced that

Plato's theory of Forms could help us know things any better, saying that "they help in no wise towards the knowledge of other things...." Since presumably the Forms are motionless, Aristotle concluded that they could not help us understand things as we know them, which are full of motion, nor could they, being immaterial, explain objects of which we have sense impressions. Again, how could the immaterial Forms be related to any particular thing? That things *participate* in the Forms was not a satisfactory explanation for Aristotle, leading him to conclude that "to say that they are patterns and that other things share in them, is to use empty words and poetical metaphors."

When we use the words *matter* and *form* to describe any specific thing, we seem to have in mind the distinction between what something is made of and what it is made into. This, again, disposes our minds to assume that what things are made of, matter, exists in some primary and unformed state until it is made into a thing. But, again, Aristotle argues that we shall not find anywhere such a thing as "primary matter," that is, matter without form. Consider the sculptor who is about to make a statue of Venus out of marble. He or she will never find marble without some form; it will always be this marble or that, a square piece or an irregular one, but he or she will always work with a piece in which form and matter are already combined. That the sculptor will give it a different form is another question. The question here is, how does one thing become another thing? What, in short, is the nature of *change?*

The Process of Change: The Four Causes   In the world around us we see things constantly changing. Change is one of the basic facts of our experience. For Aristotle, the word *change* means many things, including motion, growth, decay, generation, and corruption. Some of these changes are *natural,* whereas others are the products of *human art.* Things are always taking on new form; new life is born and statues are made. Because change always involves taking on new form, several questions can be asked concerning the process of change. Of anything, says Aristotle, we can ask four questions, namely (1) what is it? (2) what is it made of? (3) by what is it made? and (4) for what end is it made? The four responses to these questions represent Aristotle's four *causes.* Although the word *cause* refers in modern use primarily to an event prior to an effect, for Aristotle it meant an *explanation.* His four causes represent therefore a broad pattern or framework for the total explanation of anything or everything. Taking an object of art, for example, the four causes might be (1) a statue (2) of marble (3) by a sculptor (4) for a decoration. Distinguished from objects produced by human art, there are those things which are produced *by nature.* Although nature does not, according to Aristotle, have "purposes" in the sense of "the reason for," it does always and everywhere have "ends" in the sense of having built-in ways of behaving. For this reason, seeds sprout and roots go down (not up!) and plants grow and, in this process of change, move toward their "end," i.e., their distinctive function or way of being. In nature, then, change will involve these same four elements. Aristotle's *four causes* are therefore (1) the *formal* cause, which determines *what* a thing is, (2) the *material* cause, or that out of which it is made, (3) the *efficient* cause, by what a thing is made, and (4) the *final* cause, the "end" for which it is made.

Aristotle looked at life through the eyes of a biologist. For him, nature is *life*. All things are in motion, in the process of becoming and dying away. The process of reproduction was for Aristotle a clear example of the power inherent in all living things to initiate change and to reproduce their kind. Summarizing his causes, Aristotle said that "all things that come to be come to be by some agency and from something, and come to be something." From this biological viewpoint, Aristotle was able to elaborate the notion that form and matter never exist separately. In nature, generation of new life involves, according to Aristotle, first of all an individual who already possesses the specific form which the offspring will have (the male parent); there must then be the matter capable of being the vehicle for this form (this matter being contributed by the female parent); from this comes a new individual with the same specific form. In this example, Aristotle indicates that change does not involve bringing together formless matter with matterless form. On the contrary, change occurs always in and to something that is already a combination of form and matter and that is on its way to becoming something new or different.

Potentiality and Actuality   All things, said Aristotle, are involved in processes of change. Each thing possesses a power to become what its form has set as its end. There is in all things a dynamic power of striving toward their "end." Some of this striving is toward external objects, as when a man builds a house. But there is also the striving to achieve ends that pertain to one's internal nature, as when one fulfills one's nature as a human being by the act of thinking. This self-contained end of anything Aristotle called its *entelechy*. All things have their own entelechy.

That things have ends led Aristotle to consider the distinction between *potentiality* and *actuality*. This distinction is used by Aristotle to explain the processes of change and development. If the *end* of an acorn is to be a tree, in some way the acorn is only potentially a tree but not actually so at this time. A fundamental mode of change, then, is the change from potentiality to actuality. But the chief significance of this distinction is that Aristotle argues for the priority of actuality over potentiality. That is, although something actual emerges from the potential, there could be no movement from potential to actual if there were not first of all something actual. A child is potentially an adult, but before there could be a child with that potentiality, there had to be an actual adult.

As all things in nature are similar to the relation of a child to an adult, or an acorn to a tree, Aristotle was led to see in nature different levels of being. If everything were involved in change, in generation and corruption, everything would partake of potentiality. But, as we have seen, for there to be something potential, there must already be something actual. To explain the existence of the world of potential things, Aristotle thought it was necessary to assume the existence of some actuality at a level above potential or perishing things. This led to the notion of a Being that is pure actuality, without any potentiality, at the highest level of being. Since change is a kind of motion, Aristotle saw the visible world as one composed of things in motion. But motion, a mode of change, involves potentiality. Things are potentially in motion but must be moved by something that is actually in motion. Again, to explain motion ultimately led Aristotle to speak of the Unmoved Mover.

The Unmoved Mover   For Aristotle, the Unmoved Mover did not mean the same thing as a *first* mover, as though motion could be traced back to a *time* when motion began. Nor was the Unmoved Mover considered by him a *creator* in the sense of later theology. From his previous distinction between potentiality and actuality, Aristotle concluded that the only way to explain how motion or change can occur is to assume that something actual is *logically* prior to whatever is potential. The fact of change must imply the existence of something actual, something *purely* actual without any mixture of potentiality. This *Mover* is not, according to Aristotle, an *efficient* cause in the sense of exerting a power or force, or as expressing a *will.* Such acts would imply potentiality, as when one says that God "willed" to create the world. This would mean that *before* God created the world, he was potentially capable or intended to create it.

Aristotle did not think of the Unmoved Mover as a Being that *thinks* or prescribes *purposes* for the world. In a sense, the Unmoved Mover does not know anything precisely because it is not a kind of being as much as it is a way of explaining the fact of motion. All of nature is full of striving toward fulfilling all of its particular entelechies. Each thing is aiming at perfecting its possibilities and its *end,* aiming, that is, at becoming the perfect tree, the perfectly good person, and so on. The aggregate of all these strivings constitutes the large-scale processes of the world order so that it can be said that all of reality is in the process of change, moving from its potentialities and possibilities to the ultimate perfection of these potentialities. To explain this comprehensive or general motion, to make it intelligible, Aristotle referred to the Unmoved Mover as the "reason for" or the "principle of" motion. For this reason, the Unmoved Mover stood for the actual, and, because there is here no potentiality, the *eternal* principle of motion. Since this explanation of motion implies an eternal activity, then, there was never a "time" when there was not a world of things in process. For this reason, too, Aristotle denied that there was a "creation" in time. Although there are passages in Aristotle that have a distinctly religious and theistic flavor, the dominant mood of his thought on this matter is less religious than it is scientific. Still, to speak of an Unmoved Mover involved Aristotle in certain metaphorical language. In explaining how an Unmoved Mover can "cause" motion, he compared it to a beloved who "moves" the lover just by being the object of love, by the power of attraction and not by force. In a more technical way, Aristotle considered the Unmoved Mover as the *form* and the world as the substance. From the point of view of his four causes, Aristotle considered the Mover as the *final* cause, in the way that the *form* of the adult is in the child, directing the motion of change toward a *final,* that is, fixed or appropriate, natural *end.* By being a final cause, the Unmoved Mover thereby, in relation to the world, becomes also *efficient* cause, through the power of attraction, by being desired and loved, by inspiring the striving toward natural ends, a process that goes on eternally. What in Aristotle's thought was the unconscious principle of motion and immanent form of the world, the Unmoved Mover, became, especially at the hands of Aquinas in the thirteenth century, the philosophical description of the God of Christianity. Aristotle's Unmoved Mover could be said to be pure understanding, pure *nous,* and since it must think the best, it "thinks itself...and its thinking is a thinking of thinking... throughout all eternity." Such a "God" is not the religious God who becomes involved in the affairs of man. Aristotle's "God" is immanent in the world, making the world an intelligible order.

THE PLACE OF MAN: PHYSICS, BIOLOGY, AND PSYCHOLOGY

Aristotle placed humans in the nature of things in such a way as to distinguish their position in the hierarchy of being from inanimate things and animals. He points out in his *Physics* that "Of things that exist, some exist by nature, some from other causes. 'By nature' the animals and their parts exist, and the plants and the simple bodies (earth, fire, air, water)." In the order of nature, there are, then, first of all, simple bodies, plants, and animals. What is significant about all these things in nature is, as Aristotle states, that they all "present a feature in which they differ from things which are *not* constituted by nature. Each of them has *within* itself a principle of motion and of rest." This internal motion is the decisive aspect of things, for through this motion Aristotle explains the whole process of generation and corruption.

Physics   Limiting our concern only to the question of how things come to be in the natural world, Aristotle begins with the notion of *prime matter.* We have already said that Aristotle rejected the position that either pure forms or pure matter could exist separately. There is no *primary matter* existing by itself anywhere. By *prime matter* Aristotle must have meant the substratum in things that is capable of changing, of becoming other substances or things, of assuming novel forms. The processes of nature, then, involve the continuous transformation of matter from one form to another. When the sculptor makes a statue, his material, let us say marble, already has some form, and he will then transform it. In this same sense, Aristotle says that there are certain materials out of which *nature* makes things and he calls these *simple bodies,* namely air, fire, earth, and water. In one way or another, he says, all things are analyzable down to these. Still, when these bodies combine with one another, they form novel substances. Unlike the statue, however, the genesis of these new forms is a product of nature itself, since these bodies have within themselves a "principle of motion and rest." For this reason, fire tends to rise and become air, water to fall and become earth, the solid to become liquid, and the wet to become dry. In any case, to say that things *change* is to say that these basic simple bodies are constantly being transformed into things through their internal principle of motion and by the motion of other things.

Biology   What confers life upon certain kinds of bodies? Aristotle accounts for the transition from inorganic to organic bodies by considering the nature of the *soul.* All bodies, he says, are a combination of the primary elements, but some have life and others do not. By life Aristotle means "self-nutrition and growth (with its correlative decay)." Matter as such is not the principle of life, since material substance is said to be only potentially alive. Matter is always potentiality, whereas form is actuality. A body, then, that is actually alive has its life from the source of actuality, namely, *form.* The soul, then, is the form of an organized body. Neither can exist without the other, nor are they identical, and, says Aristotle, "that is why we can wholly dismiss as unnecessary the question whether the soul and body are one: it is as meaningless as to ask whether the wax and the shape given to it by the stamp are one." The soul, as Aristotle defines it, is "the first grade of actuality of a natural organized body." When a body is "organized," its parts have set motions to perform: Thus, in a living plant, "the leaf serves to shelter the pericarp, the pericarp to shelter the fruit, while the roots of plants are analogous to the mouth of animals...serving for the absorption of food." The soul is "the definitive formula of a thing's essence." The soul exists when there is a particular kind of body, namely, "one having *in itself* the power of setting itself in movement and arresting itself." Soul and body are not two separate things but are rather the matter (body) and form (soul) of a single unity; and, "from this it indubitably follows that the soul is inseparable from its body." Without the body, the soul could not exist, any more than there could be vision without an eye.

Aristotle distinguished between three types of soul in order to indicate the three different ways a body can be organized. He called these the *vegetative, sensitive,* and *rational* souls. They represent various capacities of a body for activity, the first being simply the act of living, the second both living and sensing, and the third a body that includes living, sensing, and thinking.

Psychology   The sensitive soul is found at the animal level. Its chief characteristic lies in its power to absorb qualities and *forms* of things without taking in their *matter.* This is in contrast to the lower nutritive soul, which takes in the *matter* (e.g., food) but has no capacity to absorb its *form.* The basic sense is tactile, or touch, and is capable of absorbing what all bodies have in common. For the other senses, Aristotle says that "each sense has one kind of object which it discerns, and never errs in reporting that what is before it is color or sound." Again, the sensitive soul absorbs only the form and not the matter, "in the way," says Aristotle, "in which a piece of wax takes on the impress of a signet ring without the iron or gold...in a similar way the sense is affected by what is coloured or flavoured or sounding, but it is indifferent to what in each case the *substance* is."

Just how the sensitive soul senses was explained by Aristotle by a special interpretation of *potentiality.* The sense organs must be capable of sensing many different forms. They must therefore be potentially capable of adjusting to any quality. The eye, for example, must be composed of material that potentially can become blue and that in fact does become blue when a certain kind of object is sensed. This neutral material of the eye must possess potentially all colors as well as all shapes. Our various other senses have similar potentialities with respect to other qualities. Moreover, the five senses have a way of combining their information into a unified whole, reflecting the single object or world from which these "sensibles" come. Errors are possible, as when something will "look" hard but "feel" soft. The qualities we sense can continue even after we are no longer directly perceiving an object, and this Aristotle explains in terms of *memory* and also *imagination.* Much of what we remember retains its associations with other things, suggesting that neither sensation nor memory is a random act but rather tends to reproduce what in fact exists in the real world. From the power of memory and imagination comes finally the higher form of soul, the human or the rational soul.

Human Rationality   The human soul combines in itself all the lower forms of soul, the vegetative, nutritive, and sensitive, having in addition to these the *rational soul.* The rational soul has the power of scientific thought. The *reason* is capable not only of distinguishing between different kinds of things, which is the power of analysis, it is able also to understand the relationships of things to each other. Besides scientific thought, the rational soul has the power of *deliberation.* Here the mind not only discovers what truth is in the nature of things, it discovers the guides for human behavior.

Again, for Aristotle, the soul forms the *entelechy,* the definitive form, of the body. Without the body, the soul could neither be nor exercise its functions. This is in sharp contrast to Plato's explanation of the body as the prison house of the soul. By contrast, Aristotle says that the body and soul together form one substance. Because he separated soul and body, Plato could speak of the preexistence of the soul. He could also describe knowledge or learning as the process of recollection of what the soul knew in its previous state. Moreover, Plato could also speak of the immortality of the individual soul. Aristotle, on the other hand, tied soul and body so closely together that with the death of the body, the soul, its organizing principle, also perished. Also, for him the mind begins as a blank tablet.

The rational soul of man, like the sensitive soul, is characterized by potentiality. Just as the eye is capable of seeing a red object but will only see it when it actually confronts a red object, so, also, the rational soul is capable of understanding the true nature of things. But reason has its knowledge only potentially; it must reason out its conclusions. Human thought, in short, is a possibility and not a continuous actuality, for if it is *possible* for the human mind to attain knowledge, it is also possible for it *not* to attain knowledge. Human thought is therefore intermittent between *actually* and *potentially* knowing. Truth is never continuously present in the human intellect.

The continuity of truth is implied by the continuity of the world. What the human mind has as potential knowledge must therefore be perfect and continuous knowledge in some mind. Aristotle had spoken of the Unmoved Mover as the soul (*nous*) of the world and its intelligible principle. In his *De Anima* he speaks of the Active Intellect, saying that "*Nous* does not at one time function and at another not." Here he appears to compare the individual human intellect, which knows only intermittently, with the Active Intellect, which is in some sense independent of particular people and is eternal. If this intellect is indeed purely active, it possesses no potentiality. But this is what Aristotle had described as the Unmoved Mover. The distinctive activity of the Unmoved Mover is pure act, which is an exercise of the mind in complete harmony with the truth about the whole of reality. The whole system of Forms taken as the intelligible structure of all things must therefore constitute the continuous knowledge of the *nous* of the world, the Unmoved Mover, the Active Intellect. This Intellect is immortal, and to the extent that our passive and potential intellects know any truth, they have in them what the Active Intellect always knows. What is immortal when we die is what belongs to the Active Intellect, but as this is not a part of *us,* our own individual souls perish with the matter for which it was the form. Only what is pure act is eternal, and our substance, being an admixture of potentiality, does not survive.

ETHICS

Aristotle's theory of morality centers around his belief that people, as everything else in nature, have a distinctive "end" to achieve or a function to fulfill. For this reason, his theory is rightly called *teleological.* He begins his *Nicomachean Ethics* by saying that "Every art and every inquiry, and similarly every action and pursuit, is thought to aim at some good...." If this is so, the question for ethics is, "What is the *good* at which human behavior aims?" Plato had answered this question by saying that people aim at a knowledge of the Idea of the Good. For him this supreme principle of Good was separated from the world of experience and from individuals and was to be arrived at by the mind's ascent from the visible world to the intelligible world. For Aristotle, on the other hand, the principle of good and right was imbedded within each person; moreover, this principle could be discovered by studying the essential nature of humanity and could be attained through actual behavior in daily life. Aristotle warns his reader, however, not to expect more precision in a discussion of ethics than "the subject-matter will admit." Still, just because this subject is susceptible of "variation and error" does not mean, said Aristotle, that ideas of right and wrong "exist conventionally only, and not in the nature of things." With this in mind, Aristotle set out to discover the basis of morality in the structure of human nature.

Types of "Ends"   Aristotle sets the framework for his ethical theory with a preliminary illustration. Having said that all action aims toward an end, he now wants to distinguish between two major kinds of ends, which can be called *instrumental* ends (acts that are done as *means* for other ends) and *intrinsic* ends (acts that are done for their own sake). These two types of ends are illustrated, for example, in "every action connected with war." When we consider step by step what is involved in the total activity of a war, we find, says Aristotle, that there is a series of special kinds of acts, which have their own ends but which, when they are completed, are only means by which still other ends are to be achieved. There is, for one thing, the art of the bridle maker. When the bridle is completed, its maker has achieved his end as a bridle maker. But the bridle is a means for the horseman to guide his horse in battle. Also, a carpenter builds a barrack, and when it is completed, he has fulfilled his function as a carpenter. The barracks also fulfill their function when they provide safe shelter for the soldiers. But the ends here achieved by the carpenter and the building are not ends in themselves but are instrumental in housing soldiers until they move on to their next stage of action. Similarly, the function of the builder of ships is fulfilled when the ship is successfully launched, but again this end is in turn a means for transporting the soldiers to the field of battle. The doctor fulfills his function to the extent that he keeps the soldiers in good health. But the "end" of health in this case becomes a "means" for effective fighting. The officer aims at victory in battle, but victory is the means to peace. Peace itself, though sometimes taken mistakenly as the final end of war, is the means for creating the conditions under which humans, *as humans,* can fulfill their function as humans. When we discover what humans aim at, not as carpenters, doctors, or generals, but as *humans,* we will then arrive at action *for its own sake,* and for which all other activity is only a means, and this, says Aristotle, "must be the Good of Man."

How shall the word *good* be understood? As Plato before him, Aristotle tied the word *good* to the special function of a thing. A hammer is good if it does what hammers are expected to do. A carpenter is good if he or she fulfills his or her function as a builder. This would be true for all the crafts and professions. But here Aristotle distinguishes between one's craft or profession and one's activity as a person. To be a good doctor, for example, did not for Aristotle mean the same thing as being a good person. One could be a good doctor without being a good person, and vice versa. There are two different functions here, the function of doctoring and the function of acting as a person. To discover the good at which a person should aim, Aristotle said we must discover the distinctive function of human nature. The good person, according to Aristotle, is the person who is fulfilling his or her function as a person.

The Function of Man   Aristotle asks, "Are we then to suppose that while carpenter and cobbler have certain works and courses of action, Man as Man has none, but is left by Nature without a work?" Or, if "the eye, hand, foot and in general each of the parts evidently has a function, may one lay it down that man similarly has a function apart from all these?" Surely, humanity too has a distinctive mode of activity, but what is it? Here Aristotle analyzes humanity's nature in order to discover its unique activity, saying, first of all, that humanity's end "is not mere life," because that plainly is shared even by vegetables, and, says Aristotle, "we want what is peculiar to [humanity]." Next there is the life of sensation, "but this again manifestly is common to horses, oxen and every animal." There remains then "an active life of the element that has a rational principle... if the function of man is an activity of soul which follows or implies a rational principle... then the human good turns out to be activity of soul in accordance with virtue."

Since a human's function as a human means the proper functioning of the soul, Aristotle sought to describe the nature of the soul. The soul is the form of the body. As such, the soul refers to the total person. Accordingly, Aristotle said that the soul has two parts, the irrational and the rational. The irrational part in turn is composed of two subparts, the vegetative and the desiring or "appetitive" parts. For the most part, these are "something contrary to the rational principle, resisting and opposing it." The conflict between the rational and irrational elements in man is what raises the problems and subject matter of morality.

Morality involves action, for nothing is called *good* unless it is functioning. Thus Aristotle says that "as at the Olympic games it is not the finest and strongest men who are crowned, but they who enter the lists, for out of these the prize-men are selected; so too in life, of the honourable and good, it is they who act who rightly win the prizes." The particular kind of action implied here, if one has in mind Aristotle's analysis of the soul, is the rational control and guidance of the irrational parts of the soul. Moreover, the good person is not the one who does a good deed here or there, now and then, but the one whose whole life is good, "for as it is not one swallow or one fine day that makes a spring, so it is not one day or a short time that makes a man blessed and happy."

Happiness as the End   Human action should aim at its proper end. Everywhere people aim at pleasure, wealth, and honor. But none of these ends, though they have value, can occupy the place of the chief good for which people should aim. To be an ultimate end an act must be *self-sufficient* and *final,* "that which is always desirable in itself and never for the sake of something else," and it must be *attainable by people.* Aristotle seems certain that all people will agree that *happiness* is the end that alone meets all the requirements for the ultimate end of human action. Indeed, we choose pleasure, wealth, and honor only because we think that "through their instrumentality we shall be happy." Happiness, it turns out, is another word or name for *good,* for like good, happiness is the fulfillment of our distinctive function; or, as Aristotle says, "Happiness . . . is a working of the soul in the way of excellence or virtue."

How does the soul work to attain happiness? The general rule of morality is "to act in accordance with Right Reason." What this means is that the rational part of the soul should control the irrational part. That the irrational part of the soul requires guidance is obvious when we consider what it consists of and what its mechanism is. Referring now only to the appetites, or the "appetitive" part of the soul, we discover first that it is affected or influenced by things outside of the self, such as objects and persons. Also, there are two basic ways in which the appetitive part of the soul reacts to these external factors, these ways being *love* and *hate,* or through the *concupiscent* and *irascible* "passions." The concupiscent passion leads one to desire things and persons, whereas the irascible passion leads one to avoid or destroy them. It becomes quickly apparent that these passions or capacities for love and hate, attraction or repulsion, creation or destruction, taken by themselves could easily "go wild." In themselves they do not contain any principle of measure or selection. What should a person desire? How much? Under what circumstances? How should one relate oneself to things, wealth, honor, and other persons?

We do not automatically act the right way in these matters; as Aristotle says, "none of the moral virtues arises in us by nature; for nothing that exists by nature can form a habit contrary to its nature." Morality has to do with developing habits, the habits of right thinking, right choice, and right behavior.

Virtue as the "Golden Mean"   Since the passions are capable of a wide range of action, all the way from too little to too much, a person must discover the proper meaning of excess and defect and thereby discover the appropriate *mean.* Virtue is concerned with our various feelings and actions, for it is in them that there can be excess and defect. For example, it is possible, says Aristotle, to feel the emotions of fear, confidence, lust, anger, compassion, pleasure, and pain, too much or too little, and in either case wrongly. To feel them when we ought to, on which occasions, toward whom, and as we should is the *mean;* that is the best state for people to be in, and this is *virtue.* Vice, again, is either extreme, excess or defect, and virtue is the mean. It is through the rational power of the soul that the passions are controlled and action is guided. The virtue of *courage,* for example, is the mean between two vices: namely, cowardice (defect) and foolhardiness (excess). Virtue, then, is a state of being, "a state apt to exercise deliberate choice, being in the relative mean, determined by reason, and as the man of practical wisdom would determine." Therefore, virtue is a habit of choosing in accordance with a mean.

The mean is not the same for every person, nor is there a mean for every act. Each mean is relative to each person inasmuch as the circumstances will vary. In the case of eating, the mean will obviously be different for an adult athlete and a little girl. But for each person, there is nevertheless a proportionate or relative mean, *temperance,* clearly indicating what extremes—namely, gluttony (excess) and starvation (defect)—would constitute vice for that person. Similarly, when one gives money, *liberality,* as the mean between prodigality and stinginess, is not an absolute figure but is relative to one's assets. Moreover, for some acts there is no mean at all; their very nature already implies badness, such as spite, envy, adultery, theft, and murder. These are bad in themselves and not in their excesses or deficiencies. One is always wrong in doing them.

Deliberation and Choice   There are in the rational soul two kinds of reasoning. The first is theoretical, giving us knowledge of fixed principles or philosophical wisdom. The other is practical, giving us a rational guide to our action under the particular circumstances in which we find ourselves, and this is practical wisdom. What is important about the role of reason is that without this rational element, we would not have any moral capacity. Again, Aristotle stressed that although we have a natural capacity for *right* behavior, we do not act rightly *by nature.* Our life consists of an indeterminate number of possibilities. Goodness is in us *potentially;* but unlike the acorn out of which the oak will grow with almost mechanical certitude, we must move from what is potential in us to its actuality by knowing what we must do, deliberating about it, and then choosing in fact to do it. Unlike Plato and Socrates, who thought that to know the good was sufficient to do the good, Aristotle saw that there must be deliberate choice in addition to knowledge. Thus, Aristotle said that "the origin of moral action—its efficient, not its final cause—is choice, and (the origin) of choice is desire and reasoning with a view to an end." There cannot be *choice* without reason. And again, "intellect itself...moves nothing, but only the intellect which aims at an end and is practical."

Morality and moral choice imply human responsibility. If some ways of behaving are right and others wrong, it is necessary to discover why a person acts in a wrong instead of a right way. If we are to praise or blame, praise virtue and blame vice, a person must be truly capable of making a choice. Aristotle assumed that an act for which a person could be held responsible must be a *voluntary* act. A genuine choice is a voluntary action. But not all our actions are voluntary. Thus, Aristotle said that "praise and blame arise upon such as are voluntary, while for the involuntary allowance is made, and sometimes compassion is excited." The distinction, as he saw it, between voluntary and involuntary acts was in general this: *Involuntary* acts are those for which a person is not responsible because they are (1) done out of ignorance of particular circumstances, (2) done as a result of external compulsion, or (3) done to avoid a greater evil. *Voluntary* acts are those for which a person is responsible because none of these three extenuating circumstances obtain.

The Virtues   In a general way we have already defined virtue as the fulfillment of humanity's distinctive function and as the mean between extremes. Another way to describe Aristotle's concept of virtue is to consider each virtue as the product of the rational control of the passions. In this way we can combine all aspects of human behavior. Human nature consists for Aristotle not simply in rationality but in the full range covered by the vegetative, sensitive or appetitive, and the rational souls. Virtue does not imply the negation or rejection of any of these natural capacities. The moral person employs all of his or her capacities, *physical* and *mental.* Corresponding to these two broad divisions in humanity there are two functions of reason, the intellectual and the moral, and each has its own virtues. There are accordingly *intellectual virtues* and *moral virtues.*

The intellectual virtues are philosophical wisdom and understanding and owe their birth and growth to teaching and learning. Moral virtue comes about as a result of habit, whence comes the name *ethics* (*ethike*), "formed by a slight variation from the word *ethos* (habit)." All the moral virtues have to be learned and practiced, and they become virtues only through action, for "we become just by doing just acts, temperate by doing temperate acts, brave by doing brave acts." The "cardinal" moral virtues are courage, temperance, justice, and wisdom. In addition to these, Aristotle considered also the virtues of magnificence, liberality, friendship, and self-respect. And although he acknowledged the central role of reason as a guide to practical and moral action, he nevertheless concluded that philosophic wisdom is superior to practical wisdom, that *contemplation* is most likely to lead to happiness.

Contemplation   Aristotle concludes that if happiness is the product of our acting according to our distinctive nature, it is reasonable to assume that it is acting according to our highest nature, and "that this activity is contemplative we have already said." This activity is the best, says Aristotle, "since not only is reason the best thing in us, but the objects of reason are the best of knowable objects." Moreover, contemplation "is most continuous, since we can contemplate truth more continuously than we can *do* anything." Finally, "we think happiness has pleasure mingled with it, but the activity of philosophic wisdom is admittedly the pleasantest of virtuous activities."

POLITICS

In *Politics,* as in *Ethics,* Aristotle stresses the element of purpose. The state, as humanity, is endowed by nature with a distinctive function. Combining these two ideas, Aristotle says that "it is evident that the State is a creature of nature, and that man is by nature a political animal." So closely does he relate humanity and the state as to conclude that "he who is unable to live in society, or who has no need because he is sufficient for himself, must be either a beast or a god." Not only is humanity by nature destined to live in a state, but the state, as every other community, "is established with a view to some good," exists for some end. The family exists primarily to preserve life. The state comes into existence in the first instance to preserve life for families and villages, which in the long run are not self-sufficing. But beyond this economic end, the function of the state is to ensure the supreme good of humanity, namely, its moral and intellectual life.

Unlike Plato, Aristotle did not create a blueprint for an ideal state. Even though Aristotle viewed the state as the agency for enabling people to achieve their ultimate goals as human beings, he nevertheless realized that any practical theory of the state must take note of "what kind of government is adapted to particular states...[that] the best is often unattainable..." and that the legislator must be acquainted with "which is best relatively to circumstances...how a state may be constituted under any given conditions...[and] how it may be longest preserved," concluding that "political writers, although they have excellent ideas, are often unpractical." For these reasons, Aristotle had little patience with Plato's most radical ideas. Ridiculing Plato's arrangement for the abolition of the family for the guardian class and providing a public nursery for their children, Aristotle said that "there is no reason why the so-called father should care about the son, or the son about the father, or brothers about one another." The communal ownership of property would likewise destroy certain basic human pleasures as well as engender inefficiency and endless disputes.

Types of States   Aristotle was willing to recognize that under appropriate circumstances, a community could organize itself into at least three different kinds of government. The basic difference among them is primarily the number of rulers each has. A government can have as its rulers *one,* a *few,* or *many.* But each of these forms of government can have a true or a perverted form. When a government is functioning rightly, it governs for the common good of all the people. A government is perverted when its rulers govern for their own private gain or interests. The true forms of each type of government, according to Aristotle, are *monarchy* (one), *aristocracy* (few), and *polity* (many). The perverted forms are *tyranny* (one), *oligarchy* (few), and *democracy* (many). His own preference was aristocracy, chiefly because even though ideally an individual of exceptional excellence would be desirable, such persons do not exist with sufficient frequency. In an aristocracy, there is the rule of a group of people whose degree of excellence, achievement, and ownership of property makes them responsible, able, and capable of command.

Differences and Inequalities   Because he relied so heavily upon his observation of things, it was inevitable that Aristotle would make some mistakes. Nowhere is this more true than in his estimate of slavery. Observing that slaves invariably were strong and large, he concluded that slavery was a product of nature. "It is clear," said Aristotle, "that some men are by nature free, and others slaves, and that for these slavery is both expedient and right." To be sure, Aristotle took great care to distinguish between those who become slaves by nature, a mode he accepted, and those who become slaves by military conquest, a mode he rejected. Aristotle rejected slavery by conquest on the highly defensible grounds that to overpower someone does not mean that one is superior to him in nature. Moreover, the use of force may or may not be justified, in which case enslavement could very well be the product and extension of an unjust act. At the same time, speaking of the "proper treatment of slaves," he proposed that "it is expedient that liberty should be always held out to them as the reward of their services." The fact is that in his own last will and testament, Aristotle provided for the emancipation of some of his slaves.

Aristotle also believed in the inequality of citizenship. He held that the basic qualification for citizenship was a person's ability to take his share in ruling and being ruled in turn. A citizen had the right and the obligation to participate in the administration of justice. Since a citizen would therefore have to sit in the assembly and in the law courts, he would have to have both ample time as well as an appropriate temperament and character. For this reason, Aristotle did not believe that laborers should be citizens, as they had neither the time nor the appropriate mental development, nor could they benefit from the experience of sharing in the political process.

Good Government and Revolution   Over and over again Aristotle made the point that the state exists for the sake of everyone's moral and intellectual fulfillment. "A state," he said, "exists for the sake of a good life, and not for the sake of life only"; also, "the state is the union of families and villages in a perfect and self-sufficing life, by which we mean a happy and honourable life." Finally, he said, "our conclusion...is that political society exists for the sake of noble actions, and not mere companionship." Still, whether a state produces the good life depends upon how its rulers behave. We have already said that the perverted forms of government are distinguished from the true forms by this, that the good rulers seek to achieve the good of all, whereas the perverted rulers seek their own private gain.

Whatever form a government has, it will rest upon some conception of justice and proportionate equality. But these conceptions of justice can bring disagreement and ultimately revolution. Democracy, as Aristotle knew it, arises out of the assumption that those who are equal in any respect are equal in all respects; "because men are equally free, they claim to be absolutely equal." On the other hand, Aristotle said *oligarchy* is based upon the notion that "those who are unequal in one respect are in all respects unequal." Hence, "being unequal...in property, they suppose themselves to be unequal absolutely." For these reasons, whenever the democrats or oligarchs are in the minority and the philosophy of the incumbent government "does not accord with their preconceived ideas, [they] stir up revolution....Here then...are opened up the very springs and fountains of revolution."

Aristotle concludes that "the universal and chief cause of this revolutionary feeling [is] the desire of equality, when men think they are equal to others who have more than themselves." He did not overlook other causes such as "insolence and avarice" as well as fear and contempt. Knowing these causes of revolution, Aristotle said that each form of government could take appropriate precautions against it; for example, a king must avoid despotic acts, an aristocracy should avoid the rule by a few rich men for the benefit of the wealthy class, and a polity should provide more time for its abler members to share in the government. Another precaution is to guard against the beginning of change. Most important of all, Aristotle urged that "there is nothing which should be more jealously maintained than the spirit of obedience to law." In the end, people will always criticize the state unless their conditions of living within it are such that they can achieve happiness in the form of what they consider the good life.

PHILOSOPHY OF ART

Aristotle had a far more sympathetic interest in art than did Plato. For Plato, as for Aristotle, art was essentially a matter of imitation, an imitation of nature. What made Plato so contemptuous of some forms of art was his notion that a work of art is at least three steps removed from truth. The true reality of humanity, let us say, is the eternal Form of Humanity. A poor copy of this Form would be any particular person—Socrates, for example. A statue or portrait of Socrates would then be a copy of a copy. Plato was particularly concerned with the cognitive aspect of art, feeling that it had the effect of distorting knowledge because it was removed several steps from reality. Aristotle, on the other hand, believing that the universal Forms exist only in particular things, felt that the artist is dealing directly with the universal when he studies things and translates them into art forms. For this reason Aristotle affirmed the cognitive value of art, saying that since art does imitate nature, it therefore communicates information about nature.

In his *Poetics,* he stresses the cognitive aspect of poetry by contrasting poetry with history. Unlike the historian, who is concerned only with particular persons and events, the poet deals with basic human, and therefore universal, experience. The true difference between them is that history relates what has happened, whereas poetry considers what may happen. "Poetry, therefore," says Aristotle, "is a more philosophical and a higher thing than history: for poetry tends to express the universal, history the particular." By universality, Aristotle means "how a person of a certain type will on occasion speak or act, according to the law of probability or necessity," and it is "this universality at which poetry aims."

In addition to its cognitive value, art has in Aristotle's view considerable psychological significance. For one thing, art reflects a deep facet of human nature by which people are differentiated from animals, this being their implanted instinct for imitation. Indeed, from earliest childhood learning takes place through imitation. In addition to this instinct, there is also the fact of pleasure people feel upon confronting art. Thus, "the reason men enjoy seeing a likeness is, that in contemplating it they find themselves learning or inferring, and saying perhaps, 'Ah, that is he.' "

Although Aristotle gave detailed analyses of *epic, tragedy,* and *comedy,* indicating what each consists of and what its function is, it was his remarks about tragedy that became most famous in subsequent thought. He particularly emphasized the emotional aspect of tragedy, centering upon the notion of *catharsis.* "A tragedy," says Aristotle, "is the imitation of an action that is serious and also, as having magnitude, complete in itself; in language with pleasurable accessories, each kind brought in separately in the parts of the work; in a dramatic, not a narrative form; with incidents arousing pity and fear, *wherewith to accomplish its catharsis of such emotions.*" Does the term *catharsis* imply that through tragedy we "get rid of" our feelings? Or, does it mean that we are given an occasion to express or give vent to our deepest emotions in a vicarious way? In either case, what Aristotle seems to be saying is that the artistic representation of deep and great suffering arouses in the audience genuine terror and pity, thereby purging and in a sense purifying the hearers' spirit. Thus, Aristotle says that "tragedy is an imitation of an action...through pity and fear effecting the proper purgation of these emotions."

5

Classical Philosophy After Aristotle

fter Aristotle had completed his great speculative system, philosophy moved toward a new emphasis. Four groups of philosophers helped to shape this new direction, namely, the Epicureans, the Stoics, the Skeptics, and the Neoplatonists. They were, of course, greatly influenced by their predecessors, so we find that Epicurus relied upon Democritus for his atomic theory of nature, the Stoics made use of Heraclitus' notion of a fiery substance permeating all things, the Skeptics built a method of inquiry upon the Socratic form of doubt, and Plotinus drew heavily upon Plato. What made their philosophy different, however, was not so much its subject matter as its mood and its emphasis. Its emphasis was practical, and its mood was self-centered. Philosophy became more practical by emphasizing the art of living. To be sure, each of these new movements of thought did involve speculative descriptions of the structure of the universe. But instead of working out blueprints for the ideal society and fitting individuals into large social and political organizations, as Plato and Aristotle had done, these new philosophers led people to think primarily of themselves and how they as individuals in a scheme of nature could achieve the most satisfactory personal life.

These new directions in ethics were brought about to a great extent by the historical conditions of the times. After the Peloponnesian War and with the fall of Athens, Greek civilization declined. With the breakdown of the small Greek city-state, individual citizens lost the sense of their own importance and their ability to control or perfect their social and political destiny. Individuals increasingly felt this loss of personal control over collective life as they were absorbed into the growing Roman Empire. When Greece became a mere province of Rome, men lost interest in pursuing the speculative questions concerning the ideal society. What was needed was a practical philosophy to give life direction under changing conditions. And at a time when events overwhelmed people, it seemed idle to try to change history. But if history was beyond humanity's control, at least a person's own life could be managed with some success. Philosophy, therefore, shifted to this practical emphasis in a mood of increasing concern for the more immediate world of the individual.

The Epicureans turned in the direction of an ideal for living through what they called *ataraxia,* or tranquillity of soul. The Stoics sought to control their reactions to inevitable events, while the Skeptics sought to preserve personal freedom by refraining from any basic commitment to ideals whose truth was doubtful, and Plotinus promised salvation in a mystical union with God. They looked to philosophy for a source of meaning for human existence, and it is no wonder that their philosophy, particularly Stoicism, was later to compete with religion for the allegiance of humanity. They sought to discover ways in which individual persons could successfully achieve happiness or contentment in a world that was not altogether friendly and filled with many pitfalls.

EPICURUS: PERFECTING THE PLEASURE PRINCIPLE

Epicurus was born about five or six years after Plato's death, when Aristotle was forty-two years old. Born in 342 or 341 B.C. on the island of Samos in the Aegean Sea, he was exposed in his teens to the writings of Democritus, whose ideas about nature had a permanent influence upon his own philosophy. When the Athenians were driven out of Samos, Epicurus went to Asia Minor, where he became a teacher in several schools. About the year 306 B.C. he moved to Athens and here founded his own school. The meeting place of his school was his own garden, which in time ranked with Plato's Academy, Aristotle's Lyceum, and Zeno's Stoa as one of the influential schools of ancient times. Here Epicurus attracted a close group of friends, who were attached to him by deep affection and reverence and to each other by the love of cultivated conversation. In spite of the loss of the bulk of his prolific writings there emerged from this school a definite approach to philosophy, which survived Epicurus' death in 270 B.C. The lasting impact of his teaching is shown by its continuous appearance in Athens and its spread to Rome, where the poet Lucretius (98–55 B.C.) embodied the major thoughts of Epicurus in his memorable poem *On the Nature of Things* (*De rerum natura*), which has survived to our day.

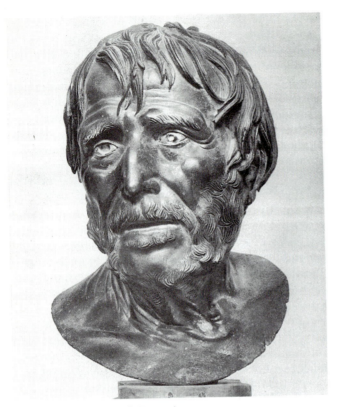

Lucretius *(MuseoNazionale Romano)*

Epicurus was a practical philosopher. He thought that ideas should have as much effect upon the control of life as medicine has upon the health of the body. Indeed, he considered philosophy as the medicine of the soul. He did not deal at length with the intricate aspects of questions such as "what is the world made of?" The picture of the world as consisting of atoms, or bits of matter, which had been developed by Democritus, seemed to Epicurus a reasonable answer. If that is what the world consists of, thought Epicurus, what consequences follow from that for human behavior?

To Epicurus, the chief aim of human life is pleasure. But it is ironic that his name should be linked even today with the indulgent gourmand or voluptuary, for nothing could be further from the teaching of Epicurus than the notion that pleasure consists in the triple formula of eat, drink, and be merry. Instead, he took great pains to distinguish between various types of pleasures, as, for example, between those that are intense but last only a short while and those that are not so intense but last longer, or between those pleasures which have a painful aftermath and those which bestow a sense of calm and repose. He tried to refine the principle of pleasure as the basis of conduct.

Physics and Ethics   What made Epicurus turn to the pleasure principle was the "science" or physics inherited from Democritus. This science had the effect of eliminating the notion that God has created everything and that human behavior should be based upon obedience to principles whose source is God. Building upon this "atomic theory," Epicurus concluded that everything that exists must be made up of eternal atoms, small, indestructible bits of hard matter. Apart from these clusters of atoms, nothing else exists. This would mean that if God or gods exist, they too must be material beings. Most important of all, God is not the source or the creator of anything but is himself the result of a purposeless and random event.

The origin of everything is explained by the notion that there is no beginning to the atoms. Atoms have always existed in space. As raindrops, they were at one time separately falling in space, and since they encountered no resistance, they always remained the same distance apart from each other. During this vertical drop, thought Epicurus, one atom instead of falling perfectly straight had developed a slight easing to one side, a lateral "swerve." In time, this atom moved into the path of an oncoming atom, and the resulting impact forced both of these atoms into the paths of other atoms, thereby setting in motion a whole series of collisions until all the atoms had been formed into clusters. These clusters or arrangements of atoms are the things we see even now, including rocks, flowers, animals, human beings, in short, the world. Since there was an infinite number of atoms, there must now be an infinite number of worlds. In any case, human beings are not part of a created or purposeful order caused or ruled by God but rather the accidental product of the collision of atoms.

God and Death   With this explanation of the origin of human beings, and for that matter of all beings including "divine beings," Epicurus thought that he had liberated humanity from the fear of God and from the fear of death. One no longer had to fear God because God did not control nature or human destiny and was, therefore, unable to intrude into people's lives. As for death, this, said Epicurus, need not bother anyone, because only a living person has sensation either of pain or pleasure. After death, there is no sensation, since the atoms that make up both the body and mind come apart, so there is no longer this particular body or mind but only a number of distinct atoms that return, as it were, to the primeval inventory of matter to continue the cycle of new formations. Only matter exists, and in human life all we know is this body and this present moment of experience. The composition of human nature includes atoms of different sizes and shapes, the larger atoms making up our bodies, with the smaller, smoother, and swifter atoms accounting for sensation and thinking. No other principle is needed to explain a person's nature, no God and, therefore, no afterlife. To be liberated from the fear of God and of death sets the stage for a way of life completely under a person's own control.

This was a new direction in moral philosophy, for it focused upon the individual and his immediate desires for bodily and mental pleasures instead of upon abstract principles of right conduct or considerations of God's commands. Just as his physical theory made the individual atom the final basis of all being, so also Epicurus singled out the individual person as the arena of the moral enterprise.

The Pleasure Principle   Although he portrayed the origin of all things in a mechanical way and placed humans into the nature of things as just another small mechanism whose nature led them to seek pleasure, Epicurus, nevertheless, reserved for humans both the power and the duty to regulate the traffic of their desires. Even though he had liberated humanity from the fear of God's providence, he had no intention, thereby, of opening the floodgates of passion and indulgence. He was certain that pleasure was the standard of goodness, but he was equally certain that not every kind of pleasure had the same value.

If one were to ask Epicurus how he knew that pleasure was the standard of *goodness,* he would answer simply that all people have an immediate feeling of the difference between pleasure and pain and of the desirability of pleasure, "For we recognize pleasure as the first good innate in us, and from pleasure we begin every act of choice and avoidance, and to pleasure we return again." Feeling, Epicurus said, is as immediate a test of goodness or badness as sensation is the test of truth. To our senses, pain is always bad and pleasure always good, just as seeing tells us whether something is in front of us or not.

Still, Epicurus laid his greatest emphasis upon the distinction between various kinds of pleasures in order to guide people to the happiest life. It was clear that some desires were both natural and necessary, as in the case of food; others natural but not necessary, as in the case of some types of sexual pleasure; and still others neither natural nor necessary, as, for example, any type of luxury or popularity. It was because he could make these clear distinctions that he concluded that "when...we maintain that pleasure is the end, we do not mean the pleasures of profligates and those that consist of sensuality, as is supposed by some who are either ignorant or disagree with us or do not understand, but freedom from pain in the body and from trouble in the mind. For it is not continuous drinkings and revellings, nor the satisfaction of lusts, nor the enjoyment of fish and other luxuries of the wealthy table, which produce a pleasant life, but sober reasoning, searching out the motives for all choice and avoidance, and banishing mere opinions, to which are due the greatest disturbance of the spirit."

Epicurus did not mean to deprecate the pleasures of the body but meant only to emphasize that too great a concern with these pleasures was both unnatural and the surest way to unhappiness and pain. Certain kinds of bodily pleasures could never be fully satisfied, he said, and if such pleasures required continuous indulgence it followed that people pursuing such pleasures would by definition always be unsatisfied and would, therefore, constantly suffer some pain. If, for example, they wanted more money, or more public acclaim, or more exotic foods, or a higher position, they would always be dissatisfied with their present situation and would suffer some internal pain. The wise person, on the other hand, is able to determine what is the minimum his or her nature requires, and is able easily and quickly to satisfy these needs. When these needs are satisfied, a person's constitution is in balance. The wise person's diet of bread and water is far more likely to bring happiness than the gourmet's surplus of fancy foods, for the wise person has learned not only to consume little but, also, and this is the clue, to need little.

The ultimate pleasure human nature seeks is repose, by which Epicurus means the absence of bodily pain and the gentle relaxation of the mind. This sense of repose can be most successfully achieved by scaling down our desires, overcoming useless fears, and, above all, turning to the pleasures of the mind, which have the highest degree of permanence. In a sense these pleasures of the mind are physical pleasures inasmuch as they have the effect of preventing overindulgence in matters of the flesh and, therefore, preventing their ensuing pain.

Individual Pleasure versus Social Duty   In the end, Epicurus had fashioned a self-centered moral philosophy, for his concern was not primarily with human society but with individual pleasure. Even the life of the philosopher is looked upon as a means to avoiding pain and not as an influence for creating a good society. Just as Epicurus sought to detach himself from the tyranny of exotic foods, so also did he seek to detach himself from entanglements with other people and particularly with poor people, whose needs and problems are many. For him the good life was not to be found in service to one's fellow man but in the pleasant, decent company of intellectually fascinating friends. The only function of civil society that Epicurus would recognize was to deter those who might inflict pain upon individuals. His theory of physics, which rules out all purpose and any realm of rational order, left him without a firm idea of justice. There was, for Epicurus, no higher value than the absence of pain and the control of desires by the mind. We shall see that for centuries to come this moral philosophy fashioned by Epicurus challenged and in turn was challenged by alternative concepts of the moral life.

STOICISM: DISTINGUISHING BETWEEN WHAT WE CAN AND CANNOT CONTROL

Stoicism as a school of philosophy includes some of the most distinguished intellectuals of antiquity. Founded by Zeno (334–262 B.C.), who assembled his school on the Stoa (Greek for *porch,* hence the term *stoic*), this philosophical movement attracted Cleanthes (303–233 B.C.) and Aristo in Athens and later found such advocates in Rome as Cicero (106–43 B.C.), Epictetus (60–117 A.D.), Seneca (4 B.C.?–65 A.D.), and the Emperor Marcus Aurelius (121–180 A.D.). Zeno had been inspired as a youth by the ethical teachings and particularly by the courageous death of Socrates. This influence helped to fix the overwhelming emphasis of Stoic philosophy upon ethics, although the Stoics addressed themselves to all three divisions of philosophy formulated by Aristotle's Lyceum, namely, logic, physics, and ethics.

Stoa—the corridor where Zeno delivered his lectures. His new school of philosophy, named Stoicism after this meeting place, was founded here. *(Agora Excavations, American School of Classical Studies at Athens)*

Wisdom and Control versus Pleasure In their moral philosophy, the Stoics aimed at happiness, but unlike the Epicureans they did not expect to find it in pleasure. Instead, the Stoics sought happiness through wisdom, a wisdom by which to control what lay within human power and to accept with dignified resignation what had to be. They were profoundly influenced by Socrates, who had faced death with serenity and courage. This example of superb control over the emotions in the face of the supreme threat to one's existence, the threat of death, provided the Stoics with an authentic model after which to pattern their lives. Centuries later the Stoic Epictetus said that "I cannot escape death, but cannot I escape the dread of it?" Developing this same theme in a more general way, he wrote, "Demand not that events should happen as you wish; but wish them to happen as they do happen, and you will go on well." We cannot, that is, control all events, but we can control our attitude toward what happens. It is useless to fear future events, for they will happen in any case. But it is possible by an act of will to control our fear. We should not, therefore, fear events—in a real sense we have "nothing to fear but fear itself."

There is an elegant simplicity to this moral philosophy, and yet it was a

Epictetus–a Stoic philosopher *(New York Public Library Picture Collection)*

philosophy for an intellectual elite. The conclusion was simple enough, to control one's attitudes, but how did the Stoics arrive at this conclusion in a philosophical way? They did it by creating a mental picture of what the world must be like and how man fits into this world. The world, they said, is an orderly arrangement where humans and physical things behave according to principles of *purpose*. They saw throughout all of nature the operation of *reason* and *law*. The Stoics relied upon a special idea of God to explain this view of the world, for they thought of God as a rational substance existing not in some single location but in all of nature, in all things. It was this kind of God, a pervading substantial form of *reason* that controls and orders the whole structure of nature, that the Stoics said determines the course of events. Herein lay the basis for moral philosophy, but the direction in which Stoic thought moved on these matters was set by their theory of the nature of knowledge.

Stoic Theory of Knowledge The Stoics went into great detail to explain how human beings are able to achieve knowledge. They did not entirely succeed in doing this, but their theory of knowledge was nevertheless important for at least two reasons. First, it laid the foundation for their materialistic theory of nature, and, secondly, it provided the basis for their conception of truth or certainty.

Both of these consequences of the Stoics' theory of knowledge stem from their account of the origin of ideas. Words, they said, express thoughts, and thoughts are originated by the impact of some object upon the mind. The mind is blank at birth and builds up its store of ideas as it is exposed to objects. These objects make impressions upon the mind through the channel of the senses. A tree, for example, impresses its image upon the mind through the sense of vision in the same way that a seal leaves its imprint in wax. Repeated exposure to the world of things increases the number of impressions, develops our memory, and enables us to form more general conceptions beyond the objects immediately before us.

The real problem the Stoics faced was how to explain this last point, that is, how to account for our general ideas. They had to show how our thinking is related to our sensations. It is one thing to prove that our idea of a tree comes from our vision of trees. But how can we account for general ideas, ideas that refer to things beyond our senses, as, for example, the idea of goodness? To this the Stoics in effect replied that all thought is in some way related to the senses, even thoughts that represent judgments and inferences. A judgment or an inference that something is good or true is the product of the mechanical process of impressions. Our thinking in all its forms starts with impressions, and some of our thinking is based upon impressions that start from within us, as in the case of feelings. Feelings can, therefore, give us knowledge; they are the source of "irresistible perceptions," which, in turn, are the ground of our sense of certainty. As the Skeptics later pointed out, this explanation could not stand up to all the critical questions one could raise against it. But the Stoics not only found in it a basis for truth, they had also, through this theory of knowledge, imposed a most distinctive slant upon their general philosophy. For to argue as they did that all thought derives from the impact of objects on the senses is to affirm that nothing real exists except things that possess some material form. Stoic logic had cast Stoic philosophy into a materialistic mold.

Matter as the Basis of All Reality   This materialism provided Stoicism with an ingenious conception of the physical world and the nature of humanity. The broad picture the Stoics drew of physical nature followed from their logic that all that is real is material. Everything in the whole universe is, therefore, some form of matter. But the world is not just a pile of inert or passive matter—it is a dynamic, changing, structured, and ordered arrangement. Besides inert matter, there is force or power, which represents the active shaping and ordering element in nature. This active power or force is not different from matter but is rather a different form of matter. It is a constantly moving, subtle thing, like an air current or breath. The Stoics said it was fire, and this fire spread to all things, providing them with vitality. This material fire had the attribute of rationality, and since this was the highest form of being, it was inevitable that the Stoics should understand this rational force to be God.

God in Everything   The pivotal idea of Stoicism was the notion that God is in everything. To say that God is fire, or force, or logos, or rationality and then to say that God is in everything is to conclude that all of nature is filled with the principle of reason. In a detailed manner the Stoics spoke of the permeability of matter, by which they meant that different types of matter are mixed up together. The material substance of God, they said, was mixed with what would otherwise be motionless matter. Matter behaves the way it does because of the presence in it of the principle of reason. The continued behavior of matter in accordance with this principle is what is meant by *natural law,* the law or principle of a thing's nature. When we recall that the Stoics ascribed the origin of nature to God, the warm, fiery matrix of all things, and that all things immediately receive the impress of God's structuring reason and continue to behave as they were arranged to behave, we can see how the Stoics also developed from these ideas their other notions of fate and providence.

Fate and Providence   To the Stoics, *providence* meant that events occur the way they do because all things and persons are under the control of the Logos, or God. The order of the whole world is based upon the unity of all its parts, and what unifies the whole structure of matter is the fiery substance that permeates everything. Nothing "rattles" in the universe, for nothing is loose. It was against this background of a material universe that is totally controlled that the Stoics fashioned their moral philosophy.

Human Nature   The Stoics knew that to build a moral philosophy it is necessary to have a clear view of what human nature is like. They shaped their view of human nature by simply transferring to the study of humanity the very same ideas they had used in describing nature at large. Just as the world is a material order permeated by the fiery substance called reason or God, so also a person is a material being who is permeated by this very same fiery substance. When the Stoics said that people contain a spark of the divine within them, they meant that in a real sense a person contains part of the substance of God. God is the soul of the world, and each person's soul is part of God. This spark of the divine is a very fine and pure material substance that permeates a person's body, causing it to move and to be capable of all sensations. The soul is corporeal, comes from God, and is transmitted by parents to children in a physical way. The Stoics thought that the soul was centered in the heart and that it circulated through the bloodstream. What the soul added to the body was the delicate mechanisms of the five senses as well as the powers of speech and reproduction. But since God is the Logos, or reason, the soul of man is also rooted in reason and consequently human personality finds its unique expression in its rationality. For the Stoics, however, human rationality did not mean simply that people are able to think, or to reason about things, but rather that a person's nature participates in the rational structure and order of the whole of nature. Human rationality represents a person's awareness of the actual order of things and of his or her place in this order. It is the awareness that all things obey law. To relate human behavior to this order of law was the chief concern of Stoic moral philosophy.

Ethics and the Human Drama   Moral philosophy in Stoic thought rested upon a simple insight, wherein each person was viewed as an actor in a drama. What Epictetus meant when he used this image was that an actor does not choose a role, but on the contrary it is the author or director of the drama who selects people to play the various roles. In the drama of the world, it is God, or the principle of reason, who determines what each person shall be and how he or she will be situated in history. Human wisdom, said the Stoics, consists in recognizing what one's role in this drama is and then performing the part well. Some people have "bit parts," while others are cast into leading roles. "If it be [God's] pleasure that you should act a poor person, see that you act it well; or a cripple or a ruler, or a private citizen. For this is your business," says Epictetus, "to act well the given part." The actor develops a great indifference to those things over which he or she has no control, as, for example, the shape and form of the scenery as well as who the other players will be. The actor especially has no control over the story or its plot. But there is one thing the actor can control, and that is his or her attitude and emotions. The actor can sulk because of a bit part, or be consumed with jealousy because someone else was chosen to be the hero, or feel terribly insulted because the makeup artist has provided a particularly ugly nose. But neither sulking nor jealousy nor feeling insulted can in any way alter the fact that he or she has a bit part, is not a hero, and must wear an ugly nose. All these feelings can do is rob the actor of happiness. If he or she can remain free from these feelings, or develop what the Stoics called *apathy,* a serenity and happiness that are the mark of a wise person will be achieved. The wise person is the one who knows what his or her role is.

The Problem of Freedom   There is, however, a persistent problem in Stoic moral philosophy, and this concerns the nature of human freedom. The whole Stoic analysis of the structure of nature as being fixed, that is, caused or ordered by God's reason, is rather easy to follow, especially when we think of this grand scheme as a cosmic drama. It may be true that actors do not choose their roles. But what is the difference between choosing your role in the drama, on the one hand, or choosing your attitude on the other? If you are not free to choose one, how can you be free to choose the other? It could very well be that God not only chose you to be a poor person, but also cast you as a particularly disgruntled poor person. Do attitudes float freely waiting to be chosen by the passing parade of humanity, or are they as much a part of a person as eye color?

The Stoics stuck doggedly to their notion that attitudes are under the control of a person's choice, that by an act of will we can decide how we shall react to events. But they never provided a satisfactory explanation for the fact that providence rules everything while at the same time providence does not rule our attitudes. The closest they came to an explanation was to imply that whereas everything in the whole universe behaves according to law or reason, or the Logos, it is the special feature of human beings that they behave according to their knowledge of the law. For example, water evaporates from the heat of the sun and later condenses and returns in the form of rain. But one drop never says to the other, "here we go again," as if to register disgust at being uprooted from the blue sea. A human being undergoes a similar process of change when he or she begins to age and face death; but people know what is happening, for in addition to the mechanical process of aging, they *know* that it is happening. No amount of additional knowledge will change the fact that a person is mortal, but the Stoics built their whole moral philosophy on the conviction that if someone knows the rigorous law and understands one's role as inevitable, he or she will not strain against the inevitable but will move cheerfully with the pace of history. Happiness is not a product of choice; it is rather a quality of existence, which follows from acquiescing or agreeing to what has to be. Freedom, therefore, is not the power to alter our destiny but rather the absence of emotional disturbance.

Cosmopolitanism and Justice   It was inevitable that the Stoics should have also developed a strong notion of cosmopolitanism, the idea that all persons are citizens of the same human community. To look at the world process as a drama was to admit that everyone had a role in it. Human relations were viewed by the Stoics as having the greatest significance, for human beings were the bearers of the divine spark. What related persons to each other was the fact that each person shared a common element. It was as though the Logos were a main telephone line and all people had their own phone and the entire circuit was on a party line, thereby connecting God to all people and all people to each other. Or, as Cicero put it: "...since reason exists both in man and God, the first common possession of man and God is reason. But those who have reason in common must also have right reason in common. And since right reason is Law, we must believe that men have Law also in common with the Gods. Further, those who share Law must also share Justice, and those who share these are to be regarded as members of the same commonwealth." Universal brotherhood and the doctrine of a universal natural law of justice were among the most impressive contributions made to the Western mind by the Stoics. They had injected basic themes into the stream of thought that were to have a decisive impact, particularly upon the development of Christian philosophy in the next period.

Although Stoicism shared many of the characteristics of Epicurean philosophy, it had made some radical innovations. With the Epicureans, the Stoics put their chief emphasis upon the practical concerns of ethics, regarded self-control as the center of ethics, viewed all of nature in materialistic terms, and sought happiness as the end. The most significant variation injected by the Stoics was that they viewed the world not as the product of chance but as the product of an ordering mind, or reason. This view involved the Stoics in a highly optimistic attitude regarding the possibilities of human wisdom. Yet it was against this claim to wisdom, a claim that we can know so much about the detailed operation of the world, that there developed the critical philosophy of the Skeptics.

SKEPTICISM: HOW TO BEHAVE WITHOUT A CRITERION OF TRUTH

Today we refer to skeptics as those whose basic mood is that of doubt. But the old Greek word, *skeptikoi,* from which *skeptics* is derived, meant something rather different, namely, *seekers* or *inquirers.* To be sure, the Skeptics were doubters, too. They doubted that Plato and Aristotle had succeeded in discovering the truth about the world, and they had these same doubts about the Epicureans and Stoics. But for all their doubt, they were nevertheless seekers after a method for achieving a tranquil life. Their founder was Pyrrho (361–270 B.C.), and early Skepticism was known also as *Pyrrhonism.* They were also known as *Academics,* after Arcesilaus (ca. 316–241 B.C.), who became head of Plato's Academy in the third century, rejected Plato's metaphysics, and developed the doctrine of probabilism. Among the many other notable Skeptics the names Carneades (214–129 B.C.) and Sextus Empiricus (ca. 200 A.D.) are outstanding. As Skepticism moved through its different periods of development, it took on many variations in its point of view. While many of the original documents written by the Skeptics are now lost, some of the works of the authoritative codifier of Greek Skepticism, Sextus Empiricus, have survived. In the early sections of his *Pyrrhonic Sketches,* Sextus offers an illuminating account of the meaning and purposes of the viewpoint of Skepticism.

What gave rise to Skepticism? Sextus says that Skepticism originated in the hope of attaining mental peace or calmness. People have been disturbed, he says, by the contradiction in things and plagued by doubt as to which alternative they should believe. Accordingly the Skeptics thought that if they could by investigation determine truth from falsehood they could then attain tranquillity of mind. The Skeptics were struck, however, by the different conceptions of truth different philosophers had proposed. They also noticed that people who searched for truth could be placed into three groups, those who think they have discovered the truth (and these the Skeptics called *dogmatists*), those who confess they have not found it and also assert that it cannot be found (and this they also considered a dogmatic position), and finally those who persevere in the search for it. Unlike the first two, says Sextus, "the Skeptics keep on searching." Skepticism is not a denial of the possibility of finding truth, nor is it a denial of the basic facts of human experience. It is rather a continuous process of inquiry in which every explanation of experience is tested by a counterexperience. The fundamental principle of Skepticism, says Sextus, is that to every proposition an equal proposition is opposed. It is in consequence of this principle, he says, that "we end by ceasing to dogmatize."

The Skeptics were greatly impressed by the fact that "appearances" call forth such a variety of explanations from those who experience them. They discovered also, says Sextus, that arguments opposed to each other seem to have equal force. By equality of force he meant equality in respect of the credibility of probability of alternative explanations. Accordingly, the Skeptics were led to suspend judgment and to refrain from denying or affirming anything. From this suspension of judgment they hoped to achieve an undisturbed and calm mental state.

Clearly, the Skeptics did not give up the enterprise of vigorous thought and debate. Nor did they deny the evident facts about life, that people become thirsty and hungry and that they are in peril when they come near a precipice. That people must be careful about their behavior was very clear to the Skeptics. They had no doubt that they lived in a "real" world. They only wondered whether this world had been accurately described. No one, says Sextus, will dispute that objects have this or that appearance; the question is whether "the object is in reality such as it appears to be." Therefore, even though the Skeptics refused to live dogmatically, they did not deny the evident facts about experience. "We pay due regard to appearances," says Sextus. Daily life seemed to the Skeptics to require careful recognition of four items, which Sextus calls (1) the guidance of nature, (2) the constraint of the feelings, (3) the tradition of laws and customs, and (4) the instruction of the arts. Each of these contributes to successful and peaceful living and not one of them requires any dogmatic interpretation or evaluation, only acceptance. Thus, it is by Nature's guidance that we are naturally capable of sensation and thought. Also, it is by the force of the feelings that hunger drives us to food and thirst to drink. And it is the tradition of laws and customs that constrains us in everyday life to accept piety as good and impiety as evil. Finally, says Sextus, it is by virtue of the instruction of the arts that we engage in those arts in which we choose to participate.

There can be no doubt, therefore, that the Skeptics were far from denying the evident facts of sense perception. Indeed, Sextus says that those who say that the Skeptics deny appearances "seem to me to be unacquainted with the statements of our School." They did not question appearances but only "the account given of appearances." As an example, Sextus says that honey appears to be sweet, and "this we grant, for we perceive sweetness through the senses . . . ." But the real question is whether it is really, in essence, sweet. Thus, the arguments of the Skeptics about appearances are expounded not with the intention of denying the reality of appearance but in order to point out the "rashness" of the "Dogmatists." The moral Sextus drew from this treatment of the objects of sense was that if human reason can be so easily deceived by appearances, "if reason is such a trickster as to all but snatch away the appearances from under our very eyes," should we not be particularly wary of following reason in the case of nonevident matters and thus avoid rashness?

Nonevident matters had a central place in the great philosophical systems of Plato, Aristotle, and the Stoics. Here the Skeptics found elaborate theories, especially about the nature of physical things. But how can any theory of physics, an inquiry which deals with nonevident matters, give us reliable truth? The Skeptics had a double attitude toward the study of physics. On the one hand, they refused to theorize about physics as if to give "firm and confident opinions on any of the things in physical theory about which firm doctrines are held." Nevertheless, they did touch on physics "in order to have for every argument an equal argument to oppose it, and for the sake of mental tranquillity." Their approaches to matters of ethics and logic were similar. In each case their pursuit of mental tranquillity was not a negative approach, a refusal to think, but rather an active approach. Their mode of "the suspension of judgment" involved the activity of "setting things in opposition." As Sextus says, "we oppose appearances to appearances, or thoughts to thoughts, or appearances to thoughts."

The Skeptics, then, distinguished between two types of inquiry, between those dealing with evident and nonevident matters. Evident matters, such as whether it is night or day, raise no serious problems of knowledge. In this category, too, are evident requirements for social and personal tranquillity, for we know that customs and laws bind society together. But nonevident matters, as, for example, whether the stuff of nature is made of atoms or some fiery substance, do raise intellectual controversies. Whenever we go beyond the sphere of what is evident in human experience, our quest for knowledge should proceed under the influence of creative doubt. Thus, if we ask how we know what the universe is like, the Skeptics would answer that we do not yet know. It may be, they said, that people can attain the truth; it may also be that they are in error. But whether they have the truth or are in error cannot be decided, because there is available as yet no reliable criterion for determining the truth in nonevident matters.

The Senses Are Deceptive   If, as the Stoics had argued, our knowledge comes to us from our experience or sense impressions, all the more reason is there to doubt the adequacy of all knowledge. For the fact is that our senses give us different information about the same object at different times and under different circumstances. From a distance, a square building looks round. Landscape looks different at different times of day. To some people honey is bitter. Painted scenery at a theater gives the impression of real doors and windows when only lines exist on a flat surface. That we do have impressions is certain, as, for example, when we "see" a bent oar in the water. But what we can never be certain about is whether in fact the oar is bent. Although the oar can be taken out of the water and the error of perception discovered, not every perception affords such an easy test for its accuracy and truth. Most of our knowledge is based upon perceptions for which we have no criterion of truth. The conclusion of the Skeptic, therefore, is that we cannot be certain that our knowledge of the nature of things is true or not true.

Moral Rules Raise Doubts   Moral conceptions as well as physical objects are subject to doubt. People in different communities have different ideas of what is good and right. Customs and laws differ with each community and in the same community at different times. The Stoics said that there is a universal reason in which all people share, leading to a general consensus of all people regarding human rights. The Skeptics challenged both the theory and the fact, saying that there was no proof that all people have the capacity to agree upon the truth of universal moral principles and adding that there is no evidence that people in fact exhibit this universal agreement. The fact is that people disagree. Moreover, those who disagree can all make equally strong cases for their own points of view. On matters of morality there is no absolute knowledge; there is only opinion. Whereas the Stoics had argued that on certain matters the test for truth was the "irresistible perception," the Skeptics responded by saying that the sad fact is that however strongly an opinion is held, it is, after all, still only an opinion, and one can with as much evidence support an opposite opinion. When people take a dogmatic stand, their conclusions always seem to them to be irresistible, but this is no guaranty that their conceptions are true.

The outcome of this skeptical attitude toward our knowledge of the nature of things and our knowledge of moral truth is that we have a right to doubt the validity of knowledge. Since we lack sure knowledge, it behooves us to withhold judgment on all matters. But there is a matter about which it is difficult for people to withhold judgment, and that is the matter of ethics. When one faces a problem of behavior, one wants to know what is the right thing to do, and this requires knowledge of the right. It would appear, therefore, that the Skeptics had made ethics impossible and had removed from men any guide for human behavior.

Morality Possible without Intellectual Certainty The Skeptics argued, however, that it was not necessary to have knowledge in order to behave sensibly. It is enough, they said, to have reasonable assurance, or what they called *probability*. There could never be absolute certainty, but if there was a strong probability that our ideas would lead us to a life of happiness and peacefulness, we should be justified in following these ideas. We are able from daily experience to distinguish between notions that are not clear and those that have a high degree of clarity. When notions of right have a high degree of clarity, they create in us a strong belief that they are right, and this is all we need to lead us to action. For this reason customs, the laws of the land, and our basic appetites are for the most part reliable guides. But even here the Skeptic wants to retain a certain amount of caution, so that we will not mistake appearance for reality and above all avoid fanaticism and dogmatism. Although we are able to act enthusiastically even without a criterion of truth, our psychological safety requires that we leave open the channels of inquiry. The only safe attitude to take is one of doubt about the absolute truth of any idea. And one who can maintain a sense of imperturbability under this mood of doubt has the best chance of achieving the happy life.

If we ask whether the Skeptics had a "system," Sextus answers "No," if by a *system* is meant "an adherence to a number of dogmas which are dependent both on one another and on appearances" and where *dogma* is taken to mean "assent to a non-evident proposition." But if by a *system* is meant "a procedure which, in accordance with appearance, follows a certain line of reasoning...indicating how it is possible to seem to live rightly...," then the Skeptic did have a system. For, as Sextus says, "we follow a line of reasoning which-...points us to a life conformable to the customs of our country and its laws and institutions, and to our own instinctive feelings."

PLOTINUS: SALVATION IN MYSTICAL UNION WITH GOD

At the culmination of classical philosophy stands the influential figure of Plotinus (ca. 204–270 A.D.). He lived at a time when there was no single compelling philosophical doctrine that could satisfy the special concerns of his age. The great variety of religious cults attested to the desperate attempt by people in the second and third centuries of the Roman world to lay hold of an explanation of life and its destiny. It was an age of syncretism, when ideas were taken from several sources and put together as philosophies and religions. The cult of Isis combined Greek and Egyptian ideas of the gods; the Romans developed the Imperial Cult and worshiped their emperors, living and dead; devotees of the Mithraic cult worshiped the sun; and there was the Phrygian worship of the Great Mother of the Gods. Christianity was still considered a cult, even though there had already emerged some Christian thinkers, such as Justin Martyr (100–165), Clement of Alexandria (ca. 150–220), Tertullian (ca. 160–230), and Origen (185–254), who sought to give the Christian faith a systematic character and an intellectual defense. Origen had tried to provide a Platonic and Stoic framework for Christianity. Earlier, Clement of Alexandria had also tried to join Christian thought with philosophic ideas. But Christian theology would not achieve its full strength until Augustine had formulated his powerful synthesis of Christian and Platonic thought. The decisive bridge between classical philosophy and Augustine would be the writings of Plotinus. But Plotinus nowhere mentions Christianity; his original contribution consisted of a fresh version of Plato's philosophy, and for this reason is known as Neoplatonism.

Plotinus was born in Egypt about 204 A.D. He was the pupil of Ammonius Saccas in Alexandria. Alexandria was at this time an intellectual crossroads of the ancient world, and here Plotinus developed a wide grasp of classical philosophy, including the ideas of Pythagoras, Plato, Aristotle, Epicurus, and the Stoics. Out of all these strands he selected Platonism as the surest source of truth and indeed criticized the others by using his version of Plato's thoughts as his standard. From Alexandria he went, at the age of forty, to Rome, where the atmosphere was charged by considerable chaos in morality and religion and by social and political unrest. At Rome he opened his own school, to which he attracted some of that city's elite, including the emperor and his wife. For a while he planned to develop a city based upon the doctrines of Plato's *Republic* to be called Platonopolis, but this plan was never realized. He wrote fifty-four treatises with no particular order and in a style less eloquent than his speech. These treatises were assembled after Plotinus' death by his ablest pupil, Porphyry, who arranged them into six sets of nines, or, as they are now called, *Enneads*. Plotinus had been a brilliant lecturer and at the same time a man of spiritual idealism. Indeed, it was his moral and spiritual force combined with his intellectual rigor that influenced not only his contemporaries but especially St. Augustine. Later, Augustine said that Plotinus would have to change "only a few words" to become a Christian. In any case, the thought of Plotinus became a major strand in most of medieval philosophy.

What made Plotinus' philosophy distinctive was that he combined a speculative description of the system of reality with a religious doctrine of salvation. He not only described the world, but also gave an account of its source, of people's place in it, and of how people overcome their moral and spiritual difficulties in it. In short, Plotinus developed a doctrine about God as the source of all things and as that to which people must return. In formulating his thought, Plotinus successively analyzed and rejected as inadequate the views of the Stoics, Epicureans, Pythagoreans, and Aristotelians. Among his objections to these schools of thought was his conviction that they did not understand the true nature of the soul. The Stoics had described the soul as a material body, a physical "breath." But Plotinus argued that neither the Stoics nor Epicureans, both materialists, understood the essential independence of the soul from the material body. Likewise, the Pythagoreans, who had said that the soul is the "harmony" of the body, would have to admit that when the body is not in harmony, it has no soul. Finally, Aristotle's notion that the soul is the form of the body, that it cannot exist without a body, was rejected by Plotinus on the ground that if part of the body loses its form, this would mean that to that extent the soul would also be deformed. This would make the body primary, whereas, said Plotinus, it is the soul that is primary, that gives life to the body as a whole. Everything for Plotinus turned upon the accurate understanding of a person's essential nature.

To understand human nature, Plotinus pursued the line of thought Plato had set forth in his vivid myths and allegories. He was struck by Plato's comprehensive treatment of reality, including his account of the Demiurge fashioning matter into the world, the doctrine that the Idea of the Good is like the rays of light emanating from the sun, the notion that the soul has an existence before it enters the body, is a prisoner in the body, and struggles to escape from this captivity and return to its source, and that the true reality is to be found not in the material but in the spiritual world. Plotinus took these basic ideas, emphasizing particularly the central Platonic theme that only the spirit is true reality, and reformulated Plato's ideas into a new kind of Platonism.

God as the One The material world, with its multiplicity of things, cannot be the true reality, Plotinus thought, because it is always changing. Only that can really *be* that does not change, and this unchanging reality must therefore be something different from the material world. The true reality is God, about whom nothing specifically descriptive can be said except that He absolutely transcends or lies beyond everything in the world. For this reason God is not material, is not finite, is not divisible, has no specific form either as matter, soul, or mind, each of which undergoes change, cannot be confined to any idea or ideas of the intellect and for this reason cannot be expressed in any human language, and is accessible to none of the senses but can be reached only in a mystical ecstasy that is independent of any rational or sense experience. For this reason, Plotinus spoke of God as the One, signifying thereby that in God there is absolutely no complexity, that God is Absolute Unity. The One signifies, moreover, that God does not change, is indivisible, has no variety, is uncreated, and is in every way unalterable.

The One cannot be the sum of particular things because it is precisely these things whose finite existence requires explanation and a source. Plotinus held that the One "cannot be any existing thing, but is prior to all existents." There are no positive attributes that we can ascribe to the One because all our ideas of attributes are derived from finite physical things. It is not possible therefore to say that God is this and not that since this procedure would fasten upon God certain limits. To say, then, that God is One is to affirm that God *is,* that God transcends the world, that He is simple, without any duality, potentiality, or material limitation, and that He transcends all distinctions. In a sense, God cannot engage in any self-conscious activity since this would imply complexity through thinking *particular* thoughts *before* and *after,* thus implying change. God in no way resembles man. He is indeed simply One, Absolute Unity.

The Metaphor of Emanation If God is One, He cannot create, for creation is an act, and activity, said Plotinus, implies change. Then how can we account for the many things of the world? Striving to maintain a consistent view of the Unity of God, Plotinus explained the origin of things by saying that they come from God, not through a free act of creation but through necessity. To express what he meant by "necessity," Plotinus used several metaphors, especially the metaphor of *emanation.* Things emanate, they flow from God, the way light emanates from the sun, the way water flows from a spring that has no source outside itself. The sun is never exhausted, it does not *do* anything, it just *is;* and being what it is, it necessarily emanates light. In this way, God is the source of everything, and everything manifests God. But nothing is equal to God, any more than the rays of light equal in any way the sun. Plotinus, in short, is not a pantheist. On the contrary, his theory of emanation formed the basis for the hierarchic view of nature. Just as the light closest to the sun is the brightest, so also the highest form of being is the first emanation. Plotinus described this first emanation from the One as *mind (nous).* It is most like the One but is not absolute and can therefore be said to have a specific attribute or character. This *nous* is *thought* or *universal intelligence* and signifies the underlying rationality of the world. It is the nature of rationality to have no spatial or temporal boundaries. But rationality does imply multiplicity in that thinking contains the ideas of all particular things.

The World Soul Just as light emanates from the sun in ever-diminishing intensity, so also the gradations of being, which emanate from God, represent a decline in the degrees of perfection. Moreover, each succeeding emanation is the cause of the next-lower emanation, as if there were a principle at work requiring that every nature bring into being that which is immediately subordinate to it. In this way, the *nous* is in turn the source of the Soul. The Soul of the World has two aspects: looking upward, as it were, toward *nous* or pure rationality, the Soul strives to contemplate the eternal ideas of all things; looking downward, it emanates by reasoning one thing at a time, providing thereby the life principle to all of nature, bridging the gap between the ideas of things and the actual realm of the natural order. The activity of the Soul accounts for the phenomenon of *time,* since now there is the emergence of things, and the relations of things to each other results in events, and events come *after* one another, and this relationship of events is what is meant by time. To be sure, the One, the *nous,* and the World Soul are all coeternal; it is that below the World Soul lies the realm of nature, of particular things, reflecting in a changing way, in time, the eternal ideas.

The Human Soul   The human soul is an emanation from the World Soul. Like the World Soul, it also has two aspects. Again, looking upward, the human soul shares in the *nous* or universal reason, and looking downward, the soul becomes connected with, but is not identical with, the body. Here Plotinus reaffirmed Plato's doctrine of the preexistence of the soul, believing also that the union of the soul with the body is a product of a "fall." Moreover, after death the soul survives the body, conceivably enters a sequence of transmigrations from one body to another, and, being spiritual and therefore truly real, will not be annihilated but will join all other souls again in the World Soul. While in the body, it is the soul that provides the power of rationality, sensitivity, and vitality.

The World of Matter   At the lowest level in the hierarchy of being, that is, at the farthest remove from the One, is matter. Recalling that there is a principle at work in emanation, which requires that the higher grades of being overflow in accordance with the next realm of possibilities, it follows, then, that after ideas and souls comes the world of material objects organized into a mechanical order whose operation or movement is the work of reason, subjecting all objects to the laws or rules of cause and effect. Once again, the material world displays a higher and lower aspect, the higher being its susceptibility to the laws of motion but the lower, its bare material nature, being a dark world of gross matter moving aimlessly with sluggish discord toward collision and extinction. Plotinus compared matter to the dimmest, the farthest, reach of light, the most extreme limit of light, which is darkness itself. Darkness, clearly, is the very opposite of light; similarly, matter is the opposite of spirit and is therefore the opposite of the One. Again, insofar as matter exists in conjunction with the soul, either the individual or the World Soul, to this extent matter is not complete darkness. But just as light tends to emanate finally to the point of utter darkness, so also matter stands at the boundary line of nothingness, where it tends to disappear into non-being.

What Causes Evil?   By the doctrine of emanation, Plotinus argued that

God necessarily overflows in order to share His perfection as much as possible. Since God could not reduplicate Himself perfectly, He did so in the only possible way, namely, by representing, in the emanations, all the possible degrees of perfection. For this reason, it was necessary to have not only the *nous* but also the lowest level of being, matter. Still, there is moral evil, sin, pain, and the continued warfare of the passions, and, finally, death and sorrow. How could the Perfect One, from whom everything ultimately emanates, permit this kind of imperfection to exist among human beings? Plotinus explained the problem of evil in various ways. For one thing, he said that evil in its own way occupies a place in the hierarchy of perfection, since without evil something would be lacking in the scheme of things. Evil is like the dark shadings of a portrait, which greatly enhance the beauty of the image. Moreover, all events occur with rigorous necessity, as the Stoics had argued earlier, so that the good person does not look upon them as evil, whereas for the sinner they could be considered just punishment. But Plotinus finds the best explanation of evil in his account of matter.

For Plotinus, matter is the necessary and final reach of the emanation from the One. The very nature of emanation as we have seen is that the higher levels necessarily move toward the lower, that the One generates the *nous*, and, finally, that the individual soul generates a body, matter. Matter itself, however, continues the process of emanation, as if moving farther and farther from the One, the way the light grows dimmer and dimmer, the farther it moves from the sun. There is, then, the tendency for matter to move beyond, or separate itself from, the activity of the soul and to engage in motion that is not rationally directed. Again, as matter faces upward, it encounters the soul or the principle of rationality; for objects in nature this accounts for the orderliness of their movements, whereas for an individual person it means that the body responds to the activity of the soul at the levels of rationality, sensitivity, appetite, and vitality. But as matter faces downward, which is its natural tendency because of the downward momentum of emanation, it encounters darkness itself and at this point matter is separated from rationality.

The clue to the problem of moral evil is, then, that the soul is now united with a material body, and, in spite of the rational character of the soul, it must contend with the body, whose material nature disposes it to move downward and away from rational control. When the body reaches the level below rationality, it becomes subject to an indefinite number of possible ways of acting. Now the passions move the body to respond to all kinds of appetites. Evil is the discrepancy between the soul's right intentions and its actual behavior; it is an imperfection in the soul-body arrangement, and much of the cause for this imperfection is ascribed to the final irrational movement of the material body.

Matter, or body, is the principle of evil in the sense that matter is at the fringe of emanation, where the absence of rationality results in formlessness and the least degree of perfection. But since matter comes from God in the sense that everything emanates from the One, it could be said that God is the source of evil. Still, evil, for Plotinus, is not a positive destructive force; it is not a "devil" or rival god contending with the good God; nor, as the Persians thought, is it a contest between the coequal forces of light and darkness. Evil, for Plotinus, is simply the absence of something, the lack of perfection, the lack of form for the material body, which is not itself essentially evil. A person's moral struggle is therefore a struggle not against some outside force but against the tendency to be undone within, to become disordered, to lose control of the passions. Evil, again, is no *thing,* but rather the absence of order. The body *as such* is not evil. Evil is the formlessness of matter as darkness is the absence of light. Throughout his analysis, Plotinus tries simultaneously to argue that the soul is responsible for its acts and that all events are determined. Just how these two views can be reconciled is not exactly clear. At the same time, much of Plotinus' appeal came from the promise of salvation, which he thought his philosophy could provide.

Salvation   Plotinus moved from his philosophical analysis of emanation to the religious and mystical program of salvation. Unlike the mystery cults of his day, which offered a swift fulfillment of a person's desire to unite with God, Plotinus described the soul's ascent to unity with God as a difficult and painful task. This ascent required that a person develop successively the moral and intellectual virtues. Since the body and the physical world were not considered evil per se, it was not necessary to reject them altogether. The key insight was rather that the physical things of the world must not distract the soul from its higher aims. The world is therefore renounced as a means of facilitating the soul's ascent to intellectual activity, as in philosophy and science. One must discipline himself in rigorous and correct thinking. Such thinking lifts a person out of his individuality, and with a broad knowledge of things, one tends to relate the self to the whole arrangement of the world. But all the steps up the ladder of knowledge lead toward the final union of the self with the One or with God in a state of ecstasy, where there is no longer any consciousness of the self's separation from God. This ecstasy is the final result of right conduct, correct thinking, and the proper disposition of the affections.

To achieve this union, said Plotinus, could require many incarnations of each soul. Finally the soul is refined and purified in its love, as Plato had indicated in his *Symposium,* and is capable of the fullest self-surrender. At this point the process of emanation is fully reversed, and the self merges once again with the One. For many, Plotinus' Neoplatonism had all the power of a religion and represented a strong alternative to Christianity. Although its intricate intellectual scheme prevented it from becoming widely popular, Neoplatonism made a considerable impact upon the emerging Christian theology of this era. It was St. Augustine who saw in the *Enneads* of Plotinus a strikingly new explanation of evil and of salvation through orderly love. Through Augustine, Neoplatonism became a decisive element in the intellectual expression of the Christian faith during the Middle Ages.

THE MEDIEVAL PERIOD: THE CONFLUENCE OF PHILOSOPHY AND THEOLOGY

6

St. Augustine's Christian Philosophy

S t. Augustine's intense concern over his personal destiny provided the driving force for his philosophic activity. From his early youth, he suffered from a deep moral turmoil, which drove him to a life-long quest for true wisdom and spiritual peace. He was born in Tagaste in the African province of Numidia in 354 A.D. His father was a pagan, but his mother, Monica, was a devout Christian. At the age of sixteen, Augustine began the study of rhetoric in Carthage, a port city given to licentious ways. Though his mother had instilled in him the ways of Christian thought and behavior, he threw off this religious faith and morality, taking at this time a mistress by whom he had a son and with whom he lived for a decade. At the same time, his thirst for knowledge impelled his extremely able mind to rigorous study, and he became a successful student of rhetoric.

A series of personal experiences led him to his unique approach to philosophy. He was nineteen years old when he read the *Hortensius* of Cicero, which was an exhortation to achieve philosophical wisdom. These words of Cicero kindled his passion for learning, but he was left with the problem of where to find intellectual certainty. His Christian ideas seemed unsatisfactory to him. He was particularly perplexed by the ever-present problem of moral evil. How can one explain the existence of evil in human experience? The Christians had said that God is the creator of all things and also that God is good. How, then, is it possible for evil to arise out of a world that a perfectly good God had created? Because Augustine could find no answer in the Christianity he learned as a youth, he turned to a group called the Manichaeans, who were sympathetic to much of Christianity but who, boasting of their intellectual superiority, rejected the basic monotheism of the Old Testament and with it the doctrine that the Creator and Redeemer of humanity are one and the same. Instead, the Manichaeans taught a doctrine of dualism, according to which there were two basic principles in the universe, the principle of light or goodness, on the one hand, and the principle of darkness or evil, on the other. These two principles were held to be equally eternal and were seen as eternally in conflict with each other. This conflict was reflected in human life in the conflict between the soul, composed of light, and the body, composed of darkness. At first this theory of dualism seemed to provide the answer to the problem of evil; it overcame the contradiction between the presence of evil in a world created by a good God. Augustine could now attribute his sensual desires to the external power of darkness.

Although this dualism seemed to solve the contradiction of evil in a God-created world, it raised new problems. For one thing, how could one explain why there are two conflicting principles in nature? If no convincing reason could be given, is intellectual certitude possible? Far more serious was his awareness that it did not help to solve his moral turmoil to say that it was all engendered by some external force. The presence of fierce passion was no less unsettling just because the "blame" for it had been shifted to something outside of himself. What had originally attracted him to the Manichaeans was their boast that they could provide him with truth that could be discussed and made plain, not requiring, as the Christians did, "faith before reason." He therefore broke with the Manichaeans, feeling that "those philosophers whom they call Academics [Skeptics] were wiser than the rest in thinking that we ought to doubt everything, and that no truth can be comprehended by man." He was now attracted to Skepticism, though at the same time he retained some belief in God. He maintained a materialistic view of things and on this account doubted the existence of immaterial substances and the immortality of the soul.

Hoping for a more effective career in rhetoric, Augustine left Africa for Rome and shortly thereafter moved to Milan, where he became municipal professor of rhetoric in 384. Here he was profoundly influenced by Ambrose, who was then Bishop of Milan. From Ambrose Augustine derived not so much the techniques of rhetoric, but somewhat unexpectedly a greater appreciation of Christianity. While in Milan, Augustine took another mistress, having left his first one in Africa. It was here also that Augustine came upon certain forms of Platonism, especially the Neoplatonism found in the *Enneads* of Plotinus. There was much in Neoplatonism that caught his imagination, particularly the conception of an immaterial world totally separate from the material world and the belief that people possess a spiritual sense that enables them to know God and the immaterial world. Moreover, from Plotinus Augustine derived the conception that evil is not a positive reality but is rather a matter of privation, the absence of good. Above all, Neoplatonism overcame Augustine's former skepticism, materialism, and dualism. Through Platonic thought he was able to understand that not all activity is physical, that there is a spiritual as well as a physical reality. He could now see the unity of the world without having to assume the existence of two principles behind soul and body, for Plotinus had presented the picture of reality as a single graduated system in which matter is simply on a lower level.

Intellectually, Neoplatonism provided what Augustine had been looking for, but it left his moral problem still unsolved. What he needed now was moral strength to match his intellectual insight. This he found by way of Ambrose's sermons. Neoplatonism had finally made Christianity reasonable to him, and now he was also able to exercise the act of faith and thereby derive the power of the spirit without feeling that he was lapsing into some form of superstition. His dramatic conversion occurred in 386, when he gave "real assent" to abandoning his profession of rhetoric and giving his life totally to the pursuit of philosophy, which, for him, also meant the knowledge of God. He now saw Platonism and Christianity as virtually one, seeing in Neoplatonism the philosophical expression of Christianity, saying that "I am confident that among the Platonists I shall find what is not opposed to the teachings of our religion." He therefore set out on what he called "my whole program" of achieving wisdom, saying that "from this moment forward, it is my resolve never to depart from the authority of Christ, for I find none that is stronger." Still, he emphasized that "I must follow after this with the greatest subtlety of reason."

For Augustine, true philosophy was inconceivable without a confluence of faith and reason. To him, wisdom was Christian wisdom. Reason without revelation was certainly possible, but it would never be complete. This was true particularly for Augustine, since he came to believe that there is no such thing as a purely natural person without some ultimate spiritual destiny. Consequently, to understand the concrete condition of people, they must be considered from the point of view of the Christian faith, and this in turn requires that the whole world be considered from the vantage point of faith. There could be, for Augustine, no distinction between theology and philosophy. Indeed, he believed that one could not properly philosophize until his will was transformed, that clear thinking was possible only under the influence of God's grace. In this way, Augustine set the dominant mood and style of Christian wisdom of the Middle Ages, although Aquinas in the thirteenth century altered some of its assumptions.

It is therefore not possible to discuss Augustine's philosophy without at the same time considering his theological viewpoint. Indeed, Augustine wrote no purely philosophical works in the contemporary sense of that term. He was an incredibly prolific writer, and as he became a noted leader in the Catholic church, he was inevitably involved in writing as a protagonist of the faith and a defender against heresy. In 396 he became bishop of Hippo, the seaport near his native town of Tagaste. Among his many opponents was Pelagius, with whom he entered into a celebrated controversy. Pelagius had taught that all people possess the natural ability to achieve a righteous life, thereby denying the doctrine of original sin. This led, according to Augustine, to misunderstanding the true nature of people by assuming that their will is capable of achieving salvation and thereby minimizing the function of God's grace. This controversy illuminates Augustine's mode of thought perfectly, for it indicates again his insistence that all knowledge upon all subjects must take into account the revealed truth of Scripture along with the insights of philosophy. Since all knowledge is aimed at helping humanity understand God, this religious dimension had clearly a priority in his reflections. As Aquinas said about him later, "Whenever Augustine, who was imbued with the doctrine of the Platonists, found in their writings anything consistent with the faith, he adopted it; and whatever he found contrary to the faith, he amended." Still, it was Platonism that had rescued Augustine from skepticism, made the Christian faith reasonable and, indeed, powerful for him, and set off one of the great literary achievements in theology and philosophy. As if to symbolize his tempestuous life, Augustine died in 430 at the age of seventy-five in the posture of reciting the Penitential Psalms as the Vandals besieged Hippo.

HUMAN KNOWLEDGE

Overcoming Skepticism   Augustine had taken the Skeptics (Academics) seriously for a time, agreeing with them that "no truth can be comprehended by man." But after his conversion, his problem was no longer *whether* people can attain certainty, but rather *how* they can attain it. Augustine therefore sought to answer the Skeptics, and he did this first of all by showing that human reason does indeed have certainty about various things. Specifically, human reason is absolutely certain of the principle of contradiction. We know that a thing cannot both be and not be at the same time. Using this principle, we can be certain, for example, that there is either one world or many worlds; that if there are many, their number is either finite or infinite. What we know here is simply that both alternatives cannot be true. This is not yet any substantive knowledge, but it meant for Augustine that the mind is not hopelessly lost in uncertainty. Not only does the mind know that both alternatives cannot be true simultaneously, it knows also that this is always, eternally, the case. In addition, he said that even the Skeptics would have to admit that the act of doubting is itself a form of certainty, for a person who doubts is certain that he doubts. Here, then, is another certainty, the certainty that I exist, for if I doubt, I must exist. Whatever else one can have doubts about, he cannot doubt that he doubts. To object, as the Skeptics did, that a person could be asleep and only dreaming that he sees things or is aware of himself, did not seem to Augustine to be a formidable argument, for in reply he said "whether he be asleep or awake he lives." Any conscious person is certain that he exists, that

St. Augustine *(Scala, Editorial Photocolor Archives, Art Resource)*

he is alive, and that he can think, "for we are," says Augustine, "and we know we are, and we love our being and our knowledge of it.... These truths stand without fear in the face of the arguments of the Academics." Unlike Descartes, who formulated a similar argument in his classic "I think, therefore I am" and then proceeded to use it as a foundation for his system of philosophy, Augustine was content merely to derive from the fact of doubt a refutation of the Skeptics' basic premise. Instead of proving the existence of external objects, Augustine referred to these objects chiefly in order to describe in some detail how the mind achieves knowledge in relation to things.

Knowledge and Sensation   When a person senses objects, he or she derives some knowledge from this act of sensation. But according to Augustine, such sense knowledge is at the lowest level of knowing. Still, the senses do give us a kind of knowledge. What puts sense knowledge at the lowest level is that it gives us the least amount of certainty. What reduces the certainty of sense knowledge is two things: first, that the objects of sense are always changing, and, second, that the organs of sense change. For these two reasons, sensation varies from time to time and between persons. Something can taste sweet to one person and bitter to another, warm to one and cold to another. Still, Augustine believed that the senses are always accurate as such. It is unjust, he said, to expect or demand more from the senses than they can provide. For example, there is nothing wrong with our senses when the oar in the water appears bent to us. On the contrary, there would be something wrong if the oar appeared straight, since under these circumstances the oar ought to seem bent. The problem arises when we have to make a judgment about the actual condition of the oar. One would be deceived if assent were given to the notion that the oar was in fact bent. To avoid this error, says Augustine, "don't give assent to more than the fact of appearance, and you won't be deceived." In this way, Augustine affirmed the reliability of the senses while also indicating their limitations. Just how the senses give us knowledge Augustine indicated by analyzing the nature or mechanics of sensation.

What happens when we sense an object? To answer this question Augustine relied upon his Platonic interpretation of humanity. A person is a union of body and soul. He even suggested that the body is the prison of the soul. But when he described how the soul attains knowledge, he departed from the Platonic theory of recollection. Knowledge is not an act of remembering. It is an act of the soul. When we see an object, the soul (mind) fashions out of its own substance an image of the object. The object cannot make a physical "impression" upon the mind the way a signet ring leaves its mark in wax because the soul is spiritual, not material. Accordingly, it is the mind itself that produces the image. Moreover, when we sense an object, we not only sense an image but also make a judgment. We look at a person and say that she is beautiful. This act of judgment indicates that I not only see the person with my senses, but also compare her with a standard to which my mind has access in some realm other than that in which I sense the person. Similarly, when I see seven boys and three boys I know that they can be added to make ten boys. As other things in nature are mutable, these ten boys, being mortal, will eventually pass away. But we are able to separate the numbers from the boys and discover that seven and three do not depend upon the boys or any other things and that their making ten by addition is always and necessarily true.

Sensation, then, gives us some knowledge, but its chief characteristic is that it necessarily points beyond its objects. From the sensation of an oar we are moved to think about straightness and bentness, from the person to beauty, and from the boys to the eternal truths of mathematics. Here the description of humanity becomes again decisive, since the explanation of the mechanics of sensation leads to a distinction between body and soul. Sensation involves the body insofar as some physical organ is required to sense things, but, unlike animals, humans not only sense things, they have some rational knowledge of them and make rational judgments about them. When rational people make such judgments, they are no longer dependent solely upon the senses but have directed their minds to other objects, such as Beauty and the truths of mathematics. A careful analysis shows therefore that the act of human sensation involves at least four elements, namely (1) the object sensed, (2) the bodily organ upon which sensation depends, (3) the activity of the mind in formulating an image of the object, and (4) the immaterial object, e.g., Beauty, which the mind uses in making a judgment about the sensed object. What emerges from this analysis is that there are two different kinds of objects that human beings encounter, namely, the objects of the bodily sense and the objects of the mind. With the physical eye people see things, and with the mind they apprehend eternal truths. These different objects account for the different degrees of intellectual certainty, for a person will derive less reliable truth when the mutable sense organs are directed toward changing physical objects than when the mind is contemplating eternal truths independently of the senses. Also, sensation directs the trail of knowledge to an activity within people and not to things outside of them. Knowledge moves from the level of sensed things to the higher level of general truth. The highest level of knowledge is for Augustine the knowledge of God. Sensation plays its part in attaining this knowledge in that it directs the mind upward. Hence, Augustine says that we move toward God "from the exterior to the interior, and from the inferior to the superior."

The Doctrine of Illumination   In his account of the relation between sensation and knowledge, Augustine was left with the problem of how the mind could make judgments involving eternal and necessary truths. What makes it possible for the mind to know that seven and three, which at first the mind confronts in relation to things, always and necessarily make ten? Why, as a matter of fact, is there a problem here? The problem exists because so far in his account of human knowledge, all the elements involved are mutable or imperfect, hence finite and not eternal. The sensed objects are mutable, and the bodily organs of sense are also subject to change. The mind itself is a creature and is therefore finite and not perfect. How, then, can these elements be deployed in such a way as to rise above their own imperfection and mutability and discover eternal truths about which the mind has no doubts, truths that indeed confront the mind with the coercive power of certitude, truths so superior to what the human mind could produce that the mind must adjust or conform to them? Plato had answered this question by his doctrine that knowledge is recollection, whereby the soul is made to remember what it once knew before it entered the body. Aristotle, on the other hand, argued that the eternal universal ideas were abstracted by the intellect from particular things. Augustine accepted neither one of these solutions, though he did follow Plato's other insight contained in the analogy between the sun in the visible world and the Idea of the Good in the intelligible world.

Augustine was not so much concerned with the origin *as with our awareness of the certitude* of some of our ideas. Rejecting recollection and some form of innate Ideas, he came closer to the notion of abstraction. Actually, Augustine says that humans are made in such a way that when the eye of one's body sees an object, the mind can form an image of it provided the object is bathed in light. Similarly, the mind is capable of "seeing" eternal objects provided that they too are bathed in their own appropriate light. As Augustine says, we ought to believe "that the nature of the intellectual mind was so made that, by being naturally subject to intelligible realities, according to the arrangement of the Creator, it sees these truths [such as mathematical truth] in a certain incorporeal light of a unique kind, just as the eye of the body sees the things all around it in this corporeal light." The human mind, in short, requires illumination if it is to "see" eternal and necessary truths. We cannot anymore "see" the intelligible objects or truths of the intellect without some illumination than we can see the things in the world without the light of the sun.

Augustine states his doctrine of *illumination* in succinct form when he says that "there is present in [us]...the light of eternal reason, in which light the immutable truths are seen." Just what he means by this doctrine is not altogether clear. What is clear is that for Augustine the illumination comes from God just as light is shed abroad by the sun. If this analogy or metaphor is taken seriously, the divine light must illuminate something that is already there. By the light of the sun we can see the trees and houses. If the divine light performs the same kind of function, this light must also illuminate something—our ideas. This light is not so much the source of our ideas as it is the condition under which we recognize the quality of truth and eternity in our ideas. In short, divine illumination is not a process by which the content of ideas is infused into our minds; it is, rather, the illumination of our judgment whereby we are able to discern that certain ideas contain necessary and eternal truth. God, the source of this light, is perfect and eternal, and the human intellect operates under the influence of God's eternal ideas. It could not be said that the human mind knows God, but the doctrine of illumination does mean that the limitations of knowledge caused by the mutability of physical objects and the finitude of the human mind are overcome by the divine illumination. With this doctrine, then, Augustine solved to his satisfaction the problem of how the human intellect is able to go beyond sense objects and make judgments about necessary and eternal truths.

GOD

Augustine was not interested in mere speculations about the existence of God. His philosophical reflections about God were the product of his intense pursuit of wisdom and spiritual peace. His deep involvement in sensual pleasures had given him dramatic evidence that the soul cannot find its peace among the pleasures of flesh or sensation. Similarly, in his quest for certainty of knowledge, he discovered that the world of things was full of change and impermanence. His mind, too, he discovered, was imperfect, since it was capable of error. At the same time, he had the experience of knowing certain truths that were eternal. He was able to compare the experience of contemplating truth with the experience of having pleasure and sensations. Of these two experiences he found that the activities of the mind could provide more lasting and profound peace. When he considered the technical question of how it was that his finite human mind was capable of attaining knowledge beyond the capacity of his mind, he concluded that this knowledge could not have come from finite things outside of him; nor could it be produced fully by his own mind. Since the knowledge available to him was superior to the workings of his mind, that is, since this knowledge was eternal and could not come from his limited or finite mind, he was led to believe that immutable truth must have its source in God. What led to this conclusion was the similarity between the characteristics of some of his knowledge and the attributes of God, namely, that both are eternal and true. The existence of eternal truth meant for Augustine the existence of the Eternal Truth, which God is. In this way, Augustine moved through various levels of personal experience and spiritual quest to what amounted to a "proof" of the existence of God.

Since God is Truth, God in some sense is within a person, but since God is eternal, He also transcends humanity. But what else can a person say by way of describing God? Actually, Augustine found it easier to say what God is not than to define what He is. Still, to say that God is superior to finite things was a major step. Taking the scriptural name for God given to Moses, namely, "I Am That I Am," Augustine transposed this to mean that God is *being itself.* As such He is the highest being, not the beingless One of Plotinus but the "something than which nothing more excellent or more sublime exists," a phrase that influenced Anselm to formulate his famous ontological argument. As the highest being, God is perfect being, which means that He is self-existent, immutable, and eternal being. As perfect, He is also "simple," in that whatever plural attributes are assigned to Him turn out to be identical; His knowledge, wisdom, goodness, and power are all one and constitute His essence. Further, Augustine reasoned that the world of everyday things reflects the being and activity of God. Although the things we see are mutable in that they gradually cease to be, nevertheless insofar as they exist they have a definite form, and this form is eternal and is a reflection of God. Indeed, that things possess any being at all is ascribed by Augustine to God, who is the source of all being.

But unlike the things of the world, God, as Augustine says, "is...in no interval or extension of place" and similarly "is in no interval or extension of time." In short, Augustine described God as pure or highest being, suggesting thereby that in God there is no change either from non-being to being or from being to non-being. God *is*; "I Am That I Am." Again, the force of this line of thought is to be found not so much in its philosophic rigor, though Augustine was convinced it had that too, as in its relevance in solving Augustine's spiritual problem. God as the source of being and truth and the one eternal reality now became for Augustine the legitimate object both of thought and affection. From God there comes both enlightenment for the mind and strength for the will. Moreover, all other knowledge is possible because God is the standard for truth. His essence is to be, and to be is to act, and to act is to know, and being both eternal and all-knowing, God always knew all the possible ways in which He could be reflected in creation. For this reason, the various forms in which the world is shaped were always in God as Exemplars. All things therefore are finite reflections of God's eternal thought. If God's thought is "eternal," difficulties arise in our language when it is said that God "foresees" what will happen. What is important to Augustine, however, is that the world and God are intimately related, that the world reflects God's eternal thought even though God is not identical with but transcends the world. Because there is this relation between God and the world, to know one is to know something of the other. This is why Augustine was so convinced that the person who knew most about God could understand most deeply the true nature of the world and especially the true nature and destiny of humanity. Finally, although Augustine saw everywhere evidences of the Trinity, his language about God revolves chiefly around the Father, since the other persons, the Word and the Spirit, being of the same substance, are one and share the same being.

THE CREATED WORLD

Even though Augustine concluded that God is the most appropriate object of thought and affection and that the physical, mutable world could not provide humanity with true knowledge or spiritual peace, he nevertheless paid considerable attention to the material world. After all, human life must be lived in the physical world, and one needs to know how to understand this world in order to relate oneself appropriately to it. From what he had already said about the nature of knowledge and about God, it was inevitable that Augustine should see the world as the creation of God. Wherever one looks, says Augustine in his *Confessions,* all things, for example, the flowers, say, "We made not ourselves, but He made us that abideth forever." Finite things, that is, demand that there should be some permanent being to explain how they could come into existence. Just how God is related to the world was explained by Augustine in his unique theory of creation.

Creatio Ex Nihilo   Augustine's distinctive doctrine was that God created all things *ex nihilo,* out of nothing. This was in contrast to Plato's account of the world which was not "created" but was the Demiurge's combining of the Forms and the receptacle, which always existed independently. Augustine also departed from the Neoplatonic theory of Plotinus, which explained the world as an emanation from God. Plotinus had said that there was a *natural necessity* in God to overflow, since the Good must necessarily diffuse itself. Moreover, this theory held that there is a continuity between God and the world, that the world is merely an extension of God. Against all these notions, Augustine stressed that the world is the product of God's free act, whereby He brings into being, out of nothing, all the things that make up the world. All things, then, owe their existence to God. There is, however, a sharp distinction between God and the things He created. Whereas Plotinus saw the world as the overflowing and therefore continuation of God, Augustine speaks of God as bringing into being what did not exist before. He could not have created out of an existing matter because matter, even in a primary form, would already be something. To speak of a formless matter is really to refer to nothing. Actually, according to Augustine, everything, including matter, is the product of God's creative act. Even if there were some formless matter that was capable of being formed—even this would have its origin in God and would have to be created by Him out of nothing. That matter is created by God meant for Augustine that matter is good, because nothing evil is created by God. The essential goodness of matter was to play an important role in Augustine's theory of morality, for this doctrine was in sharp contrast to the teachings of the Manichaeans, who said that the body was composed of darkness and therefore embodied the principle of evil. Indeed, Augustine was to reject the notion that anything in the created order can be intrinsically evil since everything is created by the goodness of God.

The Rationes Seminales   Augustine was struck by the fact that the various species in nature never produce new species. Horses produce horses, and flowers produce flowers; at the human level, parents produce more children. What fascinated Augustine about all this was its relevance to the general question about *causality.* Although in a sense the parents are the cause of the children and the flowers the cause of the new flowers, still, none of these things is able to introduce new forms into nature. In the created order, existing things are able only to animate existing forms into completed beings. Augustine drew from this fact (for which he admittedly did not have decisive empirical information) the conclusion that the causality behind the formation of all things is God's intelligence. There is no original causal power in things capable of fashioning new forms. How then do things, animals, and people produce anything? Augustine's answer was that in the act of creation, God had implanted seminal principles (*rationes seminales*) into matter, thereby setting into nature the potentiality for all species to emerge. These *rationes seminales* are the germs of things; they are invisible and have causal power. Thus, all species bear the invisible, potential power to become what they are not yet at the present time. When species begin to exist, their seminal principle, that is, their potentiality, is fulfilled, and subsequently actual seeds transmit the continuation of the fixed species from potentiality to actuality. Originally, God, in a single act of complete creation, furnished the germinating principles of all species.

With this doctrine, Augustine explained the origin of species, locating their cause in the mind of God, whence came the seminal principles. By this doctrine of *rationes seminales,* Augustine thought he also solved a problem in the

Scriptures, where it is said in Genesis that God created the world in six days. That God should have to create step by step seemed inconsistent with Augustine's view of God. There was some question, too, about what is meant here by six days, especially since the sun was not "created" until the fourth day. What the doctrine of *rationes seminales* enabled Augustine to say was that God had created all things at once, meaning by this that he had implanted the seminal principles of all species simultaneously. But, since these germs are principles of potentiality, they are the bearers of things that are to be but that have not yet "flowered." Accordingly, though all species were created at once, they did not all exist fully formed simultaneously. They each fulfilled their potentiality in a sequence of points in time. Although Augustine did not try to do so, his notion of seminal principles could conceivably be extended into a doctrine of the evolution of species.

MORAL PHILOSOPHY

Every philosophical notion developed by Augustine pointed in one way or another to the problem of humanity's moral condition. For him, therefore, moral theory was not some special or isolated subject. Everything culminates in morality, in clarifying for humanity the sure road to happiness, which is the goal of human behavior. In fashioning his ideas about morality, then, Augustine brought to bear his major insights about the nature of human knowledge, the nature of God, and the doctrine of creation. From the vantage point of these ideas, he focused upon the nature of humanity's moral constitution.

Humanity's moral quest is the inevitable outcome of a specific and concrete condition. The condition is that humanity is made in such a way that one seeks happiness. Although the ancient Greeks had also considered happiness as the culmination of the good life, Augustine's theory provided a novel estimate of what constitutes happiness and just how it is to be achieved. What differentiated him from, say, Aristotle was that whereas Aristotle said that happiness is achieved when a person fulfills natural functions through a well-balanced life, Augustine held that happiness required that a person go beyond the natural to the supernatural. He expressed this view both in religious and philosophical language. In his *Confessions* he wrote, "Oh God Thou hast created us for Thyself so that our hearts are restless until they find their rest in Thee." In more philosophical language he makes this same point by saying that human nature is so made that "it cannot itself be the good by which it is made happy." There is, in short, no purely "natural" person. The reason there is no purely natural person, says Augustine, is that nature did not produce people. God did. Consequently, humanity always bears the marks of its creation, which means, among other things, that there are some permanent relations, actual and possible, between humanity and God. It is not by accident that a person *seeks* happiness. That he or she seeks it is a consequence of his or her incompleteness, finitude. That he or she can find happiness only in God is also no accident, since he or she was made by God to find happiness only in God.

Augustine elaborates this aspect of humanity's nature through the doctrine of love.

The Role of Love A person inevitably loves. To love is to go beyond oneself and to fasten one's affection upon an object of love. What makes it inevitable that people will love is, again, incompleteness. There is a wide range of objects that people can choose to love, reflecting the variety of ways in which people are incomplete. A person can love (1) physical objects, (2) other persons, or even (3) oneself. From those one can derive satisfaction for some desires and passions. Augustine stressed that all things in the world are good because all things come from God, who is goodness itself. Consequently, all things are legitimate objects of love. Everything that people love will provide them with some measure of satisfaction and happiness. Nothing is evil in itself; evil is not a positive thing but the absence of something. Humanity's moral problem consists not so much in loving or even in the objects humans love as in the *manner* in which they attach themselves to these objects of love and in their *expectations* regarding the outcome of this love. Everyone expects to achieve happiness and fulfillment from love, yet people are miserable, unhappy, and restless. Why? Augustine lays the blame upon "disordered" love.

Evil and Disordered Love Each object of love is different, and for this reason the consequences of loving each will be different. Similarly, the human needs which prompt the act of love are also different. Augustine thought that there is some sort of correlation between various human needs and the objects that can satisfy them. Love is the act that harmonizes these needs and their objects. What constitutes the chief fact about humans is that the range of their needs includes not only (1) objects, (2) other persons, and (3) themselves, but also, and most of all, (4) God. There is no way to unmake this fact about humanity. Augustine formulates this point in virtually quantitative terms. Each object of love can give only so much satisfaction and no more. Each of a person's needs likewise has a measurable quantity. Clearly, satisfaction and happiness require that an object of love contain a sufficient amount of whatever it takes to fulfill or satisfy the particular need. Thus, we love food and we consume a quantity commensurate with our hunger.

But our needs are not all physical in that primary sense. We love objects of art too for the aesthetic satisfaction they give. At a higher level we have the need for love between persons. Indeed, this level of affection provides quantitatively and qualitatively more in the way of pleasure and happiness than love of mere physical things, such as the various forms of property, can. From this it becomes clear that certain human needs cannot be met by an interchange of objects; the deep human need for human companionship cannot be met any other way than by a relationship with another person. Things can't be a substitute for a person because things do not contain within themselves the unique ingredients of a human personality. Therefore, although each thing is a legitimate object of love, one must not expect more from it than its unique nature can provide. The basic need for human affection cannot be satisfied by things.

But this is particularly the case with humanity's spiritual need. A person was made, said Augustine, to love God. God is infinite. In some way, then, a person's nature was made so that only God, the infinite, can give the person ultimate satisfaction or happiness. "When," says Augustine, "the will which is the intermediate good, cleaves to the immutable good...man finds therein the blessed life" for "to live well is nothing else but to love God." To love God is, then, the indispensable requirement for happiness, because only God, who is infinite, can satisfy that peculiar need in people that is precisely the need for the infinite.

If objects are not interchangeable, if things cannot substitute for a person, neither can any finite thing or person substitute for God. Yet, all people confidently expect that they can achieve true happiness by loving objects, other persons, and themselves. While these are all legitimate objects of love, people's love of them is disordered when these are loved for the sake of ultimate happiness. Disordered love consists in expecting more from an object of love than it is capable of providing. Disordered love produces all forms of pathology in human behavior. Normal self-love becomes pride, and pride is the cardinal sin that affects all aspects of people's conduct. The essence of pride is the assumption of self-sufficiency.

Yet the permanent fact about people is precisely that they are not self-sufficient, neither physically, emotionally, nor spiritually. People's pride, which turns them away from God, leads them to many forms of overindulgence, since they try to satisfy an infinite need with finite entities. People therefore love things more than they should in relation to what they can do for themselves. Their love for another person can become virtually destructive of the other person, since they try again to derive from that relationship more than it can possibly give. Appetite flourishes, passion multiplies, and there is a desperate attempt to achieve peace by satisfying all desires. The soul becomes seriously disfigured and is now implicated in envy, greed, jealousy, trickery, panic, and a pervading restlessness. It does not take long for disordered love to produce a disordered person, and disordered persons produce a disordered community. No attempt to reconstruct an orderly or peaceful community or household is possible without reconstructing each human being. The rigorous and persistent fact is that personal reconstruction, salvation, is possible only by reordering love, by loving the proper things properly. Indeed, Augustine argued that we can love a person properly only if we love God first, for then we will not expect to derive from human love what can be derived only from our love of God. Similarly, we can love ourselves properly only as we subordinate ourselves to God, for there is no other way to overcome the destructive consequences of pride than by eliminating pride itself.

Free Will as the Cause of Evil   Augustine did not agree with Plato that the cause of evil is simply ignorance. To be sure, there can be some circumstances under which a person does not know the ultimate good, is not aware of God. Still, Augustine says that "even the ungodly" have the capacity to "blame and rightly praise many things in the conduct of men." The overriding fact is that in daily conduct people understand praise and blame only because they already understand that they have an obligation to do what is praiseworthy and to abstain from what is blameworthy. Under these circumstances, people's predicament is not that they are ignorant but that they stand in the presence of alternatives. People must choose to turn toward God or away from God. They are, in short, free. Whichever way a person chooses, it is with the hope of finding happiness. People are capable of directing their affections exclusively toward finite things, persons, or themselves and away from God. Augustine says that "this turning away and this turning to are not forced but voluntary acts." Evil, or sin, is a product of the will. It is not, as Plato said, ignorance, nor, as the Manichaeans said, the work of the principle of darkness permeating the body. In spite of the fact of original sin, all humanity still possesses the freedom of the will. This freedom (*liberum*) of the will is not, however, the same as spiritual freedom (*libertas*), for true spiritual liberty is no longer possible in its fullness in this life. A person now uses free will to choose wrongly; but even when people choose rightly, they do not, says Augustine, possess the spiritual power to do the good they have chosen. A person must have the help of God's grace. Whereas evil is caused by an act of free will, virtue, on the other hand, is the product not of people's will but of God's grace. The moral law tells people what they must do, but in the end it really shows them what they can't do. Hence, Augustine concludes that "the law was . . . given that grace might be sought; grace was given that the law might be fulfilled." He also says that "sin is quelled when it is beaten down by the love of God, which none but He gives, and He only, by Jesus Christ the Mediator of God and Man, who made Himself mortal that we might be made eternal."

JUSTICE

For Augustine, public or political life was under the same rule of the moral law as was a person's individual or personal life. There is a single source of truth for both realms, and this truth he considered "entire, inviolate and not subject to changes in human life." All people recognize this truth and know it, for the purposes of conduct, as natural law or natural justice. Augustine considered natural law as humans' intellectual sharing in God's truth, or God's *eternal law*. Augustine's notion of *eternal law* had already been anticipated by the Stoics when they spoke of the diffusion of the principle of reason throughout all of nature, ascribing to this reason the role and power of ruling everything. Their theory was that *nous,* the principle of reason, constituted the laws of nature. Whereas the Stoics, then, considered the laws of nature to be the working of the *impersonal* force of rational principles in the universe, Augustine interpreted the eternal law as the reason and will of the personal Christian God, saying that "the eternal law is the divine reason and the will of God which commands the maintenance (observance) of the natural order of things and which forbids the disturbance of it." Since *eternal law* is God's reason commanding orderliness, a person's intellectual grasp of the eternal principles is called *natural law*. When a political state makes a law, said Augustine, such temporal laws must be in accord with the principle of natural law, which in turn is derived from the eternal law.

Augustine's chief argument regarding law and justice was that the political state is not autonomous, that in making laws the state does not merely express its power to legislate; the state must also follow the requirements of justice. Justice is a standard, moreover, which precedes the state and is eternal. What made Augustine's argument unique was his novel interpretation of the meaning of justice. He accepted the formula that said that "justice is a virtue distributing to every one his due." But, he asked, what is "due" to anyone? He rejected the notion that justice is conventional, that it will differ with each society. For him, justice was to be discovered in the structure of human nature with its relation to God. Hence, he said that justice is "the habit of the soul which imparts to every man the dignity due him. . . . Its origin proceeds from nature . . . and this notion of justice . . . is not the product of man's personal opinion, but something implanted by a certain innate power." To require the state to follow such a standard was obviously to place heavy moral limitations upon political power. Indeed, Augustine argued that if the laws of the state were out of harmony with natural law and justice, they would not have the character of laws, nor would there be a state. He said, "If then a commonwealth be an estate of the people, and that they be no people that are not united in one consent of the law: nor is that a law which is not grounded in justice: then it must follow, where no justice is, there no commonwealth is."

By relating justice to the moral law, Augustine argued that justice is not limited merely to the relations between people. The primary relationship in justice is between a person and God. For this reason, Augustine said, "if man serve not God what justice can be thought to be in him? seeing that if he serve not Him the soul has neither lawful sovereignty over the body nor the reason over the affections." Moreover, collective justice is impossible apart from this individual justice, for "if this justice is not found in one man, no more then can it be found in a whole multitude of such like men. Therefore, amongst such there is not that consent of law which makes a multitude of people." Again, "Is he not [unjust who] takes himself away from his Lord God, and gives himself to the service of the devil?" To serve God is to love God, but this means also to love one's fellowman. Still, "what justice is that which takes man from the true God?" To serve God and to love one's fellowman are, among other things, to recognize that all people should also have this inviolate right and opportunity to love and serve God. All of ethics, then, is based upon a person's love for God and love for his fellowman. Love is the basis of justice.

Although Augustine's thoughts about law raised the church and religion to a position of superiority over the temporal state, he did concede to the state the right to use coercive force. Indeed, the state is the product of humanity's sinful condition and therefore exists as a necessary agency of control. Even so, Augustine would never concede that the principle of force was higher than the principle of love, for he says that ". . . a society cannot be ideally founded unless upon the basis and by the hand of faith and strong concord, where the object of love is the universal good which in its highest and truest character is God Himself and where men love one another with complete sincerity in Him, and the ground of their love for one another is the love of Him from whose eyes they cannot conceal the spirit of love." The earthly state still has a function even though its force cannot match the creative power of love, for the state's action can at least mitigate some evils: "When the power to do hurt is taken from the wicked," says Augustine, "they will carry themselves better being curbed." For this reason, the state "had not been designed in vain."

THE TWO CITIES AND HISTORY

Augustine made the love of God the central principle of morality. He also accounted for evil by his doctrine of disordered love. From this he concluded that the human race can be divided between those who love God, on the one hand, and those who love themselves and the world, on the other. These groups form in their own way a society, since they are, so Augustine says, "an association of rational beings united by a unanimous agreement upon the things they love." There being two basically different kinds of love, there are, then, two opposing societies. Those who love God Augustine called the *City of God,* and those who love self and the world he called the *City of the World.*

These two cities were not considered by Augustine to be identical with the church and state, respectively. Having stressed that the decisive element in the formation of a society is the dominant love of its members, he pointed out that those who love the world are found both in the state and in the church. It does not follow therefore that the church contains the whole society called the City of God. Similarly, there are in the state those who love God. These two cities therefore cut across both church and state and have an independence of them in an invisible way. Hence, wherever those people are who love God, there will be the City of God, and wherever there are those who love the world, there will be the City of the World.

History Augustine saw in the conflict between the two cities the clue to a philosophy of history. What he meant by a *philosophy* of history was that history has a meaning. The early Greek historians saw no pattern in the events of humanity other than, perhaps, the fact that kingdoms rise and fall and that there are cycles of repetition. Aristotle, it will be recalled, considered history as hardly capable of teaching people any important knowledge about humanity because, unlike drama, history deals with individual persons, nations, and events, whereas drama deals with universal conditions and problems. But Augustine thought that the greatest drama of all is human history. Its author, moreover, is God. History begins with Creation, is punctuated by such decisive events as the Fall of man and the Incarnation of God in Christ. The present historic moment is involved in the tension between the City of God and the City of the World. Nothing happens without reference to God's ultimate providence. Moreover, what happens is a consequence of human actions, particularly actions of sin and vice. Thus, when the barbarian Goths sacked Rome in 410, the pagans laid the blame upon the Christians, saying that their excessive emphasis upon loving and serving God had the effect of diluting patriotism and weakening the defenses of the state. To answer such charges and many others, Augustine wrote his book *The City of God* in 413. In it he argued that the fall of Rome was due not to the subversive activities of the Christians but, on the contrary, to the rampant vice throughout the Empire, which the Christian faith and love of God could have prevented. The fall of Rome was for Augustine just another example of God's providential intrusion into history, whereby He was seeking to establish the City of God and curb the City of the World. In this drama there was for Augustine a universal meaning and relevance, for all humanity must know that their own destinies, as well as the destinies of their societies, are inevitably linked with the two cities and with the providence of God. There is an all-embracing destiny for humanity and the world, and it will be achieved in God's good time and when the love of God reigns. With these views, Augustine took what he considered otherwise random persons and events and supplied them with a comprehensive meaning, a "philosophy of history."

Philosophy in the Dark Ages: Boethius, Pseudo-Dionysius, Erigena

The fall of the Roman Empire in 476 ushered in a period of intellectual darkness. The barbarians who destroyed the political might of Rome also shattered the institutions of culture in Western Europe. Learning came almost to a halt. Virtually the whole body of ancient literature was lost. For the next five or six centuries, philosophy was kept alive by Christian scholars who became the channels through which the works of the ancient Greeks were transmitted to the West.

BOETHIUS

One of the most prominent philosophic figures in the early Middle Ages was Anicius Manlius Severinus Boethius (ca. 480–524), of Rome and Pavia, Italy. He grew up in the kingdom of Theodoric as a Christian. At an early age he was sent to Athens, where he mastered the Greek language and encountered Aristotelianism, Neoplatonism, and Stoicism. Later, in 510, he was elevated to the position of consul in the court of Theodoric and was eventually showered with honors. In spite of his fame and his impressive political status, he was sus-

Boethius visited in prison by Philosophia—tenth-century manuscript illumination *(The Granger Collection)*

pected of high treason, stripped of his honors, subjected to a long imprisonment, and, in 524, finally executed. During his imprisonment, in Pavia, he wrote his famous *The Consolation of Philosophy,* a book that was widely circulated in the Middle Ages and had such lasting influence that Chaucer translated it and patterned some of his *Canterbury Tales* on its contents. In the early pages of this book Boethius offered an allegorical description of philosophy, which can still be seen carved on the façades of many cathedrals in Europe. What led him to see philosophy in these allegorical terms was his attempt to overcome his melancholy by writing poetry as he languished in prison. At this point he was struck by a new vision of philosophy, which he set down with considerable imaginative force. Philosophy came to him as a noble woman with eyes of such keenness as to suggest that philosophy has powers higher than human nature. She gives the impression of having no specific age, indicating that philosophy is perennial. On her robe appear the Greek letters phi (ϕ), symbolizing practical philosophy, and theta (θ), symbolizing theoretical philosophy, and a ladder between them indicates the ascent on the steps to wisdom. Boethius is consoled by philosophy when he discovers from it that no earthly goods and pleasures can give him true happiness, that one must turn to the Supreme Good to whom philosophy leads. But in addition to this allegorical interpretation, Boethius formulated a more technical definition of philosophy, calling it the "love of wisdom." The word *wisdom* carried the whole freight of his definition. To Boethius *wisdom* meant a reality, something that exists in itself. Wisdom is the living thought that causes all things. In loving wisdom, one loves the thought and cause of all things. In the end, the love of wisdom is the love of God.

Boethius became the most important channel through which Greek thought, especially some of Aristotle's works, was transmitted to the West in the early Middle Ages. Being an accomplished student of the Greek language, Boethius had originally intended to translate the works of Plato and Aristotle into Latin and to show how their apparent differences could be harmonized. Although he did not accomplish this ambitious project, he nevertheless did leave a considerable legacy of philosophical writings, consisting of translations of some of Aristotle's works, commentaries on these works, and some original treatises. In addition he was the author of theological works of considerable importance, as well as of treatises concerning each of the four liberal arts—arithmetic, geometry, astronomy, and music—to which he gave the name *quadrivium* to distinguish them from the other three liberal arts, the *trivium*, consisting of grammar, logic, and rhetoric.

Boethius translated Aristotle's logical treatises, including the *Prior* and *Posterior Analytics*, the *Topics*, and the *Categories*. He also translated Porphyry's *Introduction (Isagoge) to Aristotle's Categories*. His commentaries were on Porphyry's *Isagoge*, on Aristotle's *Categories, Topics*, and *On Interpretation*. In addition, he wrote a commentary on Cicero's *Topics*. His original treatises covered several aspects of logic. He also wrote on mathematics and music, and his aforementioned *The Consolation of Philosophy*, a dialogue between himself and a personification of philosophy, ranged over the subjects of God, fortune, freedom, and evil.

In his original treatises, Boethius drew upon a wide variety of authors, indicating his familiarity with Plato, Aristotle, the Stoics, Plotinus, Augustine, and others, though clearly under the dominant influence of Aristotle. His works achieved the status of classics and were later used by the leading philosophers, including St. Thomas Aquinas, as authoritative guides for interpreting ancient authors and basic philosophic problems. In particular, Boethius became the great interpreter of Aristotle's thought, exhibiting in this work his own immense philosophical skill. In his original treatises, Boethius worked out with great care some preliminary formulations of problems that later received more elaborate treatment. These problems covered such significant topics as the proof for God's existence, the problem of universals, and the nature of *being*, which ultimately became the center of Aquinas' philosophy. Though he wrote some specifically theological works, he tried to distinguish between faith and reason, and in his *Consolation* he makes no mention of Christianity but rather formulates a natural theology based upon what the unaided human reason can provide. At the same time, he considered the problem of knowledge, somewhat unexpectedly accepting Plato's doctrine of reminiscence, which held that learning consists in the soul's recovery of what it once knew but forgot. Boethius also departed from Aristotle's theory of universals, saying that we do not abstract the universal from particular things, that the mind is able to think universals "separate from bodies." At the same time, Boethius gave evidence of being a student of St. Augustine, employing some of his insights concerning evil and the cause of human restlessness, the relation between human freedom and God's providence, and our intuitive consciousness of God.

What Boethius gave the early Middle Ages in the form of translations, commentaries, and original treatises gave him a stature comparable to Aristotle and Augustine for centuries to come. His chief significance lies in his having taught the fundamentals of Aristotle's thought and in having formulated the basic philosophical definitions and terms that were destined to become the keys to the intellectual activity of the West.

PSEUDO-DIONYSIUS THE AREOPAGITE

A large and influential body of Neoplatonic writing, whose origin has been traced to the Byzantine world but whose author is still unknown, appeared in the West around 500 A.D. For a while, these writings were attributed to the disciple of St. Paul, Dionysius the Areopagite. But since their contents embody ideas developed by Proclus (ca. 410–485) and were appealed to at the Council of 533, it is now thought that they were written probably in Syria close to 500 and that the author used a pseudonym. The treatises of Pseudo-Dionysius attempt to relate Christian thought systematically with Neoplatonic philosophy. These works consist of *The Divine Names, The Celestial Hierarchy, The Ecclesiastical Hierarchy, The Mystical Theology,* and also ten letters. They were all translated into Latin frequently, and several commentaries were written on them. The influence of Pseudo-Dionysius was very great throughout the Middle Ages. Philosophers and theologians concerned with quite different problems made considerable use of his writings. The mystics drew heavily upon his elaborate theory of the hierarchy of beings, as it afforded a rich source for describing the ascent of the soul to God. Aquinas used his theories in accounting for the great chain of being and the analogical relation between humanity and God. Above all, he was one of the most powerful sources of Neoplatonism, influencing philosophical thought regarding the origin of the world, the knowledge of God, and the nature of evil.

Pseudo-Dionysius gave an account of the relation of the world to God in which he combined the Neoplatonic theory of *emanation* and the Christian doctrine of *creation.* He wanted to avoid the pantheism latent in the theory that says that all things are emanations from God. At the same time he wanted to establish that whatever exists comes from God, though he apparently had no clear conception of God's creative act as an act of free will. The world, nevertheless, is the object of God's providence. God has placed between Himself and humanity a virtual ladder or hierarchy of beings called heavenly spirits. From the lowest level of being to the highest, where God is at the summit, there are various degrees of being. Though he came close to pantheism and monism because of this continuous scale or chain of being, which he sometimes described as a shaft of light, Dionysius did maintain a pluralistic view of things. God is the goal of all created things. He attracts all things to Himself by His goodness and the love He inspires.

The knowledge of God, says Dionysius, can be approached in two ways, a *positive* and a *negative* way. When the mind takes the positive way, it ascribes to God all the perfect attributes discovered by a study of creatures. In this way the *divine* can be given such *names* as goodness, light, being, unity, wisdom, and life. Dionysius indicates that these names belong in their perfection to God and only in a derivative sense to humanity, depending upon the degree to which the creature participates in these perfections. Dionysius thought it was fair to assume that these attributes would be found actually to exist in God in the literal sense, since surely God *is* goodness, life, wisdom, and so on. By contrast, humans *have* these to a lesser degree. Still, God and humanity are more alike than God and a stone, about which it cannot be said that it is good, wise, and alive.

More important, however, was the *negative* way, which Dionysius developed under the influence of Proclus. Dionysius considered it more significant than the positive way, and St. Thomas Aquinas made considerable use of it in the thirteenth century. In the negative way, the mind considers God's nature by denying of God whatever seems least compatible with Him, such as "drunkenness and fury." Then, by a process of "remotion," various categories of attributes are "removed" from our conception of God. Dionysius was aware that people unavoidably develop anthropomorphic conceptions of God, and for this reason he undertook to remove from God all the attributes of creatures. To him it was obvious that what characterized God was precisely that He did not have the attributes of finite creatures. Step by step he removed from the conception of God all the things we say about creatures. Since all we know is the world of creatures, the negative process of "remotion" leads the human mind not to a clear conception of God but only to a "darkness of unknowing," the only positive aspect of which is the assurance of knowing what God is *not* like. Because God is no object, He is beyond the knowable. This view became of paramount influence among the later mystics, who believed that as humanity ascended closer to God, the ordinary forms of human knowledge were annihilated by the blindness caused by the excess of God's light.

In Neoplatonic terms, Dionysius denied the positive existence of *evil.* If evil were something positive, had some substantial being, it would have to be traced back to God as its cause, for all being is from God. For Dionysius, being and goodness were identical terms, for whatever is, is good, and something that is good, certainly is. In God goodness and being are one, and therefore whatever comes from God (and everything that is *does* come from God) is therefore good. The corollary would not necessarily be true, namely, that evil is synonymous with non-being. Still, it is in fact non-being in the sense of the absence or "privation" of being *where it rightly belongs* that constitutes evil. The absence of being amounts to evil because it means the absence of good. Evil people are good in all the ways in which they possess positive being but are evil in whatever respect they are lacking some form of being, particularly in the operation of their will. Ugliness and disease in physical nature are called evil for the same reason that acts in the province of morality are, namely, because they suffer deficiency in form or the absence of some being. Blindness is the absence of sight and not the presence of some evil force.

All three of these doctrines refined by Pseudo-Dionysius in an attempt to combine Neoplatonism and Christianity were to play a strong role in the rest of medieval philosophy, as writers continued to speculate about the origin of the world, about what can be known of God's nature, and about how to account for the presence of evil.

JOHN SCOTUS ERIGENA

Three centuries passed from the time of Boethius and Pseudo-Dionysius before another philosopher of stature appeared in the West. He was a remarkable Irish monk, John Scotus Erigena, who produced the first full-scale philosophical system in the Middle Ages. Born in Ireland in 810, he studied in a monastery and was one of the few scholars of his day who had mastered Greek, as the study of Greek in the ninth century was virtually limited to the Irish monasteries. Even the great educator from York, Alcuin, who crossed the Channel to become headmaster in the Palace School under Charlemagne and who sought to restore the school system of Western Europe, which had been destroyed by the barbarians, knew very little Greek. By any standard, Erigena was an unusually able Greek scholar, and given the philosophical material at his disposal at that time, his systematic writing set him apart as the most impressive thinker of his century.

Erigena left Ireland and appeared in the court of Charles the Bald around 851. His studies at this time were devoted chiefly to Latin authors, especially St. Augustine and Boethius, on whose *The Consolation of Philosophy* he wrote a commentary. At the request of Charles the Bald, Erigena translated the Greek texts of Pseudo-Dionysius into Latin in 858 and in addition wrote commentaries on these texts. He also translated works by Maximus the Confessor and St. Gregory of Nyssa. After this work of translation, Erigena produced his celebrated treatise on *The Division of Nature,* a book written in dialogue form around 864. In this work, Erigena undertook the complicated task of expressing Christian thought and Augustine's philosophical views in terms of the Neoplatonism of Pseudo-Dionysius. Although it became a landmark in medieval thought, it attracted little attention from Erigena's contemporaries. Various later writers appealed to this book to corroborate theories, such as pantheism, that were inimical to orthodoxy, leading Pope Honorius III to condemn Erigena's *The Division of Nature* on January 25, 1225, and order it to be burned, in spite of which several manuscript copies have survived even to the present time.

The Division of Nature   The complicated argument of Erigena's *The Division of Nature* revolves around his special understanding of the two words in the title of his book. First of all, by *Nature* Erigena meant "everything there is." In this sense Nature includes both God and creatures. Secondly, when he talks about the *division* of Nature, he has in mind the ways in which the whole of reality, God and creatures, is divided. In addition, the word *division* has a special meaning. Erigena says that there are two ways of understanding the structure of reality: one is by *division* and the other is by *analysis.* By *division* he means moving from the more universal to the less universal, as when one divides *substance* into *corporeal* and *incorporeal.* In turn, *incorporeal* can be divided into *living* and *inanimate,* and so on. On the other hand, by *analysis* the process of division is reversed, and the elements divided off from substance are worked back into the unity of substance. Underlying Erigena's method of division and analysis was his conviction that the human mind works in accordance with the metaphysical realities. The mind is not simply dealing with *concepts* when it "divides" and "analyzes"; it is describing how things really exist and behave. If God is the ultimate unity, things and the world are divisions of this basic unity, and analysis is the process by which things return to God. The laws of thought, according to Erigena, parallel the laws of reality.

With these distinctions in mind, Erigena argued that there is only one true reality and that all other things depend upon it and return to it, and this reality is God. Within the total reality of Nature, a fourfold division is possible as follows: there is, first, nature that creates and is not created; second, nature that is created and creates; third, nature that is created and does not create; and fourth, nature that neither creates nor is created. Erigena goes into considerable detail to elaborate each of these divisions, using Christian, Augustinian, and especially Neoplatonic concepts to formulate his philosophy about them. Some of his central ideas about each division will indicate the mode of his thought.

Nature That Creates and Is Not Created   By this Erigena meant God, who is the cause of all things but does not Himself need to be caused. He brought all creatures into existence out of nothing. Our knowledge of God, following the distinction made by Pseudo-Dionysius, is *negative,* since none of the attributes we derive from objects in our experience apply in any proper sense to God, who possesses all the perfections in His infinity. To make sure that not even the likely attributes of wisdom and truth are ascribed to God without qualification, Erigena adds the term *super* to them, so that about God one would say that He is superwisdom and supertruth. None of Aristotle's predicates or categories applies to God, for these predicates assume some form of substance—as, for example, "quantity" implies dimension—but God does not exist in a definable place. Most of what Erigena says about God's nature and of creation "out of nothing" follows generally along Christian and Augustinian lines. But as he pursues the subject of the relation between God and creatures, his Neoplatonism seems to become dominant, and it is difficult to avoid the conclusion that for Erigena there is no sharp distinction between God and creatures. "When we hear that God made all things," says Erigena, "we should understand nothing else but that God is in all things." This follows because only God "truly is," and therefore whatever is in anything is God.

Nature That Is Created and Creates   This division refers to the divine Ideas, which become the prototypes of all created things. They are the *exemplary causes* of all the created species. To say that they are *created* does not mean, according to Erigena, that they come to be at some point of time. He has in mind a logical and not a chronological sequence. In God there is the full knowledge of everything, including the primordial causes of all things. These primordial causes are the divine Ideas and prototypes of things, and they are said to *create* in the sense that all creatures "participate" in them, as, for example, humanity's wisdom participates in superwisdom. Though he uses the word *creation* here, his Neoplatonism once again dominates, particularly since creation for Erigena does not occur in time but is an eternal relation between God's Ideas and creatures.

Nature That Is Created and Does Not Create   This is the world of things as we experience it. Technically, it refers to the collective external effects of the primordial causes. These effects, whether incorporeal (for example, angels or intelligence) or corporeal (such as people and things), are *participations* in the divine Ideas. Erigena emphasizes that these things, this full range or hierarchy of beings, contain God as their essence, even though specific things give the impression of being individual. He compares this apparent plurality of things to the many varied reflections of light on the feathers of a peacock. Each color is a real one, but it depends upon the feathers, and therefore, in the end, the color is not an independent reality. In the created world, each individual is real by virtue of its primordial cause, which is in God's mind. But God is, if anything, a unity, and to speak of Ideas, prototypes, and archetypes in His mind is to speak metaphorically, for these all constitute a unity. For this reason, the world is also a unity, as the peacock, and between the world and God, finally, there is also a comprehensive unity, since God is in everything. All things depend upon and are infused with the suprasensible; they exhibit a rhythm of "going out" into species and genera, but only as reflections, as the colors, of the divine Ideas and then "returning." What Erigena appears to say is that the divine *Ideas* stand midway between God and creatures, as though they could look "up" toward God and "down" toward these externalized forms. But in the end his Neoplatonism leads him to erase the "spaces" between the *Ideas* and God and creatures, fusing them all into a unity and eventually a pantheism.

Nature That Neither Creates Nor Is Created   This last division refers to God again, this time as the goal or end of the created order. As all things proceed from God, they also all return to God. Using Aristotle's metaphor, Erigena compares God to a beloved who, without moving, attracts the lover. Whatever starts from a principle returns again to this same principle, and in this way the universal cause draws to itself the multitude of things that have risen from it. With this return there is an end to all evil, and man finds his union with God.

Erigena's *The Division of Nature* displayed his wide knowledge of Neoplatonism but also his inevitable pantheism. Again, his book did not receive immediate attention or acclaim but became, nevertheless, one of the decisive documents in the development of medieval philosophy. This book, along with his translations of Pseudo-Dionysius, Maximus, and Gregory of Nyssa, amounted to a substantial contribution by Erigena to the tradition of theology and philosophy.

Early
Statements of Major
Problems

ith the aggressive revival of learning under Charlemagne and with the appearance of Erigena's large-scale and systematic work *The Division of Nature,* it might have been expected that philosophy had emerged from the Dark Ages and that it would soon flourish again in Western Europe. This early promise of continued revival was delayed, however, by several historical events. After Charlemagne's death, the Empire was decentralized into feudal divisions, the papacy entered a period of moral and spiritual weakness, the monasteries exerted no effective leadership in their special province of education and learning, and the invasions by the Mongols, Saracens, and Norsemen added to these forces, making for cultural darkness. For almost a hundred years, during most of the 900s, very little philosophical activity was carried on. When philosophy did revive in the next century, its main feature for the next two hundred years, from about 1000 to 1200, was its preoccupation with particular problems, including the problems of universals, of proving God's existence, and of relating the domains of faith and reason. In the discussion of these problems, several sources of philosophy were stimulated, producing a confluence of Greek, Christian, Jewish, and Arabian thought.

THE PROBLEM OF UNIVERSALS

The problem of universals, by no means a new one, struck the medieval think-ers as fundamental, because in their judgment the enterprise of thought rested to a great extent upon its solution. The central issue in this problem is how to relate the objects of human thought and the objects that exist outside the mind. Objects outside the mind are individual and many, whereas objects in the mind are single or universal. For example, in human discourse we use words such as *tree* or *person,* but such words refer to the actual and particular trees and people that we observe with our senses. To *see* a tree is one thing; to *think* it is an-other. We see particulars but we think universals. When we see a particular thing, our minds place it into either a species or a genus. We never see *tree* or *person,* only "this oak" or "John." *Tree* stands in our language for all the ac-tual trees, oak, elm, and so on, whereas *person* includes John, Jane, and every other specific person. What, then, is the relation between these words and these trees and persons? Is the word *tree only* a word, or does it refer to something that exists someplace? If the word *tree* refers to something in this oak that be-longs to all trees, the word refers to something universal. The universal, then, is a general term, but the objects that exist outside our mind are single or par-ticular and specific. If the universal is merely an idea in our mind, what is the connection between the way we think, on the one hand, and the actual par-ticular objects outside our mind, on the other? How does the mind go about forming a universal concept? Is there anything *outside* the mind corresponding to the universal idea *in* the mind?

Boethius States the Problem   Boethius had translated Porphyry's *Intro-duction (Isagoge) to Aristotle's Categories.* There he found a discussion of the problem of universals in terms of certain questions raised by Porphyry. These questions centered around the relation between generic and specific notions. What, in short, is the relation between genera or species and specific objects? Porphyry raised these three questions: (1) Do genera and species really exist in nature, or are they merely constructions of the mind? (2) If they are realities, are they material or immaterial? (3) Do they exist apart from sensible things or somehow in them? While Porphyry did not answer his own questions, Boe-thius formulated a solution chiefly in terms of Aristotle's approach to the prob-lem.

Boethius was aware of the immense difficulty of the problem. If the issue is to discover whether human thought conforms to realities outside the mind, we can quickly discover some ideas in our mind for which there is no corre-sponding external object. We can think of a centaur, but such a combination of man and horse does not exist. Or, again, we can think of a line, the way a geometer does. But we do not find this kind of line existing as such anywhere. What is the difference between the idea of the centaur and of the line? One can say about the concept of the centaur that it is *false,* whereas the concept of the line is *true.* What Boethius wants to illustrate here is that there are two fundamentally different ways in which the mind forms concepts, namely, by *composition* (putting together horse and man) and *abstraction* (drawing from a particular object some of its predicates). He wanted to say that universal ideas, such as genera and species, are abstracted by the mind from actual individual things and are, therefore, *true* ideas.

Saying that universals are abstracted from individuals led Boethius to conclude that genera or species *exist in* the individual things and that they are universals when they are *thought* by the mind. In this way, universals (not only genera and species, to which Boethius limited his analysis, but other qualities such as *just, good, beautiful*) are simultaneously in the object and in the mind, *subsisting* in the thing and *thought* in the mind. What makes two trees both trees is that, as objects, they resemble each other because they contain a universal or the same substance or foundation to their being; at the same time, they can both be *thought* as trees because the mind discovers the same universal element in both of them. This, then, was Boethius' way of answering the first question, namely, whether universals exist in nature or only in the mind. For him, they exist both in things and in the mind. To the second question, whether the universals are material or immaterial, he could now say that they exist concretely in things and immaterially or abstractly in the mind. Similarly, his reply to the third question, whether universals exist apart from individual objects or are realized in them, was that they exist both in things and apart from them in the mind.

When these questions, which were formulated by Porphyry and answered by Boethius, came under discussion almost five hundred years later, they precipitated a vigorous debate for centuries to come. Although the issues were formulated in relatively restricted and seemingly unimportant terms, the participants saw serious theological as well as philosophical consequences hinging on the outcome of the debate. At least three major approaches were developed to this problem of universals.

Exaggerated Realism   The problem had resolved itself into the simple question of whether a universal is a real *thing* or not. Those who said universals are in fact real things were known as *exaggerated realists*. These people said that genera or species exist in reality and that individual things *share* in these universals. They did not go so far as Plato, who said, in addition, that the universals were Forms or Ideas and existed separately from individual things. Rather, he said, for example, that *humanity* and *man* exist but that these exist in the plurality of human beings.

Why should this form of realism seem such an important matter? One answer is found in the works of Odo of Taurnai, who taught in the Cathedral School of Tours, founded the Abbey of St. Martin, was Bishop of Cambrai, and died in the Monastery at Anchin in 1113. For him realism was the foundation of certain orthodox theological doctrines. For example, the doctrine of original sin, according to him, requires the realistic description of human nature. Realism says that there exists a universal substance, which is contained in every member of a species. If we are to understand the condition of human nature accurately, he said, we must realize that in the sin of Adam and Eve, the universal substance of *man* or *humanity* was affected and infected so that all subsequent generations have inherited the consequence of their acts. If one denied *realism,* what Adam and Eve did would pertain only to themselves, in which case the force of the doctrine of original sin would be lost. In a similar way, St. Anselm (1033–1109) thought that the doctrine of the Trinity required the viewpoint of *realism.* If one denied that an identical substance exists in several members, the Trinity would amount to tritheism, where each member is a totally separate and different being. Replying to this line of reasoning developed by Roscellinus (1050–1125), Anselm, an advocate of exaggerated realism, said that "He who does not understand how many men are specifically one only man cannot understand that several persons, each one of which is God, are one only God."

Another exaggerated realist was Guillaume de Champeaux (1070–1121), who had formulated two different views: First, in his *identity* theory, he held that the universal, say *humanity,* is identical in all members, in this case in all persons. The *whole* reality of the universal is contained in each person. What differentiates Jane and John is merely certain secondary or accidental modifications of their essence or substance. Abelard (1079–1142) ridiculed this line of reasoning by saying that if each person is the whole human species, humanity exists in Socrates in Rome and in Plato in Athens. If Socrates is present wherever the human essence is found, and since it is both at Rome and Athens, Socrates must be at the same moment in Rome and in Athens, and this, said Abelard, is not only absurd but leads to pantheism. Guillaume was forced by this and other criticisms to adopt a second theory, that of *indifferentism,* an antirealist view, in which he now argued that the individuals of a species are the same thing not through some common essence but because in certain respects they are not different, they are *indifferent.*

Nominalism   One of the most formidable critics of exaggerated realism was Roscellinus (or Roscelin), who was born in Compiègne; traveled to England, Rome, and Tours; taught at Taches, Compiègne, and Besançon; and was a teacher of Abelard. His central argument was that only individuals exist in nature. Species and genera are not real things. A general term, a universal such as a word, does not refer to anything; it is only a word (*voces*), or a name (*nomen*), composed of letters and expressed as a *vocal emission* and therefore only air. Logic, in Roscellinus' view, deals only with words. For this reason, discussions about universals are about words and not real things. Roscellinus was willing to draw certain obvious conclusions from his argument, particularly that the three persons of the Trinity are three separate beings and that all they have in common is a word but nothing really essential, hence they can be considered three Gods. For these views he was accused by the council at Soissons (1092) of tritheism, and when he was threatened with excommunication, he denied this doctrine. Nevertheless, Roscellinus served a decisive function in the history of the problem of universals in that he deflected thought from exaggerated realism by holding that universals, or any kind of abstraction, must not be made into a thing.

Conceptualism or Moderate Realism   Roscellinus seemed to be as extreme in his nominalism as others had been in their realism. Both were exaggerated views. Avoiding both of these extremes was the position developed by Peter Abelard, who was born in Le Pallet in 1079 of a military family. During his tempestuous life, he quarreled with his teachers, had a celebrated romance with Heloïse, was abbot of the monastery in Brittany, was a famous lecturer in Paris, was condemned for his heretical teachings by Innocent II, and finally retired at Cluny, where he died in 1142.

On the problem of universals, Abelard said that universality must be ascribed principally to words. A word is *universal* when it is applied to many individuals. The word *Socrates* is not universal because it applies only to one person, whereas the word *man* is universal because it can be applied to all persons. The function of a universal term, says Abelard, is to denote individual things in a special way. The question then is, how does it come about that we formulate these universal terms? To this Abelard answers that certain individual things, because of the *way* they exist, cause anyone observing them to conceive a likeness in all these individuals. This so-called likeness is not what the realists called an *essence* or *substance*. It consists simply in the way things agree in likeness. When we experience an individual, we *see* it but also *think* or *understand* it. Unlike the eye, which requires an object, the mind does not require a physical object since it can form *conceptions*. Thus, the mind is capable of doing two things, namely, forming concepts of individuals, Plato or Socrates, and forming concepts of universals, such as *humanity*. The conception of the individual is clear, whereas the conception of the universal is blurred. We cannot clearly focus on the precise meaning of the universal even though we do in fact know what it means. As conceptions of the mind, the universals exist apart from the individual sensible bodies; but as words applied to these individuals they exist only in these bodies. The same word can be applied commonly to several individuals because each individual already exists in such a way as to cause it to be conceived the way others like it are conceived. The universal is therefore abstracted from the individual. The process of abstraction tells us how we understand the universal but not how the universal subsists. We understand things properly insofar as we abstract from them those properties that they truly possess. Abelard concluded, therefore, that the universal is a word and concept representing some reality that supplies the ground for this concept. This ground is the way similar things exist and strike our minds. To this extent, there is an objective ground for the universals, but this ground is not, as the realist held, something *real* in the sense of a *thing*. Nor would Abelard agree with the strict nominalist who would say that the universal is *only* a subjective idea or word for which there is no objective ground.

Abelard's theory of universals carried the day, defeating both extremes of realism and nominalism. For the most part, St. Thomas Aquinas accepted

Abelard's moderate realism. Using Avicenna's formulation of the status of universals, Aquinas, following Abelard, agreed that universals exist outside of things (*ante rem*) but as such only as the divine Ideas in God's mind, in things (*in re*) as the concrete individual essence in all members of a species, and in the mind (*then post rem*) after abstracting the universal concept from the individual. The problem of universals had one more major treatment in the Middle Ages, and this time it was given a different solution by William of Ockham.

PROVING THE EXISTENCE OF GOD: ANSELM'S ONTOLOGICAL ARGUMENT

St. Anselm is famous in the history of thought primarily for his celebrated *ontological* argument for the existence of God. He was born in Piedmont in 1033, entered the Benedictine Order, and eventually became Archbishop of Canterbury, where he died in 1109. For Anselm, there was no clear line between philosophy and theology. Like Augustine before him, he was particularly concerned with providing rational support for the doctrines of Christianity, which he already accepted as a matter of faith. He was convinced that faith and reason lead to the same conclusions. Moreover, Anselm believed that human reason can create a natural theology or metaphysics that is rationally coherent and does not depend upon any authority other than rationality. This did not mean, however, that Anselm denied any connection between natural theology and faith. On the contrary, his view was that natural theology consists of giving a rational version of what is believed. In this he was thoroughly Augustinian, saying that he was not trying to *discover* the truth about God through reason alone, but wanted rather to employ reason in order to *understand* what he was believing. His method therefore was *faith seeking understanding;* "I do not seek to understand in order that I may believe," he said, "but I believe in order that I may understand." He made it particularly clear that his enterprise of proving God's existence could not even begin unless he had already believed in His existence. The human mind cannot penetrate into the profundity of God, "for I deem my intellect in no way sufficient thereunto." From the rational proof of God's existence, Anselm had a limited expectation, as he said that "I desire only a little understanding of the truth which my heart believes and loves."

Before he composed the ontological argument, which appears in his book entitled *Proslogion,* he formulated three other arguments in an earlier book called *Monologion.* These three arguments indicate his philosophical orientation, namely, his acceptance of *realism* and his rejection of *nominalism.* His realism comes out in his belief that words are not simply sounds or grammatical conventions but stand for real things outside of the mind. Stated briefly, his three early arguments proceed as follows: (1) Men seek to enjoy what they consider *good.* Since we can compare things with each other as being *more* or *less* good, these things must share in one and the same goodness. This goodness must be good-in-itself and as such the supreme good. One could use the same argument as applied to *greatness.* There must therefore be something which is the best

De A. Theuet, Liure III. 130

ANSELME ARCHEVESQVE DE
Cantorbie.　*Chap.63.*

Anselm—French engraving, 1584 (*The Granger Collection*)

and greatest of all. (2) Everything that exists, exists either through something or through nothing. Obviously, it cannot come out of nothing. The only remaining alternative, then, is to say that a thing is caused either by something else or by itself. It cannot be caused by itself because before it is, it is nothing. To say that it is caused by something else could mean that things cause each other, which is also absurd. There must therefore be one thing that alone is from itself and that causes all other things to be, and this is God. (3) There are various *degrees* or *levels* of being, whereby animals have a *higher* being than plants, and people have a higher being than animals. Using a line of reasoning similar to the first argument, Anselm concluded that unless one continued to move up through an infinite number of levels, one must arrive at a *highest* and most perfect being, than which there is none more perfect. All three of these arguments start from an existing finite thing and move up through a hierarchy until they reach the summit of the scale of Being. Again, Anselm's realism is evident here, as is the influence of Plato and Augustine, since he assumes throughout that when a finite thing shares in what our language calls *good, great, cause, being,* these words refer to some existing reality; finite things therefore share not only in a *word* but in *being,* which somewhere exists in maximum perfection. Still, Anselm was aware that these arguments did not have the clarity or power of a mathematical proof. Moreover, his fellow monks wondered whether he could simplify these arguments. Accordingly, after much thought on the matter, Anselm thought he had discovered a single, clear, and virtually flawless argument, which he published in the *Proslogion; or, Faith Seeking Understanding.*

Ontological Argument The first thing to notice about this proof is that Anselm's thought proceeds from within his mind, rather than starting, as Aquinas did, with the assumption that each proof must begin with some empirical evidence from which the mind can then move logically to God. Anselm followed Augustine's doctrine of divine illumination, which gave him direct access to certain truths. Indeed, Anselm asks the reader, before beginning the ontological argument, to "enter the inner chamber of your mind" and to "shut out all things save God and whatever may aid you in seeking God." Clearly, Anselm is assured of the existence of God before he begins, saying, again, that "unless I believe, I shall not understand."

The argument itself moves swiftly. We believe, says Anselm, that God is "that than which nothing greater can be thought." The question then is, does this than which nothing greater can be thought really exist? There are those who would deny God's existence. Anselm quotes Psalms 14:1, where it says that "The fool has said in his heart: There is no God." What is meant by the word *fool* in this context? It means that one who denies God's existence is involved in a flat contradiction. For when the fool hears the words "something than which nothing greater can be thought," he understands what he hears, and what he understands can be said to be in his intellect. But it is one thing for something to be in the intellect; it is another to understand that something actually exists. A painter, for example, thinks in advance what he is about to portray. At this point, there is in his intellect an understanding of what he is about to make, though not an understanding that the portrait, which is still to be made, actually exists. But when he has finally painted it, he both has in his understanding and understands as existing the portrait he has finally made. What this proves is that something can be in the intellect even before the intellect knows it to exist. There is, then, in the fool's intellect an understanding of what is meant by the phrase "something than which nothing greater can be thought," even though he does not yet necessarily understand that this something does in fact exist. It is in his intellect because when the fool hears this phrase, he understands it, and whatever is understood is in the understanding. Hence, even the fool knows that there is at least in his intellect a being than which nothing greater can be thought. This brings Anselm to the crux of his argument, which is this: Anyone, even the fool, can think of something greater than a being which is only in the intellect as an *idea,* and this something is the *actual existence* of that than which there is no greater. The contradiction in which the fool finds himself is in understanding what is meant by the word *God,* namely, a being than which nothing greater can be thought, realizing that its actual existence is greater than just having an idea of it in the intellect, and still denying that God exists. Therefore, says Anselm, "there exists beyond doubt something than which a greater cannot be thought, both in understanding and in reality." In a concluding prayer, Anselm thanks God "because through your divine illumination I now so understand that which, through your generous gift, I formerly believed."

Gaunilon's Rebuttal   In the Abbey of Marmontier near Tours, another Benedictine monk, Gaunilon, came to the defense of the "fool." Gaunilon did not want to deny God's existence but simply to argue that Anselm had not constructed an adequate proof. For one thing, Gaunilon argued that the first part of the "proof" is impossible to achieve: It requires that there be in the understanding an idea of God, that upon hearing this word the fool is expected to have a conception of that than which there is no greater. But, says Gaunilon, the fool cannot form a concept of such a being since there is nothing among other realities he experiences from which this concept can be formed, in addition to which Anselm has already argued that there is no reality like Him. Actually, if the human mind could form such a concept, no "proof" would be necessary, for one would then already connect existence as an aspect of a perfect being. Gaunilon's other major objection is that we often think of things that in fact do not exist. We can imagine a perfect island, an island than which no greater can exist, but there is no way to prove that such a perfect island exists.

Anselm's Reply to Gaunilon   Anselm gave two replies. First, he said that we, along with the fool, are able to form a concept of that than which there is no greater. We do this whenever we compare different degrees of perfection in things and move upward to the maximum perfection, than which there is no more perfect. Secondly, he thought Gaunilon's reference to a perfect island showed that he had missed the point of the argument. Anselm points out that we can move from an idea to its necessary existence in only one case, namely, in the case of that Being whose nonexistence cannot be thought. An island does not *have to be,* it is a *possible* or *contingent* kind of being. This would be similarly true of every finite thing. There is only one something through which everything else has its being but that is itself not derived from anything else but has its existence necessarily from itself, and this is God.

FAITH AND REASON IN ARABIAN AND JEWISH THOUGHT

Most of medieval thought is an attempt to reconcile the domains of philosophy and theology, of faith and reason. The leading writers were Christians, who wrote philosophy with an admixture of theology. Their religious orientation stemmed from the mainstream of the Christian tradition and was therefore, for the most part, the same for all of them. Their philosophical orientations, however, were quite diverse, since at different times and at different places they were exposed to different philosophers. Even when they relied upon the same philosopher—Aristotle, for example—they were exposed to different interpretations of his writings. What makes the Arabian philosophers highly important in the Middle Ages is that they had produced influential commentaries on Aristotle upon which many Christian writers depended for their understanding of Aristotle. As it turned out, these Arabian interpretations of Aristotle were the source of much knowledge about Aristotle but also the cause of serious difficulties in harmonizing the domains of faith and reason.

Arabian Philosophy Under the leadership of Muhammad (570–632) there was established the vast Moslem Empire with cultural centers in Persia and Spain, where during the ninth through the twelfth centuries significant philosophic activity took place. During these centuries, the Moslem world was far more advanced in its knowledge of Greek philosophy, science, and mathematics than was the Christian world. Moreover, the Moslem world had access to the chief works of Aristotle centuries before Western Europe finally received them. Many texts of the Greek philosophers had been translated into the Arabic, from which later Latin translations were made in the West. By 833, philosophy was well established in Baghdad, where a school had been established for translating Greek manuscripts on philosophy and science, and for creative scholarship as well. A distinguished line of thinkers worked here, especially Avicenna (980–1037). The other focal point of Moslem culture was Cordova, Spain, where the other leading Arabian philosopher, Averroës, wrote much of his philosophy. Although Avicenna and Averroës wrote in Arabic and were Moslems, they were not Arabs. Avicenna was a Persian, and Averroës a Spaniard. Both of them wrote interpretations of Aristotle's philosophy. These interpretations were accepted by some Christian writers as the authentic doctrines of Aristotle. Because these interpretations showed Aristotle to be at variance with Christian doctrine, some medieval writers, such as Bonaventura, thought it necessary to reject Aristotle to avoid errors. St. Thomas Aquinas, on the other hand, contended with the leading exponent at the University of Paris of Averroës' views, Siger de Brabant, but Aquinas had access to other versions of Aristotle. For this reason, Aquinas' debates with Brabant were not to reject Aristotelianism but to interpret Aristotle in a way compatible with Christian doctrine. The significance of the Arabian philosophers was therefore twofold in that they were transmitters of Aristotle and other Greek thinkers to the West and were also the authors of interpretations of Aristotle that became the basis of controversy in medieval philosophy.

Avicenna Avicenna, born in Persia in 980, was a phenomenal scholar. He had studied geometry, logic, jurisprudence, the Koran, physics, theology, and medicine, becoming a practicing physician at the age of sixteen. He was the author of many works, and although his thought centered around Aristotle, it shows some Neoplatonic influences as well as original formulations of problems.

Of particular importance was Avicenna's formulation of the doctrine of creation. Here he combined Aristotelian and Neoplatonic views and arrived at a theory that was hotly debated in the thirteenth century. Avicenna begins with the assumption that whatever begins to be (as is the case with everything we experience) must have a cause. Things that require a cause are called *possible* beings. A cause which is also a *possible* being must be caused by a prior being. This too must have a cause, but there cannot be an infinite series of such causes. There must therefore be a First Cause, whose being is not simply *possible* but is *necessary,* having its existence in itself and not from a cause, and this is God. (Aquinas would later make much of this line of reasoning in his *third proof.*)

God is at the apex of Being, has no beginning, always is in act (i.e., is always expressing His full Being), and therefore has always created. According to Avicenna, then, creation is both necessary and eternal. This conclusion struck Bonaventura in the thirteenth century as a serious error and in conflict with the Biblical notion of creation, whose two chief features were that creation is a product of God's free will, not of necessity, and that creation occurred at a point in time, not from eternity. Aquinas would agree, however, that philosophically there is no way to decide whether creation occurred in time or from eternity, that this must ultimately be a matter of faith.

If Avicenna's metaphysics caused Christian philosophers difficulties because of his doctrine of creation, his psychology caused even more serious concern. In his psychology, Avicenna wanted particularly to account for humanity's intellectual activity. Central to his theory was the distinction between the *possible* intellect and the *Agent Intellect.* To account for this distinction, Avicenna employed his Neoplatonic view of the gradations of beings, placing people under the lowest level of angelic beings or Intelligences. That is, God creates a single effect, and this effect is called an *Intelligence,* the highest angel, but this Intelligence in turn creates a subordinate Intelligence. There are nine such Intelligences in descending order, each one creating (1) the one below it and (2) the soul of the successive sphere. The ninth Intelligence, then, creates the tenth and final Intelligence, and this is the Agent Intellect. It is the Agent Intellect that creates the four elements of the world and the individual souls of people. The Agent Intellect not only creates the souls or minds of men, it also "radiates forms" to these created minds.

What Avicenna was saying is that since a person's mind has a beginning, it is a *possible* being; therefore, a person has a *possible intellect.* Here Avicenna made a sharp distinction between existence and essence, saying that there are two different things in creatures. That is, because a creature's essence is distinct from his existence, his *essence* is not automatically fulfilled, and it is certainly not given existence by itself. The essence of the human mind is to know, but it does not always know. The intellect is capable of knowing, its essence is to know, but its knowing is only *possible.* The intellect is actually created without any knowledge but with an essence or possibility for knowledge. The *existence* of knowledge in the human intellect requires two elements, namely, (1) the bodily senses through which we perceive sensible objects externally and the powers of retaining images of objects in the memory or imagination internally, and

(2) the power to discover the essence or universal in individual things through the power of abstraction. But, and here was Avicenna's unique point, this abstraction is not performed by the human intellect but is the work of the Agent Intellect, which illuminates the human mind to enable it to *know,* thereby adding existence to the mind's essence. Since the Agent Intellect is the creator of the souls of all people and, in addition, is the active power in human knowledge, there is, then, only one active intellect in all people, in which all people share.

What concerned Bonaventura so much about this psychology, which Siger de Brabant was teaching at the University of Paris, was that it threatened the notion of the discrete individuality of each person. Avicenna had not meant to imply this, for he actually had a doctrine of the immortality of each soul, since each returned to its source, the Agent Intellect. Still, Christian writers tended to see in the doctrine of the Agent Intellect the annihilation of the individual soul as well as serious separation between humanity and God, since the Agent Intellect, and not God, confers enlightenment upon the human intellect. Individual people exist only insofar as matter is formed into their bodies, and the soul is the form of the body. But, again, the active part of the intellect is not *theirs.* In these ways, then, Avicenna injected into medieval philosophy some very provocative themes, including (1) the eternity and necessity of creation, (2) the gradations and emanations of a hierarchy of beings, (3) the doctrine of the Agent Intellect who both creates the human soul and illuminates the *possible intellect,* and (4) the distinction between essence and existence as related to possible and necessary being.

Averroës   Like Avicenna before him, Averroës was a prodigious scholar. He was born in 1126 in Cordova, Spain, where he studied philosophy, mathematics, jurisprudence, medicine, and theology. After serving, as his father had, as a judge, he became a physician, but spent much of his time writing his famous commentaries, for which reason he became known in the Middle Ages as The Commentator. He spent his last days in Morocco, where he died in 1198 at the age of seventy-two.

Averroës considered Aristotle the greatest of all philosophers, going so far as to say that nature had produced him as the model of human perfection. For this reason, Averroës structured all his work around Aristotle's texts and ideas. At some points he disagreed with Avicenna. For one thing, whereas Avicenna argued that creation is eternal and necessary, Averroës denied altogether the idea of creation, saying that philosophy knows no such doctrine, that this is merely a teaching of religion. Averroës also rejected the distinction between essence and existence, saying that there is no *real* distinction between them (such as led Avicenna to distinguish between the *possible* and *active intellects*), but only a logical distinction for purposes of analysis. Moreover, Averroës held that the form of a person is the soul, but that the soul is a material and not a spiritual form. As such, the material soul has the same mortality as the body, so that upon death nothing survives. What confers special status to humans among animals is that, unlike the lower animals, humans are united through knowledge with the Agent Intellect. Unlike Avicenna, who said that each person has a possible intellect, a unique spiritual power, whereas for all people there was one and the same Agent Intellect, Averroës denied that people have separate *possible* intellects. He therefore explicitly located human knowledge in the universal Agent Intellect and denied the doctrine of immortality. It is no wonder that the Christian thinkers thought his teachings impious. But his influence was immense, and Aquinas frequently quotes from his works. Still, Averroës had little respect for theology and went to great lengths to distinguish the domains of philosophy and theology, of faith and reason.

Philosophy and theology each have a function, said Averroës, because there are different kinds of people whom they respectively serve. He envisioned three groups of people: (1) The majority of people live by imagination and not by reason. They are kept virtuous through fear communicated by eloquent preachers. By contrast, the philosopher needs no threat, but is motivated by his knowledge. Although religion and philosophy work generally for the same end, they communicate different contents and, in this sense, different truths. These truths do not necessarily contradict each other; they simply are different kinds. Hence, the first group is composed of those who are governed more by dramatic forms of thought than by reason. (2) The second group is of theologians, who differ from the first group only in that while they have the same religious beliefs, they attempt to devise intellectual supports for them as their justification. But, having prejudiced their thinking by resting it upon inflexible assumptions, they cannot arrive at truth even though they have some notion of the power of reason. (3) The third and superior group consists of the philosophers, who constitute a small minority. They are able to appreciate the truth for which religious persons and rational theologians are seeking, but they see no reason for trying to see this truth *through* the unavoidably indirect perspective of religion. The philosophers know truth directly. Actually, Averroës thought that religious beliefs had a social function in that they made philosophical truths accessible to minds that were incapable of philosophical thought. He thought, however, that the theologians, as compared with the masses, should have known better than to employ the powers of sophisticated reasoning upon a subject matter, religion, that is by nature a deviation from, though not necessarily contrary to, reason.

Jewish Philosophy: Moses Maimonides　　Both Jewish and Arabian thought were more advanced than and therefore superior to Christian thought in the twelfth century. The reason is that at this time the Christian philosophers did not have access to the rich apparatus of Greek philosophic concepts. As we have seen, the Arabians had been working with Aristotle's texts since the ninth century. The great Jewish philosopher Maimonides owed his acquaintance with Aristotle to the Arabians. Both the Arabian and Jewish philosophers exerted a powerful influence upon the development of thirteenth-century scholastic philosophy because they had worked out some preliminary solutions to the major philosophical problems and had, moreover, transmitted considerable learning to that century. Maimonides had a special influence upon the succeeding generations of Christian thinkers because he shared with them a common belief in the Old Testament. And Maimonides' attempt to harmonize Old Testament thought with Greek philosophy and science served as a model for Thomas Aquinas in reconciling Biblical and secular learning.

Moses ben Maimonides was born in 1135 at Cordova and was a contemporary of Averroës who was also born there. He was forced to leave Spain, and he went first to Morocco and then to Egypt, where he earned his livelihood by practicing medicine. He died in Cairo in 1204 at the age of sixty-nine. His principal work was his book entitled *Guide of the Perplexed.* In it he set out to prove that the teachings of Judaism harmonize with philosophic thought and, in addition, that Biblical thought offers certain valid insights that reason alone cannot discover. To accomplish this end, Maimonides drew on an astonishing amount of literature, being dominated, however, by the works of Aristotle. Again, that he had so effectively utilized Aristotle as a rational foundation for Jewish theology had a strong influence upon others, notably Aquinas, who undertook the similar task of harmonizing Christian thought with philosophy.

Apart from expressing many of Aristotle's views, which others had also learned and taught, Maimonides proposed certain distinctive notions. Among these are the following: *First,* Maimonides believed that there can be no basic conflict between theology, philosophy, and science, between faith and reason. His *Guide of the Perplexed* was addressed principally to those believing Jews who had studied the sciences of the philosophers and had become perplexed by the literal meaning of the Law. The science of the Law (Torah) and philosophy, he said, are distinct forms of knowledge. Although they do not conflict, their range and content are not the same. For this reason, not every religious doctrine will have a rational or philosophical explanation.

Second, the doctrine of the creation of the world is a matter of religious belief. Although Aristotle's philosophy suggests that the world existed from eternity, that there was no creation in time, Maimonides points out that on this matter the philosophic proof is not decisive; that is, philosophically the arguments for and against the doctrine of creation are of equal weight. Aquinas later took this same view, saying, as Maimonides had, that on this matter, the religious view must prevail, since it does not conflict with rational thought.

Third, Maimonides thought that conflicts between faith and reason were produced by two things, namely, the anthropomorphic language of religion and the disorderly way in which the problems of faith are approached by the perplexed. One must proceed step by step, moving from mathematics, the natural sciences, to the study of the Law, and then to metaphysics or technical philosophical theology. With this kind of methodical training it becomes easier to understand the allegorical nature of much Biblical language. But to reduce the anthropomorphic element in religious language one must be trained in the categories of scientific and philosophical concepts.

Fourth, Maimonides agreed with Avicenna regarding the structure of human nature. Like Avicenna, he accepted the theory of the Agent Intellect as the source of a person's substantive knowledge. Each person has only a *possible* or *passive* intellect belonging uniquely to him or her. Each person *acquires* an active intellect, which *is* the Agent Intellect, or comes from the Agent Intellect in varying degrees, depending upon each person's degree of merit. Upon death, a person's soul, which is the form of the body, perishes, and the only element that survives is the active intellectual ingredient that came from the Agent Intellect and that now returns to it. If this is a doctrine of immortality, it is one in which the unique characteristics of each individual have been greatly diminished.

Fifth, Maimonides anticipated three of Aquinas' proofs for the existence of God. Using portions of Aristotle's *Metaphysics* and *Physics,* he proved the existence of a Prime Mover, the existence of a *necessary* Being (relying here also on Avicenna), and the existence of a primary cause. Whether the world was created out of nothing or existed from eternity did not, Maimonides thought, affect the enterprise of natural theology. But having proved the existence of God, Maimonides, unlike Aquinas, rejected the possibility of saying *what* God is like. No positive attributes can be ascribed to God but only negative ones, by saying what God is *not* like.

Sixth, the goal of human life is to achieve humanity's appropriate perfection. The philosophers, says Maimonides, have made it clear there are four kinds of perfections that a person can attain; there are, in ascending order, the perfection of possessions, the perfection of the bodily constitution and shape, the perfection of the moral virtues, and, finally, the highest, which is the acquisition of the rational virtues. By rational virtues, says Maimonides, "I refer to the conception of intelligibles, which teach true opinions concerning the divine things. That is in true reality the ultimate end; thus what gives the individual true perfection...through it man is man." This rational account of a person's perfection had its counterpart also in faith, for Maimonides concluded by saying that "the prophets too have explained the self-same notions—just as the philosophers have interpreted them." Faith and reason are in harmony.

The Apex of
Medieval Philosophy:
The
Scholastic System
of St. Thomas Aquinas

The great achievement of St. Thomas Aquinas (1225–1274) was that he brought together into a formidable synthesis the insights of classical philosophy and Christian theology. More specifically, Aquinas "Christianized" the philosophy of Aristotle. Although his philosophical orientation was dominated by Aristotle, he was aware of the vast scope of thought produced by the ancients, the Christian fathers, and the earlier medieval writers, including the Arabian and Jewish writers. By the time he began his literary work, a large part of Plato's and Aristotle's writings had become available in Western Europe. Augustine had formulated an earlier synthesis of philosophy and theology by combining the Christian faith with elements of Plato's thought, which he had discovered in the writings of the Neoplatonist Plotinus. Shortly after Augustine, in the sixth century, Boethius made a portion of Aristotle's works available in Latin for the first time and thereby stimulated philosophical speculation again. From about the seventh to the thirteenth century there were several lines of development, leading toward differences and controversies between Platonists and Aristotelians. This conflict continued after the thirteenth century as a controversy between Augustinians and Thomists, insofar as Augustine and Thomas built their thoughts around Plato and Aristotle, respectively. In these formative centuries, medieval thinkers wrestled with the problem of relating philosophy and theology, expressing this problem as the relation between faith and reason. There was also the problem of *universals,* which not only reflected the different viewpoints of Plato and Aristotle but also had important ramifications for the Christian faith. On all these matters, Aquinas now exerted a decisive influence by clarifying the precise questions involved, acknowledging alternative solutions offered by different authorities, and answering the major objections to his Aristotelian-Christian solutions. In this way, Aquinas perfected the "scholastic method."

The term *scholasticism* in this context is derived from the intellectual activity carried on in the medieval cathedral *schools,* and its proponents were called *doctores scholastici.* Eventually, scholasticism came to refer to the dominant system of thought developed by the doctors in the schools and to the special method they utilized in teaching philosophy. Scholastic philosophy was an attempt to put together a coherent system of *traditional* thought rather than a pursuit of genuinely novel forms of insight. The content of this system was for the most part a fusion of Christian theology and the philosophies of Plato and especially Aristotle. Most distinctive in scholasticism was its *method,* a process relying chiefly upon strict logical deduction, taking on the form of an intricate *system* and expressed in a *dialectical* or disputational form in which theology dominated philosophy. Again, Aquinas perfected what "the first scholastic," Boethius (480–524), established as the "scholarly" point of view regarding theological subjects. Boethius had urged that "as far as you are able, join faith to reason." This conjunction of faith with reason was raised to its highest form by Aquinas, who, while accepting revealed and traditional theological truths, endeavored simultaneously to provide rational argumentation in order to make these revealed truths comprehensible to the rational mind.

Thomas was born in 1225 near Naples. His father was a Count of Aquino who had hoped that his son would someday enjoy high ecclesiastical position. For this reason, Thomas was placed in the Abbey of Monte Cassino as a boy of five, and for the next nine years he pursued his studies in this Benedictine abbey. At the age of fourteen, he entered the University of Naples, but while in that city he was fascinated by the life of some Dominican friars at a nearby convent and decided to enter their order. As the Dominicans were particularly dedicated to teaching, Thomas had, upon entering their order, resolved to give himself to a religious and also a teaching vocation. Four years later, in 1245, he entered the University of Paris, where he came under the influence of a prodigious scholar whose enormous intellectual achievements had earned him the names "Albert the Great" (Albertus Magnus) and the "Universal Teacher." During his long and intimate association with Albert both at Paris and Cologne, Thomas' mind was shaped in decisive ways by the vast range of Albert's learning and by his views on particular problems.

Albert had recognized the significance of philosophy and science for grounding Christian faith and for developing the capacities of the human mind.

St. Thomas Aquinas *(The Bettmann Archive)*

While other theologians looked askance at secular learning, Albert concluded that the Christian thinker must master philosophical and scientific learning in all its forms. He had respect for all intellectual activity, and his writings attest to his acquaintance with a vast amount and variety of learning. He knew virtually all the ancient, Christian, Jewish, and Arabian writers. His mind was encyclopedic rather than creative. Still, it was Albert who had recognized the fundamental difference between philosophy and theology, sharpening more accurately than his predecessors had the boundaries between them. Albert thought that such writers as Anselm and Abelard, for example, had ascribed too much competence to reason, not realizing that from a rigorous point of view much of what they ascribed to reason was in fact a matter of faith. Albert's particular objective was to make Aristotle clearly understandable to all of Europe, hoping to put into Latin all of Aristotle's works. He considered Aristotle the greatest of all philosophers, and much of the credit for the dominance of Aristotle's thought in the thirteenth century must be given to him. It was inevitable, under these circumstances, that his pupil Thomas Aquinas would also see in Aristotle the most significant philosophical support for Christian theology.

Unlike Albert, who did not change anything in the philosophers he quoted in his works, Thomas used Aristotle more creatively, systematically, and with a more specific recognition of the harmony between what Aristotle said and the Christian faith. After an interval of teaching under the auspices of the Papal Court from 1259 to 1268, Thomas returned once again to Paris and became involved in the celebrated controversy with the Averroists. In 1274, Pope Gregory X called him to Lyons to participate in a council, and while on his way there, he died in a monastery between Naples and Rome, at the age of forty-nine.

Thomas left a huge literary legacy, the vastness of which is all the more remarkable when one recalls that it was all composed within a twenty-year span. Among his principal works are his commentaries on many of Aristotle's writings, careful arguments against the errors of the Greeks and the Averroists, a brilliant early work on essence and existence, a political treatise on rulers, and many other notable works. His most renowned literary achievements are his two major theological works, the *Summa contra Gentiles* and *Summa Theologica*.

The University of Paris   The first universities grew out of what were called "cathedral schools." The University of Paris evolved from the Cathedral School of Notre Dame, its formal rules of organization and procedures being approved officially by the Papal representative in 1215. Originally, like all early universities, Paris consisted of masters and students without any special buildings or other features we now associate with universities, such as libraries and endowments. These were added in the fourteenth and fifteenth centuries. But the most important ingredients were there, namely, masters and students with a passion for learning. Being originally church institutions, universities shared a common theological doctrine. This meant, too, that of the four faculties, theology, law, medicine, and arts, the theological faculty enjoyed undisputed supremacy.

Besides its theological orientation, the University of Paris had a receptivity to universal knowledge. This accounts for the gradual acceptance and triumph of Aristotle's philosophy at Paris. It is easily apparent, however, that the invasion of Aristotelianism would raise problems of orthodoxy. There was, however, not only the concern over the impact of Aristotle's philosophy upon Christian thought, but also serious questions over whether Aristotle had been faithfully and accurately interpreted by the Arabians. In addition, whereas Augustine and Platonism had triumphed at Oxford, this mode of thought, although not dominant at Paris, was nevertheless strongly represented there at this time by Bonaventura, a contemporary of Aquinas. Bonaventura was critical of Aristotle, holding that by denying the Platonic doctrine of Ideas, Aristotle's thought would, if incorporated into theology, produce serious errors. For example, to deny the Platonic Ideas would mean that God does not possess in Himself the Ideas of all things and would therefore be ignorant of the concrete and particular world. In turn, this would deny God's providence or His control over the universe. This would also mean that events occur either by chance or through mechanical necessity. Even more serious was Bonaventura's charge that if God does not think the Ideas of the world, He could not have created it. On this point Aquinas was later to have serious difficulties with the church authorities, for in following Aristotle, he could discover no decisive reason for denying that the world always existed instead of being created at a point in time. But, said Bonaventura, if the world always existed, there must have existed an infinite number of human beings, in which case there must be either an infinite number of souls, or, as Averroists argued, there is only one soul or intellect, which all human beings share. If this Averroist argument were accepted, it would annul the doctrine of personal immortality. This was strongly urged by the leading Averroist of the thirteenth century, Siger de Brabant, who said that there is only one eternal intellect and that while individual people are born and die, this intellect or soul remains and always finds another human being in which to carry out its functions of organizing the body and the act of knowing. In short, there is only one intellect, which all people have in common.

Against Aristotelian philosophy, which Bonaventura considered dangerous to Christian faith because of all these errors it engendered, he offered the insights of Augustine and Platonism. Still, because Aristotle's thought was so formidable and so systematic, particularly concerning matters of nature and science, its forward march was irresistible, and its triumph virtually inevitable. If most parts of the University were to be oriented to Aristotle's thought, the theologians could not avoid coming to terms with this monumental thinker. If Aristotle was to be accepted, the specific task of the theologians would now be to harmonize his philosophy with Christianity, that is, they would have to "Christianize" Aristotle. This is what Aquinas set out to do, contending at the same time against Bonaventura's Augustinianism and Siger de Brabant's version of Aristotle.

PHILOSOPHY AND THEOLOGY

Aquinas thought and wrote as a Christian. He was primarily a theologian. At the same time, he relied heavily upon the philosophy of Aristotle in writing his theological works. That he brought together philosophy and theology did not mean that he confused these two disciplines. On the contrary, it was his view that philosophy and theology played complementary roles in humanity's quest for truth. Like his teacher Albert the Great, Aquinas went to great pains to delineate the boundaries between faith and reason, indicating what philosophy and theology respectively could and could not provide to the human mind. That he wished to combine the insights of these two disciplines reflected the dominant religious orientation of thirteenth-century thought, in that knowledge of God was considered of decisive importance. What made the correct knowledge of God so essential was that any basic errors on this subject could affect the direction of a person's life, directing one either toward or away from God, who is humanity's ultimate end. Philosophy and theology were therefore viewed in relation to humanity's end, being distinguished by their different ways of contributing to humanity's knowledge of God. Philosophy proceeds from principles discovered by human reason, whereas theology is the rational ordering of principles received from authoritative revelation and held as a matter of faith. Aquinas' philosophy, then, consists for the most part in that portion of his theology that we should call *natural theology* and that Aquinas considered rationally demonstrable.

Faith and Reason

Aquinas saw specific differences between philosophy and theology, between reason and faith. For one thing, philosophy begins with the immediate objects of sense experience and reasons upward to more general conceptions until, as in Aristotle's case, the mind fastens upon the highest principles or first causes of being, ending in the conception of God. Theology, on the other hand, begins with a faith in God and interprets all things as creatures of God. There is here a basic difference in method, since the philosopher draws his conclusions from his rational description of the essences of things, whereas the theologian rests the demonstration of his conclusions upon the authority of revealed knowledge. Again, theology and philosophy do not contradict each other, but not everything that philosophy discusses is significant for a person's religious end. Theology deals with what people need to know for their salvation, and to ensure this knowledge, it was made available through revelation. Some of the truths of revelation could never be discovered by natural reason, whereas other elements of revealed truth could be known by reason alone but were revealed to ensure their being known. For this reason, there is some overlapping between philosophy and theology. For the most part, however, philosophy and theology are two separate and independent disciplines. Wherever reason is capable of knowing something, faith, strictly speaking, is unnecessary, and what faith uniquely knows through revelation cannot be known by natural reason alone. Both philosophy and theology deal with God, but the philosopher can only infer that God exists and cannot by reflecting upon the objects of sensation understand God's essential nature. There is, nevertheless, a coalescence of the object of philosophy and theology since they are both concerned with truth. Aristotle had considered the object of philosophy the study of first principles and causes, the study of being and its causes, and this led to a First Mover, which he understood as the ground of truth in the universe. This is the philosophical way of saying what the theologian has set as his object of knowledge, namely, God's being and the truth this reveals about the created world. To discover the chief aspects of Aquinas' philosophy, then, it is necessary to take from his theological writings those portions of it in which he attempts to demonstrate truths in a purely rational way. His philosophical approach is particularly evident in his attempts to demonstrate the existence of God.

PROOFS OF GOD'S EXISTENCE

Aquinas formulated five *proofs* or ways of demonstrating the existence of God. His approach was the opposite of Anselm's. Anselm began his proof with the *idea* of a perfect being "than which no greater can be conceived," from which he inferred the existence of that being inasmuch as the actual existence is greater than the mere idea of a perfect being. By contrast, Aquinas said that all knowledge must begin with our experience of sense objects. Instead of beginning with innate ideas of perfection, Aquinas rested all five of his proofs upon the ideas derived from a rational understanding of the ordinary objects that we experience with our senses. The chief characteristic of all sense objects is that their existence requires a *cause*. That every event or every object requires a cause is something the human intellect knows as a principle whenever, but not until, it comes in contact with experience. By the light of natural reason, the intellect knows, by experiencing events, that for every effect there must be a cause, that *ex nihilo nihil fit,* nothing comes from nothing. To demonstrate that God exists, Aquinas relied, then, first upon his analysis of sense objects and secondly upon his notion that the existence of these objects requires a finite series of causes and ultimately a First Cause, or God.

Proof from Motion   We are certain, because it is evident to our senses, that in the world some things are in motion. It is equally clear to us that whatever is in motion was moved by something else. If a thing is at rest, it will never move until something else moves it. When a thing is at rest, it is only potentially in motion. Motion occurs when something potentially in motion is moved and is then actually in motion; motion is the transformation of *potentiality* into *actuality.* Imagine a series of dominoes standing next to each other. When they are set up in a row, it can be said that they are all potentially in motion, though actually at rest. Consider a particular domino. Its potentiality is that it will not move until it is knocked over by the one next to it. It will move only if it is moved by something actually moving. From this fact, Aquinas drew the general conclusion that nothing can be transformed from a state of potentiality by something that is also in a mere state of potentiality. A domino cannot be knocked over by another domino that is standing still. Potentiality means the absence of something and is therefore *nothing;* for this reason, potential motion in the neighboring domino cannot move the next one because it is *nothing,* and you cannot derive motion from nonmotion. As Aquinas says, "nothing can be reduced from potentiality to actuality except by something in a state of actuality." Moreover, it is not possible for the same thing, for example a domino, to be *at the same time* in actuality and potentiality regarding motion. What is actually at rest cannot be simultaneously in motion. This means that the particular domino cannot be simultaneously the thing that is moved and also the mover. Something potentially in motion cannot move itself. Whatever is moved must be moved by another. The last domino to fall was potentially in motion, but so was the next to the last. Each domino could become a *mover* only after it had been moved by the one prior to it. Here we come to Aquinas' decisive point: If we are to account for motion, we cannot do so by going back in an infinite regress. If we must say about each mover in this series that it in turn was moved by a prior mover, we would never discover the source of motion, because every mover would then be only potentially in motion. Even if such a series went back infinitely, each one would still be only potential, and from that no actual motion could ever emerge. The fact is, however, that there *is* motion. There must therefore be a Mover, which is able to move things but which does not itself have to be moved, and this, says Aquinas, "everyone understands to be God."

Two things need to be noticed about this proof. First, Aquinas does not limit his concept of motion to things such as dominoes, that is, to locomotion. He has in mind the broadest meaning of motion so as to include the idea of *generation* and creation. Secondly, for Aquinas the First Mover is not simply the first member of a long series of causes, as though such a Mover was just like the others, its only distinction being that it is the first. Clearly, this could not be the case, for then this Mover would also be only potentially in motion. The First Mover must therefore be pure Actuality without potentiality and is therefore First not in the series but in actuality.

Proof from Efficient Cause   We experience various kinds of effects, and in every case we assign an efficient cause to each effect. The efficient cause of the statue is the work of the sculptor. If we took away the activity of the sculptor, we should not have the effect, the statue. But there is an order of efficient causes; the parents of the sculptor are his or her efficient cause. Workers in the quarry are the efficient cause of this particular piece of marble's availability to the sculptor. There is, in short, an intricate order of efficient causes traceable in a series. Such a series of causes is demanded because no event can be its own cause; sculptors do not cause themselves, and statues do not cause themselves. A cause is prior to an effect. Nothing, then, can be prior to itself; hence, events demand a prior cause. Each prior cause must itself have its own cause, as parents must have their own parents. But it is impossible to go backward to infinity, because all the causes in the series depend upon a first efficient cause that has made all the other causes to be actual causes. There must then be a first efficient cause "to which everyone gives the name of God."

Proof from Necessary versus Possible Being   In nature we find that things are possible to be and not to be. Such things are *possible* or *contingent* because they do not always exist; they are *generated* and are *corrupted.* There was a time when a tree did not exist; it exists, and finally it goes out of existence. To say, then, that it is *possible* for the tree to exist must mean that it is also possible for it *not* to exist. The possibility for the tree *not* to exist must be taken two ways: First, it is possible for the tree *never* to come into existence, and secondly, once the tree is in existence, there is the possibility that it will go out of existence. To say, then, that something is *possible* must mean that at both ends of its being, that is, before it comes into being and after it goes out of being, it does not exist. *Possible* being has this fundamental characteristic, namely, that it can *not-be*. It can *not-be* not only after having existed but more importantly *before* it is generated, caused, or moved. For this reason something that is possible, which can not-be, in fact "at some time is not."

All *possible* beings, therefore, at one time did not exist, will exist for a time, and will finally pass out of existence. Once possible things *do* come into existence, they can cause other similar possible beings to be generated, as when parents beget children, and so on. But Aquinas is making this argument, namely, that possible beings do not have their existence in themselves or from their own essence; and that if *all* things in reality were only *possible,* that is, if about *everything* one could say that it could not-be *both* before it is and after it is, then at one time there was nothing in existence. But if there was a time when nothing existed then nothing could start to be, and even now there would be nothing in existence, "because that which does not exist begins to exist only through something already existing." But since our experience clearly shows us that things do exist, this must mean that not all beings are *merely possible.* Aquinas concludes from this that "there must exist something the existence of which is necessary." We must therefore admit, he says, "the existence of some being having of itself its own necessity, and not receiving it from another, but rather causing in others this necessity. This all men speak of as God."

Proof from the Degrees of Perfection   In our experience we find that some beings are more and some less good, true, and noble. But these and other ways of comparing things are possible only because things resemble in their different ways something that is the maximum. There must be something that is truest, noblest, and best. Similarly, since it can be said about things that they have more or less being, or a lower or higher form of being, as when we compare a stone with a rational creature, there must also be "something which is most being." Aquinas then argues that the maximum in any genus is the cause of everything in that genus, as fire, which is the maximum of heat, is the cause of all hot things. From this, Aquinas concludes that "there must also be something which is to all beings the cause of their being, goodness, and every other perfection; and this we call God."

Proof from the Order of the Universe   We see that things such as parts of the natural world or parts of the human body, which do not possess intelligence, behave in an orderly manner. They act in special and predictable ways to achieve certain ends or functions. Because these things act to achieve ends always, or nearly always, in the same way and to achieve the best results, "it is plain that they achieve their end, not fortuitously, but designedly." But things that lack intelligence, such as an ear or a lung, cannot carry out a function unless it be directed by something that does have intelligence, as the arrow is directed by the archer. Aquinas concludes, therefore, that "some intelligent being exists by whom all natural things are directed to their ends; and this being we call God."

Summary   The two major characteristics of these five proofs are (1) their foundation in sense experience and (2) their reliance upon the notion of causality. In addition, the first three proofs do not as obviously lead to the idea of what all men call God, a personal being. These are, however, proofs that Aquinas considered philosophical corroborations of the religious notion of God, and they, it must be remembered, were composed in the context of his theological task. Moreover, many of Aquinas' illustrations, as, for example, that fire is the maximum of heat, and his assumptions, that order, for example, presupposes an intelligence independent of the natural process, raise for the modern mind critical questions. Still, Aquinas was deliberately employing the insights he had derived from Aristotle, Maimonides, and Albert the Great in order, by means of these philosophical arguments, to make the religious claim of God's existence intellectually defensible. His own view was that the argument from motion was the most obvious of all. The third one, comparing possible and necessary being, appears, however, to contain the most philosophical rigor and the basic assumption of all the other proofs, namely, that possible beings must derive their existence from something that has its existence necessarily in itself.

KNOWLEDGE OF GOD'S NATURE

To prove *that* God is does not tell us positively *what* God is. There is a vast gulf between the powers of human knowledge and the infinitude of God's nature. Aquinas was always aware of this virtually unbridgeable gulf, saying that "the divine reality surpasses all human conceptions of it." But each of the five proofs adds something to the conception of God. As First Mover, God is seen as unchangeable and therefore eternal. As First Cause, God is seen as all powerful to create. To say that God is a necessary rather than a possible being is to say that God is pure actuality. As the ultimate truth and goodness, God is perfection itself. And as the orderer or designer of the universe, God is the supreme intelligence directing things.

The Negative Way (*Via Negativa*)   The knowledge about God derived from the five proofs does not clarify positively what the essence of God is. We know what we do about God only in a negative way by knowing what God is not. The proof shows only that God is *un*moved, and that therefore he must be *un*changeable. This must mean that God is *not* in time, and is therefore eternal. Similarly, to account for motion, it is necessary that there be something that does *not* have potentiality—it is matter in particular that has potentiality—therefore, in God there is nothing material. God is pure act and *im*material. Since there is neither matter nor potentiality in God, He is then *simple, without* any composition. This idea of God's *simplicity* is achieved not by our direct apprehension of it but via the negative way, whereby we *remove* from our conception of God such notions as compositeness and corporeality. Philosophically, God's simplicity means that unlike creatures that possess both potentiality and actuality, God is simply pure act. Whereas a creature *has* its being, God *is* His being. Whereas in creatures existence is one thing and essence another, God's essence is His existence. But even these positive-sounding attributes of God are in the end ways of saying what God is not, saying that God is other than creatures.

Knowledge by Analogy   All human language is inevitably derived from our experience with things in our sensed world. For this reason, as Aquinas realized, the names men apply to God are the same ones they use when describing human beings and things. These names, such as *wise* or *loving,* certainly cannot mean the same thing when applied to finite people on the one hand and to the infinite God on the other. If, then, these names and words mean different things to us when we use them respectively to describe creatures and God, the critical question is whether we can know anything at all about God from our knowledge about creatures.

Aquinas distinguishes among three ways in which God might be related to human beings. The first type of relation would be *univocal,* in which case words, such as *wise,* used about God and humanity would mean exactly the same thing and would imply that God and humanity are alike in nature. This clearly cannot be the case since God and humanity are not alike. God is infinite, and humanity is finite. A second type of relation might be what Aquinas calls *equivocal,* where terms applied to both would mean totally different things for each, implying that God and humanity are totally unlike. In this case our knowledge of humanity would give us no knowledge whatsoever about God. Aquinas insists, however, that insofar as humanity is a creature of God, humans must in some degree, even though imperfectly, reflect the nature of God. The third and final possibility is that humanity and God are neither totally alike nor totally unlike, that their relationship is *analogical.* When a word such as *wise* is used to describe both God and humanity, it does not mean that God and humanity are wise in exactly the same sense, nor does it mean that they are wise in completely different ways.

Analogy for Aquinas is an ontological term; it means that what is in God is also in humanity. This is more than mere metaphor or simile. To say that there is an analogical relationship between God and humanity is to say that man resembles God. *Resembles* here means that humanity has in some degree or certain proportion what God uniquely is. For example, Aquinas says that humanity *has* a certain mode or degree of being. God, on the other hand, *is* Being. What makes the relationship between God and humanity analogical is, therefore, the fact that God and humanity are linked together by common attributes. Humanity derives its very existence from God, and this fact accounts for the common elements in both God and humanity. When we use a word such as *wise,* we refer to (but do not fully comprehend) an attribute perfectly realized in God and only partially realized in humanity. Wisdom is something that exists both in God and humanity, and the relationship between the two wisdoms is analogical, which is midway between univocal and equivocal. What makes wisdom different in people is that their mind is located in their physical body and is dependent upon the senses. When people think and speak, they do so discursively, saying and thinking a word or an idea at a time. God, being pure act with no material substance, knows all things simultaneously. Analogy would mean, then, that humanity knows what God knows but not everything that God knows and not the way God knows it. Again, what makes this analogical relation possible is that God's creatures bear a likeness to God. Analogy means, then, that humanity is simultaneously like and unlike God. To know what humanity is like is to have *some* degree of knowledge about God. For this reason, names and terms that people formulate first of all about human beings have some meaning when applied to God, provided that the meanings in each case are adjusted to reflect the different degrees and modes of being of God and humanity.

CREATION

Throughout his discussion of the proofs of God's existence and of God's nature, Aquinas assumes the doctrine of creation. The objects of our sense experience, according to the proofs, cannot derive their existence from themselves but must have it from the First Mover, First Cause, Necessary Being, Perfect Being, and Orderer of the Universe. There are, however, certain specific problems concerning the doctrine of creation that Aquinas considers from a philosophical point of view.

Is the Created Order Eternal?   According to biblical revelation, creation occurred at a point in time. How could this doctrine of faith be supported by philosophical reasoning? Aquinas did not think that it is possible to decide in a philosophical manner whether the world has existed from eternity or whether it was created in time. That it was created must follow from the revealed nature of God. Being pure act and free, God willed to create. Creation, as a free act, is distinguished by Aquinas from a *necessary* emanation, as taught by Plotinus. But since God is pure act, He could have acted to create the world from eternity. In short, there is no contradiction in saying that God created and that He created eternally. There might be a more serious question of contradiction if one argued that God created in time, since this could imply potentiality in God in that before He created things He was potentially a creator. That Aquinas was somewhat inconclusive on this point raised questions about his orthodoxy. But he maintained that Aristotle, who had argued that God had created from eternity, could not be refuted, in spite of Bonaventura's attempts to do so. In the end, Aquinas settled the question by accepting the authority of revelation, concluding that philosophically either solution is possible.

Ex Nihilo What does it mean to say that God creates out of nothing, *ex nihilo?* Again, Aquinas thought that if God is the source of all being, there cannot be any other source of being. There is, in short, no useful comparison between God and an artist at this point. An artist rearranges already existing materials, as when a sculptor fashions a statue. Prior to creation there is only God: God does not act upon any existing material since no such primary matter exists. Only God exists originally, and whatever comes to be derives its existence from God. Everything, then, is related to God, is a creature of God, because it came ultimately from God, there being no independent source of being other than God.

Is This the Best Possible World? Aquinas argued that to answer such a question requires that one bear in mind two things. First, unlike God, who is infinite, a person is finite, and a person's perfection will therefore be less than God's. Secondly, the universe cannot be any better than or any different from what creatures are capable of by their nature. Throughout this discussion, Aquinas stresses that certain limitations must pervade the universe only because to create certain kinds of beings sets limits on others. The world is the best only in the sense that it contains the best arrangement possible of the kinds of things that have been created.

Evil as Privation The problem of evil is aggravated by the argument that everything that exists comes from God. Since there is evil in the world, it would appear that evil, too, comes from God. But Aquinas accepted Augustine's solution of the problem of evil, saying that evil is not anything positive. God is not the cause of evil because evil is not a thing. Moral evil represents the absence or privation in something that in itself is good. In this sense, absence or privation consists of an inappropriate mode of action where the action as such is not evil. The act of the adulterer, says Aquinas, is evil not in its physical aspects but in that which makes it adultery, namely, the absence of propriety. Similarly, in the natural order evil is not a positive thing but a privation, as in the case of blindness, which consists of the absence of sight. Still, in the moral realm, there appear to be those who choose to indulge in ways that are obviously wicked. Like Plato, Aquinas argues that people always will their acts, however diabolical they may seem, under the assumption, and with the hope, that some good will come out of them. The adulterer never wills his or her act solely as an evil but rather for that aspect of the act that is good and affords pleasure. The question remains, however, why God should permit defects both in physical nature and in people's moral behavior. Aquinas replies that the perfection of the universe required the existence of various kinds of beings, including corruptible as well as incorruptible beings, thus providing the possibility, but not the necessity, for defect and suffering. But having created corruptible things, there will be corruption, that is, alteration in things.

In the moral order, the primary fact is that people possess freedom. Without freedom people could not love God; with freedom they possess the capacity to choose for or against God, right, just, and good. Evil is the possibility for wrong choice that accompanies a person's freedom. Its actual occurrence was not willed by God even though God willed that people should have freedom. The possibility of evil is the unavoidable corollary of the greater good that comes from people's freedom to love and serve God. Aquinas therefore concludes that God is not the cause of evil even though by creating human beings with freedom He permitted the possibility of it. Moral evil, under these circumstances, is the product of the will whereby the essentially good element in the willed act lacks its true end.

The Range of Created Being: the Chain of Being Aquinas describes the universe as consisting of a full range, or hierarchy, of different things, as if there existed a great *chain of being*. These beings differ in species and in the degree of their being. That such a full range of beings exists is required so that God's perfection can be most adequately represented in the total created order. Because no single creature could ever reflect God's perfection suitably, God created many levels of being, which overlap in such a way that there are no gaps in the structure of being. Thus, below God is the hierarchy of angels. Aquinas calls these *intelligences* and says that they are immaterial. These can be known to exist both by revelation (the Bible speaks of them in various terms, such as *principles, powers, seraphim,* etc.) and reason. Reason requires their existence in order to account for the full continuity of beings from the lowest to the highest without any unaccounted-for spaces. Below these angels are human beings, whose nature includes both material and spiritual aspects. Then come animals, plants, and finally the four elements of air, earth, fire, and water.

Aquinas points out that there are no gaps between the various levels of beings: they interlock like links in a chain. For example, the lowest species of animals overlap with the highest forms of plants, the highest forms of animals correspond to the lowest form of human nature, and the highest element in man (intelligence) corresponds to what uniquely constitutes angels. What distinguishes the beings on all these levels is their particular composite nature, or the way their form and matter are related. In a person, the soul is the form, and the body is the material substance. Angels have no material substance, and because they do not possess the kind of matter that designates the particular qualities of a specific individual, each angel is its own species. Each angel, then, occupies a separate grade in the hierarchy of being, differing from other angels in the degree or amount of its being. The highest angel is nearest God and the lowest nearest humanity, and below humanity are the animals, plants, and single elements, all representing the full range of created beings.

MORALITY AND NATURAL LAW

Aquinas built upon Aristotle's theory of ethics. Like Aristotle, he considered ethics or morality a quest for happiness. Moreover, following Aristotle's lead, Aquinas argued that happiness is connected closely with a person's end or purpose. To achieve happiness one must fulfill one's purpose. But whereas Aristotle envisioned a *naturalistic* morality whereby people could achieve virtue and happiness by fulfilling their natural capacities or end, Aquinas added to this his concept of a person's *supernatural* end. As a Christian, Aquinas viewed human nature as having both its source and ultimate end in God. For this reason, human nature does not contain its own standards of fulfillment. It is not enough for a person to simply be human and to exercise his or her natural functions and abilities in order to achieve perfect happiness. Aristotle thought such a naturalistic ethics was possible. Aquinas agreed with most of this claim, adding only that the Aristotelian ethics is incomplete. Aquinas therefore argued that there is a double level to morality corresponding to a person's natural end and to his or her supernatural end.

The ingredients of humanity's moral experience are provided by humanity's nature. For one thing, the fact that a person has a body inclines one to certain kinds of acts. One's senses become the vehicle for appetites and passions. One's senses also provide a certain level of knowledge about sensible objects so that one is attracted to some objects, which one perceives as pleasurable and good (concupiscent appetite), and repels some objects, which one perceives as harmful, painful, or bad (irascible appetite). This attraction and rejection are the rudiments of humanity's capacity for love and pleasure, and hate and fear.

In animals these irascible and concupiscent appetites immediately control and direct behavior. In a person, however, the will, in collaboration with the power of reason, consummates the human act. The will is the agency that inclines a person toward the achievement of good. That is, humanity's full range of appetites seeks to be satisfied, and the process of satisfaction requires that choices be made between alternative objects. This choice must be made by the will under the direction of reason. If the right choices are made, a person achieves happiness. But not every choice is a correct one. For this reason, the will by itself cannot always make the right move; the intellect must be the guide. Nor is the intellect the final source of knowledge, for a person's supernatural end requires God's grace and revealed truth. Still, the will represents a person's appetite for the good and right, whereas the intellect has the function and capacity for apprehending the general or universal meaning of what is good. The intellect is a person's highest faculty, and a natural end requires that the intellect, as well as all the other faculties, seek its appropriate object. The appropriate object of the intellect is truth, and truth in its fullness is God. When the intellect directs the will, then, it helps the will choose the good. The intellect knows, however, that there is a hierarchy of goods, that some goods are limited and must not be mistaken for a person's most appropriate and ultimate good. Riches, pleasure, power, and knowledge are all goods and are legitimate objects of the appetites, but they cannot produce a person's deepest happiness because they do not possess the character of the universal good that a person's soul seeks. The perfect happiness is found not in created things but in God, who is the supreme good.

Moral constitution consists, then, of sensuality, appetites, the will, and reason. What confers upon a person the attributes of morality is that these elements are the ingredients of *free* acts. If a person were moved to act by his or her appetites in a mechanical or rigorously determined way, his or her acts would not be free and could not be considered from a moral point of view. Not only is freedom a prerequisite for an act to be considered *moral;* Aquinas adds that an act is *human* only if it is free. For freedom is possible only where there is knowledge of alternatives and the power of will to make choices. Virtue, or goodness, consists in making the right choices, the mean between extremes. Aquinas agreed with Aristotle that the virtues of the natural person are achieved when the appetites are duly controlled by the will and reason. The dominant or cardinal natural virtues are courage, temperance, justice, and prudence. In addition to these particular virtues, the natural end of a person is further realized through humanity's knowledge of the natural law or the moral law.

Natural Law   Morality, as Aquinas viewed it, is not an arbitrary set of rules for behavior. The basis of moral obligation, he thought, is found, first of all, in the very nature of humanity. Built into humanity's nature are various inclinations, such as the preservation of life, the propagation of species, and, because people are rational, the inclination toward the search for truth. The basic moral truth is simply to "do good and avoid evil." As a rational being, then, a person is under a basic natural obligation to protect his or her life and health, in which case suicide and carelessness are wrong. Secondly, the natural inclination to propagate the species forms the basis of the union of man and wife, and any other basis for this relation would be wrong. And thirdly, because humanity seeks for truth, people can do this best by living in peace in society with all others who are also engaged in this quest. To ensure an ordered society, human laws are fashioned for the direction of the community's behavior. All these activities of preserving life, propagating the species, forming an ordered society under human laws, and pursuing the quest for truth—all these, again, pertain to people at their natural level. The moral law is founded upon human nature, upon the natural inclinations toward specific modes of behavior, and upon the reason's ability to discern the right course of conduct. Because human nature has certain fixed features, the rules for behavior that correspond to these features are called *natural law.*

Much of this theory of natural law was already developed by Aristotle. In his *Ethics,* Aristotle distinguished between natural justice and conventional justice. Some forms of behavior, he said, are wrong only because, and only after, a law has been made to regulate such behavior. To use a modern example, it is wrong to drive a vehicle at certain speeds only because a speed limit has been set, but there is nothing in nature that requires that vehicles travel at that speed. Such a law is therefore not natural but conventional, because before the law was passed, there was nothing wrong with traveling at speeds exceeding the new limit. On the other hand, there are some laws the precepts of which are derived from nature, so that the behavior they regulate has always been wrong, as in the case of murder. But Aquinas did not limit his treatment of natural law to the simple notion that in some way humanity's reason is able to discover the natural basis for human conduct. Instead, he reasoned that if humanity's existence and nature can be fully understood only when seen in relation to God, then natural law must be described in metaphysical and theological terms, as the Stoics and St. Augustine had done.

Law, says Aquinas, has to do primarily with reason. The rule and measure of acts is the reason, because it belongs to reason to direct a person's whole activity toward his or her end. Law consists of these rules and measures of human acts and therefore is based upon reason. The natural law is dictated by the reason. But Aquinas argues that since God created all things, human nature and the natural law are best understood as the product of God's wisdom or reason. From this standpoint, Aquinas distinguishes *four* kinds of law.

Eternal Law   This law refers to the fact that "the whole community of the universe is governed by Divine Reason. Wherefore the very Idea of the government of things in God the Ruler of the universe, has the nature of a law. And since the Divine Reason's conception of things is not subject to time but is eternal...therefore it is that this kind of law must be called eternal."

Natural Law   For Aquinas, natural law consists of that portion of the eternal law that pertains particularly to people. His reasoning is that "all things partake somewhat of the eternal law...from its being imprinted on them" and from this all things "derive their respective inclinations to their proper acts and ends." This is particularly true of people, because their rational capacity "has a share of the Eternal Reason, whereby it has a natural inclination to its proper act and end." And, says Aquinas, "this participation of the eternal law in the rational creature is called the natural law," and, again, "the natural law is nothing else than the rational creature's participation of the eternal law." We have already indicated the basic precepts of the natural law as being the preservation of life, propagation and education of offspring, and pursuit of truth and a peaceful society. Thus the natural law consists of broad general principles that reflect God's intentions for man in creation.

Human Law   This refers to the specific statutes of governments. These statutes or human laws are derived from the general precepts of natural law. Just as "we draw conclusions of the various sciences" from "naturally known indemonstrable principles," so also "from the precepts of the natural law... the human reason needs to proceed to the more particular determination of certain matters." And "these particular determinations, devised by human reason, are called human laws...." What was so far-reaching about this conception of human law was that it repudiated the notion that a law was a law only because it was decreed by a sovereign. Aquinas argued that what gives a rule the character of law is its moral dimension, its conformity with the precepts of natural law, its agreement with the moral law. Taking St. Augustine's formula, namely, that "that which is not just seems to be no law at all," Aquinas said that "every human law has just so much of the nature of law, as it is derived from the law of nature." But, he adds, "if in any point it deflects from the law of nature, it is no longer a law but a perversion of law." Such laws no longer bind in conscience but are sometimes obeyed to prevent an even greater evil. Aquinas went further than simply denying the character of law to a command of a government that violated the natural moral law; such a command, he said, should not be obeyed. Some laws, he said, "may be unjust through being opposed to the Divine Good: such are the laws of tyrants inducing to idolatry, or to anything else contrary to the Divine Law.... " He concluded that "laws of this kind must nowise be observed, because...*we ought to obey God rather than men."*

Divine Law The function of law, said Aquinas, is to direct people to their proper end. Since people are ordained to an end of eternal happiness, in addition to their temporal happiness, there must be a kind of law that can direct them to that supernatural end. Here, in particular, Aquinas parted company with Aristotle, for Aristotle knew only about humanity's natural purpose and end, and for this purpose the natural law known by human reason was considered a sufficient guide. But the eternal happiness to which people are ordained, said Aquinas, is "in proportion to man's natural faculty." Therefore, "it was necessary that besides the natural and the human law, man should be directed to his end by a law given by God." The *divine law,* then, is available to a person through revelation and is found in the Scriptures. It is not the product of humanity's reason but is given to humanity through God's grace to ensure that all people know what they must do to fulfill both their natural and, especially, their supernatural ends. The difference between the natural law and divine law is this: The natural law represents humanity's rational knowledge of the good, by which the intellect directs the will to control humanity's appetites and passions, leading people to fulfill their natural end by achieving the cardinal virtues of justice, temperance, courage, and prudence. The divine law, on the other hand, comes directly from God through revelation, a gift of God's grace, whereby people are directed to their supernatural ends, having obtained the higher or theological virtues of faith, hope, and love, not through any of humanity's natural powers, for these virtues are "infused" into humanity by God's grace. In this way, Aquinas completed and surpassed the naturalistic ethics of Aristotle, showed how the natural desire of humanity to know God can be assured, indicated how revelation becomes the guide for reason, and described the manner in which humanity's highest nature is perfected through God's grace.

THE STATE

The state, said Aquinas, is a natural institution. It is derived from the nature of humanity. In this view, Aquinas was following the political theory of Aristotle, from whom he had taken the phrase that "man is by nature a social animal." But insofar as Aquinas had a different view of human nature, he was bound to have a somewhat different political philosophy also. The difference lay in the two conceptions of the role or task of the state. Aristotle supposed that the state could provide for all the needs of humanity because he knew only about humanity's natural needs. Aquinas, on the other hand, believed that in addition to its material or natural needs, humanity also has a supernatural end.

The state is not equipped to deal with this more ultimate end of humanity. It is the church that directs humanity to this end. But Aquinas did not simply divide these two realms of human concern, giving one to the state and the other to the church. Instead, he looked upon the state, and explained its origin, in terms of God's creation.

The state, in this view, is willed by God and has its God-given function. It was required because of the social nature of humanity. The state is not, for Aquinas, as it was for Augustine, a product of people's sinfulness. On the contrary, Aquinas says that even "in the state of innocence man would have lived in society." But even then, "a common life could not exist, unless there were someone in control, to attend to the common good." The state's function is to secure the common good by keeping the peace, organizing the activities of the citizens into harmonious pursuits, providing for the resources to sustain life, and preventing, as far as possible, obstacles to the good life. This last item concerning threats to the good life gives to the state not only a function tied to humanity's ultimate end; it also accounts for the state's position in relation to the church.

The state is subordinate to the church. To say this did not mean that Aquinas considered the church a superstate. Aquinas saw no contradiction in saying that the state has a sphere in which it has a legitimate function and that at the same time it must subordinate itself to the church. Within its own sphere the state is autonomous. But, insofar as there are aspects of human life that bear upon humanity's supernatural end, the state must not put arbitrary hindrances in the way to frustrate humanity's spiritual life. The church does not challenge the autonomy of the state; it only says that the state is not absolutely autonomous. Within its own sphere, the state is what Aquinas calls a "perfect society," having its own end and the means for achieving it. But the state is like a person; neither the state nor a person has only a natural end. Humanity's spiritual end cannot be achieved, as Aquinas says, "by human power, but by divine power." Still, because a person's destiny does include attaining to the enjoyment of God, the state must recognize this aspect of human affairs: in providing for the common good of the citizens, the sovereign must pursue the community's end with a consciousness of humanity's spiritual end. Under these circumstances, the state does not become the church, but it does mean that the sovereign "should order those things which lead to heavenly beatitude and prohibit, as far as possible, their contraries." In this way, Aquinas affirmed the legitimacy of the state and its autonomy in its own sphere, subordinating it to the church only to ensure that the ultimate spiritual end of a person be taken into account.

As the state rules the behavior of its citizens through the agency of law, the state is in turn limited by the requirements of just laws. Nowhere is Aquinas' rejection of the absolute autonomy of the state so clearly stated as when he describes the standards for the making of human or positive law. We have already analyzed the different types of law: eternal, natural, human and divine. The state is particularly the source of human law. Each government is faced with the task of fashioning specific statutes to regulate the behavior of its citizens under the particular circumstances of its own time and place. Lawmaking, however, must not be an arbitrary act but must be done under the influence of the natural law, which is humanity's participation in God's eternal law. Positive laws must consist of particular rules derived from the general principles of natural law. Any positive human law that violates the natural law loses its character as law, is a "perversion of law," and loses its binding force in the consciences of humanity. The lawmaker has authority to legislate from God, the source of all authority, and is responsible to God. If the sovereign decrees an unjust law by violating God's divine law, such a law, says Aquinas, "must nowise be observed."

The political sovereign has this authority from God, and the purpose of this authority is to provide for the common good. Authority is never to be used as an end in itself or for selfish ends. Nor must the common good be interpreted in such a way that the individual is lost sight of in the collective whole. The common good must be the good of concrete persons. Thus Aquinas says that "the proper effect of law is to lead its subjects to their proper virtue...to make those to whom it is given good...." The only "true ground" of the lawgiver is his intention to secure "the common good regulated according to divine justice," and thus it follows that "the effect of the law is to make men good...." This is to say that the phrase *common good* has no meaning for Aquinas except insofar as it results in the good of individuals. At the same time, Aquinas says that "the goodness of any part is considered in comparison with the whole. . . . Since then every man is a part of the state, it is impossible that a man be good unless he be well proportionate to the common good." The entire scheme of society and its laws is characterized by the rational elements in it. Law itself, says Aquinas, is "an ordinance of reason for the common good, made by him who has care of the community, and promulgated." Thus, although the sovereign has authority and power, the laws must not reflect this power in a naked sense but as domesticated by reason and aimed at the common good.

HUMANITY AND KNOWLEDGE

Humanity Aquinas had a distinctive conception of humanity. Humanity, he said, is a physical substance. What made this a unique conception was that Aquinas insisted upon the *unity* of human nature. Plato had talked about the soul as being imprisoned in the body. Similarly, Augustine considered the soul as a spiritual substance. Both Plato and Aristotle agreed that the soul is the form of the body but did not see, as Aquinas thought he did, that the soul of a person is as dependent upon the body as the body is upon the soul. To say, as Aquinas did, that a person is a physical substance underscored the substantial unity of humanity. Humanity *is* a unity of body and soul. Without the soul, the body would have no form. Without the body, the soul would not have its required organs of sense through which to gain its knowledge. As a physical substance, a person is a composite of soul and body. The angels are pure intelligence and have no body, but although people, too, are rational creatures, their special attribute is to exist and function as persons only when unified as body and soul. Since the soul confers upon a person bodily form, it is the soul that gives a person life, understanding, and special physical functions. The soul accounts also for humanity's capacity for sensation and the powers of intellect and will. Humanity's highest capacity is located in the intellect, making people rational animals and conferring upon them the means by which to attain the contemplation of God.

Knowledge   Aquinas followed Aristotle's theory of knowledge. He was especially impressed with Aristotle's answer to those who doubted that the human mind could arrive at certainty on any subject. Some ancient philosophers had argued that since humanity's knowledge is limited to sense perception, there could be no certainty because each person senses things differently and the objects of sense are always in flux. Plato agreed with this estimate of sense knowledge, saying that it could give us no certainty. But he avoided intellectual pessimism by assuming the existence of a separate world, the intelligible world, contrasting it with the visible world, saying that in it there existed Ideas or Forms, which possess eternal being and provide the basis for knowledge. St. Augustine adapted this Platonic theory of Ideas to Christian thought by saying that God possesses these Ideas in His mind and that human beings are able to know the truth insofar as these Ideas illumine their minds through the divine light. But Aquinas accepted Aristotle's approach, saying that the human mind knows what it does through its confrontation with actual concrete objects. The mind is able to grasp what is permanent and stable within sensible things. When we sense things or persons, we *know* their essence, for example, *tree* and *man,* even though they are in the process of change. What we know about them, given the fact that they are in flux, is that they are either more or less a tree or a man, but we are not in doubt about what they are. In short, the intellect *sees* the universal *in* the particular thing; it *abstracts* the universal from the particular. The mind does not possess any innate ideas, but is rather in potentiality to knowledge. Unlike angelic intelligences, the human mind, set in the composite of soul and body, has as its natural object of knowledge the essential properties of physical things. A person's active intellect is able, says Aquinas, to recognize the intelligible aspect of sense objects, discovering in individual things the universal essence. Aquinas denied that the universal, for example *humanity,* has any existence separate from particular concrete humans. There is only the abstracted concept, not an existing Idea, which the actual intellect formulates and which makes knowledge possible. It was Aquinas' view that there could be no knowledge without sense experience, for nothing could be in the intellect that was not first in the senses (*nihil in intellectu quod prius non fuerit in sensu*).

SOME REACTIONS TO AQUINAS: VOLUNTARISM, NOMINALISM, AND MYSTICISM

If Aquinas' most important achievement was to synthesize theology and philosophy, the most significant reactions to his work were those that tended to dissolve this synthesis. Among those whose thinking led to the gradual dissolution of the thirteenth-century synthesis was John Duns Scotus (1265–1308), William of Ockham (ca. 1280–1349), and Johannes Eckhart (ca. 1260–1327). These people did not disagree with everything Aquinas had taught. Indeed, on many matters they were in general agreement with his ideas. At the same time, they each set forth a basic criticism that had the effect of driving a wedge between philosophy and theology, between faith and reason. Against Aquinas' notion of the supremacy of reason, Scotus argued that in God the will is supreme, and this became known as the doctrine of *voluntarism.* Against Aquinas' notion that universals as such have some form of existence, Ockham argued that universals are only words, and this view became known as *terminism* or *nominalism.* And against the highly rational and technical articulation of theology as he found it in both Albert the Great and Aquinas, Eckhart urged the more immediate experience of the divine reality in the spiritual exercise of *mysticism.*

Voluntarism

Why should these three developments have the effect of separating philosophy and theology? The problem becomes at once clear when we consider some of the implications of voluntarism. Aquinas had argued that both in humanity and God the will is subordinate to the intellect, that reason guides or determines the will. Scotus maintained, however, that if God's will were subordinate to reason, or were limited by an eternal truth, God Himself would appear to be limited. He cannot do whatever He wills since He is bound or *determined* by a norm in some sense *above* Him. If God is to be *free,* He must be conceived as having an absolutely free will, in which case His will is His dominant faculty.

The consequence of saying that God's will, and not His intellect, is primary is that God's actions and moral commands are acts of will and as such irrational. If God's actions in creation and in the giving of the moral law do not represent His adherence to the standards of rationality, the created world is not the embodiment of God's rational nature. God, in this view, could have willed any kind of universe and whatever moral rules He chose. Both murder and adultery could, strictly speaking, become good actions if God commanded them. Moreover, where there is no ethical good there can be no merit and no reward. In this view, neither dispensation of beatitude nor damnation bears any strict causal relationship to behavior in this world, since God is absolutely free and can reward any behavior He chooses. But, Aquinas said that God commands certain moral rules *because they are good* and His wisdom recognizes them as good. Scotus, on the contrary, maintained that a moral rule is good *because God willed or commanded it.* Morality therefore cannot be discovered rationally. Aquinas had made much of the point that moral principles are known by a *natural light,* that people habitually contain these principles in their conscience. Most important of all, Aquinas assumed that morality is capable of an intellectual discipline insofar as the principles of good can be discovered rationally. Scotus and Ockham both argued, however, that morality is grounded not in reason but in will. Consequently, morality cannot be a subject of philosophy, of rational inquiry, but only a matter of faith and acceptance.

Nor could there be a *natural theology* whereby, for example, human reason could discover a rational order in which cause and effect are linked in such a way that reason could move reliably, by inference, from effect to cause. Aquinas had assumed that his demonstrations had rational rigor and were therefore valid. Scotus, on the other hand, would not agree that reason could discover a rational relationship between the world of experience and God. The existence of God, apart from merely *probable* demonstrations, became for Scotus and Ockham a matter of faith, and the domain of reason was limited to the empirical world. In this way, the subject matter and the concerns of philosophy were separated from those of theology. Religious *knowledge* was now seen again more in Platonic and Augustinian terms as a product of divine illumination or *revelation* and not attainable by philosophical discovery.

Nominalism

In a similar way, Ockham's nominalism separated faith and reason. Ockham had raised critical questions about the status of universal terms. The central question was whether such terms as *humanity* refer to any reality other than particular humans, James and John. Is there a *substance* in addition to these *particular* humans to which the *universal* term *humanity* refers? To a keen logician such as Ockham these critical questions had far-reaching consequences. Most important of all was his conclusion that in using universal terms, the mind is not doing anything more than thinking in an orderly way about particular things. Only concrete individual things exist. Universal terms such as *humanity* refer equally to James and John not because there is some real substance of "human-ness" in which both James and John *share* or *participate*, but only because the nature that is James is like the nature that is John. Universal terms such as *humanity* are simply *signs* or *names* (hence *nominalism*) for designating those concepts that particular things engender in human reason. Human reason, then, is limited to the world of individual things. Ockham's view was genuinely empirical. The mind, he said, does not know anything more than individual things and their qualities even though the mind is able to use universal terms. Such terms are nothing more than terms or names for classes of individual things: Above all, universal terms do not refer to a realm of reality *above* or *beyond* the world of concrete individual things.

How did this view differ from Aquinas' treatment of the problem of universals? For the most part Ockham's view was in harmony with what Aquinas had said, inasmuch as Aquinas argued that universals are found *in re,* in particular things, and are abstracted from things *post rem,* after our experiences of them. But Aquinas also accorded universals a metaphysical status when he said that they exist before individual things do as Ideas in the mind of God, as universals *ante rem.* If universals exist in the mind of God, two people are alike because they share in this metaphysical reality in God's mind. Also, the human mind, when it thinks universals, shares in some way in God's thought. This was the point Ockham wished to reject. He rejected the doctrine of divine Ideas for the same reason Scotus had, holding that in God the will has supremacy. People are what they are because God chose to make them that way and not because they reflect an eternal pattern that exists in God's mind as an Idea. Hence, says Ockham, "no universal is anything existing in any way outside the [mind of man]."

If people's thoughts are restricted to individual things in experience, their knowledge of these things does not lead them in any logical way to any reality beyond experience. Those who believed that universal terms signified something real as existing beyond individual things were confident that their use of such terms gave them reliable knowledge about reality beyond the empirical scene. And if one assumed that universals were Ideas in God's mind, one would conclude that philosophical reasoning about the origin, nature, and relationships of individual things could lead to various theological truths. There could be a *natural,* that is, rational, theology. But Ockham's strict interpretation of universals had the effect of severing (hence, Ockham's razor) philosophy from metaphysics, making out of philosophy something more like science. Theology and religious truth could not be achieved by philosophy or science. Indeed, his position implied the doctrine of *double truth,* that one kind of truth is available through science or philosophy, and another kind of truth is received through revelation. The first truth is the product of human reason, and the other is a matter of faith. One kind of truth, moreover, cannot influence the other kind. The ultimate consequence of the double-truth doctrine was that theological and philosophical truths were not only independent and not derivable from each other but that these different truths could even contradict each other. This was the explicit teaching of the followers of Averroës who held, for example, that while it is true in philosophy that there is no personal immortality, such a doctrine is false for theology. Ockham had not gone that far in separating faith and reason. He had, nevertheless, set the stage for an empirical and scientific way of thinking about the facts of experience. His nominalism had the effect of separating science from metaphysics. The study of natural things became more and more independent of metaphysical or theological explanations. His celebrated formula, which we know as *Ockham's razor,* included one of his guiding principles, namely, that "what can be explained on fewer principles is explained needlessly by more." Thus, universal terms, he felt, can be adequately explained as being simply names for concepts that similar individual things engender in the human mind. Such terms do not refer to reality beyond visible things. Hence, the combined force of Ockham's nominalism and Scotus' voluntarism did much to dismantle the medieval synthesis by separating philosophy and theology, faith and reason.

Mysticism

Finally, Eckhart's mysticism shifted the medieval emphasis from reason to feeling. Actually, he appeared simply to carry to a further extreme what Albert the

Great and Thomas Aquinas had done. While these great masters, especially Aquinas, constructed elaborate rational systems of theology, Eckhart attempted to articulate as far as possible his deep feeling of piety. Eckhart was not a careful systematic philosopher. Though he considered in great detail many systematic questions concerning God's nature, creation, and the nature of humanity, he was primarily a mystic who wanted to share with others his rich experiences of unity with God. In translating his piety into theological language, he made many bold statements, as for example that God is "above being," and that apart from God there is "nothing." More important was his notion that *being* and *knowledge* are one. If therefore God is above being, He is also above knowledge; He is particularly beyond human concepts and categories. Consequently, the union of humanity and God is an experience beyond rationality, and Eckhart is forced to use such terms as *wilderness* or *darkness* to express this mystical union. And this union cannot be reached except by liberating oneself from the objects of the world. Whereas Aquinas built his demonstrations of God's existence upon his explanation of finite things, Eckhart urged people to pass beyond sensory knowledge, which is after all limited to material objects. But union with God is not achieved by human effort. Only through God's grace and illumination is union consummated, and only in the deepest reaches of the soul does one grasp God in His fullness. When this happens, says Eckhart, people become one with God, for "we are transformed totally into God and are converted into Him in a similar manner as in the sacrament the bread is converted into the body of Christ."

Eckhart's teachings contained many contradictions; he was not a precise philosopher or a highly systematic theologian. His use of earlier ideas gained from Albert and Aquinas shows the strong influence of Neoplatonism into which he cast most of his thought. What is significant about his writings is that they focused upon the inner world of mysticism, where faith and piety are dominant. There followed after Eckhart a flowering of mystical writers, among whom some of the more notable were Johannes Tauler (1300–1361), Heinrich Suso (1300–1366), and John Ruysbroeck (1293–1381). The element of feeling that mysticism exalted and the scientific mood that the empiricism of Ockham required received new emphasis as the Middle Ages merged into the Renaissance.

Galileo *(The Bettman Archive)*

THREE

THE
MODERN PERIOD:
PHILOSOPHY
AND THE
UNFOLDING
WORLD
OF SCIENCE

10

The Renaissance Interlude

For most philosophers in the Middle Ages, the sky hung low, suggesting a close bond between heaven and earth, and, accordingly, between philosophy and theology. Indeed, philosophy in the Middle Ages was virtually the handmaiden of theology, supplying religious thought with a reasoned account of its various doctrines. To be sure, Plato and Aristotle had also concerned themselves with the question of how the daily affairs of people could and should be related to the permanent structures of reality and to God. But the synthesis of theology and philosophy in the Middle Ages was a precarious one. For one thing, there was some serious question about the compatibility, for example, of Aristotle's nontheistic philosophy and the belief in a personal God in Christianity. Moreover, much of Aristotle's thought was made available at this time through Moslem Arabian thinkers, who had construed Aristotle in ways that could hardly be accepted by Christians. Aquinas sought to reinterpret and Christianize Aristotle to overcome this incompatibility. Yet, philosophy now found itself to a great extent doing a task that it had not originally set out to do, namely, providing an intellectual and metaphysical foundation for revealed religion. Nor had philosophy been previously domesticated, as it were, by an institution the way it was by the church in the Middle Ages. To be sure, philosophers were from the earliest days in mortal jeopardy when their teachings threatened the *status quo*. Socrates was, after all, put to death for just this reason, and in Aristotle's case Athens almost "sinned against philosophy a second time." Generally, classical philosophy had been free to move wherever the pursuit of truth led it. Philosophy could dwell upon the subjects of humanity, nature, ethics, God, and political authority by referring only to what human thought discovered about these matters. The spirit of medieval philosophy was different in that its starting point was now virtually fixed by the doctrines of Christian theology. In addition, the whole cultural atmosphere was affected by the predominance of the church so that moral theory, political doctrine, the institutions of society such as the family and work, the arts and literature, and much of science—all these bore the imprint of theology.

Just how closely daily life followed the ideals of this synthesis in the Middle Ages is not altogether clear. That there was a widening gap between the set structure of thought of Christendom and humanity's yearning for a freer encounter with all the possibilities of life, art, and thought is attested by the eventual decline of the medieval synthesis. Within the church itself, the debates over the appropriateness of employing philosophy as the handmaiden of theology led finally to the conclusion that as a discipline philosophy is wholly separate from theology and religion. Although Ockham sought to preserve the medieval synthesis by employing his theory of the "double truth," according to which some truths are known by faith and others by reason, this same double-truth theory ultimately provided a virtually decisive impetus for the destruction of the fragile synthesis by showing that in no way can the human mind rise above the realm of human experience, that philosophy cannot produce a "natural theology." For example, Ockham says that "there is no way of knowing with clear certainty either by reason or experience that such and such a form is within us, or such and such a soul is in us, or that such and such a soul is the form of the body. We hold these three truths by faith only." Accordingly, religion was reconceived as primarily a matter of faith, a point of view that found its great culmination in the Reformation, and philosophy was reinstated, most dramatically by the father of modern philosophy, Descartes, as an autonomous discipline. It may be argued that Descartes had not really created a new foundation for philosophy after all, but what is significant at this point is that he thought he had.

With the dissolution of the synthesis between Aristotle's philosophy and Christian theology, Aristotle became only one thinker among many to whom people would now turn. During this period called the Renaissance, spanning roughly the fifteenth and sixteenth centuries, there was a revival of classical learning, and many of the philosophies of antiquity once again became available. Although the Middle Ages had known Plato through the Neoplatonists and especially Augustine, Plato was now being read for himself without particular reference to theology. Stoicism became widespread again, influencing such eminent writers as Montaigne and Charron. Even the skepticism of Sextus Empiricus and of Pyrrho became strongly felt and in some cases employed as a ground for viewing religion as a matter of faith rather than reason. The separation of philosophy from theology also brought about a far greater accent upon the strictly human dimensions of life. Artists now paid more attention to the human body and form. Nature itself became the object of fresh and free inquiry. This humanism and natural science did not involve the rejection of religion but only the affirmation that areas of humanity and nature could be fruitfully studied by methods and assumptions not directly derived from religion. Philosophical thought in the Renaissance centuries, then, included Platonism, Aristotelianism, Skepticism, Epicureanism, Stoicism, humanism, and the influence of those natural philosophers, including Copernicus, Kepler, and Galileo, who were so influential in ushering in the enterprise of modern science.

The Renaissance was a time of discovery and emancipation. On every hand new worlds were being opened. While Columbus' bold adventure led him to discover a new continent, others opened up new worlds of the mind and spirit. Giotto's (ca. 1276–1337) paintings and Dante's (1265–1321) literature had earlier facilitated the transition from medieval symbolism to the exaltation of nature. Petrarch (1304–1374) turned to a description of the joys and sorrows of natural humanity, expressing deep dimensions of feeling as opposed to the brittle logic of doctrine. Boccaccio (1313–1375) was even more frank in his account of humanity's sensual capacities. Curiosity and the desire for beauty led others to explore the structure and subtleties of the human body. Even while serving the church with the genius of his art, Michelangelo (1475–1564) managed to give strong expression to the new humanism of the time. His painting of Adam is a striking description of physical beauty and strength all the more powerful in its unashamed nakedness and resolute poise toward light and life. Leonardo da Vinci (1452–1519), that universal genius, looked behind beauty with care to the more minute ingredients of human anatomy, a mode of curiosity that later led William Harvey (1578–1657) to discover the circulation of the blood.

Such concern with natural humanity led also to a new-found basis of human dignity. In his *Oration on the Dignity of Man*, Pico della Mirandola (1463–1494) imagined God as saying to humanity, his creation, that "we have set thee at the world's center that thou mayest from thence more easily observe whatever is in the world. . . so that with freedom of choice and with honor, as though the maker and molder of thyself, thou mayest fashion thyself in whatever shape thou shalt prefer." Enhancing the dignity of the individual was his ready access to information. There was much enthusiasm over the discovery of original texts of classical writers, which could now be read in place of garbled translations and revised versions which had been rearranged to suit special purposes. Greek manuscripts were brought back from Athens to Rome. In Florence, Cosimo de' Medici founded an academy where Plato's philosophy was the chief subject of study. This academic influence, reinforced by similar academies in Naples and Rome, further diluted the preeminence of Aristotelian thought and scholastic methodology. Direct access to texts also created a deep fascination for language.

The discovery of ancient Greek and Roman literature had the effect of encouraging a new style of writing, which was less formal than the original texts of medieval authors and had its expression increasingly in the vernacular. With the use of the vernacular, literature became more and more the property of the people. Wycliffe's rendering of the Bible into the vernacular would in time set off widespread reverberations in religious thought as the masses acquired direct access to the contents of the Scriptures. The extensive diffusion of culture was most effectively facilitated by Johann Gutenberg's invention in the 1440s of movable type, which made books readily available, smaller and easier to handle, and cheaper to buy. Printing presses soon appeared in Paris, London, Madrid, and in Italy at the monastery of Subiaco. The making of books and the use of the vernacular inevitably affected the mode of writing philosophy in that the sense of liberation implied in these activities led philosophers to engage more in original formulations rather than in writing commentaries on authoritative thinkers. In time, the modern philosophers would write their treatises in the language of their own people, so that Locke and Hume would write in English, Voltaire and Rousseau in French, and Kant in German.

If the Renaissance were regarded simply as the decisive influence of classical literature upon the modern world, one might be tempted to say that Erasmus *was* the Renaissance. But the Renaissance was not limited to literary activity. Equally important, as we have seen, was the new art with its preoccupation with human nature and its purely natural qualities. At the same time, new theories of political authority and behavior were fashioned, particularly by Machiavelli, who shifted the base of political thought away from the moral ground prepared by Thomas Aquinas' theory of natural law toward a new secular theory of the state. Religion, the chief element in the medieval synthesis, took a sharp turn in this period when the Reformers added immense power to a view already suggested by Scotus and Ockham that Christianity is a matter of faith and not reason. Although the crosscurrents of thought in this period were still in somewhat unsystematic disarray, many of the new modes of thinking were gathered up in the extraordinary person of Michel de Montaigne. And inevitably, the new intellectual mood of the Renaissance engendered a new mode of analyzing the structure of nature. Natural science was now to be born in its modern form with its stress upon observation and mathematics, an approach employed chiefly by Copernicus, Kepler, and Galileo. The Renaissance was, therefore, a time when many individuals from many lands exhibited many new modes of freedom and expression, causing at points some discontinuity with the past while changing the emphasis in areas in which continuity with the past was preserved. Although the extraordinary richness of the Renaissance can hardly be captured in this brief space, some additional comments can be made concerning the impact of Erasmus, the Reformation, Machiavelli, Montaigne, and the scientists upon the unfolding of modern thought.

ERASMUS AND LUTHER

Erasmus

Born in Rotterdam in 1466, the illegitimate son of a priest, Desiderius Erasmus had a considerable influence upon the development of humanism. He was the foe of scholastic theology though he had no intention of rejecting the Christian faith. Through his humanistic learning, especially in the Greek language, he sought to uncover the pure and simple elements of Christianity that had been overlaid and obscured by the excessive rationalism of scholastic doctrine. His earliest training began in the school of the Brethren of the Common Life, from which he later entered the Augustinian monastery of Steyn. At the monastery, life was miserable for Erasmus as he was unfitted mentally, physically, and temperamentally for a regime that offered little physical comfort and virtually no intellectual freedom. Through good fortune, he was invited by the Bishop of Cambrai to become his Latin secretary. The Bishop sent him to study for a while at the Collège Montaigue in Paris, where again he felt only contempt for scholastic methods of instruction. It was here, nevertheless, that his enthusiasm for classical literature was stimulated, and it was here, too, that he began his first book, which would in time become one of his famous volumes, a book of proverbs entitled *Adagiorum Chiliades*. In 1499, Erasmus visited England, where he soon came under the influence of John Colet, a Biblical scholar, and Sir Thomas More. Erasmus thought it strange that Colet should lecture on the Bible without a knowledge of Greek. He therefore set out to become proficient in this language, eventually publishing a widely accepted Greek Testament with a new Latin translation. During a second visit to England in 1511, Erasmus became a member of the academic community of Cambridge, where he had been appointed Lady Margaret Professor. He had little respect for his colleagues, whom he called "Cyprian bulls and dung-eaters," nor did he have any good words for the English beer or climate. After a few years he went to Basel, where he made his home until his death in 1536 at the age of seventy.

Erasmus made several contributions to the spirit of the Renaissance. His enthusiasm for classical learning was a decisive influence at this time. He realized that the invention of printing now made it possible to popularize the ancient classics by bringing inexpensive editions within the reach of large numbers of intelligent readers. These books opened up new worlds of classical learning that had not been available in the Middle Ages. But Erasmus was not simply an editor, even though his work in making available these classic Greek and Latin editions would have secured his reputation and significance in the history of thought. More important was his contribution to the development of a new style of literary expression. Erasmus loved words and spent much thought in selecting just the right word or phrase to express his insights. As painters would display genius in their use of colors, Erasmus, long a foe of the incredible lifelessness of scholastic discourse, found deep joy and freedom in fashioning a new and pure literary style marked by the elegance of each phrase.

Erasmus criticized scholastic jargon not only because of its lack of elegance but even more because it obscured the true teachings of the Gospels. It appeared to Erasmus that the ideas of the great classical writers were in basic harmony with the Gospels. In particular, he saw a close similarity between Plato's philosophy and the teachings of Christ. He sensed a deep incongruity between the simple teachings of Christ and the opulence and arrogance of the Papal Court. This moved him to write the satirical *Julius Exclusus* in which Pope Julius II is forbidden by St. Peter to enter the heavenly gates. His own earlier experience with life in the monasteries prompted him to write a trenchant criticism of the clergy in a book called *Praise of Folly*, which Luther made much use of in his decisive argument with the church. But Erasmus was neither a religious skeptic nor did he become a Lutheran. His was a lover's quarrel with the church. He wished to harmonize the church's teachings with the new humanistic learning.

Erasmus' *Praise of Folly* was both an ironic and a serious treatment of two kinds of folly. It was the clergy's folly that felt the weight of Erasmus' irony and invective as he lashed out at the priests for their intricate calculations over pardons and indulgences and the exact duration of a soul's residence in purgatory. He ridiculed the disputations of the theologians as they struggled valiantly with each other over the doctrines of the Incarnation, Trinity, and transubstantiation. His chief complaint was that the whole point of religion had been lost, that too much emphasis was being put on trivial and irrelevant details, especially in the monasteries where matters of dress and minutiae of discipline deflected people from the central aim of Christianity. Imagining how these priests would stand before the judgment seat seeking to enter heaven by calling attention to all their good works, Erasmus, going beyond good humor to invective, describes a priest who points to "so many bushels of prayers, another brags of not having touched a penny without at least two pairs of gloves on." To all these Christ answers, "I left you but one precept, of loving one another, which I do not hear anyone plead that he has faithfully discharged." Closely connected with this criticism of monastic life was Erasmus' abiding dislike of the hair-splitting logic of scholastic doctrine. Whereas his praise of the priests' folly was ironic, he now quite seriously praised that other kind of folly that he identified with the simplicity of faith. True religion, he felt, is a matter of the heart and not of the head, a view that became central for the Reformers and was again expressed with great force by Pascal, who wrote that "the heart has reasons which the reason does not know."

But while Luther became a passionate Reformer, Erasmus remained only a critic. In his moderate book *Essay on Free Will* he expressed the Renaissance view that humanity has great capacities for moral improvement. To this book

Luther replied with his bristling *De Servo Arbitrio*, affirming the Pauline doctrine of the corruption of human nature and dismissing Erasmus as a "babbler," a "skeptic," or "some other hog from the Epicurean sty." In this debate Erasmus was the great exponent of the spirit of the Renaissance. With unfaltering optimism he continued to believe that education would eventually conquer stupidity and ignorance. His interest in classical literature and philosophy did not lead him to formulate a new scholasticism or to subordinate Christian faith to the philosophy of Plato. Rather, he used his knowledge of the classical languages to discover the real words of the Gospels, saying that "if there is any fresh Greek to be had, I had rather pawn my coat than not get it, especially if it is something Christian, as the Psalms in Greek or the Gospels." As it turned out, Erasmus exerted an enormous influence simultaneously upon the development of humanistic learning and, though he remained a son of the church, upon the Reformation.

If Erasmus looked back to antiquity for the treasure of the classics, the Reformers, particularly Luther, looked back to the primitive community of Christians for the original spirit of Christianity. In this way the Renaissance and the Reformation both epitomized a revival of the past. Though Erasmus and Luther could agree on many points in their mutual attacks upon the state of Christianity in the sixteenth century, Luther pushed his argument to the point of causing a sundering explosion within the church. The significance of Luther's vigorous revolt was that it altered the mode of thought for a substantial number of people in Western civilization. Whereas Erasmus could balance classical humanistic learning with a simplified Christian faith, Luther's exaltation of faith had the effect of throwing serious doubt upon the capacity of human reason to lead humanity to salvation.

Luther

Luther had been deeply influenced philosophically by William of Ockham, whom he called "my beloved Master William." It was Ockham who had earlier rejected St. Thomas Aquinas' impressive system of natural theology based primarily upon the notion of causality. Natural reason, said Aquinas, leads us to God by way of an analysis of the causal relations of all things, an analysis that ends by requiring a First Cause, which is God. Ockham had developed a strictly empirical and, in a sense, skeptical view regarding knowledge. He argued that "from the fact that one thing is known to exist, it cannot be inferred that another thing exists." To say that some things are caused by other things gives one no warrant to argue that God is the cause of the natural order. Ockham concluded not that we can know nothing about God but only that the unaided reason cannot discover God. Knowledge of God is a gift of grace and is assured by an act of faith. Luther built on this foundation, finding impressive support for this view in the writings of St. Augustine.

From St. Augustine Luther also drew his heavy emphasis upon the

Pauline conception of sin, which located the human predicament not in ignorance or undeveloped reason but rather in the bondage of the will. It is therefore *faith*, not reason, that overcomes this predicament. Moreover, said
Luther, "it is the quality of faith that it wrings the neck of reason." What
seems impossible to reason becomes feasible to faith. The difficulty with reason is that being the faculty of finite humanity it tends to reduce everything
to its own limited perspective. This is especially true when the natural reason
contemplates the nature and capacities of God. Here human reason tends to
limit God to strictly human estimates of what God is and can do. Luther was
particularly struck by the intellectual difficulties faced by Abraham when
God promised that from his barren wife Sarah he would give him seed.
"There is no doubt," said Luther, that "faith and reason mightily fell out in
Abraham's heart about this matter, yet at last did faith get the better, and
overcame and strangled reason, that all-cruelest and most fatal enemy of
God." The element of faith reveals the limited scope not only of reason but
also of so-called good works.

Luther's version of the Christian life had the effect therefore of challeng-
ing not only the medieval system of scholastic theology but also those optimistic visions of individual and social perfection based upon good works. Luther
said, "all manner of works, even contemplation, meditation and all that the soul
can do, avail nothing." Only one thing is necessary for righteousness, liberty,
and the Christian life, and "that one thing is the most holy word of God, the
Gospel of Christ." If someone asks "what then is this word of God, and how
shall it be used, since there are so many words of God?" Luther answers, "the
Apostle explains that in Romans I:17 'The just shall live by faith.'... It is clear
then that a Christian man has in his faith all that he needs, and needs no works
to justify him."

Luther's emphasis upon faith in religious matters had its counterpart in
his political thought. Government, according to Luther, is ordained of God.
For this reason, he viewed the functions of government as the "preservation of
the peace." The recalcitrance of people caused by their sinful nature requires
a strong ruler, and for this reason "God has subjected them to the sword, so
that even though they would do so, they cannot practice their wickedness."
The counterpart of faith in the political realm was therefore the attitude of obedience. The individual must obey the ruler in spite of what the ruler commands,
since his commands are directed toward the preservation of peace and order.
Without the power of the ruler, self-centered people would produce anarchy
"and thus the world would be reduced to chaos." Life upon earth is in any case
not the most important consideration; what counts most is the salvation of one's
soul. Whatever a ruler or sovereign does "cannot harm the soul but only the
body and property." Consequently, said Luther, "the temporal power is a very
small thing in God's sight, and far too slightly regarded by Him, that for its
sake, whether it do right or wrong, we should resist, become disobedient and
quarrel." Indeed, says Luther, "to suffer wrong destroys no one's soul, nay, it
improves the soul, although it inflicts loss upon the body and property."

fact," he says, "it is vain to look for anything good from those countries which we see nowadays so corrupt, as is the case above all others with Italy." This fact of human corruption was therefore the decisive starting point for Machiavelli's political thought. A basically corrupt society requires a strong government, preferably in the hands of a single person since it happens rarely or not at all that a republic or kingdom is well-ordered or reformed "if this is not done by one man." It is therefore necessary that "there should be one man alone who settles the method and on whose mind any such organization depends." In short, there is a need for an absolute legislator.

Machiavelli envisioned a double standard of behavior, one for rulers and the other for the people. Although he thought it would be disastrous for the rulers to adapt their acts to Christian ethics, he considered religion to be a very important element for uniting people in peace and order. This was a cynical and pragmatic view of religion, since Machiavelli was not particularly concerned with its truth but only with its social usefulness. The ruler, on the other hand, must have the freedom to adjust his acts to the requirements of each occasion without feeling bound to any objective moral rules. There is some question whether *The Prince* was in any sense intended to be a *philosophy* of politics. Since it grew out of the particular circumstances of Machiavelli's day, the recommendations to rulers contained therein constitute instead a practical program of action for existing rulers. Still, the drift of Machiavelli's thought is in the direction of equating the right with the expedient. The ruler should keep faith only if his best interests are served thereby. He will at times therefore be faithless, "but it is necessary," says Machiavelli, "to be able to disguise this character well, and to be a great feigner and dissembler." Thus, while it is not necessary for the ruler to have all the virtues, "it is very necessary to seem to have them." Even ruthlessness has its place. Machiavelli speaks approvingly of Caesar Borgia's treatment of Ramiro d'Orco, a subordinate whose stern treatment of the people caused him, and therefore Caesar Borgia, to become unpopular. To overcome the damage which d'Orco's unpopularity might have upon him, Caesar Borgia "caused him to be executed and left on the Piazza at Cesaria, with the block and a bloody knife at his side. The barbarity of this spectacle caused the people to be at once satisfied and dismayed."

Machiavelli was well aware of the shifting mood of the people and believed that their inconstancy must be matched by shrewdness and swift adaptability on the part of the ruler. Moreover, he said, "men are ungrateful, fickle, false, cowards, covetous and as long as you succeed they are yours entirely." But when the ruler really needs help, "they turn against you." Machiavelli was therefore repelled by any notions that would require the ruler to be domesticated by morality. He recognized no higher law such as Aquinas had propounded but urged a thoroughly secular approach to politics. He valued skill in cunning higher than moral conviction. But again, Machiavelli was not unmindful of the desirability of certain political ends. His chief point was, however, that the ruler should choose only those means that could guarantee that the ends be in fact achieved. In the context of unscrupulous and egotistical people, morality must

This is a far cry from the medieval view that St. Thomas formulated whe
said that if a positive law of the state is contrary to the natural law, it is r
law but a perversion of the law and need not be obeyed. Still, Luther tho
that he had given a theological basis for his justification of the power o
temporal ruler and his laws. It was Machiavelli who went the next step
shifted political thought to a thoroughly secular base, anticipating the m
theories of sovereignty and power politics.

MACHIAVELLI (1469–1527)

Niccolò Machiavelli, the son of an Italian lawyer, was a young man in his
ties when the great preacher Savonarola was at the height of his influ
Florence. That such an influential man came to such a miserable end
Machiavelli an early lesson about the relative power of good and evil f
society. During his own career in government and diplomacy, and with
toration of the Medici in 1512, he gave considerable thought to the
principles of effective political behavior, recording his unsystematic
in two books, *The Prince* and *The Discourses*. In *The Discourses*, Ma
writes approvingly of the Roman Republic, expressing enthusiasm
government and liberty. In *The Prince*, however, his emphasis is upon
for an absolute monarch. The clue to Machiavelli's thought lies in th
for his apparent inconsistency in these two books. By expressing a p
for an absolute monarch in *The Prince*, he had not intended to reje
sirability of self-government about which he spoke so approvingly in
courses. His argument was, rather, that given the condition of mora
Italy when he was writing *The Prince* (1513), the kind of popular g
exemplified in the Roman Republic could not be successfully estab

If Machiavelli urged rulers to develop the art of deception, it w
he was convinced that only the shrewdest and most crafty indivic
survive in the precarious art of governing. Basing his thought upon a
inspection of the actual behavior of his contemporaries, he quickly
that to think of political behavior in moral terms would be to expos
all the dangers that clever opponents could create. For this reaso
oped an indifference to the claims of morality. Indeed he argued
ligion places the supreme happiness in humility, lowliness and a
worldly objects, whilst the...[religion of antiquity] on the contra
supreme good in grandeur of soul, strength of body and all such o
as render men formidable." His chief criticism against Christian e
it had "made men feeble, and caused them to become an easy
minded men."

That people are evil was a fact only too obvious to Mach
was corruption at the highest levels; even the popes of his day
bad repute that Machiavelli could write that "we Italians then ow
of Rome and to her priests our having become irreligious and ba
particularly struck by the general social decadence of Italy

give way to sheer power if the ruler is to succeed. Only those elements in society that have superior power can prevail.

Machiavelli thought his views were supported by past history, where political "Machiavellianism" was far more prevalent than idealistic theorists would be candid enough to admit. It was one of Machiavelli's achievements that he translated politics into the vernacular and anticipated others, notably Thomas Hobbes, who would amplify with more philosophical sophistication the secular and totalitarian implications of Machiavelli's reflections. Unhappily, too, history in the twentieth century produced rulers who carried Machiavelli's recommendations to extremes he might never have imagined.

MONTAIGNE (1533–1592)

In his celebrated *Essays*, Michel de Montaigne expressed for the Renaissance a captivating version of classical Skepticism. Montaigne had discovered in the ancient writings of the Skeptics a prescription for an emancipated mode of daily life. The Skeptics of antiquity, such as Pyrrho, Skepticism's founder, and Sextus Empiricus, meant by *skepticism* something quite different from what that word means in modern usage. The word *skepticism* has over the centuries come to mean chiefly the mood of doubt, a doubt that anything can ever be known with certainty. The corollary of such doubt is an indifference to the drift of events and, in extreme cases, an indifference to the physical conditions of life, not unlike the Stoic sense of resignation. But these were not the chief characteristics of classical Skepticism or of Montaigne's thought. Pyrrho had formulated no strict doctrine about what people could or could not know, what did or did not exist. Central to classical Skepticism was the mood of inquiry coupled with a desire to live a thoroughly exemplary human life. This also was Montaigne's chief concern. He was particularly attracted to a way of life that permitted him constantly to discover new insights and at the same time enjoy all the powers he possessed as a human being. Montaigne wrote that "Pyrrho did not want to make himself into a stone; he wanted to make of himself a living man, discoursing and reasoning, enjoying all pleasures and natural commodities, using all of his corporeal and spiritual parts regularly and properly."

Above all, Montaigne looked upon himself, as he said, as "an unpremeditated philosopher," one who was not confined intellectually to some rigid set of ideas within which his thought and life must be expressed. His desire to live a happy life could not be fulfilled if he committed himself to doctrines about which perfectly reasonable objections could be raised. Many problems, he felt, had no clear solutions. On such questions as what is the true nature of things, which so preoccupied the pre-Socratics, Montaigne accepted the judgment of the Skeptics, who said that there is "no more likelihood that this is true than that that is true." But, again, this formula of Skepticism was not intended to deny what common sense tells us is the case. In a curious way Montaigne saw in Skepticism a liberating force, which would in the end make doubt superfluous because one would never make any permanent commitment to any doc-

Michel de Montaigne *(The Bettmann Archive)*

trines but would assume a perpetual mood of inquiry. Contentment, said Montaigne, is possible only as one achieves tranquillity of mind. What disturbs this tranquillity is the attempt to go beyond our ordinary experiences and penetrate the inner nature of things. The saddest spectacle of all is to find people formulating final answers on questions that are far too subtle and variable for such treatment. The final folly of this attempt to capture the perfect and permanent truth is the mood of fanaticism and dogmatism.

Montaigne knew well the frightful outcome of fanaticism. In his lifetime he saw wars and fierce religious persecution. He wrote of his "neighborhood grown so old in riot" that he wondered whether his society could be held together. "I saw," he wrote, "common and general behavior so ferocious, above all in inhumanity and treachery, that I cannot think of it without blenching in horror." This he blamed upon the fires of fanaticism. The loss of inner peace of mind would in time, he felt, be reflected in social turmoil. He genuinely believed that a mood of constructive skepticism could prevent such outbursts of cruelty. In the mood of true skepticism, human energies would be directed toward manageable subjects and purposes. Rather than struggling with riddles about the universe and its destiny, Montaigne would counsel people to start their philosophy of life by reflecting upon matters close at hand.

A good place to begin, said Montaigne, is with one's own personal experiences: "Every man carries within himself the whole condition of humanity." For this reason he was convinced that whatever proved useful to himself might also serve usefully for someone else. In the true spirit of the Renaissance, Montaigne sought an open and clear form of expression about the most natural and normal actions of men, rejecting the obscurity of technical jargon. "My page," he writes, "makes love and knows what he is doing. But read to him Leo Hebraeus or Ficino where they speak of the actions and thoughts of love, and he can't make head or tail of it." Montaigne complained that "I can't recognize most of my daily doings when they appear in Aristotle. They are decked out or hidden in another cloak for the benefit of schoolmen." What Montaigne thought was needed was to "do as much to make art natural as they do to make nature artificial." The art of life is to recognize what it means to be human, he says, for "there is nothing so handsome as to play the man properly and well. Of all our diseases, the worst is to despise our own being." Nothing disfigures human nature more than a man's attempt to think higher of himself than he should. Whenever this happens, says Montaigne, "I have always observed a singular accord between supercelestial ideas and subterranean behavior." Whenever men "would flee from themselves and escape from being men [they] engage in folly. Instead of transforming themselves into angels, they turn themselves into beasts."

For Montaigne, *skepticism* did not mean either pessimism as a mood or license as a rule for behavior. On the contrary, he saw in skepticism a source for a positive affirmation of all the facets of human life. Although he saw serious limits to the power of technical reason, he glorified the human capacity for judgment. To be a human being in the deepest sense, he thought, is to have fully conscious experiences, experiences in which a person consciously weighs alternatives and controls his behavior through an act of judgment. Judgment, in contrast to reason, permits a fuller expression of the faculties of a person, including the affections and emotions, and is far more willing to allow the soul to be "warned and awakened by occasions foreign, present and fortuitous," inasmuch as "agitation is [the soul's] life and its grace." But although Montaigne could say that "chance has a greater right over me" than the stricture of doctrine, he nevertheless thought it to be a matter of good judgment to accept the basic conditions of life as he found them. He thought that "for men the height of wisdom is to take things as they are, and look upon the rest with confidence."

He adopted as his own the central insight of classical Skepticism, using this formula: "I stop—I examine—I take for my guide the ways of the world and the experience of the senses." The senses give people sufficiently reliable information about themselves and the physical world to ensure physical survival and genuine pleasure. The ways of the world also have value almost irrespective of their objective rightness or truth. Religion and laws are positive facts about the world, and to deny or reject them is virtually the same as saying that one is in no danger as one stands at the edge of a precipice. Practical judgment requires one to accept the formal conditions and organization of the country of which one is a citizen. Again, judgment can distinguish between appropriate and inappropriate restrictions upon one's life. For these reasons, Montaigne's skepticism did not lead him to revolutionary or anarchic behavior. He became a true conservative who believed that social change must not be abrupt, that since there are no absolute truths, there are no specific ends toward which society must be forced to move. Custom acquires therefore a higher claim upon people's allegiance. In matters of religion also the person of good judgment will respect the authority of tradition, seeing in the stability of the organized religious community the condition for continued inquiry that anarchy would render impossible.

Thus Montaigne sought to remind his generation that wisdom lies in accepting life as it is and realizing how difficult it is to know anything with certainty. He wanted particularly to direct people's attention to the richness of human life that respectful acceptance of human capacities could make possible. In this he was a true representative of the main current of the Renaissance. It was not long, however, before Descartes once again saw philosophy's task as the quest for certainty and thereby employed human doubt for purposes quite foreign to Montaigne's intentions. Moreover, Montaigne's preoccupation with human instead of cosmic questions did not deflect other Renaissance thinkers from pursuing questions about the physical world. Indeed, one of the significant aspects of the Renaissance was the gradual emergence during this period of the method of modern science.

SCIENCE

The scientists of the Renaissance brought about the most fundamental alterations in the world of thought, and they accomplished this feat by devising a new method for discovering knowledge. Unlike the medieval thinkers who proceeded for the most part by reading traditional texts, the early modern scientists laid greatest stress upon observation and the formation of temporary hypotheses. The method of observation implied two things: namely, that traditional explanations of the behavior of nature should be empirically demonstrated, the new assumption being that such explanations could very well be wrong, and that new information might be available to scientists if they could penetrate beyond the superficial appearances of things. People now began to look at the heavenly bodies with a new attitude, hoping not solely to find the confirmation of Biblical statements about the firmament but, further, to discover the principles and laws that describe the movements of bodies. Observation was directed not only upon the stars but also in the opposite direction, toward the minutest constituents of physical substance.

To enhance the exactness of their observations, they invented various scientific instruments. Tippershey, a Dutchman, invented the telescope in 1608, although Galileo was the first to make dramatic use of it. In 1590 the first compound microscope was created. The principle of the barometer was discovered by Galileo's pupil Torricelli. The air pump, which was so important in creating a vacuum for the experiment that proved that all bodies regardless of their weight or size fall at the same rate when there is no air resistance, was invented by Otto von Guericke (1602–1686). With the use of instruments and imaginative hypotheses, fresh knowledge began to unfold. Galileo discovered the moons around Jupiter, and Anton Leeuwenhoek (1632–1723) discovered spermatozoa, protozoa, and bacteria. Whereas Nicolaus Copernicus (1473–1543) formed a new hypothesis of the revolution of the earth around the sun, Harvey (1578–1657) discovered the circulation of the blood. William Gilbert (1540–1603) wrote a major work on the magnet, and Robert Boyle (1627–1691), the father of chemistry, formulated his famous law concerning the relation of temperature, volume, and pressure of gases. Added to these inventions and discoveries was the decisive advance made in mathematics, especially by Sir Isaac Newton and Leibniz, who independently invented differential and integral calculus. The method of observation and mathematical calculation now became the hallmarks of modern science.

The new scientific mode of thought in time influenced philosophic thought in two important ways. First, the assumption that the basic processes of nature are observable and capable of mathematical calculation and description had the effect of engendering another assumption, namely, that everything consists of bodies in motion, that everything conforms to a mechanical model. The heavens above and the smallest particles below all exhibit the same laws of motion. Even human thought was soon explained in mechanical terms, not to mention the realm of human behavior, which the earlier moralists described as the product of *free will*.

A second consequence of scientific thought was a new estimate of the place of humanity in the universe. Medieval thought had placed humanity at the apex of creation, locating it upon the earth, which stood in the center of the universe. But the ancient Ptolemaic astronomy, which had envisioned an earth-centered universe, was shattered in the Renaissance. The Polish astronomer Copernicus formulated a new hypothesis in his *De Revolutionibus Orbium Coelestium*, which said that the sun is at the center of the universe and that the earth rotates daily and revolves around the sun annually. Copernicus was a faithful son of the church and had no thought of contradicting any orthodox Biblical doctrines. His work expressed rather his irrepressible desire to work out a theory of the heavens that would conform to the available evidence. As an hypothesis, it was startling enough, but more facts were required before confirmation could be achieved. Tycho Brahe (1546–1601) made additional and corrective observations, and his young associate Johannes Kepler (1571–1630) formulated three important laws of planetary motion in which he added mathematical equations to support mere observation. It was Galileo (1564–1642) who provided the greatest theoretical precision to the new astronomy and, in the course of this endeavor, formulated his important laws of acceleration and dynamics.

But Galileo's scientific impact was not limited to his brilliant calculations in the realm of astronomy or to his formulations of the laws of acceleration and dynamics. Of equally far-reaching influence upon the development of modern philosophy and science were the assumptions and methods he employed in the study of nature in general. We have already seen that Democritus as early as the fifth century B.C. reduced all things in the universe to atoms in motion, in short, to matter. Later, Lucretius (98–55 B.C.) showed how deceptive appearances can be: He described how a person standing on one side of a valley might see on the other side something that looked like a white cloud only to find upon going there that the "cloud" was a flock of sheep. Similarly, Galileo stressed the distinction between appearance and reality, where appearance is made up of *secondary* qualities while reality consists of *primary* qualities. We cannot trust appearances as a reliable path to truth. For example, our notion based upon appearances leads us to the erroneous conclusion that the sun moves around the earth. Or, a tree or a rock appears to be a single solid thing but in reality is composed of a multitude of atoms. The most accurate knowledge available to us is produced by the mathematical analysis of moving bodies, not only as in astronomy but also closer to hand as in physics.

The rigor of Galileo's thinking lay in his method of focusing strictly upon exact mathematical demonstrations and avoiding secondhand information based simply upon tradition and opposing conjectures contained in books. "To demonstrate to my opponents the truth of my conclusions," Galileo said, "I have been forced to prove them by a variety of experiments." Some notion of the stubborn mood of the established scholars of his day who held to older ways of knowing is found in Galileo's letter to his fellow astronomer Johannes Kepler: "My dear Kepler, what would you say of the learned here, who, replete with the pertinacity of the asp, have steadfastly refused to cast a glance through the telescope? What shall we make of all this? Shall we laugh or shall we cry?"

Having in mind the distinction between primary and secondary qualities, Galileo certainly gave the impression that only those qualities that belong to bodies or matter have true reality. Primary qualities, such as size, position, motion, and density, are truly real because they can be dealt with mathematically. By contrast, secondary qualities, such as color, taste, emotions, and sounds, "reside only in consciousness; if the living creature were removed, all these qualities would be wiped away and annihilated." A human being can be defined as a body with physical organs. But when one is defined as a person, it turns out that most personal characteristics are represented by secondary qualities. This would mean that either these secondary qualities must be explained mathematically as being aspects of the primary qualities of matter or that the secondary qualities do not participate at all in the realm of reality. In either case, the unique dignity, value, or special status of human beings in the nature of things is severely diminished.

Sir Isaac Newton (1642–1727), accepting the view that nature is composed of "particles and bodies," expressed the wish that all the phenomena of nature could be explained "by the same kind of reasoning derived from mechanical principles, for I am induced by many reasons to suspect that they may all de-

pend upon certain forces by which the particles or bodies...are either mutually impelled towards one another and cohere in regular figures, or are repelled
and recede from one another." Accordingly, Newton refined the earlier formulations of the laws of motion in his great work *Principia,* a work which had
enormous influence for generations to come. Although Newton still spoke of
God as the one who created the machine of nature, it became increasingly unnecessary to refer to God when explaining the phenomena of nature. The whole
drift of the new scientific method was toward a new conception of humanity,
of nature, and of the whole mechanism of human knowledge.

As the universe was now viewed as a system of bodies in motion, so now
all other aspects of nature were described as bodies in motion. Humanity and
human thought also were soon to be viewed in mechanical terms. If all things
consist of bodies in motion, this mechanical behavior, it was thought, must be
capable of mathematical description. Thus, again, observation and the use of
mathematics emerged in the Renaissance as the ingredients of the new method
of scientific thought. With this method, it was assumed that new knowledge
could be discovered. It was the view of Renaissance scientists that medieval
thinkers had simply worked out explanatory systems for what people already
knew but had provided no method for discovering new information. But the
spirit of discovery, dramatized by Columbus' discovery of a new continent and
by the discovery of new worlds in the arts, in literature, and in the unused
faculties and capacities of people, was now impelling scientists to open up new
worlds in the structure of nature. And it was this new attitude of science that
had the most immediate effect upon the development of modern philosophy,
especially upon Francis Bacon and Thomas Hobbes, to whom we now turn.

11

Advocates
of the Method
of Science:
Bacon and Hobbes

s the world of science began to open, it was inevitable that philosophy would be affected by this new way of discovering facts. Among the early modern thinkers who saw in the methods of science a fresh way of developing knowledge and who therefore sought to utilize these methods for the enterprise of philosophy were Sir Francis Bacon and Thomas Hobbes. The old and the new ways of thinking had not yet been clearly separated, so science still clung to some traditional ways of thinking and philosophy had not adjusted itself to the methods and assumptions of science. What had to be done now was to make science and philosophy consistent with each other, and it was in doing just this that Bacon and Hobbes launched philosophy upon its modern course.

FRANCIS BACON: METHOD AS THE KEY TO KNOWLEDGE

Francis Bacon assigned himself the task of reforming the philosophy and science of his day. His central criticism was that learning had become stagnant. Science was identified with learning, and learning meant reading ancient texts.

The study of medicine, for example, was chiefly literary and was practiced by poets, rhetoricians, and clergymen, whose qualification to practice was their ability to quote Hippocrates and Galen. Philosophy was still dominated by Plato and Aristotle, whose teachings Bacon denounced as "shadows" and "phantoms." Because he emphasized the utility of knowledge, having said that "Knowledge is power," he was particularly agitated by the "uselessness" of traditional learning. What made this learning useless was that science had become mixed up with "superstition," unguided speculation, and theology. Bacon challenged this approach to science as having no adequate method for discovering what nature and its workings are really like. The one ancient thinker for whom he did have respect was Democritus, whose materialism he adopted. But the teachings of the Schoolmen of the Middle Ages he considered as "degenerate" versions of Aristotle and of no merit because, instead of deriving substantial evidence from the actual nature of things, they worked upon their own imaginations and as spiders brought forth "cobwebs of learning, admirable for the fineness of thread and work, but of no substance or profit."

Bacon advocated wiping the slate of human knowledge clean and starting over again, using a new method for assembling and explaining facts. He was convinced that he had discovered such a method, which would unlock all the secrets of nature. He was aware of other attempts to correct the inadequacies of traditional learning, particularly attempts by Gilbert, Copernicus, and Galileo to amend Aristotle's physics. But what impressed him most was Galileo's construction and use of telescopes, an event he considered one of the most important in the history of astronomy because it made possible an advancement of learning. Whereas the ancients did not know the composition of the Milky Way, the telescope made it evident that the Milky Way is a collection of distant stars. Bacon considered the mind as being like a glass or mirror, which had been made rough and uneven both by natural tendencies of passions as well as by the errors of traditional learning. In such a condition, the mind cannot reflect truth accurately. Bacon's method, and his hope, was to make the mind's surface clean and smooth and to supply it with new and adequate instruments so that it could observe and understand the universe accurately. To achieve this, he would have to free science from entrenched and traditional learning, separate scientific truth from revealed truths of theology, and fashion a new philosophy based upon a new method of observation and a new interpretation of nature.

By birth and breeding, Bacon was destined to live, work, and think in a style befitting one of high station. He was born in 1561, the son of Sir Nicholas Bacon, who was then Lord Keeper of the Great Seal. He entered Cambridge at the age of twelve and at the age of sixteen was admitted at a relatively senior status to the legal world of Gray's Inn. Through the succeeding years, he was honored by Queen Elizabeth and King James I as a member of Parliament, the House of Lords, and in time became Solicitor-General, Lord Keeper, and finally Lord Chancellor. When one considers that Bacon engaged in a full legal and political career and in addition wrote philosophical works of great breadth and significance, among which his *Advancement of Learning* and *Novum Organum* are the best known, his precocious nature can be all the more appreciated. But he was aware that his political life had interfered with his primary objectives as a thinker, saying that "I reckoned that I was by no means discharging my duty, when I was neglecting that by which I could of myself benefit man." To add further misery to his last years, he was, shortly after being named Lord Chancellor, accused of accepting bribes and was thereupon fined, sentenced to a short imprisonment, and barred from public office forever. The end came when, pursuing his zeal for experimentation, wondering whether the putrefaction of flesh could be halted by freezing, he went out in the cold and stuffed a chicken with snow, getting badly chilled, from which affliction he died in a few days in 1626 at the age of sixty-five.

Bacon's ideal objective was, as he said, "the total reconstruction of the sciences, arts and all human knowledge," and this he called his "great instauration." But before he could proceed with his creative task, he leveled some fierce criticisms against Oxford, Cambridge, and universities in general, and also against the reigning schools of philosophy, denouncing them for their slavish attachment to the past. It was Bacon who gathered up the rising discontent with medieval philosophy and sounded the call for a break with the lingering influence of Aristotle. The mood in which Bacon carried out his attack upon the past ways of thinking can best be discovered in his treatment of the "distempers of learning" and the Idols that proceed from the mind, which "are not sincere, but of an ill and corrupt nature."

Distempers of Learning   Bacon named the three distempers of learning, *fantastical* learning, *contentious* learning, and *delicate* learning. These he considered the vices or major diseases of learning, and he described how they distort knowledge. In fantastical learning, people concern themselves with words, emphasizing texts, languages, and style, and "hunt more after words than matter, and more after choiceness of phrase... than after the weight of matter." Contentious learning is even worse, he said, because it begins with the fixed positions or points of view taken by earlier thinkers, and these views are used as the starting point in contentious argumentation. Finally, there is delicate learning, wherein earlier authors, who claim more knowledge than can be proved, are accepted by readers as knowing as much as they claim, and this accounts for the acceptance of Aristotle, for example, as the dictator of science. These three diseases, he argued, must be cured in order to relieve the mind of the errors they engender.

Idols of the Mind   Likewise, the human mind is corrupted by Idols. Bacon refers to four Idols, which he metaphorically calls the Idols of the *Tribe*, the *Cave*, the *Market Place*, and the *Theatre*. These Idols, or "false phantoms," are distortions of the mind, like distortions of beams of light reflected from an uneven mirror: "For from the nature of a clear and equal glass, wherein the beams of things should reflect according to their true incidence, it is rather like an enchanted glass, full of superstition and imposture." The only way to correct this wayward mode of thought is through observation and experimentation, through the inductive method. These Idols, or "false opinions," "dogmas," "superstitions" and "errors," distort knowledge in many ways.

The Idols of the Tribe are humanity's preoccupation with opinions, following from "the false assertion that the sense of man is the measure of things." Here Bacon wanted to make the point that simply looking at things is no guarantee we shall see them as they really are, because we all bring our hopes and fears, prejudices, and impatience to things and thereby affect our understanding of them.

The Idols of the Cave were taken by Bacon from the Platonic allegory and again suggest the limitations of the untrained mind, which is shut in the cave of its own environment of customs and opinions, reflecting the kinds of books one reads, the ideas one considers significant, and the intellectual authorities to whom one defers.

The third class of Idols is very aptly designated as the Idols of the Market Place, for it stands for the words people use in the commerce of daily life, words that are common coin in daily conversation. In spite of their usefulness, words can weaken knowledge, because they are not created with care or precision but framed so that the common person will understand their use. And even philosophers are diverted by these Idols, for they often give names to things that exist only in their imagination and, in addition, fashion names for abstractions derived from things, such as *element of fire* or *fortune*, or such names of qualities as *heavy, rare*, or *dense*.

Finally, the Idols of the Theatre are the grand systematic dogmas of long philosophic treatises, "representing worlds of their own creation after an unreal and scenic fashion." Bacon wants to include here not only whole systems, but all principles or axioms in science that "by tradition, credulity and negligence have come to be received."

Inductive Method Having duly warned his generation that the understanding can be distorted by these Idols, Bacon set forth a new method for acquiring knowledge. In order to "penetrate into the inner and further recesses of nature," he said, "it is necessary that our notion... be derived from things in a more sure and guarded way." This way would include ridding oneself of his prejudices ("unless one become as a child") and looking at things as they are: "We must lead men to the particulars themselves, and their series and order." To guide and help observation it is necessary to supply "rectifications to correct its errors; and this I endeavour to accomplish not so much by instruments as by *experiments*. For the subtlety of experiments is far greater than that of sense itself."

Bacon's concept of experiment and his method of observation, however, did not lead to what we today know as the scientific method. He relied too much upon pure induction, that is, upon the possibility of deriving "laws" from the simple observation of particulars and their series and order. Bacon knew the limitations of "induction by simple enumeration," for example, concluding that all horses are black because the first eighteen counted were black; but in going beyond this type of induction, he ironically lapsed back into a search for a "substance," a procedure more appropriate to an Aristotelian.

The example he gave of his inductive method was the outline of how one could investigate the cause of heat. The first step is to draw up a list of all the forms in which we encounter heat, producing a *Table of Essence and Presence.* Next, another list must be compiled to include items that resemble those on the first list but that do not have heat, and this second list he called the *Table of Deviation.* Thus, the first list would include the sun, and the second would include the moon. A third, the *Table of Comparison*, is a further attempt to discover the nature of heat by analyzing the different degrees of heat to be found in different things, "as in fishes, quadrupeds, serpents, birds,...man,... planets." The fourth step is the *Process of Exclusion*, whereby, setting "induction to work," we try to find some "nature" that is present whenever there is heat and absent when heat is absent. Is light the cause of heat? No, because the moon is bright but is not hot. This process of exclusion was central to Bacon's method of science, and this process he called "the foundation of true induction." He assumed that "the Form of a thing is to be found in each and all the instances, in which the thing itself is to be found." Applying this assumption to the problem of heat, Bacon concluded that "from a survey of all instances, all and each, the nature of which heat is a particular case appears to be Motion." This conclusion has an Aristotelian sound when Bacon says that "Heat itself, its essence and quiddity, is Motion and nothing else," for essences are what Aristotle talked about. This suggests that Bacon's break with Aristotle was not complete, for he clung to the concept of substance. The final step, however, does have a modern ring, for Bacon wanted to verify his conclusions by checking them against all the items produced in his tables.

The major weakness in Bacon's method is that he had no grasp of what modern scientists mean by an hypothesis. Bacon assumed that if one simply looked at enough facts, an hypothesis would suggest itself, whereas a modern scientist knows it is necessary to have an hypothesis before one inspects facts in order to have some guide in the selection of facts relevant to the experiment. Furthermore, only if one begins with an hypothesis does deduction as well as induction play a large part in science. Bacon also underestimated the importance of mathematics for science. But he had, nevertheless, dislodged the grip of scholastic thought and provided the impetus for making philosophy scientific. The addition of mathematical and deductive reasoning to scientific philosophy was achieved in England by Bacon's friend and countryman, Thomas Hobbes.

THOMAS HOBBES: A SINGLE METHOD FOR KNOWING MATTER, MAN, AND THE STATE

The life of Thomas Hobbes spans ninety-one eventful years, from 1588 to 1679. He was born at Westport near Malmesbury, England, the son of a vicar. His education at Oxford stirred in him a fascination for classical literature, whereas his exposure to Aristotelian logic left him bored. In 1608 he left Oxford and had the good fortune of becoming the tutor of the Earl of Devonshire, William Cavendish. This association with the Cavendish family was to influence Hobbes' development significantly, as it afforded him the opportunity to travel widely on the Continent and to meet many leading thinkers and personages of the day. In Italy he met Galileo, and in Paris he formed a lasting friendship with Descartes' admirer Mersenne and also Descartes' antagonist Gassendi. There is some question whether he ever met Descartes in person, but his carefully reasoned objections to the *Meditations* indicate Hobbes' close familiarity with Descartes' philosophy. In England, Hobbes was much admired by Bacon, who, as Lord Chancellor, enjoyed conversation with him and frequently dictated his thoughts to Hobbes during "delicious walkes at Gorambery." Hobbes' early interest in classics led him to translate Thucydides, but his discovery of Euclid's *Elements* in his early forties shifted his interest to mathematics and analysis. The next stage of his development, which was to persist for the rest of his life, witnessed the publication of his brilliant philosophical treatises, among which the most renowned is his *Leviathan*.

Influence of Geometry upon Hobbes' Thought Although the *Leviathan* is primarily a book on social and political philosophy, Hobbes had not intended to restrict his attention to that subject. Caught up in the rising tide of scientific discovery, he was deeply impressed by the precision of science and above all by the certainty of scientific knowledge. The intellectual atmosphere of the sixteenth and seventeenth centuries had been undergoing a radical alteration as one area of inquiry after another yielded to the probing method of science. Copernicus (1473–1543) had called into question the traditional view of astronomy, which had remained virtually unchanged and unchallenged since Ptolemy (second century, Egypt) had argued that the earth is the center of the universe. Against this Ptolemaic view, Copernicus held, "at length by much and long observation" of the "motions of the other planets," and having "calculated as for the revolution of that planet [the earth]," that the earth revolves on its axis and moves in a circular path around the sun, thus making the sun the center, instead of the earth. This was a major development, but equally important was the method Copernicus had employed, a method characterized by two salient features, namely, the observation of moving bodies and the mathematical calculation of the motion of bodies in space.

By the time Hobbes appeared on the intellectual scene, what Copernicus had begun was now considerably refined by Kepler (1571–1630) and particularly by Galileo (1564–1642), who not only emphasized the importance of observation, which led to his discovery of the satellites around the planet Jupiter, but who sought to give astronomy the precision of geometry. By using the model of geometry for his reasoning about astronomy, Galileo assumed that he could demonstrate the accuracy of his conclusions if he could, as one does in geometry, produce basic axioms from which to deduce his conclusions. Moreover, he assumed that empirical facts correspond to geometric axioms, or that the axioms that the mind formulates correspond to the actual characteristics of ob-

Title page, Hobbes' ***Leviathan,*** **1652** *(The Bettmann Archive)*

servable moving bodies. To think in terms of geometry is to know how things actually behave. Specifically, Galileo formulated, for the first time, a geometric representation of the motion of bodies and their acceleration. Galileo helped to perfect a method that, in their own way, Francis Bacon in his *Novum Organum* (1620) and Descartes in his *Discourse on Method* (1637) had attempted. What most of these thinkers had in common was their belief that human knowledge about the nature of things is available to anyone who used the appropriate method in its pursuit. Instead of looking back to tradition or to the testimony of ancient authorities, individuals can have direct access to the truth about nature, and this truth would most likely be discovered if one took the information received through observation and organized it into a system of axioms.

Hobbes caught the spirit of the times. His initial fascination with mathematics came from his encounter with Euclid's *Elements*, a book that "made [him] in love with geometry." Hobbes joined that small but eloquent company of thinkers who saw in geometry the key to the study of nature. With a razor-sharp intellect and a fervor that caused him to exaggerate the possibilities of this method, Hobbes undertook to recast the whole gamut of knowledge in accordance with this single approach. Hobbes assumed that it mattered little what the object of study was, that the method of observation and deductive reasoning from axioms, formed from observation, would yield exact knowledge. He therefore set out an ambitious project, which was to recast the study of physical nature, the nature of humanity, and the nature of human society, using the same method throughout. He published *De Cive* (*The Citizen*) in 1642, *De Corpore* (*Concerning Body*) in 1655, and *De Homine* (*Concerning Man*) in 1658. In the end, it was his political philosophy that made him famous, for it was here that his application of rigorous logic and the scientific method produced startling new results.

As a political philosopher, Hobbes is frequently, though not accurately, called the father of modern totalitarianism. His books *De Cive* and *Leviathan* read like grammars of obedience. He describes the relation between citizen and sovereign in such severe terms that it is no wonder he brought upon himself widespread criticism. Two considerations led Hobbes to formulate his unique theory of political obligation. The first was the political turbulence of his times, which saw Cromwell preparing to lead his people in a savage civil war. This experience of violence growing out of deep disagreements on political matters contrasted sharply in Hobbes' mind with the relatively quick agreements people achieved in mathematical and scientific matters. Secondly, Hobbes looked at political philosophy as a variation of the science of physics. He assumed that from a thoroughly materialistic view of human nature, in which human behavior could be explained simply in terms of bodies in motion, he could formulate an accurate political philosophy. It was his hope that if political theory could be formulated with logical precision, men would be more likely to achieve agreement among themselves and thereby arrive at what Hobbes longed for most of all, namely, peace and order. There is some question whether Hobbes was logically consistent in his systematic political philosophy, and there is even greater question about his assumption that people would become orderly in their relations to each other just because they had been provided a logical plan for harmonious behavior. In any case, his theory of humanity and society took its novel turn mainly because he built it according to a mechanical model, the chief ingredients of which were bodies and motion. And because Hobbes' political theory depends so much upon his unique theory of knowledge and his mechanical model of reality, these aspects of his philosophy need to be considered in some detail as the background to his views on political community.

Bodies in Motion: The Object of Thought   Philosophy, according to Hobbes, is concerned chiefly with the causes and characteristics of bodies. There are three major types of bodies, physical bodies such as stones, the human body, and the body politic. Philosophy is concerned with all three types, inquiring into their causes and characteristics. There is one principal characteristic that all bodies share and that alone makes it possible to understand how they came to be and do what they do, and that characteristic is motion. Motion is a key concept in Hobbes' thought. Equally important is the assumption Hobbes makes that only bodies exist, that knowable reality consists solely of bodies. He will not admit that anything such as *spirit* or *God* exists if these terms refer to beings that have no bodies, or are incorporeal. Of God's existence, Hobbes writes that "by the visible things in this world, and their admirable order, a man may conceive there is a cause of them, which men call God: and yet not have an idea or image of him in his mind." Hobbes was willing to concede *that* God exists but argued that people do not know *what* God is. Still, it made no sense to Hobbes that there could be something with an *incorporeal substance*, as the theologians characterized God. Substance, he argued, could be only corporeal, wherefore God would possess some form of body. But Hobbes did not wish to pursue theological subtleties and appears to have dealt with God's nature in this connection only to make the broader point that whatever exists is corporeal and that the scope of philosophy is limited to the study of bodies in motion.

Hobbes set out to explain both physical and mental events as nothing more than bodies in motion. "Motion," says Hobbes, "is a continual relinquishing of one place and acquiring of another." Anything that moves is changing its location, and, similarly, whatever is caused to move changes its place. If something is at rest, it will always be at rest unless something moves it. Only a moving body can cause a resting body to move, for "by endeavoring to get into its place by motion [it] suffers it no longer to remain at rest." Similarly, a body in motion tends to stay in motion unless its movement is halted by some other body. This account of motion appears to be restricted to locomotion, for such concepts as inertia, force, impetus, resistance, and endeavor, terms that Hobbes uses to describe motion, all seem to apply to things in space that occupy or change their location. But since Hobbes started with the premise that only bodies exist, it was inevitable that he would have to explain all of reality and all processes in terms of moving bodies. Motion is therefore not only locomotion in the simple sense but is also what we know as the process of change. Things become different because something in them has been moved by something else, and this refers not only to physical but also to mental change.

Besides the kind of motion Galileo described as he charted the course of the stars and planets, or the more obvious modes of locomotion, Hobbes refers to two kinds of motion that are peculiar to animals or people, namely, *vital* and *voluntary* motions. Vital motions begin with the process of birth, continue through life, and include such motions as pulse, nutrition, excretion, the course of the blood, and breathing, "to which motions there needs no help of imagination." On the other hand, voluntary motions, such as going, speaking, and the deliberate movement of our limbs, are first of all movements in our minds, and "because *going, speaking* and the like voluntary motions, depend always upon a precedent thought of *whither, which way*, and *what*; it is evident that the imagination is the first internal beginning of all voluntary motion." Imagination is the cause of voluntary acts, but imagination itself and the human activity we call *thought* are also explained as being effects of prior causes, as being consequences of prior motions.

Mechanical View of Human Thought   The human mind works in various ways, ranging from *perception, imagination, memory*, to *thinking*. All of these modes of mental activity are fundamentally the same because they are all motions in our bodies. That perception, imagination, and memory are alike was particularly obvious to Hobbes. Perception, by which he meant our ability to "sense" things, is our basic mental act, and the others are "derived from that original." The whole structure and process of human thought is explained as bodies in motion, and the variations in mental activity are accounted for by designating the location of each type of mental act along a describable causal chain. Thus, the thought process begins when a body external to us moves and causes a motion inside of us, as when we *see* a tree, and seeing the tree is *perception* or *sensation*. When we look at an object, we see what Hobbes called a *phantasm*. A phantasm is the image within us caused by an object outside of us. Perception is not the sensation *of* motion, or the sensation of the exact qualities an object actually possesses. We see the green tree, but *green* and *tree* are two *phantasms*, a *quality* and an *object*, and these represent the *ways* we experience the motion caused by the body external to us. The initial impact upon us caused by an external object creates not only our immediate sensation but more lasting effects as well, just as on the ocean, though the wind cease, "the waves give not over rolling for a long time after." And, "so also it happeneth in that motion, which is made in the internal parts of man...for after the object is removed, or the eye shut, we still retain an image of the thing seen, though more obscure than when we see it." This retention of the image within us after the object is removed is what Hobbes means by imagination. Thus, imagination is simply a lingering, or what Hobbes called a *decaying*, sensation. When, later, we wish to express this decay and indicate that the sense is fading, we call this *memory,* "so that imagination and memory are but one thing, which for divers considerations hath divers names."

It would appear that thinking, as when we have conversation with each other, is something quite different from sensation and memory. In sensation the sequence of images in our mind is determined by what is happening, moving, outside of us, whereas in thinking we seem to put ideas together whichever way we wish. But, using his mechanical model, Hobbes explained thinking in exactly the same terms that he used in his account of sensation, so that thinking, for him, is a variation of sensation. Ideas follow each other in thought because they first followed each other in sensation, for "those motions that immediately succeeded one another in sense, continue also together after sense." Our ideas have a firm relationship to each other for the reason that in any form of continued motion, and thought is such a motion, "one part follows another by cohesion." But the mechanism of thought is not all that perfect, and people are always thinking in ways that do not mirror their past sensations exactly. Hobbes was aware of this, but he tried to explain even the broken sequences as the invasions of more dominant sensations into the stream of imagination and memory, as when the thought of the civil war might remind him of a personal experience and thereby break the chain of events for which the civil war stood in his memory. He wanted to establish the view that nothing happens in thinking that cannot be accounted for by sensation and memory.

Still, there is a difference between the mind of an animal and the mind of a human being, even though both have sensation and memory. What distinguishes them is that people are able to form *signs* or *names* to mark their sensations. With these names people are able to recall their sensations. Moreover, science and philosophy are possible because of the human capacity to formulate words and sentences. Knowledge, then, takes on two different forms, one being knowledge of *fact* and the other knowledge of *consequences*. Knowledge of fact is simply memory of past events. Knowledge of consequences is hypothetical or conditional, but still based upon experience, for it affirms that *if A is true, B* will also be true, or, using Hobbes' illustration, "If the figure shown be a circle, then any straight line through the center shall divide it into two equal parts." Scientific knowledge, or philosophy in the broad sense, is possible only because of the human capacity to use words and speech. Although Hobbes spoke of signs and names as "word(s) taken at pleasure to serve for a mark," these words represent our experiences. Words and sentences point to the actual way things behave. Reasoning with words is therefore not the same as playing with words, for once the meaning of words is established, certain consequences follow for their use, mirroring the reality they help our imaginations recall. Thus, to say that *a human is a living creature* is a true proposition for the two reasons that the word *human* already includes the idea of living and that the word *human* is a mark for the sensation we have when we see an actual human being. The relation of words to each other is based upon the relations between the events for which the words stand as representations. Reasoning, then, is "nothing but *reckoning*, that is adding and subtracting, of consequences of general names...." And even if the word *human* does not refer to any general or universal reality but only to particular people, Hobbes still maintains that we have reliable knowledge, that although "experience concludeth nothing universally," science, based on experience, does "conclude universally." This is Hobbes' *nominalism*, which led him to say that universal terms such as *human* are merely words and point to no general reality, and his *empiricism*, which led him to argue that we can know things about all people because of what we know from our experience about some people.

Political Philosophy and Morality   When we turn directly to Hobbes' political philosophy, we find that he employed as much of his theory of motion and his logic, as well as the method of geometry, as this subject would permit. Just as he looked to the concepts of motion and bodies to describe the nature of people, and particularly to describe human knowledge, so also he now analyzes the structure and nature of the state in terms of moving bodies. Moreover, his account of the state is the most impressive example of his conception of philosophy, for if philosophy is a matter of "*reckoning*, that is adding and subtracting, of consequences of general names," it is preeminently in his political philosophy that he exhibits his skill and rigor with the meanings of words.

What strikes one first about Hobbes' theory of state is that he approaches the subject not from an historical point of view but from the vantage point of logic and analysis. He does not ask, "*when* did civil societies emerge?" but asks rather, "*how* do you explain the emergence of society?" He is concerned to discover the *cause* of civil society, and in harmony with his general method sets out to explain the cause of the state by describing the motion of bodies. His thought about political philosophy resembles the method of geometry only in the sense that from axiomlike premises he deduces all the consequences or conclusions of his political theory, and most of these premises cluster around his conception of human nature.

The State of Nature Hobbes describes people, first of all, as they appear in what he calls the *state of nature*, which is the condition of people before there is any state or civil society. In this state of nature all humans are equal and equally have the right to whatever they consider necessary for their survival. Equality here means simply that people are capable of hurting their neighbors and taking what they judge they need for their own protection. Differences in strength can in time be overcome and the weak can destroy the strong. The "right of all to all" which prevails in the state of nature does not mean that one person has a right whereas others have corresponding duties. The word *right* in the bare state of nature is a person's *freedom* "to do what he would, and against whom he thought fit, and to possess, use and enjoy all that he would, or could get." The driving force in a person is the will to survive, and the psychological mood pervading all people is fear, the fear of death and particularly the fear of violent death. In the state of nature all people are relentlessly pursuing whatever acts they think will secure their safety. The picture one gets of this state of nature is of people moving against each other, bodies in motion, or the anarchic condition Hobbes called "the war of all against all."

Why do people behave this way? Hobbes analyzes human motivation by saying that everyone possesses a twofold *endeavor*, namely *appetite* and *aversion*. These two endeavors account for a person's motions to and from persons or objects, and have the same meanings as the words *love* and *hate*. People are attracted to what they think will help them survive, and they hate whatever they judge to be a threat to them. The words *good* and *evil* have whatever meaning each individual will give them, and people will call *good* whatever they love and *evil* whatever they hate, "there being nothing simply and absolutely so." Humans are fundamentally egotistical in that they are concerned chiefly about their own survival and identify goodness with their own appetites. It would appear therefore that in the state of nature there is no obligation for humanity to respect others or that there is no morality in the traditional sense of goodness and justice. Given this egotistical view of human nature, it would appear also that humanity did not possess the capacity to create an ordered and peaceful society.

But Hobbes argued that several logical conclusions or consequences can be deduced from humanity's concern for its survival, among these being what Hobbes called *natural laws*. Even in the state of nature, people *know* these natural laws, which are logically consistent with people's principal concern for their own safety. A natural law, said Hobbes, "is a precept, or general rule, found out by reason," telling what to do and what not to do. If the major premise is that I want to survive, I can logically deduce, even in the state of nature, certain rules of behavior that will help me to survive. The first law of nature is therefore that every man ought to "seek peace and follow it." Now this law that urges me to seek peace is natural because it is a logical extension of my concern for survival. It is obvious that I have a better chance to survive if I help to create the conditions of peace. My desire for survival therefore impels me to seek peace. From this first and fundamental law of nature is derived the second law, which states that "a man be willing, when others are so too, as farforth as for peace, and defense of himself he shall think it necessary, to lay down his right to all things; and be contented with so much liberty against other men, as he would allow other men against himself."

Obligation in the State of Nature   If people know these and other natural laws even in the state of nature, do they have an obligation to obey them? Hobbes answers that these laws are always binding, in the state of nature as well as in civil society. But he distinguishes between two ways in which these natural laws are applicable in the state of nature, saying that "the laws of nature oblige *in foro interno*; that is to say, they bind to a desire they should take place: but *in foro externo*; that is, to putting them in act, not always." Thus, it isn't as if there were no obligation in the state of nature; rather, the circumstances for living by these laws in the state of nature are not always present. People have a right to all things in the state of nature not because there is no obligation, but because if a person were modest, tractable, and kept his promises "in such time and place where no man else should do so, [he] should but make himself a prey to others, and procure his own ruin, contrary to the ground of all laws of nature, which tend to nature's preservations." And even when people act to preserve themselves, they are not free from rational natural laws, for even in the state of nature they ought to act in good faith: "If any man *pretend* somewhat to tend necessarily to his preservation, which yet he himself doth not confidently believe so, he may offend against the laws of nature."

Hobbes was aware that the logical outcome of egotistical individuals all deciding how best to survive would be anarchy, where there were "no arts; no letters; no society; and which is worst of all, continual fear, and danger of violent death; and the life of man solitary, poor, nasty, brutish, and short...." To avoid such a condition of anarchy, the chief cause of which is the conflict of individual and egotistical judgments of right, people, following the dictates of natural law, seeking peace, renounce some of their rights or freedoms and enter into a social contract and thereby create an artificial person, that great *le-viathan*, called a *commonwealth*, or *state*.

The Social Contract   The contract by which people avoid the state of na-ture and enter civil society is an agreement between individuals, "as if every man should say to every man, *I authorize and give up my right of governing myself, to this man, or to this assembly of men, on this condition, that thou give up thy right to him, and authorize all his actions in like manner*." Two things stand out clearly in this contract. First, the parties to the contract are individuals who promise each other to hand over their right to govern them-selves to the sovereign; it is not a contract between the sovereign and the citi-zens. The sovereign has absolute power to govern and is in no way subject to the citizens. Secondly, Hobbes clearly states that the sovereign can be either "this man" or "this assembly of men," suggesting that in theory, at least, his view of sovereignty was not identified with any particular form of government. It may be that he had a preference for a single ruler with absolute power, but he recognized the possible compatibility of his theory of sovereignty with "de-mocracy." But whatever form the sovereign would take, it is clear that Hobbes saw the transfer of the right to rule from the people to the sovereign as both absolute and irrevocable.

Hobbes was particularly anxious to demonstrate with logical rigor that sovereign power is indivisible. Having shown that in the state of nature anar-chy is the logical consequence of independent individual judgments, he con-cluded that the only way to overcome such anarchy is to make a single body out of the several bodies of the citizens. The only way to transform multiple wills into a single will is to agree that the sovereign's single will and judgment represent the will and judgment of all the citizens. In effect, this is what the contract says when people agree to hand over their right to govern themselves. The sovereign now acts not only on behalf of the citizens but *as if* he embod-ied the will of the citizens, thereby affirming an identity between the wills of the sovereign and citizens. Resistance against the sovereign by a citizen is there-fore illogical on two counts, first because it would amount to resistance to him-self, and secondly, to resist is to revert to independent judgment, which is to revert to the state of nature or anarchy. The power of the sovereign must there-fore be absolute in order to secure the conditions of order, peace, and law.

Civil Law versus Natural Law   Law begins only when there is a sovereign. This is a logical truism, for in the judicial or *legal* sense, a *law* is defined as a command of the sovereign. It follows that where there is no sovereign, there is no law. To be sure, Hobbes affirmed that even in the state of nature people have knowledge of the natural law, and in a special sense the natural law is binding even in the state of nature. But only after there is a sovereign can there be a legal order, because only then is there the apparatus of law in which the power of enforcement is central. Without the power to enforce, said Hobbes, covenants are "mere words." Hobbes identifies law with sovereign command and makes the additional point that "there can be no unjust law."

Nowhere does Hobbes' severe authoritarianism express itself in more startling form than when he argues that there can be no unjust law. It appears that justice and morality begin with the sovereign, that there are no principles of justice and morality that precede and limit the acts of the sovereign. Hobbes affirmed this in a notable passage: "To the care of the sovereign, belongeth the making of good laws. But what is a good law? By good law, I mean not a just law: for no law can be unjust." Hobbes gives two reasons for saying no law can be unjust: first, because justice means obeying the law, and this is why justice comes into being only after a law has been made and cannot itself be the standard for law; secondly, when a sovereign makes a law, it is as though the people were making the law, and what they agree upon cannot be unjust. Indeed, the third natural law Hobbes speaks of is *that men perform their covenants made*," and he indicated that this is the "fountain of justice." Hence, to keep the contract in which you agreed to obey the sovereign is the essence of Hobbesian justice.

It is evident that Hobbes forces the reader to take each word seriously and "reckon" all the "consequences" that can be deduced from it. If law means the sovereign's command and if justice means obeying the law, there can be no *unjust* law. But there can be a *bad* law, for Hobbes was enough of an Aristotelian to recognize that a sovereign has a definite purpose "for which he was trusted with the sovereign power, namely, the procuration of *the safety of the people*; to which he is obliged by the law of nature, and to render an account thereof to God." But even in such a case, where the sovereign has commanded a "bad" law, the citizens are not the ones to judge it as such, nor does this justify their disobedience. The sovereign has the sole power to judge what is for the safety of the people; if the people disagreed with him, they would revert to anarchy. If the sovereign engages in iniquitous acts, this is a matter between the sovereign and God, not between the citizens and the sovereign. And because he feared anarchy and disorder so deeply, Hobbes pushed his logic of obedience to the point of making religion and the church subordinate to the state. To the Christian who felt that the sovereign's command violated the law of God, Hobbes gave no comfort but insisted that if such a person could not obey the sovereign, he must "go to Christ in martyrdom."

With these bold strokes, Hobbes altered the course of philosophy. He was among the first to apply the methods of science to the study of human nature, providing novel explanations for human knowledge and moral behavior, departing also from the medieval notion of natural law, and arriving in the end at a highly authoritarian concept of sovereignty. Although Hobbes did not win widespread approval in his day, and even though there is much in his philosophy to question and criticize, his enduring influence was assured by the precision of his formulation of the problems of philosophy.

12

Rationalism on the Continent: Descartes, Spinoza, and Leibniz

Although philosophy rarely alters its direction and mood with radical suddenness, there are times when its new concerns and emphases clearly separate it from its immediate past. Such was the case with seventeenth-century Continental rationalism, whose founder was René Descartes and whose new program initiated what is called *modern philosophy*. In a sense, much of what the Continental rationalists set out to do had already been attempted by the medieval philosophers and by Bacon and Hobbes. But Descartes, Spinoza, and Leibniz fashioned a new ideal for philosophy. Influenced by the progress and success of science and mathematics, their new program was an attempt to provide philosophy with the exactness of mathematics. They set out to formulate clear rational principles that could be organized into a system of truths from which accurate information about the world could be deduced. Their emphasis was upon the rational capacity of the human mind, which they now considered the source of truth both about man and about the world. Although they did not reject the claims of religion, they did consider philosophical reasoning something independent of supernatural revelation. Although they saw little value in subjective feeling and enthusiasm as means for discovering truth, they did believe that the mind of an individual is structured in such a way that simply by operating according to the appropriate method it can discover the nature of the universe. This was an optimistic view of human reason, which offset the recent attempts, by Montaigne and Charron, at reviving ancient skepticism. The rationalists assumed that what they could think clearly with their minds did in fact exist in the world outside their minds. Descartes and Leibniz even argued that certain ideas are innate in the human mind, that, given the proper occasion, experience would cause these innate truths to become self-evident. That the highly optimistic program of rationalism was not altogether successful is indicated by the differences in the three systems it produced. To be sure, all the rationalists finally interpreted the natural world after the mechanical model of physics and ascribed determinism to all physical events. But Descartes described reality as a dualism consisting of two basic substances, thought and extension; Spinoza proposed a monism, saying that there is only a single substance, Nature, which has various attributes and modes; Leibniz was a pluralist, saying that although there is only one kind of substance, the monad, there are nevertheless different kinds of monads accounting for the various elements in nature. The British empiricists, Locke, Berkeley, and Hume, who can be considered a second group of modern philosophers following closely after the rationalists, asked some searching questions about the premises of the rationalists; some of these questions have not been satisfactorily answered to this day.

DESCARTES

René Descartes, usually called the "father of modern philosophy," was born in Touraine in 1596. His father, Joachim Descartes, was a councillor of the Parliament of Brittany. From 1604 to 1612 young Descartes studied in the Jesuit college of La Flèche, where his education included mathematics, logic, and philosophy. He was most impressed, during these years, with the certainty and precision of mathematics, as compared with philosophy, whose teachings invariably produced doubts and disputes. For a time he was a soldier in the army of Maximilian of Bavaria. After traveling widely throughout Europe, he decided, in 1628, to settle down in Holland, and it was here that Descartes wrote his principal works, including his *Discourse on Method* (1637), *Meditations on First Philosophy* (1641), *Principles of Philosophy* (1644), and *The Passions of the Soul* (1649). He went to Sweden in 1649 at the invitation of Queen Christina, who wanted Descartes to instruct her in his philosophy. As the queen could see him only at five o'clock in the morning, this unaccustomed encounter with the bitter cold of that hour made him easy prey to illness. Within a few months he suffered an attack of fever, and in February, 1650, he died at the age of fifty-four.

Descartes was concerned chiefly with the problem of intellectual certainty. He had been educated, as he says, "at one of the most celebrated schools in Europe...." And yet, "I found myself embarrassed with...many doubts and

Classroom, University of Paris—1600s, in the time of Descartes *(Snark International, Art Resource)*

errors." Looking back on his studies, he saw that ancient literature provided him charming fables that stimulated his mind but could not guide his behavior, because these fables portrayed behavior beyond the power of human beings to perform. He spoke kindly of poetry, saying that the poet gives us knowledge through his "imaginative force," even making truth "shine forth the more brightly" than could the philosophers. Still, poetry is a gift of the mind and not the fruit of study and therefore gives us no method for consciously discovering truth. Though he honored theology, he concluded that its "revealed truths... are quite above our intelligence" and that if one were to be successful in thinking about them, "it was necessary to have some extraordinary assistance from above and to be more than a mere man." He did not want to deny these truths, for he apparently remained a pious Catholic to the end, but he did not find in theology a method by which these truths could be arrived at solely through the powers of human reason. Nor was the philosophy he learned at college any more helpful in this regard, for "no single thing is to be found in it which is not subject of dispute, and in consequence which is not dubious."

His quest for certainty led Descartes to turn from his books to that "great book of the world," where through travel he met "men of diverse temperaments and conditions" and collected "varied experiences." It was his thought that among men of the world, he would discover more exact reasoning, since in practical life, as compared with scholarly activity, a mistake in reasoning has harmful consequences. But, he says, he found as much difference of opinion among practical people as among philosophers. From this experience with the book of the world, Descartes decided "to believe nothing too certainly of which I had only been convinced by example and custom." He resolved to continue his search for certainty, and on a memorable night, November 10, 1619, he had three dreams, which unmistakably convinced him that he must construct the system of true knowledge upon the powers of human reason alone.

Descartes broke with the past and gave philosophy a fresh start. In particular, since his system of truth would have to be derived from his own rational powers, he would no longer rely on previous philosophers for his ideas, nor would he accept any idea as true only because it was expressed by someone with authority. Neither the authority of Aristotle's great reputation nor the authority of the church could suffice to produce the kind of certainty he sought. Descartes was determined to discover the basis of intellectual certainty in his own reason. He therefore gave philosophy a fresh start by using only those truths he could know through his own powers as the foundation for all other knowledge. He was well aware of his unique place in the history of philosophy, for he writes that "although all the truths which I class among my principles have been known from all time and by all men, there has been no one up to the present, who, so far as I know, has adopted them as the principles of philosophy . . . as the sources from which may be derived a knowledge of all things else which are in the world. This is why it here remains to me to prove that they are such."

His ideal was to arrive at a system of thought whose various principles were true and were related to each other in such a clear way that the mind could move easily from one true principle to another. But in order to achieve such an organically connected set of truths, Descartes felt that he must make these truths "conform to a rational scheme." With such a scheme he could not only organize present knowledge but could "direct our reason in order to discover those truths of which we are ignorant." His first task therefore was to work out his "rational scheme," his *method*.

Descartes' Method   Descartes' method consists of harnessing the powers of the mind with a special set of rules. He insisted upon the *necessity* of method, upon systematic and orderly thinking. He was appalled at scholars who sought aimlessly for truth, comparing them to people who, "burning with an unintelligent desire to find treasure, continuously roam the streets, seeking to find something that a passerby might have chanced to drop. . . . It is very certain that unregulated inquiries and confused reflections of this kind only confound the natural light and blind our mental powers." Our minds naturally possess two powers, namely, *intuition* and *deduction*, "mental powers by which we are able, entirely without fear of illusion, to arrive at the knowledge of things." But by themselves these powers can lead us astray unless they are carefully regulated.

René Descartes *(New York Public Library Picture Collection)*

Method consists, therefore, in those rules by which our powers of intuition and deduction are guided in an orderly way.

The Example of Mathematics   Descartes looked to mathematics for the best example of clear and precise thinking. "My method," he writes, "contains everything which gives certainty to the rules of arithmetic." Indeed, Descartes wanted to make all of knowledge a "universal mathematics." For he was convinced that mathematical certainty is the result of a special *way of thinking*, and if he could discover this *way*, he would have a method for discovering true knowledge "of whatever lay within the compass of my powers." Mathematics is not *itself* the method but merely exhibits the method Descartes is searching for; geometry and arithmetic, he says, are only "examples" or "the outer covering" and not "the constituents" of his new method. What then is there about mathematics that led Descartes to find in it the basis of his own method?

In mathematics, Descartes discovered something fundamental about the operation of the human mind. Specifically, he fastened upon the mind's ability to apprehend directly and clearly certain basic truths. He was not so much concerned with explaining the mechanics of the formation of our ideas from experience as he was with affirming the fact that our minds are capable of knowing some ideas with absolute clarity and distinctness. Moreover, mathematical reasoning showed him that we are able to discover what we do not know by progressing in an orderly way from what we do know. If we can discover the mathematical values of certain terms (e.g., the degree of an angle) from our knowledge of other terms (e.g., the length of lines and degrees of other angles in a triangle), why can we not use this same method of reasoning in other fields as well? Descartes was convinced that we could, for he claimed that his method contained "the primary rudiments of human reason" and that with it he could elicit the "truths in every field whatsoever." To him all the various sciences are merely different ways in which the same powers of reasoning and the same method are used. In each case it is the orderly use of intuition and deduction.

    Intuition and Deduction   Descartes placed the whole edifice of knowledge upon the foundation of intuition and deduction, saying that "these two methods are the most certain routes to knowledge," adding that any other approach should be "rejected as suspect of error and dangerous." By *intuition*, Descartes means an intellectual activity or vision of such clarity that it leaves no doubt in the mind. Whereas the fluctuating testimony of our senses and the imperfect creations of our imaginations leave us confused, intuition provides "the conception which an unclouded and attentive mind gives us so readily and distinctly that we are wholly freed from doubt about that which we understand. . . . " Intuition gives us not only clear notions but also some truths about reality, as, for example, that *I think*, that *I exist*, and that *a sphere has a single surface*, truths that are basic, simple, and irreducible. Moreover, it is by intuition that we grasp the connection between one truth and another: for example, that two things equal to a thing are equal to each other (if $A = B$ and $C = B$, then $A = C$) is made clear to us by intuition.

    By *deduction* Descartes means something similar to intuition, describing it as "all necessary inference from facts that are known with certainty." What makes intuition and deduction similar is that both involve truth: By intuition we grasp a simple truth completely and immediately, whereas by deduction we arrive at a truth by a process, a "continuous and uninterrupted action of the mind." By tying deduction so closely with intuition, Descartes gave a new interpretation of deduction, which up to his time had been identified with a mode of reasoning called the syllogism. Deduction, as Descartes described it, is different from a syllogism, for whereas a syllogism indicates the relationship of *concepts* to each other, deduction for Descartes indicates the relation of *truths* to each other. It is one thing to move from a fact that is known with certainty to a conclusion that that fact implies, as Descartes indicates we must do by deduction. But it is something different to go from a *premise* to a conclusion as one does in a syllogism. Descartes emphasized this difference between reasoning from a *fact* and from a *premise*, for the central point of his method was at stake here. Descartes was aware that one can reason *consistently* from a premise but argued that the value of the conclusion would depend upon whether the premise was *true* or not. His quarrel with earlier philosophy and theology was

that conclusions were drawn syllogistically from premises that were either untrue or else based only upon authority. Descartes wanted to rest knowledge
upon a starting point that had absolute certainty in the individual's own mind.
Knowledge requires the use, therefore, of intuition and deduction, where "first
principles are given by intuition alone while the remote conclusions... are furnished only by deduction." Still, Descartes' *method* does not consist only of
intuition and deduction, but also in the rules he formulated for their guidance.

Rules of Method The chief point of Descartes' rules is to provide a clear
and orderly procedure for the operation of the mind. It was his conviction that
"method consists entirely in the order and disposition of the objects toward
which our mental vision must be directed if we would find out any truth." The
mind must begin with a simple and absolutely clear truth and must move step
by step without losing clarity and certainty along the way. Descartes spent many
years at the task of formulating rules for helping the mind choose appropriate
starting points for reasoning and to direct the mind in the ordered process of
reasoning. Of the twenty-one rules found in his *Rules for the Direction of the
Mind*, the following are among the most important. Rule III: When we propose
to investigate a subject, "our inquiries should be directed, not to what others
have thought, nor to what we ourselves conjecture, but to what we can clearly
and perspicuously behold and with certainty deduce." Rule IV: This is a rule
requiring that other rules be adhered to strictly, for "if a man observe them
accurately, he shall never assume what is false as true, and will never spend
his mental efforts to no purpose." Rule V: We shall comply with the method
exactly if we "reduce involved and obscure propositions step by step to those
that are simpler, and then starting with the intuitive apprehension of all those
that are absolutely simple, attempt to ascend to the knowledge of all others by
precisely similar steps." Rule VIII: "If in the matters to be examined we come
to a step in the series of which our understanding is not sufficiently well able to
have an intuitive cognition, we must stop short there."

In a similar way, Descartes formulated four precepts in his *Discourse on
Method*, which he believed were perfectly sufficient, "provided I took the firm
and unwavering resolution never in a single instance to fail in observing them":
"The *first* was never to accept anything for true which I did not clearly know
to be such;... to comprise nothing more in my judgment than what was presented to my mind so clearly and distinctly as to exclude all ground of doubt.
The *second*, to divide each of the difficulties under examination into as many
parts as possible, and as might be necessary for its adequate solution. The *third*,
to conduct my thoughts in such order that by commencing with objects the
simplest and easiest to know, I might ascend by little and little, and, as it were,
step by step, to the knowledge of the more complex.... And the *last*, in every
case to make enumerations so complete, and reviews so general, that I might
be assured that nothing was omitted."

Compared with Bacon and Hobbes, Descartes puts very little emphasis
in his method upon sense experience and experiment in achieving knowledge.
How is it that we know the essential qualities, for example, of a piece of wax,

Descartes asks? At one time a piece of wax is hard, has a certain shape, color, size, and fragrance. But when we bring it close to the fire its fragrance vanishes, its shape and color are lost, and its size increases. What remains in the wax that permits us still to know it is wax? "It cannot," says Descartes, "be anything that I observed by means of the senses, since everything in the field of taste, smell, sight, touch, and hearing is changed, and still the same wax nevertheless remains." It is "nothing but my understanding alone which does conceive it... solely an inspection by the mind," which enables me to know the true qualities of the wax. And, says Descartes, "what I have said here about the wax can be applied to all other things external to me." He relies for the most part upon the truths contained in the mind, "deriving them from [no] other source than certain germs of truth which exist naturally in our souls." Descartes assumed that we possess certain innate ideas, in the sense that we are "born with a certain disposition or propensity for contracting them." Because we can know these truths, we can be assured of a reliable foundation for our deductions. Descartes was confident that he could start from the beginning and rethink and rebuild all of philosophy by having recourse solely to his own rational powers, and directing them in accordance with his rules. He therefore set out to show that we can have certainty of knowledge not only about mathematical concepts but also about the nature of reality.

Methodic Doubt   Descartes used the method of doubt in order to find an absolutely certain starting point for building up our knowledge. Having set out in his *Rules* that we should never accept anything about which we can entertain any doubt, Descartes now tries to doubt everything, saying that "because I wished to give myself entirely to the search after truth, I thought it was necessary for me... to reject as absolutely false everything concerning which I could imagine the least ground of doubt." His intention is clear, for he wants to sweep away all his former opinions, "so that they might later on be replaced, either by others which were better, or by the same, when I had made them conform to the uniformity of a rational scheme."

By this method of doubt, Descartes shows how uncertain our knowledge is, even of what seems most obvious to us. What can be clearer than "that I am here, seated by the fire... holding this paper in my hands...." But when I am asleep, I dream that I am sitting by the fire, and this makes me realize that "there are no conclusive indications by which waking life can be distinguished from sleep." Nor can I be sure that *things* exist for I cannot tell when I am imagining or really knowing, for "I have learned that [my] senses sometimes mislead me." But surely arithmetic, geometry, or sciences that deal with things must contain some certainty, for "whether I am awake or asleep, two and three together will always make the number five." Here Descartes refers to his long-held belief that there is a God who can do anything: but "how can I be sure but that [God] has brought it about that there is no earth, no sky, no extended bodies... and that nevertheless I have impressions of these things.... And ... that I am always mistaken when I add two and three...." We cannot be certain that

God is supremely good, for "He may be an evil genius not less powerful than deceitful," so that all things I experience "are nothing but illusions and dreams." Descartes is therefore "constrained to confess that there is nothing in what I formerly believed to be true which I cannot somehow doubt."

Reversal of Doubt   At this point, Descartes says that "if I am fortunate enough to find a single truth which is certain and indubitable," that will suffice to reverse doubt and establish a philosophy. Like Archimedes, who demanded only an immovable fulcrum to move the earth from its orbit, Descartes searched for his one truth and found it in the very act of doubting.

Cogito and the Self   Though I can doubt that my body exists, or that I am awake, or that I am being deceived, in short that all is illusion or false, one thing remains about which I can have no doubt at all, that *I think*. To doubt is to think, and "it must necessarily be that I who [think am] something; and re-marking that this truth, *I think*, therefore I am [*cogito ergo sum*], was so solid and so certain that all the most extravagant suppositions of the skeptics were incapable of upsetting it, I judged that I could receive it without scruple as the first principle of the philosophy that I sought." So clear was the truth of his own existence that again Descartes says, "this conclusion, *I think, therefore I am*, is the first and most certain of all which occur to one who philosophizes in an orderly way." Accordingly, Descartes employed this basic truth for revers-ing his doubts about the self, things, true ideas, and God.

At first, nothing more is proved by this truth, *I think, therefore I am*, than the existence of my thinking self. My doubts still remain about the exist-ence of my own body and about anything else that is other than my thinking. To say *Cogito ergo sum* is to affirm *my* existence: "But what then am I? A thing which thinks. What is a thing which thinks? It is a thing which doubts, understands, affirms, denies, wills, refuses and which also imagines and feels." Throughout, Descartes assumes that because thinking is a fact, there must also be a thinker, "a thing which thinks." This "thing" is not the body, for "I knew that I was a substance the whole nature of which is to think, and that for its existence there is no need of any place, nor does it depend on any material thing." This much then seems absolutely certain, namely, that I, an ego, exist, "for it is certain that no thought can exist apart from a thing which thinks." But so far, the thinker is alone, a Robinson Crusoe, enclosed in his ideas.

Criterion of Truth   To go beyond the certainty of his own existence as a thinking being, Descartes asks again how we know something to be true. "What," he asks, "is required in a proposition for it to be true and certain?" What is there about the proposition, *Cogito ergo sum* that makes it certain? "I came to the conclusion that I might assume as a general rule that the things which we conceive very *clearly* and *distinctly* are all true." In this context *clear* means "that which is present and apparent to an attentive mind," in the same way that objects are clear to our eyes, and *distinct* refers to "that which is so precise and different from all other objects that it contains within itself nothing but what is clear." The reason, then, that the proposition *I think, therefore I am*, is true is simply that it is clear and distinct to my mind. This is the reason, too, that mathematical propositions are true, for they are so clear and distinct that we cannot help accepting them. But to guarantee the truth of our clear and distinct ideas, Descartes had to prove that God exists and that He is not a deceiver who makes us think that false things are true.

The Existence of God   Descartes cannot use Aquinas' proofs for the existence of God because those proofs are based upon the very facts which are still subject to Descartes' doubt, namely, facts about the external world such as *motion* and *cause* among physical things. Instead, Descartes must prove God's existence solely in terms of his rational awareness of his own existence and internal thoughts. He therefore begins his proof by examining the various ideas that pass through his mind.

Two things strike him about these ideas, that they are caused, and that according to their content they differ markedly from each other. Ideas are effects, and their causes must be discovered. Some of our ideas seem to be "born with me," some "invented" by me, whereas others "come from without." Our reason tells us that "something cannot be derived from nothing" and also that "the more perfect...cannot be a consequence of...the less perfect." Our ideas possess different degrees of reality, but "it is manifest by natural light that there must be at least as much reality in the efficient and total cause as in the effect." Some of our ideas, judging by the degree of their reality, could have their origin in myself. But the idea of God contains so much "objective reality" that I wonder whether I could have produced that idea by myself. For "by the name God I understand a substance which is infinite, independent, all-knowing, all-powerful and by which I myself and everything else, if anything else exists, have been created." How can I, a finite substance, produce the idea of an infinite substance? Indeed, how could I know that I am finite unless I could compare myself with the idea of a perfect being? The idea of perfection is so clear and distinct that I am convinced that it could not proceed from my imperfect nature. Even if I were *potentially* perfect, the idea of perfection could not come from that potentiality, for an actual effect must proceed from a being that *actually* exists. For these reasons, Descartes concludes that since ideas have causes, and since the cause must have at least as much reality as the effect, and finally since he is finite and imperfect, it must be that the cause of his idea of a perfect and infinite Being comes from outside himself, from a perfect Being who exists, from God. In addition, Descartes concludes that God cannot be a deceiver, "since the light of nature teaches us that fraud and deception necessarily proceed from some defect," which could hardly be attributed to a perfect Being.

In addition to this argument from causation, by which he proved the existence of God, Descartes, following Augustine and Anselm, offered his version of the ontological argument. Whereas in the argument from causation he reasoned that his idea of a perfect Being could not have come from himself because of his own known imperfection, in the ontological argument Descartes sought to demonstrate the existence of God by exploring what the very idea of God implies. He says that if "all which I know clearly and distinctly as pertaining to this object really does belong to it, may I not derive from this an argument demonstrating the existence of God?" How is it possible to move from an analysis of an idea to the certainty that God exists?

Some of our ideas, says Descartes, are so clear and distinct that we immediately perceive what they imply. One cannot, for example, think of a triangle without at once thinking of its lines and angles. Although one cannot think about a triangle without also thinking about its attributes of lines and angles, it does not follow that to think about a triangle implies that it exists. But just as the idea of a triangle implies certain attributes, so also the idea of God implies attributes, and specifically the attribute of existence. The idea of God signifies a perfect Being. But the very idea of perfection implies existence. To speak of a nonexistent perfection is to engage in contradiction. One cannot coherently conceive of a Being who is supremely perfect in all respects and at the same time nonexistent. Just as one cannot think the idea of triangle without recognizing its attributes, so also one cannot think the idea of God, says Descartes, without recognizing that this idea clearly implies the attribute of existence. Descartes says, "That which we clearly and distinctly understand to belong to the true and immutable nature of anything, its essence or form, can be truly affirmed of that thing. But after we have with sufficient accuracy investigated the nature of God, we clearly and distinctly understand that to exist belongs to His true nature. Therefore we can with truth affirm of God that He exists." Against this line of reasoning, Descartes' critic Gassendi said that perfection does not imply existence, since existence is not a necessary attribute of perfection. To lack existence, he said, implies no impairment of perfection, only the lack of reality. Kant, as we shall see, went into considerably greater detail in his criticism of these attempts to prove the existence of God.

Existence of Things   From his own existence, Descartes has proved God's existence. Along the way he has also established the criterion of truth and provided thereby the foundation for mathematical thought and for all rational activity. Now, Descartes takes another look at the physical world, at his own body, and other things, and asks whether he can be certain that they exist. To be a thinking thing does not of itself prove that my body exists, for my thinking self "is entirely and absolutely distinct from my body and can exist without it." How then can I know that my body and other physical things exist?

Descartes answers that we all have the clear and distinct experiences of changing our position and moving about, activities that imply a body, or what he calls "an extended substance." We also receive sense impressions, of sight, sound, and touch, frequently even against our will, and these lead us to believe that they come from bodies other than our own. This overwhelming inclination to believe that these impressions "are conveyed to me by corporeal objects" must come from God; otherwise, He could not "be defended from the accusation of deceit if these ideas were produced by causes other than corporeal objects. Hence we must allow that corporeal objects exist." For Descartes, then, knowledge of the self is prior to knowledge of God, and both the self and God are prior to our knowledge of the external world.

Descartes has now reversed all his doubts and has satisfied himself absolutely that the self, things, and God exist. He has concluded that there are thinking things and things that are extended, have dimension. Since a person has both a mind and body, Descartes is left with the problem of indicating how body and mind are related.

Mind and Body   The whole drift of Descartes' thought is in the direction of *dualism*—the notion that there are two different kinds of substances in nature. We know a substance by its attribute, and since we clearly and distinctly know two quite different attributes, namely, *thought* and *extension*, there must be two different substances, the spiritual and the corporeal, mind and body. Because Descartes defines a *substance* as "an existent thing which requires nothing but itself to exist," he considers each substance as thoroughly independent of the other. To know something about the mind, therefore, we need make no reference to the body, and similarly, the body can be thoroughly understood without any reference to the mind. One of the consequences of this dualism was that Descartes hereby separated theology and science and assumed that there need be no conflict between them. Science would study physical nature in isolation of any other discipline, since material substance possessed its own sphere of operation and could be understood in terms of its own laws.

If thought and extension are so distinct and separate, how can one account for living things? Descartes reasoned that because living bodies partake of extension, they are part of the material world. Consequently, living bodies operate according to the same mechanical and mathematical laws that govern other things in the material order. Speaking, for example, of animals, Descartes considered them to be automata, saying that "the greatest of all prejudices we have retained from infancy is that of believing that brutes think." We assume animals think, says Descartes, only because we see them act as humans do on occasion, as when dogs do acrobatic tricks. Because *humans* have two principles of motion, one physical and the other mental, we assume that when animals perform humanlike acts, their physical movements are caused by their mental powers. But Descartes saw no reason for attributing mental powers to animals, because all of their motions, or actions, can be accounted for by mechanical considerations alone, since it is "nature which acts in them according to the disposition of their organs, just as a clock, which is only composed of wheels and weights." Thus animals are machines or automata. But what about human beings?

Many activities of the human body, said Descartes, are as mechanical as those of animals. Such physical acts as respiration, circulation of the blood, and digestion are automatic. The workings of the human body could be reduced, he thought, to physics. Every physical event can be adequately accounted for by a consideration of mechanical or efficient causes; there is no need to consider a final cause when describing the physical processes of the body. Moreover, as Descartes believed that the total quantity of motion in the universe is constant, he was led to conclude that the movements of the human body could not *originate* in the human mind or soul; the soul, he said, could only affect or alter the direction of the motion in certain elements and parts of the body. Just how the mind could do this was difficult to explain precisely, because thought and extension, mind and body, were for Descartes such different and separate substances. He said that the soul does not move the various parts of the body directly but, having "its principal seat in the brain," in the pineal gland, comes first of all in contact with the "vital spirits," and through these the soul interacts with the body. Clearly, Descartes tried to give the human body a mechanical explanation and at the same time preserve the possibility of the soul's influence, through the activity of the will, upon human behavior. Humans, therefore, unlike animals, are capable of several kinds of activities: They can engage in pure thought, their minds can be influenced by physical sensations and perceptions, their bodies can be directed by their minds, and their bodies are moved by purely mechanical forces.

But Descartes' strict dualism made it difficult for him to describe how the mind and body could interact upon each other. If each substance is completely independent, the mind must dwell in the body as a pearl in an oyster, or, to use Descartes' own metaphor, as a pilot in a ship. Scholastic philosophy had described humans as a unity, in which mind is the form and body is the matter, and said that without one there could not be the other. Hobbes had reduced mind to bodies in motion and achieved human unity in that way. But Descartes aggravated the separation of mind and body by his novel definition of "thinking," for he included in the act of thinking some experiences that had traditionally been referred to the body, namely, the whole sphere of sense perceptions, for example, "feeling." When Descartes defines "what I am" as "a thing which thinks," he makes no mention of the body, for everything is included in "thinking": a thinking thing "is a thing which doubts, understands, affirms, denies, wills, refuses, and which also imagines and *feels*." Presumably the self could feel heat without a body. But here Descartes cannot, apparently, accept his own dualism, for he admits that "nature also teaches me by these sensations of pain, hunger, thirst, etc., that I am not lodged in my body as a pilot in a vessel, but that I am very closely united to it, and, so to speak, so intermingled with it that I seem to compose with it one whole." He even tried to locate the mind in the pineal gland, though even there the technical problem of interaction remains, for if there is interaction, there would have to be contact, and so mind would have to be extended. On this problem, his rules of method did not lead him to any clear and distinct conclusion.

Some of Descartes' followers struggled with this mind-body problem and proposed some ingenious solutions. Among them, Arnold Geulincx is most notable for his theory of *occasionalism* or *parallelism*. Geulincx maintained Descartes' strict dualism and denied that there is any interaction between mind and body, for they are two separate substances. Still, it is a fact that when I *decide* or *will* to move my arm, it actually moves. But, said Geulincx, my will did not *cause* my arm to move. Rather, there are two parallel series of acts going on simultaneously, one physical and the other mental. When I will to move my arm, on that occasion God moves it and thereby creates an action parallel to my thought. It may even be, he said, that God has decreed this parallelism from the beginning of time. However cumbersome this explanation may seem, it does no violence to Descartes' thought, for Descartes was willing to accept a deterministic explanation of physical nature and also animal nature, and there seems to be nothing to prevent the inclusion here of human nature.

SPINOZA

Spinoza was the greatest of Jewish philosophers. His originality of mind is suggested by his expulsion from the Synagogue of Amsterdam for his unorthodox views. His refusal to accept the chair of philosophy at Heidelberg was further evidence of his desire to preserve his freedom to pursue his ideas wherever the search for truth might lead him. Though he was content to live in simplicity, to earn a modest living grinding lenses, his fame as a thinker spread abroad and aroused both admiration and condemnation. Baruch Spinoza was born in Amsterdam in 1632 in a family of Portuguese Jews who had fled from persecution in Spain. He was trained in the study of the Old Testament and the Talmud and was familiar with the writings of the Jewish philosopher Maimonides. Having been forced to leave Amsterdam, he eventually went, in 1663, to The Hague, where he carried on his literary career, of which his *Ethics* is the crowning work. In 1677 he died of consumption at the age of forty-five.

Spinoza was influenced by Descartes' rationalism, by his method, and by his choice of the major problems of philosophy. But their similarity of interest and even terminology does not mean that Spinoza was a follower of Descartes. At many points Spinoza brought something new to Continental rationalism, which Descartes had begun.

Method   In common with Descartes, Spinoza thought that we can achieve exact knowledge of reality by following the method of geometry. Descartes had worked out the basic form of this method for philosophy, starting with clear and distinct first principles and attempting from these to deduce the whole content of knowledge. What Spinoza added to Descartes' method was a highly systematic arrangement of principles and axioms. Whereas Descartes' method was simple, Spinoza almost set out literally to write a geometry of philosophy, that is, a complete set of axioms or theorems (about 250 altogether) that would explain the whole system of reality the way geometry explains the relations and movement of things. In geometry, conclusions are demonstrated, and Spinoza believed that our theory of the nature of reality could also be demonstrated. Hobbes questioned whether Spinoza had accomplished anything by arranging his vast number of axioms and theorems into a system of knowledge. Hobbes argued that it is certainly possible to draw consistent conclusions from axioms but that since these axioms consist of nothing more than arbitrary definitions, they do not tell us about reality. Spinoza would not agree that his definitions were arbitrary, for he believed, as did Descartes, that our rational powers are

Spinoza

capable of forming ideas that reflect the true nature of things: "Every definition or clear and distinct idea," says Spinoza, "is true." It must follow, therefore, that a complete and systematic arrangement of true ideas will give us a true picture of reality, for "the order and connection of ideas is the same as the order and connection of things."

The order of things also provides the pattern for the order in which the philosopher should arrange his subjects. It is of utmost importance to observe this order carefully if we are to understand the various aspects of nature accurately. If, for example, we say that things depend for their nature upon God, we must first know all that we can about God before we can understand things. For this reason Spinoza could find little value in Francis Bacon's method, which consisted of enumerating observations of visible events and drawing conclusions from these observations by induction. Nor would he use Aquinas' method of accounting for the existence of God by first of all analyzing the nature of our ordinary experience with things and persons. At this point, too, Spinoza rejects Descartes' approach, for Descartes started with a clear and distinct idea of his *own* existence and from the formula *I think, therefore I am,* proceeded to deduce the other parts of his philosophy. Because in the true nature of things God is prior to everything else, Spinoza believed that philosophy must formulate ideas about God first so that these ideas could appropriately affect the conclusions we draw about such matters as human nature, ways of behaving, and the relation between mind and body. And because Spinoza had such novel things to say about God, it was inevitable that he would say novel things also about human nature. Spinoza, therefore, begins his philosophy with the problem of the nature and existence of God.

God   Spinoza offered a strikingly unique conception of God, in which he identified God with the whole cosmos. His famous formula was *Deus sive Natura*, God or Nature, as if to say that these two words are interchangeable. Although this pantheism could be found in such Biblical descriptions of God as He "in whom we live and move and have our being," Spinoza stripped the idea of God of earlier meanings by emphasizing not the *relation* between God and humanity but a basic *unity* between them: "Whatever is," he said, "is in God, and nothing can exist or be conceived without God." The clue to Spinoza's unique conception of God is found in his definition: "God I understand to be a being absolutely infinite, that is, a substance consisting of infinite attributes, each of which expresses eternal and infinite essence." Spinoza's special thoughts revolve around the ideas of *substance* and its *attributes.*

Substance and Attributes   Through an intricate sequence of arguments Spinoza arrives at the conclusion that the ultimate nature of reality is a single substance. This substance is infinite. That such a substance does exist and that it is infinite follow from our ability to think certain ideas clearly and distinctly. Spinoza defines *substance* as "that which is in itself and is conceived through itself: I mean that the conception of which does not depend on the conception of another thing from which it must be formed." Substance, then, has no external cause but has the cause of itself within itself. So far this is only a *conception*, an idea of a self-caused infinite substance. This idea, however, includes not only what this substance is like but also that it exists. The very idea of substance includes its existence, for "existence appertains to substance," and "therefore from its mere definition its existence can be concluded." This resembles Anselm's *ontological* argument and raises the same problems. Still, Spinoza was certain that we can go with assurance from our idea of this perfect substance to its existence, saying that "if anyone says that he has a clear and distinct, that is, a true idea of substance and nevertheless doubts whether such a substance exists, he is like one who says that he has a true idea and yet doubts whether it may not be false." That this substance is one and infinite follows from the previous definition Spinoza has given of substance. There is therefore a single substance with infinite attributes.

An *attribute,* says Spinoza, is "that which an intellect perceives as constituting the essence of substance." If God is defined as a "substance consisting of infinite attributes," it would appear that there would be an infinite number of substances or that God would possess infinite essence. But Spinoza could very well mean here that since an attribute is "that which an intellect perceives," it is possible for the intellect to perceive the single substance in an infinite number of ways. Actually, says Spinoza, we can know only two attributes of substance, namely, thought and extension. Descartes thought that these two attributes indicated the existence of two substances, thereby leading him to affirm the dualism of mind and body. Spinoza saw these two attributes as different ways of expressing the activity of a single substance. God is therefore substance perceived as infinite thought and infinite extension. Being infinite, God contains everything.

God and the World: The Modes Spinoza does not contrast God and the world as if they were as different and distinct as cause and effect, as though God were the immaterial cause and the world the material effect. He has already established that there is only one substance and that the word *God* is interchangeable with *Nature.* But Spinoza does distinguish between two aspects of Nature, using for this purpose the two expressions *natura naturans* and *natura naturata.* By *natura naturans* Spinoza means substance and its attributes, or God insofar as He is considered to act by the requirements of His own nature. On the other hand, by *natura naturata*, he means "everything which follows from the necessity of the nature of God, or of any one of God's attributes." Further, "by *natura naturata* I understand... all the modes of God's attributes in so far as they are considered as things which are in God, and which without God can neither be nor can be conceived." What in earlier language was called the *world*, Spinoza now calls the *modes* of God's attributes. The *world* is not distinct from God but *is* God expressed in various modes of thought and extension, of thought and corporeality.

Modes and Necessity As the *world* consists of the modes of God's attributes, everything in the world acts in accordance with necessity—that is, everything is determined—for the modes in which thought and extension take form in the world are determined by God's substance, or, as Spinoza says, these modes represent "everything which follows from the necessity of the nature of God." Spinoza gives us a picture of a tight universe where every event unfolds in the only possible way in which it can occur, for "in the nature of things nothing contingent is granted, but all things are determined by the necessity of divine nature for existing and working in a certain way." In a special way God is free, not that He could have created a different kind of world but that though He had to create just what He did, He was not forced to do this by some external cause, only by His own nature. On the other hand, people are not even that free, for they are determined to exist and behave according to God's substance, of whose attributes humanity is a mode. All modes of God's attributes are fixed from eternity, for "things could not have been produced by God in any other manner or order than that in which they were produced." All the things we experience "are nothing else than modifications of the attributes of God [Nature], or modes by which attributes are expressed in a certain and determined manner." Thus, everything is intimately connected, the infinite substance providing a continuity through all things, particular things being simply modes or modifications of the attributes of substance, or Nature, or God.

No Final Cause   Because everything is eternally as it must be, and because particular events are simply finite modifications of substance, there is no direction toward which things are moving, no *end*, no *purpose*, no final cause. From our human vantage point, we try to explain events as either fulfilling or frustrating some purpose of history. Ideas of purpose, says Spinoza, are derived from our tendency to act with an end in view. From this habit we tend to look at the universe as though it too had some goal. But this is a wrong way of looking at the universe and indeed at our own behavior. For neither the universe nor human beings are pursuing purposes; they are only doing what they must. This "truth might have lain hidden from the human race through all eternity, had not mathematics, which does not deal with final causes but with the essences of things, offered to men another standard of truth." And the truth is that all events are a continuous and necessary set of modifications of the eternal substance, which simply *is*. Thus Spinoza reduced the biological to the mathematical.

The Levels of Knowledge   But how can Spinoza claim to know the ultimate nature of reality? He distinguishes between three levels of knowledge and describes how we can move from the lowest to the highest. We begin with the things most familiar to us, and, says Spinoza, "the more we understand individual things the more we understand God." By refining our knowledge of things, we can move from (1) *imagination*, to (2) *reason*, and finally to (3) *intuition*.

At the level of *imagination* our ideas are derived from sensation, as when we see another person. Here our ideas are very concrete and specific, and the mind is passive. Though our ideas on this level are specific, they are vague and inadequate, for we know things only as they affect our senses—I know that I *see* a person, but as yet I do not know simply by looking what this person's essential nature is. I can form a general idea, such as *human*, by seeing several people, and the ideas I form from experience are useful for daily life, but they do not give me true knowledge.

The second level of knowledge goes beyond imagination to *reason*. This is scientific knowledge. Everyone can participate in this kind of knowledge because it is made possible by a sharing in the attributes of substance, in God's thought and extension. There is in humanity what is in all things, and since one of these common properties is mind, the human mind shares in the mind that orders things. At this level a person's mind can rise above immediate and particular things and deal with abstract ideas, as it does in mathematics and physics. At this level, knowledge is *adequate* and *true*. If we ask Spinoza how we know that these ideas of reason and science are true, he replies in effect that truth validates itself, for "he who has a true idea knows at the same time that he has a true idea, nor can he doubt concerning the truth of the thing."

The third and highest level of knowledge is *intuition*. Through intuition we can grasp the whole system of nature. At this level we can understand the particular things we encountered on the first level in a new way, for at that first level we saw other bodies in a disconnected way, and now we see them as part of the whole scheme. This kind of knowing "proceeds from an adequate idea of the formal essence of certain attributes of God to the adequate knowledge of the essence of things." When we reach this level we become more and more conscious of God and hence "more perfect and blessed," for through this vision we grasp the whole system of Nature and see our place in it, giving us an intellectual fascination with the full order of Nature, of God.

Mind and Body Descartes was left with the difficult problem of explaining how the mind interacts with the body. This was for him virtually insoluble because he assumed that mind and body represent two distinct substances. For Spinoza, however, this was no problem at all because he viewed mind and body as attributes of a single substance. There is only one order of Nature, to which both the body and mind belong. Humankind is a single mode. It is only because we are able to consider humanity as a mode of extension that we speak of a body, and as a mode of thought that we speak of a mind. There can be no separation of mind and body because they are aspects of the same thing. For every body there is a corresponding idea, and, in general, Spinoza says that the mind is the idea of the body, which is his way of describing the relationship of the mind to the body. The structure within which the mind and body operate is the same. Thus, humanity is a finite version of God, for it is a mode of God's attributes of thought and extension. This interpretation of both humanity and God set the stage for Spinoza's distinctive theory of ethics.

Ethics The central feature of Spinoza's account of human behavior is that he treats people as an integral part of Nature. When Spinoza says that he looks upon "human actions and desires exactly as if I were dealing with lines, planes, and bodies," his point is that human behavior can be explained just as precisely in terms of causes, effects, and mathematics as any other natural phenomenon. Although people think they are *free* and are able to make *choices*, they are victims of an illusion, for it is only human ignorance that permits us to think we possess freedom of the will. People like to think that in some special way they stand outside the rigorous forces of cause and effect, that though their wills can cause actions, their wills are themselves not affected by prior causes. But Spinoza argued for the unity of all Nature, with people as an intrinsic part of it. Spinoza therefore develops a naturalistic ethics whereby all human actions, both mental and physical, are said to be determined by prior causes.

All people possess as a part of their nature the *endeavor* to continue or persist in their own being, and this endeavor Spinoza calls *conatus*. When this *conatus* refers to the mind and body, it is called *appetite*, and insofar as appetite is conscious, it is called *desire*. As we become conscious of higher degrees of self-preservation and perfection, we experience pleasure, and with a reduction of such perfection, we experience pain. Our ideas of good and evil are related to our conceptions of pleasure and pain, for as Spinoza says, "By good I understand here all kinds of pleasure and whatever conduces to it, and more especially that which satisfies our fervent desires, whatever they may be. By bad I understand all kinds of pain, and especially that which frustrates our desires." There is no intrinsic *good* or *bad*, for we call something *good* if we desire it and *bad* if we dislike it. Goodness and badness reflect a subjective evaluation. But because our desires are determined, so are our judgments.

If all our desires and actions are determined by external forces, how can there be any occasion for morality? Here Spinoza resembles the Stoics, who also argued that all events are determined. The Stoics called for resignation and acquiescence to the drift of events, saying that though we cannot control events, we can control our attitudes. In a similar way, Spinoza tells us that through our knowledge of God we can arrive at "the highest possible mental acquiescence." Morality, therefore, consists of improving our knowledge by moving from the level of confused and inadequate ideas up to the third level of intuition, where we have clear and distinct ideas of the perfect and eternal arrangement of all things in God. Only knowledge can lead us to happiness, for only through knowledge can we be liberated from the bondage of our passions. We are enslaved by passions when our desires are attached to perishable things and when we do not fully understand our emotions. The more we understand our emotions, the less excessive will be our appetites and desires. And "the mind has greater power over the emotions and is less subject thereto, in so far as it understands all things as necessary." We must study not only our emotions but the whole order of Nature, for it is only from the perspective of eternity that we can really understand our own particular lives, for then we see all events through the idea of God as cause. Spiritual unhealthiness, says Spinoza, can always be traced to our "excessive love for something which is subject to many variations and which we can never be masters of." But we possess by nature the desire for and the capacity for higher degrees of perfection, and we achieve levels of perfection through our intellectual powers. Passions enslave us only when we lack knowledge. But "from this kind of knowledge necessarily arises the intellectual love of God. From this kind of knowledge arises pleasure accompanied by the idea of God as cause, that is, the love of God; not in so far as we imagine Him as present, but in so far as we understand Him to be eternal; this is what I call the intellectual love of God." This love of God is of course not the love of a divine person but is more akin to the mental pleasure we have when we understand a mathematical formula or a scientific operation. That the way to morality described here is "exceedingly hard" Spinoza was willing to admit, adding that "all things excellent are as difficult as they are rare."

LEIBNIZ

From his early youth, Leibniz showed unmistakable signs of a brilliant mind. At the age of thirteen, he was reading difficult scholastic treatises with the same ease that others would be reading novels. He developed the infinitesimal calculus and published his results three years before Sir Isaac Newton, who claimed to have made the discovery first, had released his manuscript to the printers. He was a man of the world, courting the favor and receiving the patronage of eminent people. He was personally acquainted with Spinoza, whose philosophy impressed him, though he departed from Spinoza's ideas in decisive ways. Leibniz engaged in extensive correspondence with philosophers, theologians, and men of letters. Among his grand projects were attempts to achieve a reconciliation between Protestantism and Catholicism and an alliance between Christian states, which in his day would have meant a United States of Europe. He became the first president of the Society of the Sciences at Berlin, which was later to become the Prussian Academy.

Gottfried Wilhelm von Leibniz was born at Leipzig in 1646 and entered the university there at the age of fifteen. At Leipzig he studied philosophy, going next to Jena to study mathematics and then to Altdorf, where he completed the course in jurisprudence and received the doctorate in law at the age of twenty-one. With extraordinary vigor he lived actively in the two worlds of action and thought. He was the author of several significant works, including *New Essays on Human Understanding*, in which he examines systematically Locke's *Essay, Essays in Theodicy*, which deals with the problem of evil, *Discourse on Metaphysics*, the *New System of Nature and the Interaction of Substances*, and the *Monadology*. He was in the service of the House of Hanover, but when George I became King of England, Leibniz was not invited to go with him, possibly because of his quarrel with Newton. His public influence declined, and in 1716, neglected and unnoticed even by the learned society he founded, he died at the age of seventy.

Substance Leibniz was dissatisfied with the way Descartes and Spinoza had described the nature of substance, because he felt they had distorted our understanding of human nature, freedom, and the nature of God. To say, as Descartes did, that there are two independent substances, thought and extension, was to produce the impossible dilemma of trying to explain how those two substances could interact as body and mind either in humanity or in God. Spinoza had tried to solve the dilemma by saying that there is only one substance with two knowable attributes, thought and extension. But to reduce all reality to a single substance was to lose the distinction between the various elements in nature. To be sure, Spinoza spoke of the *world* as consisting of many *modes*, in which the attributes of thought and extension appear. Still, Spinoza's monism was a pantheism in which God was everything and everything was part of everything else. To Leibniz, this conception of substance was inadequate because it blurred the distinctions among God, humanity, and nature, each of which Leibniz wanted to keep separate. Paradoxically, Leibniz accepted Spinoza's single-substance theory and his mechanical model of the universe but presented such a unique theory of this one substance that he was able to speak of the individuality of persons, the transcendence of God, and the reality of purpose and freedom in the universe.

Extension versus Force   Leibniz challenged the fundamental assumption upon which both Descartes and Spinoza had built their theory of substance, namely, that *extension* implies actual size and shape. Descartes assumed that *extension* refers to a material substance that is extended in space and is not divisible into something more primary. Spinoza, too, considered extension as an irreducible material attribute of God or Nature. Leibniz disagreed. Observing that the bodies or things we see with our senses are divisible into smaller parts, why can we not assume, asked Leibniz, that all things are compounds or aggregates? "There must be," he said, "simple substances, since there are compound substances, for the compound is only a collection or *aggregatum* of simple substances."

There is nothing new in saying that things must be made of simple substances, for Democritus and Epicurus had argued centuries before that all things consist of small atoms. But Leibniz rejected this notion of atoms, because Democritus had described these atoms as extended bodies, as irreducible bits of matter. Such a particle of matter would have to be considered lifeless or inert and would have to get its motion from something outside itself. Rejecting the idea of matter as primary, Leibniz argued that the truly simple substances are the *monads*, and these are "the true atoms of nature...the elements of things." The monads differ from atoms in that atoms were viewed as extended bodies, whereas Leibniz described the monad as being *force* or *energy*. Leibniz therefore said that matter is not the primary ingredient of things but that monads with their element of force constitute the essential substance of things.

Monads   Leibniz wanted to emphasize that substance must contain life or a dynamic force. Whereas Democritus' material atom would have to be acted upon from outside itself in order to move or become a part of a large cluster, Leibniz said that simple substance, the monad, is "capable of action." He added that "*compound* substance is the collection of *monads. Monas* is a Greek word which signifies unity, or that which is one.... Simple substances, lives, souls, spirits are unities. Consequently all nature is full of life."

Monads are unextended, they have no shape or size. A monad is a point, not a mathematical or a physical point but a metaphysically existent point. Each monad is independent of other monads, and monads do not have any causal relation to each other. It is difficult to imagine a *point* that has no shape or size, yet Leibniz wanted to say just this in order to differentiate the monad from a material atom. Actually his thinking here resembles the twentieth-century notion that physical particles are reducible to energy, or that particles are a special form of energy. Essentially Leibniz was saying that monads are logically prior to any corporeal forms. True substances, then, are monads, and these

Leibniz also calls *souls* to emphasize their nonmaterial nature. Each monad is different from the others, and each possesses its own principle of action, its own force, and, says Leibniz, "there is a certain sufficiency which makes them the source of their internal actions and, so to speak, incorporeal automata." Monads are not only independent and different. They also contain the source of their activity within themselves. Moreover, in order to emphasize that the rest of the universe does not affect their behavior, Leibniz says that the monads are *windowless*. But there must be some relation between all the monads which make up the universe, some explanation for their orderly actions. This explanation Leibniz finds in his idea of a *preestablished harmony*.

Preestablished Harmony Each monad behaves in accordance with its own created purpose. These *windowless* monads, each following its own purpose, form a unity or the ordered universe. Even though each is isolated from the other, their separate purposes form a large-scale harmony. It is as though several clocks all struck the same hour because they keep perfect time. Leibniz compares all these monads to "several different bands of musicians and choirs, playing their parts separately, and so placed that they do not see or even hear one another...nevertheless [they] keep perfectly together, by each following their own notes, in such a way that he who hears them all finds in them a harmony that is wonderful, and much more surprising than if there had been any connection between them." Each monad, then, is a separate world, but all the activities of each monad occur in harmony with the activities of the others. In this way it can be said that each monad mirrors the whole universe (but from a unique perspective), in the sense that if anything "were taken away or supposed different, all things in the world would have been different" from what they are like at present. Such a harmony as this could not be the product of an accidental assortment of monads but must be, said Leibniz, the result of God's activity, whereby this harmony is preestablished.

God's Existence To Leibniz, this fact of a universal harmony of all things provided a "new proof of the existence of God." He had accepted, for the most part, the earlier attempts to prove God's existence, saying that "nearly all of the means which have been employed to prove the existence of God are good and might be of service, if we would perfect them." But he was particularly impressed by "this perfect harmony of so many substances which have no communication with each other," saying that this harmony pointed to the existence of God with "surprising clearness," because a harmony of many windowless substances "can only come from a common cause." This resembles the argument from design and from a first cause, although Leibniz modified the argument from cause with his principle of *sufficient reason*.

Principle of Sufficient Reason Any event, said Leibniz, can be explained by referring to a prior cause. But that prior cause must itself be explained by a still earlier cause. If all the causes we refer to are alike in that they must be caused, we could never truly explain the reason for any event. It is not sufficient to point to the immediate or proximate cause, for we are left with the problem of explaining *its* existence. Only by referring to some cause outside the series of causes, or outside the complex organization of the universe, can the solution be found for the existence of any particular thing. The final reason, or the sufficient reason, for all things is found in a substance whose own existence is necessary, whose existence requires no cause or further explanation, a Being "whose essence involves existence, for this is what is meant by a necessary Being." The sufficient reason for the ordinary things we experience in the world of fact lies therefore in a Being outside the series of obvious causes, in a Being whose very nature or essence is a sufficient reason for its own existence, requring no prior cause, and this Being is God.

    Evil and the Best of All Possible Worlds   The harmony of the world led Leibniz to argue not only that God had preestablished it but also that in doing this God has created the best of all possible worlds. Whether this is the best or even a good world is open to question because of the disorder and evil in it. Indeed, Schopenhauer thought that this is, if anything, the worst of all possible worlds and that consequently we are not justified in concluding that God exists or that the world with all its evil is the creation of a good God. Leibniz was aware of the fact of evil and disorder but considered it compatible with the notion of a benevolent Creator. In his perfect knowledge, God could consider all the possible kinds of worlds he could create, but his choice must be in accord with the moral requirement that the world should contain the greatest possible amount of good. Such a world would not be without imperfection. On the contrary, the world of creation consists of limited and imperfect things, "for God could not give the creature all without making it God; therefore there must needs be... limitations also of every kind." The source of evil is not God but rather the very nature of things God creates, for as these things are finite or limited, they are imperfect. Evil, then, is not something substantial but merely the absence of perfection. Evil for Leibniz is privation. This is why Leibniz could say that "God wills *antecedently* the good and *consequently* the best," since the most that God can do, in spite of his goodness, is to create the best possible world. As a final consideration, Leibniz agrees that we cannot rightly appraise evil if we consider only the particular evil thing or event. Some things that in themselves appear to be evil turn out to be the prerequisites for good, as when "sweet things become insipid if we eat nothing else; sharp, tart and even bitter things must be combined with them, so as to stimulate the taste." Again, events in our lives, taken by themselves, lose their true perspective. Leibniz asks, "If you look at a very beautiful picture, having covered up the whole of it except a very small part, what will it present to your sight, however thoroughly you examine it... but a confused mass of colors, laid on without selection and without art? Yet if you remove the covering, and look at the whole picture from the right point of view, you will find that what appeared to have been carelessly daubed on the canvas was really done by the painter with very great art."

    Freedom   How can there be any freedom in the determined world Leibniz portrays, where God preestablishes an orderly arrangement by infusing specific purposes into the several monads? Each monad is involved in developing its built-in purpose, and "every present state of a simple substance is naturally a consequence of its preceding state, in such a way that its present is big with its future." Each person, whose identity centers around a dominant monad, his soul, must represent in this mechanical view an unfolding of a life that has been set from the beginning. Yet, since the basic nature of this person is thought, his development through life consists in overcoming confused thoughts and arriving at true ideas, which lie in all of us in the murky form of potentiality seeking to become actual. When our potentialities become actual, we see things as they really are, and this, says Leibniz, is what it means to be free. For him freedom does not mean volition, the power of choice, but rather self-development, so that although one is determined to act in specific ways, it is his own internal nature that determines his acts and not outside forces. Freedom in this sense means the ability to become what one is destined to be without obstructions, and it also means a quality of existence whereby one's knowledge has passed from confusion to clarity. The free man is one who knows why he does what he does. It was along these lines that Leibniz thought he had succeeded in reconciling his deterministic view of nature with freedom.

Whether Leibniz succeeded in reconciling his world of monads with the notion of freedom is certainly questionable. Although he does at one point speak of freedom in terms of "choice in our will" and say that "free and voluntary mean the same thing," still his dominant emphasis appears to be upon determinism, upon the notion of a mechanical-like universe, a spiritual machine. Actually, Leibniz does not use the mechanical model in describing the universe, for if he did, he would have to say that the various parts of the universe act upon each other the way parts of a clock affect the movements of each other. In a sense, Leibniz's explanation is even more rigorously deterministic than the mechanical model suggests, for his monads are all independent of each other, are not affected by each other, but behave in accordance with their original purpose which they received from the beginning through God's creation. This kind of determinism is more rigorous because it does not depend upon the vagaries of external causation but upon the given and permanently fixed internal nature of each monad.

Knowledge and Nature This deterministic view of nature is further supported by Leibniz's theory of knowledge. A person, for example, is for Leibniz similar to a subject in the grammatical sense. For any true sentence or proposition, the predicate is already contained in the subject. Thus, to know the subject is already to know certain predicates. "All men are mortal" is a true proposition because the predicate *mortal* is already contained in the notion of *men*. Leibniz therefore says that in any true proposition "I find that every predicate, necessary or contingent, past, present, or future, is comprised in the notion of the subject." Similarly, in the nature of things, all substances are, so to speak, subjects, and the things they do are their predicates. Just as grammatical subjects contain their predicates, so also existing substances already contain their future behavior. Thus, Leibniz concludes that "in saying that the individual notion of Adam involves all that will ever happen to him, I mean nothing else but what all philosophers mean when they say that the predicate is in the subject of a true proposition." Leibniz patterned his theory of substance or metaphysics after his theory of knowledge or logic. At the center of his argument is his special treatment of the notion of truth.

Leibniz distinguished between truths of reason and truths of fact. We know truths of reason purely by logic, whereas we know truths of fact by experience. The test of a truth of reason is the law of contradiction, and the test for a truth of fact is the law of sufficient reason. A truth of reason is a necessary truth in that to deny it is to be involved in a contradiction. Truths of fact, on the other hand, are contingent, and their opposite is possible. A truth of reason is a necessary truth because the very meaning of the terms used and the mode of human understanding require that certain things be true. For example, that a triangle has three sides is true because to have three sides is what a triangle means. To say that a triangle has four sides is clearly to be involved in a contradiction. That 2 and 2 equals 4, that A is A, that A is not not-A, that heat is not cold—all these propositions are true because to deny their truth would be contradictory. Truths of reason are tautologies, because in such propositions the predicate simply repeats what is already contained in the subject. Once the subject is clearly understood, there needs to be no further proof about the truth of the predicate. Truths of reason do not require or affirm that the subject of the proposition exists. It is true, for example, that a triangle has three sides even though one does not refer to any specific existing triangle. Truths of reason tell us what would be true in any case where a subject, in this case triangles, is involved. They deal with the sphere of the possible. That a triangle should be a square is never possible, would be contradictory, and therefore cannot be true.

Mathematics is a striking example of the truths of reason, since its propositions are true when they pass the test of the law of contradiction. Thus Leibniz says that "the great foundation of mathematics is the principle of contradiction...that is, that a proposition cannot be true and false at the same time.... This single principle is sufficient to demonstrate every part of arithmetic and geometry." In short, truths of reason are self-evident truths. They are *analytic* propositions, the predicate of which is contained already in the subject, and to deny the predicate is to be involved in a contradiction.

What about truths of fact? These truths are known through experience. They are not necessary propositions. Their opposites can be considered possible without contradiction, and for this reason their truth is contingent. The statement "Mary exists" is not a truth of reason; its truth is not a priori. There is nothing in the subject *Mary* that necessarily implies, or makes it possible for us to deduce, the predicate *exists*. We know the predicate that she exists only *a posteriori*, after an experience. This truth of fact, as is the case with all truths of fact, is based upon the law of sufficient reason, which says that "nothing happens without a reason why it should be so rather than otherwise." As it stands, the proposition "Mary exists" is contingent upon some sufficient reason. In the absence of any sufficient reason, it would be just as true to say that "Mary does not exist." When a sufficient reason is present, other propositions have a basis of truth, so that we say "if A, then B." This hypothetical character of A indicates that although there may be a necessary connection between A and B, it is not absolutely necessary that A exist. The existence of A is contingent, that is, is *possible*. Whether it will in fact exist depends upon whether there is or will be a sufficient reason for it to exist. About every truth of fact one can think of its opposite as possible without contradiction.

When one considers all the possibilities that propositions about facts imply, a principle of limitation emerges. Whereas some events can be considered possible, simply as the opposite of others, they cannot be possible once certain other possibilities have become actual. That is, some possibilities are *compossible* with some events though not with others. Thus Leibniz says that "not all possible species are compossible in the universe, great as it is, and that this holds not only in regard to things which exist contemporaneously but also in regard to the whole series of things."

The universe of facts, as we know it, is only a collection of certain kinds of compossibles, that is, the collection of all the existent possibles. There could be other combinations of possibles than the ones our actual universe contains. The relation of the various possibles to each other requires us to understand the sufficient reason that connects each event to another event. Physical science, unlike mathematics, cannot, however, be a deductive discipline. The truths of mathematics are analytic. But in propositions concerning facts, the subject does not contain the predicate. The law of sufficient reason, which governs truths of fact, requires that these truths be verified. But this verification is always partial, since each preceding event in the causal chain of events must also be verified. However, no human being is able to account for the infinite sequence of causes. If the cause of A is B, it is then necessary to account for the cause of B and to go back as far as the beginning. The first fact about the universe is like any other fact; it does not contain, so far as the power of human analysis is capable of discovering, any clearly necessary predicate. To know its truth requires that we discover the sufficient reason for its being what it is.

The final explanation of the world, says Leibniz, is that "the true cause why certain things exist rather than others is to be derived from the free decrees of the divine will." Things are as they are because God willed them to be that way. Having willed some things to be what they are, He limited the number of other possibilities and determined which events can be compossible. God could have willed other universes, other combinations of possibilities. But having willed this universe, there now exist certain necessary connections between specific events. Although from the perspective of human reason, propositions concerning the world of facts are *synthetic*, or require experience and verification, if we are to know their truth, these propositions are, from God's perspective, *analytic*. Only God can deduce all the predicates of any substance. And only our ignorance prevents us from being able to see in any particular person all the predicates connected with that person. In the end, truths of fact are also analytic, according to Leibniz. A person does already contain his predicates, so that if we really comprehended the complete notion of a person, we could deduce these predicates, as, for example, "the quality of king, which belongs to Alexander the Great." Thus, "God, seeing the individual notion of Alexander, sees in it at the same time the foundation and the reason of all the predicates which can be truly attributed to him, as, for example, whether he would conquer Darius and Porus, even to knowing *a priori* [and not by experience] whether he died a natural death or by poison which we [with our limited human intellects] can only know by history."

For Leibniz, then, logic is a key to metaphysics. From the grammar of propositions, he inferred conclusions about the real world. In the end, he argued that all true propositions are analytic. For this reason, substances and persons are for Leibniz equivalent to subjects of an analytic proposition; they really contain, he said, all their predicates. He also applies his *law of continuity* to his notion of substance in order to confirm his theory that each substance unfolds its predicates in an orderly and (from God's perspective) predictable way. The *law of continuity* states that "Nature makes no leaps." Among created things, every possible position is occupied, so that all change is continuous. According to the law of continuity rest and motion are aspects of each other, merging into each other through infinitesimal changes, "so much so that the rule of rest ought to be considered as a particular case of the rule of motion." The *windowless* monads, then, bear in themselves all their future behavior. And as this is true of each monad, all the combinations and possibilities of events already contained in the world also contain the whole future of the world, and the sufficient reason for this order is ". . . the supreme reason, which does everything in the most perfect way." Although the human mind cannot know all reality as God knows it, still, says Leibniz, it contains certain innate ideas, self-evident truths. A child does not know all these truths at once but must wait until maturity and for specific occasions in experience when these ideas are called forth. That these ideas become known only on such occasions makes them *virtually* innate. Still, this doctrine of innate ideas, along with Leibniz's general treatment of the relation of logic to reality, reflected his optimistic appraisal of the capacity of reason to know reality and his belief that from innate self-evident truths considerable knowledge of the real world could be deduced.

13

Empiricism in Britain: Locke, Berkeley, and Hume

lthough the school of empiricism came upon the scene in an unpretentious way, it was destined to alter the course and concerns of modern philosophy. Whereas Bacon aimed at "the total reconstruction of... all human knowledge," Locke, who was the founder of empiricism in Britain, aimed at the more modest objective of "clearing the ground a little, and removing some of the rubbish that lies in the way to knowledge." But in the process of "clearing" and "removing," Locke hit upon a bold and original interpretation of how the mind works and, from this, described the kind and extent of knowledge we can expect from the human mind.

The scope of our knowledge, Locke said, is limited to, and by, our experience. This was not a new insight, for others before him had said much the same thing. Both Bacon and Hobbes had urged that knowledge should be built upon observation, and to this extent they could be called *empiricists*. But neither Bacon nor Hobbes raised any critical question about the intellectual powers of man. Although both uncovered and rejected modes of thought that they considered fruitless and erroneous, they nevertheless accepted without challenge the general view that the mind is capable of producing certainty of knowledge about nature provided only that the proper method is used. Similarly, Descartes assumed that there was no problem that human reason could not solve if the correct method was employed. This was the assumption Locke called into critical question, namely, the assumption that the human mind has capabilities that enable it to discover the true nature of the universe. David Hume pushed this critical point even further and asked whether any secure knowledge at all is possible. In their separate ways, the British empiricists Locke, Berkeley, and Hume challenged not only their English predecessors but also the Continental rationalists, who had launched modern philosophy upon an optimistic view of our rational powers that the empiricists could not accept.

LOCKE

John Locke was born in 1632 at Wrington, Somerset, and died seventy-two years later in 1704. He grew up in a Puritan home, trained in the virtues of hard work and the love of simplicity. After a thorough training in the classics at Westminster School, Locke became a student at Oxford University, where he took the bachelor's and master's degrees and was appointed Senior Student and later Censor of Moral Philosophy. He spent thirty years of his life in the city of Oxford. Though he continued his studies of Aristotle's logic and metaphysics, he was gradually drawn toward the newly developing experimental sciences, being influenced in this direction particularly by Sir Robert Boyle. His scientific interests led him to pursue the study of medicine, and in 1674 he obtained his medical degree and was licensed to practice. As he pondered what direction his career might take, there was added to the considerations of medicine and Oxford Tutor an alternative, diplomacy. He actually served in various capacities, eventually becoming the personal physician and confidential adviser to the Earl of Shaftesbury, one of the leading politicians of London. But earlier influences, among them his reading of Descartes' works while at Oxford, confirmed his desire to devote his creative powers to working out a philosophical understanding of certain problems that perplexed his generation. He wrote on such diverse topics as *The Reasonableness of Christianity, An Essay concerning Toleration,* and the *Consequences of the Lowering of Interest and Raising the Value of Money,* indicating his active participation in the public affairs of his day.

In 1690, when he was fifty-seven years old, Locke published two books which were to make him famous as a philosopher and as a political theorist: *An Essay concerning Human Understanding* and *Two Treatises on Civil Government.* Although other philosophers before him had written about human knowledge, Locke was the first one to produce a full-length inquiry into the scope and limits of the human mind. Similarly, others had written important works on political theory, but Locke's second of the *Two Treatises* came at a time when it could shape the thoughts of an era and later affect the course of events. The *Two Treatises* and *Essay* indicate Locke's way of combining his practical and theoretical interests and abilities. The *Two Treatises* were expressly formulated to justify the revolution of 1688. Some of its ideas took such strong

John Locke *(New York Public Library Picture Collection)*

hold upon succeeding generations that phrases contained in it, as, for example, that we are "all equal and independent" and possess the natural rights to "life, health, liberty and possessions," worked their way into the Declaration of Independence and affected the shaping of the American Constitution. Regarding his *Essay*, he tells us that it grew out of an experience that occurred about twenty years before this work was published. On that occasion, five or six friends met to discuss a point in philosophy, and before long they were hopelessly snarled, "without coming any nearer a resolution of those doubts which perplexed us." Convinced that the discussion had taken a wrong turn, Locke decided that before one could move directly into such a subject as "the principles of morality and revealed religion," it was necessary "to examine our own abilities, and see what *objects* our understandings were, or were not, fitted to deal with." From this examination Locke eventually composed his *Essay on Human Understanding*, which became the foundation of empiricism in Britain.

Locke's Theory of Knowledge   Locke set out "to enquire into the origin, certainty, and extent of human knowledge." He assumed that if he could describe what knowledge consists of and how it is obtained, he could determine the limits of knowledge and decide what constitutes intellectual certainty. His conclusion was that knowledge is restricted to *ideas*, not Plato's Ideas or Forms, but ideas that are generated by objects we experience. The origin of ideas is *experience*, and experience takes two forms, *sensation* and *reflection*. Without exception, then, all our ideas come to us through the senses, whereby we experience the world external to us, and through reflection upon these ideas, which is an experience internal to us. What Locke wanted to make quite clear was that we cannot have the experience of *reflection* until we have had the experience of *sensation*. For reflection means simply the mind's taking notice of its own operations; but its operations begin when the mind is provided with ideas, and these ideas come from without through the senses. This means that each person's mind is in the beginning like a blank sheet of paper upon which experience alone can subsequently write knowledge. Before he could elaborate these conclusions, Locke felt that he must lay to rest the persisting theory of innate ideas, the notion that in some way we all come into the world with a standard stock of ideas built into the mind.

No Innate Ideas   It is obvious that if Locke is going to say that all ideas come from experience, he must reject the theory of innateness. He points out that "It is an established opinion among some men, that there are in the understanding certain innate principles...stamped upon the mind of man, which the soul receives in its very first beginning, and brings into the world with it." Not only does Locke reject this as not true, but he considers this doctrine a dangerous tool in the hands of those who could misuse it. If a skillful ruler could convince people that certain principles are innate, this could "take them off from the use of their own reason and judgment, and put them on believing and taking them upon trust without further examination," and "in this posture of blind credulity, they might be more easily governed." But there were those whose interest in the theory of innate ideas was not so malignant, as in the case of Cudworth, the Cambridge Platonist, who published *The True Intellectual System of the Universe* in 1678, just at the time when Locke was trying to sort out his thoughts on these problems. Cudworth took the position that the demonstration of the existence of God rested upon the premise that certain principles are innate in the human mind. It was his contention that the famous empiricist formula that "nothing exists in the intellect which was not first in the senses" leads to atheism. He reasoned that if knowledge consists solely of information supplied to the mind by objects external to it, the external world existed before there was knowledge. In that case, knowledge could not have been the cause of the world. Locke disagreed with this view, saying that it was indeed possible to prove the existence of God without recourse to the notion of innate principles. He was particularly concerned to expose the groundless claim for innate ideas in order to keep clear the distinction between prejudice, enthusiasm, and opinion, on the one hand, and knowledge on the other. He therefore set out a series of arguments against this claim to innate ideas.

Those who argued for the theory of innate ideas did so on the grounds that people universally accept as true and certain various rational principles. Among these are the principles that "What is, is," which is the principle of identity, and that "It is impossible for the same thing to be, and not to be," which is the principle of noncontradiction. But are these innate? Locke denies that they are, though he does not question their certainty. These principles are certain not because they are innate but because the mind, reflecting on the nature of things as they are, will not let us think otherwise. To enforce this line of reasoning, Locke suggests first of all that even if it were true that these principles were accepted as true by all, this would not prove that they were innate, provided that an alternative explanation could be given for this universal consent. Moreover, there is some question whether there is universal knowledge of these principles. "Seldom," says Locke, are these general principles "mentioned in the huts of Indians, much less are they found in the thoughts of children." If it is argued that such principles can be apprehended only after the mind matures, then why call them *innate?* If they were truly innate, they must always be known, for "No proposition can be said to be in the mind, which it never yet knew, which it never yet was conscious of." As Locke saw the matter, the doctrine of innate ideas was superfluous because it contained nothing that he could not explain in terms of his empirical account of the origin of ideas.

Simple and Complex Ideas   Locke assumed that knowledge could be explained by discovering the raw materials out of which it was made. Of these ingredients he spoke this way: "Let us then suppose the mind to be, as we say, white paper, void of all characters, without any ideas:—How comes it to be furnished?... Whence has it all the *materials* of reason and knowledge? To this I answer, in one word, from EXPERIENCE." Experience gives us two sources of ideas, sensation and reflection. From the senses we receive into our minds several distinct perceptions and thereby become conversant about objects external to us. This is how we come to have the ideas of yellow, white, heat, cold, soft, hard, bitter, sweet, and all other sensible qualities. Sensation is the "great source of most of the ideas we have." The other facet of experience is reflection, an activity of the mind that produces ideas by taking notice of previous ideas furnished by the senses. Reflection involves perception, thinking, doubting, believing, reasoning, knowing, willing, and all those activities of the mind that produce ideas as distinct as those we receive from external bodies affecting our senses. All the ideas we have can be traced either to sensation or to reflection, and these ideas are either simple or complex.

Simple ideas constitute the chief source of the raw materials out of which our knowledge is made. These ideas are received passively by the mind through the senses. When we look at an object, ideas come into our minds single file. Even though an object has several qualities blended together, such as a white lily that has the qualities of whiteness and sweetness without any separation, the mind receives the ideas of *white* and *sweet* separately because each idea enters through a different sense, namely the sense of sight and the sense of smell. But even if different qualities entered by the same sense, as when both the hardness and coldness of ice come through the sense of touch, the mind sorts out the difference between them because there are in fact two different qualities involved. Simple ideas originate first of all, then, in sensation. But they also originate in reflection. Just as the senses are affected by objects, so also the mind is *aware* of the ideas it has received. In relation to the ideas received through the senses, the mind can develop other simple ideas by reasoning and judging, so that a simple idea of reflection might be pleasure or pain, or the idea of power obtained from observing the effect natural bodies have on one another.

Complex ideas, on the other hand, are not received passively but are rather put together by the mind as a compound of simple ideas. Here the emphasis is upon the activity of the mind, which takes three forms as the mind *joins* ideas, *brings* ideas together but holds them separate, and *abstracts*. Thus, the mind joins the ideas of whiteness, hardness, and sweetness to form the complex idea of a lump of sugar. The mind also brings ideas together but holds them separate for the purpose of thinking of relationships, as when we say the grass is greener than the tree. Finally, the mind can separate ideas "from all other ideas that accompany them in their real existence [as when we separate the idea of *man* from John and Peter]; and thus all its general ideas are made."

Primary and Secondary Qualities   To describe in even more detail how we get our ideas, Locke turned his attention to the problem of how ideas are related to the objects that produce them. Do our ideas reproduce exactly the objects we sense? If, for example, we consider a snowball, what is the relation between the ideas that the snowball engenders in our minds and the actual nature of the snowball? We have ideas such as round, moving, hard, white, and cold. To account for these ideas, Locke says that objects have *qualities*, and he defines a quality as "the power [in an object] to produce any idea in our mind." The snowball, then, has qualities that have the power to produce ideas in our minds.

Locke attempts here an important distinction between two different kinds of qualities in order to answer the question of how ideas are related to objects. He terms these qualities *primary* and *secondary*. Primary qualities are those that "really do exist in the bodies themselves"; thus our ideas, caused by primary qualities, resemble exactly those qualities that belong inseparably to the object. The snowball looks round and *is* round, appears to be moving and *is* moving. Secondary qualities, on the other hand, produce ideas in our mind that have no exact counterpart in the object. We have the idea of *cold* when we touch the snowball and the idea *white* when we see it. But there is no whiteness or coldness in the snowball; what *is* in the snowball is the quality, the power to create in us the ideas of cold and white. Primary qualities, then, refer to solidity, extension, figure, motion or rest, and number, or qualities which belong to the object. Secondary qualities, such as colors, sounds, tastes, and odors, do not belong to or constitute bodies except as powers to produce these ideas in us.

The importance of Locke's distinction between primary and secondary qualities is that through it he sought to distinguish between appearance and reality. Locke did not invent this distinction. Democritus had long ago suggested something similar when he said that colorless atoms are the basic reality and that colors, tastes, and odors are the results of particular organizations of these atoms. Descartes also separated secondary qualities from the basic substance he called *extension*. Locke's distinction reflected his interest in the new physics and the influence of the "judicious Mr. Newton's incomparable book" upon his thought. Newton explained the appearance of *white* as the motions of invisible minute particles. Reality, then, is found not in whiteness, which is only an effect, but in the motion of something, which is the cause. His discussion of primary and secondary qualities assumed throughout that there was *something* that could possess these qualities, and this he called *substance*.

Substance   Locke approached the question of substance from what he regarded as a common-sense point of view. How can we have ideas of qualities without supposing that there is something, some substance, in which these qualities subsist? If we ask what has shape or color, we answer something solid and extended. *Solid* and *extended* are primary qualities, and if we ask in what they subsist, Locke answers *substance*. However inevitable the idea of substance may be to common sense, Locke was unable to describe it with precision, admitting that "if any one will examine himself concerning his notion of pure substance in general, he will find he has no other idea of it at all, but only a supposition of he knows not what support of such qualities which are capable of producing simple ideas in us." Still, Locke saw in the concept of substance the explanation of sensation, saying that sensation is caused by substance. Similarly, it is substance that contains the powers that give regularity and consistency to our ideas. Moreover it is substance, Locke held, that constitutes the object of sensitive knowledge.

Locke was impelled by the simple logic of the matter: If there is motion, there must be something that moves; qualities cannot float around without something that holds them together. We have ideas of *matter* and of *thinking*, but "we shall never be able to know whether any mere material being thinks or no." But if there is thinking, there must be something that thinks. We also have an idea of God, which, like the idea of substance in general, is not clear and distinct. Yet, "if we examine the idea we have of the incomprehensible supreme being, we shall find that we come by it in the same way, and that the complex ideas we have both of God and separate spirits are made up of the simple ideas that we receive from reflection." The idea of God, as the idea of substance, is inferred from other simple ideas and is the product not of immediate observation but of demonstration. But the idea of substance, being "something we know not what," does raise for Locke the question of just how far our knowledge extends and how much validity it has.

The Degrees of Knowledge   How far our knowledge extends and how much validity it has depend, according to Locke, upon the relations our ideas have to each other. Indeed, Locke finally defines *knowledge* as nothing more than "the perception of the connexion of and agreement, or disagreement and repugnancy of any of our ideas." Our ideas enter single file into our minds, but once they are inside they can become related to each other in many ways. Some of the relations our ideas have to each other depend upon the objects we experience. At other times, our imagination can rearrange our simple and complex ideas to suit our fancy. Whether our knowledge is fanciful or valid depends upon our *perception* of the relationships of our ideas to each other. There are three modes of perception, namely, *intuitive, demonstrative*, and *sensitive*, and each one leads us to a different degree of knowledge regarding reality.

Intuitive knowledge is immediate, leaves no doubt, and is "the clearest and most certain that human frailty is capable of." Such knowledge "like sunshine forces itself immediately to be perceived as soon as ever the mind turns its view that way." Instantly we know that a circle is not a square or that 6 is not 8 because we can perceive the repugnancy of these ideas to each other. But besides these formal or mathematical truths, intuition can lead us to a knowledge of what exists. From intuition we know that we exist: "Experience then convinces us, that we have intuitive knowledge of our own existence, and an internal infallible perception that we are."

Demonstrative knowledge occurs when our minds engage in trying to discover the agreement or disagreement of ideas by calling attention to still other ideas. Ideally, each step of the demonstration must have intuitive certainty. This is particularly the case in mathematics, but again Locke thought that demonstration is a mode of perception that leads the mind to a knowledge of some form of existing reality. Thus "man knows, by an intuitive certainty, that bare nothing can no more produce any real being than it can be equal to two right angles." From this starting point Locke argued that since there are in fact existing things that begin and end in time, and since a "nonentity cannot produce any real being, it is an evident demonstration, that from eternity there has been something." Reasoning in a similar way, he concludes that this eternal Being is "most knowing" and "most powerful" and that "it is plain to me we have a more certain knowledge of the existence of God, than of anything our senses have not immediately discovered to us."

Sensitive knowledge is not knowledge in the strict sense of the term; it only "passes under the name of knowledge." Locke did not doubt that things outside of us exist, for, otherwise, where did we get our simple ideas? But sensitive knowledge does not give us certainty, nor does it extend very far. We sense that we see another person and have no doubt that the person exists, but our certainty ends when that person leaves us. "For if I saw such a collection of simple ideas as is wont to be called *man,* existing together one minute since, and am now alone, I cannot be certain that the same man exists now, since there is no *necessary connexion* of his existence a minute since with his existence now." And therefore, "though it be highly probable that millions of men do now exist, yet, whilst I am alone, writing this, I have not that knowledge of it which we strictly call knowledge; though the great likelihood of it puts me past doubt." Since experience simply makes us aware of qualities, we have no assurance of the connections between qualities, and in particular sensitive knowledge does not assure us that qualities which appear to our senses to be related are *necessarily* connected. We simply sense things as they are, and as we never sense *substance*, we never know from sensation how things are *really* connected. Nevertheless, sensitive knowledge gives us *some* degree of knowledge but not certainty. Intuitive knowledge gives us certainty that we exist, demonstrative knowledge indicates that God exists, and sensitive knowledge assures us that other selves and things exist but only as they are when we experience them.

Locke's Moral and Political Theory   Locke placed our thoughts about morality into the category of demonstrative knowledge. To him morality could have the precision of mathematics: "I am bold to think that morality is capable of demonstration, as well as mathematics: since the precise real essence of the things moral words stand for can be perfectly known, and so the congruity and incongruity of the things themselves be perfectly discovered." The key word in ethics, namely *good*, is perfectly understandable, for everybody knows what the word *good* stands for: "Things are good or evil only in reference to pleasure or pain. That we call good which is apt to cause or increase pleasure, or diminish pain in us...." Certain kinds of behavior will bring us pleasure, whereas other kinds will bring us pain. Morality, then, has to do with choosing or willing the good.

As a further definition of *ethics*, Locke says that "moral good and evil, then, is only the conformity or disagreement of our voluntary actions to some law," and he speaks of three kinds of laws, namely, the *law of opinion*, the *civil law*, and the *divine law*. The real issue here is to ask how Locke knows that these laws exist and also how he understands the relation of all three of them to each other. Bearing in mind that he saw no difficulty in demonstrating the existence of God, he now wants to draw further deductions from that demonstrative knowledge, saying that "...the idea of a supreme being infinite in power, goodness and wisdom, whose workmanship we are and on whom we depend, and the idea of ourselves as understanding rational beings, being such as are clear in us, would, I suppose, if duly considered and pursued, afford such foundations of our duty and rules of actions, as might place morality amongst the sciences capable of demonstration: wherein I doubt not but from self-evident principles, by necessary consequences, as incontestable as those in mathematics, the measures of right and wrong might be made out to anyone that will apply himself with the same indifferency and attention as he does to the other of those sciences."

Locke is here suggesting that by the light of nature, that is, by our reason, we can discover the moral rules that conform to God's law. He did not elaborate this program into a system of ethics, but he did indicate what relation the different kinds of laws should have to each other. The law of opinion represents a community's judgment of what kind of behavior will lead to happiness: Conformity to this law is called *virtue*, though it must be noticed that different communities have different ideas of what virtue consists of. The civil law is set by the commonwealth and enforced by the courts. This law tends to follow the first, for in most societies the courts enforce those laws that embody the opinion of the people. Divine law, which people can know either through their own reason or revelation, is the true rule for human behavior: "That God has given a rule whereby men should govern themselves, I think there is nobody so brutish as to deny." And "this is the only true touchstone of moral rectitude." In the long run, then, the law of opinion and also the civil law should be made to conform to the divine law, the "touchstone of moral rectitude." The reason there is a discrepancy between these three kinds of laws is that men everywhere tend to choose immediate pleasures instead of choosing those that have more lasting value. However ambiguous this moral theory may seem to us, Locke believed that these moral rules were eternally true, and upon the insights derived from the divine law he built his theory of natural rights.

The State of Nature   In his *Second Treatise of Government*, Locke begins his political theory as Hobbes did, with a treatment of "the state of nature." But he describes this condition in a very different way, even making Hobbes the target of his remarks. For Locke, the state of nature is not the same as Hobbes' "war of all against all." On the contrary, Locke says that "men living together according to reason, without a common superior on earth with authority to judge between them is properly the state of nature." According to Locke's theory of knowledge, people were able even in the state of nature to know the moral law. He said that "reason, which is that law, teaches all mankind who will but consult it, that, being all equal and independent, no one ought to harm another in his life, health, liberty or possessions." This natural moral law is not simply the egotistical law of self-preservation but the positive recognition of each person's value by virtue of his or her status as a creature of God. This natural law implied natural rights with correlative duties, and among these rights Locke emphasized particularly the right of private property.

Private Property   For Hobbes, there could be a right to property only after the legal order had been set up. Locke said that the right to private property precedes the civil law, for it is grounded in the natural moral law. The justification of private ownership is labor. Since one's labor is one's own, whatever one transforms from its original condition by one's labor becomes one's own, for one's labor is now mixed with those things. It is by mixing his or her labor with something that a person takes what was common property and makes it private property. There is consequently also a limit to that amount of property one can accumulate, namely, "as much as anyone can make use of to any advantage of life before it spoils, so much he may by his labour fix a property in." Locke assumed also that as a matter of natural right a person could inherit property, for "every man is born with...a right, before any other man, to inherit with his brethren his father's goods."

Civil Government   If people have natural rights and also know the moral law, why do they desire to leave the state of nature? To this question Locke answered that "the great and chief end of men's uniting into commonwealths and putting themselves under government is the preservation of their property."

By the term *property* Locke meant people's "lives, liberty and estates, which I call by the general name, property." It is true that people know the moral law in the state of nature, or rather they are capable of knowing it if they turn their minds to it. But through indifference and neglect they do not always develop a knowledge of it. Moreover, when disputes arise, people tend to decide them in their own favor. It is desirable therefore to have both a set of written laws and also an independent judge to decide disputes. To achieve those ends, people create a political society.

Locke put great emphasis on the inalienable character of human rights, and this led him to argue that political society must rest upon people's *consent,* for "men being... by nature all free, equal and independent, no one can be put out of this estate and subjected to the political power of another without his consent." But to what do people consent? They consent to have the laws made and enforced by society, but since "no rational creature can be supposed to change his condition with an intention to be worse," these laws must be framed so as to confirm those rights that people have by nature. They consent also to be bound by the majority, since "it is necessary the body should move that way whither the greater force carries it, which is the consent of the majority." For this reason Locke considered absolute monarchy as "no form of civil government at all." Whether in fact there was a time when we entered a compact is considered by Locke to be of no great consequence, for the important thing is that logically our behavior indicates that we have given our consent, and this Locke calls "tacit consent." For if we enjoy the privilege of citizenship, own and exchange property, rely upon the police and the courts, we have in effect assumed also the responsibilities of citizenship and consented to the rule of the majority. The fact that a person stays in his country, for after all he could leave and go to another one, confirms his act of consent.

Sovereignty Locke gives us a different picture of the sovereign power in society from the one we find in Hobbes. Hobbes' sovereign was absolute. Locke agrees that there must be a "supreme power," but he carefully placed this in the hands of the legislature, for all intents the majority of the people. He emphasized the importance of the division of powers chiefly to ensure that those who execute or administer the laws do not also make them, for "they may exempt themselves from obedience to the laws they make, and suit the law, both in its making and execution, to their own private advantage." The executive is therefore "under the law." Even the legislature is not absolute, although it is "supreme," for legislative power is held as a *trust* and is therefore only a fiduciary power. Consequently, "there remains still in the people a supreme power to remove or alter the legislative when they find the legislative act contrary to the trust reposed in them." Locke would never agree that people had irrevocably transferred their rights to the sovereign. The right to rebellion is retained, though rebellion is justified only when the government is *dissolved.* For Locke, government is dissolved not only when it is overthrown by an external enemy but also when internally there has been an alteration of the legislature. The legislative branch can be altered, for example, if the executive substitutes his law for the legislature's or if the executive neglects the execution of the official laws; in these cases rebellion is justified. Whereas Hobbes placed the sovereign under God's judgment, Locke stated that "the people shall judge."

BERKELEY

George Berkeley was born in Ireland in 1685. At the age of fifteen he entered Trinity College, Dublin, where he studied mathematics, logic, languages, and philosophy. He became a Fellow of the College a few years after he took his B.A. degree and was also ordained a clergyman in the Church of England, becoming a bishop in 1734. Beginning his famous literary career in his early twenties, his most important philosophical works include, among others, his *Essay towards a New Theory of Vision* (1709), *A Treatise Concerning the Principles of Human Knowledge* (1710), and *Three Dialogues between Hylas and Philonous* (1713). He traveled in France and Italy, and in London became friends with Steele, Addison, and Swift. While in London he sought to interest Parliament in his project of creating a college in Bermuda, whose purpose would be "the reformation of manners among the English in our western plantations, and the propagation of the Gospel among the American savages." With his new bride, he sailed in 1728 for America and for three years stayed in Newport, Rhode Island, making plans for his college. As the money for his college was never raised, Berkeley returned to London, leaving his influence upon American philosophy through frequent associations with Jonathan Edwards. Shortly thereafter he returned to Ireland, where for eighteen years he was Bishop of Cloyne. At the age of sixty-seven, he settled down in Oxford with his wife and family; a year later, in 1753, he died and was buried in Christ Church Chapel in Oxford.

It is ironic that Locke's common-sense approach to philosophy should have influenced Berkeley to formulate a philosophical position that at first seems so much at variance with common sense. He became the object of severe criticism and ridicule for denying what seemed most obvious to anyone. Berkeley had set out to deny the existence of matter. Dr. Samuel Johnson must have expressed the reaction of many when he kicked a large stone and said about Berkeley, "I refute him thus."

Berkeley's startling and provocative formula was that "to be is to be perceived," *esse est percipi.* Clearly this would mean that if something were not perceived, it would not exist. Berkeley was perfectly aware of the potential nonsense involved in this formula, for he says, "Let it not be said that I take away Existence. I only declare the meaning of the word so far as I comprehend it." Still, to say that the existence of something depends upon its being perceived does raise for us the question whether it exists when it is not being perceived. For Berkeley the whole problem turned on how we interpret or understand the word *exists*: "The table I write on I say exists; that is, I see and feel it: and if I were out of my study I should say it existed; meaning thereby

George Berkeley with family group in Newport, Rhode Island, during his brief stay in America *(Yale University Art Gallery)*

that if I were in my study I might perceive it, or that some other spirit actually does perceive it." Here Berkeley is saying that the word *exists* has no other meaning than the one contained in his formula, for we can know no instance where the term *exists* is used without at the same time assuming that a mind is perceiving something. To those who argued that material things have some kind of *absolute* existence without any relation to their being perceived, Berkeley replied, "that is to me unintelligible." To be sure, he said, "the horse is in the stable, the books in the study as before, even if I am not there. But since we know of no instance of anything's existing without being perceived, the table, horse, and books *exist* even when I do not perceive them because someone does perceive them."

How did Berkeley come upon this novel view? In his *New Theory of Vision* he argued that all our knowledge depends upon actual vision and other sensory experiences. In particular Berkeley argued that we never sense *space* or *magnitude*; we only have different visions or perceptions of things when we see them from different perspectives. Nor do we *see* distance; the distance of objects is *suggested* by our experience. All that we ever see are the qualities of an object that our faculty of vision is capable of sensing. We do not see the *closeness* of an object; we only have a different vision of it when we move toward or away from it. The more Berkeley considered the workings of his own mind and wondered how his ideas were related to objects outside of his mind, the more certain he was that he could never discover any object independent of his ideas. "When we do our utmost to conceive the existence of external bodies," he said, "we are all the while contemplating our own ideas." Nothing seems easier for us than to imagine trees in a park or books in a closet without anyone's looking at them. But what is all this, says Berkeley, except "framing in your mind certain ideas which you call *books* and *trees*.... But do not *you* yourself perceive or think of them all the while?" It is impossible, he concluded, ever to think of *anything* except as related to a mind. We never experience something that exists outside of us and separate from us as our ideas of *close* and *far* might suggest. There is nothing *out there* of which we do not have some perception.

It was Locke's philosophy that had raised doubts in Berkeley's mind about the independent existence of things, about the reality of matter. Locke had failed to push his own theory of knowledge to conclusions that to Berkeley seemed inevitable. When Locke spoke of substance as "something we know not what," he was only a short step from saying that it was nothing, which Berkeley did say. Locke's treatment of the relation between ideas and things assumed there is a real difference between primary and secondary qualities, between an object's size and shape on the one hand and its color, taste, and smell on the other. He assumed that whereas color exists only as an idea in the mind, size has to do with an object's *substance*, that reality that exists "behind" or "under" such secondary qualities as color and is therefore independent of a mind, is inert matter.

Berkeley, however, argued that size, shape, and motion "abstracted from all other qualities, are inconceivable." What, for example, is a cherry? It is soft, red, round, sweet, and fragrant. All these qualities are ideas in the mind that the cherry has the power to produce through the senses, so that the softness is felt, the color is seen, the roundness is either felt or seen, the sweetness is tasted, and the fragrance smelled. Again, the very existence of all these qualities consists in their being perceived. And, apart from these qualities, there is no sensed reality, in short, nothing else. The cherry, then, consists of all the qualities we perceive; the cherry (and all things) represents a complex of sensations. To say that besides the qualities perceived by the senses there are more primary qualities such as shape and size is to assume, says Berkeley, that primary and secondary qualities can be divided. It is impossible, he said, even to conceive of shape or size as independent of perception and therefore independent of secondary qualities. Is it possible, he asks, to separate primary and secondary qualities "even in thought"? He adds, "I might as easily divide a thing from itself. ... In truth, the object and the sensation are the same thing, and cannot therefore be abstracted from each other." A thing *is*, therefore, the sum of its perceived qualities, and it is for this reason that Berkeley argued that to be is to be perceived. Since substance, or matter, is never perceived or sensed, it cannot be said to exist. If substance does not exist and if only sensed qualities are real, then only thinking or, as Berkeley says, *spiritual* beings exist.

Besides leading Locke's empirical philosophy to what he thought were obvious conclusions, Berkeley was also contending with a complex of problems, to which he referred in his *Principles of Human Knowledge* as "...*the chief causes of error and difficulty in the Sciences, with the grounds of Scepticism, Atheism and Irreligion...inquired into.*" It was the notion of *matter* that caused all the difficulties, for if an inert material substance is admitted as really existing, where is there any place for spiritual or immaterial substances in such a universe? Also, would not scientific knowledge, based upon general ideas drawn from the behavior of things, give us a complete philosophy without requiring the idea of God, leading to "the monstrous systems of atheists"? This is not to say that Berkeley arbitrarily denounced the idea of matter because of these theological consequences but that he had additional reasons for pressing his views, which, he was convinced, were intrinsically right.

Matter a Meaningless Term   Locke had said that substance, or matter, *supports* or acts as a *substrate* to the qualities we sense. In Berkeley's *First Dialogue between Hylas and Philonous*, Hylas expresses Locke's view: " I find it necessary to suppose a material *substratum*, without which [qualities] cannot be conceived to exist." Philonous replies that the word *substratum* has no clear meaning for him and that he would want to "know any sense, literal or not literal, that you understand in it." But Hylas admits that he cannot assign any definite meaning to the term *substratum*, saying, "I declare I know not what to say." From this the conclusion is drawn that "The *absolute* existence of unthinking things [matter] are words without meaning." This is not to say that sensible things do not possess reality but only that sensible things exist only insofar as they are perceived. This of course implies that only ideas exist, but Berkeley adds that "I hope that to call a thing 'idea' makes it no less real." Aware that his idealism can be ridiculed, Berkeley writes: "What therefore becomes of the sun, moon, and stars? What must we think of houses, rivers, mountains, trees, stones; nay even of our own bodies? Are all these so many chimeras and illusions of fancy?" By his principles, he says, "we are not deprived of any one thing in nature. Whatever we see, feel, hear, or any wise conceive or understand, remains as secure as ever, and is as real as ever. There is a *rerum natura*, and the distinction between realities and chimeras retains its full force." If this is the case, why say that only *ideas*, instead of *things*, exist? In order, says Berkeley, to eliminate the useless concept of matter: "I do not argue against the existence of any one thing that we can apprehend, either by sense or reflexion.... The only thing whose existence we deny, is that which philosophers call matter or corporeal substance. And in doing of this, there is no damage done to the rest of mankind, who, I dare say, will never miss it."

Science and Abstract Ideas   Since it was the science of his day, particularly physics, that relied so heavily upon the notion of matter, Berkeley had to come to terms with its assumptions and methods. Science had assumed that we can, and must, distinguish between appearance and reality. The sea appears blue but is really not. Berkeley challenged the scientist to show whether there is any other reality than the sensible world. In this analysis Berkeley was pursuing the principle of empiricism and was trying to refine it. Physicists, he said, were obscuring science by including metaphysics in their theories: They used such words as *force, attraction, gravity* and thought they referred to some real physical entity. Even to speak of minute particles, whose motions cause the quality of color, is to engage in a rational and not empirical analysis. What disturbed Berkeley most was that scientists used general or abstract terms as though these terms accurately referred to real entities, particularly to an underlying material substance in nature. Nowhere, Berkeley argues, do we ever come upon such a substance, for substance is an abstract idea. Only sensed qualities really exist, and the notion of substance is a misleading inference drawn from observed qualities: "As several of these [qualities] are observed to accompany each other, they come to be marked by one name, and so to be reputed as one *thing*. Thus, for example, a certain colour, taste, smell, figure and consistence having been observed to go together, are accounted one distinct thing, signified by the name apple; other collections of ideas constitute a stone, a tree, a book and the like sensible things." Similarly, when scientists observe the operations of things, they use such abstract terms as *force* or *gravity* as though these were things or had some real existence in things. But *force* is simply a word describing our sensation of the behavior of things and gives us no more knowledge than our senses and reflections give us.

Berkeley did not mean to destroy science any more than he wanted to deny the existence of the "nature of things." What he did want to do was to clarify what scientific language was all about. Terms such as *force, gravity*, and *causality* refer to nothing more than clusters of ideas which our minds derive from sensation. We experience that heat melts wax, but all we know from this experience is that what we call *melting wax* is always accompanied by what we call *heat*. We have no knowledge of any single thing for which the word *cause* stands. Indeed, the only knowledge we have is of particular experiences. But even though we do not have firsthand knowledge of the causes of all things, we do know the order of things. We experience order, that *A* is followed by *B*, even though we have no experience of *why* this occurs. Science gives us a description of physical behavior, and many mechanical principles can be accurately formulated from our observations that are useful for purposes of prediction. Thus Berkeley would leave science intact, but he would clarify its language so that nobody would think that science was giving us more knowledge than we can derive from the sensible world. And the sensible world shows us neither substance nor causality.

God and the Existence of Things   Since Berkeley did not deny the existence of things or their order in nature, it was necessary for him to explain how things external to our minds exist even when *we* don't perceive them and how they achieve their order. Thus, elaborating his general thesis that to be is to be perceived, Berkeley says that "When I deny sensible things an existence out of the mind, I do not mean my mind in particular, but all minds. Now it is plain they have an existence exterior to my mind, since I find them by experience to be independent of it. There is therefore some other mind wherein they exist, during the intervals between the time of my perceiving them." And because all human minds are intermittently diverted from things "there is an *omnipresent eternal Mind*, which knows and comprehends all things, and exhibits them to our view in such a manner and according to such rules as he himself hath ordained, and are by us termed the *Laws of Nature*." The existence of things therefore depends upon the existence of God, and God is the cause of the orderliness of things in nature.

Again, Berkeley did not want to deny, for example, that even if he left the room, the candle would still be there, and that when he returned after an interval of time, it would have burned down. But this meant for Berkeley only that experience has a certain regularity that makes it possible for us to predict what our future experiences will be. To say that candles burn even when *I* am not in the room still does not prove that material substance exists independently from a mind. It seemed a matter of common sense to Berkeley to say that one can know about the candle only because he actually experiences a perception of it. In a similar way, we know that we exist because we have an awareness of our mental operations.

If, then, I try to describe or interpret reality in terms of my experience, I come first to the conclusion that there are other persons like myself who have minds. From this it can be assumed that as I have ideas, other persons likewise have ideas. Apart from my finite mind and the finite minds of others, there is a greater Mind analogous to mind, and this is God's Mind. God's ideas constitute the regular order of nature. The ideas that exist in our minds are God's ideas, which He communicates to us, so that the objects or things that we perceive in daily experience are caused not by *matter* or *substance* but by God. It is God, too, who coordinates all experiences of finite minds, assuring regularity and dependability in experience, which, in turn, enables us to think in terms of the "laws of nature." Thus the orderly arrangement of ideas in God's mind is communicated to the finite minds or spirits of humans, allowance being made for the differences in competence between the Divine and finite minds. The ultimate reality, then, is spiritual, (God), and not material, and the continued existence of objects when *we* are not perceiving them is explained by God's continuous perception of them.

To say, as Berkeley does, that our ideas come from God implies a special interpretation of causation. Again, Berkeley did not deny that we have an insight into causation; he only insisted that our sense data do not disclose to us a unique causal power. We do not, for example, when considering how and why water freezes, discover any power in cold that forces water to become solid. We do, however, understand causal connections through our mental operations. We are, for example, aware of our volition: we can will to move our arm, or, what is more important here, we can produce imaginary ideas in our minds. Our power to produce such ideas suggests that perceived ideas are also caused by a mental power. But whereas imaginary ideas are produced by finite minds, perceived ideas are created and caused to be in us by an infinite Mind.

Berkeley was confident that through his treatment of the formula *esse est percipi* he had effectively undermined the position of philosophical materialism and religious skepticism. Locke's empiricism inevitably implied skepticism insofar as he insisted that knowledge is based upon sense experience and that substance, or the reality behind appearances, could never be known. Whether Berkeley's arguments for the reality of God and spiritual beings successfully refuted materialism and skepticism remains a question, for his arguments contained some of the flaws he held against the materialists. His influence was nevertheless significant, but it was his empiricism and not his idealism that had lasting influence. Building upon Locke's empiricism, Berkeley made the decisive point that the human mind reasons only and always about particular sense experiences, that abstract ideas refer to no equivalent reality. Hume, who was to carry empiricism to its fullest expression, spoke of Berkeley as "a great philosopher [who] has disputed the received opinion in this particular, and has asserted that all general ideas are nothing but particular ones.... I look upon this to be one of the greatest and most valuable discoveries that has been made of late years in the republic of letters."

HUME

David Hume took the genuinely empirical elements in the philosophy of Locke and Berkeley, rejected some lingering metaphysics from their thought, and gave empiricism its clearest and most rigorous formulation. Born in Edinburgh in 1711 of Scottish parents, his early interest in literature soon indicated to his family that he would not follow their plan for him to become a lawyer. Though he attended the University of Edinburgh, he did not graduate. He was a gentle person with a tough mind who regarded "every object as contemptible except the improvement of my talents in literature," feeling "an insurmountable aversion to everything but the pursuits of philosophy and general learning." He spent the years 1734–1737 in France, under conditions of "rigid frugality," composing his *A Treatise of Human Nature*. When this book appeared in 1739, Hume was disappointed in its reception, remarking later that "never literary attempt was more unfortunate," for the book "fell deadborn from the press." His next book, *Essays Moral and Political*, published in 1741–1742, was an immediate success. Hume then revised his *Treatise* and eventually gave it the new title *An Enquiry Concerning Human Understanding*, by which it is known today. Besides his extensive books on the history of England, Hume wrote three other works that were to enhance his fame, namely, *Principles of Morals (1751), Political Discourses (1752),* and the book published after his death, *Dialogues concerning Natural Religion.*

Hume played a part in public life, going to France in 1763 as secretary to the British ambassador. His books had given him a wide reputation on the Con-

David Hume *(New York Public Library Picture Collection)*

tinent, and among his European friends was the philosopher Rousseau. For two years, 1767 to 1769, he was Under-Secretary of State, and in 1769 he returned to Edinburgh, where his house became the center for the most distinguished persons of that society. Being now "very opulent," he lived a quiet and contented life among friends and admirers, among them Adam Smith. He died in Edinburgh in 1776.

Hume wanted to build a "science of man," to study human nature by using the methods of physical science. His wide acquaintance with literature had shown him how often conflicting opinions are offered to readers on all subjects. He considered this conflict of opinions the symptom of a serious philosophical problem: How can we know the true nature of things? If artful authors can lead readers to accept conflicting ideas about morality, religion, and the true nature of physical reality, are these ideas equally true, or is there some method by which to discover the reason for this conflict of ideas? Hume shared the optimism of his day, which saw in scientific method the means for solving all the problems of the universe. He believed that such a method could lead us to a clear understanding of human nature and, in particular, the workings of the human mind.

As it turned out, Hume discovered that this optimism about the possibilities of using scientific methods for describing the mechanics of human thought could not be justified. His early faith in reason led, in the end, to skepticism. For as he traced the process by which ideas are formed in the mind, he was startled to discover how limited is the range of human thought. Both Locke and Berkeley had come to this same point, but neither one took his own account of the origin of ideas seriously enough to rest his theory of knowledge wholly upon it. They still had recourse to people's "common-sense" beliefs, which they were not willing to give up entirely. Although they argued that all our ideas come from experience, they felt confident that experience can give us certainty of knowledge on many subjects. Hume, on the other hand, concluded that if we take seriously the premise that all our ideas come from experience, we must accept the limits to knowledge that this explanation of ideas forces upon us, no matter what our customary beliefs may suggest.

Hume's Theory of Knowledge   The only way, says Hume, to solve the problem of disagreements and speculations regarding "abstruse questions" is to "enquire seriously into the nature of human understanding, and show from an exact analysis of its powers and capacity, that it is by no means fitted for such remote and abstruse subjects." Accordingly, Hume carefully analyzed a series of topics that led him to his skeptical conclusion, beginning with an account of the contents of the mind.

Contents of the Mind   Nothing seems more unbounded, says Hume, than our thought. Although our body is confined to one planet, our mind can roam instantly into the most distant regions of the universe. Nor, it may seem, is the mind bound by the limits of nature or reality, for without difficulty the imagination can conceive the most unnatural and incongruous appearances, such as flying horses and gold mountains. But, though the mind seems to possess this wide freedom, it is, says Hume, "really confined within very narrow limits." In the last analysis, the contents of the mind can all be reduced to the materials given us by the senses and experience, and those materials Hume calls *perceptions*. The perceptions of the mind take two forms, which Hume distinguishes as *impressions* and *ideas*.

Impressions and *ideas* make up the total content of the mind. The original stuff of thought is an *impression*, and an *idea* is merely a copy of an impression. The difference between an impression and an idea is only the degree of their vividness. The original perception is an impression, as when we hear, see, feel, love, hate, desire, or will. These impressions are "lively" and clear when we have them. When we reflect upon these impressions, we have ideas of them, and those ideas are less-lively versions of the original impressions. To feel pain is an impression, whereas the memory of this sensation is an idea. In every particular, impressions and their corresponding ideas are alike, differing only in their degree of vivacity.

Besides merely distinguishing between impressions and ideas, Hume argues that without impressions there can be no ideas. For if an idea is simply a copy of an impression, it follows that for every idea there must be a prior impression. Not every idea, however, reflects a corresponding impression, for we have never seen a flying horse or a golden mountain even though we have ideas of them. But Hume explains such ideas as being the product of the mind's "faculty of compounding, transposing, or diminishing the materials afforded us by the senses and experience." When we think of a flying horse, our imagination joins two ideas, wings and horse, which we originally acquired as impressions through our senses. If we have any suspicion that a philosophical term is employed without any meaning or idea, we need, says Hume, "but enquire, *from what impression is that supposed idea derived?* And if it be impossible to assign any, this will serve to confirm our suspicion." Hume subjected even the idea of God to this test and concluded that it arises from reflecting on the operations of our own minds "augmenting without limit" the qualities of goodness and wisdom that we experience among human beings. But if all our ideas follow from impressions, how can we explain what we call *thinking*, or the patterns by which ideas group themselves in our minds?

Association of Ideas It is not by mere chance that our ideas are related to each other. There must be, says Hume, "some bond of union, some associating quality, by which one idea naturally introduces another." Hume calls it "a gentle force, which commonly prevails...pointing out to every one those simple ideas, which are most proper to be united in a complex one." It is not a special faculty of the mind that associates one idea with another, for Hume has no impression of the structural equipment of the mind. But by observing the actual patterns of our thinking and analyzing the groupings of our ideas, Hume thought he had discovered an explanation for the association of ideas.

His explanation was that whenever there are certain qualities in ideas, these ideas are associated with each other. These qualities are three in number: resemblance, contiguity in time or place, and cause and effect. Hume believed that the connections of all ideas to each other could be explained by these qualities and gave the following examples of how they work: "A picture naturally leads our thoughts to the original [*resemblance*]: the mention of one apartment in the building naturally introduces an enquiry...concerning the others [*contiguity*]: and if we think of a wound, we can scarcely forebear reflecting on the pain which follows it [*cause and effect*]." There are no operations of the mind that differ in principle from one of these three examples of the association of ideas. But of these, the notion of cause and effect was considered by Hume to be the central element in knowledge. He took the position that the causal principle is the foundation upon which the validity of all knowledge depends. If there is any flaw in the causal principle, we can have no certainty of knowledge.

Causality Hume's most original and influential ideas deal with the problem of causality. Neither Locke nor Berkeley challenged the basic principle of causality; though Berkeley did say that we cannot discover efficient causes *in* things, his intention was to look for the cause of phenomena and therefore the predictable order of nature in God's activity.

For Hume, the very idea of causality is suspect, and he approaches the problem by asking the question, "What is the origin of the idea of causality?" Since ideas are copies of impressions, Hume asks what impression gives us the idea of causality. His answer is that there is no impression corresponding to this idea. How then does the idea of causality arise in the mind? It must be, said Hume, that the idea of causality arises in the mind when we experience certain relations between objects. When we speak of cause and effect, we mean to say that *A* causes *B*. But what kind of a relation does this indicate between *A* and *B?* Experience furnishes us with three relations: first, there is the relation of *contiguity*, for *A* and *B* are always close together; secondly, there is *priority in time,* for *A,* the "cause," always precedes *B,* the "effect"; and thirdly, there is *constant conjunction,* for we always see *A* followed by *B.* But there is still another relation that the idea of causality suggests to common sense, namely, that between *A* and *B* there is a "necessary connexion." But neither contiguity, priority, nor constant conjunction implies "necessary" connection between objects. There is no object, says Hume, that implies the existence of another when we consider objects individually. No amount of observation of oxygen can ever tell us that when mixed with hydrogen it will give us water. We know this only after we have seen the two together: "It is therefore by *experience* only that we can infer the existence of one object from another." While we do have impressions of contiguity, priority, and constant conjunction, we do *not* have any impression of *necessary connections.* Thus, causality is not a quality in the objects we observe but is rather a "habit of association" in the mind produced by the repetition of instances of *A* and *B.*

Insofar as Hume assumed that the causal principle is central to all kinds of knowledge, his attack on this principle undermined the validity of all knowledge. He saw no reason for accepting the principle that *whatever begins to exist must have a cause of existence* as either intuitive or capable of demonstration. In the end, Hume considered thinking or reasoning "a species of sensation," and as such our thinking cannot extend beyond our immediate experiences.

What Exists External to Us?   Hume's extreme empiricism led him to argue that there is no rational justification for saying that bodies or things have a continued and independent existence external to us. Our ordinary experience suggests that things outside of us do exist. But if we take seriously the notion that our ideas are copies of impressions, the philosophical conclusion must be that all we know is impressions. Impressions are internal subjective states and are not clear proof of an external reality. To be sure we always act as though there is a real external world of things, and Hume was willing to "take for granted in all our reasonings" that things do exist. But he wanted to inquire into the reason why we think there is an external world.

Our senses do not tell us that things exist independent of us, for how do we know that they continue to exist even when we interrupt our sensation of them? And even when we sense something, we are never given a double view of it whereby we can distinguish the thing from our impression of it; we have only the impression. There is no way for the mind to reach beyond impressions or the ideas they make possible: "...let us chase our imagination to the heavens, or to the utmost limits of the universe; we never advance a step beyond our selves, nor can we conceive any kind of existence, but those perceptions which have appeared in that narrow compass. This is the universe of the imagination, nor have we any idea but what is there produced."

Constancy and Coherence   Our belief that things exist external to us, says Hume, is the product of our imagination as it deals with two special characteristics of our impressions. From impressions our imagination becomes aware of both *constancy* and *coherence*. There is a constancy in the arrangement of things when, for example, I look out of my window: There are the mountain, the house, and the trees. If I shut my eyes or turn away and then later look at the same view again, the arrangement is still the same, and it is this constancy in the contents of my impressions that leads my imagination to conclude that the mountain, house, and trees exist whether I think of them or not. Similarly, I put a log on the fire before I leave the room, and when I return it is almost in ashes. But even though a great change has taken place in the fire, I am accustomed to finding this kind of change under similar circumstances: "This coherence...in their changes is one of the characteristics of external objects." In the case of the mountain, there is a constancy of our impressions, whereas in respect to the fire our impressions have a coherent relation to the processes of change. For these reasons, the imagination leads us to believe that certain things continue to have an independent existence external to us. But this is a *belief* and not a rational proof, for the assumption that our impressions are connected with things is "without any foundation in reasoning." Hume extends this skeptical line of reasoning beyond objects or things to consider the existence of the *self, substance*, and *God*.

The Self   Hume denied that we have any idea of *self*. This may seem paradoxical, that *I* should say that I do not have an idea of myself, yet here again Hume wants to test what we mean by a self by asking, "from what impression could this idea be deriv'd?" Is there any continuous and identical reality which forms our ideas of the self? Do we have any one impression that is invariably associated with our idea of *self?* "When I enter most intimately into what I call *myself*," says Hume, "I always stumble on some particular perception or other, of heat or cold, love or hatred, pain or pleasure. I never can catch *myself* at any time without a perception and never can observe anything but the perception." Hume denies the existence of a continuous self-identity and says about the rest of humanity that "they are nothing but a bundle or collection of different perceptions." How then do we account for what we think is the self? It is our power of memory that gives the impression of our continuous identity. Hume compares the mind to "a kind of theatre where several perceptions successively make their appearance," but adds that "we have not the most distant notion of the place where these scenes are represented."

Substance   What led Hume to deny the existence of a continuous self that in some way retains its identity through time was his thorough denial of the existence of any form of *substance*. Locke retained the idea of substance as that *something,* which has color or shape, and other qualities, though he spoke of it as "something we know not what." Berkeley denied the existence of substance underlying qualities but retained the idea of spiritual substances. Hume denied that substance in any form exists or has any coherent meaning. If what is meant by the *self* is some form of substance, Hume argued that no such substance can be derived from our impressions of sensation. If the idea of substance is conveyed to us by our senses, Hume asked, "which of them; and after what manner? If it be perceiv'd by the eyes, it must be a colour; if by the ears, a sound; if by the palate, a taste.... We have therefore no idea of substance, distinct from that of a collection of particular qualities."

God   It was inevitable that Hume's rigorous premise, that "our ideas reach no further than our experience," would lead him to raise skeptical questions about the existence of God. Most attempts to demonstrate the existence of God rely upon some version of causality. Among these, the argument from *design* has always made a powerful impact upon the mind. Hume is aware of the power of this argument, but he quickly sorts out the elements of the problem, leaving the argument with less than its usual force.

The argument from design begins with the observance of a beautiful order in nature. This order resembles the kind of order the human mind is able to impose upon unthinking materials. From this preliminary observation, the mind concludes that unthinking materials do not contain the principle of orderliness within themselves: "Throw several pieces of steel together, without shape or form; they will never arrange themselves so as to compose a watch." Order, it is held, requires the activity of a mind, an orderer. Our experience tells us that neither a watch nor a house can come into being without a watchmaker or an architect. From this it is inferred that the natural order bears an analogy to the order fashioned by human effort and that just as the watch requires an ordering cause, so the natural order of the universe requires one. But such an inference, says Hume, "is uncertain; because the subject lies entirely beyond the reach of human experience."

If the whole argument from design rests upon the proposition "*that the cause or causes of order in the universe probably bear some remote analogy to human intelligence,*" then, says Hume, the argument cannot prove as much as it claims. Hume's criticism of the idea of causality has particular force here. Since we derive the idea of cause from repeated observations of the contiguity, priority, and constant conjunction of two things, how can we assign a cause to the universe when we have never experienced the universe as related to anything we might consider a cause. The use of analogy does not solve the problem because the analogy between a watch and the universe is not exact. Why not consider the universe the product of a vegetative process instead of a rational designer? And even if the cause of the universe is something like an intelligence, how can moral characteristics be ascribed to such a being? Moreover, if analogies are to be used, which one should be selected? Houses and ships are frequently designed by a group of designers: Should we say there are many gods? Sometimes experimental models are built with no present knowledge of what the finished form will be like: Is the universe a trial model or the final design? By this line of probing, Hume wished to emphasize that the order of the universe is simply an empirical fact and that we cannot infer from it the existence of God. This does not make Hume an atheist. He is simply testing our idea of God the way he had tested our ideas of the *self* and *substance* by his rigorous principle of empiricism. He ends, to be sure, as a skeptic, but finally makes the telling point that "to whatever length any one may push his speculative principles of scepticism, he must act and live and converse like other men.... It is impossible for him to persevere in total scepticism, or make it appear in his conduct for a few hours."

ETHICS

Hume's skepticism did not prevent him from taking ethics seriously. On the contrary, in the opening passage of the third book of his *Treatise of Human Nature,* Hume writes that "morality is a subject that interests us above all others." His interest in ethics was so strong that he hoped to do for that subject what Galileo and Newton did for natural science, saying in the first section of his *An Enquiry Concerning the Principles of Morals* that "moral philosophy is in the same condition as... astronomy before the time of Copernicus." Just as the older science with its abstract general hypotheses had to give way to a more experimental method, so also the time had come, Hume writes, when philosophers "should attempt a like reformation in all moral disquisitions; and reject every system of ethics, however subtle or ingenious, which is not founded on fact and observation."

For Hume, the central fact about ethics is that moral judgments are formed not by reason alone but by the sentiment of sympathy. There is no doubt that reason plays a considerable role in our discussions about ethical decisions. But, says Hume, reason "is not sufficient alone to produce any moral blame or approbation." What limits the role of reason in ethics is that reason makes judgments concerning *matters of fact* and *relations* whereas moral judgments of good and evil are not limited to matters of fact or relations.

Why, for example, do we judge murder to be a crime? Or, to use Hume's words, "where is that matter of fact which we here call *crime?*" If you describe the action, the exact time at which it occurred, the weapon used, in short, if you assemble all the details about the event, the faculty of reason would still not isolate that fact to which the label of crime is attached. After all, this act cannot always and in all circumstances be considered a crime. The same action might be called self-defense or official execution. The judgment of good or evil is made *after* all the facts are known. The goodness or badness of an act is not a new fact discovered or deduced by reason. Nor is moral discourse similar to mathematical reasoning. From a few facts about a triangle or circle, additional facts and relations can be inferred. But goodness, like beauty, is not an additional fact inferred or deduced by reason. "Euclid has fully explained all the qualities of the circle," says Hume, "but has not in any proposition said a word of its beauty. The reason is evident. The beauty is not a quality of the circle. It lies not in any part of the line, whose parts are equally distant from a common center. It is only the effect which that figure produces upon the mind, whose peculiar fabric of structure renders it susceptible of such sentiments."

Hume presses this point by asking us to "see if you can find that matter of fact, or real existence, which you call *vice*," and he argues that "in whichever way you take it, you find only certain passions, motives, volitions and thoughts. There is no other matter of fact in the case.... You can never find it, till you turn your reflection into your own breast and find a sentiment of disapprobation which arises in you toward this action. Here is a matter of fact; but it is the object of feeling, not reason. It lies in yourself, not in the object."

Hume realized that to build a system of ethics upon the faculty of feeling, sentiment, or sympathy is to run the risk of reducing ethics to a matter of taste, where moral judgments are subjective and relative. Moreover, to designate feeling or sentiment as the source of praise or blame is to imply that our moral judgments flow from a calculus of our individual self-interest or self-love. Hume rejects these assumptions by affirming that moral sentiments are found in all men, that men praise or blame the same actions and that praise or blame is not derived from a narrow self-love. The sentiment of sympathy, or fellow-feeling, writes Hume, must be acknowledged as a "principle in human nature beyond which we cannot hope to find any principle more general." It is through this human capacity, he writes, that "we frequently bestow praise on virtuous actions, performed in very distant ages and remote countries; where the utmost subtilty of imagination would not discover any appearance of self-interest, or find any connection of our present happiness and security with events so widely separated from us." Moreover, adds Hume, "a generous, a brave, a noble deed, performed by an adversary, commands our approbation; while in its consequences it may be acknowledged prejudicial to our particular interest." Hume was convinced that this capacity for sympathy provides a complete explanation for our judgments of praise or blame.

Hume's conception of moral sentiment and sympathy is in sharp contrast to the traditional ethical theory which holds that morality consists in the relation of actions to a rule of right. That theory defines an action as good or evil depending upon whether the action agrees or disagrees with the rule. But Hume rejects the hypothesis that there are moral rules, saying that such an hypothesis is "abstruse" and "can never be made intelligible." By contrast, Hume offers an alternative hypothesis for ethics which, he says, "defines virtue to be *whatever mental action or quality gives to a spectator the pleasing sentiment of approbation; and vice the contrary.*" Among those qualities which give the spectator the pleasing sentiment of approbation are "discretion, caution, enterprise, industry, economy, good-sense, prudence and discernment." Also, there is virtually universal agreement, even among the most cynical of the world, concerning "the merit of temperance, sobriety, patience, constancy, considerateness, presence of mind, quickness of conception and felicity of expression." What is there about these qualities which generates our praise? It is, says Hume, that these qualities are *useful* and *agreeable*. But useful for what? Hume replies, "for somebody's interest, surely. Whose interest then? Not our own only: For our approbation frequently extends farther. It must, therefore, be the interest of those, who are served by the character or action approved of." *Usefulness* is defined by Hume as "a tendency to a natural end." He also argues that the distinction between what is useful and what is pernicious is the essential moral distinction. Therefore, says Hume, "if usefulness...be a source of moral sentiment, and if this usefulness be not always considered with reference to self; it follows, that everything which contributes to the happiness of society, recommends itself directly to our approbation and good-will. Here is a principle which accounts in great part for the origin of morality: And what need we seek for abstruse and remote systems, when there occurs one so obvious and natural?"

Hume acknowledges the intermingling of self-interest and sympathy in his analysis of justice. Indeed, he argues that justice, which he describes as "a general peace and order" or "a general abstinence from the possessions of others," reflects the self-interest of each person who desires to be secure in person and property. This security and happiness can be achieved only in society, in an arrangement of justice. To this extent, justice is a reflection of self-interest. The usefulness of justice is that it satisfies self-interest. For this reason, Hume is able to say that public utility is the *sole* origin of justice, and that reflections on the beneficial consequences of this virtue are the *sole* foundation of its merit. But although social utility or self-interest drive us into society or into a scheme of justice, it is something besides self-interest which provides the *moral* basis for justice. What gives justice the quality of a moral virtue and injustice that of vice is not self-interest but rather the sentiment of sympathy. We condemn injustice not only when our own personal interests are involved but whenever it produces pain or disagreeableness in others which we can share through sympathy. "Thus," says Hume, "self-interest is the original motive to the establishment of justice: but a sympathy with public interest is the source of the moral approbation which attends that virtue."

14

Rousseau: A Romantic in the Age of Reason

ousseau's career unfolded during the French Enlightenment, that Age of Reason which in eighteenth-century France was dominated by Voltaire (1694–1778), Montesquieu (1689–1755), Diderot (1713–1784), Condorcet (1743–1794), Holbach, and others who were known as *philosophes*. These people were, for the most part, dissident voices who challenged the traditional modes of thought concerning religion, government, and morality. Believing that human reason provides the most reliable guide to man's destiny, they held that "Reason is to the *philosophe* what grace is to the Christian." This was the theme of the remarkable *Encyclopédie* (1751–1780), which contained the distinctive ideas of the *philosophes* and which, under the editorship of Diderot and d'Alembert, consisted by 1780 of thirty-five volumes. Into this vigorous intellectual climate Rousseau entered with the most unlikely credentials. Despite little formal education, he fashioned a set of ideas about human nature with such compelling power that his thought ultimately prevailed over the most impressive thinkers of his time.

Jean Jacques Rousseau was born in Geneva in 1712. His mother died a few days after his birth, and his father, a watchmaker, left him at age ten in the

Jean Jacques Rousseau *(The Bettmann Archive)*

care of an aunt, who raised him. After two years in a boarding school where, he says in his *Confessions,* "we were to learn...all the insignificant trash that has obtained the name of education," he was recalled to his aunt's household and thus, at the age of twelve, his formal education came to an end. After a short apprenticeship as an engraver of watchcases, he left Geneva and wandered from place to place, meeting a series of people who alternately helped him make a meager living or referred him to still other potential benefactors. Along the way he read books and developed his skills in music. Eventually he wandered into France and there came under the care of a noblewoman, Mme. de Warens, who sought to further his formal education, an attempt which failed, and to arrange for his employment. His most consistent work was copying music, though he was for a while tutor to the children of M. de Mably, who was grand provost of Lyons, and later secretary to the French Ambassador to Venice. Rousseau was a precocious child and learned to read at an early age. In his twenties he read portions of the classic works of Plato, Virgil, Horace, Montaigne, Pascal, and Voltaire, which in their variety strongly influenced his imagination. From Lyons he went, armed with letters of introduction from the Mablys, to Paris, where he met some of the most influential persons of this capital city. Here he was struck by the contrasts between noble wealth and sweaty artisans, the majesty of cathedrals and bishops who read the heretical ideas of Voltaire, the gaiety of the salons and the tragic themes of Racine's plays. Although he met many notables, including Diderot, and moved increasingly in the upper circles of French society, he retained his childhood shyness, especially with women, and in 1746 eventually formed a lifelong relationship with an uneducated young servant girl, Thérèse Le Vasseur, whom he finally married in 1768.

Rousseau's literary career began with his prize-winning essay entitled *Discourse on the Arts and Sciences* (1750). With strong emotional power he argued that morals had been corrupted by the replacement of religion by science, by sensuality in art, by licentiousness in literature, and by the emphasis upon logic at the expense of feeling. The essay made Rousseau instantly famous, leading Diderot to say that "never was there an instance of a like success." There followed in 1752 an operetta, *Le Devin du Village,* performed before the King and his court at Fontainebleau, and a comedy, *Narcisse,* played by the Comédie-Française. Two important works appeared in 1755, his discourse entitled *What Is the Origin of the Inequality Among Men, and Is It Authorized by Natural Law?* and *Discourse on Political Economy,* which appeared in the *Encyclopédie.* In 1761 Rousseau published a love story, *Julie, ou La Nouvelle Héloïse,* which became the most celebrated novel of the eighteenth century. His book *Émile,* published in 1762, offered an elaborate proposal for a new approach to education and contained also a provocative section, "The Confession of Faith of a Savoyard Vicar," which was critical of institutional religion while advocating the importance of religion to mankind. In the same year he published his most famous work, *The Social Contract,* in which he sought to describe the passage from the "state of nature" to the civil state and to answer why it is that laws governing people are legitimate.

Rousseau's last days were unhappy as he was in failing health and suffered from profound paranoia. Moreover, his books were severely criticized by the leaders of both church and state, and word went out that "J.-J. Rousseau shall be apprehended and brought to the Concierge prison in the Palace [of Justice]." He became a fugitive, and at one point accepted David Hume's invitation to visit him in England, where he spent sixteen months. He returned to France convinced that his enemies were plotting to defame him. When he was told that Voltaire was dying, he said, "Our lives were linked to each other; I shall not survive him long." In July 1778, Rousseau died at the age of sixty-six. His remarkably frank and detailed autobiography was published after his death in his *Confessions.*

THE PARADOX OF LEARNING

When Rousseau read the announcement by the Academy of Dijon that a prize would be given for the best essay on the question of "Whether the restoration of the arts and sciences has had the effect of purifying or corrupting morals" he reacted with passionate excitement at the prospect of writing just such an essay. Looking back upon that moment, he said, "I felt myself dazzled by a thousand sparkling lights. Crowds of vivid ideas thronged into my mind with a force and confusion that threw me into unspeakable agitation." He was already thirty-eight years old, had read widely in classical and contemporary literature, had traveled in Switzerland, Italy, and France, had observed the ways of different cultures, and had spent enough time in the social circles of Paris to have nothing but contempt for that sophisticated society. "If ever I could have written a quarter of what I saw and felt," he continued, "with what clarity I should have brought out all the contradictions of our social system." What he did set out to show was that "man is by nature good, and that only our institutions have made him bad." This turned out to be the underlying theme of Rousseau's future writings. But in this essay, the theme lacked precision and clarity, for, as Rousseau himself admitted, "though full of force and fire, [this first *Discourse*] was absolutely wanting in logic and order... and it is the weakest in reasoning of all the works I ever wrote." For this reason, Rousseau's *Discourse on the Arts and Sciences* was an easy target for his critics. It was inevitable that his readers would have difficulty with his paradoxical argument that civilization is the cause of unhappiness or that the corruption of society is caused by learning in the arts and sciences.

Rousseau begins his *Discourse* with high praise for the achievements of human reason, saying that "it is a noble and beautiful spectacle to see man raising himself... from nothing by his own exertions; dissipating by the light of reason all the thick clouds by which he was by nature enveloped." Only a few sentences later, his essay becomes a slashing attack upon the arts, literature, and sciences which, he says, "fling garlands of flowers over the chains which weight men down" in their common life and "stifle in men's hearts that sense of original liberty for which they seem to have been born." Rousseau recognizes that human nature was not really any better in earlier times but believed that the arts and sciences produced some significant changes making people worse. Before art and literature molded our behavior and taught our passions to speak an artificial language, our morals, says Rousseau, were rude but natural. Modern manners have made everyone conform in speech, dress, and attitude, always following the laws of fashion, never the promptings of our own nature, so that we no longer dare appear to be what we really are. The herd of humanity all act exactly alike and thus we never know even among our friends with whom we are dealing. Human relationships are now full of deceptions, whereas earlier people could easily see through one another, an advantage which prevented their having many vices.

Rousseau directed his attack also against luxury and against political leaders who emphasized the economic aspects of politics. He reminded his contemporaries that "the politicians of the ancient world were always talking about morals and virtue; ours speak of nothing but commerce and money." His argument against luxury was that it could produce a brilliant but not a lasting society, for although money "buys everything else, it cannot buy morals and citizens." Artists and musicians pursuing luxury will lower their genius to the level of the times, composing mediocre works that will be immediately admired. This is the evil consequence of learning in the arts and sciences where morals no longer have their rightful place and where taste has been corrupted. One way to confront this matter is to acknowledge the role of women for, says Rousseau, "men will always be what women choose to make them. If you wish then they should be noble and virtuous, let women be taught what greatness of soul and virtue are." But, says Rousseau, the question is no longer whether people are honest but whether they are clever, not whether a book is useful but whether it is well written. Rewards are lavished on ingenuity, but virtue is left unhonored.

Rousseau pointed to historical evidence for the notion that progress in the arts and sciences always leads to the corruption of morals and the decay of society. Egypt, he said not altogether correctly, was "the mother of philosophy and the fine arts; soon she was conquered by Cambyses, and then successively by the Greeks, the Romans, the Arabs and finally the Turks." Similarly, Greece, once peopled by heroes, "always learned, always voluptuous, and always a slave, has experienced amid all its revolutions no more than a change of masters." It was for this reason that in Greece "not all the eloquence of Demosthenes could breathe life into a body which luxury and the arts had once enervated." Rome developed a great empire when she was a nation of barbarians and soldiers, but when she relaxed the stoic discipline and fell into epicurean indulgence, she was scorned by other nations and derided even by the barbarians. Only Sparta, where patriotism was the supreme virtue and where arts, artists, science, and scholars were not tolerated, emerged as Rousseau's ideal state.

To see Rousseau praising ignorance during the height of the Enlightenment is an astonishing spectacle. But he did not mean to say that philosophy and science had no value. He quoted approvingly the words of Socrates, who also had praised ignorance. For Athens had its sophists, poets, orators, and artists who had made extravagant claims to knowlege while in fact they knew very little, whereas, says Socrates, "I am at least in no doubt of my ignorance." What Rousseau was concerned about was the danger to morals and society caused by the confusion of contending theories or points of view. If everyone is allowed to pursue his own thoughts about moral values or even about scientific truth, it is inevitable that there will be serious differences of opinion. If differences of opinion are to be found everywhere, it will not be long before a deep skepticism will spread throughout the population.

A stable society is based upon a set of opinions or values which the majority accept as the rule for their thought and behavior. Rousseau believed that these firmly held opinions can be undermined by philosophy and science for several reasons. For one thing, each society is unique, and its genius is its special local set of values. But science and philosophy seek to discover universal truth. The very pursuit of such universal truth exposes the local opinion as less than the truth and thereby destroys its authority. To compound this problem, science emphasizes the requirement of proof and evidence, yet the dominant opinions about the most important subjects cannot be demonstrated beyond a doubt and, therefore, lose their binding force. Moreover, science requires an attitude of doubt which is contrary to the mood of ready acceptance of opinion. What keeps society together is faith, not knowledge. Both the scientist and the philosopher suspend faith, during their pursuit of knowledge. So long as this suspension of faith is restricted to certain special individuals there is no great harm. What disturbed Rousseau was the damage done by the wide diffusion among the population of the spirit of doubt which culminates in skepticism. The step from skepticism to the loosening of morality in turn inevitably causes a weakening of public virtue, which Rousseau understood chiefly as the virtue of patriotism. The very spirit of science undermines patriotism since the scientist tends to be a cosmopolitan, whereas the patriot has a strong attachment to his own society. To counteract these disintegrating trends in society, strong governments become necessary and this, according to Rousseau, paves the way to despotism.

In the end, Rousseau's quarrel was not so much with philosophy and science as with the attempt to popularize these disciplines. He had great respect for Sir Francis Bacon, Descartes, and Sir Isaac Newton, whom he considered great teachers of mankind. But, he said, "It belongs only to a few to raise monuments to the glory of human learning," and it is proper to allow some people to apply themselves to the study of the arts and sciences. His attack was upon those who would distort knowledge by trying to make it popular, "those compilers who have indiscreetly broken open the door to the sciences and introduced into their sanctuary a populace unworthy to approach it." People need to know, said Rousseau, that "nature would have preserved them from science, as a mother snatches a dangerous weapon from the hands of her child." Ordinary people should build their happiness upon the opinions which "we can find in our own hearts." Virtue, says Rousseau, is the "sublime science of simple minds," for the true philosophy is to "listen to the voice of conscience."

THE SOCIAL CONTRACT

Although Rousseau compares natural humanity in the "state of nature" with humanity as citizens of a civil society, he admits that he cannot give a specific account of how the transition from the earlier condition to the later one occurred. The purpose of his book *The Social Contract* is therefore not to describe the change from humanity's natural state to the subsequent membership in a political society but rather to provide an answer to the question why it is that a person ought to obey the laws of government. Thus, Rousseau begins his book with the famous phrase that "Man is born free; and everywhere he is in chains." "How," he continues, "did this change come about? I do not know. What can make it legitimate? That question I think I can answer."

In the state of nature, people were happy, not because they were angels but because they lived entirely for themselves and therefore possessed an absolute independence. Rousseau rejected the doctrine of original sin and instead believed that the origin of evil is to be found in the later stages of human development in society. In the state of nature, says Rousseau, people are motivated by "a natural sentiment [*amour de soi*] which inclines every animal to watch over his own preservation, and which, directed in man by reason and pity, produces humanity and virtue." By contrast, as people develop social contacts, they also develop vices, for now they are motivated by "an artificial sentiment [*amour propre*] which is born in society and which leads every individual to make more of himself than every other," and "this inspires in men all the evils they perpetrate on each other," including intense competition for the few places of honor, envy, malice, vanity, pride, and contempt. Ultimately, it was impossible to live alone, for in all probability, says Rousseau, it was the steady growth in numbers that first brought people together into society. How, then, were people to reconcile the independence into which they were born with the inevitability that they would have to live together? The problem, says Rousseau, is "to find a form of association which will defend and protect with the whole common force the person and goods of each associate, and in which each, while uniting himself with all, may still obey himself alone." The solution to this problem is "the total alienation of each associate, together with all his rights, to the whole community." While this solution appears on the surface to be a prescription for despotism, Rousseau was convinced that it was the road to freedom.

The idea of a "social contract" seems to imply that such a contract was entered into at some point in the historic past. Rousseau did not view the contract in historical terms since he admitted that there is no way to discover evidence for such an event. For him, the social contract is a living reality which will be found to be present wherever there is a legitimate government. This living contract is the fundamental principle underlying a political association; this principle helps to overcome the lawlessness of absolute license and assures liberty, because people willingly adjust their conduct to harmonize with the legitimate freedom of others. What they lose by the social contract is their "natural liberty" and an unlimited right to everything; what they gain is "civil liberty" and a property right in what they possess. The essence of the social contract, says Rousseau, is that "each of us puts his person and all his power in common under the supreme direction of the general will, and, in our corporate capacity, we receive each member as an indivisible part of a whole." This contract tacitly assumes that whoever refuses to obey the *general will* shall be compelled to do so by the whole body; in short, "this means that he will be forced to be free."

What is the justification for saying that citizens can be "forced to be free"? The law is, after all, the product of the "general will." In turn, the general will is, says Rousseau, the will of the "sovereign." For Rousseau, the sovereign consists of the total number of citizens of a given society. The general will of the sovereign is therefore the single will which reflects the sum of the wills of all the individual citizens. The many wills of the citizens can be considered one general will because all people who are parties to the social contract (as every citizen is) have agreed to direct their actions (to limit their actions) to achieving the common good. All citizens by thinking of their own good realize that they should refrain from any behavior that would cause others to turn upon and injure them. In this way, all citizens understand that their own good and their own freedom is connected with the common good. Ideally, therefore, each individual's will is identical with every other individual's since they are all directed to the same purpose, namely, the common good. Because in this ideal setting all the individual wills are identical or at least consistent, it can be said that there is only one will, the general will. For this reason it can also be said that if laws are the product of the sovereign general will, each individual is really the author of those laws and in this way one obeys only oneself. The element of force or compulsion enters Rousseau's formula only when someone refuses to obey a law.

Rousseau distinguishes between the "general will" and the "will of all," saying that "there is often a great deal of difference between the will of all and the general will." What differentiates these two forms of the collective wills is the purpose each attempts to achieve. If the "will of all" had the same purpose as the "general will," namely, the common good or justice, there would be no difference between them. But, says Rousseau, there is often a different purpose pursued by the "will of all," where "all" refers to the voters of a group, even if by chance they are in the majority. Such a deviant purpose reflects special or private interests as opposed to the common good. When this happens, society no longer has a general will; it now has as many wills as there are groups or "factions." If, therefore, the general will is to be able to express itself, there must not be factions or partial societies within the state. Rousseau was convinced that if the people were given adequate information and had the opportunity to deliberate, and even if the citizens had no communication with one another and simply thought their own thoughts, they would arrive at the general will. They would choose the path leading to the common good or justice. Only the common good would provide the setting for the greatest possible freedom for each citizen.

At this point there could be someone who chooses not to obey the law. If the law was made with the common good or justice in mind, as opposed to special interests, then the law truly expresses the general will. The person who votes against this law or chooses to disobey it is in error: "When therefore the opinion that is contrary to my own prevails, this proves neither more nor less than that I was mistaken, and that what I thought to be the general will was not so." When a law is proposed, the citizens are not asked to approve or reject the proposal: They are asked to decide whether it is in conformity with the general will, that is, with the common good or justice. Only when the question is put this way can it be said that "the general will is found by counting the votes." Only under these circumstances is there any justification for forcing someone to obey the law. In effect he is then being forced to behave in accordance with a law he would have been willing to obey if he had accurately understood the requirements of the common good, which alone provides him with the greatest amount of freedom. Only under these circumstances, says Rousseau, is it legitimate to say that "he will be forced to be free."

Rousseau was under no illusion that it would be easy to establish all the conditions for making just laws in the modern world. For one thing, much of his thought reflected the conditions in his small native Geneva, where participation by the citizens could be more direct. In addition, his vision included certain assumptions that would require considerable human virtue. If everyone were required to obey the laws, then everyone would be entitled to participate in deciding upon those laws. When making the laws, those persons involved in the decisions would have to overcome special interests or the concerns of factions and self-consciously think of the common good. Rousseau also believed that all the citizens should be equally involved in the making of the laws, that the laws should not be made even by representatives, for "the people cannot, even if it wishes, deprive itself of this incommunicable right." But as the modern state has continued to grow in size and complexity, a development that Rousseau had already seen happening in his own day, his assumptions and conditions for achieving the just society appeared to be more of an ideal than an immediate possibility.

Taken as a whole, Rousseau's writings attacked the Age of Reason, gave impetus to the Romantic movement by emphasizing feeling (leading Goethe to say that "feeling is all"), revived religion even though he had doubts about some traditional teachings, provided a new direction for education (his book *Émile* was considered by some the best work on education since Plato's *Republic*), inspired the French Revolution, made a unique impact upon political philosophy, and, more than the writing of any of his contemporaries, influenced several subsequent philosophers, especially Immanuel Kant. On one occasion, Kant was so absorbed in reading Rousseau's *Émile* that he forgot to take his celebrated daily walk. While Kant admitted that it was David Hume who awakened him from his dogmatic slumbers regarding the theory of knowledge, it was Rousseau who showed him the way to a new theory of morality. So impressed was Kant by the insights of Rousseau that he hung a picture of him on the wall of his study, convinced that Rousseau was the Newton of the moral world.

15

Kant:
Critical Mediator
between
Dogmatism
and Skepticism

Immanuel Kant lived all of his eighty years (1724–1804) in the small provincial town of Königsberg in East Prussia. His parents were of modest means, and their religious spirit, nurtured by a sect known as Pietists, was to have a permanent influence upon Kant's thought and personal life. His education began at the local Collegium Frederi-cianum, whose director was also a Pietist, and in 1740 Kant entered the University of Königsberg. At the university he studied the classics, physics, and philosophy. The German universities were at this time dominated by the philosopher Christian von Wolff (1679–1754), who was neither a great nor an original thinker but whose achievement was that he stimulated philosophic activity by developing a comprehensive system of philosophy along the lines of Leibniz's rationalism and metaphysics. Kant's professor at Königsberg, Martin Knutzen, had come under the influence of this Wolff-Leibnizian approach to philosophy, and inevitably Kant's university training laid much emphasis upon the power of human reason to move with certainty in the realm of metaphysics. Although Martin Knutzen had thus slanted Kant's early thought toward the tradition of Continental rationalism, it was also Knutzen who stimulated

Kant's interest in Newtonian physics, an interest that played a very important part in the development of Kant's original and critical philosophy. Upon completion of his university course, Kant spent about eight years as a family tutor, and in 1755 became a lecturer at the university. In 1770 he was appointed to the chair of philosophy that had been held by Knutzen.

Although Kant's personal life contains no remarkable events, as he did not travel and developed no notable political or social connections, he was, nevertheless, immensely successful as a lecturer and was an interesting conversationalist and charming host. He is often pictured as an old bachelor whose every activity was scheduled with such precision that neighbors could set their watches when he stepped out of his house each day at half past four to walk up and down his small avenue eight times. Without this discipline, however, he could hardly have produced such a striking succession of famous books as his monumental *Critique of Pure Reason* in 1781, *Prolegomena to Any Future Metaphysics* in 1783, *Principles of the Metaphysics of Ethics* in 1785, *Metaphysical First Principles of Natural Science* in 1786, the second edition of the *Critique of Pure Reason* in 1787, the *Critique of Practical Reason* in 1788, the *Critique of Judgment* in 1790, *Religion within the Limits of Bare Reason* in 1793, and the small work *Perpetual Peace* in 1795.

THE SHAPING OF KANT'S PROBLEM

Kant revolutionized philosophy. What prompted this revolution in Kant's mind was his profound concern over a problem that the philosophy of his day could not deal with successfully or adequately. The elements of his problem are suggested by his famous comment that "two things fill the mind with ever new and increasing admiration and awe... *the starry heavens above and the moral law within.*" To him the starry heavens were a reminder that the world, as pictured earlier by Hobbes and Newton, is a system of bodies in motion, where every event has a specific and determinate cause. At the same time, all people experience the sense of moral duty, an experience which implies that people, unlike some other elements of nature, possess freedom in their behavior. The problem, then, was how to reconcile the two seemingly contradictory interpretations of events, one holding that all events are the product of *necessity* and the other saying that in certain aspects of human behavior there is *freedom.*

As Kant viewed the drift of scientific thought, he saw in it an attempt to include *all* of reality, including human nature, in its mechanical model. This would mean that all events, being parts of a unified mechanism, could be explained in terms of cause and effect. Moreover, this scientific approach would eliminate from consideration any elements that could not fit into its method, a method that placed greatest emphasis upon limiting knowledge to the realm of actual sense experience and to generalizations that could be derived by induction from such experience. Pursuing this method, science would have no need for, nor could it account for, such notions as freedom and God.

Kant was impressed by the obvious success and the constant advance of scientific knowledge. What the success of Newtonian physics did for Kant was to raise some serious questions about the adequacy of the philosophy of his day. The two major traditions of his day were Continental rationalism and British empiricism, and Newtonian physics enjoyed an independence from both of these philosophical systems. Since Continental rationalism had been built upon a mathematical model, this mode of philosophizing emphasized the relation of *ideas* to each other and therefore had no clear connection with things as they really are. Rationalism could not produce the kind of knowledge Newtonian physics represented, and for this reason its metaphysical speculations about reality beyond experience were considered dogmatic. Kant was to say with some respect that Christian Wolff, whose Leibnizian metaphysics had influenced Kant's prerevolutionary thought, was "the greatest of all dogmatic philosophers." This contrast between rationalism and science raised for Kant the question whether metaphysics can increase our knowledge the way science obviously can. The dogmatic character of metaphysics was made clear particularly by the variety of conclusions to which metaphysicians had come in their systems of thought, as indicated by the differences between Descartes, Spinoza, and Leibniz. But the heart of the matter was that the scientists were proceeding successfully in unraveling the nature of reality and were showing less and less concern about such metaphysical notions as freedom and God and the possibility of moral and valuational truth.

At the same time, science proceeded independently of the other major philosophical tradition of Kant's day, namely, British empiricism. Hume's most striking philosophical argument was that since all our knowledge comes from experience, we cannot have any knowledge of "causality" or necessary connections because we do not experience causality, and, therefore, we cannot infer or predict any future event from our experience of the present. What we call *causality,* said Hume, is simply our habit of associating two events because we experience them together, but this does not justify the conclusion that these events have any necessary connection. Thus, Hume denied inductive inference. And yet, it is precisely upon the notion of causality and inductive inference that science is built, for it assumes that our knowledge of particular events in the present gives us reliable knowledge about an indefinite number of similar events in the future. The logical outcome of Hume's empiricism was that there cannot be any scientific knowledge, and this leads to philosophical skepticism. Kant was left, therefore, with great admiration for science but with serious questions about philosophy because of the dogmatism of rationalism and the skepticism of empiricism.

Although Newtonian physics impressed Kant, science itself raised two major questions for him. The first we have already mentioned, namely, that as the scientific method was applied to the study of all of reality, including human behavior, the whole realm of moral values with its attendant notions of freedom and God was threatened by absorption into a mechanical universe. A second problem raised by science for Kant was how to explain, or to justify, scientific knowledge. That is, did the scientist give an adequate explanation of what makes his understanding of nature possible? As it turned out, these two problems were very closely related, because Kant discovered that in principle scientific knowledge is similar to metaphysical knowledge, and, therefore, the justification or explanation of scientific thought on the one hand and metaphysical thought concerning freedom and morality on the other are the same. Kant, therefore, rescued metaphysics not by attacking science but by discovering that what the scientist is doing in describing nature is similar to what the metaphysician is doing when he discusses freedom and morality. Both in science and in metaphysics, the mind starts with some given datum, which gives rise to a judgment in human reason. For this reason, says Kant, "the genuine method of metaphysics is fundamentally the same kind which Newton introduced into natural science and which was there so fruitful." By thus interpreting the nature of scientific and moral thought, Kant provided a new function and a new life for philosophy. This function is suggested by the title of Kant's major work, the *Critique of Pure Reason,* for now the task of philosophy became the critical appraisal of the capacities of human reason. In pursuing this new critical function, Kant achieved what he called his Copernican revolution in philosophy.

KANT'S CRITICAL PHILOSOPHY
AND HIS COPERNICAN REVOLUTION

The turning point in Kant's intellectual development was his encounter with Hume's empiricism. He tells us that "I openly confess, the suggestion of David Hume was the very thing, which many years ago first interrupted my dogmatic slumber and gave my investigations in the field of speculative philosophy quite a new direction." Hume had argued that all our knowledge is derived from experience and that therefore we cannot have knowledge of any reality beyond our experience. This argument struck at the very foundation of rationalism, whose advocates had argued confidently that human reason can derive knowledge about realities beyond experience simply by moving from one idea to another as one does in mathematics. The rationalist proofs for the existence of God were a case in point, and Spinoza's and Leibniz's explanation of the structure of reality was another. Kant eventually turned his back on rationalist metaphysics, calling it "rotten dogmatism," but he did not accept Hume's entire argument, saying that "I was far from following him in the conclusions at which he arrived."

Kant refused to follow Hume all the way not merely because this would lead to skepticism but because he felt that although Hume was on the right track, he had not completed the task of explaining how knowledge is acquired. Nor did Kant wish to give up some of the subjects that concerned the rationalist metaphysicians, such as freedom and God, about which it is impossible to be "indifferent," even though he was prepared to say that we cannot have demonstrative knowledge of objects beyond our experience. Kant, therefore, sought to build upon what he thought was significant both in rationalism and empiricism and to reject what could not be defended in these systems. He did not simply combine the insights of his predecessors, but rather embarked upon a genuinely new approach, which he called *critical philosophy.*

The Way of Critical Philosophy   Kant's *critical* philosophy consists of an analysis of the powers of human reason, by which he meant "a critical inquiry into the faculty of reason with reference to all the knowledge which it may strive to attain independently of all experience." The way of critical philosophy is, therefore, to ask the question "What and how much can understanding and reason know, apart from all experience?" Thus, whereas earlier metaphysicians engaged in disputes about the nature of the supreme being and other subjects that took them beyond the realm of immediate experience, Kant asked the critical question whether the human reason possessed the powers to undertake such inquiries. From this critical point of view Kant thought it foolish for metaphysicians to engage in attempts to construct systems of knowledge even before they had inquired into whether by pure reason alone one can apprehend what is not given to him in experience. Critical philosophy for Kant was therefore not the negation of metaphysics but rather a preparation for it. If metaphysics has to do with knowledge that is developed by reason alone, that is, prior to experience, or a priori, the critical question is how is such a priori knowledge possible.

The Nature of a Priori Knowledge   Kant affirmed that we possess a faculty that is capable of giving us knowledge without an appeal to experience. He agreed with the empiricists that our knowledge begins with experience, but he added that "though our knowledge begins *with* experience, it does not follow that it all arises *out of* experience." This was the point that Hume had missed, for Hume had said that all our knowledge consists of a series of impressions, which we derive through our senses. Yet we clearly possess a kind of knowledge that does not come *out of* experience even though it begins *with* experience. Hume was right that we do not, for example, experience or sense *causality,* but Kant rejected his explanation that *causality* is simply a psychological habit of connecting two events that we call cause and effect. Kant believed that we have knowledge about causality and that we get this knowledge not from sense experience but directly from the faculty of rational judgment and, therefore, a priori.

What, more specifically, is a priori knowledge? Kant replies that "if one desires an example from the sciences, one needs only to look at any proposition in mathematics. If one desires an example from the commonest operations of the understanding, the proposition that every change must have a cause can serve one's purposes." What makes a proposition of mathematics, or the proposition that every change must have a cause, a priori knowledge? It is, says Kant, that this kind of knowledge cannot be derived from experience. Experience cannot show us that *every* change must have a cause since we have not yet experienced every change. Nor can experience show us that connections between events are *necessary,* for the most experience can tell us is "that a thing is so and so, but not that it cannot be otherwise." Experience, then, cannot give us knowledge about *necessary* connections or about the *universality* of propositions. Yet we do in fact have this kind of knowledge about causality and universality for these are the notions that characterize mathematics and scientific knowledge. We confidently say that all heavy objects will fall in space or that all instances of five added to seven will equal twelve. That there is such a priori knowledge is clear, but what concerned Kant was how such knowledge can be accounted for. How, in short, can Hume's skepticism be answered? But it was not simply a question of how a priori knowledge is possible, but how "synthetical judgments *a priori*" are possible. To answer this question, Kant had first to discover what constitutes a synthetical judgment a priori.

The Synthetic a Priori   Kant distinguishes between two kinds of judgments, the *analytic* and the *synthetic.* A *judgment,* he said, is an operation of thought whereby we connect a subject and predicate, where the predicate qualifies in some way the subject. When we say that "The building is tall," we make a judgment, for the mind is able to understand a connection between the subject and the predicate. Subjects and predicates are connected to each other in two different ways, thereby leading the mind to make two different kinds of judgments.

In *analytic judgments,* the predicate is already contained in the concept of the subject. The judgment that all triangles have three angles is an analytic judgment. Because the predicate is already implicit in the subject of an analytic judgment, such a predicate does not give us any new knowledge about the subject. Again, the judgment that "all bodies are extended" is analytic, for the idea of extension is already contained in the idea of body. An analytic judgment is true only because of the logical relation of subject and predicate. To deny an analytic judgment would involve a logical contradiction.

A *synthetic judgment* differs from the analytic in that its predicate is not contained in the subject. Thus, in a synthetic judgment the predicate adds something new to our concept of the subject. To say that "the apple is red" joins two independent concepts, for the concept apple does not contain the idea of redness. Similarly, for Kant, "all bodies are heavy" is an example of a synthetic judgment, for the idea of heaviness is not contained in the concept of body, that is, the predicate is not contained in the subject.

At this point, Kant makes a further distinction, this time between judgments that are a priori and judgments that are a posteriori. All analytic judgments are a priori: their meaning does not depend upon our experience of any particular cases or events since they are independent of any observations, as in the case of mathematics. As "necessity and strict universality are sure marks of *a priori* knowledge," Kant has no trouble showing that analytic judgments represent a priori knowledge. Synthetic judgments, on the other hand, are for the most part a posteriori, that is, they occur after an experience of observation. To say, for example, that all boys in school *X* are six feet tall is a syn-

Immanuel Kant *(The Bettmann Archive)*

thetic judgment a posteriori, for this proposition regarding their height is contingently and not necessarily true of all the present or future members of that school. That judgment cannot be made without experience with the particular details of this school. Thus, while all analytic judgments are a priori, most synthetic judgments are a posteriori.

There is, however, still another kind of judgment besides the analytic a priori and the synthetic a posteriori, and this is the *synthetic a priori*. This is the kind of judgment Kant was most concerned about because he was certain that we make these judgments and yet there was the persistent question how such judgments are possible. The question arises because by definition synthetic judgments are based upon experience, but if that is the case, how can they be called a priori, since this implies independence of experience? Still, Kant showed that in mathematics, physics, ethics, and metaphysics, we do make judgments that are not only a priori but also synthetic. For example, the judgment 7 plus 5 equals 12 is certainly a priori because it contains the marks of necessity and universality; that is, 7 plus 5 *has* to equal 12, and it *always* has to do so. At the same time, this judgment is synthetic and not analytic because 12 cannot be derived by a mere analysis of the numbers 7 and 5. The act of intuition is necessary in order to achieve a synthesis of the concepts 7, 5, and plus. Kant shows that in propositions of geometry also the predicate is not contained in the subject even though there is a necessary and universal connection between subject and predicate. Thus, propositions of geometry are at once a priori and synthetic: For example, says Kant, "that a straight line between two points is the shortest, is a synthetic proposition. For my concept of *straight* contains no notion of quantity, but only of quality. The concept of *the shortest* is thus wholly an addition, and it cannot be derived by any analysis from the concept of a straight line. Intuition must, therefore, lend its aid here, by means of which alone is this synthesis possible." In physics, too, we find synthetic a priori judgments; Kant says that "natural science contains within itself synthetic *a priori* judgments as principles." The proposition "in all changes of the material world the quantity of matter remains unchanged" is a priori, for we make this judgment before we have experienced every change, and it is synthetic, for the idea of permanence is not discoverable in the concept of matter. In metaphysics, we assume that we are extending or increasing our knowledge. If this is so, the propositions of metaphysics, such as the judgment "man is free to choose" must be synthetic, for here the predicate adds new knowledge to the concept of the subject. At the same time, this metaphysical judgment is a priori, for the predicate *is free* is connected to our idea of all people even before we have experience of all people.

What Kant wanted to show by these illustrations is that it is not only in metaphysics but also in mathematics and physics that we make synthetic a priori judgments. If these judgments create difficulties in metaphysics, they create the same ones for mathematics and physics. Kant believed, therefore, that if synthetic a priori judgments could be explained or justified in mathematics and physics, they would, thereby, also be justified in metaphysics.

Kant's Copernican Revolution   Kant solved the problem of the synthetic a priori judgment by substituting a new hypothesis concerning the relation between the mind and its objects. It was clear to him that if we assume, as Hume did, that the mind, in forming its concepts, must conform to its objects, there could be no solution to the problem. Hume's theory would work for our ideas of things we have actually experienced, but these are a posteriori judgments. If I ask, "How do I know that the chair is brown?" my answer is that I can see it; and if my assertion is challenged, I refer to my experience. When I thus refer to my experience, that settles the question, because we all agree that experience gives us a kind of knowledge that conforms to the nature of things. But a synthetic *a priori* judgment cannot be validated by experience; if I say, for example, that every straight line is the shortest way between two points, I certainly cannot say that I have had experience of every possible straight line. What makes it possible for me to make judgments about events before they even occur, judgments that are universally true and can always be verified? If, as Hume believed, the mind is passive and simply receives its information from the objects, it follows that the mind would have information only about that particular object. But the mind makes judgments about all objects, even those that it has not yet experienced, and, in addition, objects do in fact behave in the future according to these judgments we make about them. This scientific knowledge gives us reliable information about the nature of things. But since this knowledge, which is both synthetic and a priori, could not be explained on the assumption that the mind conforms to its objects (how could it conform to every straight line...every change?), Kant was forced to try a new hypothesis regarding the relation between the mind and its objects.

Kant's new hypothesis was that it is the objects that conform to the operations of the mind, and not the other way around. He came to this hypothesis with a spirit of experimentation, consciously following the example of Copernicus, who, "failing of satisfactory progress in explaining the movements of the heavenly bodies on the supposition that they all revolved round the spectator, he tried whether he might not have better success if he made the spectator to revolve and the stars to remain at rest." Seeing an analogy here with his own problem, Kant says that "hitherto it has been assumed that all our knowledge must conform to objects. But all our attempts to extend our knowledge of objects by establishing something in regard to them *a priori* by means of concepts, have, on this assumption, ended in failure. We must, therefore, make trial whether we may not have more success in the tasks of metaphysics, if we suppose that objects must conform to our knowledge.... If intuition must conform to the constitution of the objects, I do not see how we could know anything of the latter *a priori;* but if the object (as object of the senses) must conform to the constitution of our faculty of intuition, I have no difficulty in conceiving such a possibility."

Kant did not mean to say that the mind creates objects, nor did he mean that the mind possesses innate ideas. His Copernican revolution consisted rather in his saying that the mind brings something to the objects it experiences. With Hume, Kant agreed that our knowledge begins with experience, but unlike Hume, Kant saw the mind as an active agent doing something with the objects it experiences. The mind, says Kant, is structured in such a way that it imposes its way of knowing upon its objects. By its very nature, the mind actively organizes our experiences. That is, thinking involves not only receiving impressions through our senses but also making judgments about what we experience. Just as a person who wears colored glasses sees everything in that color, so every human being, having the faculty of thought, inevitably thinks about things in accordance with the natural structure of the mind.

THE STRUCTURE OF RATIONAL THOUGHT

Kant says that "there are two sources of human knowledge, which perhaps spring from a common but to us unknown root, namely sensibility and understanding. Through the former objects are *given* to us; through the latter they are *thought.*" Knowledge is, therefore, a cooperative affair between the knower and the thing known. But, although I am able to distinguish the difference between myself as a knower and the thing I know, I can never know that thing as it is in itself, for the moment I know it, I know it as my structured mind permits me to know it. If colored glasses were permanently fixed to my eyes, I should always see things in that color and could never escape the limitations placed on my vision by those glasses. Similarly, my mind always brings certain ways of thinking to things, and this always affects my understanding of them. What does the mind bring to the *given* raw materials of our experience?

The Categories of Thought and the Forms of Intuition   The distinctive activity of the mind is to synthesize and to unify our experience. It achieves this synthesis first by imposing on our various experiences in the "sensible manifold" certain forms of intuition: space and time. We inevitably perceive things as being in *space* and *time.* But space and time are not ideas derived from the things we experience, nor are they concepts. Space and time are encountered immediately in intuition and are, at the same time, a priori or, to speak figuratively, lenses through which we always see objects of experience.

In addition to space and time, which deal particularly with the way we sense things, there are certain categories of thought which deal more specifically with the way the mind unifies or synthesizes our experience. The mind achieves this unifying act by making various kinds of judgments as we engage in the act of interpreting the world of sense. The manifold of experience is judged by us through certain fixed forms or concepts, such as *quantity, quality, relation,* and *modality.* When we assert *quantity,* we have in mind one or many; when we make a judgment of *quality,* we make either a positive or a negative statement; when we make a judgment of *relation,* we think of cause and effect, on the one hand, or of the relation of subject and predicate on the other; and when we make a judgment of *modality,* we have in mind that something is either possible or impossible. All these ways of thinking are what constitute the act of synthesis through which the mind strives to make a consistent single world out of the manifold of sense impressions.

The Self and the Unity of Experience   What makes it possible for us to have a unified grasp of the world about us? From his analysis of the way our minds work, Kant's answer is that it is the mind that transforms the raw data given to our senses into a coherent and related set of elements. But this leads Kant to say that the unity of our experience must imply a unity of the self, for unless there was a unity between the several operations of the mind, there could be no knowledge of experience. To have such knowledge involves, in various sequences, sensation, imagination, memory, as well as the powers of intuitive synthesis. Thus, it must be the same self that at once senses an object, remembers its characteristics, imposes upon it the forms of space and time and the category of cause and effect. All these activities must occur in some single subject; otherwise, there could be no knowledge, for if one subject had only sensations, another only memory, and so on, the sensible manifold could never be unified.

Where and what is this single subject that accomplishes this unifying activity? Kant calls it the "transcendental unity of apperception," what we should call the *self.* He uses the term *transcendental* to indicate that we do not experience the self directly even though such a unity, or self, is implied by our actual experience. Thus, the idea of this self is a priori as a necessary condition for the experience we do have of having knowledge of a unified world of nature. In the act of unifying all the elements of experience, we are conscious of our own unity, so that our consciousness of a unified world of experience and our own self-consciousness occur simultaneously. Our self-consciousness, however, is affected by the same faculties that affect our perception of external objects. I bring to the knowledge of myself the same apparatus and, therefore, impose upon myself as an object of knowledge the same "lenses" through which I see everything. Just as I do not know things as they are apart from the perspective from which I see them, so also I do not know the nature of this "transcendental unity of apperception" except as I am aware of the knowledge I have of the unity of the field of experience. What I am sure of is that a unified self is implied by any knowledge of experience.

Phenomenal and Noumenal Reality   A major impact of Kant's critical philosophy was his insistence that human knowledge is forever limited in its scope. This limitation takes two forms. In the first place, knowledge is limited to the world of experience. Secondly, our knowledge is limited by the manner in which our faculties of perception and thinking organize the raw data of experience. Kant did not doubt that the world as it appears to us is not the ultimate reality. He distinguished between *phenomenal* reality, or the world as we experience it, and *noumenal* reality, which is purely intelligible, or nonsensual, reality. When we experience a thing, we inevitably perceive it through the "lenses" of our a priori categories of thought. But what is a thing like when it is not being perceived? What is a thing-in-itself (*Ding an sich*)? We can obviously never have an experience of a nonsensuous perception. All objects we know are sensed objects. Still, we know that the existence of our world of experience is not produced by the mind. The mind, rather, imposes its ideas upon the manifold of experience, which is derived from the world of things-in-themselves. This means that there is a reality external to us that exists independently of us but that we can know only as it appears to us and is organized by us. The concept of a thing-in-itself does not, then, increase our knowledge but reminds us of the limits of knowledge.

Transcendental Ideas of Pure Reason as Regulative Concepts   Besides the general concept of the noumenal realm, there are three regulative ideas that we tend to think about, ideas that lead us beyond sense experiences but about which we cannot be indifferent because of our inevitable tendency to try to unify all our experience. These are the ideas of the *self,* of the *cosmos,* and of *God.* They are *transcendental* because they correspond to no object in our experience. They are produced not by intuition but by pure reason alone. They are, however, prompted by experience in the sense that we think those ideas in our attempts to achieve a coherent synthesis of all our experience. Kant says that "the first [regulative] idea is the "I' itself, viewed simply as thinking nature or soul... endeavoring to represent all determinations as existing in a single subject, all powers, so far as possible, as derived from a single fundamental power, all change as belonging to the states of one and the same permanent being, and all *appearances* in space as completely different from the actions of thought." In this way our pure reason tries to synthesize the various psychological activities we are aware of into a unity, and it does this by formulating the concept of the *self.*

Similarly, pure reason tries to create a synthesis of the many events in experience by forming the concept of the *world* so that "the second regulative idea of merely speculative reason is the concept of the world in general.... The absolute totality of the series of conditions... an idea which can never be completely realized in the empirical employment of reason, but which yet serves as a rule that prescribes how we ought to proceed in dealing with such series. ... The cosmological ideas are nothing but simply regulative principles, and are very far from positing... an actual totality of such series."

Kant continues, "The third idea of pure reason, which contains a merely relative supposition of a being that is the sole and sufficient cause of all cosmological series, is the idea of *God.* We have not the slightest ground to assume in an absolute manner the object of this idea.... It becomes evident that the idea of such a being, like all speculative ideas, seems only to formulate the command of reason, that all connection in the world be viewed in accordance with the principles of a systematic unity—*as if* all such connection had its source in one single all-embracing being as the supreme and sufficient cause."

Kant's use of these regulative ideas exemplifies his way of mediating between dogmatic rationalism and skeptical empiricism. With the empiricists, Kant agrees that we can have no knowledge of reality beyond experience. The ideas of the self, the cosmos, and God cannot give us any theoretical knowledge of realities corresponding to these ideas. The function of these ideas is simply and solely regulative. As regulative ideas, they give us a reasonable way of dealing with the constantly recurring questions raised by metaphysics. To this extent Kant acknowledged the validity of the subject matter of rationalism. His critical analysis of the scope of human reason, however, led him to discover that earlier rationalists had made the error of treating *transcendental* ideas as though they were ideas about *transcendent* or actual beings. Kant emphasizes that "there is a great difference between something given to my reason as an *object absolutely,* or merely as an *object in the idea.* In the former case our concepts are employed to determine the object [transcendent]; in the latter case there is in fact only a scheme for which no object, not even a hypothetical one, is directly given, and which only enables us to represent to ourselves other objects in an indirect manner, namely in their systematic unity, by means of their relation to this idea. Thus, I say, that the concept of a highest intelligence is a mere idea [transcendental]."

The Antinomies and the Limits of Reason   Because regulative ideas do not refer to any objective reality about which we can have knowledge, we must consider these ideas as being the products of our pure reason. As such we cannot bring to these ideas the a priori forms of time and space or the category of cause and effect since these are imposed by us only upon the sensible manifold. Science is possible because all people, having the same structure of mind, will always and everywhere order the events of sense experience in the same way; that is, we all bring to the *given* of sense experience the same organizing faculties of understanding. But there can be no science of metaphysics because there is not the same kind of *given* when we consider the ideas of self, cosmos, and God as when we consider "the shortest distance between two points." What *is* given in metaphysics is the felt need to achieve a synthesis of the wide variety of events in experience at ever-higher levels and of discovering an ever-wider explanation of the realm of phenomena.

There is a difference for Kant between a priori or theoretical scientific knowledge, on the one hand, and speculative metaphysics on the other. The difference is that we can have scientific knowledge of phenomena but cannot have scientific knowledge of the noumenal realm, or the realm that transcends experience. Our attempts to achieve a "science" of metaphysics, says Kant, are doomed to failure. Whenever we try to discuss the self, the cosmos, or God as though they were objects of experience, the inability of the mind ever to do so successfully is indicated by what Kant calls the *antinomies* into which we fall. These four antinomies show us that when we discuss the nature of the world beyond experience, we can argue with equal force on opposite sides of various propositions, namely, that (1) the world is limited in time and space, or that it is unlimited; that (2) every composite substance in the world is made up of simple parts, or that no composite thing in the world is made up of simple parts since there nowhere exists in the world anything simple; that (3) besides causality in accordance with the laws of nature there is also another causality, that of freedom, or that there is no freedom since everything in the world takes place solely in accordance with the laws of nature; and, finally, that (4) there exists an absolutely necessary being as a part of the world or as its cause, or an absolutely necessary being nowhere exists.

These antinomies reflect the disagreements generated by dogmatic metaphysics, disagreements that occur only because they are based upon "nonsense," that is, upon attempts to describe a reality about which we have, and can have, no sense experience. Kant did, however, believe that these antinomies have positive value; namely, that they provide an additional argument for saying that the world of space and time is phenomenal only and that in such a world freedom is a coherent idea. This follows because if the world were a thing-in-itself, it would have to be either finite or infinite in extent and divisibility. But the antinomies show that there can be no demonstrative proof that either alternative is true. Insofar, then, as the world is phenomenal only, we are justified in affirming moral freedom and human responsibility.

As regulative ideas, the concepts of the self, the world, and God have a legitimate function, for they help us to synthesize our experience. Also, to speak of a noumenal realm, or the realm of the thing-in-itself, is to respond to certain given experiences and tendencies of our thought. For this reason we can think of a person in two different ways, as a phenomenon and as a noumenon. As a phenomenon, a person can be studied scientifically as a being in space and time and in the context of cause and effect. At the same time, our experience of moral obligation suggests that people's noumenal nature, what they are like beyond our sense perception of them, is characterized by freedom. In this context, the concept of freedom, as the idea of the self, or God, is a regulative idea. There can never be any demonstrative proof either that people are free or that God exists because these concepts refer us beyond sense experience, where the categories of the mind have no data upon which to work.

Proofs of God's Existence   With this critical estimate of the powers and scope of human reason, it was inevitable that Kant would reject the traditional proofs for the existence of God, namely, the *ontological, cosmological,* and *teleological* proofs. His argument against the *ontological* proof is that it is all a verbal exercise, for the essence of this proof is the assertion that since we have the idea of a most perfect being, it would be contradictory to say that such a being does not exist. Such a denial would be contradictory because the concept of a perfect being necessarily includes the predicate of *existence.* A being, that is, that does not exist can hardly be considered a perfect being. But Kant argues that this line of reasoning is "taken from judgments, not from things and their existence," that the idea of God is made to have the predicate of existence by simply fashioning the concept in such a way that existence is made to be included in the idea of a perfect being. This argument nowhere indicates why it is necessary to have the subject, *God.* There would be a contradiction if a perfect being did exist and we denied that such a being was omnipotent. But to say that we avoid a contradiction by agreeing that a supreme being is omnipotent does not by itself demonstrate that such a being exists. Moreover, to deny that God exists is not simply to deny a predicate but to abandon the subject and thereby all the predicates that go with it, and "if we reject subject and predicate alike, there is no contradiction; for nothing is then left to be contradicted." Kant concluded, therefore, that "all the trouble and labour bestowed on the famous ontological or cartesian proof of the existence of a supreme Being from concepts alone is trouble and labour wasted. A man might as well expect to become richer in knowledge by the aid of mere ideas as a merchant to increase his wealth by adding some noughts to his cash account."

Whereas the ontological proof begins with an idea (of a perfect being), the *cosmological* proof "takes its stand on experience," for it says that "I exist, therefore, an absolutely necessary being exists" on the assumption that if anything exists an absolutely necessary being must also exist. The error of this argument, according to Kant, is that while it begins with experience, it soon moves beyond experience. Within the realm of sense experience it is legitimate to infer a cause for each event, but "the principle of causality has no meaning and no criterion for its application save only in the sensible world." Here is the direct application of Kant's critical method, for he argues that we cannot employ the a priori categories of the mind in trying to describe realities beyond sense experience. The cosmological argument cannot, therefore, securely lead us to a first cause of all things, for the most we can infer from our experience of things is a regulative idea of God. Whether there actually is such a being, a ground of all contingent things, raises the same question posed by the ontological argument, namely, whether we can successfully bridge the gap between our idea of a perfect being and demonstrative proof of its existence.

Similarly, the *teleological* argument begins with considerable persuasiveness, for it says that "in the world we everywhere find clear signs of an order in accordance with a determinate purpose.... The diverse things could not of themselves have cooperated, by so great a combination of diverse means, to the fulfillment of determinate final purposes, had they not been chosen and designed for these purposes by an ordering rational principle in conformity with underlying ideas." To this argument Kant replies that it may very well be that our experience of order in the universe suggests an orderer, but order in the world does not demonstrate that the material stuff of the world could not exist without an orderer. The most this argument from design can prove, says Kant, "is an *architect* of the world who is always very much hampered by the adaptability of the material in which he works, not a *creator* of the world to whose idea everything is subject." To prove the existence of a creator leads us back to the cosmological argument with its idea of causality, but since we cannot use the category of causality beyond the things in experience, we are left simply with an idea of a first cause or creator, and this takes us back to the ontological argument, with its deficiencies. Kant's conclusion, therefore, is that we cannot use transcendental ideas or theoretical principles, which have no application beyond the field of sense experience, to demonstrate the existence of God.

It follows from Kant's critical remarks about the "proofs," however, that just as we cannot demonstrate God's existence, neither can we demonstrate that God does *not* exist. By pure reason alone we can neither prove nor disprove God's existence. If, therefore, the existence of God cannot be effectively dealt with by the theoretical reason, which Kant has gone to such lengths to show has relevance only in the realm of sense experience, some other aspect of reason must be considered as the source of the idea of God. Thus, the idea of God has importance in Kant's philosophy, as do other regulative ideas.

PRACTICAL REASON

Besides the "starry heavens above," it was also the "moral law within" that filled Kant with wonder. He was aware that human beings not only gaze upon a world of things but become participants in a world of action. Reason is, therefore, alternately concerned with theory about things and with practical behavior. But there is "ultimately only one and the same reason which has to be distinguished in its application," says Kant, and of the objectives of reason, "the first is *theoretical*, the second *practical* rational knowledge." It was Kant's way of explaining the scope and powers of pure theoretical reason that made possible his account of the practical reason.

The tendency of scientific thought in Kant's day was to identify reality with what we can know from sense experience, from appearance. If this were a true account of reality, knowledge would consist only of a sensible manifold understood as things strictly related to each other by causality. Reality would then be viewed as a large mechanism whose every activity was the product of prior causes, and man would also be viewed as a part of this mechanical system. If this were the case, says Kant, "I could not...without palpable contradiction say of one and the same thing, for instance the human soul, that its will is free and yet is subject to natural necessity, that is, not free." Kant avoided this contradiction by saying that a person's phenomenal self, or the self we can observe, is subject to natural necessity or causality, whereas the noumenal self as a thing-in-itself possesses freedom. It is in a negative way, by limiting the scope of theoretical reason to the sensible manifold, that Kant made way for the positive use of practical reason: insofar as "our Critique limits speculative reason, it is indeed *negative*, but since it thereby removes an obstacle which stands in the way of the employment of practical reason, nay threatens to destroy it, it has in reality a positive and very important use." Morality becomes possible because even though we cannot know things-in-themselves, or objects in the noumenal realm, "we must yet be in a position at least to *think* them as things-in-themselves; otherwise we should be landed in the absurd conclusion that there can be appearance without anything that appears." But "if our Critique is not in error in teaching that the object [e.g., a human being] is to be taken *in a twofold sense*, namely as appearance and as a thing-in-itself...then there is no contradiction in supposing that one and the same will is, in the appearance, that is, in visible acts, necessarily subject to the law of nature, and so far not free, while yet, as belonging to a thing-in-itself, is not subject to that law, and is, therefore *free*." To be sure, the soul cannot be *known* by speculative reason as being free, "but though I cannot *know,* I can yet *think* free-dom." Kant has, therefore, provided the basis for moral and religious discourse by distinguishing two kinds of reality, the phenomenal and the noumenal, and by limiting the scope of science to the phenomenal and justifying the use of practical reason in connection with the noumenal world.

The Basis of Moral Knowledge   The task of moral philosophy, according to Kant, is to discover how we are able to arrive at principles of behavior that are binding upon all humanity. He was sure that we cannot discover these prin-ciples simply by studying the actual behavior of people, for although such a study would give us interesting anthropological information about how people *do* behave, it would not tell us how they *ought* to behave. Still, we do make moral judgments when we say, for example, that we ought to tell the truth, and the question is how we arrive at such a rule of behavior. For Kant, the moral judgment that "we ought to tell the truth" is on principle the same as the sci-entific judgment that "every change must have a cause." What makes them similar is that both of these judgments come from our reason and not from the objects we experience. Just as our theoretical reason brings the category of causality to visible objects and thereby explains the process of change, so also the practical reason brings to any given moral situation the concept of duty, or "ought." Both in science and in moral philosophy we use concepts that go be-yond any particular facts we experience at any one time. Experience in both cases is the occasion for triggering the mind to think in universal terms. When we experience a given example of change, our minds bring to this event the category of causality, which makes it possible to explain the relation of cause and effect not only in this case but in all cases of change. Similarly, in the con-text of human relations, the practical reason is able to determine how we should behave not only at this moment but what should be the principle of our behav-ior at all times. Like scientific knowledge, moral knowledge is based upon a priori judgments. Just as Kant discovered that scientific knowledge is possible because of the a priori categories that the mind brings to experience, so he now says that "the basis of obligation must not be sought in human nature or in the circumstances of the world in which [humanity] is placed, but *a priori* simply in the concepts of reason."

Morality for Kant is, therefore, an aspect of rationality and has to do with our consciousness of rules or "laws" of behavior, which we consider both uni-versal and necessary. The qualities of *universality* and *necessity* are the marks of a priori judgments, and this further confirms Kant's view that the principles of behavior are derived by the practical reason a priori. Instead of searching for the quality of "goodness" in the effects of our actions, Kant focuses upon the rational aspect of our behavior.

Morality and Rationality   As a rational being, I not only ask the question "What shall I do?" but am also conscious of being under an obligation to act in particular ways, that I "ought" to do something. These rational activities reflect the powers of practical reason, and I can assume that all rational beings are aware of the same problems. When I consider what I must do, therefore, I am also considering what all rational beings must do, for if a moral law or rule is valid for me as a rational being, it must be valid for all rational beings. A major test of a morally good act is, therefore, whether its principle can be applied to all rational beings and applied consistently. Moral philosophy is the quest for these principles that apply to all rational beings and that lead to behavior that we call *good*.

"Good" Defined as the Good Will   Kant says that "Nothing can possibly be conceived in the world, or even out of it, which can be called good, without qualification, except a good will." He would admit, of course, that other things can be considered good, such as moderation of the passions, "and yet one can hardly call them unreservedly good... for without the principles of a good will they may become evil indeed. The cold-bloodedness of a villain not only makes him far more dangerous, but also directly makes him seem more despicable to us than he would have seemed without it." Kant's chief point is that the essence of the morally good act is the principle that a person affirms when he wills an act. "The good will is good not because of what it causes or accomplishes, not because of its usefulness in the attainment of some set purpose, but alone because of the willing, that is to say, it is good of itself."

A rational being strives to do what *ought* to be done, and this Kant distinguishes from an act that a person does either from *inclination* or *self-interest*. We can all compare the differences in these motives, for to act either from inclination or self-interest appears to us to be on a different level morally from acting out of *duty* to the moral law. The reason Kant makes the rather startling statement that the "good will is good not because of what it accomplishes" is that he wants to emphasize the dominant role of the will in morality. It is not enough for the effects or consequences of our behavior to *agree with* the moral law; the truly moral act is done *for the sake of the moral law*, "for all these effects—even the promotion of the happiness of others—could have been also brought about by other causes, so that for this there would have been no need of the will of a rational being." The seat of moral worth is in the will, and the good will is one that acts out of a sense of duty; and "an action done from duty must wholly exclude the influence of inclination, and with it every object of the will, so that nothing remains which can determine the will except objectively the *law* and subjectively *pure respect* for this practical law."

Duty implies that we are under some kind of obligation, a moral law, and Kant says that as rational beings we are aware of this obligation as it comes to us in the form of an *imperative*. Not all imperatives or commands are connected with morality, for they are not in every case directed to all people and therefore lack the quality of universality that a moral rule requires. There are, for example, *technical* imperatives or rules of skill, which command us to do certain things *if* we want to achieve certain ends: *if* we want to build a bridge across the river, we *must* use materials of certain strength. But we do not absolutely have to build a bridge. We can either build a tunnel or use surface craft to get to the other side. Similarly, there are certain *prudential* imperatives, which say, for example, that if I want to be popular with certain people, I *must* say or do certain things. But again, it is not absolutely necessary that I achieve this popularity. The technical and prudential imperatives are, therefore, *hypothetical* imperatives because they command us only if we decide to enter their sphere of operation.

The Categorical Imperative   Unlike the technical and prudential imperatives, which are hypothetical in nature, the truly moral imperative is *categorical.* This categorical imperative applies to all people and commands "an action as necessary of itself without reference to another end, that is, as objectively necessary." It commands certain conduct immediately, without having any other purpose as a condition. Actually, the categorical imperative commands a law that forms the basis of particular actions. It is *categorical* because it instantly applies to all rational beings, and it is *imperative* because it is the principle on which we *ought to act.* The basic formulation of the categorical imperative is this: "*Act only on that maxim whereby thou canst at the same time will that it should become a universal law.*" Kant had said that "everything in nature works according to laws. Rational beings alone have the faculty of acting according *to the conception* of laws." Now he wants to indicate that the categorical imperative is our conception of the law of nature as it pertains to human behavior, and, therefore, he expresses the imperative of duty in an alternate way, namely, "*Act as if the maxim of thy action were to become a universal law of nature.*"

It is clear that the categorical imperative does not give us specific rules of conduct, for it appears to be simply an abstract formula. Still, this was precisely what Kant thought moral philosophy should provide us in order to guide our moral behavior, for once we understand the fundamental principle of the moral law, we can then apply it to specific cases. To illustrate how the categorical imperative enables us to discover our moral duties, Kant gives the following example: A man "finds himself forced by necessity to borrow money. He knows that he will not be able to repay it, but sees also that nothing will be lent to him unless he promises stoutly to repay it in a definite time. He desires to make this promise, but he has still so much conscience as to ask himself: Is it not unlawful and inconsistent with duty to get out of a difficulty in this way? Suppose, however, that he resolves to do so, then the maxim of his action would be expressed thus: When I think myself in want of money, I will borrow money and promise to repay it, although I know that I never can do so. Now this principle of self-love or of one's own advantage may perhaps be consistent with my whole future welfare; but the question now is, Is it right? I change then the suggestion of self-love into a universal law, and state the question thus: How would it be if my maxim were a universal law? Then I see at once that it could never hold as a universal law of nature, but would necessarily contradict itself. For supposing it to be a universal law that everyone when he thinks himself in a difficulty should be able to promise whatever he pleases, with the purpose of not keeping his promise, the promise itself would become impossible, as well as the end that one might have in view in it, since no one would consider that anything was promised to him, but would ridicule all such statements as vain pretenses."

If one were still to ask why one must tell the truth, or why one should avoid the contradiction involved in a false promise, Kant answers that there is something about human beings that makes them resist and resent being treated as *things* instead of *people*. What makes us persons is our rationality, and to be a person, or a rational being, is therefore an end in itself. We become a thing when someone uses us as a means for some other end, as when one tells us a lie; but however necessary such use of us may be at times, we nevertheless consider ourselves as being of absolute intrinsic worth as persons. The individual human being as possessing absolute worth becomes the basis for the supreme principle of morality: "the foundation of this principle is: *rational nature exists as an end in itself.* All men everywhere want to be considered persons instead of things for the same reason that I do, and this affirmation of the absolute worth of the individual leads to a second formulation of the categorical imperative which says: *So act as to treat humanity, whether in thine own person or in that of any other, in every case as an end withal, never as means only.*"

There is a third formulation of the categorical imperative, which is already implied in the first two but which Kant wants to make explicit by saying that we should "always so act that the *will could regard itself at the same time as making universal law through its own maxim.*" Here Kant speaks of the *autonomy* of the will, that each person through an act of will legislates the moral law. Kant distinguishes autonomy from *heteronomy,* the determination (of a law or action) by someone or something other than the self. Thus an heteronomous will is influenced or even determined by desires or inclination. An autonomous will, on the other hand, is free and independent, and as such is the "supreme principle of morality." Central to the concept of the autonomy of the will is the idea of *freedom,* the crucial regulative idea, which Kant employed to distinguish between the worlds of science and morality, the phenomenal and noumenal worlds; he says that "the *will* is a kind of causality belonging to living beings in so far as they are rational, and *freedom* would be this property of such causality that it can be efficient, independently of foreign causes determining it, just as *physical necessity* is the property that the causality of all irrational being has of being determined to activity by the influence of foreign causes." And again, "I affirm that we must attribute to every rational being which has a will that it has also the idea of freedom and acts entirely under this idea. For in such a being we conceive a reason that is practical, that is, has causality in reference to its objects." The categorical imperative, therefore, speaks of the universality of the moral law, affirms the supreme worth of each rational person, and assigns freedom or autonomy to the will. Our experience of the moral law suggested to Kant some further insights concerning the postulates of freedom, immortality, and God.

The Moral Postulates   Kant did not think it possible to prove or demonstrate that God exists or that the human will is free. Freedom is an idea that it is necessary to assume because of our experience of moral obligation, that is, "because I must, I can." Though we cannot demonstrate that our wills are free, we are intellectually compelled to assume such freedom, for freedom and morality "are so inseparably united that one might define practical freedom as independence of the will of anything but the moral law alone." How could people be responsible or have a duty if they were not able or free to fulfill their duty or respond to the moral command? Freedom must be assumed, and as such it is the first postulate of morality.

A second moral postulate for Kant is *immortality*. The line of reasoning by which Kant was led to postulate immortality begins with his conception of the supreme good, or the *summum bonum*. Although virtue is the supreme good, we as rational beings are fully satisfied only when there is a union between virtue and happiness. Though it does not always happen so, we all assume that virtue ought to produce happiness. Kant had rigorously maintained that the moral law commands us to act not so that we be happy, but so that our actions will be *right*. Still, the full realization of a rational being requires that we think of the supreme good as including both virtue and happiness. But our experience indicates that there is no necessary connection between virtue and happiness. If we were to limit human experience to this world, it would then appear impossible to achieve the supreme good in its fullness. Still, the moral law does command us to strive for perfect good, and this implies an indefinite progress toward this ideal, "but this endless progress is possible only on the supposition of the unending duration of the existence and personality of the same rational being, which is called the immortality of the soul."

The moral universe also compels us to postulate the existence of God as the grounds for the necessary connection between virtue and happiness. If we mean by happiness "the state of a rational being in the world with whom in the totality of his experience *everything goes according to his wish and will*," then happiness implies a harmony between a person's will and physical nature. But a person is not the author of the world, nor is he or she capable of ordering nature so as to effect a necessary connection between virtue and happiness. But since we do conclude from our conception of the supreme good that virtue and happiness must go together, we must postulate "the existence of a cause of the whole of nature which is distinct from nature and which contains the ground of this connection, namely, of the exact harmony of happiness with morality," and thus "it is morally necessary to assume the existence of God." This is not to say that there cannot be morality without religion, for Kant has already indicated that a person can recognize moral duty without the idea of God and that the law must be obeyed simply out of respect for the law, "for duty's sake." But Kant does say that "through the idea of the supreme good as object and final end of the pure practical reason the moral law leads to religion, that is to the recognition of all duties as divine commands, not as sanctions, that is, as arbitrary commands of an alien will...but as essential laws of every free will in itself, which, however, must be looked on as commands of the supreme Being, because it is only from a morally perfect and at the same time all-powerful will...that we hope to attain the highest good, which the moral law makes it our duty to take as the object of our endeavor."

Whether Kant succeeded in reaching the objectives he set for his new critical philosophy, his achievement was monumental. It may very well be that his mistakes along the way were more important than most people's successes, but what is beyond question is that although it is not necessary to accept everything Kant said, it is nevertheless virtually impossible to philosophize today without taking his views into account.

AESTHETICS: THE BEAUTIFUL

As we have seen, Kant developed a specific set of rules of morality by which one could determine whether an action can rightly be called "good." These rules apply to all persons, so that the test for morally good behavior is a universal or objective standard. Similarly, Kant argued that the human mind can develop reliable scientific knowledge, that nature must be considered uniform throughout, and that scientific laws must be valid or "true" for everyone. However, when he turns to the problems of aesthetics, Kant says that "there can be no rule according to which anyone can be compelled to recognize anything as *beautiful.*" There are, says Kant, no reasons or principles which signify that a dress, a house, or a flower is beautiful. Nevertheless, we do say about things that they are beautiful, and we like to think that what *we* call beautiful should also be called beautiful by others. In the end, Kant shows that even though our judgment of the beautiful is based upon our subjective feeling, the beautiful is defined as "that which pleases universally." Just how he moves from our subjective feeling of the beautiful to the conclusion that the beautiful is what pleases universally provides us with some of Kant's key insights into the nature of our aesthetic experience.

The Beautiful as Independent Pleasant Satisfaction

The first step in discovering the nature of our aesthetic judgment is to see it as a matter of subjective taste. When we express the judgment that an object is beautiful, this judgment is subjective because upon experiencing the object, our imagination refers our sensation of the object to us as subjects, to our feeling of pleasure or displeasure. This feeling of pleasure or displeasure denotes nothing in the object but is simply the manner in which the object affects us. Kant's key point here is that the judgment of taste is not a logical matter involving a knowledge of concepts. If I want to say about an object that it is "good," I have to know what kind of thing the object is intended to be. That is, I must have a concept of it. But it is not necessary for me to have a concept of an object to enable me to see beauty in it. For example, "flowers, free patterns, lines aimlessly intertwining—technically termed foliage—have no signification, depend upon no definite concept, and yet please." My judgment of beauty, my taste, is simply *contemplative,* which means that I do not need to know anything more about the object other than how its character affects my feelings of pleasure or displeasure. An aesthetic judgment is not a cognitive judgment; that is, it rests upon neither theoretical nor practical knowledge.

Kant insists that for an aesthetic judgment to be "pure," it must be independent of any special interest; it must be "disinterested." To be disinterested is of course not the same as being uninteresting. It means that the judgment that an object is beautiful is not biased by a prejudice for or against an object. The judgment that a house is beautiful or not must be independent of my prejudice against either large or small houses or of my desire to own such a house. The pure aesthetic judgment affirms that the form of the object is pleasing without reference to any special interest I may have in it. Of course it is possible that I can have an interest in or a desire for the object, but my judgment that it is beautiful is independent of that interest or desire. For this reason, Kant defines the beautiful as follows: "*Taste* is the faculty of estimating an object or a mode of representation by means of a delight or aversion *apart from any interest.* The object of such a delight is called *beautiful.*"

The Beautiful as an Object of Universal Delight

If my judgment that an object is beautiful is independent of any private interest or prejudice of mine, then my judgment does not depend upon nor is it influenced by any other interest. When I express the judgment that an object is beautiful and I am conscious when I do this that I am not depending upon nor influenced by any other interest, whether an appetite, a desire, or a bias, then my judgment is "free," that is, my judgment is arrived at freely. Because no interest peculiar or private to me is influencing my judgment, I have every reason to believe that others, similarly free of their private interests, would arrive at the same judgment of the beautiful. The aesthetic judgment is universal.

Kant is aware that not all uses of the word *taste* refer to universal aesthetic judgments. It is possible to have good taste regarding things about which different people disagree. Someone will say, "canary-wine is agreeable," but a friend will remind him to say "agreeable *to me.*" A violet color may impress someone as soft and lovely; to someone else it appears dull and faded. One person likes the sound of wind instruments, while another likes that of string instruments. On these matters, where something is or is not "agreeable" to us, it is true that "everyone has his own taste." But "agreeable" must not be confused with the beautiful. For if something is agreeable to or even pleases only one person, that person must not call it beautiful. As Kant says, many things possess for us charm and agreeableness. But if we put something on a pedestal and call it beautiful, we imply that everyone should make the same judgment, everyone should have the same delight in the object. Those who judge differently can be "blamed" and denied that they have taste. And to this extent, says Kant, "it is not open to men to say: Every one has his own taste. This would be equivalent to saying that there is no such thing at all as taste; i.e., no aesthetic judgment capable of making a rightful claim upon the assent of all men."

The ambiguous use of the word *taste* is clarified by distinguishing between the taste of our senses and the taste of reflection or contemplation. It is the taste of the senses, for example the taste of foods and drinks, which is frequently merely private. But taste which involves a judgment of the beautiful implies universal agreement. This aesthetic judgment is not based on logic because it does not involve our cognitive faculties, only the feelings of pleasure or displeasure in every subject. The judgment of the beautiful does not rest on any concept but rather upon feeling. Kant therefore defines the beautiful in yet another way: "The *beautiful* is that which, apart from a concept, pleases universally."

Finality versus Purpose in the Beautiful Object

There are two kinds of beauty: (1) free beauty and (2) beauty which is merely dependent. Free beauty presupposes no concept of what the object should be. By contrast, dependent beauty presupposes a concept of what that object should be, and that concept makes it possible for us to determine whether that object is perfect or not.

A flower is a free beauty of nature. Just by looking at it we can tell whether it is beautiful or not. We need no further knowledge about it. There is no other concept connected with the flower, such as its purpose, that would help us determine whether it is beautiful. The manner in which the flower presents itself to us is final. The flower's form as we see it represents its "finality," and this finality provides the basis for the judgment of its beauty. Surely something is going on in our consciousness and understanding when we make this judgment, but our feeling and not our reasoning powers are in control here. Kant says therefore, that "A judgment is called aesthetic precisely because its determining ground is not a concept but the feeling of that harmony in the play of the mental powers, so far as it can be experienced in feeling." To be sure, a botanist can know many things about the flower, but his concepts have no bearing on the judgment whether the flower is beautiful. Similarly, in painting, sculpture, horticulture, and even music, the design is what is essential, so that what pleases by its form is the fundamental prerequisite for taste.

But the beauty of a man, woman, or child, the beauty of a building such as a church or a summerhouse, all these presuppose a concept of the "end" or purpose which defines what each is supposed to be. We can say about each person or building that it is beautiful. But here our judgment of beauty takes into account the concepts of ends or purposes. Moreover, the judgment of beauty becomes dependent upon the fulfillment or lack of fulfillment of the proper end or purpose of the object in question. Here we do not have a pure aesthetic judgment based solely upon feeling. Instead there is an admixture of conceptual knowledge concerning the nature and purpose of a person or the purpose or function of the building. For example, someone might judge that a building excites displeasure because its form (although exquisite) is inappropriate for a church. One person might be judged beautiful because he or she behaves in a moral manner, in which case the judgment of the beautiful becomes confused or at least combined with the judgment of the good (which is a cognitive judgment). If our judgment that a person or building is beautiful depends upon the purpose of human nature or of the building, then our judgment is placed under a restriction and is no longer a free and pure judgment of taste. Accordingly, Kant defines the beautiful in a third way: "Beauty is the form of finality in an object, so far as perceived in it apart from the representation of an end (or purpose)."

Necessity, Common Sense, and the Beautiful

There is something about the beautiful that leads to "a necessary reference on its part to delight (pleasure)." This does not mean, says Kant, that I can know ahead of time "that every one *will in fact feel* this delight in the object that is called beautiful by me." The *necessity* which combines the judgment of the beautiful with delight is neither a theoretical nor a practical necessity. Even though I claim that my aesthetic judgment is universal, I cannot assume that everyone will actually agree with it. Indeed, because I am not even capable of clearly formulating a rule which defines the beautiful in terms of concepts, I am left with my own feeling of beauty which also includes my delight or pleasure. That my delight is referred to in the judgment of beauty does not mean that the element of delight is logically deduced from the concept of beauty. The "necessity" that delight is involved in the experience of the beautiful is, says Kant "a necessity of a special kind." The necessity which is thought in an aesthetic judgment "can only be termed *exemplary*." It is "a necessity of the assent of *all* to a judgment regarded as exemplifying a universal rule incapable of formulation." My judgment, in short, is an example of a universal rule regarding beauty.

If I cannot formulate the principle of beauty in a rational or cognitive form, how is it possible for me to communicate to others the necessary components of the judgment of the beautiful? Two times two necessarily equals four for everyone. How can it be that the judgment of the beautiful also contains the element of necessity? I must have, says Kant, "a subjective principle and one which determines what pleases or displeases, by means of feeling only and not through concepts, but yet with universal validity." For this reason, the judgment of taste depends upon our presupposing the existence of a common sense. Only under such a presupposition of a common sense can I lay down a judgment of taste. This does not mean that everyone will agree with my judgment, but rather that everyone *ought* to agree with it. Just as we can assume, when we communicate that two and two equals four, that others can or even must understand the universal truth of this judgment (even though in this case we are dealing with an objective principle), so also can we assume that there is a common sense in everyone to which we can communicate the subjective judgment of the beautiful. For this reason Kant gives as his fourth definition that "The Beautiful is that which, apart from a concept, is cognized as object of a *necessary* delight."

Although no less a thinker than Hegel found in Kant's theory of aesthetics "the first rational word concerning beauty," Kant was himself aware, as he points out in the preface to his *Critique of Judgment,* that "the difficulty of unraveling a problem so involved in its nature may serve as an excuse for a certain amount of hardly avoidable obscurity in its solution."

16

Hegel: Absolute Idealism

egel's historical significance lies in the fact that he accomplished with extraordinary and systematic thoroughness what Kant had so recently said could not be done. Kant had argued that metaphysics is impossible, that it is impossible for the human mind to achieve theoretical knowledge about all of reality. Hegel, on the other hand, set forth the general proposition that "what is rational is real and what is real is rational," and from this concluded that everything that is, is knowable. Here was an elaborate metaphysics, which provided a new basis for thinking about the very structure of reality and about its manifestations in morality, law, religion, art, history, and above all thought itself. It might be argued that the eventual decline of Hegelian philosophy was more a matter of abandonment than of studied attack, more like deserting a mansion than capturing a stronghold. But to imply that Hegel's successors merely decided to ignore his elaborate metaphysical system is to misjudge the impact and grip his ideas had upon the generations that followed him. The power of Hegel's thought can be measured by the fact that most twentieth-century philosophy represents ways of revising or rejecting aspects of his absolute idealism.

Hegel *(The Bettmann Archive)*

Georg Wilhelm Friedrich Hegel was born at Stuttgart in 1770 and lived through Germany's most brilliant intellectual period. This was the year when Beethoven was born and when the poet-scientist Goethe, that "complete civilization in himself," was twenty years old. Kant was forty-six years old and had not yet written his classic philosophical works. The Englishman Wordsworth was also born in this year, and his poetry in time formed a part of that romanticism that shared some of the attitudes of German idealism. At an early age, Hegel was deeply impressed by the Greek writers, coming eventually to believe that Plato and Aristotle were not only the sources of modern philosophy but even now its life-giving roots. After being a rather ordinary pupil at school in Stuttgart, Hegel enrolled at age eighteen in the theological school at the University of Tübingen. Here he became friends with Hölderlin and Schelling and was caught up in lively discussions over the issues of the French Revolution. During his five years at Tübingen his interest gradually turned to the relation between philosophy and theology. It was after he left the university that his interest in philosophy finally flowered. He became a family tutor for six years, in Berne and in Frankfurt, and during these years wrote some minor works that nevertheless contained germs of the major problems he eventually made central in his philosophical works.

By this time German idealism had found two influential spokesmen in Fichte and Schelling. In 1801, when Hegel was appointed to the faculty of the University of Jena, he published his first work, on the *Difference between the Philosophical Systems of Fichte and Schelling,* in which he expressed a dislike for Fichte's identification of the ego and the nonego in the Absolute. While he was more sympathetic with Schelling in these early days, it was not long before his independent and original approach to philosophy was made public in his first major work, *The Phenomenology of Mind,* which, he says, he finished at midnight before the Battle of Jena in 1807. As this battle closed his university, Hegel supported himself and his wife, whom he married in 1811, by becoming rector of the secondary school at Nürnberg, where he remained until 1816. It was here that he wrote his influential *Science of Logic,* which brought him invitations from several universities. In 1816 he joined the faculty at Heidelberg, where in the following year he published his *Encyclopaedia of the Philosophical Sciences in Outline,* the work in which Hegel presents the grand structure of his philosophy in its threefold aspect, namely, logic, philosophy of nature, and philosophy of mind. Two years later, Hegel was given the chair of philosophy at the University of Berlin, where he remained until his death from cholera in 1831 at the age of sixty-one. At Berlin Hegel's writing was massive, although most of it was published after his death. His works during this period included his *Philosophy of Right* and lectures, published posthumously, on *Philosophy of History, Aesthetics, Philosophy of Religion,* and *History of Philosophy.*

DEALING WITH THE LEGACY OF KANT

Following closely upon Kant's *critical* philosophy was the movement of nineteenth-century German *idealism* as formulated by Fichte, Schelling, and Hegel. Kant had reacted against the pretentions of the rationalist metaphysicians who assumed that human reason could penetrate the secrets of ultimate reality. Against these assumptions Kant set forth his critical conception of philosophy, which consisted in describing the limits beyond which the human mind could never proceed. His argument was that the mind is structured in such a way that it is forever barred from going beyond the realm of sense experience, the realm of phenomena or appearances. Moreover, our interpretation of the world of experience is permanently fixed by the categories that the mind imposes upon the objects of experience. These categories—such as cause and effect, existence and negation, and others—said Kant, are concepts that the mind possesses prior to experience and employs in relation to objects, and this is what makes knowledge possible.

The impact of Kant's critical method, however, derived from his argument that in addition to the world of experience, the world of phenomena, there is also the world "behind" phenomena called the *noumenal world.* The noumenal aspect of any object is what that object is *as such,* what the object is like when the categories of the mind are not imposed on it. We experience only the *appearance* of the red apple but not what the apple is *as such.* We can *never* experience anything except the appearance of a thing. Still, Kant said, we can *think* of that aspect of objects that *has* the appearances. Behind the redness of the apple there must be something to which the color red is related or which can *have* the color red. But, again, though we can say there is, besides the appearance of the red apple, the thing-as-such, we can never know anything about this thing-in-itself. We cannot *know* anything about the thing-in-itself because the categories of the mind apply only to the phenomenal world and not to the thing-in-itself. Since knowledge is possible, according to Kant, only when the categories of the mind are imposed upon the objects we experience through our senses, and since we do not sense the thing-in-itself, we cannot have any knowledge about it. Finally, since ultimate reality was for Kant the thing-in-itself, to say that we cannot have knowledge about it meant that we cannot have knowledge about reality.

The idealists, especially Fichte, quickly recognized the glaring contradiction in Kant's argument concerning the thing-in-itself. How is it possible to say that something exists but that we can know nothing about it? Do we not already know something about it when we say that it exists? Moreover, Kant had asserted the existence of the thing-in-itself in order to account for our experiences of sensation, saying in effect that the thing-in-itself is the *cause* of any given sensation. But he had clearly argued that the categories of the mind, such as cause and effect, could not be used to give us knowledge about the noumenal world. For Kant to say, then, that the thing-in-itself is the cause of our sensations is to contradict his own rule for limiting the use of the categories to our judgments about the objects of sense experience. Even to say that the thing-in-itself *exists* is to go beyond the limits Kant had set for knowledge because *existence* is a category of the mind, a concept, which applies only to objects that we experience through our senses. Indeed, Kant's strongest argument against the earlier metaphysicians was that they had wrongly ascribed *existence* to supposed beings and realities beyond sense experience. Now with his doctrine of the thing-in-itself, Kant appeared to have retained just what his critical philosophy was supposed to eliminate. Not only is it impossible, on Kant's terms, to ascribe the category of existence to the thing-in-itself, it is also a clear contradiction to say that there can be something in existence that is unknowable. We can, of course, distinguish between something that is at the moment unknown (but knowable) and what is unknowable. But to say that something is unknowable is contradictory, because such a statement implies that we already know that something *is* and to that extent it is knowable. The conception of the thing-in-itself collapsed, therefore, because it violated Kant's own rules for limiting the categories of cause and existence to objects of sense experience.

Now the idealists put forward the opposite thesis, namely, that whatever is, is knowable. At the same time, the first idealist, Fichte, had no intention of reverting to the kind of metaphysics Kant had rejected. Fichte believed that Kant had achieved genuine progress in philosophy, and he intended to carry forward what Kant had begun. What Fichte tried to do, therefore, was to use Kant's method, now stripped of the concept of the unknowable thing-in-itself, and transform Kant's critical idealism into a metaphysical idealism. That is, Fichte and the other German idealists took Kant's theory that the mind imposes its categories upon experience and transformed this into the theory that every object and therefore the entire universe is a product of mind.

Hegel joined with Fichte and Schelling in the enterprise of transforming Kant's critical philosophy into a metaphysical idealism. But each of these philosophers approached this enterprise in his own and somewhat different way. What they did agree on, however, was that there can be no unknowable thing-in-itself. Moreover, knowledge, as Kant had shown, was possible because the mind itself produced the forms of knowledge through its various categories. But while Kant had assumed that these forms of knowledge received their material content from the *given* of our experience, from an external thing-in-itself, the idealists now argued that the content as well as the forms of knowledge must be the product of mind. In this way, they came to the conclusion that every object of knowledge, including *things,* is the product of mind. This would mean also, as Hegel did assert, that every reality is rational and that the rational is real. And, since there can be nothing unknowable, the idealists were confident that they could know the inner secrets of absolute reality. This reality must be some form of rationality because it had just been argued that there is no independent and essentially unknowable external thing-in-itself that causes consciousness, that only mind produces the objects of knowledge. We do experience a world of things external to us, which we recognize as existing independently of us and which we did not create. If all objects of our knowledge are the products of mind, but not *our* minds, it must be assumed that they are the products of an intelligence other than that of a finite individual. The idealists concluded that all objects of knowledge, and therefore all objects, and indeed the whole universe, are the products of an absolute subject, an Absolute Mind.

Whereas for Kant the categories of the mind merely make knowledge possible, for Hegel the categories have a mode of *being* that is independent of any individual's mind. Again, for Kant, the categories represented the mental process of an individual and provided for Kant the critical explanation of the modes and limits of human knowledge. The categories, he said, are concepts in the human mind that the mind brings to experience and by which the mind can understand the world of experience. Hegel, on the other hand, considered the categories not only as mental processes but as objective realities possessing *being* independent of the thinking individual. The transformation of Kant's critical philosophy into metaphysical idealism consisted in Hegel's saying that the categories, which Kant thought were merely concepts of the human mind, had objective status, that is, possessed a mode of being independent of any individual's thought. The categories, said Hegel, have their being in the Absolute

Mind. But, as we shall see, Hegel did not mean to say that there were categories or ideas, on the one hand, and things, such as chairs and apples, on the other. Such a distinction would suggest that ideas have a separate existence and that things have a separate existence and that knowledge consists in somehow fitting the appropriate idea to the appropriate thing, the way Plato connected his Forms to things. Hegel, unlike Plato, did not ascribe any independent existence to the categories or universals. What he said was that they have *being* and have their being independently of a person's mind or thought. Hegel wanted to say that the real world is more than the subjective conceptions of men's minds. At the same time, he was saying that reality is rationality, or Thought.

Take, for example, a chair. What is a chair, or what does it consist of? Hegel said that if we take seriously the conclusion that there can be no unknowable thing-in-itself, as we must, a chair must consist of the sum of the ideas we can have about it. On this basis a chair must consist of all the universals we find in it when we experience it. We say that the chair is hard, brown, round, and small. These are all universal ideas, and when they are related to each other this way, they are a chair. These universals have their being in the chair; universals or categories never exist singly or independently. Since there is no unknowable aspect of the chair, that is, nothing in addition to the qualities we experience, it follows that the chair *is* what we know about it, and what we know about it is that it consists of a combination of universals or ideas. To say, then, that the categories and universals have objective status means that they have their being independent of the knowing subject. At the same time, as the example of the chair indicates, Hegel says that the object of thought consists after all in thought itself. There is, he said, an identity between knowing and being. Knowing and being are simply two sides of the same coin. To be sure, Hegel recognized that there is a subject and an object, a person and the world. But the essence of his idealism consisted in his notion that the object of our consciousness, the *thing* we experience and think about, is itself *thought*. In the end, Hegel arrived at the notion that reality is to be found in the Absolute Idea.

So far, two major points in Hegel's argument have been set forth, namely, that we must reject the notion of an unknowable thing-in-itself and that the nature of reality is thought, rationality, and that ultimate reality is the Absolute Idea. To indicate some of the steps by which Hegel came to this conclusion that reality is Thought, we turn next to a few of the basic elements in his intricate system of philosophy.

THE NATURE OF REALITY

Hegel looked upon the world as an organic process. We have already seen that for him the truly real is what he called the Absolute. In theological terms, this Absolute is called God. But Hegel was particularly concerned to indicate that he was not here referring to a Being separate from the world of nature or even from individual persons. Whereas Plato made a sharp distinction between appearance and reality, Hegel argued in effect that appearance *is* reality. Nothing, said Hegel, is unrelated. For this reason, whatever we experience as separate things will, upon careful reflection, lead us to other things to which they are related until at last the process of dialectical thought will end in the knowledge of the Absolute. Still, the Absolute is not the unity of separate things. Hegel rejected the premise of materialism, which held that there are separate, finite particles of hard matter, which, when arranged in different formations, make up the whole nature of things. Nor did Hegel accept the extreme alternative put forward in the ancient world by Parmenides and more recently by Spinoza, namely, that everything is One, a single substance with various modes and attributes. Hegel described the Absolute as a dynamic process, as an organism having parts but nevertheless unified into a complex system. The Absolute is therefore not some entity separate from the world but *is* the world when viewed in a special way.

Hegel believed that the inner essence of the Absolute could be reached by human reason because the Absolute is disclosed in Nature as well as in the working of the human mind. What connects these three, the Absolute, Nature, and the mind, is Thought itself. A person's way of thinking is, as it were, fixed by the structure of Nature, by the way things actually behave. Things behave as they do, however, because the Absolute is expressing itself through the structure of Nature. Thus, a person thinks about Nature the way the Absolute expresses itself in Nature. Just as the Absolute and also Nature are dynamic processes, so also human thought is a process, a dialectic process.

Logic and the Dialectic Process   Hegel laid great stress upon logic. To be sure, he understood logic to mean virtually the same thing as metaphysics. This was inevitable in his case inasmuch as he believed that knowing and being coincide. Still, it was Hegel's view that we can know the essence of reality by moving logically step by step and avoiding all self-contradiction along the way. Descartes had advocated a similar method, whereby certainty in knowledge would follow from the movement from one clear idea to the next. Unlike Descartes, however, whose emphasis was upon the relations of ideas to each other, Hegel argued that thought must follow the inner logic of reality itself. That is, since Hegel had identified the rational with the actual, he concluded that logic and logical connections must be discovered *in* the actual and not in some "empty ratiocination." He argued that "since philosophy is the exploration of the rational, it is for that very reason the apprehension of the present and the actual, not the erection of a beyond, supposed to exist, God knows where." Logic, then, is the process by which we deduce, from our experiences of the actual, the categories that describe the Absolute. This process of deduction is at the very heart of Hegel's dialectic philosophy.

Hegel's dialectic process exhibits a *triadic* movement. Usually this triadic structure of the dialectic process is described as a movement from *thesis* to *antithesis* and finally to *synthesis,* after which the synthesis becomes a new thesis, and this process continues until it ends in the Absolute Idea. What Hegel emphasized in his dialectic logic was that thought *moves* and that *contradiction,* rather than bringing knowledge to a halt, acts as a positive moving force in human reasoning.

To illustrate Hegel's dialectic method, we can take the first basic triad of his logic, namely, the triad of *Being, Nothing,* and *Becoming.* Hegel said that the mind must always move from the more general and abstract to the specific and concrete. The most general concept we can form about things is that they are. Although various things have specific and different qualities, they all have one thing in common, namely, their being. Being, then, is the most general concept the mind can formulate. Also, Being must be logically prior to any specific thing, for things represent determinations or the shaping of what is originally without features. Thus, logic (and reality) begins with the indeterminate, with "the original featurelessness which precedes all definite character and is the very first of all. And this we call Being." Hegel's system begins, therefore, with the concept of Being, and this is the thesis. The question now is, how can thought move from such an abstract concept to any other concept? More important still is the question, how is it possible to *deduce* any other concept from such a universal idea as Being?

It was here that Hegel believed he had discovered something new about the nature of thought. Ever since the time of Aristotle, logicians had thought that nothing could be deduced from a category that was not contained in that category. To deduce *B* from *A* requires that in some way *B* already be contained in *A.* Hegel accepted this. But what he rejected in Aristotelian logic was the assumption that nothing could be deduced from a *universal* term. For example, Aristotle argued that everything is a distinct thing and that logic, therefore, provides us only with specific universal terms from which no other universal terms could be deduced. Thus, for example, there is either *blue* or *not-blue;* there is no way to deduce any other color from blue. If blue is blue, you cannot at the same time say that it is something else, a non-blue. This principle of noncontradiction is very important in any formal logic. Still, Hegel believed that it is not true that a universal does not contain another concept. Returning, then, to the concept of Being, Hegel said that we have here an idea which contains none of the particular qualities or characteristics of the many things that have being. The idea of Being has no content, for the moment you give it some content, it would no longer be the concept of pure Being but the concept of something. Unlike Aristotle, however, Hegel believed that from this concept of Being it is possible to deduce another concept. He argued that because pure Being is mere abstraction, it is therefore absolutely negative. That is, since the concept of Being is wholly indeterminate, it passes into the concept of not-Being. Whenever we try to think of Being without any particular characteristics, the mind moves from Being to not-Being. This, of course, means that in some sense Being and not-Being are the same. Hegel was aware, as he said, that "the proposition that Being and Nothing are the same is so paradoxical to the imagination or understanding, that it is perhaps taken for a joke." Indeed, to understand Being and Nothing as the same, said Hegel, "is one of the hardest things thought expects itself to do." Still, Hegel's point is that Nothing is deduced from Being. At the same time, the concept of Nothing easily leads the mind back to the concept of Being. Of course Hegel is not implying here that we can say of particular things that they simultaneously are the same as nothing. His argument is limited to the concept of pure Being, which, he says, contains the idea of Nothing. He has, then, deduced the concept of Nothing from the concept of Being. The antithesis, Nothing, is contained in the thesis, Being. In Hegel's logic, the antithesis is always deduced from, because it is contained in, the thesis.

The movement of the mind from Being to Nothing produces a third category, namely *Becoming*. The concept of Becoming is formed by the mind when it understands that Being, for the reasons already mentioned, is the same as Nothing. Becoming, says Hegel, is "the unity of Being and Nothing." It is, he says, "*one* idea." Becoming is therefore the *synthesis* of Being and Nothing. If we ask how something can both be and not be, Hegel would answer that it can both be and not be when it becomes.

Throughout his vast and intricate system, Hegel employs this same dialectic method of logic. At each step, he sets forth a thesis from which is deduced its antithesis; this thesis and antithesis then find their unity in a higher synthesis. In the end, Hegel arrives at the concept of the Absolute Idea, which he describes, in accordance with his dialectic method, as Becoming, as a process of self-development. Beginning, then, at the lowest level of knowledge, with the sensation of qualities and characteristics of particular things, Hegel sought to expand the scope of knowledge by discovering the ever-widening interrelationships of all things, always making sure that the mind takes no flight of fancy but rather moves rigorously by way of deduction from one concept to the other that the mind finds as categories in actuality. Single facts, for Hegel, are irrational; only when such single facts are seen as aspects of the whole do they become rational. Thinking is forced to move from one fact to another by the very nature of each concept that facts engender. As an example, which does not accurately illustrate Hegel's point but does suggest how single facts acquire a rational quality, one can consider the parts of an engine. By itself, a spark plug has no rational character; what confers rationality upon it is its relation to the other parts of the engine. To discover the essence of the spark plug is, thus, to discover truth about the other parts and, eventually, the entire engine. The human mind, then, moves dialectically, constantly embracing an ever-increasing scope of reality, discovering the truth of anything only after discovering its relation to the whole, to the *Idea*.

The *Idea* of which Hegel speaks is deduced in his logic by the same method that yielded Becoming out of Being. The category of *subjectivity* is deduced from the fact that a person can have a notion of a thing, make a judgment about it, and be able to reason out logical connections. But from *subjectivity* there can be deduced its opposite, namely, *objectivity*. That is, the notion of subjectivity already contains the idea of objectivity. To say that I am a self (subjectivity) implies that there is a not-self (objectivity). Subjectivity consists of thought in its formal sense. Objectivity, on the other hand, is thought that is, as it were, *outside* itself and *in* things. Describing the objective character of a person's notion, Hegel says that it consists of *mechanism, chemism,* and *teleology.* What a subject knows about nature as mechanical laws, for example, objects express in their behavior. The synthesis of the subjective and the objective, says Hegel, is their unity in the Idea. That is, in the Idea, the subjective (formal) and the objective (material) are brought together in unity. The Idea, however, contains its own dialectic, namely, life, cognition, and the Absolute Idea. Thus, the Idea is the category of self-consciousness; it knows itself in its objects. The whole drift of Hegel's logic, therefore, has been to move from the initial concept of Being finally to the notion of the Idea. But this Idea must also be understood as being in a dynamic process, so that the Idea is itself in a continuous process of self-development toward self-perfection.

The Philosophy of Nature   From the Idea is derived the realm of Nature. As Hegel puts it, Nature represents the Idea "outside itself." This expression is somewhat misleading, because it implies that the Idea exists independently of the world. In addition, Hegel ascribes "absolute freedom" to the Idea as it "goes forth freely out of itself as Nature." Recalling, however, Hegel's premise that the real is rational, it must follow here that Nature is simply rationality, or the Idea, in *external* form, somewhat the way a watchmaker's idea is found outside of himself in the watch. But Hegel's view is more subtle than the relation of the watchmaker to the watch would suggest inasmuch as Hegel does not really refer to two separately existing things, Idea and Nature. Ultimate reality is a single organic and dynamic whole. Hegel's distinction between the logical Idea "behind" all things, on the one hand, and Nature, on the other, is his attempt simply to distinguish between the "inner" and "outer" aspects of the self-same reality. Nature, in short, is the opposite, the antithesis, of the rational Idea (thesis). Our thought moves dialectically from the rational (Idea) to the nonrational (Nature). The concept of Nature leads our thought finally to a synthesis represented by the unity of Idea and Nature in the new concept of Spirit (*Geist,* translated as either Spirit or Mind). What drives our thought from Nature back to Spirit is the dialectic movement within the concept of Nature. Just as logic begins with the most abstract concept, namely, Being, so the philosophy of Nature begins with the most abstract thing, which is, says Hegel, space. Space is empty (just as Being is indeterminate). At one "end," then, Nature touches emptiness. At the other end, it passes over into Spirit. Between space and Spirit is the diversity of particular things, which is what Nature is. Nature exhibits the laws of mechanics, physics, and organics. Each of these aspects of Nature is in turn analyzed by Hegel into its dialectic terms.

Much of what Hegel says about Nature is somewhat outmoded by the developments of science since his day. But it was not his intention to take over the work of the scientists. He was concerned, rather, to discover through the philosophy of Nature a rational structure and pattern in all of reality. At the same time, he tried to show the difference between *freedom* and *necessity,* saying that Nature is the realm of necessity whereas Spirit is freedom. Nature, says Hegel, "is to be considered as a system of stages, of which one proceeds necessarily from the other." Freedom, on the other hand, is the act of Spirit. There is, then, a dialectic opposition between Spirit and Nature, between freedom and necessity. Indeed, the "career" of reality, the teleological movement of history, represents the gradual and continuous unfolding of the Spirit, of the Idea of freedom.

The Philosophy of Spirit   The third part of Hegel's system, following his logical Idea and his philosophy of Nature, is the philosophy of Spirit or Mind. Here again, Hegel sets forth the elements of his dialectic in which the thesis is subjective spirit, the antithesis is objective spirit, and the synthesis is Absolute Spirit. He goes into considerable detail, piling triad upon triad to illustrate that the Absolute is Spirit and that this Spirit finds its manifestation in the minds of individuals, in the social institutions of family, civil society, and the state, and finally in art, religion, and philosophy. The subjective spirit refers to the inner workings of the human mind, whereas the objective spirit represents the mind in its external embodiment in the social and political institutions. At the apex of knowledge are art, religion, and philosophy, which are the achievement of Absolute Spirit.

Most of what made Hegel's philosophy famous was that portion of his thought that he developed around his concept of objective spirit. Here we come upon the unity of Hegel's thought as he now attempts to connect his moral, social, and political thought with the rest of his system. The whole sphere of human behavior, both individual and collective, is described by him as part of the actual and therefore is essentially rational. Moreover, as part of the actual this objective side of the Spirit is seen as involved in the dialectic process. Human behavior and social and political organisms contain or embody the Spirit, just as Nature is the objective embodiment of the Absolute Idea. For this reason, Hegel looked upon institutions not as the creations of humanity, but as the product of the dialectic movement of history, of the objective manifestation of rational reality. Speaking, for example, about his book on the *Philosophy of Right,* Hegel writes that "containing as it does the science of the state, [it] is to be nothing other than the endeavor to apprehend and portray the state as something inherently rational. As a work of philosophy, it must be poles apart from an attempt to construct a state as it ought to be." This identification of the actual state with the very grounds of reality is what caused Hegel's political theory to have such a captivating influence among those who wished to think about the state in totalitarian or at least nondemocratic terms. We turn, then, to some of the "moments" in the dialectic process by which Hegel seeks to indicate the natural movement from the individual's concept of right to the state's authority over society. The basic triadic movement here is from *right* (thesis) to *morality* (antithesis) and then to *social ethics* (synthesis).

ETHICS AND POLITICS

The Concept of Right   Human behavior must, of course, be understood first of all as the actions of individuals. Individuals, says Hegel, are aware of freedom. They express their freedom most concretely by an act of will. Hegel looked upon will and reason as virtually synonymous, saying that "only as thinking intelligence, will is free will." A person expresses freedom chiefly in relation to material things, appropriating them, using them, and exchanging them. "To appropriate," says Hegel, "is at bottom only to manifest the majesty of my will towards things, by demonstrating that they are not self-complete and have no purpose of their own." The basis of the right to property is for Hegel the free will of the individual in the act of appropriation. Inasmuch as this will resides in the individual, property is a private right. Free people, however, are able to "alienate" themselves from property, and this they do through "contract." A contract is the product of two free wills agreeing to exchange property. It also indicates the development of a duty, which the terms of the contract now embody. Hegel's central point here is that insofar as individual persons act rationally, their free acts conform to the rationality of the universe. Their individual wills harmonize with the universal will. But among free people, the harmony of wills is precarious. Thus, there is always the possibility of the opposite of right; the negation of right is exemplified in violence and fraud. "Wrong" consists in the breakdown of harmony between the individual will and the universal will. The dialectic relation between "right" and "wrong" produces the tension between the way the "wrong" will acts and the way the will should act in order to be universal, that is, rational. This tension or conflict between right and wrong is what gives rise to morality.

Morality, said Hegel, is fundamentally a matter of purpose and intention in the ethical life of humanity. There is more to "goodness," in other words, than merely obeying laws and keeping contracts. Morality has to do with those deeds for which people can themselves be held responsible. Only those consequences that a person intends and that constitute the purpose of his or her act can affect the goodness or badness of this act. It appears, then, that for Hegel the essence of morality is found internally in a person's intention and purpose. But Hegel argues that although moral responsibility begins with those acts that can be assigned to a free will, a will that intends the act, the full scope of morality is not exhausted by this subjective aspect of the act. After all, human behavior takes place always in a context, especially in a context of other persons, hence other wills. Moral duty or responsibility is therefore broader than the concerns or intentions of the individual. Moral duty derives from the requirement of identifying a person's individual will with the universal will. Although it is perfectly legitimate for people to be concerned with their own happiness and welfare, the principle of rationality requires that they must exercise their own will in such a way that the wills of other persons, also acting freely, can achieve their welfare as well. Morality is therefore an element in the dialectic process: the thesis is the abstract right of each individual; the antithesis is morality, for morality represents the duties that the universal will raises as limitations to the individual will. The relation between these two wills is the relation between freedom and duty, subjectivity and objectivity. The dialectic process in this ethical sphere is constantly moving toward a greater harmony between the subjective and objective, and in this regard Hegel described the *good* as "the realization of freedom, the absolute final purpose of the world." But the realization of freedom, for Hegel, had to occur within the limits of duty. In this sense the freest person is the one who most completely fulfills his or her duty. It was inevitable, then, that Hegel should discover the synthesis of the individual's freedom and right on the one hand, and the universal will, on the other, in the concrete institutions of humankind, particularly in the state.

The State   Between the individual and the state there are two dialectic steps, according to Hegel, namely, the *family* and *society*. The family is, as it were, the first stage of the objective will. In marriage, two persons give up their individual wills to some degree in order to become one person. Because the family is a single unit, its property becomes a common possession, even though, for legal reasons, the husband might be said to own it. Again, the family, united by a bond of feeling, or love, constitutes the logically first moment of the embodiment of the universal will. At the same time, the family contains its own antithesis, namely, individuals who will eventually grow up, leave the family, and enter into that larger context of similar individuals that is called *civil society*. These individuals now chart out their own lives and have their own purposes. We need to remember at this point that Hegel is here analyzing the dialectic development of the state and is not giving an historical account of its emergence. The state is the synthesis of the family and of civil society. The family, in this analysis, stands for the embodied universal, whereas civil society represents particularity insofar as each individual, unlike the members of a family, sets his or her own goals. These two elements, universality and particularity, cannot exist independently, for they are contained in each other; their unity, therefore, is found in the state, which is the synthesis of universality and particularity. The state is a unity in difference. This does not seem to be a genuine deduction, but Hegel does conclude that the synthesis of the universal and the particular consists in the individual. In this context, the state is conceived as an individual, the true individual, an organic unity of partial individuals.

Hegel did not conceive of the state as an authority imposed from the outside upon the individual. Nor did he consider the state the product of the general or majority will. The state, said Hegel, "is absolutely rational—substantial will," and again, "the state is the actuality of the ethical idea." Hegel conferred upon the state the characteristic of a person, saying that the state represents universal self-consciousness. A particular individual, he said, is conscious of himself insofar as he is a part of this larger self. And, says Hegel, "since the state is mind objectified, it is only as one of its members that the individual himself has objectivity, genuine individuality, and an ethical life." A person's spiritual reality is also found in the state, for as Hegel says, a human being's "spiritual reality consists in this, that his own essence—Reason—is objectively present to him, that it has objective immediate existence for him." Recalling that Hegel was not interested in formulating a theory of the *ideal* state, his descriptions of the *actual* state are all the more striking. It was the actual living state about which he said that "the state is the embodiment of rational freedom," and, most striking of all, that "the State is the Divine Idea as it exists on earth."

All these highly exalting descriptions of the state would make it appear that Hegel had advocated the totalitarian state. He did insist, however, that insofar as the state is the synthesis of particularity and universality, of the family and the individual, there be the preservation by the state of individual liberty, that liberty which the individual possesses as a member of civil society. Neither the family nor civil society is destroyed by the state; they continue to exist within the state. The laws of the state and, in general, the legislative and executive arms of the state do not issue arbitrary commands. Laws are universal rules, which have their application in individual cases involving individual persons. Moreover, laws must be rational and directed at rational persons. The reason for laws is that people, in their ability to make free choices, are capable of choosing ends that harm others. Insofar as their acts harm others, their behavior is irrational. The function of law is therefore to bring rationality into behavior. What makes an act rational is that it at once achieves a person's private good as well as the public good. Only a person who acts rationally can be free, because only rational acts can be permitted in society, because only rational acts avoid social harm. The function of the state is therefore not to compound personal harm or misery by issuing arbitrary and therefore irrational commands, but rather to increase, through its laws, the aggregate of rational behavior. The state is thus an organism that is seeking to develop the Idea of freedom to its maximum, and to achieve objective freedom only as its individual members do. In this way, the laws of the state, rather than being arbitrary, are rational rules of behavior that the individual would choose if he or she were acting rationally. The only limitation upon the individual will that reason allows is the limitation required by the existence of other wills. The sovereign acts in the name of the universal will and reason and not arbitrarily. The state then, "is the Idea of Spirit in the external manifestation of human Will and its Freedom."

When it comes to the relations between states, Hegel emphasizes the autonomy and absolute sovereignty of each state. The relation of one state to another is different for Hegel from the relation of one person to another in civil society. Above two persons who disagree in society, there is the state as a higher power capable of resolving the dispute. But as between two states, there is no higher entity. Each nation, says Hegel, "is mind in its substantive rationality and immediate actuality and is therefore the absolute power on earth." For this reason, "every state is sovereign and autonomous against its neighbors. It is a fundamental proposition of international law that obligations between states ought to be kept." But, says Hegel, "states are... in a state of nature in relation to each other," and for this reason there is no universal will binding upon them. The "rights of states are actualized only in their particular wills," insofar as there are no constitutional powers over them. There is no one to judge between states.

Why Hegel did not carry his dialectic movement to the next level, at which individual states would be united into a community of nations, is not clear. He was of course aware that Kant had an idea of securing "perpetual peace" by a League of Nations to adjust every dispute. But he said that such an arrangement could not work because it would still be necessary for each state to *will* to obey the international tribunal. But a state will always *will* its own welfare. Indeed, says Hegel, "welfare is the highest law governing the relation of one state to another." There can be no moral limitations upon the state, for the state *is* "the ethical substance." It follows, says Hegel, that "if states disagree and their particular wills cannot be harmonized, the matter can only be settled by war."

World History In Hegel's view, the history of the world is the history of nations. The dynamic unfolding of history represents the "progress in the consciousness of freedom." This progress is not a matter of mere chance but is rather a rational process. "Reason," says Hegel, "dominates the world and ...world history is thus a rational process." In a special way, the state is the bearer of reason, and it was for this reason that Hegel had said that the state is "the Idea of Spirit" in external form and that the state is "the Divine Idea as it exists on earth." But the dialectic of the historical process consists in the opposition between states. Each state expresses a national spirit and indeed the world spirit in its own collective consciousness. To be sure, only individual minds are capable of consciousness. Still, the minds of a particular people develop a spirit of unity, and for this reason it is possible to speak of a "national spirit." Each national spirit represents a moment in the development of the world spirit, and the interplay between national spirits represents the dialectic in history.

The conflict between nations is inevitable inasmuch as the historical process is the very stuff of reality, is the gradual working out of the *Idea of Freedom*. Nations are carried along by the wave of history, so that in each epoch a particular nation is "the dominant people in world history for this epoch...." A nation cannot choose when it will be great, for "it is only once that it can make its hour strike." At decisive points in history, says Hegel, special world-historical persons emerge as agents of the world spirit. These persons lift nations to a new level of development and perfection. Hegel thought that such individuals could hardly be judged in terms of a morality that belonged to the epoch out of which a nation is being led, that the value of such persons consists in their creative responsiveness to the unfolding Idea of Freedom.

The time process of history was for Hegel the logical process of the dialectic. History is moving toward a purposive end, namely, freedom. To illustrate the dialectic of history, Hegel used examples of various peoples, which, he thought, indicated the three *moments* in the development of freedom. The Orientals, he thought, knew nothing of freedom except that the potentate alone could do what he wished. Although the Greeks and Romans knew the concept of citizenship, they limited this status only to a few and regarded others as being by nature slaves. It was the *Germanic* peoples who, under the influence of Christianity, developed the insight that humanity as such is free. Thus, Hegel says that "The East knew and to the present day knows, only that *One* is free; the Greek and Roman world, that *some* are free; the German world knows that *All* are free." The highest freedom, we have seen, occurs, according to Hegel, when the individual acts according to the universal, rational will of the whole society.

ABSOLUTE SPIRIT

Hegel's philosophy has its culmination in knowledge of the Absolute. In the process of dialectic, knowledge of the Absolute is the synthesis of subjective spirit and objective spirit. Because reality is rationality, Thought, Idea, it followed for Hegel that a person's knowledge of the Absolute is actually the Absolute knowing itself through the finite spirit of humanity. Just how this moment of self-consciousness of the Absolute occurs in the spirit of humanity is described by Hegel in a final dialectic.

Our consciousness of the Absolute, says Hegel, is achieved progressively as the mind moves through the three stages from art, to religion, and finally to philosophy. Art provides "a sensuous semblance of the Idea" by providing the mind with an object of sense. In the object of art, the mind apprehends the Absolute as beauty. The object of art, moreover, is the creation of Spirit and, as such, contains some aspect of the Idea. Hegel saw in the movement from Oriental symbolic art to classical Greek art and finally to romantic Christian art an ever-deepening insight into the Absolute.

Art leads beyond itself to religion. What differentiates religion from art is that religion is an activity of thought, whereas an aesthetic experience is primarily a matter of feeling. Although art can direct consciousness toward the Absolute, religion comes closer to it precisely because the Absolute is Thought. At the same time, religious thought, said Hegel, is pictorial thought. In early religions this pictorial element looms large. "The Greek God," for example, "is the object of naïve intuition and sensuous imagination. His shape is therefore the bodily shape of man." At the apex of religion is Christianity, which is the religion of the Spirit.

Hegel regarded Christianity as the pictorial representation of philosophy. He believed that religion and philosophy have basically the same subject matter, that both represent "knowledge of that which is eternal, of what God is, and what flows out of his nature," so that "religion and philosophy come to the same things." Philosophy leaves behind the pictorial forms of religion and rises to the level of pure thought. But philosophy does not offer the knowledge of the Absolute at any particular moment, for such knowledge is the product of the dialectic process. Philosophy itself has a history, a dialectic movement, where the major periods and systems of philosophy are not mere haphazard developments. These systems in the history of philosophy represent the necessary succession of ideas required by the progressive unfolding of the Idea. The history of philosophy is for Hegel, therefore, the development of the Absolute's self-consciousness in the mind of humanity.

17

Schopenhauer: Prophet of Pessimism

A contemporary of Hegel, Schopenhauer refused to acknowledge that Hegel was an appropriate or adequate successor to Kant. So great was Schopenhauer's disrespect for Hegel that he could say that "there is no philosophy in the period between Kant and myself; only mere University charlatanism." This criticism aimed at Hegel was in the same vein as Schopenhauer's comment that "out of every page of Hume's there is more to be learned than out of [all] of the philosophical works of Hegel." But Hegel was not the only target of Schopenauer's withering criticism. He expressed his broader disdain in the judgment that "I should like to see the man who could boast of a more miserable set of contemporaries than mine." Schopenhauer became aware of his own genius as his intellectual powers developed in depth and clarity. What appears as egotism to others was to Schopenhauer simply the recognition by him of his unique gifts just as, he says, a person knows whether he is taller or shorter than the average person. He had no hesitation therefore in saying that "I have lifted the veil of truth higher than any mortal before me."

Arthur Schopenhauer was born in Danzig in 1788. Although his family

Schopenhauer *(The Granger Collection)*

was of Dutch extraction, it had for a long time been settled in this German city with its ancient traditions and its Hanseatic commercial connections. His ancestors enjoyed considerable prominence and wealth. When Russia's Peter the Great and Empress Catherine visited Danzig, Arthur's great-grandfather's house was selected as the place where these distinguished visitors would stay. His father was a wealthy merchant and wanted Arthur to follow in his footsteps as a businessman. As a child Arthur accompanied his parents on their many travels, which introduced him to a wide variety of cultures and customs and developed in him a distinctly cosmopolitan point of view. Although he gained much from these travels in France, Italy, England, Belgium, and Germany, his systematic early education was disrupted. But his capacity to learn was so great that he was able to make up his lack of ordinary knowledge very quickly. His early schooling began in France at age nine; after two years he returned to Germany, where his education focused upon the requirements for a career as a merchant, with little or no emphasis upon the classics. But soon Schopenhauer showed a strong inclination toward philosophy, a development not at all pleasing to his father, who worried that such a career could only lead to poverty. After more travel and study in England and Switzerland, Schopenhauer returned to Danzig and entered a merchant's office as a clerk. Shortly thereafter his father died, and at age seventeen he was on his own without even a close or helpful bond between his mother and himself. He and his mother had opposite temperaments, she being full of optimism and the love of pleasure while he, from an early age, was inclined toward pessimism. This difference between the two made it impossible for them to live in the same house. Later, when his mother moved to Weimar, she wrote to Arthur about the battle of Jena and the occupation of Weimar saying that "I could tell you things that would make your hair stand on end, but I refrain, for I know how you love to brood over human misery in any case."

By the age of twenty-one, Schopenhauer had more than adequately repaired his sketchy earlier education and had enriched his mind with a deep study of the classics, while his considerable aptitude for languages led him comfortably through Greek, Latin, and history, and mathematics was not neglected along the way. He was now ready to embark on a career, and in 1809 he enrolled in the medical school at Göttingen University. But the following year he transferred from medicine to the faculty of philosophy, captivated by Plato "the divine" and "the marvelous Kant." In due course he completed his studies, and for his doctoral dissertation at the University of Jena he wrote a significant book entitled *On the Fourfold Root of the Principle of Sufficient Reason* which was published in 1813. The highest praise for this book came from the poet Goethe who recognized in this early work Schopenhauer's genius. In spite of Goethe's praise for it, the book attracted virtually no attention from readers and remained unsold.

At Goethe's suggestion, Schopenhauer was encouraged to study the problem of light, which at this time was approached from different points of view by Goethe and Newton. From this study Schopenhauer produced a brief work entitled *On Vision and Colours* which tended to support Goethe's view.

Schopenhauer's masterpiece is his *The World as Will and Idea,* which he wrote during 1814 and 1818 while living quietly in Dresden and which he published in 1819. Once again, this book aroused little notice and generated the sale of only a few copies. It contains Schopenhauer's complete system of philosophical ideas. He was convinced that in this work he had made his most distinctive contribution and was further convinced that he had discovered the solution to many long-standing philosophical problems, or, as he wrote, "Subject to the limitation of human knowledge, my philosophy is the real solution of the enigma of the world." As if to prepare for shallow criticism or even a brutal disregard of his major book, he wrote, "whoever has accomplished an immortal work will be as little hurt by its reception from the public or the opinions of critics, as a sane man in a madhouse is affected by the upbraidings of the insane."

From Dresden Schopenhauer went to Berlin and began to lecture at the University of Berlin with the hope of winning acceptance or at least recognition of his systematic philosophy. This endeavor was a failure not only because of the continued indifference of the academic world to his ideas but also partly because of his audacious setting of the time of his lectures at exactly the hour when the giant Hegel gave his lectures. In 1831 Schopenhauer left Berlin, urged on by a cholera epidemic which included Hegel among its victims. He settled in Frankfurt-am-Main, and wrote other works which further explored and confirmed the fundamental ideas in *The World as Will and Idea*. Among these was *On the Will in Nature* (1836), in which he sought to provide scientific knowledge to support his theory of metaphysics. In 1838 he won a prize given by a scientific society in Norway for his essay on "whether free will could be proved from the evidence of consciousness." A second essay on the source or foundation of morals followed the announcement of a prize competition by the Royal Danish Academy. But even though Schopenhauer was the only one to submit an essay, he did not win this prize. Nevertheless, these two essays were published in 1841 as *The Two Fundamental Problems of Ethics*. In 1851 he published another major book entitled *Parerga and Paralipomena* which was a collection of essays on a variety of subjects. It included "On Women," "On Religion," "On Ethics," "On Aesthetics," "On Suicide," "On the Suffering of the World," and "On the Vanity of Existence." This was the book that first brought him wide popularity.

The sources of Schopenhauer's philosophy are to be found in his concentrated learning and equally in his unique personal temperament. At an early stage, one of his teachers urged him to concentrate his study of philosophy on Plato and Kant, and the influence of these two seminal philosophers is to be felt throughout his major work. In addition, Schopenhauer discovered another powerful but unlikely source of insight, or at least support, for his theory of metaphysics, namely, the classic of India the *Upanishads*. This work was brought to his attention by an Oriental scholar, Friedrick Mayer, the author of *Brahma, or the Religion of the Hindus*. This strand of Oriental philosophy supports Schopenhauer's combination of intellectual and temperamental conclusions that there is no more to experience than appearance, as if to the questions "is this all?" and "is this life?" the answer is a pessimistic "yes." Schopenhauer's pessimism was a matter of temperament, but he wished to draw a distinction between his pessimism, which he considered the product of his mature judgment based upon "an objective recognition of folly," on the one hand, and "malevolence of the wicked," on the other. He called his pessimism "a noble displeasure that arises only out of a better nature revolting against unexpected wickedness," adding that such pessimism as his is not directed at particular individuals only but "it concerns all, and each individual is merely an example." It can even be said that Schopenhauer's metaphysical system is not simply another way of dealing with the problems of metaphysics but rather an elaborate metaphysical justification for a pessimistic outlook upon life and reality. His understanding of the nature of the contents of the "world," his description of the function of the "will" in the world, and the status of "idea" in relation to the world lead him to the inevitable conclusion that pessimism is the only plausible point of view that a thoughtful person can take regarding human existence.

THE PRINCIPLE OF SUFFICIENT REASON

As is frequently the case with a genius, Schopenhauer arrived quickly and at an early age at his major philosophical insights. The foundation for his systematic thought was formulated at age twenty-five in his doctoral dissertation *On the Fourfold Root of the Principle of Sufficient Reason.* In this work, Schopenhauer sought answers to the questions "what can I know?" and "what is the nature of things?" If this sounds grandiose, he intended to give nothing less than a thorough account of the whole realm of reality, and to accomplish this he relied upon the Principle of Sufficient Reason.

In its simplest form, the Principle of Sufficient Reason states that "nothing is without a reason" (or "cause" or "because"). The most obvious application of this principle is found in the field of science, where the behavior and the relationships of physical objects are explained in a manner that is sufficient to satisfy the demands of reason or rationality. But Schopenhauer discovered that there are other variations besides this scientific form of the Principle of Sufficient Reason. This is so, he said, because there are objects other than those with which the scientist deals and these other objects require unique forms of this governing principle.

Altogether, Schopenhauer set forth four basic forms of the Principle of Sufficient Reason corresponding to the four different kinds of ideas which comprise the whole range of human thought. The four kinds of objects which give rise to different kinds of ideas are as follows:

1. *Physical objects.* These exist and are causally related in space and time, which we know through our ordinary experience of things, and this provides the subject matter of the material sciences, such as, for example, physics. At this point, Schopenhauer follows closely Kant's basic theory that knowledge begins with experience but is not limited, as Hume thought, to what is empirically given or presented to us. Instead, the elements of our experience are organized by the human mind, which brings to our experience a priori categories of space, time, and causality as though these categories are lenses through which we look at objects. In this realm of Phenomena, the Principle of Sufficient Reason explains *becoming* or *change.*

2. *Abstract concepts.* These objects take the form of conclusions we draw from other concepts, as when we apply the rules of inference or implication. The relationship between concepts and the conclusions they infer or imply is governed by the Principle of Sufficient Reason. This is the realm of logic, and here the Principle of Sufficient Reason is applied to the ways of *knowing.*

3. *Mathematical objects.* Here we encounter, for example, arithmetic and geometry as they are related to space and time. Geometry is grounded in the principle which governs the various positions of the parts of space. Arithmetic, on the other hand, involves the parts of time, for as Schopenhauer says, "on the connection of the parts of time rests all counting." He concludes that "the law according to which the parts of space and time...determine one another I call the principle of sufficient reason of *being.*"

4. *The self.* "How can the self be an object?" Schopenhauer says that the self is the subject that wills and that this willing (or behaving) subject is the "object for the knowing subject." This we can call *self-consciousness.* The principle which governs our knowledge of the relation between the self and its acts of will is "the principle of...sufficient reason of acting...more briefly, the *law of motivation.*"

The striking observation drawn from these four forms of the Principle of Sufficient Reason is that everywhere there is the presence of necessity. Through the whole range of objects, whether they be physical objects, the abstract concepts of logic, mathematical objects, or the self as the object of a knowing subject, in all these Schopenhauer stresses the fact of *necessity* or *determinism.* Thus we encounter physical necessity, logical necessity, mathematical necessity, and moral necessity. This element of necessity in the very nature of things is what led Schopenhauer to hold that people behave in daily life by necessity, that they simply react to the motives produced by their character, leaving aside the question whether people are capable of altering their character. The pervasiveness of necessity inevitably produced in Schopenhauer a deep sense of pessimism, which permeates all his writings concerning human existence. His pessimism becomes clearly understandable when we consider his account of the place of human beings in the universe, an account which is the central concern of his major work.

THE WORLD AS WILL AND IDEA

Schopenhauer's famous book *The World as Will and Idea* opens with the astonishing sentence "The world is my idea." What makes this sentence astonishing is that each word in it, as is the case also with each word in the title of the book, is capable of conveying a strange impression if the word is given its ordinary everyday meaning. What Schopenhauer meant by the "world" and the definition and role he ascribed to "will," as well as the account he gives of our "ideas," gives these words unique meanings and constitutes the major insights of his theory of metaphysics.

The World

For Schopenhauer, the term *world* has the widest possible meaning. It includes human beings, animals, trees, stars, moon, the earth, planets, and indeed the whole universe. But why call it *my* idea? Why not simply say that the world is there, "out there." Earlier the philosopher Berkeley had formulated the proposition that *esse est percipi,* or to be is to be perceived. If something has to be perceived for it to be, what happens to that thing when you are not perceiving it? If you go out of your library, are the books still there? But Schopenhauer insists that anyone who reflects carefully about his experience of the world discovers that "what he knows is not a sun and an earth but only an eye that sees a sun, a hand that feels an earth; that the world which surrounds him is there only as idea...." This means, he says, that "all that exists for knowledge, and therefore this whole world, is only object in relation to subject, perception of a perceiver, in a word, idea."

The World as Idea

The English word *idea* does not convey the meaning of the German word *vorstellung* used by Schopenhauer, and the difference between the two meanings helps to explain why the sentence "The world is my idea" strikes one as strange. As used by Schopenhauer, the word *vorstellung* means, literally, anything that is "set in front of" or "placed before," or that is a "presentation." This refers to everything that is placed before or presented to our consciousness or understanding, so that the "world as idea" or "my idea" refers not only to what we *think* about (i.e., ideas in the narrow view) but equally to what we hear, feel, or perceive in various other ways. There is no other object out there besides what we perceive, or, as Schopenhauer says, "The whole actual, that is active world is determined as such through the understanding and apart from it is nothing." The world presents itself to a person as an object to a subject, and we as subjects know only the world we perceive and thus "the whole world of objects is and remains idea, and therefore wholly and forever determined by the subject." It may be that no person's idea of the world is perfect, that therefore "my idea" will not be the same as "your idea." But each person can say that "the world is my idea" for the simple reason that no one knows anything about the world other than what he perceives or what is placed before his understanding. Moreover, the "world" surely continues to exist even if I no longer exist. Nevertheless, no one knows a more real world than the one of which he and everyone else has a perception. Perceptions are the basis of knowledge. In addition to perceptions we are able to formulate abstract conceptions. These abstract conceptions, for example the ideas of "tree" and "house," have a very practical function because, as Schopenhauer says, "by means of them the original material of knowledge is more easily handled, surveyed, and arranged." These abstract conceptions are therefore not simply flights of fancy. Indeed, says Schopenhauer, the value of abstract conceptions depends upon whether they rely upon or are "abstracted" from original perceptions, that is, from actual experience, for "conceptions and abstractions which do not ultimately refer to perceptions are like paths in the woods that end without leading out of it." To say, therefore, that "the world is my idea" does not suggest that my idea of the world is an abstract conception unless this conception is, as it is for Schopenhauer, firmly based upon perceptions. Hence the world is my idea because it is an objective or empirical presentation to me as an understanding subject.

The World as Will

Nowhere is it more important to clarify Schopenhauer's language than in his use of the term *will*. Ordinarily, we use the word *will* to signify a conscious and deliberate choice to behave in a certain way. We consider the will an agent of our intellect, that is, an attribute or faculty possessed by a rational person. The will, we think, is guided by reason. There can be no question that the will is influenced by reason. But this account does not prepare us for Schopenhauer's use of the term *will,* a use so novel and significant as to constitute the central theme or essence of his systematic philosophy.

Schopenhauer's concept of the will represents his major disagreement with or alteration of Kant's theory of the thing-in-itself. Kant had said that we can never know things as they are in themselves. We are always on the outside of things and can never penetrate their inner nature. But Schopenhauer thought he had found a "single narrow door to the truth." There is, he said, a major exception to the notion that we are forever on the outside of things. That exception is our experience or knowledge "which each of us has of his own *willing.*" Our bodily action is normally thought to be the product of willing, but for Schopenhauer willing and action are not two different things but rather one and the same thing. "The action of the body," he says, "is nothing but the act of the will objectified... it is only in reflection that to will and to act are different." What we know of ourselves within our consciousness is that "we are not merely a *knowing subject,* but, in another aspect, we ourselves also belong to the inner nature that is to be known." He concludes that "we ourselves are the thing in itself." And the thing in itself is *will,* or as Schopenhauer says, "the act of will is... the closest and most distinct *manifestation* of the thing in itself." This, then, is that single narrow door to the truth, namely, the discovery that the will is the essence of each person. While we are forever on the outside of everything else, the discovery that we ourselves belong to the inner nature that can be known leads Schopenhauer to conclude that this "way from within [ourselves] stands open for us to that inner nature belonging to things in themselves," so that "in this sense I teach that the inner nature of everything is *will....*" Since "everything" is what constitutes the world, it follows in Schopenhauer's thought that we must view the world as will.

For Schopenhauer, the will does not belong solely to rational persons. The will is to be found in everything that is, in animals and even in inanimate things. There is, in fact, only one will, and each thing is a specific manifestation of that will. Schopenhauer attributes the working of will to all of reality, saying that "The will is the agent in all the inner and unconscious bodily functions, the organism being itself nothing but the will. In all natural forces the active impulse is identical with will. In all instances where we find any spontaneous movements or any primal forces, we must regard the innermost essence as will. The will reveals itself as completely in a single oak tree as in a million." There is, then, in the whole of nature a pervasive force, energy, or what Schopenhauer calls "a blind incessant impulse." Moreover, he speaks of will as "endless striving," and this impulse, working "without knowledge" through all nature, is finally "the will to live."

THE GROUND OF PESSIMISM

Here we come upon the reason for Schopenhauer's pessimism. His concept of the will portrays the whole system of nature as moving in response to the driving force in all things. All things are like puppets "set in motion by internal clockwork." The lowliest being, for example the amoeba, or the highest, that is, a human being, is driven by the same force, the will. The blind will which produces human behavior "is the same which makes the plants grow." Every individual bears the stamp of a "forced condition." The assumption that human beings are superior to animals because animals are controlled only by instincts whereas men are rational beings is rejected by Schopenhauer. The intellect, he says, is itself fashioned by the universal will so that the human intellect is on the same level as the instincts of animals. Moreover, intellect and will in human beings are not to be thought of as two separate faculties. Instead the intellect is for Schopenhauer an attribute of the will; it is secondary or, in a philosophical sense, accidental. Intellectual effort can be sustained only for short periods of time, declines in strength and requires rest, and is, finally, a function of the body. By contrast, the will continues without interruption to sustain and support life. During dreamless sleep the intellect does not function, whereas all the organic functions of the body continue. These organic functions are manifestations of the will. While other thinkers spoke of the freedom of the will, Schopenhauer says "I prove its omnipotence."

The omnipotence of the will in all of nature has pessimistic implications for human beings because, as Schopenhauer says, "men are only apparently drawn from in front; really, they are pushed from behind; it is not life that tempts them on, but necessity that drives them forward." The primal drive in all of nature is to produce life. The will to live has no other purpose than to continue the cycle of life. Schopenhauer portrays the realm of nature as a fierce struggle where the will to live inevitably produces constant conflict and destruction. This will to live for one element of nature requires the destruction of other elements or parties. No purpose or aim is violated during this conflict; the underlying drive of the will leaves no alternative outcome. Schopenhauer tells of a report of a place in Java where, for as far as the eye can see, the land is covered with skeletons, which gives the impression of a battlefield. These are skeletons of large turtles, five feet long, three feet wide, and three feet high. They come out of the sea to lay their eggs and are then attacked by wild dogs, who lay them on their backs, strip off their armor, and eat them alive. Now, says Schopenhauer, "all this misery repeats itself thousands and thousands of times, year out, year in. For this, those turtles were born...it is thus that the will to live objectifies itself."

If we move from the animal world to the human race, Schopenhauer admits that the matter becomes more complicated, "but the fundamental character remains unaltered." Individual human beings do not have any value for nature because "it is not the individual but only the species that nature cares for." Human life turns out to be by no means a gift for enjoyment "but as a task, a drudgery to be performed." Millions of people are united into nations striving for the common good, but thousands fall as a sacrifice for it. "Now senseless delusions, now intriguing politics, incite them to wars with each other....In peace industry and trade are active, inventions work miracles, seas are navigated, delicacies are collected from all ends of the world." But, asks Schopenhauer, what is the aim of all this striving? His answer is "To sustain ephemeral and tormented individuals through a short span of time."

Life, says Schopenhauer, is a bad bargain. The disproportion between human trouble, on the one hand, and reward on the other means that life involves the exertion of all our strength "for something that is of no value." There is nothing to look forward to except "the satisfaction of hunger and the sexual instinct, or in any case a little momentary comfort...." His conclusion is that "life is a business, the proceeds of which are very far from covering the cost of it." There can be no true happiness because happiness is simply a temporary cessation of human pain; pain is caused by desire, and expression of need or want, most of which can never be fulfilled. Finally, human life "is a striving without aim or end." And, "the life of every individual...is really always a tragedy, but gone through in detail, it has the character of a comedy."

IS THERE ANY ESCAPE FROM THE "WILL"?

How is it possible for a person to escape from the overpowering force of the "will" which pervades everything in nature? Schopenhauer suggests at least two avenues of escape, namely, through ethics and aesthetics, that is, through asceticism, the denial of other passions and desire, on the one hand, and through aesthetic contemplation of artistic beauty on the other. There is, of course, the question of whether the power of the universal will is so strong that any escape from it can only be temporary.

What complicates a person's life and causes pain is the continuous will to live, which expresses itself in the form of endless desires. Desire produces aggressiveness, striving, destruction, and self-centeredness. If, then, there could be some way to reduce the intensity of human desire, a person could achieve at least periodic moments of happiness. To be sure, Schopenhauer always reminds us that "man is at bottom a dreadful wild animal...in no way inferior to the tiger or hyena." Still, a person is able from time to time to rise to a level of thought and consciousness which is above the realm of things. Problems arise when a person desires things and persons, for these objects of desire stimulate the inner will to live at the level of both hunger and procreation. But when these biological functions are satisfied, there still remains the aim of physical survival against violence and conquest. Beyond even this level a person can, says Schopenhauer, understand the difference between the specific individual objects of his desire and certain general or universal objects. A person is capable, that is, of knowing not only the individuals John and Mary but also universal humanity. This should enable a person to move from an intense desire for a person to a sense of sympathy for all mankind. To this extent desire can give way to an ethics of a more disinterested love. At this point, a person recognizes that we all share the same nature, and this awareness can produce an ethics of gentleness. Or, as Schopenhauer says, "My true inner being exists in every living creature as immediately as in my own consciousness. It is this confession that breaks forth as pity, on which every unselfish virtue rests, and whose practical expression is every good deed. It is this conviction to which every appeal to gentleness, love and mercy is directed; for these remind us of the respect in which we are all the same being."

In a similar way, aesthetic enjoyment can shift a person's attention away from those objects which stimulate the aggressive will to live and focus attention instead upon objects of contemplation that are unrelated to passion and desire. When one contemplates a work of art, he becomes a pure knowing, as opposed to a willing, subject. What is observed in art, whether in painting or even music, is the general or universal element. We see in a painting of a person not some specific person but a representation of some aspect of humanity which we all share. Here Schopenhauer expresses views very similar to Plato's concept of Ideas and shows the strong influence of the philosophy of India. Here, too, Schopenhauer's ethics and aesthetics have a similar function, for they both attempt to raise our consciousness above earthly passion-filled striving to a level beyond the activity of the will where the supreme act is restful contemplation.

In spite of these attempts through ethics and aesthetics to escape from the restricting and directing power of the universal will, Schopenhauer simply does not succeed in discovering a truly free individual will in human beings. For his last word on the subject of human behavior is that "our individual actions are...in no way free...so that every individual...can absolutely never do anything other than precisely what he does at that particular moment."

18

Comte:
The Rise
of Positivism
in France

A lthough Auguste Comte is called the founder of *positive philosophy,* he did not discover this mode of thought, for as John Stuart Mill has said, positivism was "the general property of the age." Comte had begun his serious thinking in an age and at a place that were characterized by intellectual confusion and social instability. It was the France of the early nineteenth century to which Comte brought his perceptive and independent mind. Born at Montpellier in 1798, he was educated at the École Polytechnique, for some years was secretary to the noted socialist Saint-Simon, and in his early twenties published a series of books of which his *Système de politique positive* (1824) is the best known and which, as it turned out, was an early sketch of his major work *Cours de philosophie positive,* which was written in several volumes over the period from 1830 to 1842. His deep romantic involvement with Clotilde de Vaux, which lasted two years, 1844–1846, and ended with her tragic death, led Comte to declare the all-important role the element of affection must play in life. This emphasis upon love, which became central in his new "Religion of Humanity," was to contrast sharply with the strictness of his views concerning the scientific understanding of human society. He admitted that there was this contrast between his earlier and later ideas, claiming that he was an Aristotle in the early period of his career and a St. Paul in the later.

Even though Comte's major philosophical contribution centered around his conception of the positive sciences and the positivistic theory of knowledge, it was also his concern to show that his new philosophy could provide the basis of true religion. But although his positive philosophy did attract devoted adherents, many of them, notably John Stuart Mill, regretted Comte's attempt to found a secularized version of the Roman Catholic Church from which all supernatural elements had been removed and of which he made himself the High Priest, all of which led Mill to say that "an irresistible air of ridicule" surrounds Comte's religion and while "others may laugh...we could far rather weep at this melancholy decadence of a great intellect." Comte blamed the severe specialization of university scholars for their refusal to provide him a post for teaching the history of the sciences. Living off voluntary contributions from the friends of positivism, he continued to work in Paris in a little house only a short distance from the place at the Sorbonne where there now stands a statue of him, and from this meager setting emerged Comte's other major books, his second *Le système de politique positive* (1851–1854), *Catéchisme positiviste* (1852), and the *Synthèse subjective* (1856). Before he could complete his projected series on ethics, the system of positive industrial organization, and other philosophical works, his career ended in 1857, when he died at the age of fifty-nine.

Comte's chief objective was the total reorganization of society. But he was convinced that this practical objective required first of all the reconstruction or at least reformation of the intellectual orientation of his era. As he saw the situation, the Scientific Revolution, which had been unfolding since the discoveries of Galileo and Newton, had not been sufficiently assimilated in other fields, particularly in social, political, moral, and religious thought. The achievements of science in France had been outstanding, including the work of Ampère and Fresnel in physics, Chevreul and Dumas in chemistry, Magendie in physiology, and Lamarck, Saint-Hilaire, and Cuvier in biology and zoology. What commanded so much respect for their work was that their discoveries could be employed in solving problems of everyday life, leading to new methods in medicine and surgery, and making possible new industrial techniques and transportation. Gaining a sense of authority from its spectacular accomplishments, science challenged other ways of thinking, which could not in their field match these successes. Inevitably, questions that had been raised earlier about the relation between science and religion, about the freedom of the will, about the value of metaphysics, and about the possibility of discovering objective moral standards now took on a greater degree of intensity and urgency.

This was an age, too, when the state of philosophy in France was being influenced by internal political events and external systems of thought. The French Revolution had been, for Saint-Simon as well as for Comte, a dramatic

Auguste Comte *(The Bettmann Archive)*

example of anarchy. There developed, accordingly, some antirevolutionary philosophies, especially in the writings of de Maistre and de Bonald. Some saw in
the Revolution a contest of power whose effect was to destroy the legitimate
power and authority both of the government and of the church, an effect that
could only result in the further destruction of the institutions of the family and
of private property. The cross-fire of thought that followed this event consisted
of theories of society where some argued that society rests upon the consent of
the governed as expressed in a social contract as against those who held the
notion that society is a reality that lies beyond or above particular individuals.
Added to these internal differences in thought was the gradual importation of
philosophies from other lands, which dealt not only with social philosophy
but treated the problems of the theory of knowledge and metaphysics in

such a way as to engender not a clear new trend in philosophy but rather an atmosphere of vigorous debate. The French were now reading such varied authors as Kant, Hegel, Fichte, Schelling, Strauss, Feuerbach, and Goethe. Advocates of materialism, idealism, and new metaphysical systems entered the lists, and grandiose doctrines of Humanity, Absolute, and Progress were put forth. Karl Marx was also among the social thinkers of the day.

To overcome the anarchy that political revolution brings to pass, and even more to overcome the anarchy of philosophic thought that makes political anarchy inevitable, Auguste Comte set out to reform both society and philosophy by developing a science of society, *sociology,* built upon a scientifically oriented philosophy, positive philosophy or *positivism.* He offered positivism, therefore, not simply as a way of thought, but as a major solution to the problems of society, for the issue was how to maintain social unity and order at a time when theological beliefs were no longer accepted as supports for political authority. When beliefs are no longer held in common and when anarchy of ideas threatens anarchy in society, the only solution, as Comte saw it, unless people accepted positivism, was a dictatorship of naked power. None of the usual arguments against dictatorship seemed satisfactory to Comte, for against those who would seek to reinstate the earlier balance of temporal and spiritual powers as they were before the Revolution, Comte answered that it is not possible to reverse the course of historical progress; and against those who advocated the methods of democracy, he argued that their concepts of *equality* and *rights of humanity* and especially *sovereignty of the people* were metaphysical abstractions and dogmas. Only the method of positivism, he declared, can guarantee social unity. His task of reorganizing society, therefore, required that he first of all bring about an intellectual reformation, which in turn led him to formulate his classic theory of positivism.

POSITIVISM DEFINED

Positivism is best defined as a general attitude of mind, a spirit of inquiry, an approach to the facts of human existence. Its central feature is first of all negative in that it rejects the assumption that nature has some ultimate purpose or end. Secondly, positivism gives up any attempt to discover either the "essence" or the internal or secret causes of things. On the positive side, its spirit is expressed in the attempt to study facts by observing the constant relations between things and by formulating the laws of science simply as the laws of constant relations among various phenomena. In this spirit, Newton described the phenomena of physics without going beyond useful limits in asking questions about the essential nature of things; before him Galileo had made great strides in understanding the movements and relations of stars without inquiring into their physical constitution; Fourier had discovered mathematical laws of the diffusion of heat without any theoretical assumption concerning the essential nature of heat; and the biologist Cuvier had worked out some laws concerning the structure of living things without any hypothesis about the nature of life. A corollary of this spirit of research and inquiry was the assumption that knowledge derived from science can be used in the material and social life. This was positivism's great appeal, for it promised an effective means for dealing not only with physical reality—as, for example, the disorders of the body, which concerned medicine—but with the disorders of the body politic, which must become the concern of the scientist of society, the sociologist.

The initial rigor of positivism is suggested by Comte's clear statement that "any proposition which does not admit of being ultimately reduced to a simple enunciation of fact, special or general, can have no real or intelligible sense." Counting himself a positivist and using much of Comte's own language, John Stuart Mill described the general outlook of positivism in these terms: "We have no knowledge of anything but Phenomena, and our knowledge of phenomena is relative, not absolute. We know not the essence, nor the real mode of production, of any fact, but only its relations to other facts in the way of succession or of similitude. These relations are constant; that is, always the same in the same circumstances. The constant resemblances which link phenomena together, and the constant sequences which unite them as antecedent and consequent, are termed their laws. The laws of phenomena are all we know respecting them. Their essential nature, and their ultimate causes, either efficient or final, are unknown and inscrutable to us." This was the intellectual mood and spirit that Comte and his followers brought to the study of society and religion, saying that in the end every subject must utilize the same approach to truth for only in that way could unity be achieved in thought as well as social life. To be sure, this method had its own assumptions, the foremost of them being that there is an order in the nature of things whose laws we can discover. Comte also assumed that we can overcome the pitfalls of subjectivity by "transforming the human brain into a perfect mirror of the external order." His optimism for achieving his objectives came from his interpretation of the history of ideas and from his study of the development of the various sciences, which he believed clearly pointed to the inevitability and the validity of positivism.

THE LAW OF THE THREE STAGES

The history of ideas, said Comte, indicates that there has been a clear movement of thought through three stages, each stage representing a different way of discovering truth. These stages are the *theological,* in which phenomena are explained as being caused by divine powers, the *metaphysical,* in which anthropocentric concepts of divinity are replaced by impersonal and abstract forces, and the *positivistic,* or scientific, in which only the constant relations between phenomena are considered and all attempts to explain things by references to beings beyond our experience are given up. He called this evolution from one stage to another the *law of the three stages,* because he thought he could find this threefold development at work not only in thought in general but in each particular science. Moreover, this law could be said to be at work in the political order, too, for since the structure of a society reflects the philosophical orientation of an epoch, any major change in philosophic thought will bring about a change in the political order. For example, the theological explanation of the physical world either in Greek mythology or in orthodox Christianity with frequent instances of the intervention of the gods or of God had its counterpart in political theory in the doctrines of the divine right of kings or the "two kingdoms." But this theological approach is superseded by metaphysics, which speaks of a *necessary being* or *ground of being* as the explanation for the existence of finite beings such as people and things. This concept of necessary being, says Comte, is abstract and impersonal, and although it goes beyond the idea of some capricious being acting upon the physical world, it does not overcome the uselessness of dogmatism. Its counterpart in political thought is the attempt to formulate abstract principles such as the *rights of humanity* or the *sovereignty of the people.* Comte's harsh judgment was that slavery and the military state go along with the theological stage and that the assumptions of liberal democracy, which he rejected as dogmas, are an outgrowth of the metaphysical stage. Such palpable dogmas as the *equality of all humanity,* thought Comte, must now give way to the clear scientific fact that people are unequal and have different capacities and must, therefore, have different functions in society. To deal effectively with such questions of political order required a carefully worked out science of society, which Comte did not find already available and which he, therefore, set out to create, calling it *sociology.*

Comte's creation of sociology illustrates his account of the development of knowledge, for in his theory the movement of thought is from decreasing generality to increasing complexity and from the abstract to the concrete. He makes much of the fact that of the five major sciences, mathematics came first; then, in order, came astronomy, physics, chemistry, and biology. In this sequence he saw the movement from generality and simplicity to complexity and concreteness, for mathematics deals with quantities of a general kind; to quantity, astronomy adds the elements of mass and force and some principles of attraction; physics differentiates between types of forces when it deals with gravity, light, and heat; chemistry makes quantitative and qualitative analyses of materials; and biology adds the structure of organic and animal life to the material order. A sixth science, sociology, deals with the relations of human beings to each other in society, and as such it is the necessary outcome of the previous stage of science. Dramatically, Comte indicates that mathematics and astronomy came early in the ancient world, whereas physics as a true science had to wait for Sir Isaac Newton in the seventeenth century, that chemistry begins with Lavoisier, biology with Bichat, and that it is now his own task to usher in the science of sociology. For him sociology is the queen of the sciences, the summit of knowledge, for it makes use of all previous information and coordinates it all for the sake of a peaceful and orderly society.

COMTE'S SOCIOLOGY AND "RELIGION OF HUMANITY"

Unlike revolutionary thinkers who called for a radical reconstruction of society, or idealists who fancied utopian communities, Comte moved along lines that he thought were clearly visible to the scientific mind and that referred to the actual conditions of history. Two things in particular dominate his sociological theory, namely, what he calls the *static* and the *dynamic* components of social existence. The static component consists of certain stable elements of society, such as the family, private property, language, and religion. Since these are virtually permanent, he does not advocate any revolutionary change in them. At the same time, he does recognize a dynamic component, which he understands as the force of progress. His theory of "the law of the three stages" contains the technical elaboration of this dynamic force. Progress has to do, therefore, not with any basic alteration of the social elements but simply with a continual refinement of our understanding of how we should utilize these stable structures in an optimum way. Just as the stars and constellations do not change as we move from the theological to the metaphysical and finally to the scientific way of accounting for their behavior, neither should the structures of society change as far as their basic elements are concerned. The family, for example, must remain, and indeed Comte sees in this institution the fundamental building blocks of society. But what the dynamic influence of positivism would bring to the family for example, would be the conferring upon women of a new and spiritually defensible status. Similarly, property should be utilized in such a way as to call forth the highest instincts of altruism instead of greed and envy. Religion is the key to the whole system, but instead of the worship of a supernatural being, religion should consist of the cult of *humanity*. Positivism also calls for a political organization that utilizes both temporal and spiritual powers in such a way that these two do not compete but, rather, harmoniously complement each other.

Comte frequently refers to the Middle Ages as a time when the relation between the static and dynamic components of society were most adequately attuned to each other. Indeed, he uses the medieval community as his model for the new society. He would, of course, reject the theological aspects of this period, but what struck him about it was the intimate relation between religion and society, between a body of thought and the organization of the structures of society in medieval Europe. The family, property, and government, all of these elements had a justification in and derived their motivations from a set of beliefs held in common. The key to the reorganization of nineteenth-century society is therefore not to destroy old structures and create new ones but rather to bring the permanent elements of society up to date and to overcome the contemporary anarchy by reestablishing the contact between religion and the institutions of society. Only by reorganizing the dynamic forces at work, the fact of intellectual and technological progress, could this contact between religion and society be reestablished. Much of the anarchy of this period, both intellectual and political, stemmed, as Comte saw it, from the breakdown of

theological authority brought on by the rise of science. To reestablish this earlier grip of theology upon contemporary minds was, he said, impossible. Moreover, the legacy of the Enlightenment, which was the exaltation of each person's own ideas and opinions, could not lead to any unity. Only a new religion,
based upon ideas and realities that would be so clearly obvious to everyone as
to achieve universal agreement, could create the unity between all the people
and between their thinking and their ways of living. The Middle Ages had the
correct approach to social organization, but, says Comte, they had the wrong
intellectual orientation. On the other hand, contemporary Europe seemed to
him to have the right philosophy in scientific positivism but not an adequate
organization. Although science had seriously shaken the hold of theology, it
had not yet completely eliminated it. The ensuing debates over the relation between science and religion also raised the specific question of the comparative
roles of intellect and feeling, the mind and the heart. Comte's enormous task,
therefore, was to reconceive the whole nature of religion in terms of science,
bind the new religion to the structures of society, and unify the powers of reason and affection in each individual's life and thereby infuse humanity's every
act with a sense of purpose or direction. Proceeding with this task, Comte said
that "Love, then, is our principle; Order our basis; and Progress our end."

What his new society would be like is indicated first of all by what he did
not want it to be. Although the theological stage had now been passed, new
dogmas created by metaphysics still lingered, and these would have to be rejected. To achieve the new society every old fiction would have to be given
up, whether it be the theistic God or the metaphysical dogma of equality or
popular sovereignty. Since the function of the mind now would be to *mirror*
the truly real state of things, the contents of the new religion must be drawn
from such an objectively real source, and this, says Comte, is *humanity* itself.
It is, after all, from humanity that we all draw our material, intellectual, spiritual, and moral resources. But although he did not want to retain past dogmas,
he nevertheless built his new *religion of humanity* as though it were a secularized version of Catholicism. Instead of God, Comte substituted humanity, which
he called *Grand-Être,* the Supreme Being; he became his own High Priest, in-
stituted a calendar of saints, mostly renowned scientists, and created a catechism, at the end of which Comte says, "Humanity definitely occupies the place
of God," adding that "she does not forget the services which the idea of God
provisionally rendered"; the sacraments become "social" and include *Presentation* (Baptism); *Initiation* at age fourteen; *Admission,* when at age twenty-
one a person is authorized to serve humanity; *Destination* or choice of career
at twenty-eight; *Marriage* for men at twenty-eight and for women at twenty-
one; and *Retirement* at age sixty-three.

Although there is no doubt that Comte had, from the beginning of his systematic thought, considered the goal of his positive science the creation, as he
says, of a "sound philosophy, capable of supplying the foundation of true religion," there is equally no doubt that his later writings were influenced by his
emotional crisis following his intense love affair with Clotilde de Vaux, his "in-

comparable angel." Having in his earlier career emphasized the role of the intellect, he now argued for the supremacy of the affections, claiming that "greater distinctness...is given to the truth that the affective element predominates in our nature." For this reason he now states that "where the moral excellence of true Religion is illustrated, feeling takes the first place. The disastrous revolt of Reason against Feeling will never be terminated till the new Western priesthood can fully satisfy the claims of the modern intellect. But this being done, moral requirements at once reassume the place that belongs to them; since in the construction of a really complete synthesis, Love is naturally the one universal principle." In light of this supremacy of feeling, it becomes the function of positive philosophy to fashion "a system which regulates the whole course of our private and public existence, by bringing Feeling, Reason and Activity into permanent harmony." As love is the supreme moral principle, all thought or acts of the intellect must become subordinate to it, thereby making scientists philosophers, and philosophers priests, wherein all of life becomes "a continuous and intense act of worship," and "live for others" becomes the truly human moral standard. The scientists will organize and rule society and the philosopher-priests will exercise their influence over society by the organization of public worship and by controlling education. In this way, Comte tried to achieve a modern version of the medieval separation between the spiritual and temporal powers. In this way, too, morals would be independent of politics and would, instead, be a constructive influence upon the political and economic order.

The civil order will also reflect the forces of dynamic progress, particularly as this process indicates the movement from a *military* to an *industrial* basis. Comte considered that the military phase of history had much to do with developing the industrial power and organization of the modern state by forcing people to bring together otherwise isolated material resources and human labor for the sake of survival. But now the habits of industry and discipline must be used for the sake of peace and internal order and civilization.

The central aim of all human effort, said Comte, must be the amelioration of the order of nature. Science helps us to understand nature so that we can alter it. Humanity, the new God, is worshiped not in the former posture of solemn inactivity, for in *positive religion,* "the object of worship is a Being [Humanity] whose nature is relative, modifiable and perfectible." Through such worship is *progress* achieved, for progress is "the development of Order under the influence of Love." Putting so much emphasis upon human effort was Comte's way of replacing the theological doctrine of *providence,* for he says that "we must look to our own unremitting activity for the only providence by which the rigour of our destiny can be alleviated."

Translating this concept of providence into more specific detail, Comte said that human providence has four main divisions: Women are the *moral providence,* the priesthood the *intellectual providence,* the patriciate or capitalists the *material providence,* and the proletariat the *general providence.* "The people," said Comte, "represent the activity of the Supreme Being, as women represent its sympathy, and philosophers its intellect." Of the capitalists, Comte said that they are "the nutritive reservoirs, the social efficiency of which mainly depends on their being concentrated in few hands," adding that only the influence of moral persuasion can regulate "their foolish and immoral pride." Inevitably, Comte's society would require that each person fulfill a special function by staying in the place most suited to his or her powers. Above all, there must be the supremacy of the intellectual elite, since the technical problems of administering a complex society can be understood only by specialists. For this reason, Comte thought it was just as senseless to permit free inquiry or discussion about matters of social and political administration by the masses as to allow them to voice their opinions about some technical matter in chemistry, a field in which they lack proper information, and, therefore, he called for the abolition of the "vagabond liberty of individual minds."

Again, the success of the *religion of humanity* would require the stability of the family and the inculcation by the family of the spirit of altruism and love. Comte would not accept the earlier theological appraisal of the depravity of humanity or the notion that altruism is uncongenial to human nature. To Comte, the altruistic instincts were a matter of scientific fact, citing the founder of phrenology Gall, who claimed to show that there is an "organ" of benevolence in the brain. In addition, just as the women preserved the claims of morality after the synthesis of the medieval period came apart and when men became preoccupied with practical and material ends, so now women would continue to exert their creative function in the family and would spontaneously consecrate their "rational and imaginative faculties to the service of feeling." For Comte, the very symbol of humanity on the *flag of positivism* was to be a young mother with her infant son, a final analogy between Christianity and the Religion of Humanity.

The more Comte concerned himself with the creation of a new religion, the further he seemed to depart from the very principles of the positivism he was so concerned to delineate and advocate. In the end, Comte seemed to be indicating the goal toward which society *ought* to be moving instead of describing the course which history *is* in fact taking. To be sure, Comte tried to derive his objectives from his scientific studies, from the "law of the three stages" and his hierarchical classification of the sciences. Although Comte's influence was soon to be eclipsed by the politically more captivating theories of Karl Marx, he is still to be considered a leading figure in that impressive line of thinkers that began with Bacon and Hobbes and the empiricists Locke, Berkeley, and Hume, who came before him, and included the students of scientific method such as Mach and Poincaré, as well as Russell and the other logical positivists of the present.

19

Utilitarianism of Bentham and Mill

For more than a hundred years, the moral and political philosophy of Jeremy Bentham and John Stuart Mill influenced the thinking and political action of the English. Rarely has a way of thinking captured the imagination of generations of men so completely as did this philosophy called *utilitarianism*. What attracted people to it was its simplicity and its way of confirming what most of them already believed, for it set forth the general thesis that pleasure and happiness are what everyone desires. From this simple fact that everyone desires pleasure and happiness, the utilitarians inferred that the whole moral idea of what is "good" can be best understood in terms of the principle of happiness, which they spoke of as "the greatest good of the greatest number," and by which they meant that "good" is achieved when the aggregate of pleasure is greater than the aggregate of pain. An act is good, therefore, if it is useful in achieving pleasure and diminishing pain.

Such a swift account of what is good had not only the merit of simplicity but had, according to Bentham and Mill, the additional virtue of scientific accuracy. Whereas earlier theories of ethics, which defined the good as the commands of God, or the dictates of reason, or the fulfillment of the purposes of human nature, or the duty to obey the categorical imperative, all raised vexing questions as to just what these commands, dictates, purposes, and imperatives consist of, the principle of utility seemed to measure every act by a standard everyone knows, namely, pleasure. To bypass the moral teachings of theology and the classical theories of Plato and Aristotle as well as the recently formulated ethics of Kant, the utilitarians followed in the philosophical footsteps of their own countrymen, the British empiricists.

Hobbes had already tried to construct a science of human nature and had turned his back upon traditional moral thought, emphasizing instead people's selfish concern for their own pleasure. Hume also had rejected the intricacies of traditional philosophy and theology and had instead built his system of thought around the individual, denying that people can know universal moral laws any more than they can know universal laws of physics. For Hume, the whole enterprise of ethics had to do with our capacity for "sympathy," a capacity that all people share and by which we "touch a string to which all mankind have an accord...." Sympathy, said Hume, is the pleasure we feel when we consider the pleasures of others, and for this reason our moral sentiments direct us to judge acts as worthy of approval if they produce pleasure and minimize pain. In similar words John Locke also said that "what has an aptness to produce pleasure in us is what we call good, and what is apt to produce pain in us we call evil."

In moral philosophy, Bentham and Mill were, therefore, not innovators, for the principle of utilitarianism had already been stated in its general form by their predecessors. What makes Bentham and Mill stand out as the most famous of the utilitarians is that they, more than the others, had succeeded in connecting the principle of utility with the many problems of their age, thereby providing nineteenth-century England with a philosophical basis not only for moral thought but also for practical reform.

JEREMY BENTHAM

Born in Red Lion Street, Houndsditch, London, in 1748, Bentham showed early signs of his unusual intellectual capacities. While only four years old, he was already studying Latin grammar, and at eight he was sent off to Westminster School, where, he said later, the instruction "was wretched." He entered Queen's College in Oxford when he was twelve years old, and after three years, which were not particularly happy ones as he disapproved of the vice and laziness of his fellow students, he took his B.A. degree in 1763 and entered Lincoln's Inn, in accordance with his father's wish, to prepare for a career in the legal profession. That same year he returned to Oxford for one of the decisive experiences of his intellectual life, for he went to hear the lectures on law given by Sir William Blackstone. What made this such a significant event was that as he listened to these lectures with deep concentration, he says he "immediately detected Blackstone's fallacy respecting natural rights," and this experience crystallized his own theory of law,

Jeremy Bentham *(The Bettmann Archive)*

in which he rejected the theory of "natural rights" as "rhetorical nonsense—nonsense on stilts." He took his M.A. degree in 1766 and again returned to London, but he never developed any affection for the legal profession and decided against being a lawyer. Instead, he was drawn into a vigorous literary career in which he tried to bring order and moral defensibility into what he considered the deplorable state both of the law and the social realities that the law made possible.

Bentham was therefore chiefly a reformer. His philosophical orientation had been provided, for the most part, by the empiricists Locke, whose enlightened and free thought gave Bentham a powerful weapon against ideas based upon prejudice, and Hume, whose *Treatise on Human Nature* Bentham read with such profit that he said it was "as if scales fell" from his eyes regarding moral philosophy. His first book, *A Fragment on Government,* appeared in 1776 and was an attack upon Blackstone. This *Fragment* was also in sharp contrast to another document that appeared in that year, namely the Declaration of Independence, which Bentham thought was a confused and absurd jumble of words in which the authors had all along assumed the natural rights of humanity, which was what they wanted to demonstrate. Among his later writings were *A Defence of Usury* (1787), his famous *Introduction to the Principles of Morals and Legislation* (1789), *A Plea for the Constitution* (1803), and *Catechism of Parliamentary Reform* (1809). With these writings and his personal involvement in the social and political problems of his day, Bentham remained a powerful public figure for most of his long life, until his death in 1832 at the age of eighty-four.

The Principle of Utility Bentham begins his *Introduction to the Principles of Morals and Legislation* with the classic sentence: "Nature has placed mankind under the governance of two sovereign masters, *pain* and *pleasure.* It is for them alone to point out what we ought to do, as well as to determine what we shall do." To be subject to pleasure and pain is a fact we all recognize, and that we desire pleasure and want to avoid pain is also a fact. But in a few sentences, without indicating just how he does it, Bentham moves from the *fact* that we *do* desire pleasure to the *judgment* that we *ought* to pursue pleasure, or from a psychological fact to the moral principle of utility. By the *principle of utility* he means "that principle which approves or disapproves of every action whatsoever, according to the tendency which it appears to have to augment or diminish ...happiness." In Bentham's language to *approve* or *disapprove* is the same as saying about an act that it is *good* or *bad,* or *right* or *wrong.* Between saying that people desire pleasure and saying that they *ought* to or that it is *right* that they should, there is a gap that Bentham does not fill with any careful argument. Still, he says that only about an action "that is conformable to the principle of utility [can] one always say either that it is one that ought to be done" or "that it is a right action." Tying *ought* to *pleasure,* says Bentham, is the only way "the words *ought,* and *right* and *wrong,* and others of that stamp have a meaning: when, otherwise, they have none." Bentham was aware that he had not proved that happiness is the basis of "good" and "right," but this was not an oversight. It is rather the very nature of the principle of utility, he says, that one cannot demonstrate its validity: "Is it susceptible to any proof? It should seem not, for that which is used to prove everything else cannot itself be proved; a chain of proofs must have their commencement somewhere. To give such proof is as impossible as it is needless."

But if Bentham could not *prove* the validity of the principle of utility, he felt that he could at least demonstrate that so-called "higher" theories of morality were either reducible to the principle of utility or else were inferior to this principle because they had no clear meaning or could not be consistently followed. As an example, Bentham takes the social-contract theory as an explanation for our obligation to obey the law. Apart from the difficulty of determining whether there ever was such a contract or agreement, Bentham argues that the obligation to obey, even in the contract theory itself, rests upon the principle of utility, for it really says that the greatest happiness of the greatest number can be achieved only if we obey the law. This being the case, why develop an involved and scientifically dubious theory when the whole problem can be swiftly solved by saying simply that obedience is better because disobedience does more harm than good? The case is the same when others say that goodness and right in an act are determined by our *moral sense* or *understanding* or *right reason* or the *theological* principle of the will of God. All of these, says Bentham, are similar to each other and are reducible to the principle of utility. For example, "The principle of theology refers every thing to God's pleasure. But what is God's pleasure? God does not, he confessedly does not now, either speak or write to us. How then are we to know what is his pleasure? By observing what is our own pleasure, and pronouncing it to be his." Only pains and pleasures, therefore, give us the real value of actions, and in private and public life we are in the last analysis all concerned with maximizing happiness.

The Sanctions   Just as pleasure and pain give the real values to acts, so do they also constitute the efficient causes of our behavior. Bentham distinguishes four sources from which pleasures and pains can come and identifies these as causes of our behavior, calling them *sanctions*. A sanction is what gives binding force to a rule of conduct or to a law, and these four sanctions are termed the *physical,* the *political,* the *moral,* and the *religious* sanctions. Bentham indicates the special character of each sanction by an example where "A man's goods, or his person, are consumed by fire. If this happened to him by what is called an accident, it was a calamity; if by reason of his own imprudence (for instance, from his neglecting to put his candle out), it may be styled a punishment of the *physical* sanction; if it happened to him by the sentence of the political magistrate, a punishment belonging to the *political* sanction; that is, what is commonly called a punishment, if for want of any assistance which his *neighbor* withheld from him out of some dislike to his *moral* character, a punishment of the *moral* sanction; if by an immediate act of *God's* displeasure, manifested on account of some *sin* committed by him...a punishment of the *religious* sanction."

In all these areas, then, the sanction, or the efficient cause of behavior, is the threat of pain. In public life, the legislator understands that people feel bound to do certain acts only when such acts have some clear sanction connected with them, and this sanction consists of some form of pain if the mode of conduct prescribed by the legislator is violated by the citizen. The legislator's chief concern is, therefore, to decide what forms of behavior will tend to increase the happiness of society and what sanctions will be most likely to bring about such increased happiness. The word *obligation* was given concrete meaning by Bentham's concept of *sanction,* for obligation now meant not some undefined duty but the prospect of pain if one did not obey the moral or legal rule. Unlike Kant, who argued that the morality of an act depends upon having the right motive and not upon the consequences of the act, the utilitarians took the opposite position, saying that morality depends directly upon the consequences.

Bentham admits that some motives are more likely than others to lead to more useful conduct, that is, conduct which increases happiness, but it is still pleasure and not the motive that confers the quality of morality upon the act. Moreover, Bentham took the position that, especially in the social arena where the law is at work, the law can punish only those who have actually inflicted pain, whatever their motive may be, though some exceptions were admitted. While it may be true that the legislator cannot always take account of motives, this whole question of motives does loom large in morality. Bentham, however, seemed to regard both the moral and legal obligations as being similar in that in both cases the external consequences of the action were considered more important than the motives behind them.

The Pleasure-Pain Calculus   Each individual and each legislator is concerned with avoiding pain and achieving pleasure. But pleasures and pains differ from each other and therefore have different values. With an attempt at mathematical precision, Bentham speaks of units, or what he called *lots,* of pleasure or pain, suggesting that before we act, we should, and really do, calculate the values of these lots. Their value, taken by themselves, will be greater or less depending, says Bentham, upon a pleasure's *intensity, duration, certainty,* and *propinquity* or nearness. When we consider not only the pleasure by itself but what consequences it can lead to, other circumstances must be calculated, such as a pleasure's *fecundity,* or its chances of being followed by more of the same sensations, that is, by more pleasure, and its *purity,* or the chances that pleasure will not be followed by pleasure but by pain. The *seventh* circumstance is a pleasure's *extent,* that is, the number of persons to whom it *extends* or who are affected by it.

As this calculus indicates, Bentham was interested chiefly in the quantitative aspects of pleasure, so that all actions are equally good if they produce the same amount of pleasure. Therefore, we "sum up all the values of all the *pleasures* on the one side, and those of all the pains on the other. The balance, if it be on the side of pleasure, will give the *good* tendency of the act...if on the side of pain, the *bad* tendency." Whether we actually do engage in this kind of calculation was a question Bentham anticipated, and he replies that "there are some, perhaps, who...may look upon the nicety employed in the adjustment of such rules as so much labor lost: for gross ignorance, they will say, never troubles itself about laws, and passion does not calculate. But the evil of ignorance admits of cure: and...when matters of such importance as pain and pleasure are at stake, and these in the highest degree...who is there that does not calculate? Men calculate, some with less exactness, indeed, and some with more: but all men calculate."

Law and Punishment   It was particularly in connection with law and punishment that Bentham made impressive use of the principle of utility. As it is the function of the legislator to discourage some acts and encourage others, how shall we classify those that should be discouraged as against those that should be encouraged?

The Object of Law   Bentham's method of legislation was first of all to measure the "mischief of an act," and this mischief consisted in the consequences, the pain or evil inflicted by the act, and acts that produce evil must be discouraged. There are, says Bentham, both primary and secondary evils that concern the legislator. Robbers inflict an evil upon their victims, who lose their money, and this is a case of primary evil. But robbery creates a secondary evil because successful robbery suggests that theft is easy. This suggestion is evil because it weakens respect for property, and property becomes insecure. From the point of view of the legislator, the secondary evils are frequently more important than the primary evils because, taking the example of robbery again, the actual loss to the victim may very well be considerably less than the loss in stability and security in the community as a whole.

The law is concerned with augmenting the total happiness of the community, and it must do this by discouraging those acts that would produce evil consequences. A criminal act or offense is by definition one that is clearly detrimental to the happiness of the community, and only an act that in some specific way does in fact inflict some sort of pain and thereby diminish the pleasure of some specific individual or group—only such an act ought to be the concern of the law. For the most part, the government accomplishes its business of promoting the happiness of society by punishing people who commit offenses that the principle of utility has clearly measured as evil. It was Bentham's confirmed belief that if the legislator used only the principle of utility in deciding which acts should be considered "offenses," many acts that the laws of his day controlled would have to be considered a matter of private morals to be subject only to the sanction of opinion. Utilitarianism had the effect, then, of requiring a reclassification of behavior to determine what is and is not appropriate for the government to regulate. In addition, the principle of utility provided Bentham with a new and simple theory of punishment, a theory that he thought could not only be justified more readily than the older theories but could achieve the purposes of punishment far more effectively.

Punishment   "All punishment," said Bentham, "is in itself evil" because it inflicts suffering and pain. At the same time, the "object which all laws have in common, is to augment the total happiness of the community." If punishment is to be justified from a utilitarian point of view, it must be shown, said Bentham, that the pain inflicted by punishment must in some way prevent or exclude some greater pain. Punishment must therefore be "useful" in achieving a greater aggregate of pleasure and happiness and has no justification if its effect is simply to add still more units or *lots* of pain to the community. The principle of utility would clearly call for the elimination of pure "retribution," where someone is made to suffer only because an act caused a victim pain, for no useful purpose is served by adding still more pain to the sum total society suffers. This is not to say that utilitarianism rejects the category of punishment but only that the principle of utility, particularly in the hands of Bentham, called for a reopening of the question of why society should punish offenders and urged a reclassification of cases that are "meet" and "unmeet" for punishment. Punishment should not be inflicted (1) where it is *groundless,* where, for example, there is an offense that admits of compensation and where there is virtual certainty that compensation is forthcoming; (2) where it must be *inefficacious* in that it cannot prevent a mischievous act, as when a law made after the act is retroactive, or ex post facto, or where a law has already been made but not been announced. Punishment would be inefficacious also where an infant, an insane person, or a drunkard was involved, though Bentham admitted that neither infancy nor intoxication was sufficient grounds for "absolute impunity." Nor should punishment be inflicted (3) where it is *unprofitable* or too *expensive,* "where the mischief it would produce would be greater than what it prevented," or (4) where it is *needless,* "where the mischief may be prevented, or cease of itself, without it: that is at a cheaper rate," particularly in cases "which consist in the disseminating pernicious principles in matters of duty," since in these cases persuasion is more efficacious than force.

Whether a given kind of behavior should be left to *private ethics* instead of becoming the object of *legislation* was a question Bentham answered by simply applying the principle of utility. If to involve the whole legislative process and the apparatus of punishment does more harm than good, the matter should be left to private ethics. He was convinced that attempts to regulate sexual immorality would be particularly unprofitable, since this would require intricate supervision, as would "such offenses as ingratitude or rudeness, where the definition is so vague that the judge could not safely be entrusted with the power to punish." Duties that we owe to ourselves could hardly be the concern of law and punishment, nor must we be "coerced" to be "benevolent," though we can be liable on certain occasions for failing to help. But the main concern of law must be to encourage those acts that would lead to the greatest happiness of the community. There is, then, a justification for punishment, which is that through punishment the greatest good for the greatest number is most effectively secured.

Besides providing a rationale for punishment, the principle of utility also gives us some clue to what punishment should consist of. Bentham describes the desirable properties of each unit or *lot* of punishment by considering "the proportion between punishments and offenses," and he gives the following rules: The punishment must be great enough to outweigh the profit that the offender might get from the offense; the greater the offense, the greater the punishment: where two offenses come in competition, the punishment for the greater offense must be sufficient to induce a person to prefer the less; punishments should be variable and adaptable to fit the particular circumstances, although each offender should get the same punishment for the same offense; the amount of punishment should never be greater than the minimum required to make it effective; the more uncertain that an offender will be caught, the greater should be the punishment; and if an offense is habitual, the punishment must outweigh not only the profit of the immediate offense but of the undiscovered offenses. These rules led Bentham to conclude that punishment should be *variable* to fit the particular case, *equable* so as to inflict equal pain for similar offenses, *commensurable* in order that punishments for different classes of crimes be proportional, *characteristic* so as to impress the imagination of potential offenders, *frugal* so as not to be excessive, *reformatory* in order to correct faulty behavior, *disabling* in order to deter future offenders, *compensatory* to the sufferer, and, in order not to create new problems, punishment should have *popular* acceptance and be capable of *remittance* for sufficient cause.

Bentham's Radicalism   It was inevitable that Bentham would discover elements in the law and the general social structure of England that did not fit the requirements set by the principle of utility. Bentham wanted the legislative process to operate on the principle of utility with practically the same rigor with which the stars obey the principle of gravitation. To systematic thought he wanted to add systematic action, so that wherever he found a discrepancy between the actual legal and social order on the one hand and the principle of utility on the other, he wanted to press for reforms. He traced most of the evils of the legal system to the judges who, he charged, "made the common law. Do you know how they make it? Just as a man makes laws for his dog. When your dog does anything you want to break him of, you wait till he does it and then beat him...this is the way judges make laws for you and me." Having exposed one monstrous evil after another, Bentham was impelled by his zeal to reform these evils and to become an aggressive philosophical radical.

Bentham laid the cause for the breakdown of the principle of utility to the very structure of the aristocratic society of his day. Why should social evils and evils of the legal system persist even after he had demonstrated that certain new modes of behavior would produce the "greatest happiness of the greatest number"? The answer, he thought, was that those in power did not want the "greatest happiness of the greatest number." The rulers were more concerned with their own interests. Bentham was acutely aware that people seek their own happiness. The object of government, however, is to help achieve the greatest happiness of the greatest number. Whenever those in power represent only a class or a small group, their self-interest will be in conflict with the proper end of government. The way to overcome this conflict or contradiction is to identify the rulers and the ruled, or to put the government into the hands of the people. If there is an identity between the rulers and the ruled, their interests will be the same, and the greatest happiness of the greatest number will be assured. This identity of interest cannot, by definition, be achieved under a monarchy, for the monarch acts in his own interests or at best aims at the happiness of a special class grouped around him. It is in a democracy where the greatest happiness of the greatest number is most apt to be realized, for the rulers are the people, and representatives of the people are chosen precisely because they promise to serve the greatest good. The application of the principle of utility clearly required, as Bentham saw it, the rejection of monarchy with all its corollaries, and so he would do away with king, house of peers, and the established church and would prefer to construct a democratic order after the model of the United States. Since "all government is in itself one vast evil," its only justification is to apply evil in order to prevent or exclude some greater evil.

Bentham's radicalism consisted in the desire to press for major social reforms in order to put his philosophical principles into practice, and his reforms were required in order to construct the kind of society and legal process that could most likely contribute the greatest happiness to the greatest number.

JOHN STUART MILL

The principle of utilitarianism had one of its ablest advocates in John Stuart Mill. His father, James Mill, had been closely associated with Bentham and, more than anyone, had helped to give shape and form to Bentham's philosophical doctrine. Later, young Mill wrote in his *Autobiography* that "it was my father's opinions which gave the distinguishing character to the Benthamic or Utilitarian propagandism...," and his father's ideas flowed into the thought of early nineteenth-century England through various channels, of which, says Mill, "one was through me, the only mind directly formed by his instructions, and through whom considerable influence was exercised over various young men." John Stuart Mill had not only shared his father's ideas but through him was exposed to the views of some of the leading thinkers of the day. He had known and visited the political economist Ricardo, but "of Mr. Bentham I saw much more, owing to the close intimacy which existed between him and my father." Mill adds that "my father was the earliest Englishman of any great mark, who thoroughly understood, and in the main adopted, Bentham's general views of ethics, government and law." And when young Mill read Bentham's principal work on law and administration, *Introduction to the Principles of Morals and Legislation,* it was "one of the turning points in my mental history." What impressed him most was that Bentham's "greatest happiness principle" rendered attempts to deduce morality and legislation from phrases such as *law of nature, right reason,* the *moral sense,* or *natural rectitude* unnecessary, if not impossible. As he read Bentham, Mill says that "the feeling rushed upon me, that all previous moralists were superseded, and that here indeed was the commencement of a new era of thought." Upon finishing Bentham's book, he became a different person, for "the 'principle of utility', understood as Bentham understood it ...gave unity to my conceptions of things. I now had opinions, a creed, a doctrine, a philosophy; in one among the best senses of the word, a religion; the inculcation and diffusion of which could be made the principal outward purpose of a life." When Bentham died, Mill was twenty-six years old, but already he was developing certain convictions of his own about utilitari-

John Stuart Mill *(National Portrait Gallery, London)*

anism, convictions which were to distinguish his approach from Bentham's in a significant way.

John Stuart Mill was born in 1806, and between the ages of three and fourteen he was the object of a rigorous "educational experiment" imposed upon him by his father. So intense was this personal tutoring in the classics, languages, and history that he could say later that "through the training bestowed on me by my father, I started, I may fairly say, with an advantage of a quarter of a century over my contemporaries." But this intense learning, with its emphasis not only upon memorizing but also upon critical and analytical thinking, took its toll upon young Mill, and at the age of twenty he fell into "a dull state of nerves." He attributed his breakdown to the overemphasis upon analysis without a parallel development of the emotional qualities, of feeling. There had been at this time an underrating of expressions of feeling, and Mill points out that "Bentham himself... used to say that 'all poetry is misrepresentation.'" But "the habit of analysis has a tendency to wear away the feelings... [and] I was thus, as I said to myself, left stranded at the commencement of my voyage, with a well equipped ship and a rudder, but no sail." He belatedly turned, therefore, to such writers as Coleridge, Carlyle, and Wordsworth, who were to affect his thought so deeply that he could later say that "the cultivation of the feelings became one of the cardinal points in my ethical and philosophical creed." His long romance with Mrs. Taylor, which began when he was twenty-five and which later led to their marriage, further confirmed his high valuation of the role of feeling among human faculties. His literary achievements reflect his attempt to maintain a balance among the wide range of human faculties, starting with the rigorous *System of Logic* (1843) and including *Principles of Political Economy* (1848), the essay *On Liberty* (1859), *Considerations on Representative Government* (1861), the essay *Utilitarianism* (1861), and his *Autobiography* and *Three Essays on Religion*, which were published after he died in 1873 at the age of sixty-seven.

Mill's Version of Utilitarianism   Mill's purpose in writing his famous essay on *Utilitarianism* was to defend the *principle of utility*, which he learned from his father and Bentham, against their critics. In the course of his defense, however, he made such important modifications of this theory that his version of utilitarianism turned out to be different from Bentham's in several ways. His definition of the doctrine of utility was perfectly consistent with what Bentham had taught: Mill writes that "The creed which accepts as the foundation of morals Utility, or the greatest Happiness Principle, holds that actions are right in proportion as they tend to promote happiness, wrong as they tend to produce the reverse of happiness. By 'happiness' is intended pleasure, and the absence of pain; by 'unhappiness,' pain, and the privation of pleasure." But even though he started with the same general ideas as Bentham did, especially relating *happiness* with *pleasure*, Mill soon took a different tack by his novel treatment of the role of pleasure in morality.

Qualitative versus Quantitative Approach   Bentham had said that pleasures differ only in their amount, that is, that different ways of behaving produce different *quantities* of pleasure. He had also said that "pushpin is as good as poetry," by which he meant that the only criterion for goodness is the amount of pleasure an act can produce. It would have to follow on this calculation that all modes of behavior that produce the same amount of pleasure would be equally good, whether such behavior be the game of "pushpin" or the writing or enjoyment of poetry. Bentham was so committed to the simple quantitative measurement of pleasure as the chief test of the morality of an act that he even suggested that "there ought to be a moral thermometer." Just as a thermometer measures the different degrees of heat or temperature, so also a "moral thermometer" could measure the degrees of happiness or unhappiness. This analogy reveals Bentham's exclusive emphasis upon quantity in his treatment of goodness and pleasure, for just as it is possible to achieve the same degree of heat whether one burns coal, wood, or oil, so also is it possible to achieve equal quantities of pleasure through pushpin, poetry, or other modes of behavior. Goodness, for Bentham, is not connected with any particular *kinds* of behavior but only with the amounts of pleasure as measured by his "calculus." Inevitably, the utilitarians were accused of being moral relativists who had rejected all moral absolutes in favor of each person's subjective opinion about what is good. John Stuart Mill sought to defend utilitarianism against these charges, but in the course of his defense he was drawn into the position of altering Bentham's quantitative approach to pleasure by substituting a qualitative approach.

Whereas Bentham had said that "pushpin is as good as poetry," Mill said that he would "rather be Socrates dissatisfied than a fool satisfied," or that "it is better to be a human being dissatisfied than a pig satisfied." Pleasures, said Mill, differ from each other in kind and quality, not only in quantity. He took his stand with the ancient Epicureans, who had also been attacked for their "degrading" emphasis upon pleasure as the end of all behavior. To their accusers the Epicureans replied that it was they, the accusers, who had a degrading conception of human nature, for *they* assumed that the only pleasures people are capable of are those of which only swine are capable. But this assumption is obviously false, said Mill, because "Human beings have faculties more elevated than the animal appetites, and when once conscious of them, do not regard anything as happiness which does not include their gratification." The pleasures of the intellect, of feelings and imagination, and of the moral sentiments have a higher value than the pleasures of mere sensation. Though Mill had referred to these higher pleasures originally in order to answer the critics of utilitarianism, his concern over higher pleasures led him to criticize the very foundation of Bentham's doctrine of utility: he said that "It would be absurd that... the estimation of pleasures should be supposed to depend on quantity alone." For Mill, the mere quantity of pleasure produced by an act was of secondary importance when a choice had to be made between pleasures. If a person, says Mill, is acquainted with two different kinds of pleasures and places one of these far above the other in his preference, "even though knowing it to be attended with a greater amount of discontent, and would not resign it for any quantity of the other pleasure which [human] nature is capable of, we are justified in ascribing to the preferred enjoyment a superiority in quality so far outweighing quantity as to render it, in comparison, of small account."

The qualitative aspect of pleasure, Mill thought, was as much an empirical fact as was the quantitative element on which Bentham placed his entire emphasis. Mill departed even further from Bentham by grounding the qualitative difference between pleasures in the structure of human nature, thereby focusing upon certain human faculties whose full use, instead of pleasure only, were to be the criterion of true happiness and, therefore, of goodness. For this reason, says Mill, "Few human creatures would consent to be changed into any of the lower animals for a promise of the fullest allowance of a beast's pleasures; no intelligent human being would consent to be a fool, no instructed person would be an ignoramus, no person of feeling and conscience would be selfish and base, even though they should be persuaded that the fool, the dunce, or the rascal is better satisfied with his lot than they are with theirs." Pleasures, according to Mill, have to be graded not for their quantity but for their quality. But if pleasures must be graded for their quality, pleasure is no longer the standard of morality; if, that is, only the full use of our higher faculties can lead us to true happiness, the standard of goodness in behavior has to do not with pleasure directly but with the fulfillment of our human faculties. Mill went beyond mere quantitative hedonism, to a qualitative hedonism wherein the moral value of life is found in the higher pleasures of man's higher faculties. But if it is better to be Socrates dissatisfied than a pig satisfied, morality is proportionate to the happiness we find in being truly human and not in the amount of pleasure we experience. The higher happiness, then, is the aim of all human life, a life "exempt as far as possible from pain, and as rich as possible in enjoyments...."

Pleasure-pain Calculus Impossible By preferring the higher quality of happiness over a mere quantity of pleasure, Mill struck at another of Bentham's important assumptions, namely, that pleasures and pains can be calculated or measured. Whereas Bentham based his pleasure-pain calculus on simple quantitative considerations, saying that pleasures can be measured as to their duration, intensity, or extent, Mill argued that there is no way to measure either the quantity or quality of pleasures. Whenever we have to make a choice between two pleasures, we can express a preference wisely only if we have experienced both possibilities. Mill asks, "what means are there of determining which is the acutest of two pains, or the intensest of two pleasurable sensations, except the general [feeling] of those who are familiar with both? ... What is there to decide whether a particular pleasure is worth purchasing at the cost of a particular pain, except the feelings and judgment of the experienced?" The main reason that pleasures and pains cannot be calculated along the lines Bentham suggested, says Mill, is that "neither pains nor pleasures are homogeneous, and pain is always heterogeneous with pleasure." Instead of calculating, people simply express a preference, and apart from this act of preference, "there is no other tribunal."

Moral Obligation: Desire versus Desirable Bentham had simply assumed that we *ought* to choose those acts that produce for us the greatest quantity of pleasure. He also assumed that we should naturally help other people achieve happiness because in that way we should secure our own, and this was his *greatest-happiness principle*. Mill accepted this point but added the quality of *altruism* to this principle, saying that "the happiness which forms the utilitarian standard of what is right in conduct, is not the agent's own happiness, but that of all concerned." Mill modified Bentham's egoistic pleasure seeking by indicating that "as between his own happiness and that of others, utilitarianism requires [us] to be as strictly impartial as a disinterested and benevolent spectator." Mill thus gives the impression that the true utilitarian interprets the greatest-happiness principle to mean not *my* greatest happiness but the greatest happiness of the greatest number. It is not surprising, therefore, that he could say that "in the golden rule of Jesus of Nazareth, we read the complete spirit of the ethics of utility. To do as one would be done by, and to love one's neighbor as oneself, constitute the ideal of utilitarian perfection." Mill is here trying to defend utilitarian ethics from the charge of egoism; and to emphasize further the "golden rule" character of utilitarianism, he adds that "utility would enjoin, first, that laws and social arrangements should place the happiness...or the interest of every individual, as nearly as possible in harmony with the interest of the whole; and secondly, that education and opinion, which have so vast a power over human character, should so use that power as to establish in the mind of every individual an indissolvable association between his own happiness and the good of the whole...so that a direct impulse to promote the general good may be in every individual one of the habitual motives of action."

The further Mill pursues his argument, the less utilitarian it sounds. To emphasize, as he does, that it is not merely the quantity of pleasures but their quality that counts, and, moreover, that it is not my pleasures but the "good of the whole" that we must seek, all this suggests that the ground of obligation is somewhere other than simply in our pleasures. Still, he wants to say that happiness is at the center of the moral life, that happiness is the most desirable goal of human conduct. The word *desirable* for Mill means something we *ought* to choose, and, therefore, to say that happiness is desirable is to say that it is our moral duty to pursue happiness. The words *right* and *good* are also involved here, since, according to the utilitarian principle, an act is good or right insofar as it produces happiness. When Mill was asked why we *ought* to pursue pleasure, his answer was that *we do*. This is the critical point, or even the fallacy, in his whole argument, for he tried to build a system of morality, of what people ought to do, upon what in fact they already do.

Nowhere is Mill's difficulty with the problem of moral obligation and choice more apparent than when he deals with the question of what is the *desirable* mode of conduct for humanity. Upon this question, Mill thought, hangs the basic principle of utilitarianism, for to answer it requires some proof that this principle is correct or that happiness is indeed the ultimate end of human conduct. But how can we prove that happiness is the true and desirable end of human life and conduct? Mill answers that "the only proof capable of being given that an object is visible, is that people actually see it. The only proof that a sound is audible, is that people hear it; and so of the other sources of our experience. In like manner, I apprehend, the sole evidence it is possible to produce that anything is desirable, is that people do actually desire it." No reason can be given why the general happiness is desirable except that "each person, so far as he believes it to be attainable, desires his own happiness."

Clearly, however, there is no similarity between the examples Mill has here given, since *desirable* is not related to *desired* in the same way that *visible* is to *seen*. The difference between these two terms turns upon an important moral distinction, for whereas *visible* means simply that something is *capable of being seen*, *desirable* implies that something is *worthy of being desired*, that, moreover, it *ought* to be desired. For this reason, it is quite true that a thing's being seen proves that it is visible, but it does not follow that because a thing is desired it is for that reason desirable. The logical difficulties here seem to be insurmountable, and the more so as Mill seemed to go beyond mere pleasure as the criterion of goodness to the internal region of "conscience" as the agency of moral sanction. Not happiness alone but a sense of *duty* directs our moral thought, and so Mill speaks of "The internal sanction of duty...a feeling in our own mind; a feeling of pain more or less intense, attendant on violation of duty....This feeling, when...connecting itself with the pure idea of duty ...is the essence of conscience...all encrusted over with collateral associations, derived from sympathy, from love and still more from fear; from all the forms of religious feeling, from the recollections of childhood and all of our past life; from self-esteem, desire of the esteem of others, and occasionally even self-abasement." Mill thus departed from Bentham's external standard of goodness and turned inward, concluding that the basis of morality is a "powerful natural sentiment" and "a subjective feeling in our own minds" and, finally, "the conscientious feelings of mankind."

Liberty   Mill was as much concerned with the problems of society as was Bentham. The principle of the greatest happiness inevitably led all utilitarians to consider how the individual and the government should be related. Bentham had put his faith in democracy as the great cure for social evils inasmuch as in a democracy the interests of the rulers and the ruled are the same because the rulers are the ruled. But Mill did not have the same implicit faith in democracy that Bentham had. Although Mill agreed that democracy is the best form of government, he set forth in his essay *On Liberty* certain dangers inherent in the democratic form of government. Principally, he warned that the will of the people is most often the will of the majority, and it is entirely possible for the majority to oppress the minority. In addition, there is in a democracy the tyranny of opinion, a danger as great as oppression. Even in a democracy, therefore, it is necessary to set up safeguards against the forces that would deny men their free and full self-development. In this respect, in his concern to eliminate clear social evils, Mill reflected Bentham's desire for reform. But Mill was particularly concerned to preserve liberty by setting limits to the actions of government.

Mill argued that "the sole end for which mankind are warranted, individually or collectively, in interfering with the liberty of action of any of their number, is self-protection. That the only purpose for which power can be rightly exercised over any member of a civilized community, against his will, is to prevent harm to others." There is, of course, a legitimate role for government, but, said Mill, no government should interfere with its subjects (1) when the action can be done better by private persons; (2) when, although the government could possibly do the action better than private individuals, it is desirable for the individuals to do it for their development and education; and (3) when there is danger that too much power will unnecessarily accrue to the government. Mill's argument for liberty was, therefore, an argument for individualism. Let each individual pursue his happiness in his own way. Even in the realm of ideas, people must be free to express their thoughts and beliefs, because truth is most quickly discovered when opportunity is given to refute falsehoods. Mill took the position that "there is the greatest difference between presuming an opinion to be true because, with every opportunity for contesting it, it has not been refuted, and assuming its truth for the purpose of not permitting its refutation." He assumed, however, that it is important that the truth be known, and his whole concept of liberty, unlike Bentham's, was conceived as the precondition for developing the full possibilities of human nature.

As he considered the ideal goal of humanity, Mill asked "what more or better can be said of any condition of human affairs than that it brings human beings themselves nearer to the best thing they can be?" But is it the function of government to make human beings the best thing they can be? Mill had a deep dislike for the totalitarian state even though he lived too soon to see its ugliest manifestations. When he set forth the limits beyond which the government must not go, Mill argued forcefully that a person must not, except to prevent harm, be subject to the power of government, and especially "his own good, either physical or moral, is not a sufficient warrant."

Still, Mill had departed sufficiently from Bentham's version of utilitarianism to set in motion subtle forces that moved Mill from his clear individualism to tepid forms of collectivism. If he was concerned with quality instead of quantity in pleasures, and if this quality is based upon human beings' being "the best thing they can be," and, finally, if only those persons who have experienced the higher pleasures can know them, there is the natural urge for those who know these qualitatively higher pleasures to want others to have them also. But what is to be done if those who do not know and appreciate the higher values do not want them? It is not surprising that in this situation Mill advocated, for example, compulsory education, thereby reversing his earlier view that people must not interfere with the liberty of any member of society even for "his own good." It is most often in the name of the good of the people that the state moves into the area of human freedom. What Mill said about liberty has particular relevance in the twentieth century, which has witnessed the encroachment of government upon the actions and thoughts of people everywhere. But the difficulties of stating utilitarianism as a consistent philosophy are nowhere better seen than in Mill's own attempts to defend its principle.

FOUR

THE CONTEMPORARY PERIOD: THE RESHAPING OF THE PHILOSOPHIC MIND

In Praise of Dialectic, René Magritte (1898–1967) The search for knowledge leads to a window, and when you open it you see new things, but you also confront other windows which you must open and that will lead to yet another window, and so on.

20

Pragmatism

ragmatism emerged at the end of the nineteenth century as the most original contribution of American thought to the enterprise of philosophy. This movement was given its initial theoretical formulation by Charles S. Peirce; it was given wide and popular circulation through the brilliant and lucid essays of William James; and it was methodically implemented into the daily affairs of American institutions by John Dewey. Each of these people expressed a different aspect, or even a different kind, of pragmatism. Peirce was initially interested in logic and science, James wrote about psychology and religion, and Dewey was absorbed with the problems of ethics and social thought, which he expressed especially through his philosophy of education. They were all contemporaries, they all came from New England, and, in spite of their common concern with the practical aspects of daily life, they were all highly skilled academics. What united them was their conviction that there must be a close connection between thinking and doing. The popular notion that pragmatism exalts the "practical" person who disdains theoretical thought and prefers to "get things done" is only a half-truth. The pragmatist philosophers, to be sure, saw little value in modes of thinking that did not somehow make a difference in daily life. At the same time, like Socrates, who thought that "the unexamined life is not worth living," they concluded that behavior that did not rest upon thought was lacking an important ingredient. For the original pragmatists, therefore, the term *practical* meant *the way thought works in action*.

As a movement in philosophy, pragmatism was founded for the purpose of mediating between two divergent tendencies in nineteenth-century thought. On the one hand, there was the cumulative impact of empiricism, utilitarianism, and science, to which Darwin's theory of evolution had given the most recent and striking claim to authoritative thought about humanity. The drift of this tradition was in the direction of looking at the world and humanity as parts of a mechanical or biological process in which the mind occupied the status either of observer or reflector of these natural physical processes. The mind, in short, was on the edge of things, molded by influences external to it, and was not a creative instrument capable of fashioning thought and directing history. On the other hand, there was the tradition stemming from Descartes' rationalistic philosophy and moving through the critical idealism of Kant, the absolute idealism of Hegel, and the romantic and revised idealism of the late-nineteenth-century neo-Hegelians. In this tradition, the human mind was, for the most part, accorded enormous power, so that philosophers proceeded to construct theories about the whole nature of things, the block universe.

Between these two traditions there was an ever-widening gulf. From the scientific point of view, much of the rationalistic and idealistic philosophy was rejected as lacking in objective evidence. From the rational and idealistic points of view, the assumptions of science constituted a threat to the distinctively human aspects of people, to their moral and religious convictions, which had provided them with a sense of purpose and a reason for expending their energies. Pragmatism sought to mediate between these traditions and to combine what was most significant in each of them. With the empirical tradition, the pragmatists agreed that we have no conception of the whole of reality, that we know things from many perspectives, and that we must settle for a pluralistic approach to knowledge. With the rationalists and idealists, they agreed that morality and religion and, in short, the whole realm of values constituted a significant aspect of human experience. But now, the pragmatists concluded, discussions about God, goodness, free will, and similar subjects must be approached not solely from an "intellectualistic" point of view, where one is concerned chiefly with verbal consistency; the pragmatic *maxim* would ask instead what difference it would make to accept one theory rather than another, what difference it would make to say, for example, that humans possess free will or that they do not.

The argument could be made that pragmatism represented an attempt to justify or to provide the grounds for theoretical thinking, requiring only that thought terminate in action of some sort. In this way, the legitimate claims of science regarding empirical evidence and the observation of facts could be coupled with the human enterprises of volition and belief. One would no longer face the bleak choice of either being a scientist and renouncing as pure subjectivity all moral and religious thought, on the one hand, or, on the other hand, accepting both science and moral and religious claims but refusing to consider any contradictions between them, assuming that if such contradictions did exist they must be ignored. In short, pragmatism unified for people the realms of fact and value, making it possible for them to utilize both science and philosophy in a coherent and creative way.

CHARLES SANDERS PEIRCE (1839–1914)

Peirce (pronounced *purse*) was born in Cambridge, where his father was a noted Harvard professor of mathematics. His early training consisted of rigorous work in mathematics, science, and philosophy both at home under his father's discipline and at Harvard College, where he was a student between the ages of sixteen and twenty. Later, after receiving an M.A. in mathematics and chemistry, he worked for three years at the Harvard astronomical observatory and published his photometric researches in 1878. For thirty years, from 1861 to 1891, he was associated with the United States Coastal and Geodetic Survey. He was also for a short period a lecturer in logic at Johns Hopkins University. But Peirce was never a full-time member of a university faculty, presumably because his brilliance was overshadowed by personal eccentricities. Without an academic position he encountered resistance and indifference from publishers, so that very little of his total literary output was published during his lifetime and he received virtually none of the fame to which his abilities entitled him. Decades after his death, his works were collected and organized into several volumes, which stand now as a prodigious achievement of creative thought. In his declining years, Peirce was in financial difficulties, failing health, and virtual social rejection. His loyal friend throughout these difficulties was William James, who not only assisted him, but became the channel through which Peirce's original thoughts about pragmatism found their way into the language and thought of a whole generation throughout the world.

A Theory of Meaning   At the heart of Peirce's pragmatism is a new explanation of how words acquire their meanings. He coined the word *pragmatism* from the Greek word *pragma* (meaning "act" or "deed") in order to emphasize the fact that words derive their meanings from actions of some sort. Our ideas are clear and distinct only when we are able to translate them into some mode of operation. For example, the adjectives *hard* and *heavy* have meaning only because we are able to conceive of some specific effects that are associated with these terms. Thus, *hard* means that which cannot be scratched by many other substances, and *heavy* means that which will fall if we let go of it. To underscore the decisive role of *effects* in the meanings of words, Peirce argued that there would be absolutely no difference between a hard thing and a soft thing as long as they did not test differently. From such simple examples, Peirce sought to generalize about the nature of meaning and knowledge in general. His basic point was that "our idea of anything *is* our idea of its sensible effects." That is, if words are to have any meaning, one must be able to use the operational formula, which says "if *A* then *B*," which is to say that such an object or such qualities imply that such effects can be expected. If a word refers to an object or a quality about which no practical effects can be conceived, such a word has no meaning.

Peirce was, of course, highly influenced by the language of science, for it is particularly scientific language that satisfies this pragmatic test for meaning. What he was arguing against was the kind of rationalism Descartes had firmly fixed in the theories of knowledge whose validity was based solely upon the consistency between ideas themselves. To be sure, the earlier empiricists had sought to show the shortcomings of rationalism, but Peirce found the assumptions of rationalism still very much alive. Descartes had localized all thought within the mind of each individual. Intellectual certainty for him consisted in "clear and distinct" ideas, which the mind grasped by intuition. For Descartes, the mind was a purely theoretical instrument that could operate successfully in isolation from environmental circumstances. Thinking, for him, was chiefly a matter of self-consciousness. Against all these assumptions Peirce argued that thinking always occurs in a context, not in isolation from it. Meanings are derived not by intuition but by experience or experiment. For these reasons, meanings are not individual or private but social and public. Again, if there is no way of testing ideas by their effects or public consequences, such ideas are meaningless. To be able to distinguish between meaningful and meaningless is particularly important, Peirce thought, when various and opposing systems of thought are urged upon a person.

The Role of Belief   Peirce looked upon belief as occupying the very important middle position between thought and action. Beliefs guide our desires and shape our actions. But beliefs are "unfixed" by doubts. It is when the "irritation of doubt" causes a struggle to attain belief that the enterprise of thought begins. Through thought, we try to fix our beliefs so that we shall have a guide for action. There are several ways in which we can fix our beliefs, according to Peirce. There is the method of *tenacity,* whereby people cling to beliefs, refusing to entertain doubts about them or to consider arguments or evidence for another view. Another method is to invoke *authority*, as when persons in authority require the acceptance of certain ideas as true on pain of punishment. Still another method is that of the metaphysician or philosopher such as Plato, Descartes, or Hegel, who, according to Peirce, would settle questions of belief by asking whether an idea was "agreeable to *reason.*" With all these methods Peirce found himself in disagreement precisely because they could not, in his view, achieve their intent, namely, to fix or settle belief. What they all lacked was some connection with experience and behavior.

Peirce therefore offered a fourth method, the method of *science,* whose chief virtue, he thought, was its realistic basis in experience. Unlike the methods of *tenacity, authority,* and *reason*, all of which rest upon what a person possesses within his own mind as a consequence solely of his thinking, the method of science is built on the assumption that there are real things, the characteristics of which are entirely independent of our opinions about them. Moreover, because these real things affect our senses according to regular laws, we can assume that they will affect each observer the same way. Beliefs that are grounded in such real things can therefore be verified, and their "fixation" can be a public act rather than a private one. There is in fact no way to agree or disagree with a conclusion arrived at by means of the first three methods since they refer to nothing whose consequences or real existences can be tested. The method of tenacity is clearly irrational; the method of authority precludes argument; and the method of *a priori* reasoning, because it occurs in isolation from facts, permits the affirmation of several different explanations of things, as was the case with the alternative metaphysical systems produced by the Continental rationalists.

The Elements of Method   What commended the scientific method to Peirce for settling the conflicts between alternative beliefs were those elements of this method that would overcome and avoid individual prejudice. For one thing, the method of science requires that a person state not only what truth he or she believes but also how it was arrived at. The procedures followed should be available to anyone who cares to retrace the same steps to test whether the same results will occur. Peirce again and again emphasized this public or community character of the method of science. Secondly, the method of science is highly self-critical. It subjects its conclusions to severe tests, and wherever indicated, the conclusions of a theory are adjusted to fit the new evidence and new insights. This, says Peirce, ought also to be the mental attitude of anyone in relation to his or her beliefs. Thirdly, Peirce felt that science requires that there be a high degree of cooperation among all members of the scientific community. This element of the method, this cooperation, is yet another force that prevents any individual or group from shaping truth to fit its own interests. Conclusions of science must be conclusions that all scientists can draw. Similarly, in questions of belief and truth, it should be possible for anyone to come to the same conclusions. Here Peirce laid down the method of empirical inquiry as the basis for any cooperative approach to belief. This meant that in the last analysis, there would have to be some practical consequence, that is, some consequence in practice, of any idea. As he pointed out, "the final upshot of thinking is the exercise of volition." The essence of science, as Peirce understood it, though not the way all scientists understand it, is that science is a method of doing something. For this reason, Peirce considered all thinking a way of doing something. But before people are able to *do*, they must have a *belief*; a belief, in turn, requires *thought*. Peirce had argued that only thought that is tested by the criteria of experience and experiment could provide people with the surest basis for belief, which in turn would establish their habit of action.

WILLIAM JAMES (1842–1910)

The rich flavor of William James' writings reflects the equally rich quality and breadth of his life. Born in New York City, he grew up in a highly cultured family, which produced not only the outstanding American philosopher, but also his brother Henry James, the gifted novelist. William studied at Harvard and traveled to universities throughout Europe, acquiring a broad outlook both culturally and intellectually. He received his M.D. degree from the Harvard Medical School in 1869 and was appointed to its faculty in 1872 as an instructor in physiology. From medicine, William James moved to psychology and philosophy, producing in 1890 his famous *Principles of Psychology*. He was a member of the illustrious Harvard department of philosophy, which included George Santayana and Josiah Royce. Although he did not write any philosophical treatise comparable in scope to his famous book on psychology, he published a great many definitive essays, which singly and as collections in book form were read throughout the world. By the time of his death in 1910 at the age of sixty-eight, William James had fashioned a new approach to philosophy and had managed to communicate his pragmatic principles to an unusually wide audience of readers. Starting from the work already done by Peirce, he took a fresh look at pragmatism and developed it along novel lines. Among the important topics to which James turned his attention were the questions of (1) the pragmatic method, (2) the pragmatic theory of truth, (3) the role and status of the human will, and (4) the relevance of the will to believe.

Pragmatism as a Method   William James thought that "the whole function of philosophy ought to be to find out what definite difference it will make to you and me, at definite instants of our life, if this world-formula or that world-formula be the true one." His emphasis was upon the concrete concerns of life, upon facts, upon action as it affects and displays power, and upon power and action as they affect *my* life *now* and in the determinate future. But pragmatism as such contained no substance or content, no special information about human purpose or destiny. As a philosophy, pragmatism did not have its own creed; it did not, as such, offer a world formula.

"Pragmatism," said James, "is a method only." Still, as a method, pragmatism assumed that human life has a purpose and that rival theories about man and the world would have to be tested against this purpose. There is in fact no single definition of human purpose; the understanding of human purpose is part of the activity of thinking. Philosophical thinking arises when people want to understand things and the setting in which they live; purpose derives its meaning from a sense of being at home in the universe. As a method, pragmatism rejected rationalism chiefly because, said James, it was dogmatic and presumed to give conclusive answers about the world in terms that frequently left the issues of life untouched. By contrast, pragmatism "has no dogmas and no doctrines save its method." As a method, pragmatism hovered close to life, refusing to close the process of thought prematurely, taking its cue from the proved facts of life, willing to be led to new conceptions of purpose as deeper facets of human emotion and expectations were discovered. Again, as a method, pragmatism did not specify any *particular* results, though it did orient thinking around results, fruits, and consequences. No formulation either in science, theology, or philosophy should be taken as final; all formulations of theory are

William James *(Culver Pictures)*

only approximations. In the last analysis, the meanings of all these theories are to be found not in their internal verbal consistency, but in their capacity to solve problems.

Instead of mere consistency, said James, "you must bring out of each word its practical cash value." Although pragmatism stands for no particular results, as a method in practice its essence is precisely to assure *results*. When it finds a theory that does not *make* a difference one way or another for practical life, such a theory is abandoned. If, for example, there is a dispute over whether God exists, pragmatism has no preconceived creed to offer; but it does ask whether it makes a difference to believe in God's existence. To raise that question could very well lead one to see the "truth" in the claim of God's existence even though the same person might have rejected a "rational proof" of the existence of God. By asking always what difference an idea makes, James had virtually reduced the pragmatic method to the formula "Does it work?" But supporting that formula was the combined methodological apparatus, as James said, of "nominalism—in always appealing to particulars; [of] utilitarianism in emphasizing practical aspects; [of] positivism in its disdain for verbal solutions, useless questions and metaphysical abstractions." It was inevitable that such a method should raise the question whether saying about an idea that "it works" is the same as saying that "it is true."

The Pragmatic Theory of Truth   James made the startling statement that "truth *happens* to an idea." What was so startling about this statement was that the more traditional theories of truth took virtually the opposite view, namely, that truth is a property or quality of an idea. James was rejecting what he called the *copy-view* of truth. This theory assumes that an idea "copies" *reality*, and an idea is therefore true if it copies what is "out there" accurately. Truth is that quality an idea has when it copies accurately. The assumption of the "intellectualists" who hold this theory, said James, is that "truth means essentially an inert static relation. When you've got your true idea of anything, there's an end of the matter. You're in possession; you *know*." Against this theory, James brought the whole arsenal of his pragmatism. Truth must be the cash value of an idea. What other motive could there be for saying that something is true or not true than to provide workable guides to practical behavior? James would ask, "what concrete difference will its being true make in anyone's actual life?"

By tying truth to life, to action, James rejected the view that truth is a *stagnant* property in ideas. Ideas *become* true; they are *made* true by events. That is why he wanted to say that truth *happens* to ideas. In addition, to say that truth happens to ideas is to make truth a part of experience. Whereas the *copy-view* of truth assumes that ideas really do copy what is out there, pragmatism says that there rarely is exact copying. Consider, he says, a clock on the wall. We consider it to be a clock not because we have a *copy-view* of it: we see only its face and hands, but not its internal mechanism, which makes it a clock. Still, our notion of it passes for true, not because our idea of it is an accurate copy, but because we *use* it as a clock and as such it *works*, enabling us to end a lecture "on time" and to catch the train. To be sure, we could check our idea to verify whether it is indeed a clock. But *verifiability* is as good as verification. We do not in fact verify every idea. Indeed, says James, "for one truth-process completed there are a million in our lives that function in this state of nascency." For this reason truth lives "on a credit system." We do not require in every instance of truth that we should, as it were, see the wheels of the clock. What more would be added to the truth of our idea that that is a clock than we already have in the successful regulation of our behavior?

Ideas become true insofar as they help us to make successful connections among various parts of our experience. Truth is therefore part of the process of experience, of *living*. As part of a process, truth is *made* by the process of successful experience; successful experience *is* the verification process. To say that a truth always is, that it absolutely obtains, would mean that the clock on the wall is a clock whether anyone sees it or not. But what James wants to show is that the question about the "truth" of the clock arises only in actual life when we live "as if" that thing on the wall is a clock, and the truth that it is a clock is *made* by our successful behavior. On this theory, says James, there are many *plural* truths, as many truths as there are concrete successful actions. Moreover, James would say that truth is bound up with the personal interests of concrete individuals. By this he meant that truth is not something *capricious*. As bound up with personal interests, the "truth" must lead to successful action; it must *work*. In the long run a true belief must work beneficially, just as an "untrue" one will work destructively.

If the pragmatist is asked why anyone *ought* to seek the truth, James answers that "our obligation to seek the truth is part of our general obligation to do what pays," just as one ought to seek health because it pays to be healthy. Above all, James thought that the pragmatic theory of truth could render a desperately needed service to philosophy by providing a means for settling disputes. Some disputes cannot be resolved if each party simply affirms that his views are true. James would ask, which theory fits the facts of real life? One such dispute, which has exercised philosophers through the ages, is the question of freedom versus determinism.

The Role and Status of the Will　William James was convinced that it is not possible to "prove" by any rational mode of argument that human will is either free or determined. Apparently equally good arguments could be given for each case. But he was nevertheless convinced that he could put the problem in a new light by applying the pragmatic method, by asking what difference it makes in actual life to accept one or the other side of the dispute. And the dispute was worth undertaking because it implied something momentous about life—either people were driven by external forces or they possessed "freedom" to choose their mode of behavior and therefore possessed the power to shape their lives and, thus, history.

The central issue in this dispute, said James, "relates solely to the existence of possibilities," of things that may, but need not, be. The determinist says that there are no ambiguous or uncertain possibilities, that what will be will be: "...those parts of the universe already laid down absolutely appoint and decree what the other parts shall be. The future has no ambiguous possibilities in its womb." On the other hand, the indeterminist says that there is a certain amount of "loose play" in the universe, so that the present existence of certain facts and arrangements does not necessarily determine what the future shall be; rather, there are genuine alternatives in the future from which an actual choice can be made. Here then are two contradictory points of view. What divides us into *possibility* people and *antipossibility* people? asks James. It is, he says, the postulates of rationality. For some it seems more rational to say that all events are set down from eternity, whereas for others it seems more rational to assume that people can engage in genuine choice. If both of these points of view seem equally rational to their respective proponents, how can the dispute be resolved?

This was not for James simply an interesting puzzle. His whole philosophical orientation revolved around this problem of the role and status of the will. With his basic concern about action and choosing those ideas and modes of behavior with the highest cash value, he inevitably saw philosophy in terms of human striving, and this, he was convinced, implied a certain kind of universe. The solution of the problem, therefore, was to ask the simply pragmatic question, what does a deterministic world imply? If, that is, one says that all events without exception are rigorously determined from the beginning of time so that they could not have happened in any other way, what kind of universe must this be? Using a metaphor, one could only answer that such a universe is like a machine, where each part fits tightly and all the gears are interlocked, so that the slightest motion of one part causes a motion of every other part. There is no loose play in the machine. How can such a metaphor be applied to people, James asks. A person is different from a mechanical part in a machine. What makes a person different is his or her consciousness. For one thing, a person is capable of a "judgment of regret." But how can one "regret" what could not have been otherwise? The determinist must define the world as a place where what "ought to be" is impossible. Still, we are always making not only judgments of regret, but of approval and disapproval. Moreover, we seek to persuade others to do or refrain from doing certain actions. In addition, people are punished or rewarded for certain actions. All these forms of judgment imply that a person is constantly facing genuine choices; a "forced" or "determined" act is not a *choice*.

The capacity of choice involves the capacity to recognize alternative influences upon one, to hold these alternatives in momentary suspense and then select one or the other. If one denies such a capacity for choice, the only alternative is the mechanical explanation. But no human beings ever consciously act as if this were a mechanically determined universe. Most of our language and thought processes suggest just the opposite; they suggest that at many points each person in fact faces genuine possibilities, options, real choices. James did not want to deny the reality of causal relations. Indeed, his pragmatism rested upon the operational formula that "*if* we do *A, B* will happen." But the word *if* is the clue; we are not forced to do *A*, and therefore *B* will happen only if we decide to choose *A*. James realized that if the determinist charged that his ideas about free will were determined, that his assumptions about genuine possibilities were part of the block universe, that such charges would indeed bring an end to rational discourse, that the problem could no longer be discussed. What would remain, however, would be human beings with their hopes, fears, and regrets, and in the arena of daily life the assumptions of mechanical determinism would be abandoned, and the pragmatic question would come to the forefront, the question "what should I do?" or "which alternative would be better or wiser for me?"

In actual practical life, we see ourselves and others as vulnerable. We are capable of lying, stealing, and murdering. We judge these to be wrong, not only in retrospect, but wrong because they were not rigorously inevitable when they were done; persons doing these things "could have" done otherwise. James concludes, in this vein, by saying that this problem is finally a "personal" one, that he simply cannot conceive of the universe as a place where murder *must* happen; it is a place where murder *can* happen and *ought not*. If this reflects only his "instinct" concerning the kind of universe this is, then, says James, "there are *some* instinctive reactions which I, for one, will not tamper with." As people, we remain the same whatever side of the dispute we choose. But, said James, the only consistent way to represent what in fact we do when we help, hinder, injure, hope, judge, and regret is to see the universe as one with real possibilities, where individual effort can make a difference in life and history. This was the basic theme in his classic essay on *The Will to Believe*.

The Relevance of the Will to Believe James raised this question: "Can our will either help or hinder our intellect in its perceptions of truth?" In answering this question, James did not intend to propose the fanciful thesis that "wishing will make it true." His intention was to give a defense of "our right" to believe something of which our purely logical intellect may not have been persuaded. Religious questions in particular have a way of running ahead of evidence. But if the evidence for God's existence is lacking, there is, nevertheless, the fact of human behavior. James put great store by the concrete fact that people engage in moral discourse and also religious practice. It is necessary to recognize this fact of religious behavior when considering the issue of religious truth. Moreover, pragmatism recognized the close relation between thinking and doing and therefore between belief and action. This made belief an important element in life, and what James wanted to do was to discover just how relevant the will to believe is in relation to truth.

James said that the will to believe is relevant only under highly restricted conditions. One cannot will to believe just anything under any and all circumstances. First of all, there must be a clear *hypothesis* that is proposed for our belief. Such an hypothesis must be *live* rather than *dead*; that is, it must, as an electric wire, make a connection with my life. If an American Protestant is asked to believe in the Mahdi, this makes no connection with him and arouses no credibility at all and could, therefore, be only a dead hypothesis. Further, there must be an *option*. James argued that a genuine option requires that both alternative hypotheses be *live* and not dead; the option must be *forced* and not avoidable; and it must be *momentous* and not trivial. The will to believe, then, is relevant and can operate only when we are confronted with an option that (1) is *forced* upon us, in that it is impossible not to choose one way or the other, (2) is a *living* option because both hypotheses make a genuine appeal, and (3) is a *momentous* option because the opportunity to choose might not present itself again. And, moreover, belief is relevant only where reason alone cannot settle the matter.

Having stated these conditions, James then argues that it is frequently the case that our wills influence our convictions. The clearest example, he thought, was our postulate that there is truth and that our minds can attain it. How do we know there is truth? We don't, says James; our belief that there is truth is but a "passionate affirmation of desire." We want to have truth, and we want to believe that our experiments will unfold more truth, and in this desire we have the support of the community. For these reasons, James says that "our passionate nature not only lawfully may, but must, decide an option between propositions, whenever it is a genuine option that cannot by its nature be decided on intellectual grounds; for to say, under such circumstances, 'Do not decide, but leave the question open,' is itself a passional decision... and is attended with the... risk of losing the truth."

Just how the will to believe becomes relevant, what its function really is, is suggested by the last phrase, where James speaks of the "risk of losing the truth." James argues that certain kinds of truths become possible only when we put ourselves in the position for the truth fully to materialize itself. If we fail to make ourselves "available," we risk losing the truth. Suppose a young man wants to know whether a certain young lady loves him. Let us also suppose that objectively it is a fact that she loves him but he does not *know* it. If he assumes that she does not, if, that is, he does not will to believe that she loves him, his doubt will prevent him from saying or doing what would cause her to reveal her love. In this case, he would "lose the truth." His will to believe would not necessarily create the love; That is already there. Belief has the effect of making what is already there come full circle. If the young man required evidence before he could know the truth, he would never know it, because the evidence he is looking for can become available only after he willed to believe it is true. In this case, the will to believe would have discovered a fact that already existed. Projecting this method deeper into the realm of religious experience, James did not want to argue that the will to believe would "create" the existence of God as the product of mere wish. He rather thought that the truth of religion and the power of God in human experience is the discovery, through the will to believe, of what is in fact "there." Some truths forever escape us until we plunge into the stream of experience.

Besides *discovering* facts, the will to believe can *create* facts. An individual, says James, frequently gains a promotion chiefly because he believed he could achieve it and acted resolutely on that belief. Taking his estimate of his powers as true, such a person *lives* by it, sacrifices for its sake, and takes risks. His faith *creates* its own verification. In a political campaign, the will to believe can provide the psychic energy for creating a majority for a candidate. When one person is impressed by the optimism of another, he is energized to express the same optimism about the outcome of the election, and this *energy* can eventually create the majority vote. James gives the illustration of the passengers on a train, all of whom are individually brave, but when held up by robbers each one is afraid that if he resists he will be shot. If they believed that the others would arise, resistance could begin. The robbers know that they can count on each other. The passengers, on the other hand, are paralyzed. Though they possess superior force, they are not *sure* their fellows would support their resistance. But if one passenger actually arose, that evidence could influence the others, and this will to believe would help to create the fact of total resistance.

In the end, religious experience was for James a fact that is both discovered and created through the will to believe. His pragmatism led him to distinguish between organized religion and that firsthand religion whose cash value could be realized only when a person put himself into a position to be affected by it. Religion grows out of the deep personal experience of the fragmentary or broken character of life, and this awareness leads one to discover a power that can overcome this sense of incompleteness. James thought of God in these terms, as a power able to reconstruct human life. For this reason, James concluded that "the universe is no longer a mere *It* to us, but a *Thou*, if we are religious; any relation that may be possible from person to person might be possible here."

JOHN DEWEY (1859–1952)

If William James was the most brilliant of the pragmatists, John Dewey was in the final analysis the most influential. By the time of his death at the age of ninety-two, Dewey had brought about a reconstruction of philosophy and had influenced the workings of many American institutions, particularly the schools and the legislative and judicial processes. His influence was felt beyond the boundaries of the United States, especially in Japan and China, where his lectures made a lasting impression. Born in Burlington, Vermont, John Dewey was educated at the University of Vermont and at the Johns Hopkins University, where he received his Ph.D. in philosophy in 1884. For the next ten years, except for one year when he was at Minnesota, he taught at the University of Michigan, and for the next decade at the University of Chicago, where he gained renown for his pragmatic concepts of education. As director of the Laboratory School for children at the University of Chicago, he experimented with a more permissive and creative atmosphere for learning, setting aside the more traditional and formal method of learning by listening and encouraging instead the pupil's initiative and individual involvement in projects. From 1904 to 1929 he was a member of the faculty at Columbia University. He produced an enormous number of writings even after his retirement in 1929. His interests covered a wide range, and he wrote on logic, metaphysics, and the theory of knowledge. But as Dewey's chief expressions of pragmatism were in the social rather than individual realm, his most influential works related to education, democracy, ethics, religion, and art.

The Spectator versus Experience Dewey's chief quarrel with earlier philosophy was that it had confused the true nature and function of knowledge. For the most part, he said, the empiricists had assumed that thinking refers to fixed things in nature, that for each idea there is a corresponding something in

John Dewey *(Culver Pictures)*

reality. It is as though knowing is modeled after what is supposed to happen when we look at something. This he called "a spectator theory of knowledge." Thus, to see something is to have an idea of it. But the reverse process was also thought to be true, namely, that to have a clear idea is to guarantee, as the rationalists argued, that the object of thought exists in reality. In either case, the mind was viewed as an instrument for considering what is fixed and certain in nature. Nature is one thing and the mind another, and knowing is the relatively simple activity of looking, as a spectator does, at what is there.

     Dewey considered this view of knowledge, admittedly more intricate than his oversimplification, as too static, for one thing, and too mechanical for another. Influenced as he was by Darwin's theories, Dewey looked upon humanity as a biological organism. As such, humans can best be understood in relation to their environment. As any other biological organism, a person struggles for survival. Although Dewey gave up his early Hegelian orientation, he still looked upon humanity as enmeshed in a dialectic process, not Hegel's conflict of ideas, but a conflict in the material or natural environment. Dewey's grand concept was therefore *experience*, a concept he employed for the purpose of connecting humanity as a dynamic biological entity with its precarious environment. If both humanity and its environment are dynamic, it is clear that a simple spectator-type theory of knowledge will not work. The mind, or more specifically *intelligence*, is for Dewey not a fixed substance, and knowledge is not a set of static concepts. Intelligence is the power one possesses to cope with one's environment. Thinking is not an individual act carried on in private, in isolation from practical problems. Thinking, or active intelligence, arises in "problem situations"; thinking and doing are intimately related.

All thinking, says Dewey, has two aspects, namely, "a perplexed, troubled, or confused situation at the beginning and a cleared-up, unified, resolved situation at the close." He gave his theory the name *instrumentalism* to emphasize that thinking is always instrumental in solving problems. The mind does not know simply individual things; it functions as a mediator between humanity as an organism and its environment. The mind spreads itself over a range of things as these bear upon the person's desires, doubts, and dangers. Knowing may very well consist of a "cognitive act," of an activity in the mind, but the full description of knowing must include the environmental origin of the problem or situation that calls forth the cognitive act. In this way, instrumentalism differs from empiricism and rationalism. Whereas the latter two theories of knowledge separate thinking and doing, instrumentalism holds that reflective thought is always involved in transforming a practical situation.

Thinking, therefore, is not a quest for the "truth," as though the truth were a static and eternal quality in things. Thinking, rather, is the act of trying to achieve an adjustment between man and his environment. The best test of the value of any philosophy, says Dewey, is to ask, "Does it end in conclusions which, when referred back to ordinary life-experiences and their predicaments, render them more significant, more luminous to us and make our dealings with them more fruitful?"

Habit, Intelligence, and Learning   Dewey built his theory of instrumentalism, his problem-solving theory of knowing, around his special view of human nature. Even though Dewey emphasized the social aspect of humanity, he did nevertheless recognize in individuals certain inherited structures. There are, for example, certain basic human instincts. At the same time, these instincts are not a fixed inheritance, but are "highly flexible." Dewey says that "any impulse may become organized into almost any disposition according to the way it interacts with surroundings." For example, *fear* may become cowardice, reverence for superiors, the cause for accepting superstitions, and so on. Just what an impulse will result in depends, says Dewey, upon the way an impulse is interwoven with other impulses and upon the inhibitions and outlets supplied by the environment. Dewey's central point here is that there is in fact a human psychological structure, that human nature possesses certain inherited capacities. At the same time, these capacities are flexible, so that given natural impulses will work differently under different social conditions. When impulses tend to result in the same response, this does not mean that for a given impulse there can be only that particular response. This was Dewey's decisive argument, for he seemed to reject the simple mechanical stimulus-response account of behavior. If an impulse reflects itself always in the same way time after time, said Dewey, this is not a mechanical necessity but only the product of *habit*. But habit and impulse need to be clearly distinguished. *Habit* is only the way a person deals with certain classes of "stimuli, standing predilections and aversions." But since habit is only *one* way of responding to the stimuli of one's impulses, clearly there is no *necessary* connection between a person's natural impulses and any *particular* response. This means that responses are acquired or learned through the interaction between human nature and culture. If this is the case, habits do not represent eternal forms of human behavior. They can be singled out, analyzed, and appraised. Habits can be tested for their usefulness, the criterion being whether they support life and generally facilitate the successful adaptation of a person to the environment.

Most important of all is the new insight this analysis gave Dewey of the nature of social and human "evil." Evil is not the product of some permanent instinct or impulse in human nature that cannot be altered. Evil is, rather, the product of the special ways a culture has shaped and conditioned people's impulses. In his view, evil is the product of the "inertness of established habit." *Intelligence* itself is a habit by which the human organism adjusts its relation to its environment. Habits therefore include not only ways of reacting to certain stimuli but also ways of thinking about the environment. Since all habits are only *established* but *not necessary* modes of behavior, the clue to overcoming personal and social evil is to alter a society's habits, its habits of response and its habits of thought.

Nothing is more important than *education* in remolding a society. If a person is a creature of habit, education should provide the conditions for developing the most useful and creative habits. Dewey regretted that in the past progress was achieved only when some catastrophe or major social upheaval broke the spell of long-standing habits. He would prefer a more controlled approach to change, and nothing, he thought, provides a person with more power to control than knowledge. Instead of revolution, therefore, change should be achieved through the skillful alteration of habits through education. He was convinced that "the chief means of continuous, graded, economical improvement and social rectification lies in utilizing the opportunities of educating the young to modify prevailing types of thought and desire." The spirit of education should be *experimental*, because the mind is fundamentally a problem-solving instrument, and it is therefore more important to try alternative means for successfully solving problems than to pursue neat theoretical formulations.

Dewey's instrumentalism was governed by the presuppositions of science. Like science, education should recognize the intimate connection between action and thought, between experiment and reflection. Achieving knowledge is a continuous process; it is a struggle to fashion theory in the context of experiment and thought. But if education is the key to social improvement, and if experiment is the best way to discover the instrumental *means* for solving problems, the crucial questions concern the problem of *ends*. Improvement assumes a scale of values, and means are employed toward ends. How does humanity or a society discover its ends or the foundations of its values? Dewey addressed himself to this difficult problem of relating facts to value, science to morality, and in the process fashioned a new theory of value.

Value in a World of Fact   Dewey's theory of value followed his general theory of knowledge. The mind discovers values the way it discovers facts, namely, in experience. Values do not exist as eternal entities some place to be discovered by the theoretical mind. Every person experiences the problem of choosing between two or more possibilities. The question about values arises in these experiences where choices have to be made. Choices are most often made regarding means for achieving ends. Where an end is already clear, the value judgment concerning the means can be pursued with scientific rigor. Science, or intelligent reflection, always asks how a given act will terminate. The act that will terminate most successfully is by definition the most "valuable" act. Much of Dewey's theory can be understood through the simple example of a leaking roof. For one thing, the problem of the leaking roof raises *all at once* the questions of both *ends* and *means*. A person quickly realizes that a leaky roof calls for action. Before action is begun, intelligence is used to sort out the various possibilities for stopping the leak. The function of intelligence is to appraise the consequences of various alternatives, using knowledge based upon past experience or experiment. The human intelligence did not have to be endowed or supplied with either a theory of "ultimate ends" or an elaborate "hierarchy of values" in order to deal effectively with the problem. All that was needed to solve this problem could be discovered by the functioning of intelligence. One does not need a theory of value to know that fixing a leaky roof is both desired and desirable. To a great extent Dewey would solve the problem of values by saying that intelligence can discover the best solution when the problem is analyzed in its specific practical context.

Dewey's novel approach was his rejection of any theory of values that said that the standard of value, whether moral, social, political, or economic, is to be found either in the "essences" of things or in some form of transcendent eternal truth. There is no way to grasp in any neat formula just how any act will terminate. Value must always mean that behavior or consequences are *satisfactory*. But it is not possible to decide *beforehand* upon a limited number of consequences that will be called *good*. Life is too dynamic and the circumstances of behavior too diverse to permit the making of any kind of *list* of rules. Moreover, there is, says Dewey, "only relative, not absolute, impermeability and fixity of structure," and "new individuals with novel ends emerge." This shows Darwin's influence upon Dewey's thinking about value; for value, as

Dewey conceived it, is the quality of satisfactoriness of an act that one performs in the Darwinian world, in the pursuit of successfully controlling life in his environment.

Dewey was so concerned to set the problem of values into the concrete events of daily life that he refused to consider the question of ultimate ends and the so-called hierarchy of values. He apparently assumed the ends concerning human existence could be discovered as easily as the notion that leaky roofs must be fixed. Since intelligence is the agency for bridging the gap between *any* problem and its solution, he assumed that this same experimental and instrumental approach could successfully resolve the problems of individual and social destiny. His optimism rested, of course, upon the spectacular successes of the sciences. He was convinced that science could also provide the standard for value judgments. Indeed, in asking where people could discover regulating norms for life if they gave up the traditional moral and religious standards, Dewey answered, for the most part "from the findings of the natural sciences."

In principle, the seat of value must be located in human desire and its satisfaction. Science can tell us not only that people have desires but also that these desires can be satisfied in various ways. By employing the scientific method in value problems, Dewey sought to go beyond the theory of utilitarianism. For the most part, the utilitarians concluded that something is desirable because in fact it is desired. People ought to maximize pleasure because they desire pleasure. At first glance this seems to be Dewey's approach also, especially because he had given up the classic theory of "truth" and the theory of ultimate ends by which to test or appraise what people in fact do desire. But Dewey added a rigorous element to his procedure of evaluation. For him, desire was only the starting point. It is necessary, he said, to engage in critical inquiry before one makes a choice. A moral choice will admittedly begin with a person's or a society's desire, but a desire must be submitted to the critical power of intelligence. What intelligence does under these circumstances is to consider the consequences of any given form of satisfaction of desire. Value is therefore not simply satisfaction of desire, but rather the satisfactory solution of the problem reflected by desire.

By this activity of critical intelligence, Dewey sought to achieve two purposes: first, to say that value is something that must be worked out in concrete experience and, secondly, to say that values are not wholly relative and subjective, but must be subject to critical scrutiny. In the end, Dewey's theory appears to rest on the assumption that experience gives a person or society the ends toward which life and behavior should move. Each generation should formulate its own ends in the context of democracy. Democracy itself represented Dewey's *faith* in the capacities of human intelligence. Dewey believed that apart from "pooled and cooperative experience" there is no reliable source of knowledge, wisdom, or guidance for collective action.

21

Karl Marx: Dialectical Materialism

For at least one-third of the world's population in the second half of the twentieth century, Marxism provided the official philosophical point of view, or the systematic articulation of beliefs about the world and human destiny in it. That the views of Karl Marx should have achieved such immense influence for several generations is all the more remarkable when one considers that he spent a considerable portion of his adult life in relative obscurity. He rarely spoke in public, and when he did, he displayed none of the attributes of the captivating orator. He was primarily a thinker, thoroughly absorbed in the task of elaborating the intricate details of a theory whose broad outlines he had grasped as a young man still in his twenties. He rarely mingled with the masses whose status and future occupied the center of his theoretical concern. Although he wrote an enormous amount, his writings were not read extensively during his lifetime. One finds no reference to Marx, for example, in the social and political writings of his famed contemporary John Stuart Mill. Nor was what Marx had to say entirely original. Much of his economic thought can be found in Ricardo, some of his philosophical assumptions and apparatus in Hegel and Feuerbach, the view that history is shaped by the conflict between social classes in Saint-Simon, and the labor theory of value in John Locke. But what was original in Marx was that out of all these sources he distilled a unified scheme of thought, which he fashioned into a powerful instrument of social analysis and social revolution.

Karl Heinrich Marx was born in Trier, Germany, in 1818, the oldest son of a Jewish lawyer and the descendant of a long line of rabbis. In spite of his Jewish lineage, he was brought up as a Protestant since his father had become a Lutheran, for apparently prudent reasons rather than religious convictions. The elder Marx had a strong influence on his son's intellectual development through his own rational and humanitarian inclinations. Young Marx was also influenced by Ludwig von Westphalen, a neighbor and a distinguished Prussian government official and his future father-in-law, who stimulated his interest in literature and a lifelong respect for the Greek poets and tragedians, Dante, and Shakespeare. After high school in Trier, Marx went to the University of Bonn in 1835 and began the study of law at the age of seventeen. A year later he transferred to the University of Berlin, giving up the study of law and pursuing instead the study of philosophy. In 1841, at the age of twenty-three, he received his doctoral degree from the University of Jena, for which he wrote a dissertation entitled *On the Difference between the Democritean and Epicurean Philosophies of Nature.*

At the University of Berlin, the dominant intellectual influence was the philosophy of Hegel, and accordingly Marx was, for the time being, deeply impressed by Hegel's idealism and his dynamic view of history. He became a member of a group of young radical Hegelians who saw in Hegel's approach to philosophy the key to a new understanding of humanity, the world, and history. Hegel had centered his thought around the notion of *Spirit* or *Mind.* To him, Absolute Spirit or Mind is God. God is the whole of reality. God is identical with all of Nature, and therefore God is found also in the configurations of culture and civilization. History consists in the gradual self-realization of God in the sequence of time. What makes Nature knowable is that its essence is Mind, and what produces history is the continuous struggle of Mind or Spirit or Idea to realize itself in perfect form. Thus, God and the world are one. The basic reality is therefore Spirit or Mind. For this reason, Hegel had concluded that the rational is real and the real is rational. Moreover, the rational basis of reality, the Idea, is in a continuous process of unfolding from lower to higher degrees of perfection, and this is the process we know as *history.* History is a dialectic process moving in a triadic pattern from *thesis* to *antithesis* and finally to *synthesis.*

Whether Marx ever accepted Hegel's idealism in all its fullness is not certain, but what did strike him with force was Hegel's method of identifying God and Nature or the world. Hegel had said that "Spirit [God] is alone reality. It is the inner being of the world, that which essentially is and is *per se.*" Whatever there is, and whatever there is to know, exists as the world of Nature; besides the world and its history there is nothing. This rejection of the older theology, which had separated God and the world, is what struck Marx as being so novel and significant. Although Hegel had not intended his views to destroy the foundations of religion, the radical young band of Hegelians at the University of Berlin undertook a "higher criticism" of the Gospels. David Strauss wrote a critical *Life of Jesus* in which he argued that much of Jesus' teaching was a purely mythical invention, particularly those portions which referred to another world. Bruno Bauer went even further by denying the historical existence of Jesus. Using the Hegelian method of identifying God and the world, these radical writers shattered the literal interpretation of the language of the Gospels and considered its only value to lie in its pictorial power, not in its truth. The inevitable drift of Hegelianism was to identify God with humanity, since humanity, among all things in Nature, embodies the element of Spirit or Mind in a unique way. It was then only another step, which Hegel had not taken, but which the young radicals, among them Marx, did take, to the position of philosophical atheism.

What began to take shape in Marx's mind from his exposure to Hegelianism was (1) the notion that there is only one reality, and this can be discovered as the embodiment of rationality in the world; (2) the recognition that history is a process of development and change from less to more perfect forms in all of reality, including physical nature, social and political life, and human thought; and (3) the assumption that the thoughts and behavior of people at any given time and place are caused by the operation in them of an identical spirit or mind, the spirit of the particular time or epoch. Although these were the general themes which Hegelianism seemed to be engendering in Marx's mind, other influences moved into his thought, causing him to reject portions of Hegel's philosophy and to reinterpret these three themes of Hegelianism accordingly. In particular, the appearance of Ludwig Feuerbach's writings, shortly after Marx had finished his doctoral dissertation, had a decisive effect upon the young radical Hegelians and especially upon Marx.

Feuerbach seemed to take the Hegelian viewpoint to its extreme conclusion and thereby criticized the very foundation of Hegelianism itself. He did this by rejecting Hegel's idealism, substituting instead the view that the basic reality is material. In short, Feuerbach had revived philosophical materialism, and Karl Marx instantly saw in this view a far more useful assumption than Hegel's idealism for explaining human thought and behavior. Whereas Hegel saw the thought and behavior of a particular epoch as the working in all people of an identical spirit, Feuerbach now contended that, on the contrary, the generating influence of thoughts was the total sum of the material circumstances of any historic time.

Feuerbach's view had the effect of inverting the Hegelian assumption of the primacy of Spirit and Idea, substituting for it the primacy of the material order. One finds this "inversion" developed with particular force in the *Essence of Christianity*, in which Feuerbach argued that it is humanity and not God that is the basic reality. When our ideas of God are analyzed, said Feuerbach, we find that apart from human feelings and wants there are no ideas of God. All so-called knowledge of God, he said, is humanity's knowledge about itself. God, therefore, is humanity. That is, the Spirit or our ideas of God—these are simply reflections of the modes of human existence. God is the product of human thought and not the other way around. In this way, Feuerbach had inverted Hegel's idealism, and the resulting materialism struck fire in Marx's mind, providing him with one of the most decisive and characteristic elements in his own philosophy.

Marx now acknowledged that Feuerbach was the pivotal figure in philosophy. Most important of all, Feuerbach had shifted from God to humanity the focal point of historic development. That is, whereas Hegelian thought said that it was Spirit or Idea that was progressively realizing itself in history, Feuerbach said that it is really humanity that is struggling to realize itself. Humanity, and not God, was in some way alienated from itself, and history has to do with humanity's struggle to overcome self-alienation. Clearly, if this was in fact the condition of humanity, Marx thought, the world should be changed in order to facilitate human self-realization. This is what led Marx to say that hitherto "the philosophers have only *interpreted* the world differently: the point is, however, to *change* it." Marx had grounded his thought in two major insights, Hegel's dialectic view of history and Feuerbach's emphasis on the primacy of the material order. Now he was ready to forge these ideas into a full-scale instrument of social analysis and, most important of all, to embark upon a vigorous and practical program of action.

At the age of twenty-five, Marx left Berlin and went to Paris, where he and some friends undertook the publication of the radical periodical *Deutsch-Französiche Jahrbücher*. In Paris, Marx met many radical revolutionaries and utopian thinkers and confronted the ideas of such people as Fourier, Proudhon, Saint-Simon, and Bakunin. Of lasting significance was his meeting with Friedrich Engels, the son of a German textile manufacturer, with whom Marx was to have a long and intimate association. Apart from his progressively deeper involvement in practical social action through his journalism, Marx was greatly preoccupied in Paris with the question of why the French Revolution had failed. He wanted to know whether it was possible to discover any reliable laws of history in order to avoid mistakes in the future in revolutionary activity. He read extensively on this subject and discovered several promising answers, being particularly impressed by Saint-Simon's account of class conflict, which led Marx to focus upon the classes not only as the parties to conflict but also as the bearers of the material and economic realities in which their lives are set. What Marx began to see was that revolutions do not succeed if they consist only in romantic ideas while overlooking the realities of the material order. But it was only a year after he arrived in Paris that Marx was expelled from the city, and for the next three years, from 1845 to 1848, Marx and his family settled in Brussels. Here he helped to organize a German Worker's Union, which in 1847, at a meeting in London, united with several other similar groups in Europe to form an international Communist League, whose first secretary was Engels. By this group Marx was asked to formulate a statement of principles, a statement that appeared in 1848, shortly before the Paris revolution, as *The*

Manifesto of the Communist Party. From Brussels he returned to Paris briefly to participate in some revolutionary activities and was again required to leave, and this time, in the autumn of 1849, he went to London, where he would spend the rest of his life.

England at this time was in no sense ripe for revolutionary activities, since there was no widespread organization of the mass of workers. Marx himself became an isolated figure, prodigiously studying and writing. Each day he went to the reading room of the British Museum, working there from nine in the morning until seven at night with additional hours of work after he returned to his bleak two-room apartment in the cheap Soho district of London. While his poverty was deeply humiliating, he was driven with such single-mindedness to produce his massive books that he could not deviate from this objective to provide his family with more adequate facilities. In addition to his poverty, he was afflicted with a liver ailment and, like Job, was plagued with boils. In this environment his six-year-old son died, and his beautiful wife's health failed. Some financial help came from Engels and from his writing regular articles on European affairs for the *New York Daily Tribune.* Under these incredible circumstances, Marx produced many notable works, including his first systematic work on economics, which he called the *Critique of Political Economy* (1859) and his massive *Das Kapital,* whose first volume he published in 1867 and whose second and third volumes were assembled from his manuscripts after his death and published by Engels in 1885 and 1894. Although Marx supplied the theoretical basis for the Communist movement, he participated less and less in the practical activities he had urged. Still, he had a lively hope that the great revolution would come and that his prediction of the downfall of capitalism would become a fact. But in the last decade of his life, as his name became famous around the world, he became less productive. Two years after his wife died and only two months after his eldest daughter's death, Karl Marx died in London on March 14, 1883, of pleurisy at the age of sixty-five.

Marx often protested that he was not a "Marxist," and not every idea or every strategy utilized by world communism can rightly be ascribed to him. There is, nevertheless, a central core of thought, which constitutes the essence of Marxist philosophy and which Karl Marx had formulated in the highly charged intellectual atmosphere of the mid–nineteenth-century Europe of which he was a part. This core of Marxist thought consists in the analysis of three basic elements, namely (1) the major epochs of history, (2) the causal power of the material order, and (3) the source and role of ideas. This analysis was meant not only to uncover what each of these three elements means but more importantly to show how they are related to each other.

THE EPOCHS OF HISTORY: MARX'S DIALECTIC

Already in his *Communist Manifesto,* Marx had formulated his basic doctrine, which he considered in many ways original. "What I did that was new," he said, "was to prove (1) that the *existence of classes* is only bound up with par-

Karl Marx *(The Granger Collection)*

ticular historic phases in the development of production; (2) that the class struggle necessarily leads to the dictatorship of the proletariat; (3) that the dictatorship itself only constitutes the transition to the *abolition of all classes* and to a classless society." Later, while in London, he worked out in painstaking detail his argument, which he thought provided scientific support for the more general pronouncements in his *Manifesto*. Accordingly, he stated in the preface to *Das Kapital*, that "it is the ultimate aim of this work, to lay bare the economic law of motion of modern society." This law of motion became his theory of dialectical materialism.

The Five Epochs   Marx indicated that the class struggle is bound up with "particular historic phases." He distinguished five such phases, dividing history into five separate epochs. These he called (1) the primitive communal, (2) slave, (3) feudal, (4) capitalist, and, as a prediction of things to come, (5) the socialist and communist phases. For the most part, this was a more or less conventional division of Western social history into its major periods. But what Marx wanted to do was to discover the "law of motion," which could explain not only *that* history had produced these various epochs but the *reasons why* these particular epochs unfolded as they did. If he could discover history's law of motion, he could not only explain the past but predict the future. He had assumed that the behavior of individuals and societies is subject to the same kind of analysis as are the objects of physical and biological science. He considered the commodity and value products of economics as being "of the same order as those [minute elements] dealt with in microscopic anatomy." When he analyzed the structure of each historic epoch, he either imposed upon it or abstracted from it the fact of class conflict as the decisive force at work. In time, this conflict itself would have to be analyzed in more detail. Now he looked upon history as the product of conflict and relied heavily upon the Hegelian concept of *dialectic* to explain it. He, of course, had rejected Hegel's idealism but had accepted the general theory of the dialectic movement of history, which Hegel had proposed. Hegel had argued that ideas develop in a dialectic way, through the action and reaction of thought, describing this dialectic process as a movement from *thesis* to *antithesis* and then to *synthesis*, where the synthesis becomes a new thesis and the process goes on and on. In addition, Hegel had said that the external social, political, and economic world is simply the embodiment of men's (and God's) ideas. The development or the movement of the external world is the result of the prior development of ideas. Marx, again, considered Hegel's notion of dialectic a most important tool for understanding history, but, through the powerful influence of Feuerbach, Marx supplied a materialistic basis for the dialectic. Accordingly, Marx said that "my dialectic method is not only different from the Hegelian, but is its direct opposite. To Hegel, the process of thinking...is the [creator] of the real world...with me, on the contrary, the ideal is nothing else than the material world reflected by the human mind, and translated into forms of thought." History, according to Marx, was to be seen therefore as a movement caused by conflicts in the material order, and for this reason history is a *dialectical materialism*.

Change: Quantitative and Qualitative   What history shows is that social and economic orders are in a process of change. The effect of Marx's dialectical materialism was to show, also, that since the material order is primary, since it is the basis of what is truly real, there are no stable fixed points in reality because everything is involved in the dialectic process of change. With this view, Marx had rejected the notion that somewhere there are stable, permanent structures of reality or certain "eternal verities." Materialism meant to Marx that the world as we see it is all there is, that the materialist outlook on the world "is simply the conception of nature as it is, without any reservations." Moreover, with Engels, he agreed that all of nature, "from the smallest thing to the biggest, from a grain of sand to the sun...to man, is in...a ceaseless state of movement and change." History is the process of change from one epoch to another in accordance with the rigorous and inexorable laws of historical motion.

For Marx, change was not the same as mere growth. A society does not simply mature the way a boy becomes a man. Nor does nature simply move in an eternally uniform and constantly repeated circle. It passes through a real history. Change means the emergence of new structures, novel forms. What causes change is simply the *quantitative* alteration of things, which leads to something *qualitatively* new. For example, as one increases the temperature of water, it not only becomes warmer, but finally reaches the point at which this quantitative change changes it from a liquid into a vapor. Reversing the process, by gradually decreasing the temperature of water, one finally changes it from a liquid to a solid, to ice. Similarly, a large pane of glass can be made to vibrate, the range of the vibrations increasing as the quantity of force applied to it is increased. But finally, a further addition of force will no longer add to the quantity of vibration but will, instead, cause a qualitative change, the shattering of the glass. Marx thought that history displays this kind of change by which certain quantitative elements in the economic order finally force a qualitative change in the arrangements of society. This is the process that has moved history from the primitive communal to the slave, and in turn to the feudal and capitalist epochs. Indeed, Marx's prediction that the capitalist order would fall was based upon this notion that the changes in the quantitative factors in capitalism would inevitably destroy capitalism. With the low-key expression of one who was describing how water will turn into steam as the heat is increased, Marx wrote in *Das Kapital* that "while there is a progressive diminution in the number of capitalist magnates, there is of course a corresponding increase in the mass of poverty, enslavement, degeneration and exploitation, but at the same time a steady intensification of the role of the working class." Then "the centralization of the means of production and the socialization of labor reach a point where they prove incompatible with their capitalist husk. This bursts asunder. The knell of private property sounds. The expropriators are expropriated." This, on the social level, is what Marx describes as the *quantitative leap*, which is "the leap to a new aggregate state...where consequently quantity is transformed into quality."

Determinism or Inexorable Law   There is a basic difference between the transformation of water into steam as a laboratory experiment and the movement of society from feudalism to capitalism and finally from capitalism to socialism. The difference is that one can *choose* to raise or not to raise the temperature of the water. But there are no such hypothetical qualifications surrounding history. Though one can say "*if* the temperature is raised," he cannot say "*if* the social order is thus and so." Marxism holds that there *is* a fundamental "contradiction within the very essence of things" causing the dialectic movement, and though there are ways of delaying or accelerating this inner movement in the nature of things, there is no way to prevent its ultimate unfolding. All things are related to each other *causally*; nothing floats freely. For this reason there are no isolated events either in physical nature or in human behavior or, therefore, in history. That there is a definite and inexorable process of movement and change at work producing "history" is as certain as the plain fact that nature exists.

This scientific notion that all things behave in accordance with a principle of regularity and predictability, according to "the laws of science," requires that Marxism make some careful distinctions. The laws of physics, for example, describe "mechanical determinism." History, on the other hand, displays a law of determinism but not in a strictly mechanical way. The movement of one billiard ball by another is the typical example of the mechanical mode of determinism. If one can locate an object in space and measure its distance from another object whose velocity can also be measured, it would then be possible to predict the time of the impact and the subsequent trajectories and rates of motion. This mechanical determinism is hardly applicable to such a complex phenomenon as a social order, which does not have the same kind of location in space and time. But society is nevertheless the result of necessary causation and determinism, and its new forms are capable of prediction just as the submicroscopic particles are determined in quantum mechanics, even though there is only "probable" prediction regarding particular particles. Thus, although the specific history of a particular person could not be predicted with any high degree of accuracy, the future state of a social order can be plotted. On the basis, therefore, of his analysis of the various epochs of history, Marx thought he had discovered the built-in law of change in nature, a kind of inexorable inner logic in events, causing history to move from one epoch to the next with a relentless determinism. From this basis, he predicted that capitalism would inevitably fall and would be transformed by the wave of the future, giving way to the qualitatively different social order of socialism and communism.

The End of History   For Marx, history would end with the emergence of socialism and, finally, communism. Here again, he followed Hegel's theory in an inverted way. For Hegel, the dialectic process comes to an end when the Idea of freedom is perfectly realized, for by definition this would mean the end of all conflict and struggle. Marx, on the other hand, seeing that the dialectic, or struggle of opposites, is in the material order and therefore in the struggle between the classes, predicted that when the inner contradictions between the classes were resolved, the principle cause of movement and change would disappear, a classless society would emerge where all the forces and interests would be in perfect balance, and this equilibrium would be perpetual. For this reason there could be no further development in history, inasmuch as there would no longer be any conflict to impel history on to any future epoch.

Marx's theory of the dialectic development of the five epochs of history rested upon the distinction between the order of material reality, on the one hand, and the order of human thought on the other. He was convinced that the only way to achieve a realistic understanding of history, and therefore to avoid errors in the practical program of revolutionary activity, was to assess properly the roles of the material order and the order of human thought. Accordingly, Marx made a sharp distinction between the *substructure* and the *superstructure* of society. The *substructure* is the material order, containing the energizing force that moves history, whereas the *superstructure* consists in people's ideas and simply reflects the configurations of the material order.

THE SUBSTRUCTURE: THE MATERIAL ORDER

To Marx, materialism meant the sum total of the natural environment, and this included for him all of inorganic nature, the organic world, social life, and human consciousness. Unlike Democritus, who defined matter in terms of irreducible tiny particles, atoms, Marx defines matter as "objective reality existing outside the human mind." Again, unlike Democritus, who considered the atoms as the "bricks of the universe," Marxist materialism did not take this approach of trying to discover a single form of matter in all things. The chief characteristic of Marxist materialism is that it recognizes a wide diversity in the material world without reducing it to any one form of matter. The material order contains everything in the natural world that exists outside our minds; the notion that any spiritual reality, God, for example, exists outside our minds and as something other than nature is denied. That human beings possess minds means only that organic matter has developed to the point where the cerebral cortex has become the organ capable of the intricate process of reflex action called human thought. Moreover, the human mind has been conditioned by the labor activity of humans as social beings. For this reason, relying upon the Darwinian notion of human evolution, Marxism affirms the primacy of the material order and regards mental activity as a secondary by-product of matter. The earliest forms of life were without mental activity until human ancestors developed the use of their forelimbs, learned to walk erect, and began to use natural objects as tools to procure food and to protect themselves against harm. The big transformation from animal to human being came with the ability to fashion and use tools and to control such forces as fire, which, in turn, made possible a wider variety of food and the further development of the brain. Even now, the complex material order is the basic reality, whereas the mental realm is derivative from it. In particular, the material order consists of (1) the *factors* of production and (2) the *relations* of production.

The Factors of Production   The basic fact of human life is that in order to live, people must secure food, clothing, and shelter; and in order to have these material things, people must produce them. Wherever we find any society of people, there is always at hand the factors of production, the raw materials, instruments as well as the experienced labor skill, by which things are produced to sustain life. But these factors or forces of production represent chiefly the way people are related to these material things. Of greater importance is the way people are related to each other in the process of production. What Marx wanted to emphasize was that production always takes place as a social act, where people struggle against and utilize nature not as individuals but as groups, as societies. The static analysis of what goes into production was for Marx, therefore, not as important as the dynamic relations of people to each other as a producing society. To be sure, the factors of production were seen by Marx as affecting the relations of production, inasmuch as such circumstances as the scarcity of raw materials or the ownership by some of the instruments of production could have a considerable effect upon the way people would become related to each other in the process of production. In any case, Marx centered his analysis of the material order upon the way people engaged in the act of production, upon the *relations of production*.

The Relations of Production   Marx considered his analysis of the relations of production to be virtually the core of his social analysis. It was here that he thought he had located the energizing force of the dialectic process. The key to the relations of production was the status of property or its ownership; that is, what determined how people were related to each other in the process of production was their relation to property. Under the slave system, for example, the slave owner owned the means of production, even owning the slave, whom he could purchase or sell. The institution of slavery was a necessary product of the dialectic process, since it arose at a time when advanced forms of tools made possible more stable and sustained agricultural activity and a division of labor. But in the slave epoch, as well as in the subsequent historical epochs, the laborer, slave or hired, is "exploited" in that the laborer shares in neither the ownership nor in the fruits of production. The basic struggle between the classes is seen already in the slave system, for the ownership of property divides the society between those who have and those who have not. In the feudal system, the feudal lord owns the means of production: The serf rises above the level of the former slaves, has some share in the ownership of tools, but still works for the feudal lord and, says Marx, feels exploited and struggles against his exploiter. In capitalism, the workers are free as compared with the slaves and the serfs, but they do not own the means of production, and in order to survive, they must sell their labor to the capitalist.

The shift from slave to feudal to capitalist relations of production is not the result of rational design but a product of the inner movement and logic of the material order. Specifically, the impelling force to survive leads to the creation of tools, and, in turn, the kinds of tools created affect the way people become related to each other. Thus, whereas certain tools, such as the bow and arrow, permit independent existence, the plough, on the other hand, logically implies a division of labor. Similarly, whereas a spinning wheel can be used in the home or in small shops, heavier machinery requires large factories and a new concentration of workers in a given locality. Such is the survey Marx makes of the unfolding of the epochs of history, emphasizing that this process moves in a deterministic way, impelled by basic economic drives whose direction is set by the technological requirements of the moment. The thoughts and behavior of all people are determined by their relations to each other and to the means of production. Although in all periods there is a conflict and struggle between the different classes, the class struggle is particularly violent under capitalism.

There are at least three characteristics of the class struggle under capitalism. First, the classes have been reduced basically to two, the owners, or the *bourgeoisie,* and the workers, or the *proletariat.* Secondly, the relations of those classes to each other rest upon a fundamental contradiction, namely, that although both classes participate in the act of production, the mode of distribution of the fruits of production does not correspond to the contribution made by each class. The reason for this discrepancy is that the price of labor in the capitalist system is determined by the forces of supply and demand, and the large supply of workers tends to send wages down to a subsistence level. But the products created by labor can be sold for more than it costs to hire the labor force. Marx's analysis assumed the labor theory of value, that the value of the product is created by the amount of labor put into it. From this point of view, since the product of labor could be sold for more than the cost of labor, the capitalist would then reap the difference, which Marx called *surplus value.* The existence of surplus value constituted the contradiction in the capitalistic system for Marx. For this reason, Marx argued that in the capitalistic system exploitation was not merely an isolated occurrence here or there, now or then, but always and everywhere, because of the manner in which the iron law of wages operates. Still, Marx made no moral judgment of this condition, saying that as a matter of fact the worker received what he was worth if the determination of the wage through the supply and demand of labor is the norm. "It is true," he said, "that the daily maintenance of labor power costs only half a day's labor, and that nevertheless the labor power can work for an entire working day, with the result that the value which its use creates during a working day is twice the value of a day's labor power. So much the better for the purchaser, but it is nowise an injustice to the seller [worker]."

In a sense, Marx did not "blame" the capitalist for this arrangement any more than he would attribute to him the organization of the laborers into a self-conscious and powerful group. These are rather the consequences of the material forces of history, which have determined the existence of these arrangements. Labor became a coherent group only because large-scale machinery required large factories, and suddenly the multitude of workers who were required to run the machines found themselves living close together. That history had produced the capitalist system was one thing, but that it rested upon a contradiction was something else. For this reason, Marx "excused" the capitalist but argued that for "scientific reasons" he must say that the class conflict caused by this contradiction of surplus value would force the dialectic movement to the next stage in history, namely, socialism and finally communism.

The third characteristic of this class struggle was the prediction that the condition of the workers in capitalism would become progressively more wretched, that the poor would become poorer and more numerous while the rich would become richer and fewer, until the masses would take over all the means of production. As a matter of historic fact, Marx could not have been more wrong than he was at this point, since it is precisely the workers whose condition has improved most dramatically in the highly developed capitalistic economies. Still, Marx argued that as long as the means of production remained in the hands of a few, the class struggle would continue inexorably until the contradiction was resolved, ending the dialectic movement. Meanwhile, the workers' lives would be terribly dehumanized by what Marx calls "the alienation of labor."

THE ALIENATION OF LABOR

While still in his twenties, Marx produced a brief series of manuscripts called the *Economic and Philosophical Manuscripts of 1844,* first published in 1932. The key concept of these manuscripts is that of *alienation,* a theme which moves throughout the whole system of Marx's thought. Although Marx was by no means the first to develop a theory of alienation, his views on this theme were unique because they were based upon his particular economic and philosophical assumptions, which formed the basis of his criticism of capitalism.

If people are alienated, that is, estranged or separated, they must be alienated from something. As early as biblical times, people were seen as alienated from God through "the fall." In a legal sense, alienation means selling or giving something away, or as Kant says, "the transference of one's property to someone else is its alienation." In the course of time almost everything became a saleable object. Kant spoke of the process by which a person could be used as a thing, while Balzac said ironically that "even the Holy Spirit has its quotation on the Stock Exchange." Rousseau insisted upon some severe limits to alienation. He held that although upon entering the Social Contract there is "the total alienation of each associate... to the whole community," Rousseau held that people cannot alienate their freedom. In addition, Rousseau decried the dehumanizing effect upon people of certain social values, of "civilization," saying that social corruption has introduced "from outside" various vices "alien to man's constitution" and destructive of the "original goodness of man." For Marx there is something about people that is essential to their nature and from which they can be alienated. What is novel about Marx's concept of alienation is the manner in which he identifies the causes of the alienation of labor within capitalism.

Marx calls attention to four aspects of alienation, saying that people are alienated (1) from *nature,* (2) from *themselves,* (3) from their *species-being,* and (4) from *other people.* He begins with the fundamental relation of workers to the product of their labor. Originally, people's relation to the product of their labor is identical with their relation to the *sensuous external world,* to the objects of nature. This relation to nature is intimate because a person lives from inorganic nature, for as Marx says, "nature is his *body* with which he must remain in continuous interchange in order not to die." To say that a person's relation, both physical and mental, is intimately related to nature, to the objects of nature, means that nature is interdependent with itself, because humanity is a part of nature. This intimate relation between people and nature, between people's activity and the objects of nature, is the "right" relationship between people and the objects of nature. Workers are not capable of creating without nature, that is, without the sensual external world. That world is the material into which they invest their labor, through which they produce things, and without which they cannot live. But in capitalism this relationship is broken, people are alienated from nature, from the products of their activity or work.

The contemporary economic fact is, says Marx, that the object produced by labor now stands as an "alien being" to the worker. Human labor is embodied in an object and is turned into a physical thing; this product is an "objectification of labor." The objectification of labor represents a loss to the worker as well as "servitude to the object." In short, it is the alienation of the worker from what he or she produces. Moreover, in the productive process, a person's labor becomes as much an object as the physical material being worked upon, since labor is now bought and sold. The more objects the worker produces, the fewer he or she can personally possess and therefore the greater is his or her loss. This follows from the fact that workers are related to the product of their labor as to an alien object. What is embodied, "objectified," in the product, part of themselves, their labor, is no longer their own. "The worker," says Marx, "puts his life into the object, and his life then belongs no longer to himself but to the object." And the object is appropriated, owned, by someone else. In this way, the original relation between humanity and nature is destroyed through the alienation from people of the products of their labor.

People are alienated not only from the products of their labor but also from themselves through the *process* of production. The nature of labor's productive activity results in people's self-alienation. This comes about because work is *external* to, that is, not part of the nature of, the workers. Work is not voluntary but is imposed upon them; they have a feeling of misery instead of well-being; rather than fulfilling themselves, they must deny themselves; they do not freely develop their physical and mental capacities but are instead physically exhausted and mentally debased. As a consequence, workers feel like human beings only during their leisure hours. Most important of all, workers are alienated from their work because it is not their own work but rather work for someone else. In this sense, workers do not belong to themselves but to someone else. The result is that "man [the worker] feels himself to be freely active only in his animal functions—eating, drinking and procreating—or at most also in his dwelling and personal adornment—while in his human functions he is reduced to an animal." Although eating, drinking, and procreating are genuine human functions, they become animal functions when separated, alienated, from other human functions.

At still another level, people are alienated from their *species-being*, from their truly human nature. The character of any species resides in the type of life activity it expresses. The species-character of human beings is "free, conscious activity." By contrast, an animal cannot distinguish itself from its activity. The animal *is* its activity. But, says Marx, "man makes his life activity itself an object of his will and consciousness." It is true that animals can produce nests and dwellings, as in the case of bees, ants, and beavers. But their production of these things is limited to what is strictly required for themselves or their young. Humanity, on the other hand, produces universally, that is, in a manner that is applicable and understandable to all human beings. Also, whereas animals produce only under the compulsion of specific physical need, people produce their most distinctive products only when they are free from physical need. Animals reproduce only themselves, whereas people can produce a whole world, a world of art, of science and literature. Animals are limited in their activity to the standards of the species to which they belong. Humanity, on the other hand, knows how to produce in accordance with the standards of every species. For these reasons, the whole object of people's labor is to objectify, that is, impose upon the world of nature, their species-life, their free, spontaneous, and creative activity. In this way people reproduce themselves in the things they create not only intellectually, in the realm of ideas, but also actively, seeing their own reflection in the world which they have created. This unique character of human species-life is lost when labor is alienated. Just as the object of labor is no longer theirs, so also are they shorn of their free and spontaneous activity and creativity. Their consciousness is now deflected from creativity and is transferred into simply a means to their individual existence. Thus alienated labor turns the species-life of people into an alien being and alienates their mental life and their human life.

Inevitably the alienation of people from the product of their labor, from their productive or life activity and from their species-life—all this leads to alienation from other people. The breakdown in people's relation to their fellow human beings is similar to the alienation of people from the objects of their labor. In an environment of alienated labor all people look upon other people from the point of view of workers who see other workers as objects whose labor is bought and sold, and not as full members of the human species. To say, then, that people's species nature is alienated or estranged from them means that "each man is estranged from the other, as each of them is from man's essential nature."

Marx asks, "if the product of labor is alien to me...to whom does it belong?" In an earlier age, when temples were built in Egypt and India, it was thought that the product belonged to the gods. But, says Marx, the alienated product of labor can belong only to people themselves. If it does not belong to the worker, it must belong to a person other than the worker. Thus, as a result of alienated labor the worker produces a new relationship between another person and labor, this other person being the capitalist. The final product of alienated labor is private property. Private property is both a product of alienated labor and also the means by which labor is alienated. In the wage system entailed by private property labor finds itself not as an end but as the servant of wages. Nor would a forced increase in wages restore to either the workers or to their work their human significance or value. As a statement of eventual redemption, Marx concludes that the emancipation of society from private property involves the emancipation of the workers which in turn will lead to the emancipation of humanity as a whole.

The general matter-of-fact tone of Marx's analysis of capitalism is in sharp contrast to the shrill voice of world communism. Marx was himself capable on occasion of the severest denunciation of the conditions of the capitalism to which he was exposed. He was convinced, moreover, that the dialectic process inevitably involves tragic conflicts, wars, and revolutions. He saw in history the deep tension between forces that are, in the last analysis, incompatible, each exerting its power to overcome the other. The use of revolutionary force could hardly be avoided, but force could not bring into being simply any desired utopian system. Only the relations of production toward which the inner logic of the material order was driving in a determined way could be the objective of revolution. Even when a society is aware of the so-called "natural laws of its movement," this society, says Marx, "can neither clear by bold leaps, nor remove by legal enactments, the obstacles offered by the successive phases of its normal development." What, then, is the function of the revolutionary activities of the working classes? It is, says Marx, to "shorten and lessen the birth-pangs."

With this rigorous view of the nature of the class struggle, Marx had clearly assigned to the substructure, to the material order, the supreme significance in the dialectic process of history. What, then, is the status and role of human thought? Do ideas have power and consequences? For Marx, ideas represented a mere reflection of the basic material reality, and for this reason, he described the enterprise of human thought as the *superstructure*.

THE SUPERSTRUCTURE: THE ORIGIN AND ROLE OF IDEAS

Each epoch, said Marx, has its dominant ideas. People formulate ideas in the areas of religion, morality, and law. Hegel had argued that people agreed for the most part in their religious, moral, and juristic thought because there was at work in them a universal Spirit, the Idea. Marx, on the contrary, said that the ideas of each epoch grow out of and reflect the actual material conditions of the historic period. For this reason, thinking comes *after* the material order has affected people's minds. Thus, Marx accounted for the relationship between people's conscious life and their material environment by saying that "it is not the consciousness of men that determines their being, but, on the contrary, their social being that determines their consciousness."

The source of ideas is rooted in the material order. Such ideas as justice and goodness and even religious salvation, says Marx, are only various modes of rationalizing the existing order. Justice, for the most part, represents the will of the economically dominant class and its desire to "freeze" the relations of production as they are. Marx had been impressed during his early years as a law student with the teachings of the jurist Savigny, who had defined law as the "spirit" of each epoch. Savigny argued that law is like language and is therefore different for each society. Like Savigny, but now for different reasons, Marx rejected the notion of a universal and eternal norm of justice. Indeed, he thought it followed with logical rigor that if ideas simply reflect the inner order of the relations of production, each successive epoch will have its own set of ideas, its own dominant philosophy.

The conflict of ideas within a society at a given time is due to the dynamic nature of the economic order. The dialectic process, which is a struggle of opposites, has its material aspect but also its ideological side. Since members of a society are related to the dialectic process by belonging to different classes, their interests are different, and therefore their ideas are opposed. Moreover, the greatest error, according to Marx, is to fail to realize that ideas that accurately reflected the material order at an earlier time no longer do so because, in the meantime, the substructure of reality has moved on. Those who hold on to old ideas do not realize that there is no longer any reality corresponding to them, and their desire to reverse the order of things to fit these ideas makes them "reactionaries." On the other hand, an astute observer can discover the direction in which history is moving and will adjust his thinking and behavior to it. The fact is, says Marx, that the dialectic process involves the disappearance of some things and the birth of new things; that is why one epoch dies and another is born, and there is no way to stop the process. Those who assume the objective reality of "eternal principles" of justice, goodness, and righteousness do not realize that such notions cannot refer to reality since the material order, which is the only reality, is constantly changing. "The sum total of the productive relations," says Marx, "constitutes the economic structure of society—the real foundation on which rise legal and political superstructures... [and which] determines the general character of the social, political and spiritual processes of life."

Because he believed that ideas were chiefly a reflection of the material order, Marx attributed a limited role or function to them. Ideas are particularly useless when they bear no relationship to the economic reality. Marx's impatience with reformers, do-gooders, and utopians was intense. He argued that ideas cannot determine the direction of history, that they can only hinder or accelerate the inexorable dialectic. For this reason, Marx thought that his own ideas about capitalism did not constitute a moral condemnation. He did not say that capitalism was either wicked or due to human folly; it was caused by the "law of motion of society." In the end, Marx assumed that he was proceeding in his analysis as a scientist, limiting his thought to objective reality, abstracting from it the laws of motion.

Almost every aspect of Marx's thought raises serious critical questions. He was, for one thing, apparently unaware that at the time he was writing *Das Kapital* the nature of English capitalism was undergoing modifications. His scientific style was not adequately supported with empirical observations. Marx clearly expressed a metaphysical belief in the existence of a predetermined goal for all history. His theory of knowledge solved some problems but created new ones, particularly the problem of accounting for the diversity of ideas and of erroneous ideas. If ideas reflected reality, reality and thought would have to correspond. But how does one account for the emergence of utopian thought? Moreover, to say that force is a necessary element of revolution showed that Marx had not understood how a society could move through self-criticism and change, and even revolution, without physical violence. What did come as a genuine contribution from Marx was his insight that the economic order is capable of creating an ideology whereby some are led to believe that the *status quo* rests upon eternal and immutable principles. His insistence upon self-reflection to discover the subtle disguise of self-interest was an important aspect of social analysis. Still, it is a matter of fascination that Marxism as a philosophy should have spread chiefly among underdeveloped peoples rather than in the advanced capitalist states where, presumably, it was supposed to have its greatest relevance.

22

Nietzsche

Friedrich Nietzsche died on August 25, 1900, at the age of fifty-five, leaving a legacy of brilliant writings whose impact and influence were delayed until the twentieth century. His life was full of sharp contrasts. The son and grandson of Lutheran ministers, he was nevertheless the herald of the judgment that "God is dead" and undertook a "campaign against morality." He was nurtured in an environment thoroughly dominated by females yet advocated the most masculine philosophy of the superman. He called for the fullest expression of human vitality in the name of the Will to Power, and yet believed that sublimation and control are the truly human characteristics. His writings rank among the most lucid ever written, yet he ended his days in hopeless insanity.

Named after the reigning King of Prussia, Friedrich Wilhelm Nietzsche was born in Röcken, in the province of Saxony, on October 15, 1844. His father died when he was four years old, and he grew up in a household consisting of his mother, sister, grandmother, and two maiden aunts. At age fourteen he was sent to the famed boarding school at Pforta, where for six years he underwent rigorous intellectual discipline, excelling particularly in the classics, reli-

Friedrich Nietzsche *(The Bettmann Archive)*

gion, and German literature. It was here that he came under the spell of the Greek genius, discovering it especially in Aeschylus and Plato. In October of 1864 he went to the University of Bonn but stayed only one year as he was unimpressed by the caliber of his fellow students and decided to follow his excellent teacher of classics and philology, Friedrich Ritschl, who was invited to accept a chair at the University of Leipzig. While at Leipzig he came upon the main work of Schopenhauer, whose atheism and antirationalism deeply influenced Nietzsche for a while and confirmed his own revolt against contemporary European culture, which he had come to despise as decadent. It was here also that Nietzsche came under the spell of Wagner's music. "I could not have stood my youth without Wagner's music," Nietzsche said later. "When one wants to rid oneself of an intolerable pressure, one needs hashish. Well, I needed Wagner."

When the University of Basel was looking for someone to fill the chair of philosophy, Nietzsche's name figured prominently. He had not yet completed his doctor's degree, but some of his published papers had attracted notice for their exceptional scholarship. On the additional strength of his teacher Ritschl's enthusiastic recommendation, Nietzsche was appointed a university professor at the age of twenty-four. After the University of Basel confirmed his appointment, the University of Leipzig conferred the doctor's degree upon Nietzsche without examination. In May, 1869, he delivered his inaugural lecture on *Homer and Classical Philology.* During his years at Basel, Nietzsche visited Richard Wagner frequently at his villa on Lake Lucerne. While this friendship was not destined to last, Wagner did exert an influence upon Nietzsche's thought in his first book (1872), *The Birth of Tragedy from the Spirit of Music.* Of longer duration was Nietzsche's friendship with his older colleague Jacob Burckhardt, the eminent historian, with whom he shared a common fascination for ancient Greece and Renaissance Italy. Nietzsche's wretched health and his dislike of his duties at the university led him to resign his professorship in 1879 at the age of thirty-four. For the next decade, he wandered through Italy, Switzerland, and Germany searching for some place where his health might be restored. In spite of his poor health, he wrote several books during the six-year period 1881–1887 including *The Dawn of Day, Joyful Wisdom,* the famous *Thus Spake Zarathustra, Beyond Good and Evil,* and *A Genealogy of Morals.*

In 1888, when he was forty-four, Nietzsche felt a brief period of respite from his prolonged cycle of sickness and recovery and during a span of six months produced with incredible speed five books, among which are to be found some of his best, *The Case Wagner, The Twilight of the Idols, Antichrist, Ecce Homo,* and *Nietzsche contra Wagner.* Shortly thereafter, in January, 1889, Nietzsche collapsed on a street in Turin. He was taken back to Basel to a clinic from which he was sent to an asylum in Jena and finally to the care of his mother and sister. For the last eleven years of his life, Nietzsche was irretrievably insane as a result of an infection that affected his brain. He was thus unable to complete his projected major work, the *Revaluation of All Values.* Nietzsche's books have great vivacity of style and are written with a passionate intensity; even though some of his later works show signs of impending difficulties, it is generally agreed that his writings cannot be discounted because of his subsequent mental collapse.

"GOD IS DEAD"

Nietzsche wrote philosophy in a manner calculated more to provoke serious thought than to give formal answers to questions. In this regard he resembled Socrates and Plato more than Spinoza, Kant, or Hegel. He produced no formal system because system building, he thought, assumes that one has at hand self-evident truths upon which to build. It was his conviction that building a system is to lack integrity, since honest thought must challenge precisely these self-evident truths upon which most systems are built. One must engage in dialectic and be willing at all times to declare himself against his previous opinions. Moreover, most philosophic system builders, he thought, try to solve all problems at once by acting as the "unriddler of the universe." Nietzsche believed that the philosopher must be less pretentious, pay more attention to questions of human values than to abstract systems, and concern himself with immediate human problems with an attitude of fresh experimentation and a freedom from the dominant values of his culture. Because he took a variety of positions on important problems, it was inevitable that Nietzsche's ideas should be interpreted in contradictory ways. Moreover, he expressed his views on issues with brief aphorisms instead of detailed analyses, leaving the impression of ambiguity and ambivalence. Still, Nietzsche formulated many distinctive views, which emerge from his writings with considerable clarity.

While others saw in nineteenth-century Europe the symbols of power and security, Nietzsche grasped with prophetic insight the imminent collapse of the traditional supports of the values to which modern men had committed themselves. The Prussian army had made Germany a great power on the Continent, and the mood of optimism was further animated by the astonishing advances of science and technology, yet Nietzsche boldly prophesied that power politics and vicious wars were in store for the future. What he sensed was an approaching period of *nihilism,* the seeds of which had already been sown. The greatest fact for him was neither the military power of Germany nor the unfolding advances of science but rather the incontrovertible fact that belief in the Christian God had drastically declined to the point where he could say that "God is dead."

Although Nietzsche was by temperament an atheist, he contemplated the "death" of God with mixed reactions. He was appalled at the consequences that would follow once everyone had become fully aware of all the implications of the death of God, a cultural event that he said has not yet become apparent to modern humanity. Contemplating simultaneously the collapse of religious faith and the mounting belief in the Darwinian notion of a relentless evolution of the species, he could see in this combination the destruction of any basic distinction between human and animal. If this is what people will be asked to believe, he said, then nobody should be surprised if, in the arena of the future, there will be wars such as have never been seen on earth. At the same time, the death of God meant for Nietzsche the opening of a new day, a day when the essentially life-denying ethics of Christianity could be replaced with a life-affirming philosophy. "At last," he said, "the sea, *our* sea, lies open before us. Perhaps there has never been so open a sea." His ambivalent reaction to the nihilistic consequences of the death of God turned Nietzsche's mind to the central question of human values. In his search for a new foundation for values in a day when God could no longer be the goal and sanction of human conduct, Nietzsche turned to the aesthetic dimension of human nature as the most promising alternative to religion. Only as an aesthetic phenomenon, he said, are existence and the world eternally justified. It was the Greek genius, he believed, that had originally discovered the true meaning and mode of human endeavor. He initially drew his fundamental insights about people from the Greek conceptions of Apollo and Dionysus.

APOLLONIAN VERSUS DIONYSIAN

What concerned Nietzsche at first was whether in light of the encircling nihilism it was inevitable that people must become pessimistic about life and therefore renounce it, as Schopenhauer did, or whether there was some reason neverthe-less for affirming life, as one of Nietzsche's idols, Goethe, had done in his ca-reer. Nietzsche found in Homer's account of Apollo and Dionysus that the birth of tragedy, that is, the emergence of art and the fullest development of the aes-thetic element in humanity, is the result of a fusion between the two principles that these gods respectively represent and embody. Dionysus was for Nietzsche the symbol of the dynamic stream of life, which knows no restraints or barriers and defies all limitations. In the worship of Dionysus, the individual would lapse into a drunken frenzy and thereby lose his own identity in the larger ocean of life. Apollo, on the other hand, was the symbol of order, restraint, and form, the power to create beauty through art. If the Dionysian mood was best expressed in the feeling of abandonment in some types of music, the Apollonian form-giving force found its highest expression, according to Nietzsche, in Greek sculpture. Thus Dionysus symbolized humanity's unity with life where individuality is ab-sorbed in the larger reality of the life force, whereas Apollo was the symbol of the "principle of individuation," that power that controls and restrains the dy-namic processes of life in order to create a formed work of art or a controlled personal character. From another point of view, the Dionysian represents the negative and destructive dark powers of the soul, which culminate, when un-checked, in "that disgusting mixture of voluptuousness and cruelty" typical of "the most savage beasts of nature." Again, the Apollonian represents the power to deal with the powerful surge of vital energy, to harness destructive powers, and to transmute these into a creative act.

Greek tragedy, according to Nietzsche, is a great work of art. It repre-sents the conquest of Dionysus by Apollo. But from this account Nietzsche drew the conclusion that people are not faced with a choice between the Dionysian and the Apollonian. To assume even that one has such a choice to make is to misunderstand the true nature of the human condition. The fact is that human life inevitably includes the dark and surging forces of passion. What Greek tragedy illustrates, according to Nietzsche, is that instead of abandon-ing oneself to the flood of impulse, instinct, and passion, the awareness of these driving forces becomes the occasion for producing a work of art, whether in one's own character through moderation or in literature or the plastic arts through the imposition of form upon a resisting material. Nietzsche saw the birth of tragedy or the creation of art as a response of the basically healthy element in a person, the Apollonian, to the challenge of the diseased frenzy of the Dionysian. In this view, art could not occur without the stimulus of the Dionysian; at the same time, if the Dionysian were considered either the only element in human nature or the dominant element, one might very well despair and come finally to a negative attitude toward life. But for Nietzsche, the su-preme achievement of human nature occurred in Greek culture where the Dionysian and Apollonian elements were brought together. To deny, as nineteenth-century culture seemed to do, that the Dionysian element had a right-ful place in life was to postpone, as Nietzsche saw, to some later date the in-evitable explosion of vital forces, which cannot be permanently denied expres-sion. To ask whether life should dominate knowledge or knowledge dominate

Dionysus, symbol of the power of dynamic passions, whose devotees drank the fruit of the vine and engaged in sensuous and frenzied dance *(Hirmer Fotoarchiv, Munich)*

life is to provoke the question which of these two is the higher and more decisive power. There is no doubt, said Nietzsche, that life is the higher and dominating power, but raw vital power is finally life-defeating. For this reason, Nietzsche looked to the Greek formula, the fusion of the Dionysian and Apollonian elements, by which human life is transformed into an aesthetic phenomenon. Such a formula, thought Nietzsche, could provide modern culture with a relevant and workable standard of behavior at a time when religious faith was unable to provide a compelling vision of human destiny. What disqualified religious faith, in Nietzsche's mind, was the essentially life-denying negativeness of the Christian ethics.

MASTER MORALITY VERSUS SLAVE MORALITY AND THE WILL TO POWER

Nietzsche rejected the notion that there is a universal and absolute system of morality that everyone must equally obey. People are different, he thought, and to conceive of morality in universal terms is to disregard basic differences between individuals. It is unrealistic to assume that there is only one kind of human nature, whose direction can be prescribed by one set of rules. There is,

Apollo and His Chariot with the Hours by John Singer Sargent, symbol of restraint, order, and rational control of the powerful passions *(Museum of Fine Arts, Boston)*

however, one thing that does characterize all human beings, says Nietzsche, and that is the drive to dominate the environment. This drive, so central to human nature, is the *Will to Power.* This Will to Power is more than simply the will to survive. It is, rather, an inner drive to express a vigorous affirmation of all of a person's powers. As Nietzsche says, "the strongest and highest Will to Life does not find expression in a miserable struggle for existence, but in a Will to War. A Will to Power, a Will to Overpower!" Whenever someone proposes a universal moral rule, he or she invariably seeks really to deny the fullest expression of people's elemental vital energies. In this respect, Christianity, along with Judaism, is the worst offender, for the Judeo-Christian ethics is so contrary to people's basic nature that its antinatural morality debilitates humanity and produces only "botched and bungled" lives.

How did human beings ever produce such unnatural systems of morality? There is, says Nietzsche, a "twofold early history of good and evil," which shows the development of two primary types of morality, namely, the *master morality* and the *slave morality.* In the *master morality, good* has always meant "noble" in the sense of "with a soul of high calibre," and *evil* meant "vulgar" or "plebeian." Noble people regard themselves as the creators and determiners of values. They do not look outside of themselves for any approval of their acts. They pass judgment upon themselves. Their morality is one of self-glorification. These noble individuals act out of a feeling of power, which seeks to overflow. They may help the unfortunate, but not out of pity, rather from an impulse generated by an abundance of power. They honor power in all its forms and take pleasure in subjecting themselves to rigor and toughness and have reverence for all that is severe and hard. By contrast, the *slave morality* originates with the lowest elements of society, the abused, the oppressed, the slaves, and those who are uncertain of themselves. For the slave, "good" is the symbol for all those qualities that serve to alleviate the existence of sufferers, such as "sympathy, the kind helping hand, the warm heart, patience, diligence, humility and friendliness...." This slave morality, says Nietzsche, is essentially the morality of utility, where goodness refers to whatever is beneficial to those who are weak and powerless. Whereas for the slave morality the person who arouses fear is "evil," according to the master morality it is precisely the "good" person who is able to arouse fear.

The challenge to the master morality resulted from a deep-seated *resentment* on the part of the "slaves," a resentment, says Nietzsche, "experienced by creatures who, deprived as they are of the proper outlet of action, are forced to find their compensation in an imaginary revenge." This revenge took the form of translating the virtues of the noble aristocrat into evils. Nietzsche's great protest against the dominant Western morality was that it exalted the mediocre values of the "herd," which "knows nothing of the fine impulses of great accumulations of strength, as something high, or possibly as the standard of all things." Incredibly, the "herd mentality" in time overcame the master morality by succeeding in making all the noble qualities appear to be vices and all the weak qualities appear to be virtues. The positive affirmation of life in the master morality was made to seem "evil" and something for which one should have a sense of "guilt." The fact is, says Nietzsche, that "men with a still natural nature, barbarians in every terrible sense of the word, men of prey, still in possession of unbroken strength of will and desire for power, threw themselves upon weaker, more moral, more peaceful races.... At the commencement, the noble caste was always the barbarian caste: their superiority did not consist first of all in their physical, but in their psychical power—they were *complete* men." But the power of the master race was broken by the undermining of its psychic strength. Against the natural impulse to exert aggressive strength, the weak races had erected elaborate psychic defenses. New values, new ideals, such as peace and equality, were put forward under the guise of "the fundamental principle of society." This, said Nietzsche, was a not-so-subtle desire on the part of the weak to undermine the power of the strong. The weak have created a negative psychic attitude toward the most natural drives of humanity. This slave morality is, says Nietzsche, "a Will to the *denial* of life, a principle of dissolution and decay." But a skillful psychological analysis of the herd's resentment and its desire to exact revenge against the strong will show, says Nietzsche, what must be done, namely, that one must "resist all sentimental weakness: life is essentially appropriation, injury, conquest of the strange and weak, suppression, severity, obtrusion of peculiar forms... and at the least, putting it mildest, exploitation...." Nietzsche wanted particularly to emphasize that "exploitation" is not some depraved act, that it does not belong to an imperfect or primitive society. It belongs, he said, "to the nature of the living being as a primary function." Exploitation is, he said, "a consequence of the intrinsic Will to Power, which is precisely the Will to Life—a *fundamental fact* of all history...." Come now, he said, "let us be so far honest toward ourselves!"

European morality, by denying the primacy of the Will to Power, was basically dishonest, in Nietzsche's view. He assigned primary responsibility for this dishonest morality to Judaism and Christianity. With utter directness, he said that "I regard Christianity as the most fatal and seductive lie that has ever yet existed—as the greatest and most *impious lie*." He was appalled that Europe should be subjected to the morality of that small group of wretched outcasts who clustered around Jesus. Imagine, he said, "the *morality of paltry people* as the measure of all things...." This he considered "the most repugnant kind of degeneracy that civilization has ever brought into existence." Worse yet was the fact that New Testament ethics is still hanging, under the name of "God," over people's heads. To Nietzsche it was incredible that in the New Testament "the least qualified people... have their say in its pages in regard to the greatest problems of existence." With what impudent levity "the most unwieldy problems are spoken of here (life, the world, God, the purpose of life) as if they were not problems at all, but the most simple things which these little bigots know all about!!!" Christianity contradicts nature when it requires us to love our enemies, for Nature's injunction is to *hate* your enemy. Moreover, the natural origin of morality is denied by requiring that before a person can love anything, he or she must first love God. To inject God into a person's affections, said Nietzsche, is to subvert the immediate, natural moral standard of the affirmation of life. All the vital energies of the strong are diluted by routing a person's thinking toward God. Again, this is the revenge that the resentment of the weak has engendered. Among people there is always a surplus of "dejective, diseased, degenerating, infirm, and necessarily suffering individuals." These are the "failures," which the Judeo-Christian religions seek to keep alive and preserve. Nietzsche was willing to admit that the "spiritual men" of Christianity had rendered invaluable services to Europe by offering comfort and courage to the suffering. But at what price was Christian charity achieved? asked Nietzsche. The price, he said, was "the deterioration of the European race." It was necessary "to *reverse* all estimates of value—*that* is what they had to do! And to shatter the strong, to spoil great hopes, to cast suspicion on the delight in beauty, to break down everything autonomous, manly, conquering, and imperious." In addition, all instincts that are natural to the full "men" had to be transmuted into "uncertainty, distress of conscience, and self-destruction." Christianity succeeded in inverting "all love of the earthly and of supremacy over the earth into hatred of the earth and earthly things...."

Nietzsche was willing for the weak and the herd to have their own morality, provided that they did not impose it upon the higher ranks of humanity. Why should people of great creative powers be reduced to the common level of mediocrity characteristic of the herd? When Nietzsche spoke of rising "beyond good and evil," he had in mind simply rising above the dominant herd morality of his day. He envisioned a new day, when once again the truly complete person would achieve new levels of creative activity and thereby become a higher type of person. This new person will not reject morality; he or she will reject only the negative morality of the herd. Again, Nietzsche argued that the morality based upon the Will to Power is only an honest version of what the slave morality has carefully disguised. If the superman is "cruel," said Nietzsche, one must recognize that, actually, almost everything that we now call "higher culture" is simply a spiritualized intensification of cruelty. "This is my thesis," he said, that "the 'wild beast' has not been slain at all, it lives, it flourishes, it has only been—transfigured." He refers to the Romans' pleasures in the arena, the Christian ecstasy of the cross, the Spaniards' delight at the gory sight of the bullfight, the Parisian workman's homesickness for a bloody revolution, and the Wagnerienne who "with unhinged will" *undergoes* a performance of *Tristan und Isolde*. "What all these enjoy and strive with mysterious ardour to drink in," said Nietzsche, "is the philtre of the great Circe 'cruelty.'" Looked at from the vantage point of the master morality, the word *cruelty* refers simply to the basic Will to Power, which is a natural expression of strength. People are differentiated into ranks, and it is, he says, "quanta of power, and nothing else, which determine and distinguish ranks." For this reason, such ideals as equality among people are nonsensical. There can be no equality where there are in fact different quanta of power. Equality can only mean the leveling downward of everyone to the mediocrity of the herd. Nietzsche wanted to preserve the natural distinction between the two ranks or types of people, namely, between that "type which represents ascending life and a type which represents decadence, decomposition, weakness." To be sure, a higher culture will always require as its basis a strongly consolidated mediocre herd, but only to make possible the development and emergence of the higher type of man, the "superman." If the superman is to emerge, he must go beyond good and evil as conceived by the lower ranks of men.

REVALUATION OF ALL MORALS

What would Nietzsche want to put in the place of the traditional morality, which he believed was clearly dying? His positive prescriptions are not so clear as his critical analysis. Much of the content of his new values can, however, be inferred from his rejection of the slave morality. If the slave morality originated in resentment and revenge, there must again occur a *revaluation* of all values. By *revaluation* Nietzsche did not intend the creation of a new table of moral values. He meant rather to declare war upon the presently accepted values, as Socrates, "applying the knife vivisectionally to the very virtues of the time...." Since traditional morality is a perversion of original natural morality, *revaluation* must consist in rejecting traditional morality in the name of honesty and accuracy. Revaluation implies, said Nietzsche, that all the "stronger motives are still extant, but that now they appear under false names and false valuations, and have not yet become conscious of themselves." It is not necessary to legislate new values but only to reverse values once again. Just as "Christianity was a revaluation of all the values of antiquity," so today the dominant morality must be rejected in favor of people's original and deepest nature. Thus Nietzsche's program of *revaluation* was essentially a critical analysis of modern human ideals. He showed that what modern man called "good" was not at all virtuous, that his so-called truth was disguised selfishness and weakness, and that his religion was a skillful creation of psychological weapons with which moral pygmies domesticated natural giants. Once the disguise is removed from modern morality, he thought, the true values will emerge.

Moral values must in the last analysis be built upon the true nature of humanity and its environment. Unlike Darwin, who laid great stress upon external circumstances when describing the evolution of the species, Nietzsche focused upon the internal power within an individual, which is capable of shaping and creating events, "a power which *uses* and *exploits* the environment." Nietzsche's grand hypothesis was that everywhere and in everything the Will to Power is seeking to express itself. "This world," he says, "is the Will to Power—and nothing else." Life itself is a plurality of forces, "a lasting form of processes of assertions of force...." People's psychological makeup shows that their preoccupation with pleasure and pain reflects a striving after an increase of power. Pain can be the spur for exerting power to overcome an obstacle, whereas pleasure can represent a feeling of increased power.

THE SUPERMAN

The Will to Power has its greatest relevance for Nietzsche's philosophy in his notion of the *superman.* We have already seen that Nietzsche rejected the concept of equality. He also indicated that morality must suit each rank of humanity. Even after the *revaluation* of all values, the "common herd" will not be intellectually capable of reaching the heights of the "free spirits." There can, in short, be no "common good." Great things, says Nietzsche, remain for the great, "everything rare for the rare." The superman will be rare, but he is the next stage in human evolution. History is moving not toward some abstract developed "humanity" but toward the emergence of some exceptional men: "*Superman* is the goal," says Nietzsche. But the superman will not be the product of a mechanical process of evolution. Only when superior individuals have the courage to revalue all values and respond with freedom to their internal Will to Power can the next stage be reached. "Man is something to be surpassed," and it is the superman who represents the highest level of development and expression of physical, intellectual, and emotional strength. The superman will be the truly free man for whom nothing is forbidden except what obstructs the Will to Power. He will be the very embodiment of the spontaneous affirmation of life.

Nietzsche did not contemplate that his superman would be a tyrant. To be sure, there would be much of the Dionysian element in him. But his passions would be controlled and his animal nature harmonized with his intellect, giving style to his behavior. Such a superman is not to be confused with a totalitarian bully. Nietzsche had in mind as a model his hero Goethe, suggesting also as an ideal "the Roman Caesar with Christ's soul." As Nietzsche's thought matured, his ideal man would have to possess a balanced unity of the Dionysian and Apollonian elements. Earlier, when his thought was influenced by Wagner and Schopenhauer, Nietzsche had criticized Socrates for having caused Western humanity to take a wrong turn in history, the turn toward rationality. Even at the end, Nietzsche believed that knowledge and rationality must be used in the service of life and that life must not be sacrificed for knowledge. Still, Socrates was important historically precisely because he saved people from self-destruction, which would have occurred if, says Nietzsche, "this whole incalculable sum of energy [in human striving was] *not* employed in the service of knowledge...." The lust for life, he says, would then have led to wars of annihilation. The Dionysian element by itself leads to pessimism and destruction. That it was necessary to harness people's vital energies already suggested a basic decadent tendency in people, which could be halted only by the kind of influence Socrates represented. But while the Apollonian element could subvert the vital streams of life, Nietzsche did not see how, in the end, life could be lived without its form-giving guidance. Socrates became important for Nietzsche precisely because this ancient philosopher was the first to see the proper relation between thought and life. Socrates recognized, said Nietzsche, that thought serves life, while for previous philosophers life served thought and knowledge. Here, then, was Nietzsche's ideal: the passionate person who has passions under control.

23

Two Twentieth-Century Metaphysicians: Bergson and Whitehead

J ust when modern science was reaching its most impressive heights of achievement, two bold speculative philosophers called into question the basic assumptions of the scientific mode of thought. Neither Bergson nor Whitehead wished to deny that the scientific method had given people considerable control over nature and to that extent was a brilliantly successful enterprise. What concerned them primarily was a philosophical question, namely, whether reality, the basic nature of things, was what science assumed it to be. As late as the second half of the nineteenth century, and the early decades of the twentieth, the major assumption of science was that nature consists of material objects located in space. Matter, it was held, is the final irreducible stuff out of which all things are formed. The model for thinking about the contents and behavior of nature was the model of a machine. All the particular things in nature were thought to be parts of a large mechanism. This meant that the behavior of each part could in time be described with mathematical exactness, since material objects moved in space in accordance with precise rules or laws. Moreover, as parts of a mechanism, things were related to each other in a tight sequence of cause and effect. Human nature was also viewed in these material and mechanical terms. As parts of a tightly organized cosmic machine, people were no longer thought of as being "free," as possessing freedom of the will.

Each of these assumptions raised serious philosophical problems for Bergson and Whitehead. They wondered whether nature really does consist of inert material objects located in space and whether the intellect is capable of discovering "out there" such an orderly and mechanical arrangement of things as the logical and mathematical reasoning of science portrays. How, moreover, can there be any genuine novelty in nature if the basic reality is material and its various parts organized in a tight mechanism? Can a world made of material things ever become anything more than these same objects simply rearranged from time to time? How, in short, can inert matter overcome its static status and "evolve"? How can the concrete experience of life be explained in terms of a lifeless nature? And how can human freedom be explained in a thoroughly mechanical universe? Science itself had recently been developing new concepts, as, for example, the theory of evolution, which made the mechanical model of nature less and less plausible.

Whitehead pointed out that late in the nineteenth century, the "men of science were quite unaware that the ideas they were introducing, one after the other, were finally to accumulate into a body of thought inconsistent with the Newtonian ideas dominating their thoughts and shaping their modes of expression." Whitehead moved, as it were, from within science to his metaphysics, drawing out many of the implications of the emerging new physics. Similarly, Bergson had no intention of rejecting science but thought, rather, that metaphysics and science could enrich each other. His view was that "philosophy ought then to follow science, in order to superpose on scientific truth a knowledge of another kind, which may be called metaphysical. Thus combined, all our knowledge, both scientific and metaphysical, is heightened." What Bergson and Whitehead did challenge in science, however, was the assumption that the scientific mode of thought could be the sole comprehensive source of knowledge. Accordingly, they sought to show just what the limits of science are and what unique insights could be provided by metaphysics.

BERGSON

Henri Bergson was born in Paris in 1859, the brilliant son of a Polish father and an English mother. This same year saw the publication of Darwin's *On the Origin of Species by Means of Natural Selection* and the birth of John Dewey. Bergson's rise in the academic world was rapid. At the age of twenty-two he became professor of philosophy at the Angers Lycée, and by 1900 he was appointed to the distinguished chair of modern philosophy at the Collège de France. With uncommon lucidity and a captivating style, Bergson wrote a series of works that won wide attention and stimulated considerable discussion, including *Time and Free Will* (1889), *Matter and Memory* (1897), *An Introduction to Meta-*

Henri Bergson *(New York Public Library Picture Collection)*

physics (1903), *Creative Evolution* (1907), and *The Two Sources of Morality and Religion* (1932). These last three works gained particular fame and contain his most distinctive ideas. Their publication assured him of a worldwide reputation and attracted people from many countries to hear his lectures in Paris, where he lived until his death in 1941 at the age of eighty-two.

Analysis versus Intuition   At the center of Bergson's philosophy is his conviction that there are "two profoundly different ways of knowing a thing." The first way, he says, "implies that we move around the object," and the second, that "we enter into it." Knowledge derived in the first way depends upon the vantage point from which we observe an object, and therefore this mode of knowledge will be different for each observer and, on that account, *relative.* Moreover, knowledge derived by observation is expressed in symbols, where the symbol used can refer not only to this specific object but to any and all similar objects. The second kind of knowledge, however, is *absolute,* says Bergson, because in this case, by "entering" the object, we overcome the limitations of any particular perspective and grasp the object as it really is.

The Way of Analysis　Bergson illustrates these two modes of knowing with several examples. First, there is the example of the movement of an object in space. My observation of this object, he says, will vary with the point of view, moving or stationary, from which I observe it. When I try to describe this motion, my expression of it will vary with the points of reference to which I relate it. Both in observing and describing the moving object, I am placed outside of it. In describing the object's motion, I think of a line that is divided into units and express this through the symbol of a graph with its axes, a series of points through which the object is thought to move. By contrast to this attempt to plot and chart movement in terms of discrete units of space, there is, says Bergson, the true movement, a continuous flow, where there are in reality no points being crossed. Suppose, says Bergson, that you were inside the object as it moved. You would then know the object as it really is and moves and not only as translated into the symbolic language of points and units of distances, for "what I experience will depend neither on the point of view I may take up in regard to the object, since I am inside the object itself, nor on the symbols by which I may translate the motion, since I have rejected all translations in order to possess the original." Instead of trying to grasp the movement from where I stand, from my static position, I must try to grasp the object's motion from where *it* is, from within, as the motion is in the object itself. When people raise their arms, they have a simple and single perception of the movement they have created; they have an "absolute" knowledge of this movement. But, says Bergson, for me, "watching it from the outside, your arm passes through one point, then through another, and between these points there will be still other points.... Viewed from the inside, then, an absolute is a simple thing; but looked at from the outside, that is to say, relatively to other things, it becomes, in relation to these signs which express it, the gold coin for which we never seem able to finish giving small change."

The case is the same when we take a character in a novel. The author takes great pains to describe his or her traits and to make the character engage in action and dialogue. But, says Bergson, "all this can never be equivalent to the simple and indivisible feeling which I should experience if I were able for an instant to identify myself with the person of the hero himself." The reason why descriptive traits do not help me know this particular hero is that such traits are merely symbols, "which can make him known to me only by so many comparisons with persons or things I know already." Such symbols take me outside of him, and "they give me only what he has in common with others and not what belongs to him alone." It is not possible, says Bergson, to perceive what constitutes a person's "essence" from without, because by definition his essence is internal and therefore cannot be expressed by symbols. Description and analysis require the use of symbols, but symbols are always "imperfect in comparison with the object of which a view has been taken, or which the symbols seek to express." Not all the photographs of Paris, taken from every conceivable point of view, and not even motion pictures, would ever be equivalent to the solid Paris in which we live and move. Not all the translations of a poem could render the inner meaning of the original. In every example, there is the original, which we can know absolutely only by entering into it, compared with the "translation," or copy, which we know only relatively, depending upon our vantage point and the symbols we use for expression.

What, more precisely, does it mean to "go around" an object and to "enter into it"? To go around an object is what Bergson means by that special activity of the intellect that he calls *analysis*. By contrast, to enter into an object is what is implied by his use of the term *intuition*. By intuition, Bergson means "the kind of *intellectual sympathy* by which one places oneself within an object in order to coincide with what is unique in it and consequently inexpressible." The basic contrast between science and metaphysics turns upon the difference between *analysis* and *intuition*.

Bergson contended that in the end scientific reasoning, insofar as it is based upon analysis, falsifies the nature of whatever object it analyzes. This follows, he said, from the fact that "analysis...is the operation which reduces the object to elements already known, that is, to elements common both to it and other objects." Therefore, "to analyze...is to express a thing as a function of something other than itself." To analyze a rose is to take it apart and discover its constituents. From such an analysis we do in fact derive knowledge of the rose, but in such a state of analysis, the rose is no longer the living thing it was in the garden. Similarly, the science of medicine discovers much knowledge of the human anatomy by dissecting it into parts.

In every case, says Bergson, the analytic intellect learns, ironically, by destroying the object's essence. Its essence is its dynamic, thriving, pulsing, living, continuing existence—its *duration*. Analysis, however, interrupts this essential duration; it *stops* life and movement; it separates into several independent and static parts what in true life is a unified, organic, and dynamic reality.

The language of analytic science tends, moreover, to exaggerate even further this static and disjointed conception of things through its use of symbols. Each new object is described by science by using as many symbols as there are ways of looking at a thing. And the content of each such perception is, says Bergson, *abstracted*, that is, drawn or lifted out from the object. Thus, the intellect forms a series of concepts about a thing, "cutting out of reality according to the lines that must be followed in order to act conveniently upon it." Since we think in terms of our language, that is, in terms of single concepts, we tend to analyze things into as many concepts as there are ways of looking at, moving around, an object. This is, says Bergson, the ordinary function of scientific analysis, namely, to work with symbols. Even the sciences concerned with life "confine themselves to the visible form of living beings, their organs and anatomical elements. They make comparisons between these forms, they reduce the more complex to the more simple; in short, they study the workings of life in what is, so to speak, only its visual symbol." There seem to be, says Bergson, a "symmetry, concord and agreement" between our intellect and matter, as though our intellect were made to analyze and utilize matter. Indeed, he says, "our intelligence is the prolongation of our senses"; even before there was either science or philosophy, "the role of intelligence was already that of manufacturing instruments and guiding the action of our body on surrounding bodies." If, then, the intellect has been made to utilize matter, "its structure has no doubt been modelled upon that of matter." But it is precisely for this reason that the intellect has a limited function; its very structure and function fit it for analysis, for separating what is unified into its parts. Even when it comes to the study of the most concrete reality, namely, the *self*, the intellect, proceeding analytically, is never capable of discovering the true self. As all other sciences, psychology analyzes the self into separate "states" such as sensations, feelings, and ideas, which it studies separately. To study the self by studying separately the various psychical states is, says Bergson, like trying to know Paris by studying various sketches, all of which are labelled *Paris*. The psychologists claim to find the "ego" in the various psychical states, not realizing that "this diversity of states has itself only been obtained...by transporting oneself outside the ego altogether...." And "however much they place the states side by side, multiplying points of contact and exploring the intervals, the ego always escapes them...."

The Way of Intuition   But there is another way, says Bergson, of knowing the self, and that is by *intuition*. As he says, "there is one reality, at least, which we all seize from within, by intuition and not by simple analysis. It is our own personality through time—our self which endures." As Descartes, Bergson founded his philosophy upon the immediate knowledge of the self. But whereas Descartes built a system of rationalism upon his self-knowledge, Bergson set forth the method of intuition, which was in sharp contrast to rationalism. Intuition, Bergson argued, is a kind of intellectual sympathy. It enables one's consciousness to become identified with an object; intuition "signifies ...immediate consciousness, a vision which is scarcely distinguishable from the object seen, a knowledge which is contact or even coincidence." Most important of all, says Bergson, "to think intuitively is to think in *duration*." This is the difference between analytic and intuitive thought. Analysis begins with the static and reconstructs movement as best it can with immobilities in juxtaposition. By contrast, "intuition starts from movement, posits it, or rather perceives it as reality itself, and sees in immobility only an abstract moment, a snapshot taken by our mind...." Ordinarily, analytic thought pictures the new as a new arrangement of what already exists; although nothing is ever lost, neither is anything ever created. But "intuition, bound up to a duration which is growth, perceives in it an uninterrupted continuity of unforeseeable novelty; it sees, it knows that the mind draws from itself more than it has, that spirituality consists in just that, and that reality, impregnated with spirit, is creation." Intuition, then, discovers that the self is a duration, a continuous flux.

The inner life of the self is compared by Bergson to a continual rolling up, "like that of a thread on a ball, for our past follows us, it swells incessantly with the present that it picks up on its way; and consciousness means memory." An even better way of thinking about the self, he says, is to imagine an infinitely small elastic body, which is gradually drawn out in such a manner that from that original body comes a constantly lengthening line. While even this image is not satisfactory to him, Bergson does see in it an analogy to human personality in that the drawing out of the elastic body is a continuous action representing the duration of the ego, the pure mobility of the self. But whatever images are used to describe it, "the inner life is all this at once: variety of qualities, continuity of progress, and unity of direction. It cannot be represented by images.... No image can replace the intuition of duration."

Duration Bergson centered his attention upon the process in all things that he called *duration.* His criticism of classical schools of philosophy was that they failed to take duration, or becoming, seriously. For the most part, philosophers such as Plato, Descartes, and Kant sought to interpret the world through fixed structures of thought. This was particularly the case with Plato, whose notion of the Forms provides us with a static structure of reality. Even the empiricists, in spite of their preoccupation with experience, analyzed experience into static components, as in the case of Hume, who described knowledge in terms of individual "impressions." Neither the rationalists nor the empiricists, Bergson charged, took the matter of mobility, development, becoming, and duration seriously. Just how this metaphysical notion of duration could be employed in scientific knowledge Bergson did not make entirely clear. But he was certain that to "think in duration" is to have a true grasp of reality. Such thought also gives us a more accurate notion of *time,* real, continuous time, as compared with the "spatialized" time created by the intellect.

Only when we think of time and motion in such "spatialized" terms do we encounter the paradoxes Zeno spoke of. Zeno, it will be recalled, said that a flying arrow really does not move, because at each instant the arrow occupies a single point in space, which would mean that at each instant the arrow is at rest; otherwise, it would not occupy a given space at a given instant of time. Zeno's argument would be unassailable, says Bergson, if his assumption about space and time were correct. But he argues that Zeno was in error in assuming that there are real positions in space and discrete units of time; these so-called positions are, says Bergson, merely *suppositions* of the intellect, and the units of time are only the artificial segments into which the analytic intellect slices what in reality is a continuous flow. What Zeno's paradoxes show us is that it is impossible to construct mobility out of static positions or true time out of instants. Although the intellect is capable of comprehending static parts, it is incapable of grasping movement or duration. Only intuition can grasp duration. And reality is duration. Reality, says Bergson, does not consist of *things,* but only of "things in the making, not self-maintaining *states,* but only changing states...." Rest is only apparent, for all reality "is tendency, if we agree to mean by tendency an incipient change of direction."

The "Élan Vital"   Is not the doctrine of evolution an example of how science can successfully understand duration and becoming? After examining the major conceptions of evolution, Bergson concludes that none of these scientific theories are adequate and therefore offers a theory of his own. The particular inadequacy he found in the other theories was their inability to give a convincing account of how the transition is made through the gap that separates one level from a higher level. Darwin referred to variations among members of a species, and DeVries spoke of mutations as the conditions leading some members to possess variations favorable for survival. But neither Darwin nor DeVries explained how such variations in a species could occur; both of them inferred that either slowly or suddenly a change occurs, presumably in some part of the organism. This overlooks the functional unity of an organism, which requires that any variation in one part must be accompanied by variations throughout the organism. Just how this can occur neither Darwin nor DeVries explained, leaving unanswered the question of how there can be a continuity of function in spite of successive changes of form. The neo-Lamarckian theory attributed evolution to the special "effort" employed by certain organisms, causing them to develop capacities favorable to survival. But can such acquired characteristics be transmitted from one generation to the next? Bergson insisted that although "effort" had some promising implications, it was too haphazard a notion to explain the overall process of development. Nor was Spencer's theory of the transmission of acquired characteristics such as habits satisfactory, since, again, this seemed to Bergson to be an unsuccessful attempt to construct movement or evolution out of unchanging parts.

Evolution, said Bergson, is best explained in terms of a vital impulse, the *élan vital,* which drives all organisms toward constantly more complicated and higher modes of organization. The *élan vital* is the essential interior element of all living beings—and is the creative power that moves in unbroken continuity through all things. Since the intellect can grasp only static things, it is not capable of grasping the *élan vital,* because this is the essence of duration, of movement, and "all change, all movement, [is]...absolutely indivisible." Knowing, for Bergson, is a secondary activity; more basic, and therefore primary, is living. Intuition and consciousness, not analytic intellect, grasp this primary life and discover it to be a continuous and undivided process of which all things are expressions and not parts. All things are motivated by this *élan vital;* the *élan vital* is the fundamental reality. We discover it first through the immediate awareness of our own continuous self: we discover that we *endure.*

Here finally is where intuition must challenge intellect, for intellect by its natural function transforms, and thereby falsifies, movement into static states. The truth that intuition discovers about reality is that it is continuous, that it cannot be reduced to parts, and that the creative process caused by the *élan vital* is irreversible. "To get a notion of this irreducibility and irreversibility," says Bergson, "we must do violence to the mind, go counter to the natural bent of the intellect. But that is just the function of philosophy."

Whereas the intellect would describe evolution as a single, steady line moving upward through measurable levels, intuition suggests divergent tendencies at work. The vital impulse, says Bergson, moved in three discernible directions, producing vegetative beings, anthropods, and vertebrates (including, finally, humanity). Distinguishing intellect and intuition, he says that the emergence of intellect and matter occurred together, and these were intended to work together: "our intellect in the narrow sense of the word, is intended to secure the perfect fitting of our body to its environment, to represent the relations of external things among themselves—in short, to think matter." Moreover, "matter is weighted with geometry." But neither matter nor geometrical figures represent ultimate reality. The *élan vital* must itself resemble consciousness, from whence emerges life and all its creative possibilities. Evolution is creative precisely because the future is open, there is no preordained "final" goal; duration constantly endures, producing always genuinely novel events, like artists who never know precisely what they will create until they have created their work. Bergson finally refers to the creative effort of the *élan vital* as being "of God, if it is not God himself."

Morality and Religion There are, says Bergson, two sources of morality. The first is the sheer feeling of the necessity for solidarity, and to achieve such social solidarity, a society formulates certain rules of obligation. The second source lies in a deeper seat of feeling, which is touched by the example of great moral people whose emotional appeal transcends particular cultural groups. These two sources, the pressure of social necessity and the aspiration toward higher modes of life, reflect the differences between intellect and intuition. The intellect thinks in particular terms, directing specific rules to specific people to achieve specific ends. To this extent, the intellect tends to restrict morality to a closed society. Bergson was aware that the Stoics saw in reason a source of universal morality. Still, it takes intuition, a breadth of sympathy and feeling, to develop a morality that extends beyond a closed society. Moral progress occurs, says Bergson, only when mystics and saints, obscure heroes of moral life, appear, people who raise humanity to a new destiny, "who see in their mind's eye a new social atmosphere, an environment in which life would be more worth living...." Even when the intellect formulates laws for all people, the intuition opens up richer sources of emotional power, at once inducing aspiration and providing creative power to embrace new modes of life. Thus morality moves constantly from a consideration of the self and of one's society to the larger field of humanity.

The difference between intellect and intuition is reflected also in the two modes of religion, which Bergson calls *static* and *dynamic*. Since we find that all people are religious in one way or another, religion must be due to some inherent aspect of human structure. Moreover, since the intellect is formed to aid man in preserving his survival, the intellect must be the source of religion, inasmuch as religion presumes to answer certain basic demands of life. Religious concepts seek to provide security, confidence, and a defense against fear. But these concepts soon become institutionalized, are converted into belief to protect them against critical reason, are surrounded by ceremonies and disciplines, and tend to become embedded in the social structure. This is static religion, the religion of social conformity. Dynamic religion, on the other hand, is more in the nature of mysticism. Bergson's definition of *mysticism* follows closely his notion of intuition when he says that "the ultimate end of mysticism is the establishment of a contact, consequently of a partial coincidence, with the creative effort which life itself manifests." Just as intuition grasps reality more completely than intellect does, so does dynamic religion discover God more vividly. For, says Bergson, we must consider static religion "as the crystallization, brought about by a scientific process of cooling, of what mysticism had poured, white hot, into the soul of man."

WHITEHEAD

Whitehead reacted, as Bergson had, against the analytic mode of thought, which assumed that facts exist in isolation from other facts. His main theme was that "connectedness is the essence of all things." What science tends to separate, philosophy must try to see as an organic unity. Thus, "the red glow of the sunset should be as much a part of nature as are the molecules and electric waves by which men of science would explain the phenomenon." The function of natural philosophy, he thought, is "to analyze how these various elements of nature are connected." Describing Wordsworth's romantic reaction against the scientific mentality, Whitehead says that "Wordsworth was not bothered by any intellectual antagonism. What moved him was moral repulsion." He was repulsed by the fact that scientific analysis had left something out, "that what had been left out comprised everything that was most important," namely, moral intuitions and life itself. Whitehead, agreeing with Wordsworth, went on to say that "neither physical nature nor life can be understood unless we fuse them together as essential factors in the composition of really real things whose interconnections and individual characters constitute the universe." And, he says, "it is important therefore to ask what Wordsworth found in nature that failed to receive expression in science. I ask this question in the interest of science itself." Whitehead was convinced that "the status of life in nature...is the modern problem of philosophy and science." Although he shared these same problems with Bergson, Whitehead brought a different intellectual background to their solution and produced therefore a different and novel speculative metaphysics.

Alfred North Whitehead had three careers, two in England and one in America. Born in the village of Kent in 1861, he was educated at Sherborn School and at Trinity College in Cambridge. For twenty-five years he taught mathematics at Trinity. It was here, too, that Whitehead collaborated with Bertrand Russell on their famed *Principia Mathematica,* which went to press in 1910. From Trinity he moved to London, eventually becoming associated with the University of London as a member of its faculty of science and later as the dean of this faculty. During these thirteen years at London, he also developed a strong interest in the problems of higher education, being concerned particularly with the impact of modern industrial civilization upon the enterprise of learning. But his major writings while at London represented an attempt to replace Isaac Newton's concept of nature with his own empirically grounded theory. These works on the philosophy of science include his *Enquiry Concerning the Principles of Natural Science* (1919), *The Concept of Nature* (1920), and *The Principle of Relativity* (1922).

When Whitehead was sixty-three years old and nearing retirement, he was appointed professor of philosophy at Harvard and embarked upon the third and, in many ways, most important of his careers. To his achievements as a logician, mathematician, and philosopher of science he added his works as a metaphysician, writing at this time his *Science and the Modern World* (1925), *Process and Reality* (1929), and *Adventures of Ideas* (1933). What motivated Whitehead to write these books was his conviction that scientific knowledge had arrived at a point in its history that called for a new scheme of ideas to reflect more adequately the new developments in science. Since scientific thought always relies upon some scheme of ideas, he said, the importance of philosophy is to make such schemes explicit so that they can be criticized and improved. Though his chief speculative work, *Process and Reality,* is a massive and intricate statement, Whitehead acknowledges in the preface that "there remains the final reflection, how shallow, puny, and imperfect are efforts to sound the depths in the nature of things. In philosophical discussion, the merest hint of dogmatic certainty as to finality of statement is an exhibition of folly." His metaphysical writings combine, then, a bold and creative mind tempered with a sensitive humility. In 1937, Whitehead retired but continued to live near Harvard Yard until his death in 1947 at the age of eighty-seven.

The Error of Simple Location

Whitehead was convinced that Newtonian physics was based upon a fallacy, consisting in the doctrine of *simple location,* and he called it the *fallacy of misplaced concreteness.* Newton had followed Democritus in assuming that the nature of things consists of individual bits of matter existing in space. What is fallacious about that? Whitehead says that "to say that a bit of matter has *simple location* means that, in expressing its spatio-temporal relations, it is adequate to state that it is where it is in a definite region of space and throughout a definite duration of time, apart from any essential reference of the relations of that bit of matter to other regions of space and to other durations of time." Against this view, Whitehead argues that "among the primary elements of nature as apprehended in our immediate experience, there is no element whatsoever which possesses this character of simple location." The concept of an isolated atom, he says, is the product of intellectual *abstraction.* By a process of abstraction we can, he admits, "arrive at abstractions which are the simply-located bits of material...." But these abstractions, by definition, represent the lifting out of a thing from its concrete environment. To mistake the abstraction for the concrete is the error that Whitehead calls the *fallacy of misplaced concreteness.*

Such things as instants of time, points in space, or independent particles of matter are helpful concepts for scientific thought, but when they are taken as descriptions of ultimate reality, they are distortions of concrete reality.

When it came to giving his own account of concrete reality, Whitehead developed a novel form of atomism. He sought to draw out the implications of the recent developments in quantum physics, the theory of relativity, and evolution. His units of reality differed from the atoms of Democritus and Newton in two ways, namely, in their *content* and in their *relations* to each other. Whitehead discarded the word *atom* because historically this term meant that the content of the atom is hard, lifeless matter and that being hard, atoms never penetrate each other; hence their relations to each other are always external. For the term *atoms,* Whitehead therefore substituted the term *actual entities* or its equivalent *actual occasions.* Unlike lifeless atoms, Whitehead's actual entities are "chunks in the life of nature." As such, they never exist in isolation but are intimately related to the whole field of life that throbs around them. Whereas atomistic materialism gives us a mechanical view of nature, Whitehead's actual occasions permit us to view nature as a living *organism.* Thus, whether we speak of God or "the most trivial puff of existence," there is the same principle of life in all things, for "actual entities—also termed 'actual occasions'—are the final real things of which the world is made up."

Self-consciousness

Whitehead saw in our own self-consciousness a good example of an actual occasion. He felt that the "direct evidence as to the connectedness of [my] immediate present occasion of experience with [my] immediately past occasions, can be validly used to suggest...the connectedness of all occasions in nature." Because an actual occasion is not a material thing, it is best understood as an experience. These occasions do not exist, they happen. The difference is that merely to exist implies no change, whereas to happen suggests a dynamic alteration. Whitehead's actual occasions represent continually changing entities, this change coming about through the input of entities upon each other. Consider what occurs when a person has an experience. We usually think that in this case there is, on the one hand, a permanent subject and then something "out there" that the subject experiences. Whitehead argues that the subject and the object are both in a continual process of change, that every experience the subject has affects the subject. If it is true, as Heraclitus said, that one cannot step into the same river twice, it is also true that no person can think the same way twice, because after each experience he or she is a different person. And this is true of all of nature as it consists of actual occasions or aggregates of actual occasions. Thus, if all of reality is made up of actual occasions, drops of experience, nature is a throbbing organism undergoing constant change throughout. "The universe is thus a creative advance into novelty. The alternative to this doctrine is a static morphological universe."

The doctrine of actual occasions enabled Whitehead to account for the relation of body and mind and for the presence of feeling and purpose in the universe. Democritus had not satisfactorily described how it is possible to have sensation, feeling, thinking, purpose, and life in a universe consisting solely of lifeless material atoms. Nor could Descartes ever join together his two substances, thought and extension. Leibniz did recognize that from lifeless matter it was impossible to derive life, and so he described nature as consisting of monads, which, though they resembled the atoms of Democritus in some ways, were thought by Leibniz to be individual "souls," or centers of energy. Although the Leibnizian monad was a somewhat more satisfactory concept than the atom of Democritus, Whitehead considered it inadequate. Leibniz had described the monads as "windowless," meaning thereby that each monad was completely closed or locked up within itself, that its relation to other monads was purely external, that its behavior was determined by a preestablished harmony; and although the monad was thought to undergo change, this change did not signify any truly novel process, no evolution, no creativity, but only the running of its predetermined course. By contrast, Whitehead's actual entities have no permanent identity or history. They are always in the process of becoming. They feel the impact of other actual occasions and absorb them internally. In this process, actual occasions come into being, take on a determinate form or character, and, having become actual occasions, perish. To "perish" signifies that the creativity of the universe moves on to the next birth and that in this process an actual occasion loses its unique character but is preserved in the flow of the process. Perishing, says Whitehead, is what we mean by memory or causality, that with the passage of time something of the past is preserved in the present.

Prehension

We do not ever experience a single isolated actual entity but only aggregates of these entities; an aggregate of actual entities Whitehead calls either a *society* or a *nexus* (plural *nexūs*) in which the entities are united by their *prehensions*. These are some of the novel words Whitehead invented to explain his novel ideas. "In the three notions—actual entity, prehension, nexus—[says Whitehead] an endeavor has been made to base philosophical thought upon the most concrete elements in our experience.... The final facts are, all alike, actual entities; and these actual entities are drops of experience, complex and interdependent." Whitehead visualized reality as a continual process in which actual entities are constantly becoming, a process in which *what* an actual entity becomes depends upon *how* it becomes. His emphasis is upon the notion of *creativity* as the fundamental characteristic of the process of nature. Creativity is the ultimate principle by which the many enter into complex unity. If we took each actual entity separately, we should have a disjoined universe, but the creative unity of the many constitutes the conjoined universe. And "the production of novel togetherness," says Whitehead, "is the ultimate notion embodied in the term 'concrescence'...." But the meaning of the term *concrescence* is closely related to the activity that Whitehead calls *prehension*.

Whitehead uses the term *prehension* to describe how the elements of actual entities are related to each other and how these entities are further related to other entities. Nothing in the world is unrelated; in a sense, every actual occasion absorbs, or is related to, the whole universe. Actual entities are brought together by the creative process into sets, or societies, or nexūs. In this process of becoming, actual entities are formed through the concrescence of prehensions. Every prehension, says Whitehead, consists of three factors: first, the "subject" that is prehending; secondly, the "datum which is prehended"; and thirdly, the "subjective form," which is *how* the subject prehends the datum. There are various species of prehensions: *positive prehensions,* which are termed *feelings,* and *negative prehensions,* which are said to "eliminate from feeling." The subjective forms, or the ways data are prehended, are of many species, including emotions, valuations, purposes, and consciousness. Thus, for Whitehead, emotional feeling is the basic characteristic of concrete experience. Even in the language of physics it is appropriate, according to Whitehead, to speak of *feelings,* for *physical feelings* are the physicist's idea that energy is transferred. Both physical feelings and conceptual feelings are positive prehensions, or internal relations of the elements of actual entities.

The distinction between physical and conceptual feelings does not imply the older dualism of body and mind. It is of course still meaningful to use the terms *body* and *mind.* But Whitehead insists that to assume that these terms imply a basic metaphysical difference, as Descartes said existed between his terms *thought* and *extension,* is to commit again the fallacy of misplaced concreteness. This fallacy, it will be recalled, is committed when one mistakes an abstraction for the concrete. Both body and mind are, for Whitehead, societies, or nexūs—they are sets of actual entities. The only concrete reality is an actual entity, but actual entities can be organized into different kinds of societies, such as body and mind. But in each case, the actual entities possess the same characteristic, namely, the capacity for prehension, for feeling, for internal relations. Body and mind are both abstractions in the sense that their mode of existence, their reality, is dependent upon the peculiar organization of the actual entities; hence, body and mind are not permanently or ultimately different. To speak of the body as an abstraction is similar to speaking of the *body politic* as an abstraction where only the individual citizens are the concrete reality. Whitehead insisted that "The final facts are, all alike, actual entities," and all of these are capable of being interconnected in a stream of experience.

Eternal Objects

One might ask at this point just how Whitehead accounts for the underlying process of reality, the process of creativity, which brings actual entities into being and organizes them into societies and preserves what to our experience appears as the endurance of things. Here Whitehead's thought displays a strong Platonic influence. What makes an actual entity what it is, he says, is that the entity has been stamped with a definiteness of character by certain *eternal ob-jects*. These *eternal objects,* resembling Plato's Forms, are uncreated and eter-nal; they are patterns and qualities, such as roundness or squareness, green-ness or blueness, courage or cowardice. An actual occasion acquires a definite character and not other possible characters because it selects *these* eternal ob-jects and rejects *those*. Hence, an actual event is constituted by the together-ness of various eternal objects in some particular pattern.

Eternal objects, says Whitehead, are *possibilities,* which, like the Platonic Forms, retain their identity independent of the flux of things. The relation be-tween the eternal object and an actual entity is described as *ingression,* which means that once the actual entity has selected an eternal object, the latter *in-gresses,* that is, stamps its character upon the actual entity. Thus, "the func-tioning of an eternal object in the self-creation of an actual entity is the 'in-gression' of the eternal object in the actual entity." Simple eternal objects stamp their character upon actual entities, whereas complex eternal objects give def-initeness, or the status of fact, to societies or nexūs.

To speak of eternal objects as *possibilities* required that Whitehead de-scribe how and where these possibilities exist and how they become relevant to actual occasions. Since only actual occasions exist, what is the status of eternal objects? Whitehead designated one actual entity as being timeless, and this entity he called God. For him God is not a creator, he is "not *before* all creation, but *with* all creation." God's nature is to grasp conceptually all the possibilities that constitute the realm of eternal objects. This realm of eternal objects differs from Plato's system of Forms in that whereas Plato visualized one perfect order for all things, Whitehead's God grasps virtually unlimited pos-sibilities, "all possibilities of order, possibilities at once incompatible and un-limited with a fecundity beyond imagination." What makes the creative pro-cess of the world orderly and purposive is the availability of eternal objects, of possibilities. These possibilities exist in God as his primordial nature. God, more-over, is the active mediator between the eternal objects and the actual occa-sions. It is God who selects the relevant possibilities from the realm of eternal objects. God does not impose the eternal objects upon actual entities. Rather, God presents these possibilities as *lures* of what might be. Persuasion, not com-pulsion, characterizes God's creative activity. That God always presents rel-evant possibilities is no guarantee that actual entities will select them. When God's persuasive lure is accepted, the result is order, harmony, and novel ad-vance. When it is rejected, the result is discord and evil. God is the ultimate principle striving toward actualizing all relevant possibilities. What we experi-ence as the stable order in the world and in our intuition of the permanent right-ness of things shows forth God's "consequent nature." "God's role," says White-head, "lies in the patient operation of the overpowering rationality of his conceptual harmonization. He does not create the world, he saves it: or, more accurately, he is the poet of the world, with tender patience leading it by his vision of truth, beauty and goodness."

24

Analytic
Philosophy

The dominant movement of philosophical activity in the contemporary English-speaking world is known as *analytic philosophy*. To call it a *movement* rather than a *school* underscores the fact that although analytic philosophy has certain clear distinguishing characteristics, the sources out of which it emerged, the changes it has undergone, and the variety of ways in which it is pursued are many. What unifies all analytic philosophers is their agreement concerning the central task of philosophy. The task of philosophy, they say, is to clarify the meaning of language. In his early work, the *Tractatus Logico-Philosophicus,* Ludwig Wittgenstein said that "the object of philosophy is the logical clarification of thoughts" so that "the result of philosophy is not a number of philosophical propositions, but to make propositions clear." The full force of this new way of doing philosophy is found in the negative and positive aspects of its task.

On the negative side, to say that the philosopher does not formulate "philosophical propositions" meant for the early analysts that there must be a self-imposed limit upon the scope of philosophic activity. Specifically, this meant that in contrast to the immediately past tradition of nineteenth-century idealism, especially Hegelianism, whose practitioners engaged in constructing complete systems of thought regarding the whole universe, the analysts would now undertake the more modest task of working upon individual problems. Not only would these problems be single and manageable, they would all fit into a single class: They would all be problems revolving around the meanings and usages of language. For this reason, it would no longer be the task of the philosopher to investigate the nature of reality, to build complete systems that seek to explain the universe, or to fashion moral, political, and religious philosophies of behavior. Philosophy, in this new key, "is not a doctrine but an activity" and as such it can produce "no ethical propositions," said Wittgenstein. Philosophers are no longer to consider themselves capable of discovering unique forms of information about the world and humanity. The discovery of facts is the task of the scientist. There are no facts left over for the philosophers after all the sciences have done their work.

On the positive side, the new assumption was that the philosopher can render a genuine service by carefully unpacking complex problems whose origin is found in the imprecise use of language. Scientists themselves, it was felt, had discussed their findings in language that was often misleading and in certain ways ambiguous. That is, scientific language contained ambiguities of logic, not of physical discovery, and the clarification of these logical ambiguities was required. It was assumed, also, that rigorous linguistic analysis could *prevent* the use or abuse of language in ways that would cause us, as A. J. Ayer said, "to draw false inferences, or ask spurious questions, or make nonsensical assumptions." What concerned Ayer was that we often use propositions about nations as though nations were persons, we talk about material things as though we believed in a physical world "beneath" or "behind" visible phenomena, and we use the word *is* in relation to things whose existence we could not possibly want to infer. Philosophy is called upon to remove these dangers from our use of language, said Ayer. In a somewhat similar vein, Gilbert Ryle wrote about "Systematically Misleading Expressions," saying that although he would rather allot to philosophy "a sublimer task than the detection of the sources in linguistic idioms of recurrent misconstructions and absurd theories," still, philosophical analysis consists in inquiring about "what it really means to say so and so." In this way, the new philosophy became closely related to the enterprises of science, not as a rival discipline offering propositions of what reality is like but as the proofreader of the scientists' expressions, checking the literature of science for its clarity and logical meaningfulness. It would no longer be the function of the philosopher either to propound vast systems of thought after the manner of Plato, Aristotle, and Hegel or to tell people how they ought to behave. He would instead analyze statements or propositions to discover the causes of ambiguities and the foundations of meaning in language.

What caused this dramatic shift in the enterprise of philosophy? At Cambridge, Bertrand Russell and G. E. Moore had reacted in the early decades of the twentieth century against the system building of the Hegelian philosophers such as F. H. Bradley, Bernard Bosanquet, and J. E. McTaggart, who had been

engaged in ambitious metaphysical speculation. They reacted to the extrava-
gance of the metaphysical language these Hegelians used and wondered just
what could be meant by these interpretations of the whole universe. Although
Moore did not necessarily want to give up metaphysics, he was especially disturbed by the contrast between metaphysical language and so-called "common
sense." To him, certain statements, as, for example, McTaggart's famous notion that "time is unreal," seemed "perfectly monstrous." Moore was inspired to
analyze language particularly to clarify ordinary language and to make language
fit the test of common sense in its meaning. Bertrand Russell, on the other hand,
was a brilliant mathematician, trained in precise thought, and in comparison
with the language of mathematics, metaphysical language seemed to him loose
and obscure. He did not want to reject metaphysics, any more than Moore did,
but he did want to tighten up the language of metaphysics. While Moore set
out to analyze common-sense language, Russell tried to analyze "facts" for the
purpose of inventing a new language, *logical atomism,* which would have the
exactness and rigor of mathematics because this new language would be made
to correspond exactly to the "facts." Although neither Moore nor Russell gave
up the attempt to understand reality, the way they went about their task emphasized the fact that philosophy is concerned not with discovery but with clarification and, therefore, in a sense, not with truth but with meaning.

Across the channel, a group of mathematicians, scientists, and philosophers formed a group in Vienna in the 1920s describing themselves as *logical
positivists* and known as the Vienna Circle. Their orientation was rigorously
empirical, and they proceeded to reject the whole enterprise of metaphysics.
Their ideal for philosophy was the unification of the sciences, hoping thereby
to produce a unified system of meaningful and valid knowledge. Among this
group were Moritz Schlick, Rudolph Carnap, Friedrich Waismann, Herbert
Feigl, Otto Neurath, and Kurt Gödel. A young former student of Bertrand Russell's, Ludwig Wittgenstein, lived nearby, and though he was not a member of
the Circle, he had conversations with them, since his early book, *Tractatus
Logico-Philosophicus* (1919), was considered by the Vienna Circle to express
its philosophical point of view with great accuracy. Not only had Wittgenstein
said that "whatever can be said at all can be said clearly," he concluded his
book by saying that "whereof one cannot speak, thereof one must be silent."
This dictum was less harsh than Hume's rigorous conclusion in his *Enquiry,*
where, following the implicit logic of his principles of empiricism, he wrote:
"When we run over libraries, persuaded of these principles, what havoc we
must make? If we take in our hand any volume; of divinity or school metaphysics, for instance; let us ask, Does it contain any abstract reasoning concerning quantity or number? No. Does it contain any experimental reasoning
concerning matter of fact and existence? No. Commit it then to the flames: for
it can contain nothing but sophistry and illusion." The Vienna Circle thought
of themselves as the twentieth-century heirs of Hume's empirical tradition. To
this tradition they now sought to apply the rigorous apparatus of mathematics
and science. If their ideal was to clarify the language of science and the sci-

ences, their first task would have to be the formulation of a standard for clarity, and this resulted in their famous *verification principle*. This principle would in time be shown to suffer from certain defects and require attempts at modification. These internal difficulties with their central principle as well as with other aspects of their philosophic concerns, and the scattering of the members to British and American universities in the 1930s, dissolved the Vienna Circle and gradually led to the decline of *logical positivism.*

What followed next in the history of analytic philosophy was the decisive work of the "new" Wittgenstein. Between his *Tractatus Logico-Philosophicus* (1919) and the posthumous publication of his famed *Philosophical Investigations* (1953), his thought had acquired a radically new character, and it is this version of his way of doing philosophy that has dominated the contemporary philosophic scene in the English-speaking world. The major facets of analytic philosophy are to be found, then, in Bertrand Russell's *logical atomism,* the Vienna Circle's *logical positivism,* and the later Wittgenstein's *philosophical analysis.* We shall also consider the work of Gilbert Ryle and John Austin.

BERTRAND RUSSELL

Logical Atomism

Bertrand Russell's point of departure in philosophy was his admiration for the precision of mathematics. Accordingly, he announced that "the kind of philosophy that I wish to advocate, which I call logical atomism, is one which has forced itself upon me in the course of thinking about the philosophy of mathematics." He wanted to set forth "a certain kind of logical doctrine and on the basis of this a certain kind of metaphysics." Russell thought that since it was possible to construct a logic by which the whole of mathematics could be derived from a small number of logical axioms, as he had already done with A. N. Whitehead in their *Principia Mathematica,* then why could not this logic form the basis of a language that could accurately express everything that could be clearly stated? His assumption was, recalling that in the quotation above he connected "logical atomism" and "a certain kind of metaphysics," that the world would correspond to his specially constructed logical language. The vocabulary of the new logic would, for the most part, correspond to particular objects in the world. To accomplish this task of creating a new language, Russell set out first of all to analyze certain "facts," which he differentiated from "things."

"The things in the world," said Russell, "have various properties, and stand in various relations to each other. That they have these properties and relations are *facts*." Facts constitute for Russell the complexity of the relations of things to each other, and therefore "it is with the analysis of *facts* that one's consideration of the problem of complexity must begin." Russell's basic assumption was that "facts, since they have components, must be in some sense complex, and hence must be susceptible of analysis." The complexity of facts is matched by the complexity of language. For this reason, the aim of analysis

Bertrand Russell *(UPI/Bettmann Newsphotos)*

is to make sure that every statement represents an adequate picture of the reality, of the facts, of the world.

Language, according to Russell, consists of a unique arrangement of words, and the meaningfulness of language is determined by the accuracy with which these words represent facts. Words, in turn, are formulated into propositions. "In a logically perfect language," said Russell, "the words in a proposition would correspond one by one with the components of the corresponding facts." By analysis, certain *simple* words are discovered. These are words that cannot be further analyzed into something more primary and can therefore be understood only by knowing what they symbolize. The word *red,* for example, is not capable of further analysis and is therefore understood as a simple *predicate.* Other words, similarly simple, refer to particular things, and as symbols of these things they are *proper names.* Language consists in part, then, of words, which in their simplest form refer to a particular thing and its predicate, as, for example, a *red rose.* A proposition states a fact. When a fact is of the simplest kind, it is called an *atomic fact.* Propositions that state atomic facts are called *atomic propositions.* If our language consisted only of such atomic propositions, it would amount only to a series of reports regarding atomic facts. This is what Wittgenstein said in his *Tractatus* when he wrote that "the world is everything that is the case.... What is the case, the fact, is the existence of atomic facts."

It is clear that in our language atomic propositions are put together into more complex propositions. When two or more atomic propositions are linked together with such words as *and* and *or,* the result is what Russell calls a *molecular proposition.* However, there are no "molecular" *facts,* only atomic facts. For this reason, molecular propositions cannot correspond to molecular facts. How can one test the truth or falsity, then, of molecular propositions? Their truth depends upon the truth or falsity of the atomic propositions of which they are made up. Language, on this account, consists of an indefinite number of atomic propositions, whose correspondence with actual facts is settled by empirical methods and techniques. Nothing can be said about the world that is not analyzable down to an atomic proposition, which, in turn, corresponds to an atomic fact. The grammatical independence of each atomic proposition indicates the metaphysical independence of each atomic fact. Again, in an ideal language words and propositions would correspond to facts. Moreover, it was assumed that after a careful analysis of words and propositions and their corresponding atomic facts, one would arrive at the basic character of language and of the world, and that apart from these facts there would be no residue. Thus, the ideal language would express all there is to say about the world. All of reality, on this theory, could be described in statements such as "That is green."

Underlying this thought of an ideal language for describing reality was Russell's recent work in logic and mathematics. He had devised various symbolic notations for the foundations of mathematics. Now he would try to use similar notations for metaphysical language. A proposition or statement is either true or false. Using symbolic notations, a true proposition can be called *p* and a false proposition *not-p.* A molecular proposition consists of two or more atomic propositions (*p, q,* and so on) linked together with logical connectives, such as *and* and *or.* A proposition such as *p and q* [for which symbols any facts can be supplied, such as (*p*) he is tall and (*q*) he is dark] is true, says Russell, only if the atomic propositions *p* and *q* are each true. The entire molecular proposition is what Russell calls a *truth function.* There is no single atomic fact corresponding to the entire proposition. Its truth or falsity can be determined only from the truth or falsity of each of its component atomic propositions. To say that "he is tall and dark" is therefore a truth function of "he is tall" and "he is dark." The propositions *p* and *q* (and an indefinite additional number *n*) are capable of a wide variety and intricacy of relationships. But these relationships can all be stated symbolically, and since the logical forms of language correspond to reality, it is possible to discover through the logically correct relations of propositions a true essence of things or the world.

Difficulties developed in the program of logical atomism first of all when Russell and others tried to account for *general* facts. It is one thing to say "That is a white horse," where truth or falsity is checked by connecting the *words* "white" and "horse" with the atomic *facts* of this white color and this animal, the horse. It is another thing to say "All horses are white." How would one test the truth or falsity of such a statement? According to logical atomism, one should analyze this statement into its atomic propositions and test *their* truth or falsity. There is no atomic fact corresponding to "all horses...," for this means more than just this horse and that horse, namely, all horses, and this is a *general* fact. But the whole argument of logical atomism was that only atomic facts exist, and the theory had no way of dealing adequately with so-called general facts unless general facts were accepted as a form of atomic facts. Still, if one were disposed to consider only the particular things recorded by our senses as the basis of our language, as Hume did, singular atomic facts would be the only facts available for human discourse, and language would therefore consist solely of atomic and molecular propositions.

As the revived interest in Hume's empiricism was more and more felt by the logical atomists, it was difficult for their theory to retain its metaphysical character. In addition, Wittgenstein pointed out in his *Tractatus* that from the point of view of logical atomism, propositions could be stated *significantly* only if they could correspond to an atomic fact or be truth functions of propositions that did. Therefore, only atomic or molecular propositions could be stated significantly. But most of the propositions of logical atomism were peculiar in that they said things *about* facts rather than stating facts. If only propositions that state facts are significant or sensible, the conclusion had to be that language *about* facts, as when one tries to account for the relation between words and facts, is senseless and insignificant. This would, of course, make most of philosophy insignificant, and Wittgenstein was deeply aware of this upshot of logical atomism. For this reason, he concluded that "my propositions are elucidatory in this way: he who understands me finally recognizes them as senseless, when he has used them to climb out beyond them. (He must so to speak throw away the ladder, after he has climbed up on it)." Wittgenstein became more and more convinced that philosophy must reject the metaphysical elements in logical atomism. The right method of philosophy would be "to say nothing except what can be said, i.e., the propositions of science...." This is, for the most part, just what logical positivism took as its basic theme.

RUDOLPH CARNAP AND W. V. O. QUINE

Logical Positivism

The individuals who formed the Vienna Circle were, by temperament, attracted to the methods of science and mathematics. They were disposed to reject metaphysics, as had the earlier positivists who considered metaphysics, as Comte did, as outdated by science. Now they had the additional argument, because of Russell's work in logic and Wittgenstein's powerful formulation of the relation of logic and language in the *Tractatus,* that metaphysics is impossible as shown by the logical and essential character of language. To differentiate themselves from the earlier Comtean positivists and to emphasize that they would combine the rigorous techniques of the new logic with the empirical temper of Hume, they called themselves *logical positivists,* or sometimes *logical empiricists.* For the English-speaking world, A. J. Ayer, in his brilliantly lucid and powerfully argued book *Language, Truth, and Logic* (1936) did, as he later said with considerable understatement, "something to popularize what may be called the classic position of the Vienna Circle."

This position called for a blanket rejection of metaphysics, and the grounds for this rejection were to be found in the Vienna Circle's famous *verification principle.*

Rudolph Carnap Among the foremost members of the Vienna Circle was the eminent positivist Rudolph Carnap. Born in Germany in 1891, he taught in Vienna and Prague from 1926 to 1935. After arriving in the United States in 1936, he taught for many years at the University of Chicago, and from 1954 until his death in 1970 he was associated with the University of California at Los Angeles. "The only proper task of Philosophy," Carnap wrote in his *Philosophy and Logical Syntax,* "is Logical Analysis." It is the function of logical analysis, he said, to analyze all knowledge, all assertions of science and of everyday life, in order to make clear the sense of each such assertion and the connections between them. The purpose of logical analysis is to discover how we can become certain of the truth or falsehood of any proposition. One of the principal tasks of the logical analysis of a given proposition is, therefore, to discover the method of verification of that proposition.

For Carnap, the method of verification of a proposition is either direct or indirect. If a proposition asserts something about a perception I am having—for example, that I see a house—this proposition is effectively tested or verified by my present perception. On the other hand, there are propositions which cannot be verified so directly. To say, for example, that "this key is made of iron" requires an indirect method of verification. For one way to verify the assertion that the key is made of iron is to place it near a magnet which enables one to perceive that the key is attracted. It now becomes possible to arrange a series of propositions in a tight logical sequence leading to verification as follows: A verified physical law holds that "if an iron thing is placed near a magnet it is attracted"; another verified proposition asserts that "this metal bar is a magnet"; it is verified through direct observation that "the key is placed near the bar." When the key is finally attracted by the magnet, the verification is complete. Carnap concludes that a proposition which is not directly verifiable can only be verified by the direct verification of those propositions, as indicated in the preceding example, which can be clearly and logically deduced from the original proposition together with other propositions already empirically verified. If a proposition is phrased as a prediction, as in the proposition "The key will be attracted by the magnet," its verification requires observation of the completed attraction. If the key is attracted by the magnet, there is a considerable degree of certainty about the truth of the description of the key. Statements of predictions, however, are only *hypotheses* since there is always the possibility of finding in the future a negative instance. For this reason, even though the degree of certainty is sufficient for most practical purposes, the original proposition cannot ever be completely verified so as to produce *absolute* certainty.

These two forms of verification, direct and indirect, are central to the scientific method, for in the field of science every proposition, says Carnap, asserts something about either present perceptions or future perceptions. In both cases, verification is either through direct perception or by the logical connection of already verified propositions. Thus, if a scientist were to make an assertion from which no proposition verified by perception could be deduced, it would be no assertion at all. To say, for example, that there is not only a gravitational field but also a *levitational field* could not be verified. While propositions concerning gravity can be verified by observing its effects upon bodies, there are no observable effects or laws describing levitation. Assertions about levitation are, says Carnap, no assertions at all because they do not speak about anything. They are nothing but a series of empty words—expressions with no sense.

When logical analysis is applied to metaphysics, Carnap concludes that metaphysical propositions are not verifiable, or, if an attempt at verification is made, the results are always negative. If one takes, for example, the proposition propounded by Thales that "the principle of the World is Water," one cannot deduce any propositions asserting any perceptions whatever which may be expected in the future. Such a proposition therefore asserts nothing at all. It is inevitable, says Carnap, that metaphysicians cannot avoid making their propositions nonverifiable because if they made them verifiable they would belong to the realm of empirical science since their truth or falsehood would depend upon experience. Carnap therefore rejects metaphysics by saying in Chapter I of his *Philosophy and Logical Syntax:* "Metaphysical propositions are neither true nor false, because they assert nothing, they contain neither knowledge nor error, they lie completely outside the field of knowledge, of theory, outside the discussion of truth or falsehood. But they are, like laughing, lyrics, and music, expressive. They express not so much temporary feelings as permanent emotional or volitional dispositions....The danger lies in the *deceptive* character of metaphysics; it gives the illusion of knowledge without actually giving any knowledge. This is the reason why we reject it."

Normative ethics and value judgments in general belong, according to Carnap, to the realm of metaphysics. When he applies his method of logical analysis to the propositions of normative ethics, these propositions predictably turn out to be meaningless for him. There can, of course, be a science of ethics in the form of psychological or sociological or other empirical investigations about the actions of human beings and their effects upon other people. But the philosophy of moral values or moral norms does not rest upon any facts since its purpose is to state norms for human action or for making judgments about moral values. The value statement "Killing is evil" has the grammatical form of an assertive proposition. But, says Carnap, "a value statement is nothing else than a command in a misleading grammatical form. It may have effects upon the actions of men, and these effects may be in accordance with our wishes or not; but it is neither true nor false. It does not assert anything and can neither be proved nor disproved."

Carnap was convinced that the propositions of psychology belong to the region of empirical science in just the same way as do the propositions of biology and chemistry. He was aware that many would consider it an offensive presumption to place psychology, "hitherto robed in majesty as the theory of spiritual events," into the domain of the physical sciences. Yet that is what he proceeded to do, saying in his essay on *Psychology and Physical Language* that *"every sentence of psychology may be formulated in physical language."* What he meant by this was that "all sentences of psychology describe physical occurrences, namely, the physical behavior of humans and other animals." This is an extension of the general thesis of physicalism which Carnap described as holding that "physical language is a universal language, that is, a language into which every sentence may be translated." In effect, Carnap would make psychology an aspect of physics since all science would become physics and the various domains of science would become parts of unified science. In this manner, propositions in psychology were to be tested by the criterion of verifiability by translating them into physical language. Thus, the statement "John is in pain" is translated into a statement describing the observable state S of John's body. This process of translation requires only that there be a scientific law stating that someone is in pain if and only if his or her bodily condition is in a particular state S. It is then meaningful to say that "John is in pain" and "John's body is in state S" since, while not equivalent, these are interchangeable translations. Only those statements which could be verified or translated into verifiable statements were thought to have meaning. Neither metaphysics, some aspects of psychology, theories of "reality," nor the philosophy of normative values could satisfy the criterion of verifiability and were therefore rejected as meaningless.

In time, there were objections to Carnap's early formulation of the criterion of verifiability, as we shall indicate shortly. Reacting to criticisms from Reichenbach, Popper, Lewis, and Nagel, Carnap shifted his ground from verification to *confirmation*. Carnap agreed that if verification is taken to mean a complete and definitive establishment of the truth, then the laws of science could never be verified. The number of instances to which the laws, say, of biology or physics, apply is infinite; and if strict verification required personal observation of every instance, then obviously there could not be verification as so defined. Though the universal scientific law cannot be verified in its universal application, single instances in the form of particular sentences derived from the law and from other sentences previously established can be verified. In this way, *verification* in the strict sense gives way to the gradually increasing *confirmation* of scientific laws.

As a further aid to logical clarity, Carnap made a distinction in his book *The Logical Syntax of Language* between what he called the *material* and the *formal* modes of language. It was his contention that the *material* mode, commonly used in philosophy, frequently leads to the ambiguities and errors of metaphysicians and in general is the source of meaningless philosophical controversy. To overcome these dangers, Carnap felt it necessary to translate sentences from the material idiom into the more accurate *formal* idiom. He gives the following example: The sentence "The moon is a thing" is cast in the material mode. It can be translated into the formal mode in this sentence: "The word 'moon' is a thing-designation." Every sentence which states "Such and such is a *thing*" belongs in the material mode. Carnap holds that many other words, such as *quality, relation, number,* and *event,* also function the same way as the word *thing.* Another example of this distinction is the manner in which the sentence "7 is not a thing but a number," expressed in the material mode, is translated into the formal mode by saying "The sign 7 is not a thing sign but a numerical sign." The way to avoid the "dangerous material mode," says Carnap, is to avoid the word *thing* and use instead the syntactical term *thing-designation.* Similarly, instead of using the word *number,* one should use the term *numerical-designation;* instead of *quality, quality-designation;* instead of *event, event-designation;* and so forth. Other examples would include the translation of Wittgenstein's sentence "There is also the inexpressible" in the material mode to "There are also words which are not words" in the formal mode. Or, "He lectured about Babylon" is translated into "The word Babylon occurred in his lecture." It was Carnap's hope that by this method of translation of sentences into the formal mode "we free logical analysis from all reference to extra-linguistic objects themselves," being then concerned only with the form of linguistic expressions, with *syntax.* It would appear from his distinction between the material and formal modes of language that Carnap implied that one could never speak about anything besides words. This is, of course, true to the extent that Carnap's conclusion applies to *logical analysis.* But, says Carnap, "...there is no question of eliminating reference to objects themselves from object-sciences. On the contrary, these sciences are really concerned with objects themselves, with things, not merely with thing-designations." In short, statements are not merely syntactical, they are also semantic.

The Principle of Verification   If the charge against metaphysics was that its language, its propositions or sentences, was *meaningless* or, as Wittgenstein said in the *Tractatus, senseless,* such a charge required the use of some criterion by which to test which sentences did and which did not express a genuine proposition about a matter of fact. Accordingly, the logical positivists formulated the verification principle as the basic criterion for the meaningfulness or the literal significance of a proposition. If a proposition fulfilled the requirements of this criterion, it was considered meaningful, and if a proposition failed to do so, it was considered meaningless.

The *verification principle* consisted in the notion that *the meaning of a statement is the method of its verification.* The assumption behind this principle was that verification must always rest upon empirical observation, that is, in sense experience. Any proposition, therefore, that could not be verified by the method of observation would be said to have no meaning. The case of mathematical propositions was treated in a special way, but it was clear that with such a rigorous criterion, metaphysical language could not pass the test of meaningfulness.

The positivists, following the tradition of Hume and Kant, distinguished two types of statements, namely, *analytic* and *synthetic.* Each of these types has a different ground for its meaningfulness. Analytic statements derive their meaningfulness from the definitions of their words or symbols. To say that "all men are mortals" has literal significance because the word *men* is defined in such a way as to include the idea *mortals.* In general, in analytic statements the subject already contains or implies the predicate. For the most part, analytic statements do not increase our knowledge, and for this reason they are *tautologies.* Moreover, their meaning does not depend upon experience, only upon the consistent use of their clearly defined terms. If words with clearly defined terms are used inconsistently, the result is a *contradiction.* A statement, then, that is necessarily true, true because of the meanings of its terms, is a tautology, whereas a statement that is necessarily false is a contradiction. An analytic proposition that is also a tautology is always and in every case necessarily true, because its only test is the meanings of the terms. Similarly, a contradiction is always and necessarily a false proposition since its falseness is determined by the inconsistent use of terms. Thus, the truth or falsity of an analytic proposition turns on the logical analysis of meanings. On the other hand, *synthetic* propositions are either true or false in each case, and their truth or falsity can be discovered only by reference to some nonlogical or nonlinguistic datum, a fact. Unlike analytic statements, which are *necessarily* either tautologies or contradictions, synthetic statements may be either true or false. Synthetic statements require some sense experience of the object that such a statement refers to in order to advance from its possible to its actual truth.

From this distinction between analytic and synthetic propositions, the positivists formulated their conception of *cognitive meaning* or *literal significance.* Analytic propositions, they said, have a *formal* meaning, since their meaning derives not from facts but from the logical implications of words and ideas, as in mathematics, logic, and the formal sciences. On the other hand, synthetic propositions have a factual meaning, because their meaning is based upon the empirical observation of the objects referred to in the statements. Synthetic statements are the language of the factual sciences, physics, biology, psychology, and so on. It was at this point that the principle of verification had its decisive application. For now the positivists concluded that there could be only two kinds of statements that could have any meaning at all, namely, *analytic* statements, which are universally and necessarily true because the consistent use of words would never allow them to be anything else, and *synthetic* statements, which are judged as true or false by using the verification principle. Statements that are neither analytic nor synthetic have no cognitive meaning or literal significance; they are simply *emotive*. It takes only brief reflection to realize that into this category of *emotive* or *noncognitive* language would fall not only metaphysics but also ethics, aesthetics, and religion.

W. V. O. Quine The distinction between analytic and synthetic truths was challenged by W. V. O. Quine, who was himself sympathetic to the original ideal of the Vienna Circle. In his essay "Two Dogmas of Empiricism" (Chapter II of his *From a Logical Point of View*), Quine argued that "a boundary between analytic and synthetic statements simply has not been drawn. That there is such a distinction to be drawn at all is an unempirical dogma of empiricists, a metaphysical article of faith." The other dogma is that of *reductionism*, which holds that every meaningful statement can be translated into a statement about immediate experience. Quine was aware that to reject these dogmas would mean abandoning, or at least "blurring the supposed boundary between speculative metaphysics and natural science." Not only is the notion of "analyticity" difficult to clarify, apart from some limited logical statements, but synthetic statements do not live up to their empirical verifiability as clearly as they are supposed to. After a rigorous and sustained analysis of the many ways others have sought to establish the truth of both analytic and synthetic statements, Quine draws the conclusion that "no statement is immune to revision." This would mean that both analytic and synthetic propositions contain only contingent truth and, to that extent, do not differ. Even logical statements, presumably true "no matter what," can be revised, as once proposed, for example, as a means of simplifying quantum mechanics. Quine asks: "What difference is there in principle between such a shift [in logic] and the shift whereby Kepler superseded Ptolemy, or Einstein, Newton, or Darwin, Aristotle?" As an empiricist, Quine believes that conceptual schemes, including science and logic, are tools. Indeed, the total range of our knowledge, he says, "is a man-made fabric which impinges upon experience only along the edges." Any conflict between a statement we hold to be true and a new experience at variance with it requires an adjustment not only of that one statement but ultimately of all the interconnected concepts. Just where certainty seems greatest, in the physical realm, a serious reminder must be made to the effect that physical bodies are themselves only a convenient conceptual tool. Indeed, Quine says that physical objects are simply "irreducible posits," comparing them to the gods of Homer. As an empiricist he believes that it would be an error not to believe in physical objects instead of in Homer's gods. "But," he says, "in point of epistemological footing the physical objects and the gods differ only in degree and not in kind." To argue in this manner clearly undercuts the distinction between analytic and synthetic and between metaphysics and science. In the end, this leads Quine to settle for a strongly pragmatic conception of truth, saying, "Each man is given a scientific heritage plus a continuing barrage of sensory stimulation; and the considerations which guide him in warping his scientific heritage to fit his continuing sensory promptings are, where rational, pragmatic." Besides Quine's technical argument against the analytic-synthetic distinction, a variety of reactions to the clearly iconoclastic movement of positivism emerged. Some were appalled at the incredible denial of meaning to moral language. Others took comfort in the fact that the verification principle had simply formulated the requirements whereby an utterance could be rightly called a *statement*. That is, the only consequence that followed from the inability of an utterance to be verified by sense experience was that it could not be called a genuine statement. But this, it was felt, was of little consequence, since it meant at most that the designation *statement* would merely be reserved for a special class of utterances. Still, there could be little comfort in this, since the positivists made two things very clear along the way: first, that their choice of utterances to be designated as statements was not at all arbitrary, but must be those utterances that could be empirically verified; and secondly, that only statements have cognitive meaning. At the same time, this rigorous interpretation of the verification principle encountered serious difficulties, not from its external critics but from some inherent defects, which the positivists themselves recognized.

Among the difficulties encountered was, first of all, the serious question of what constituted verification. To answer "sense experience" raised the further question "whose experience?" The assumption behind the verification principle was that whatever could be said meaningfully would be stated in atomic or elementary statements. Scientific language would be reducible ultimately to *observational statements*. But what is the "fact" that an observation statement reports? Is it a subjective experience about a physical object, or is it a pure picture of that object? The technical problem was whether it is ever possible to translate a person's internal experience into a statement about a physical object, or vice versa. This is the problem of *solipsism*, the view that the self is the only object of real knowledge and that therefore the experiences of one person cannot be the same as those of another. Each person's experience is different, and all of their experiences are different from the objectively real world. If this is the case, what does the verification principle amount to in the end? Verification statements would mean one thing to one person and something else to others.

In the second place, it was in the very area where this principle was presumed to have its greatest relevance, in the sciences, that its greatest difficulty arose. Scientific knowledge is frequently expressed in the form of universal laws. These "laws" are the basis for scientific *prediction*. But the problem the positivists faced was whether to consider scientific statements meaningful. How can a statement that makes a prediction be verified? Can my present experience, or experiment, tell me anything about the future? Obviously, literal significance or meaning is one thing when we verify the statement "There is a black cow in Smith's barn" and quite another thing when we say, as the scientist does, for example, that when a moving body is not acted upon by external forces, its direction will remain constant. The first case is specific and verifiable. The second involves an indefinite number of cases, and any single case in the future can falsify that statement. Since there is no single fact that can verify *now* the future truth of a general scientific statement, such a statement, by a rigorous application of the verification principle, would be meaningless. Schlick had said of certain utterances, "If not conclusively verifiable in principle, then not propositions." This would have to apply to scientific as well as other forms of language. For this reason, a compromise in the rigorous application of the principle was proposed, thus giving rise to the distinction between the *strong* and *weak* forms of the verification principle. The weak form said simply that a statement must be at least "verifiable in principle," or *capable* of verification, that is, confirmed in some degree by the observation of something physical.

In the third place, it turned out that the verification principle was not itself verifiable. Critics asked why it should be that the criterion of meaning should be sense experience. The Vienna Circle did not answer this question in any formal way. It may be that for them the verification principle was clearly suggested by the difference between scientific procedures, on the one hand, and metaphysical speculation on the other. Being oriented chiefly to science, the positivists assumed that only language that referred to physical objects and their interrelationships could have cognitive meaning. Moreover, the techniques of logic as they understood them implied the correspondence between words and facts and between the logical structure of language and the logical relation of facts. The positivists assumed, furthermore, that through *physicalism,* their doctrine that called for the coupling of all statements to physical facts, they could achieve the *unity of science* and that such a unified knowledge would give sciences a common language and tell us all there is to say. But the internal defects of the verification principle, namely, the difficulty of formulating the criterion of sense experience without falling into solipsism and the impossibility of verifying general scientific statements, gradually led not only to a weak form of verification but also to the recognition that statements reflect many forms of experience. For this reason, the initial iconoclastic intensity of positivism was toned down. The blanket rejection of metaphysics and morals was reversed. Instead, analysts began to ask what kind of problem the metaphysicians and moralists were driving at. Ayer described this new temper by saying that "the metaphysician is treated no longer as a criminal but as a patient: there may be good reasons why he says the strange things he does." Ethics, by this view, is no longer nonsense but a discipline whose language is analyzed both for its relation to fact and for its value in pointing to a problem. As it turns out, ethical language is, as R. M. Hare has argued, not *descriptive* but, rather, *imperative*. C. L. Stevenson has also elaborated the emotive theory of ethics, showing that ethical statements express approval and disapproval and are used particularly for purposes of persuasion. What positivism came ultimately to say about ethics was that it is not possible to derive normative statements, what *ought* to be done, from a description of facts, from what *is*. But even though the analyst still holds that it is not his or her function as a philosopher to *prescribe* or *exhort* any particular form of behavior, he or she does accept the task of creatively analyzing moral language for the purpose of clarifying it. That he or she reserves the right to make value judgments as a *person* underscores the growing recognition that there are modes of human experience besides simply the observation of physical objects and their interrelationships that have meaning and literal significance. Although logical positivism in its classical form dissolved from the weight of its inner difficulties, its impact continues in the analytic movement, which is still concerned overwhelmingly with the usages and analysis of language.

LUDWIG WITTGENSTEIN

The "New" Wittgenstein

With the appearance of Ludwig Wittgenstein's *Philosophical Investigations* (1953), analytic philosophy adjusted itself to a new point of view. It was still concerned with language, as were logical atomism and logical positivism. But now the analyst would see the nature of language in a different light. Wittgenstein, who had provided the most impressive systematic statement of logical atomism in the *Tractatus Logico-Philosophicus* (1919), had shortly thereafter repudiated a considerable portion of that book on the grounds that the theory of language upon which that book was based was now seen as inadequate. It was inadequate because it assumed that language has really only one function, namely, to state facts. It was further assumed that sentences for the most part derive their meanings from stating facts. More seriously, Wittgenstein had assumed, as did also Rudolph Carnap, that the skeleton of all language is a logical one. What struck Wittgenstein now was the somewhat obvious point that language has *many* functions besides simply "picturing" objects. Language always functions in a *context* and therefore has as many purposes as there are contexts. Words, he said, are like "tools in a tool-box; there is a hammer, pliers, a saw, a screwdriver, a rule, a glue-pot, glue, nails and screws.—The function of words is as diverse as the functions of these objects." What made him think earlier that language had only one function? He had been "held captive" by a "picture" of language as being the giving of names, as if by Adam, to all things. We are all the victims, he said, of "the bewitchment of our intelligence by means of language." Our incorrect picture of language is "produced by grammatical illusions." To analyze grammar might lead one to discover some logical structure in language. But would that justify the conclusion that all language

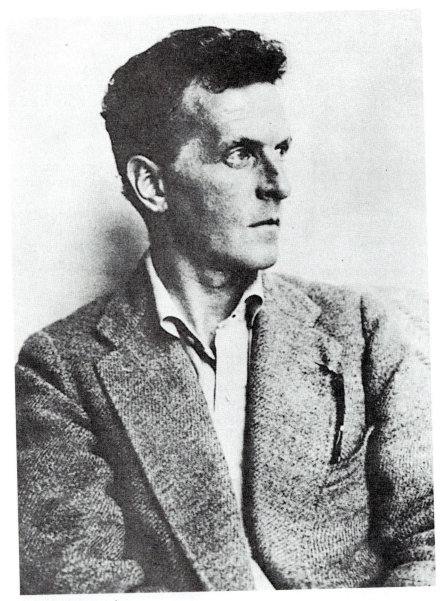

Ludwig Wittgenstein

has essentially the same rules, functions, and meanings? It occurred to Wittgenstein that the assumption that all language states facts and contains a logical skeleton was derived not by observation but by "thought." It was simply assumed that all language, in spite of certain superficial differences, is alike, the way all games are alike. Wittgenstein uncovered the flaw in this analogy by taking the case of games and asking, "What is common to them all?—Don't say: There *must* be something common, or they would not be called 'games'—but *look and see* whether there is anything common at all.—For if you look at them you will not see something that is common to *all,* but similarities, relationships, and a whole series of them at that. To repeat: don't think, but look." He was apparently saying that logical atomism was the product of thought, of theory, and not of careful observation of the way, in fact, language operates and is used. Wittgenstein therefore shifted the program of analysis from a preoccupation with logic and the construction of a "perfect" language to the study of the ordinary usages of language. He moved away from what Russell and Carnap were doing and turned now in the direction of G. E. Moore's earlier emphasis upon the analysis of ordinary language, testing it by the criterion of "common sense." Wittgenstein was now of the opinion that language does not contain one single pattern alone, that it is as variable as life itself. Indeed, he said that "to imagine a language means to imagine a form of life." For this reason, analysis should consist not in the *definition* of language or its meanings but rather in a careful *description* of its uses: "We must do away with all explanation, and *description alone* must take its place." We must, said Wittgenstein, "stick to the subjects of everyday thinking, and not go astray and imagine that we have to describe extreme subtleties." Confusions arise not when our language is "doing work," but only when it is "like an engine idling."

By recognizing the diversity of the functions of language, Wittgenstein inevitably altered the task of philosophy. For one thing, unlike the positivists, he would not reject the statements of metaphysics outright. Since the new mood was to consider the metaphysician a patient instead of a criminal the function of philosophy could now be considered as "therapeutic." Metaphysical language can indeed create confusion, and the central concern of philosophy is to deal with problems that baffle and confuse us because of the lack of clarity. Philosophy is a "battle against the bewitchment of our intelligence by means of language." Bewitchment causes confusion, and so "A philosophical problem has the form: 'I don't know my way about.'" Philosophy helps one to find his or her way, to survey the scene. "What we do," said Wittgenstein, "is to bring words back from their metaphysical to their everyday usage." His aim in philosophy, he said, was "to show the fly the way out of the fly-bottle." When the fly is out of the bottle, and when words are brought back from metaphysics to their everyday usage, and when the person who didn't know his or her way about now does know the way, what has happened? Wittgenstein says that philosophy "leaves everything as it is." Philosophy does not provide one with new or more information, but adds clarity by a careful description of language. It is as though one could see all the parts of a jigsaw puzzle but was baffled by how to put it together; one is actually looking at everything needed to solve the problem. Philosophical puzzlement is similar and can be removed by a careful description of language as we ordinarily use it. What makes us feel trapped like a fly in a bottle is the use of language in ways that it is not ordinarily used. Hence, "the results of philosophy are the uncovering of one or another piece of plain nonsense." By *nonsense* Wittgenstein did not necessarily mean the language of metaphysics, for, again, he had a basic sympathy for what some metaphysicians were trying to do. If metaphysics displayed resistance or a prejudice that obscures the ordinary usage of words, he agreed that this is "not a *stupid* prejudice." He saw in the confusions of metaphysics a deep human condition, saying that "the problems arising through a misinterpretation of our forms of language have the character of *depth*. They are deep disquietudes; their roots are as deep in us as the forms of our language and their significance is as great as the importance of our language."

How, more specifically, does one who doesn't know his way about find it, or how does the fly escape from the fly-bottle? One must not expect from Wittgenstein any single systematic answer to this question. He is too sensitive to the suppleness and variability of life and language to force upon them the straitjacket of a single method. "There is not *a* philosophical method," he says, "though there are indeed methods, like different therapies." Because philosophical problems grow out of language, it is necessary to acquire a basic familiarity with the usages of the language out of which each problem arises. As there are many kinds of games, there are many sets of rules of the games. Similarly, as there are many languages (that is, the many forms of ordinary language of work, play, worship, science, and so forth), there are many *usages*. Under these circumstances, "the work of the philosopher consists in *assembling reminders* for a particular purpose." In his *Philosophical Investigations,* Wittgenstein "does philosophy" by taking many problems and assembling many reminders of the way language is used as a means of clarifying these problems. But the philosopher, in addition to assembling these uses of language, selects and arranges them in order to get a picture of the landscape. In other words, philosophy does not consist in giving crisp abstract answers to questions. A person who has lost his way wants, rather, a map of the terrain, and this is supplied by the selection and arrangement of concrete examples of the actual use of language in ordinary experience.

But it is not enough to just look at these examples of usage, any more than it is sufficient simply to look at the pieces of the jigsaw puzzle. There must be selection and rearrangement. Then, everything is before us that we need for solving problems. Still, says Wittgenstein, we frequently "fail to be struck by what, once seen, is *most* striking and most powerful." The most important things are hidden "because of their simplicity and familiarity." But what does it mean to "fail to be struck"? There is no sure method according to Wittgenstein to guarantee that one will "be struck" and thereby find his way. Apparently the fly can frequently pass the opening of the jar without escaping. In any case, what Wittgenstein sought to do was to shift philosophy's concern from meanings, from the assumption that words carried in them as so much freight "pictures" of objects in the world. Instead, he directed attention, through the assembling, selecting, and arranging of relevant examples, to the actual usages of words. Because most *philosophical* problems were assumed to arise from puzzlements about words, the scrupulous description of their ordinary

Gilbert Ryle at Magdalen College, Oxford
(Samuel E. Stumpf)

uses would, it was assumed, eliminate this puzzlement. It was in this manner also that Gilbert Ryle (1900–1976), whose teaching at Oxford began in 1924, defined the task of the new style of philosophy.

RYLE AND AUSTIN

Gilbert Ryle

An impressive example of philosophical analysis is Gilbert Ryle's book *Concept of Mind,* published in 1949, four years before Wittgenstein's *Philosophical Investigations.* While these two books have substantially the same objectives, Ryle's book is distinctive in that it focuses in a sustained manner upon a mind-body problem, to which he applies his method of philosophical analysis. As early as 1932, Ryle had already established his commitment to this new style in philosophy in his vigorous essay "Systematically Misleading Expressions" in which he wrote that to enquire "what it means to say so and so...is what philosophical analysis is, and...this is the sole and whole function of philosophy." Philosophy, says Ryle in the introduction to *Concept of Mind,* does not give new information about minds, or for that matter about any other subject. "The philosophical arguments which constitute this book," he writes, "are not intended to increase what we know about minds, but to rectify the logical geography of the knowledge which we already possess."

The Ghost in the Machine   Ryle contends that the "official doctrine" about the nature and the place of minds is unsound and contradicts virtually everything we know about minds. In its simplest form, the official doctrine holds that every human being has both a mind and a body, that these two are coordinated, but that upon the death of the body the mind may continue both to exist and to exert its powers. Not only is this basic theory of mind-body incorrect, says Ryle, but it also leads to many other serious errors as one elaborates the implications of this doctrine.

It must follow from the official doctrine that each person has two collateral histories, one consisting of the events of the body and the other consisting of what transpires in and to the mind. Whereas human bodies are in space and are governed by mechanical physical laws, minds do not exist in space and are not subject to mechanical laws. A person's bodily life is publicly observable while the activities of the mind are not accessible to external observers and are therefore private. At this point a rather serious difficulty is encountered since the contrast between the public character of the body and the private status of the mind requires one to say that the workings of the body are external whereas the workings of the mind are internal. It is then a short step to say that the mind is *in* the body. Although this language describing the place of the mind may be "metaphorical," since the mind which occupies no space could hardly be in any particular place, it is Ryle's contention that for the most part the contrast between the outer and inner realms is taken literally. Theorists in various disciplines take this contrast between "inner" and "outer" for granted. Stimuli are assumed to come from "outside" and from far distances, generating responses inside the skull. Activity of the mind is said to produce external events such as a motion of the hand or eye; smiles suggest activities of the mind. All this suggests, too, some mode of transaction between the mind and body, but there is no method for either observing or reporting just how these transactions between mind and body take place. No laboratory experiment can discover this relationship, and physiologists and psychologists alternate in designating physical bases and mental behavior as possible explanations of how these polar oppositions are brought together. Self-analysis and introspection are special modes of perception requiring no physical eye and are so private as to be a special privilege of the mind itself to which no one else has direct access. Even though one were to assume that minds similar to one's own are located in other human bodies, there is no way to discover what they do or undergo, and so, says Ryle, "Absolute solitude is on this showing the ineluctable destiny of the soul. Only our bodies can meet." Accordingly, language that presumes to describe someone's mental activities—such as knowing, hoping, dreading, or intending—must be construed as signifying special events in the secret histories of people. No one has direct access to these mental operations, neither biographer, teacher, critic, or friend. But because we know how to use mental-conduct words and to use them with general correctness, earlier philosophers constructed their theories of the nature and place of minds in conformity with the official doctrine. They sought to identify the logical geography of their mental-conduct concepts, and thus arose what Ryle has called the basically incorrect "dogma of the Ghost in the Machine."

The Category-Mistake What Ryle finds wrong with the official doctrine of the Ghost in the Machine is not that some details here and there are ambiguous but that the very principle on which the theory rests is false. It is not even a series of particular mistakes. It is, says Ryle, one big mistake of a unique kind, and this he calls a "category-mistake." The big mistake consists in representing the facts of mental life as if they belonged to one and the same logical category whereas in fact they belong to quite different and separate ones. The official doctrine is therefore a "myth," and it is necessary to "rectify the logic of mental-conduct concepts."

To indicate what is meant by a category-mistake, Ryle describes the imaginary visit of a foreigner to Oxford for the first time. The visitor is shown the playing fields, museums, scientific laboratories, and some of the colleges. Having seen these various places, the visitor asks, "But where is the University?" The question assumes that the University is yet another institution, a counterpart to the colleges and laboratories, another entity that can be seen in the same way as the others. Actually, the University is simply the way all he has already seen is coordinated. Thus, the visitor's mistake consists in his assumption that one can correctly speak of the Bodleian Library, the Ashmolean Museum, All Souls College, *and* the University as if the University was the same kind of member in the class to which the others belong. In short, the visitor mistakenly placed the University into the wrong category, a category in which it does not belong. In a similar illustration, Ryle speaks of the mistake made by a child watching a military parade in which a division is marching by. Having been told that he was seeing battalions, batteries, and squadrons, the child wanted to know when the division was going to appear. Again, he assumed that the division is another unit similar to the others, not realizing that in seeing the battalions, batteries, and squadrons he had already seen the division. His mistake was in thinking it correct to speak of battalions, batteries, squadrons, *and* a division. He placed the division in the wrong category. The category-mistake indicates an inability to use certain elements in the English language correctly. What is more significant, says Ryle, is that people who are perfectly capable of applying concepts are nevertheless liable in their abstract thinking to allocate these concepts to logical categories to which they do not belong.

What Ryle has sought to do through these illustrations is to show, as he says, that "a family of radical category-mistakes is the source of the double-life theory." The notion that a person is a ghost mysteriously ensconced in a machine is a consequence of thinking that because a person's feeling, thinking, and purposive activities cannot be described solely in terms of physics, they must be described in a set of counterpart idioms. Moreover, because mental conduct differs so from bodily activities, the official theory sought to invest mind with its own status, though made of a different stuff and having a different structure, and possessing its own complex organization. Body and mind were thought to be separate fields of causes and effects, the body's being mechanical and the mind's nonmechanical.

How did this category-mistake originate? Although Ryle designates Descartes as the major culprit of this error, it is obvious that the mind-body dualism has a history extending very much further back than the seventeenth century. Still, Descartes' special formulation of this official doctrine for modern philosophy, says Ryle, followed Galileo's assertion that his methods of scientific discovery were capable of providing a mechanical theory which would be applicable to every occupant in space. From a strictly scientific point of view, Descartes was impressed with the mechanical description of nature, but as a religious and moral person he was reluctant to agree with the claim that human nature in its mental aspects differs only in degree of complexity from a machine. Consequently, Descartes and subsequent philosophers wrongly construed mental-conduct words to signify nonmechanical processes and concluded that nonmechanical laws must explain the nonspatial workings of minds. But what this explanation retained was the assumption that mind, though different from body, was nevertheless a member of the categories of "thing," "stuff," "state," "process," "cause," and "effect." Thus, just as the visitor expected the University to be another, extra unit, so Descartes and his heirs treated minds as additional though special centers of the causal process. From these conclusions a host of theoretical difficulties arose. How are the mind and body related? How do they cause effects in each other? If the mind is governed by strict laws analogous to the laws governing the body, does this not imply determinism, in which case such notions as responsibility, choice, merit, and freedom make no sense? Worst of all, only negative terms could be used to speak of the mind as compared with the body since minds are not in space, have no motions, are not aspects of matter, and are not observable. For these and other reasons Ryle concludes that the entire argument of the Ghost in the Machine is "broken-backed."

In a sustained and careful analysis of several assertions "about the mind," Ryle seeks to clarify these assertions by arguing in each case that mental-conduct words do indeed refer to mental acts but not to minds. The acts of knowing, exercising intelligence, understanding, willing, feeling, imagining, and the like, all these according to the official theory, were considered as being unconnected with the body and as occurring, when referred to in the present tense, in the mind. Refuting this, Ryle holds that virtually in every assertion about the mind some facts about bodily behavior are relevant. For example, in speaking of human emotions one does not infer the working of some interior and obscure forces. In favorable circumstances, says Ryle, "I find out your inclinations and your moods more directly than this. I hear and understand your conversational avowals, your interjections and your tones of voice; I see and understand your gestures and facial expressions." Or, if we consider that the act of theorizing is the distinctive act of human intelligence and that this supports the dogma of the Ghost in the Machine, Ryle gives various rejoinders, including that "to find that most people have minds...is simply to find that they are able and prone to do certain sorts of things, and this we do by witnessing the sorts of things they do." Or, "overt intelligent performances are not clues to the workings of minds; they are those workings." Ryle says, further, that "In opposition to this entire dogma, I am arguing that in describing the workings of a person's mind we are not describing a second set of shadowy operations. We are describing his one career; namely we are describing the ways in which parts of his conduct are managed." And again, in speaking about the act of *understanding*, Ryle says, "It is being maintained throughout this book that when we characterize people by mental predicates, we are not making untestable inferences to any ghostly processes occurring in streams of consciousness which we are debarred from visiting; we are describing the ways in which those people conduct parts of their predominantly public behavior." Assertions ostensibly about the mind are therefore made true or false not by inner private events but by what has or will happen publicly. To say of someone that she is intelligent appears to be an assertion about her mind, but Ryle argues that it is rather our knowledge of her public performance.

What Ryle has sought to achieve through his analysis is a new theory of mind. It may appear that he is arguing that only bodies exist, that mental-conduct words are really statements about bodily behavior and that there is no independent private inner life. It was his intention in his *Concept of Mind* to "dissipate the contrast between Mind and Matter," not by reducing the one to the other but by demonstrating that the polar opposition between Mind and Matter can be resolved by rejecting the assumption that they are terms of the same logical type. In any case, *Concept of Mind* represents one of the outstanding attempts to deal with a classic problem through the analysis of linguistic idioms wherein misconstructions and absurd theories might be detected and clarified.

John Austin

Another philosopher concerned with the analysis of language was the Englishman John Austin. During his brilliant but brief career, Austin fashioned a new way of doing philosophy. Born in 1911 and educated at Oxford, he later became a powerful figure as a scholar at Oxford through the sheer force of his intellect. At his untimely death at the age of forty-nine in 1960, he had achieved immense respect as an original thinker even though he had not yet produced what others might consider a monumental work. That he did not publish extensively was only partly a consequence of his brief life. He once said that he had to decide early on whether he was going to write books or teach people to do philosophy in a way that he had found so useful and satisfying in his own work and life. That his style of doing philosophy has not become as widespread as other more familiar ones might be due to the greater difficulty of transferring to others his unique capacities, interests, rigorous classical training, and patient temperament. Nevertheless, his mode of linguistic analysis has been highly influential and, though it is not easy to imitate, it is not difficult to understand and appreciate. One detects an unusually pleasant mood and a sense of fascination as Austin goes about his special way of doing philosophy. Early in his significant essay on "A Plea for Excuses," he tells the reader that doing it provided for him what philosophy is so often barren of, namely, "the fun of discovery, the pleasure of cooperation and the satisfaction of reaching agreement." With relief and humor, he tells how his research enabled him to consider various words and idioms "without remembering what Kant thought" and to move on by degrees to discuss "deliberation without for once remembering Aristotle or self-control without Plato." In contrast to heavy and grim philosophizing, Austin exhibited a deceptive simplicity as expressed, for example, in the opening sentence of his William James Lectures at Harvard, *How to Do Things with Words,* where he wrote, "What I shall have to say here is neither difficult nor contentious: the only merit I should like to claim for it is that of being true, at least in parts."

Austin centered his work on the analysis of ordinary language. He was aware that the use of such phrases as "the analysis of language," or "analytic philosophy" or even "ordinary language" could lead to the misunderstanding that such analysis was *only* and *solely* concerned with words. It is not only words, says Austin, "but also...the realities we use the words to talk about" that concerned him: "We are using a sharpened awareness of words to sharpen our perception of, though not the final arbiter of, the phenomena." He even wondered in passing whether his way of doing philosophy might not more usefully be called "linguistic phenomenology," a notion he gave up as being "rather a mouthful." Actually, Austin had little interest in criticizing the methods of other philosophers or putting excessive emphasis upon his own style. He had discovered a technique for studying the nature of language and found it successful in dealing with various philosophical problems. Turning to his essay on "A Plea for Excuses," we find in it some flavor of his fruitful analysis of ordinary language.

Before Austin analyzes the many uses of the word *excuses,* he elaborates in some detail just how and why he philosophizes about words. For one thing, Austin felt that philosophy can be "done" in a wide variety of ways. Unlike one of the sciences, whose subject matter and methods are highly organized, philosophy functions in those spheres where no one is sure just what is the best way to resolve a particular problem. Austin therefore developed the technique of selecting some area of discourse of interest to philosophers. For him the word *excuses* provided a rich field for the study of language as well as human behavior. Through the analysis of this word, Austin discovers distinctions of various degrees, sometimes minute, between words closely connected with *excuses.* Moreover, his analysis uncovers interesting insights into human behavior as suggested by the distinctions among a web of interrelated words.

At the outset, the word *excuses* turns out to be a term surrounded by other significant words, such as *defence, justification,* or *plea.* It is necessary, says Austin, to give a complete and clear account and to consider the largest number possible of cases of the use of the chosen word. Excuses involve, in general, a situation where people are *accused* of having done something wrong, or "bad," or "inept," and they either try to defend their conduct or establish their innocence. They can admit that they *did* what they are accused of doing and then argue that under the prevailing circumstances it was either the right or the acceptable or at least the understandable thing to do. This would be to "justify" the action. A quite different way to proceed would be for the accused to admit that the act was a bad one but that it would be unfair to say without qualification that they *did* it. It could be that their action was unintentional, an accident, or precipitated by some other event. The word "responsibility" becomes significantly related to "they did it" and to "excuses." And the distinction between an "excuse" for an action and a "justification" of it turns out to be an important one. Moreover, if the charge happens to be murder, a plea for the accused could rest on the justification of self-defense or excused as accidental. Words with finer degrees of distinction could be employed here, including "mitigation" and "extenuation." And what about the language of a defendant who says, "I didn't do it—something in me made me do it." An act can also be the result of a "fit of anger" as distinguished from a "deliberate act."

Why go through this analysis of the word *excuses* or any other term of discourse? Apart from the fact that the fashioning of excuses has occupied such an important role in human affairs and is on that account worthy of careful study, Austin believed that moral philosophy could benefit by this analysis for two reasons. For one thing, such an analysis could facilitate in developing a more accurate and up-to-date version of human conduct. Secondly, as a corollary, it could contribute toward the correction of older and prematurely settled theories. And inasmuch as moral philosophy is the study of the rightness and wrongness of conduct or the doing of actions, it becomes crucial to understand what it means to "do something" before one can properly say about it that it is either right or wrong.

"Doing an action," says Austin, is a very abstract expression. Do we mean by it "to think something," "to say something," or "to try to do something"? It is just as inaccurate, says Austin, to think that all our actions are of the same nature as it is to think that all "things" are of the same kind, that winning a war, as an action, is the same as sneezing, that a horse as a thing is equal to a bed as a thing. Do we *do* an action when we breathe or see? For what, then, is the phrase "doing an action" an appropriate substitute? What rules are there for the proper word signifying "the" action for which a person is responsible or for which he or she manufactures excuses? Can human actions be divided in order to attribute one part to the actor and the remainder to someone or something else? Moreover, is an action a simple event? Austin here emphasizes rather the complex nature of a human act, even the mere motion of the body which could involve intentions, motives, response to information, the reflection upon rules, a studied control of the motion of a limb, or a shove from someone else.

Austin believed that the questions just raised and the problems posed can be illumined by an analysis of the word *excuses*. For one thing, an excuse implies that a certain mode of behavior went wrong in some way. To determine the nature of the wrongness involves a clarification of the "right." The abnormal frequently clarifies the normal. The careful study of excuses provides the opportunity to determine when excuses are appropriate, what actions can be classified as excusable, what particular abnormalities of behavior are truly "actions," and, in a more intricate manner, determine what constitutes the very structure or mechanism of human behavior. The study of excuses can also resolve some traditional mistakes or inconclusive arguments in moral philosophy. High on the list is the problem of freedom. Here Austin compares the words *freedom* and *truth,* pointing out that just as "truth" is not a name characterizing assertions, neither is "freedom" a name characterizing actions. Freedom, says Austin, is "the name of the dimension in which action is assessed." He then says, "in examining all the ways in which each action may not be 'free', i.e., the cases in which it will not do to say simply 'X did A,' we may hope to dispose of the problem of freedom." This is, of course, just the beginning of Austin's meticulous analysis of the word *excuses,* but it suffices to suggest his style.

Besides throwing light on moral philosophy, the study of excuses provides Austin with a concrete application for his philosophical method. He begins with "ordinary language" through which he expects to discover "what we should say when" and therefore "why and what we should mean by it." Underlying his faith in the fruitfulness of the analysis of ordinary language is his conviction that such an analysis can clear up the uses and misuses of words and in that manner avoid the traps in which one can be caught by imprecise language. The analysis of ordinary language also emphasizes the differences between words and things and enables one to remove the words from the realities we use words to talk about and in that way get a fresh look at those realities. Most of all, Austin believed that "our common stock of words embodies all the distinctions men have found worth drawing, and the connections they have found worth making, in the lifetimes of many generations." This stock of words in ordinary language must, he felt, be more sound and more subtle than any we could think up for the purpose of philosophizing, inasmuch as they have stood up to the test of time and the competition of other possible words. Moreover, ordinary language provides the philosopher "a good site for fieldwork." It makes possible a different climate of philosophical discourse by disengaging individuals from frozen and rigid philosophical positions. How much easier it is to agree on the uses of words or even on how to reach agreement. Austin hoped that this method could someday be applied in the turbulent field of aesthetics, saying, "if only we could forget for awhile about the beautiful and get down to the dainty and the dumpy."

Austin was aware that ordinary language, as a basis for analysis, could present certain problems. For one thing, there is a certain "looseness" in ordinary language so that one person's usage may not be the same as another's. To this Austin replies that there is not as much disagreement in the use of words as one might think. Surface differences tend to disappear when, through analysis, it is discovered that it was not really the *same* situation about which different persons have been speaking: "The more we imagine the situation in detail," says Austin, "the less we find we disagree about what we should say." Sometimes, however, there are disagreements in the use of words, but even here, says Austin, "we can find *why* we disagree," and "the explanation can hardly fail to be illuminating." Another question about ordinary language, besides its looseness, is whether it should be construed as the "last word" on matters. While ordinary language does not claim to be the last word, it is significant that it embodies the inherited experience and insights of many generations. And although these insights have been focused particularly upon the practical affairs of men, that fact further strengthens the claim for its accuracy. For if the distinctions of words work well in ordinary life, "then there is something in it," says Austin. To be sure, scholars may have interests other than those whose language pertains to ordinary life. And there is no reason to believe that error and superstition cannot survive for long periods of time in a language. To this extent, Austin readily concedes that "ordinary language is *not* the last word: in principle it can everywhere be supplemented and improved upon and even superseded." But for Austin it *is* the first word in his program of analysis.

Austin recommended three resources which one can utilize in undertaking a full-scale analysis of the word *excuses*. Similar resources and methods would presumably be available for the analysis of other words as well. First, he advocated using the dictionary. A concise one would do, and he suggested reading through it entirely and listing all the relevant words, remarking that it would not take as long as many would suppose. Or one could make a list of obviously relevant words first and consult the dictionary to discover their various meanings, a process which would then lead to other germane words until the relevant list is complete. A second source for this purpose would be the law. Here one would be provided with a vast number of cases along with a wide variety of pleas for excuses along with many analyses of the circumstances of the particular conduct in question. The third source is psychology. The use of psychology is an interesting example of how ordinary language is supplemented and even superseded inasmuch as psychology classifies some varieties of behavior or gives explanations of ways of acting which may not have been noticed by laymen nor captured by ordinary language. Given these resources "and with the aid of imagination," Austin was confident that the meanings of a vast number of expressions would emerge and that a large number of human actions could be understood and classified, thereby achieving one of the central purposes of this whole process, namely, "explanatory definition."

RICHARD RORTY

Richard Rorty's Pragmatic Turn

The emergence of analytic philosophy gave the impression that the linguistic turn had produced a major revolution in the aims, limits, and practice of philosophy. Ever since Plato, traditional philosophers sought to discover the foun-

Richard Rorty *(David Burnett/Contact Press Images)*

dations of knowledge, to know exactly what is "out there"—outside the mind—to distinguish between mind and body, between appearance and reality, and to provide a "grounding" for absolutely certain truth.

By contrast, analytic philosophers scaled down the enterprise of philosophy to the more modest objective of discovering the foundations of meaningful language. Sentences or propositions would be considered meaningful only if they corresponded to objective and verifiable facts. In this way, philosophy would resemble the rigor of scientific knowledge.

But did this shift in the concerns of philosophy represent a major revolution? To be sure, linguistic analysis clarified some philosophical problems by demonstrating the frequent misuse of language. More dramatically, by requiring that language, to be meaningful, must accurately represent facts, it turned out that several "problems" were simply eliminated from the agenda of philosophy. What "facts" could be "represented" by language when talking about the "good" or the "beautiful" or the "just" or "God"? If there were no such facts, philosophy could no longer speak confidently, or meaningfully, about ethics, aesthetics, religion, justice, and metaphysics. Surely this represented a revolutionary departure from the traditional concerns of philosophy.

However, in a very significant way, analytic philosophy did not usher in a major change in the assumptions of philosophy, according to Richard Rorty. In his provocative book *Philosophy and the Mirror of Nature,* Rorty argues that analytic philosophy is not something new but, rather, a variation of what

Descartes and Kant had done, namely, to provide a "foundation" for knowledge. What is new in analytic philosophy, says Rorty, is the conviction that knowledge is represented by what is linguistic and not by what is mental. But to say this is to leave unchanged the assumption that as human beings we possess by our very nature some framework within which the activity of inquiry takes place. We still have, in analytic philosophy, (1) a "knowing subject," (2) "reality out there," and (3) a "theory of representation" which describes how reality is represented to the knowing subject. The old account of how we know is still the same, namely, that the mind is like a great mirror containing representations of nature, some accurate and some inaccurate, which we then study by pure "rational" methods. Analytic philosophy does not remove the assumption that the mind is like a mirror. It simply tries to increase the accuracy of the representations captured by the mind, as Rorty says, by "inspecting, repairing and polishing the mirror." Moreover, to engage in repairing and polishing the mirror implies the presence of another old assumption, namely, that there is something, "reality," which is "out there" (eternally out there) but which for some reason is inaccurately represented to the mind. For these reasons, Rorty believes that a truly revolutionary move in philosophy would require the final rejection of several assumptions, including the traditional mirror-imagery (the assumption that human beings are equipped with a structural framework which dictates how their inquiries must proceed) and the assumption that even before there is thinking or history, there is an "essence" to reality, which to know is to know the truth.

Richard Rorty was himself an analytic philosopher as a young professor at Princeton University. He was born in 1931 and raised in New York City as an only child whose parents were freelance journalists and whose maternal grandfather, Walter Raschenbusch, was an eminent liberal Protestant theologian. At age fourteen, Rorty entered the University of Chicago and later completed his graduate studies in philosophy at Yale. After a brief teaching assignment at Wellesley, he joined the faculty at Princeton, whose philosophy department at that time was strongly oriented to analytic philosophy. For a few years, Rorty immersed himself in "doing" analytic philosophy but finally grew dissatisfied with the piecemeal task of unravelling linguistic and logical puzzles. After a brief period of professional crisis during the early 1970s and to the considerable surprise of his colleagues, Rorty chose a new direction for his studies, toward the pragmatism of John Dewey.

John Dewey delivered a lecture in 1909 on "The Influence of Darwinism on Philosophy" on the occasion of the celebration of the fiftieth anniversary of Darwin's *Origin of Species* (1859). The influence it had, said Dewey, was that it introduced a new mode of thinking, a mode that influenced Dewey himself. The theory of biological evolution, Dewey said, emphasized that change is fundamental to everything that exists. This change represents not only, as Whitehead would say later, simple rearrangements of bits of matter; the biological dimension focused upon the presence of "organic systems" and their creativity with respect to the environment.

Darwin had "laid his hand upon the sacred ark of absolute permanency," writes John Randall. This meant that knowledge could no longer aim at realities lying behind any notion of the mathematical Order of Nature or any vestige of Platonic "eternality." There is no "givenness" about the world. Philosophy would no longer enquire about absolute origins and absolute final ends, as in Hegel's gradual realization of the Idea of freedom or Marx's final phase of human society. Philosophy would no longer, in some quarters, seek to prove that our life necessarily must have certain qualities or values as a result of an earlier cause, such as creation, or a specific goal. The world, in this view, is not described as reflecting an eternal pattern, out there, abstractly.

Instead, philosophical thinking would begin with our immediate concrete experiences of *life*. Human life would be seen, at least in one respect, as it was by Aristotle, namely, that although we are a part of nature and behave in certain mechanical ways as described by science, we are nevertheless *human*. And although we partake of some characteristics of other animals, we are nevertheless unique. What makes us unique is that we are aware of the processes of nature and we can know how we *function*. We know where some forms of behavior lead, what values or ends they support or frustrate. Experience tells us what things are "necessary for," or "better for" or "worse for" other things. We can evaluate things not in terms of some remote and abstract standards but rather in terms of some more obvious "ends" built into the very natural functions of our organisms. Human life in this view reveals a close relationship between the functions of human nature and the various simultaneous functions of the larger natural environment, which provides wide choices of ends and values.

It is easy to see how this "new mode of knowledge" influenced Dewey in the direction of pragmatism. Instead of pursuing a single ultimate truth about reality, his emphasis shifted to a pluralism of truths, many truths, and the characteristic that these ideas or notions are true because they "work."

Rorty was drawn to Dewey's pragmatism for these and several other reasons. For one thing, it gave him an avenue of escape from the severe limitations which linguistic analysis had placed upon the scope of his philosophic activity. Pragmatism provided for him a basis for finally rejecting the idea that the mind is a reliable mirror reflecting reality, a notion that assumed that only those thoughts and language are true which faithfully represent the real world. Since there is no way to be absolutely certain that a thought or statement accurately corresponds to reality, it is, he thought, better to think that a statement is true if it leads to successful behavior, if, that is, it "works." Statements should be looked upon as "tools" whose truth is based upon their usefulness. Since there are several types of statements, there are correspondingly several kinds of truths. To look upon truth in this manner is to bring back to philosophy the subject matter of many fields. From this point of view, science has no special claim upon truth since it is only one among many areas of practical human concerns, such as politics, ethics, art, literature, history, and religion. Scientific method cannot therefore provide the sole criterion for truth since there are several particular kinds of truth.

What especially attracted Rorty to pragmatism was that its pluralistic view of truth opened wide areas of legitimate philosophical discussion. In addition to the analysis of language, it now became philosophically useful to study novels and poetry to find there insights into human problems which philosophy had virtually abandoned. Moreover, Anglo-American philosophers could more comfortably engage in discourse with their counterparts on the Continent, where the darker themes of dread, *angst,* and solitude permeate the works of such writers as Nietzsche, Kierkegaard, and Heidegger. Rorty discovered that while analytic philosophy had isolated itself from some of the deepest concerns of life, it is possible to overcome this isolation by expanding the range and type of literature considered worthy of study. Almost inevitably, Rorty is no longer in a department of philosophy but has, since 1983, held the title of University Professor of Humanitites at the University of Virginia. Here, his mode of philosophy relies heavily upon literary and cultural criticism and acknowledges the morally illuminating power of novelists and poets. Rorty has no interest in nor does he think it is useful to engage in "systematic" philosophy. More and more, he believes, the emphasis will be on "edifying" philosophy, whose practitioners will be concerned with culture and self-transformation.

"Contingency"

If there is one theme that captures the truly radical aspect of Rorty's philosophical point of view it is his conviction that there are no eternal "essences," as, for example, "human nature," the "true nature of the self," or "universal moral law," discoverable by human reason. Instead of a timeless and stable structure in reality, what we find, says Rorty, is that everywhere we are confronted by "contingency," by the ever-presence of "chance." If everything is "contingent," how can there be any meaning to life? If there is no timeless truth, how can we know whether our lives fall short of their intended purpose or value? Rorty is aware of these consequences of his pragmatism. But instead of being intimidated by this bewildering world of chance, he sees in it wide opportunities for overcoming contingency by constant self-transformation or self-creation. Still, he insists that it is philosophically important to recognize that contingency, chance, characterizes such fundamental aspects of our experience as our *language,* our idea of our *selfhood,* and our conception of human society or *community.*

The Contingency of Language   We normally think of language as a means by which our vocabulary represents reality to the mind. How can a vocabulary represent, be the medium of, something "out there"? One way is to use the metaphor of a jigsaw puzzle. By the use of words it is assumed that we can describe various pieces of the puzzle so that as the vocabulary changes and evolves, our language will come closer and closer to what exists out there. But this assumes that out there are to be found fixed and stable realities capable of being described.

Take, for example, the language of science. Galileo created a new vocabulary when he described the behavior of the earth and the sun in relation to each other. What does this history of the change in scientific language illustrate? Does it show that Galileo's new description represents a deeper insight into the intrinsic nature of the natural world? Rorty does not think so. "We must," he says, "resist the temptation to think that the redescriptions of reality offered by contemporary physical or biological sciences are somehow closer to 'the things themselves.' " It is not as though more of the jigsaw puzzle has been filled in by the new language. Rather, we should instead use the metaphor of language as a "tool" so that the new vocabulary of science will simply enable those who create the new language to accomplish new objectives. There is no necessary line of development in language any more than there is a necessary line of evolution in nature. We cannot return to the way nature and its purposes were thought about before the time of Darwin. Contingency, chance, that is, the more or less random behavior of things, explains the changes in nature and in language. Physical evolution did not have to occur precisely as it did. Was it necessary or only by chance that orchids came upon the scene—and didn't Mendel, says Rorty, "let us see mind as something which just happened rather than as something which was the whole point of the process?" To say the opposite, namely, that the world has an intrinsic nature which the physicist or poet has glimpsed, is, he says, "a remnant of the idea that the world is a divine creation, the work of someone who had something in mind, who Himself spoke some language in which He described His own project."

Because our language is the product of random choices made by those who sought to describe the world, there is no reason now to be bound by that inherited language. That the language of the past has influenced the way we think is not a sufficient reason to assume that we should not create our own new vocabulary if that would be more useful in solving our problems. "It is essential to my view," says Rorty, "that we have no prelinguistic consciousness to which language needs to be adequate, no deep sense of how things are which it is the duty of philosophers to spell out in language." Truth, says Rorty, is no more than what Nietzsche called "a mobile army of metaphors."

The Contingency of Selfhood　Plato gave us the metaphor of two worlds, the world of time, appearance, and change, on the one hand, and the world of enduring, changeless truth on the other. A person's life represents the attempt to escape from the distractions of the flesh and dominant opinions of a particular time and place in order to enter the real world of reason and contemplation. With this vocabulary, Plato created a language designed to describe the essence of human nature, implying that there is only one true description of our human situation. As we face the contingent events of our life, we are to control our affections by the use and power of our reason and thereby achieve moral and intellectual virtue. Theologians offered basically this same metaphor, urging human beings to strive toward our "true nature." Similarly, Kant described the difference between our daily experiences with their local influences on our choices, on the one hand, and our internal moral consciousness which reveals for all human beings our timeless and universal moral laws on the other.

These versions of the two worlds which we encounter represent the true world as compared with the deceptive world which we must try to escape.

Rorty believes that the language of Plato, the theologians, and Kant have imposed labels and descriptions of "the self" upon our consciousness as if these were absolutely true descriptions. There are, after all, alternative ways of defining the self. If, for example, Nietzsche says that "God is dead," he implies that there is nothing more to reality than the flow of events, the flux of chance. Nor is there any universal moral law nor a "true self." This skepticism leaves the question of how to provide a meaning for human life. There is no other choice, says Nietzsche, to which Rorty agrees, than for each person to give meaning to his own life by writing his own language, describing his own objectives. In a real sense, each of us must be involved in transforming our "self," not by seeking the truth but by overcoming the old self, by choosing, willing a new self. According to Rorty, "we create ourselves by telling our own story."

Plato tried to describe human nature in some specific detail when he spoke of the tripartite aspect of the self, including the physical body, the passions and affections, and, highest of all, the mind. He assumed that the mind had a "clear shot" at the truth and could overcome the contingent events encountered in daily life. But Rorty finds quite different descriptions of consciousness have been offered without assuming a realm of eternal truth. On the contrary, he finds in the writings of Freud a tripartite description of the self as nothing but the product of contingent events. The sense of guilt is explained not by an innate knowledge of the moral law. Rather, as Freud says, "a regressive degrading of the libido takes place, the super-ego becomes exceptionally severe and unkind, and the ego, in obedience to the super-ego, produces strong reaction-formations in the shape of conscientiousness, pity and cleanliness. . . . " It may be that the metaphor of the two worlds has been too powerful to overcome. But Freud replies that "if one considers chance to be unworthy of determining our fate, it is simply a relapse into the pious view of the universe which Leonardo himself was on the way of overcoming when he wrote that the sun does not move . . . we are all too ready to forget that in fact everything to do with our life is chance, from our origin out of the meeting of spermatozoon and ovum onwards. . . . Everyone of us human beings corresponds to one of the countless experiments in which [the countless causes] of nature force their way into experience."

The Contingency of Community   How shall human beings live together, or, how can human beings achieve solidarity and community? Here, again, Plato drew a tight connection between "the essential nature of man" and the social and political arrangement of the community. The three classes of Plato's society were thought by him to be the necessary extensions of the three parts of the human soul or self. The artisans embody the physical element of man, the guardians express the spirited passions, and the rulers are the incarnation of the mind, reason. Plato also argued that there must first be a harmony of the three parts of the private individual if the collective harmony of the community was to be achieved. All the elements of the self must be subject to and governed by the highest faculty, by reason. Similarly, all the classes of society must be subordinate to the ruler. This whole arrangement is dictated by the structure of human nature.

Rorty disagrees with this notion that the public life of mankind must be based upon the antecedent facts of human nature. Theologians have also offered their versions of the Platonic account of the origin and justification of political authority, especially in their theory of the divine rights of kings, while Karl Marx drew from his description of history, and from the relation of human beings to the material order of nature, a theory of a classless society. These various vocabularies or languages describing the good society are contingent upon the special perspectives of each author. Each account focuses upon a different concept of "ultimate reality," a different view of the essential nature of man. It is not surprising, then, says Rorty, that there can be no single concept of community which is required by some true description of human nature.

For his part, Rorty holds that since there is no absolutely true account available about human nature, there is no point in looking in that direction for some moral basis of society. The contingency of language and the contingency of the self mean that there is no reliable objective information which can lead to the "right" kind of community. There is no theory of knowledge that can guarantee the just society—neither "rationality, the love of God, or the love of truth." Instead, Rorty agrees with the insights of Dewey as reflected by John Rawls in his Dewey Lectures:

> What justifies a conception of justice is not its being true to an order antecedent and given to us, but its congruence with our deeper understanding of ourselves and our aspirations, and our realization that, given our history and the traditions embedded in our public life, it is the most reasonable doctrine for us.

The central value on which to build a community is the value of freedom and equality, the ideal of liberal democracy. It is not helpful, says Rorty, to ask at this point, "How do you *know* that freedom is the chief goal of social organization?" any more than it is to ask, "How do you *know* that Jones is worthy of your friendship?" The preference for freedom and equality and the desire to eliminate suffering are not discovered by reason but by chance. These values were not always obvious nor always chosen. They were not always options, for example, for the Egyptians, nor can they be defended rationally against those who refuse to accept them. The social glue that holds a liberal society together consists in a consensus, says Rorty, in which everybody has an opportunity at self-creation to the extent of his abilities. From the point of view of his pragmatism, Rorty says that what matters most is the widely shared conviction that "what we call 'good' or 'true' [is] whatever is the outcome of free discussion," for if we take care of political freedom, "truth and goodness will take care of themselves."

25

Existentialism

Existentialism emerged in its contemporary form in Paris following World War II. At first it appeared to be a philosophical fad whose practitioners expounded their thoughts in cafés far removed from the professional precincts of university philosophers. Like most fads, it was expected that this one too would soon pass into oblivion. But existentialism has, if anything, gained momentum by invading virtually every form of human thought and expression, including the novel, theater, poetry, art, and theology. In the sheer scope of its influence existentialism has achieved a far wider response than any other mode of philosophy in current times, and this influence does not appear to be waning.

What appeared after World War II in the essays, plays, and novels of Jean Paul Sartre and Albert Camus was for the most part a brilliant and popular version of a mood and mode of thought that earlier philosophers had seized upon but that evoked widest response only in the historic circumstances of the twentieth century. Existentialism was one of the major currents of thought in Germany under the Weimar Republic, with Heidegger and Jaspers among its leaders. In the middle of the nineteenth century its main themes had already been worked out by the melancholy Dane Sören Kierkegaard with variations found in the works of Schelling and Marx. That writers with such diverse philosophical orientations should all have become identified with existentialism is an important indication that existentialism has many forms and that among existentialists there are probably more differences than similarities. Even William James, Bergson, Nietzsche, the German mystic Jacob Böhme, and Pascal must be counted among those who contributed to the existentialist theme. What all these philosophers had in common was a concern about existence, human existence, the conditions and quality of the existing human individual.

Existentialism was bound to happen. The individual had over the centuries been pushed into the background by systems of thought, historical events, and technological forces. The major systems of philosophy had rarely paid attention to the uniquely personal concerns of individuals. Although Aristotle, for example, wrote a major treatise on ethics, Montaigne could say that "I can't recognize most of my daily doings when they appear in Aristotle." Nietzsche also wrote that "to our scholars, strangely enough, the most pressing question does not occur: to what end is their work... useful?" To be sure, Socrates had focused upon just these matters with his insistence that all thought and activity should be directed toward enhancing the meaning of human existence. St. Augustine also engaged in profound introspective psychological analysis to discover the source of human beings' personal insecurity and anxiety. Still, philosophy for the most part dealt with the technical problems of metaphysics, ethics, and the theory of knowledge in a general and objective manner, which bypassed the intimate concerns of people about their personal destiny. Historical events, particularly wars, showed a similar disregard for the feelings and aspirations of individuals. And technology, which arose as an aid to humankind, soon gathered a momentum of its own, forcing people to fit their lives into the rhythm of machines. Everywhere men and women were losing their peculiarly human qualities. They were being converted from "persons" into "pronouns," from "subjects" into "objects," from an "I" into an "it."

Inevitably, dehumanized Western humanity began to exhibit all the symptoms of dehumanization. If learning, even philosophy and theology, talked in abstract generalities and skirted around the personal perplexities of individuals, it would be only a question of time before everyone would conclude that there is no expressible meaning for any human being's existence. If wars overwhelmed people in spite of their frantic efforts to forestall such calamities, life would be regarded as precarious, ambiguous, and insecure, and men and women would develop deep anxiety and the feeling of being abandoned in an insensitive and random universe. If technology removed much of the human dimension of existence by harnessing men and women to machines and requiring them to work as "organization people," they would find fewer occasions for expressing their existence as persons.

Religion, the traditional source of human beings' sense of worth, meaning, and moral guidance, was itself suffering from the critical impact of rational and scientific thought. Dostoevsky experimented with the implications of a non-religious estimate of humanity, wondering whether one could successfully maintain that "since there is no God, everything is permitted." For Nietzsche, the bankruptcy of religious faith appeared to be the decisive cultural fact of the day. He did not hesitate to proclaim that for all intents and purposes "God is dead." This fact, he urged, should be accepted with courage, and upon it should be built a new conception of human existence. Atheism had become an important cause of the problems that gave rise to existentialism, since the breakdown of the religious tradition of Europe greatly aggravated the growing sense of life's worthlessness and meaninglessness. In their struggle against this meaninglessness, some existentialists took a frankly atheistic position and drew out all the consequences of such a position in formulating their approach to life. Others turned once again to religion in order to rediscover there what they believed had been missed by rational and scientific thinkers.

Whether they were theists or atheists, the existentialists all agreed that traditional philosophy was too academic and remote from life to have any adequate meaning for them. They rejected systematic and schematic thought in favor of a more spontaneous mode of expression in order to capture the authentic concerns of concrete existing individuals. Although there is no "system" of existentialist philosophy, its basic themes can, nevertheless, be discovered in some representative existentialist thinkers.

SÖREN KIERKEGAARD

Many of the themes of contemporary existentialism were first expressed in the writings of Sören Kierkegaard. Born in Copenhagen in 1813, he spent his short life in a brilliant literary career, producing an extraordinary number of books before his death in 1855 at the age of forty-two. Although his books were soon forgotten after his death, they made an enormous impact upon their rediscovery by some German scholars in the early decades of the twentieth century. At the University of Copenhagen Kierkegaard was trained in Hegel's philosophy and was not favorably impressed by it. When he heard Schelling's lectures at Berlin, which were critical of Hegel, Kierkegaard agreed with this attack upon Germany's greatest speculative thinker. "If Hegel had written the whole of his Logic and then said... that it was merely an experiment in thought," wrote Kierkegaard, "then he could certainly have been the greatest thinker who ever lived. As it is, he is merely comic." What made Hegel comic for Kierkegaard was that this great philosopher had tried to capture all of reality in his system of thought and, in the process, had lost the most important element, namely, *existence*. For Kierkegaard, the term *existence* was reserved for the individual human being. To exist, he said, implies being a certain kind of individual, an individual who strives, who considers alternatives, who chooses, who decides, and who, above all, makes a commitment. Virtually none of these acts were implied in Hegel's philosophy. Kierkegaard's whole career might well be considered a self-conscious revolt against abstract thought and an attempt on his part to live up to Feuerbach's admonition: "Do not wish to be a philosopher in

Sören Kierkegaard *(Royal Danish Ministry)*

contrast to being a man...do not think as a thinker...think as a living, real being ...think in Existence."

What It Means to Think Existentially

To "think in Existence" meant for Kierkegaard to recognize that one is faced with personal choices. Human beings find themselves constantly in an "existential situation." For this reason, their thinking ought to deal with their own personal situation with a view to coming to terms with the problem of alternatives and choices. Hegel's philosophy falsified people's understanding of reality because it shifted attention away from the concrete individual to the concept of universals. It called upon individuals *to think* instead of *to be,* to think the Absolute Thought instead of being involved in decisions and commitments. Kierkegaard made a distinction between the *spectator* and the *actor,* arguing

Kierkegaard House, second from right corner *(Royal Danish Ministry)*

that only the actor is involved in existence. To be sure, the spectator can be said to exist, but the term *existence* does not properly belong to inert or inactive things, whether these be spectators or stones. Kierkegaard illustrated this distinction by comparing two kinds of people in a wagon, one holding the reins while asleep and the other fully awake. In the first case, the horse goes along the familiar road without any direction from the sleeping person, whereas in the other case the person is truly a driver. Surely, in one sense it can be said that both people exist, but Kierkegaard insists that *existence* must refer to a quality in the individual, namely, his conscious participation in an act. Only the conscious driver exists, and so, too, only a person who is engaged in conscious activity of will and choice can be truly said to exist. Thus, while both the spectator and the actor exist in a sense, only the actor is involved in existence.

Kierkegaard's criticism of rational knowledge was severe. He revolted against the rational emphasis in Greek wisdom, which, he charged, had permeated subsequent philosophy and Christian theology. His specific argument was that Greek philosophy had been too greatly influenced by a high regard for mathematics. Although he did not want to reject either mathematics or science in their proper uses, he did reject the assumption that the mode of thought characteristic of science could be successfully employed when trying to understand human nature. Mathematics and science have no place for the human individual, only for the general, the universal. Likewise, Platonic philosophy emphasizes the universal, the Form, the True, the Good. Plato's whole assumption was that if one *knew* the Good he would do it. Kierkegaard thought that such an approach to ethics was a falsification of people's real predicament. What Kierkegaard wanted to underscore was that even when a person has knowledge, he or she is still in the predicament of having to make a decision. The grand formulations of philosophical systems are, in the long run, only prolonged detours which eventually come to nothing unless they lead attention back once again to the individual. To be sure, there are problems that can be solved by mathematics and science as well as by ethics and metaphysics. But over against such universal or general problems stands life, each person's life, making demands upon the individual, and at these critical moments general and abstract thought do not help. Kierkegaard saw in the biblical story of Abraham the typical human condition: "God did tempt Abraham and said unto him, Abraham: and he said, here I am. And he said, take now thy son, thine only son, Isaac, whom thou lovest." What kind of knowledge can help Abraham decide whether to obey God, to sacrifice his son? The most poignant moments in life are personal, where one becomes aware of oneself as a subject. This subjective element is obscured if not denied by rational thought, which considers only a person's objective characteristics, those characteristics that *all* people have in common. But subjectivity is what makes up each person's unique existence. For this reason, objectivity cannot give the whole truth about the individual self. That is why rational, mathematical, and scientific thought are incapable of guiding a person to genuine existence.

Truth as Subjectivity

Truth, said Kierkegaard, *is* subjectivity. By this strange notion he meant that for existing, striving, deciding persons there is not available "out there" a prefabricated truth. Anticipating the pragmatic view of William James, who said that "truth is made" by an act of will, Kierkegaard wrote that what is "out there" is "an objective uncertainty"; he argued that "the highest truth attainable for an Existing individual" is simply "an objective uncertainty held fast in the most passionate personal experience...." Whatever may have been his criticism of Plato, he did nevertheless find in Socrates' claim to ignorance a good example of this notion of truth, saying that "the Socratic ignorance which Socrates held fast with the entire passion of his personal experience, was thus an expression of the principle that the eternal truth is related to the Existing individual." This would suggest that the cultivation of the mind is not the only important or decisive thing in life. Of more consequence is the development and maturity of personality.

The Existential Situation

In describing the human *existential situation*, Kierkegaard distinguished between people's present estate, that is, what they now *are*, and what they *ought* to be, or what they are *essentially*. There is, says Kierkegaard, a movement in one's life from one's *essential* to one's *existential* condition, a movement from *essence* to *existence*. The traditional explanation of this movement in theology is made in terms of the doctrine of sin, of the Fall. Kierkegaard translated this doctrine into a profound psychological analysis, in which he isolated people's anxiety over their own finitude as the cause of their estrangement or alienation from their essential being. Sensing their insecurity and finitude, people try to "do something" to overcome their finitude, and invariably what they do only aggravates their problem by adding guilt and despair to their anxiety. Kierkegaard has in mind throughout his analysis the Christian understanding of humankind. Humankind's *essential* nature entails its relation to God, the infinite. Its *existential* condition is a consequence of its alienation from God. If, then, a person's actions drive him or her even further from God, his or her alienation and despair are compounded. This is why it is not of any help to lose oneself in a crowd. Whatever be the nature of a crowd or collectivity, whether rich or poor or political in makeup, or even a congregation in a church—in every case, says Kierkegaard, "a crowd in its very concept is the untruth, by reason of the fact that it renders the individual completely impenitent and irresponsible, or at least weakens his sense of responsibility by reducing it to a fraction." Being in a crowd, in short, unmakes one's nature as an individual by diluting the self. From the point of view of Christian faith, being thus immersed in a crowd appears as an attempt upon a person's part to derive some meaning for his or her existence. But this is a wrong attempt, for "to relate oneself to God is a far higher thing than to be related to" any other thing, whether a person, race, or even church. Until one does actualize one's essential self in God, says Kierkegaard, one's life is full of anxiety. One's anxiety is caused by one's awareness, however obscure, of a deep alienation of one's existential from one's essential self. This alienation creates in one a dynamic drive to recover one's essential self. In describing this dynamic movement, Kierkegaard speaks of the "stages on life's way."

The Three Stages

Kierkegaard's analysis of the "three stages" represents a sharp contrast to Hegel's theory of the gradual development of a person's self-consciousness. Whereas Hegel expounded the dialectic movement of the mind as it moves from one stage of intellectual awareness to another through the process of thinking, Kierkegaard described the movement of the self from one level of existence to another through an act of will, an act of choice. Hegel's dialectic moves gradually toward a knowledge of the universal, whereas Kierkegaard's dialectic involves the progressive actualization of the individual. Whereas Hegel overcomes the antithesis by a conceptual act, Kierkegaard overcomes it by the act of personal commitment.

The Aesthetic Stage The first stage in this dialectic process, says Kierkegaard, is the *aesthetic stage*. At this level, a person behaves according to his or her impulses and emotions. Although one is not simply sensual at this stage, one is for the most part governed by the senses. For this reason, the aesthetic person knows nothing of any universal moral standards and has no specific religious belief. The chief motivation is a desire to enjoy the widest variety of pleasures of the senses. Life has no principle of limitation except one's own taste; one resents anything that would limit one's vast freedom of choice. At this stage an individual can *exist* inasmuch as he or she deliberately chooses to be an aesthetic person. But even though *existence* can be achieved at this level, Kierkegaard injects the element of *quality* into the matter of existence. Later existentialists were to speak of this quality in terms of *authenticity*. That is, an individual on the aesthetic level is aware, notwithstanding his or her variety of sense experiences, that life consists, or *ought* to consist, of more than emotive and sense experiences.

Kierkegaard distinguishes between our capacity to be *spirit* on the one hand and *sensuousness* on the other, calling the first the *building* and the second the *cellar*. A person, he says, "prefers to dwell in the cellar." To be able to make this distinction about someone else is one thing; but for each individual to have an awareness of these two possibilities within himself or herself is what triggers the dialectic movement in the individual. The antithesis of the sensual drive is the lure of the spirit. In experience, this conflict produces anxiety and despair when one discovers that one is in fact living in the "cellar" but that life at this level cannot possibly produce one's *authentic* self, cannot result in *true existence*. The individual is now face to face with an *either-or;* either one remains on the aesthetic level with its fatal attractions, whose limitations are known, or one moves to the next stage. This transition, says Kierkegaard, cannot be made by thinking alone but must be achieved by making a decision, or by an act of will, by a commitment.

The Ethical Stage   The second level is the *ethical stage*. Unlike the aesthetic person, who has no universal standards but only his or her own taste, the ethical person does recognize and accept rules of conduct that reason formulates. Moral rules give the ethical person's life the elements of form and consistency. Moreover, the ethical person accepts the limitations upon his or her life that moral responsibility imposes. Kierkegaard illustrates the contrast between the aesthetic person and the ethical person in their attitude toward sexual behavior, saying that whereas the former yields to impulses wherever there is an attraction, the ethical person accepts the obligations of marriage as an expression of reason, the universal reason of humanity. If Don Juan exemplifies the aesthetic person, it is Socrates who typifies the ethical person or the reign of universal moral law. The ethical person has the mood of moral self-sufficiency; he or she takes a firm stand on moral questions and, as Socrates argued, assumes that to know the good is to do the good. For the most part, the ethical person considers moral evil to be a product either of ignorance or of weakness of will. But the time comes, says Kierkegaard, when the dialectic process begins to work in the consciousness of ethical people. They begin to realize that they are involved in something more profound than an inadequate knowledge of the moral law or insufficient strength of will. They are, in short, doing something more serious than merely making mistakes. Ethical people ultimately come to realize that they are in fact incapable of fulfilling the moral law, that they deliberately violate that law, and therefore become conscious of their guilt. Guilt, or the sense of sin, says Kierkegaard, becomes the dialectic element, the antithesis, that places before people a new *either-or.* Now they must either remain at the ethical level and try to fulfill the moral law, or they must respond to their new awareness, the awareness of their own finitude and estrangement from God to whom they belong and from whom they must derive their strength. Again, an individual's movement from the ethical to the next stage cannot be achieved by thinking alone but by an act of commitment, by a *leap* of faith.

The Religious Stage The difference between faith and reason is particularly striking for Kierkegaard when we arrive at the third level, or the *religious stage.* Our movement from the aesthetic to the ethical level required an act of choice and commitment; it ushered us into the presence of reason inasmuch as the moral law is an expression of our universal reason. But the movement from the ethical to the religious level is quite different. The leap of faith does not bring one into the presence of a God who can be philosophically or rationally described as the Absolute and Knowable Truth (and therefore objective) but into the presence of a Subject. The secret of religious consciousness, says Kierkegaard, is that the existing individual cannot pursue God in an "objective way," or "bring God to light objectively." This, says Kierkegaard, "is in all eternity impossible because God is subject, and therefore exists only for subjectivity in inwardness." At the ethical level, it is possible for the existing individual to give his or her life, as Socrates did, for the moral law that he or she rationally understands. But when it is a question of one's relation to God, there is available no rational or conceptual or objective knowledge about this relationship.

The relationship between God and each individual is a unique and subjective experience. There is no way, prior to the actual relationship, to get any knowledge about it. Any attempt to get such objective knowledge about it is, says Kierkegaard, entirely an *approximation process.* Only an act of faith can assure the existing individual of his or her personal relation to God. That we must find our self-fulfillment in God becomes clear to us as we discover the inadequacy of our existence at the aesthetic and ethical levels. Through despair and guilt we are brought to the decisive moment in life when we confront the final *either-or* of faith. The existence of God is suggested to us in our awareness of our self-alienation, that subjective awareness of the contrast between our existential and our essential selves. That God has disclosed Himself in Christ is a further complication, indeed a *paradox.* To say, as Christian faith does, that God, the infinite, is revealed in Christ, the finite, is an extraordinary affront to human reason, "to the Jews a stumbling block and to the Greeks foolishness." But Kierkegaard wanted to maintain that the only way to cross the span between humanity and God, that "infinite qualitative distinction between time and eternity," is not through speculative reason, not even Hegel's, but through faith. Again, truth for Kierkegaard was a subjective matter, a consequence of commitment. Without risk, said Kierkegaard, there is no faith. And with faith, the existing individual realizes his or her true self.

Kierkegaard's existentialism can be summed up in his statement that "Every human being must be assumed in essential possession of what essentially belongs to being a man." This being the case, "the task of the subjective thinker is to transform himself into an instrument that clearly and definitely expresses in existence whatever is essentially human." This is Kierkegaard's central point, namely, that each person possesses an essential self, which he or she *ought* to actualize. This essential self is fixed by the very fact that human beings must inescapably become related to God. To be sure, we can *exist* at any one of the three stages along life's way. But the experience of despair and guilt creates in us an awareness of qualitative differences in various modes of existence, that some modes of human existence are more authentic than others. But arriving at authentic existence is not a matter of the intellect; it is a matter of faith and commitment, a continuous process of choice by the existing individual in the presence of varieties of *either-or*.

EDMUND HUSSERL

Husserl's Phenomenology

A major source of contemporary existentialism is the phenomenology of Edmund Husserl. The connection between existentialism and phenomenology is not always obvious since so much of Husserl's philosophy is cast in technical and even special scientific language, whereas existentialism focuses upon the immediate human concerns of our daily existence. Phenomenology is rationalistic whereas existentialism is concerned with such practical issues as making choices, decisions, and personal commitments. Moreover, a significant element in Husserl's phenomenology is the act of detachment, of standing back from the realm of experienced existence in order to understand it, whereas existentialism urges a life of thoroughgoing engagement and involvement as the surest way of creating meaning for human existence. Although there are these and other differences between existentialism and phenomenology, it is the spectacular spread of existentialism that has brought Husserl's thought before a wider audience. Husserl can rightly be called the "father" of phenomenology, but he is also the first in a line of thinkers who, together, encompass many modes of existentialism and phenomenology. Among those influenced in various ways by Husserl's insights were the philosophers Heidegger, Merleau-Ponty, and Sartre.

Edmund Husserl was born in the Moravian province of Prossnitz in 1859, the same year in which Bergson and Dewey were born. After his early education in that province, he went to the University of Leipzig where, from 1876 to

Edmund Husserl

1878, he studied physics, astronomy, and mathematics and found time to attend lectures by the philosopher Wilhelm Wundt. Husserl continued his studies at the Friederich Wilhelm University in Berlin and later, in 1881, he went to the University of Vienna where, in 1883, he earned his Ph.D. for his dissertation on "Contributions to the Theory of the Calculus of Variations." During 1884 to 1886, he attended the lectures of Franz Brentano (1838–1917), who became a most significant influence on Husserl's philosophical development, especially through his lectures on Hume and John Stuart Mill and his treatment of problems in ethics, psychology, and logic. On Brentano's advice, Husserl went to the University of Halle where in 1886 he became an assistant under Carl Stumpf (1848–1936), the eminent psychologist under whose direction he wrote his first book, *Philosophy of Arithmetic* (1891). His *Logical Investigations* appeared in 1900 and in the same year he was invited to join the philosophy faculty at the University of Göttingen. It was here that Husserl spent sixteen productive years, writing such important works as his *Lectures on Phenomenology* (1904–1905), *Lectures on Phenomenology of Inner Time Consciousness* (1905–1910), *The Idea of Phenomenology* (1906–1907), *Philosophy as a Rigorous Science* (1911), and the first volume of his *Ideas* (1913). In 1916 Husserl became a full professor at Freiburg, where he taught until 1928. Here he wrote the last two volumes of his *Ideas* (1912—), *First Philosophy* (1923—), *Phenomenological Psychology* (1925—), and *Formal and Transcendental Logic* (1928). In 1928 Husserl applied for retirement. Then, between 1929 and 1936, he published two major works, *Cartesian Meditations* (1931) and the first part of his book *Philosophy and the Crisis of European Man* (1936). Because of his Jewish origins, Husserl was forbidden to participate in academic activities after 1933. Although he was offered a professorship by the University of Southern California, Husserl declined the offer, and after several months of suffering, he died of pleurisy at the age of 79 in 1938 at Freiburg in Breisgau.

Husserl's philosophy evolved gradually through several phases. His early interest was in logic and mathematics; next, he developed an early version of phenomenology focused chiefly upon a theory of knowledge; then, he moved on to a view of phenomenology as a universal foundation for philosophy and science; and finally he entered a phase in which his life-world, *Lebenswelt,* idea became a more dominant theme in his phenomenology. It is no wonder, then, that Husserl's philosophy should have had a variety of influences upon different scholars at various times. For example, Martin Heidegger, who became Husserl's assistant at Freiburg in 1920, had been familiar during his student days with Husserl's work in logic and his earlier writings in phenomenology. As his assistant from 1920–1923, Heidegger worked closely with Husserl. Together they prepared an article on phenomenology for the *Encyclopaedia Britannica.* Heidegger also prepared some of Husserl's earlier lectures for publication. Even after Heidegger left in 1923 to become a professor at Marburg, he continued his close association with Husserl. As time passed, however, Heidegger found it difficult to share Husserl's novel developments, especially those dealing with transcendental phenomenology. In his major work, *Being and Time,* Heidegger was critical of Husserl's method and his distinctive view of the ego. By the time Heidegger succeeded to Husserl's chair at Freiburg in the fall of 1928, their relationship had begun to weaken and eventually came to an end.

Similarly, although Sartre was deeply influenced by Husserl's writings when he studied German phenomenology at Freiburg, he eventually came to believe that Heidegger's modification of Husserl's view was philosophically more significant. Nevertheless, it was Sartre who, upon his return to Paris from Germany in 1934, called Merleau-Ponty's attention to Husserl's book *Ideas* and urged him to study it carefully. Merleau-Ponty was extremely impressed by several distinctive elements in Husserl's phenomenology and was inspired to work further in Husserl's writings, being particularly influenced by Husserl's *Philosophy and the Crisis of European Man.* Although Merleau-Ponty was thoroughly familiar with Husserl's ideas as interpreted by Heidegger and Sartre, he made his own extensive study of the original documents. He even went to Louvain, where he had access to the Husserl archives. These archives, which contain over 40,000 pages of Husserl's manuscripts written in shorthand, are gradually becoming available through transcriptions and translations. What we find, then, without analyzing all the details, is that Husserl exerted a strong influence upon Heidegger, Merleau-Ponty, and Sartre, the leading exponents of phenomenology and existentialism. His influence upon these younger philosophers was different at various stages of their philosophical development. And, even though they rejected many of Husserl's key ideas, their finished works bear the imprint of his phenomenology.

Naturalism and the Collapse of Reason   Before answering the question "What is phenomenology?" it is helpful to ask, "What prompted Husserl to invent phenomenology in the first place?" Husserl's philosophy grew out of his deep conviction that Western culture had lost its true direction and purpose. His mood is reflected in the title of his last major philosophical work, *Philosophy and the Crisis of European Man*. The "crisis" consists of philosophy's departure from its true goal, which is to provide the best possible answers to people's human and humane concerns, to deal rigorously with their quest for the highest values, and, in short, to develop the unique broad-range capacities of human reason. Husserl described the "crisis" as the "seeming collapse of rationalism," and he set his lifetime objective as "saving human reason." What human reason has to be saved from, according to Husserl, provides the background for his phenomenology.

The Crisis of Western Humanity

The key to the crisis of Western humanity is the enterprise of "natural science." Husserl is profoundly impressed by the brilliant successes of natural science. Indeed, his ultimate objective is to save human reason by developing philosophy into a rigorous science. His criticism is therefore not directed at science as such but rather at the assumptions and methods of the natural sciences. Husserl believes that the natural sciences have over the years developed a faulty *attitude* in Western humanity regarding what the world is like and how best to know it. The natural sciences rest upon the fatal *prejudice* that nature is basically physical and that the realm of spirit, or "soul," the realm of knowing, valuing, and judging, in short, the realm of culture, is causally based upon corporeality. The possibility of formulating a self-contained science of the spirit is rejected by the natural scientist, and this rejection, says Husserl, explains to a large degree the crisis of modern humanity. To insist that the realm of spirit must be understood after the manner of the physical sciences reflects, says Husserl, the "naiveté" of modern scientific rationalism. What makes this rationalism naive is that it expresses the questionable assumption of the various forms of *naturalism* which is that physical nature envelops everything. This means, for example, that all psychology is psychophysical. It means, moreover, that knowledge and truth are "objective," based upon a "reality" beyond the self. Just how this "objectivism" of naturalism constitutes the naiveté of modern nalism is explained by Husserl as a fundamental departure from the original philosophical attitude developed in Greece.

The distinctive Greek attitude as exemplified in Socrates, Plato, and Aristotle was that the task of philosophy is to search for universal ideal norms for our thought and behavior. Philosophy had transformed the earlier pre-philosophical mode of human existence which was characterized as a naively direct living immersed in the world, in a world constantly there. Life in this state was practical and even the developing mythologies and early religions supported the basically practical concerns of individuals and larger groups. In this condition there was no culture of ideas in the sense of ideas reaching beyond the immediate boundaries of local experience and practical interests. What Greek philosophy did, says Husserl, was to develop a new kind of outlook or attitude, namely, a universal critique of all life and its goals. This was a critique of all systems of culture that had grown up in the life of humankind. The positive side of this critique was its aim of raising humankind through universal reason toward a radically new humanity, rising above the limited horizons of custom, geography, and social groups. What made this possible was a new conception of truth, a truth independent of tradition, universally valid, and capable of infinite refinement. Here, then, is the origin of the spiritual life, the culture, of Europe, of Western humanity. It was in ancient Greece that this new attitude grew up, orienting individuals toward their environing world. The systematic formulation of this attitude is what the Greeks called *philosophy*. Correctly translated, says Husserl, this philosophy "bespeaks nothing but universal science, science of the world as a whole, of the universal unity of all being." But it was this one science, philosophy, with its comprehensive grasp of all nature, which included the cultural as well as the physical, ideas as well as objects, which ultimately began to splinter into the several separate sciences. The intervening step was the discovery of how the world of perceived nature can be changed into a mathematical world, a discovery which eventually led to the development of the mathematical natural sciences.

Ultimately, the success of the mathematical natural sciences resulted in the gradual scientific repudiation of the spirit. By steadily focusing upon the environing world, the objective attitude was developed wherein everything was considered to be physical or derived from the physical. To be sure, such a view had been offered earlier by Democritus but had been rejected by Socrates. For Socrates, people were viewed primarily as having a spiritual life within the context of society. For Plato and Aristotle, too, people possessed the same Socratic spiritual dimension. For, while human beings belong to the universe of objective facts, they are nevertheless persons, egos, who have goals and aims. But with the later success of the mathematical natural sciences, the methods of the natural sciences were extended to the knowledge of the spirit. A person's spirit was now conceived as an objective fact founded upon corporeality, taking on, Husserl says, "a predominantly dualistic, i.e., psychophysical form." Hence, the same causality embraces the one world in such a way that all explanation of the spirit involves the physical. For this reason, Husserl said that from the attitude of natural science, "there can be no pure self-contained search for an explanation of the spiritual, no purely inner-oriented psychology or theory of spirit beginning with the ego in psychical-self-experience and extending to the other psyche. The way that must be traveled is the external one, the path of physics and chemistry." He concluded that there can be no improvement in our understanding of humankind's true purposes so long as naturalistic objectivism, with its "naive" and "absurd" dualistic interpretation of the world, looks upon spirit after the manner of spatio-temporal objects and studies spirit according to the methodology of the natural sciences. It was his desire to develop a proper method for grasping the essential nature of the spirit, to overcome naturalistic objectivism, that led Husserl to formulate his transcendental phenomenology.

What, then, is phenomenology? Some appreciation of this complex philosophy with its novel terminology can be gained by even a brief consideration of some major themes in Husserl's thought.

Husserl and Descartes Husserl says that "phenomenology must honor Descartes as its genuine patriarch." There are, of course, other influences upon Husserl's thought, notably the empiricism of Locke, the skepticism of Hume, the Copernican revolution of Kant, and the pragmatism of William James. In every case Husserl went beyond these and others whose insights shaped his own ideas. Nevertheless, Descartes' influence was decisive, for it led Husserl to begin where Descartes began, with the thinking self. However, whereas Descartes sought through systematic doubt to achieve an absolutely certain foundation for knowledge, Husserl formulated the distinctive mood of phenomenology by accepting only one part of Descartes' starting point. Husserl says, "We thus begin, everyone for himself and in himself with the decision to disregard all our present knowledge. We do not give up Descartes' guiding goal of an absolute foundation for knowledge. At the beginning, however, to presuppose even the possibility of that goal would be prejudice." Husserl thus takes an even more radical approach than Descartes did, for he tries to build a philosophy without *any* presuppositions, looking solely to "things and facts themselves, as these are given in actual experience and intuition." Husserl made it a cardinal rule "to judge only by the evidence" and not according to any preconceived notions or presuppositions. He sought to recapture humanity's prescientific life, which is filled with "immediate and mediate evidences." Thus, whereas Descartes employed systematic doubt, Husserl simply withheld any judgment about his experiences, seeking instead to describe his experiences as fully as possible in terms of the evidence of experience itself.

Experience obviously revolves around the self, the ego, and for Husserl as well as for Descartes the source of all knowledge is the ego. But while for Descartes the ego becomes the first axiom in a logical sequence which enables him to deduce, as one would in mathematics, a series of conclusions about reality, Husserl sees the ego simply as the matrix of experience. Husserl therefore puts primary emphasis upon experience instead of logic. His concern is to discover and describe the given in experience as it is presented in its pure form and found as the immediate date of consciousness. Husserl criticizes Descartes for moving beyond the conscious self, the ego, to the notion of extended substance, a body, which ties the subject to an objective reality producing thereby the mind-body dualism. Instead, Husserl believed that "pure subjectivity" more accurately describes the actual facts of human experience. Moreover, whereas Descartes emphasized the two terms in his famous *ego cogito,* Husserl believed that a more accurate description of experience is expressed in the three terms *ego cogito cogitatum.* That is, whereas Descartes emphasized the "I think," Husserl makes the point that to say "I think *something*" is the typical human experience. Indeed, Husserl's analysis rests to a significant degree upon the relation he saw between consciousness, thinking, the thing thought, and the element of intentionality which "creates" the phenomena of experience.

Phenomena   What provides Husserl the term *phenomenology* as the descriptive term for his philosophy is his refusal to go beyond the only evidence or data available, namely, the data available to consciousness, and the data derived from appearances—from phenomena. But unlike theories of knowledge which distinguish between a knowing mind, on the one hand, and the object of knowledge on the other, Husserl sees virtually no distinction, at least in the preliminary description, between consciousness and the phenomenon. Indeed, Husserl's unique point is that phenomena, or whatever is, are ultimately contained in the very subjective act whereby what is is present to consciousness. This is his novel "attitude," so contrary to the naturalistic attitude which assumes an objective physical world independently existing out there. For Husserl, knowing is not the act of a camera taking pictures of things. Nor is a simple psychological description of experience sufficient. Phenomenology goes beyond listing objects given in experience; it enlarges the act of "description" of experience to include the real object, our actual perception of it, the object as we mean it, and the act of intentionality which constitutes the object for us. Thus Husserl brings to his empiricism the element of "reflection"; that is, he moves beyond the description of the superficial aspects of phenomena or appearances to the intricate activity of consciousness whereby, as Husserl says, "consciousness makes possible and necessary the fact that such an 'existing' and 'thus determined' Object is intended in it, occurs in it as such a sense." In short, we understand the elements of our experience, phenomena, best by discovering the active role of consciousness in intending and creating phenomena.

Intentionality   For Husserl, the clearest fact about human experience is not simply the fact of consciousness but rather that consciousness is always consciousness of something. Moreover, the clearest fact about consciousness is that its essence is to point toward, or to intend, some object. Our perception of things, our experience, consists of our projection toward intended objects. Thus Husserl believed that the essence of consciousness is intentionality. By intentionality, Husserl means that any object of my consciousness, a house, a pleasure, a number, or another person, is something meant, constructed, constituted, that is, intended by me. Pure consciousness has no segments—it is a continuous stream. Our primitive perception consists of the undifferentiated world. The separate objects of perception are those parts of the stream of consciousness which we as subjects constitute by intending them. Kant described earlier how the mind organizes experience by imposing such categories as time, space, and causality upon sensory experience. Similarly, Bergson said that "in the continuity of sensible qualities we mark off the boundaries of bodies." For Husserl, too, intentionality designates the active involvement of the ego in creating our experience. Indeed, for Husserl, intentionality is the structure of consciousness itself and is also the fundamental category of being. Again, this means that phenomenology stresses the need to describe the data and activity of consciousness in the process of discovering reality, instead of looking for reality in things, for things are what we intend them to be. For example, we perceive a person from a limited perspective, a profile, or in a given setting, a concert, or at a given time, at school. From these fragments, which are parts of reality, our consciousness constitutes, "intends," *the* person in question. This process of intentionality may not be a conscious one but rather automatic. For this reason, Husserl calls the ego's constitution of the world a *passive genesis.* But the question remains, Just how does Husserl arrive at this notion of the intentionality of consciousness? The presence of intentionality is disclosed through the process Husserl calls *phenomenological epochē.*

Phenomenological Epochē   The term *epochē* is the Greek word for "bracketing." Husserl uses this term to describe his method of "detachment from any point of view regarding the objective world." Whereas Descartes began by doubting everything, including all phenomena, in short, the world, except his thinking self, Husserl in contrast "brackets" all phenomena, all the elements of experience, by refusing to assert whether the world does or does not exist. He abstains from entertaining any belief about experience. Thus Husserl "brackets" the whole stream of experienced life, including objects, other people, and cultural situations. To bracket all these phenomena means only to look upon them without judging whether they are realities or appearances and to abstain from rendering any opinions, judgments, or valuations about the world. It is this phenomenological *epochē,* this standing back from the phenomena of experience, this ridding his mind of all presuppositions and prejudices, which enabled Husserl to discover himself as the ego, the life of consciousness, in which and through which the objective world in its entirety exists. Unlike Descartes, who deduced the objective world from the residual certainty of the ego, Husserl found that the ego "contained" the world. In his *Paris Lectures,* Husserl says: "For me the world is nothing other than what I am aware of and what appears valid in such *cogitationes* (my acts of thought). The whole meaning and reality of the world rests exclusively on such *cogitationes.* My entire worldly life takes its course within these. I cannot live, experience, think, value and act in any world which is not in some sense in me, and derives its meaning and truth from me."

Husserl said that "we must not make assertions about that which we do not ourselves *see*." For this reason, Husserl rejects those portions of Descartes' and Kant's philosophies which go beyond the immediate phenomenal realm, what Husserl terms the *transcendental realm,* the world of experience. Kant's distinction between the *phenomenal* (experience) and the *noumenal* (the thing-in-itself, or the *transcendent*) is unacceptable to Husserl, notwithstanding the many similarities between his and Kant's philosophies. Husserl rigorously limits the scope of philosophy to the realm of experience, and that is why it is called *transcendental phenomenology.* By bracketing the realm of experience, that is, by affecting the transcendental *epochē,* Husserl is "reduced," that is, led back (*re-ducere*) to the center of reality, namely, the conscious self. It makes no difference, says Husserl, whether we deny or affirm the existence of the world; he says, "the *epochē*...discloses the greatest and most magnificent of facts: I and my life remain—in my sense of reality—untouched by whichever way we decide the issue of whether the world is or is not." And from his unprejudiced view of his experience, Husserl concludes that "I have discovered my true self. I have discovered that I alone am the pure ego, with pure existence....Through this ego alone does the *being of the world,* and, for that matter, any being whatsoever, make sense to me and have possible validity."

To say, as Husserl does, that only through the ego does the being of the world make any sense takes us once again to his notion of intentionality. For the ego is consciousness, and consciousness is always consciousness of something. But pure consciousness must be discovered under several layers of presuppositions and points of view developed by various cultures. It is especially necessary to overcome the presuppositions of the natural sciences, which have led us to believe that the original objects of experience are the ones as described and determined by the sciences. But the objects of science are abstractions and artificial structures as compared with our original experience. The *epochē* helps us discover the original, the primordial, mode of experience, and what we find there is consciousness and *its* objects. The irreducible element of experience is the constant presence of the ego as the source of objects and their meanings. Husserl says, therefore, that all objects appear as basically determined by the structure of thinking itself. The meaning and the being of things is primordially constituted in and through consciousness. This is the act of intentionality which Husserl held to be the characteristic property of our consciousness.

The Life-World (Lebenswelt)   In order to prepare the way for the rigorous foundation of his philosophy, Husserl again and again urged the *epochē,* the bracketing of all presuppositions and especially the presuppositions of the natural sciences. To emphasize this point, Husserl urged the reduction to, that is the leading back to, the original form of human experience, the mode of experience which is prescientific. This is the realm of one's daily world, one's life-world, the *Lebenswelt.* The life-world consists of all those experiences—the perception, response, interpretation, and synthesis or organization of the many facets of everyday affairs—in which human beings are typically involved. This life-world is the source from which the sciences must abstract their objects. To that extent they provide only a partial grasp of reality. Much of the rich and meaningful elements of experience remains after the sciences have abstracted the elements of their concern. Indeed, the very nature of being a scientist is unaccounted for by science itself. Only a rigorous analysis of the way in which the life-world functions in people's unsophisticated experience as well as in science will provide an adequate basis for philosophy. In the last analysis, the basic justification or confirmation of truth is to be found in the type of evidence that derives from events of the life-world. The totality of these events of the life-world is what Husserl calls "our world-experiencing life." Through this notion of the life-world, Husserl sought to liberate the philosopher, the phenomenologist, from a point of view which is dominated by the various natural sciences. For the purpose of an even more useful mode of science, but especially in order to liberate the spirit, Husserl fashioned a way of discovering what the world is like before it is interpreted by the scientific outlook. Through the *epochē,* the life-world emerges as a fresh terrain for the enterprise of description, opening a new way of experiencing, thinking, and even theorizing. Husserl thought he had discovered that the "world" is what we as subjects know it to be, for it is, as he says, "the correlate of the subjectivity which gives it ontic meaning, through whose validities the world 'is' at all." It was this return to the life-world and subjectivity which channeled many facets of phenomenology into existentialism.

JASPERS AND MARCEL

Karl Jaspers

Kierkegaard's writings influenced the philosopher Karl Jaspers (1883–1969), who was a professor at Heidelberg and, after World War II, at Basel. Jaspers believed that just as philosophy could not be the same again after Hume focused such a searching light upon the nature of human knowledge, so philosophy could never return to its earlier modes since Kierkegaard focused upon the human condition. Jaspers' works as a professional philosopher are placed in the setting of the predicament of twentieth-century humanity. His chief concern, he said, is the age-old question of Being, which must be studied from the vantage point of *existence philosophy.* The subject of Being and of personal existence has been obscured by the overwhelming impact of the scientific mode of thinking upon the contemporary mind. In addition, the "human condition" has deteriorated with the development of technology, the emergence of mass movements, and the loosening of the bonds of religion. In particular, Jaspers comes to the conclusion that the task of philosophy must be reconsidered in the contemporary world, especially because of the developments in the various sciences. Each of the sciences has carved out a special area for its subject matter, and each science has developed its own method. It would seem that a universal science could be formulated by bringing together in some kind of unity all the particular sciences. Could not the unified sciences constitute a single science of Being, of total reality?

Jaspers believed that there could not be a universal *science* of Being. His argument is that just as each science functions within strict subject-matter limits, so, also, the aggregate of all the sciences is characterized by a limitation of coverage. The limitation of science, says Jaspers, is self-imposed. Each science deals with *objective data*. Hence, each science deals with a particular mode of being, with *a* particular kind of object. By definition, the sciences "divide up" reality into objects. To think scientifically, then, is to have access to only one kind of data, namely, objective data. But the content of Being, total reality, Existence, is not limited to objective data. The self, the individual, the whole complex of the subject—all this subjectivity is part of Existence. And nowhere is the limitation of science more apparent than when it tries to study the individual. There can be various human sciences, such as psychology, sociology, and anthropology, but these, says Jaspers, cannot deal with a person as an *existing* self, only as an object: "Sociology, psychology and anthropology teach that man is to be regarded as an object concerning which something can be learnt that will make it possible to modify this object by deliberate organization." Jaspers recognizes the value and usefulness of each of these sciences. He cannot be considered an antirationalist. His argument is, however, that the task of philosophy is not the same as that of science, that in studying Being, philosophy must not ape the sciences by treating Being as an *object* of thought, for that would make out of Being *a* being among other beings. Science, he argues, is subphilosophic because it does not deal with the unique inner experiences of concrete individual human beings.

Jaspers believes that the task of philosophy is to deal with Existence, whose subject matter is based upon the existential thinker's immediate inner and personal experience. There is a level of Being, says Jaspers, that the existential thinker can grasp, a level that is neither purely objective nor purely subjective but is the creative *source* of experience, and this is Existence. Existence, says Jaspers, "is something that can never become a mere object; it is the 'Source' whence springs my thinking and acting." Personal existence, he continues, is the center and direction of reality; it is an error to reverse this conclusion and to say that reality consists of objects. For this reason, only someone with a consciousness of personal experience can grasp the meaning of Existence. Philosophic thinking, under these assumptions, cannot set out, as Hegel had, "to raise philosophy to a science." Instead, philosophy, says Jaspers, must reaffirm that "truth is subjectivity," that philosophizing means communicating not about objects or objective knowledge but about the content of personal awareness produced by the individual's *inner constitution*. Existential thinking, says Jaspers, is "the philosophic practice of life."

Although Jaspers does not depreciate the technical knowledge of science, he insists that the "practice of life" requires that human beings bring to this knowledge some additional reality. All the principles and laws of science, he insists, are of no avail "unless individual human beings fulfill them with an effective and valuable reality." The piling up of knowledge cannot by itself assure any particular outcome for humanity. "Decisive is a man's inward attitude," says Jaspers, "the way in which he contemplates his world and grows aware of it, the essential value of his satisfactions—these things are the origin of what he does." Philosophy, therefore, must be *existence philosophy.*

Although existence philosophy cannot be reduced to any systematic statement, one can nevertheless give, as Jaspers does, some of its characteristics. Primarily, existence philosophy is the manner of thought through which a person seeks to become himself. It is a way of thought that does not restrict itself to knowing objects but rather "elucidates and makes actual the being of the thinker." It does not discover solutions in analytic reflection but rather "becomes real" in the dialogue that proceeds from one person to another in genuine communication. Existence philosophy does not assume that "what man is" is a settled piece of knowledge, for that would make it not philosophy but, once again, anthropology, psychology, and sociology. There is the danger that existence philosophy may lapse into pure subjectivity, into a restrictive preoccupation with one's own ego, into a justification for shamelessness. But Jaspers considers these possibilities as aberrations. Where it remains genuine, existence philosophy is, he says, uniquely effective in promoting all that makes man genuinely human. Each person is "completely irreplaceable. We are not merely cases of universal Being." The concept of Being, for existence philosophy, arises only in the consciousness of each concrete human being.

If existence philosophy can be said to have a "function," it is to make the mind receptive to what Jaspers calls the *Transcendent.* The human situation is described as a movement from a knowledge of objects to a second stage, where the individual recognizes in himself or herself the foundations of existence, and finally to a third stage, where a person becomes conscious of striving toward his or her genuine self. At this last stage, one discovers one's finitude. There are certain "limiting situations" that each of us faces as, for example, death, the possibility of one's own death. When one experiences an awareness of one's own finitude, one simultaneously becomes aware of its opposite, namely, Being as the Transcendent. This awareness of the Transcendent, which traditional theology calls God, is a purely personal experience incapable of specific delineation or proof; it is simply an awareness that everything, including myself and all objects, is grounded in Being. Central to my awareness of the Transcendent is my concurrent awareness of my own *freedom.* In my striving to fulfill my genuine self, I am *free* to affirm or deny my relationship to the Transcendent. Authentic existence, however, requires that I affirm it. I stand in the presence of a choice, an either-or, without the help of any scientific proof or even knowledge, only an awareness. In the end, I must express a *philosophic faith*, not unlike Kierkegaard's *leap* of faith, which signifies not some mystical union with the Transcendent but a union with the depths of life.

Gabriel Marcel

Like Jaspers, Gabriel Marcel (1889–1973) centered his existentialist philosophy upon the problem of Being, particularly upon the human question "What am I?" Like Jaspers, also, Marcel wrote in a profuse and elusive style, making it virtually impossible to capture his thought in any brief form. There is in Marcel's works, however, a basic distinction, which provides one with a significant clue to his thought. This is the distinction between a *problem* and a *mystery*. It is not possible, he writes, to answer the question "What am I?" by reducing it to a problem, analyzing its parts, and then producing a solution. A problem implies that we lack some information or knowledge and that all we need to do is look for it, engage in "research," and thereby overcome our temporary ignorance. A problem usually revolves around an object or a relationship between objects. Information regarding objects and their relationships can be gathered and calculated. But the question "What am I?" cannot be reduced to a problem, because the *I* is not an object, an *it*. Although I am some sort of object, since I do have a body, my being is a combination of subject and object; and because the subjective part of myself can never be eliminated, I cannot be reduced to a mere object, and therefore the question about my existence is not merely a problem: It is a mystery. In this context, Marcel means by the word *mystery* certain kinds of experiences that are permanently incapable of being translated into objects "out there"; these experiences *always* include the subject, and these are therefore matters of mystery.

Marcel says that "the essence of man is to be in a situation." He means by this that a person's relation to Being is different from a stone's. For one thing, "man is the only being who can make promises," a phrase of Nietzsche's which Marcel wanted to underscore. To be able to make a promise places a person into a unique relationship with another person, a kind of relationship that could not possibly exist between two objects. This moral dimension of existence led Marcel to believe that the ultimate character of a person's relationships involves the element of fidelity. Fidelity therefore is the major clue to the nature of one's own existence, for it is through fidelity that a person continues to shape his or her life, thereby expressing faith in whatever is other than he or she is, and it is therefore in expressing fidelity that a person's life achieves a responsible and authentic continuity. Fidelity is discovered in friendship and in love, where it has the power to overcome the "objectivity" of the other and to produce a new level of intimacy. In a deeper sense, too, one affirms Being through fidelity insofar as one responds to a world that makes demands and in which one assumes responsibilities. This is the deep existentialist theme in Marcel, which he discovers in the question "What am I?" a question whose answer is illusive because it does not constitute a problem but is rather a mystery. The element of mystery is virtually irreducible precisely because human existence is a combination of "being and having." Whereas *having* things and ideas can be translated into objective and therefore cognitive terms, *being* is always the element of subjectivity. In the end, human existence derives its deepest meaning from the subjective affirmation of Being through fidelity. Although he is in no sense a narrow or even orthodox theologian, Marcel found in the Christian faith the basic spirit of his philosophy, becoming a convert to the Roman Catholic Church at the age of thirty-nine. Although Kierkegaard, Jaspers, and Marcel formulated their existential philosophies in different ways, they had in common a religious basis for existentialism. Sartre parts company with these men by frankly accepting the assumptions of atheism as the starting point and foundation for his philosophy of existentialism, a perspective Sartre derived from Heidegger.

MARTIN HEIDEGGER

Even before Heidegger ever published anything, his reputation as an extraordinary thinker spread among students in the German universities. What was extraordinary about Heidegger as a teacher was that he did not develop a "set of ideas" or a "system" of philosophy. He produced nothing in the way of a neat structure of academic ideas which a student could quickly understand and memorize. He was not interested so much in objects of scholarship as in matters of thinking. With one bold stroke, he shifted the attention of twentieth-century Continental philosophy away from traditional concerns about theories and books and focused instead upon the concerns of thinking individuals. An individual is born in the world and responds to all his experiences by thinking. What Heidegger set out to explore was the deepest nature of an individual's thinking when he is thinking as an existing human being.

Born in 1889 in Germany's Black Forest region, Heidegger received his preparatory schooling in Constance and Freiburg and was introduced to philosophy at the age of seventeen when the pastor of his church gave him Franz Brentano's book entitled *On the Manifold Meaning of Being according to Aristotle.* This book, though difficult, made such an impression upon the young Heidegger that it launched him on his lifelong endeavor to explore the meaning of Being, or "the meaning that reigns in everything that is." Along the way, Heidegger was also influenced by Kierkegaard, Dostoevski, and Nietzsche, from whom he discovered that some concerns of philosophy are most creatively clarified by paying attention to concrete and historically relevant problems. At the University of Freiburg, he began his studies in theology, but after four semesters he came under the influence of Husserl and changed his major field to philosophy. Upon completing his dissertation and some further advanced studies, Heidegger became Husserl's assistant until he was appointed in 1922 as an associate professor at the University of Marburg. Here, he pursued his studies in Aristotle, formulated a fresh interpretation of phenomenology, and was hard at work on a manuscript which was to become his most famous book. In order to facilitate his promotion, his Dean at Marburg urged him to publish this manuscript, and in 1927, deliberately leaving it incomplete, Heidegger hurriedly published his book with the title *Being and Time.* It was this book that became so influential as to be regarded as the fundamental source of modern existentialism. One year later, in 1928, Heidegger was chosen to be Husserl's successor to the chair of philosophy at Freiburg. He was elected Rector of the University in 1933, and for a brief period he was a member of the Nazi party. In less than a year, in 1934, he resigned as Rector and, for the next ten years, taught courses critical of the Nazi interpretation of philosophy. He was drafted into the "People's Militia," having been declared in 1944 the "most expendable" member of the Freiburg faculty. The French occupying forces did not permit him to return to his teaching until 1951, one year before his retirement. Even after his retirement, he published several essays and interpretations of the history of philosophy, including a two-volume study on Nietzsche (1961) and, his last work, *The Matter of Thinking* (1969). Heidegger died in 1976 in Freiburg at the age of eighty-six.

In a remarkable way, Heidegger transformed the concept of Being from a highly abstract and remote concept into a subject of intense concern to every human being. To be sure, he fashioned a new vocabulary and gave old words new meanings to convey his philosophical thought. But beneath his sometimes forbidding language, one can grasp his central objective, which is to clarify our understanding of our own being, or to elucidate the meaning of Being itself. From his fresh interpretation of the concept of Being, Heidegger produced a new conception and understanding of humanity.

Between humanity and things there is this fundamental difference: Only people can raise the question about their being or about Being itself. The error in traditional philosophy which Heidegger sought to correct was the tendency to think about humanity in the same way as we think about things. We think about things by defining them, that is, by listing their attributes or characteristics. But the essence of humanity cannot be accounted for by listing its attributes. Unlike the being of things, the being of humanity includes an awareness of being. Unlike a hammer, which is simply a kind of being, a person, says Heidegger, "always has to be (i.e., realize) his being as his own"—by which he means that one is aware of the possibility of being or not being one's own self. Whether one realizes or fails to realize this possibility of being one's unique self is a matter entirely of one's personal decision. In their awareness that they face possibilities, that they must make decisions, that they might fail to realize their true self, people become aware not only of their own being but of Being itself. Only people, unlike things, have a relation to their own being, because only people find themselves as "thrown into the world" and as having to choose how to be. For people, being their unique selves is a continuous task imposed upon them. Moreover, only a person has such urgent experiences as anxiety, fear, care, and a concern about death. These and other human experiences lead a person to ask not only the limited question about his or her own being but also the larger question of what it means to be.

Humanity as "Dasein"

The word *human* can be deceptive, says Heidegger, because in the history of philosophy, definitions of humanity have tended to resemble the definition of things. To think of humanity as, for example, Descartes did, as mind and body, placed the emphasis upon humanity as a combination of these two substances. As such, humanity was set off as a knowing subject facing a world as a known or knowable object. To view humans and their relation to the world in these terms is to have a distorted view of both people and the world. Instead, Heidegger takes the lead from phenomenology and seeks to avoid defining people in terms of properties or attributes that divide them from the world. Phenomenology focuses rather upon the full texture of experience without separating it into discrete parts. Heidegger took seriously the meaning of the Greek word *phenomenon* as "that which reveals itself." What he thought he discovered by letting our human existence reveal itself was something quite different from our conventional conception of humanity. For this reason, Heidegger coined a new word to describe more accurately the experience of human existence: That word is *Dasein,* which in German means simply "being there." A human is best described as a unique mode of being rather than defined as an object. As Heidegger points out, "because we cannot define Dasein's essence by citing a 'what' of the kind that pertains to [an object]... we have chosen to designate this entity [person] as 'Dasein,' a term which is purely an expression of its being." A person as Dasein, or "being there" in the world, is a continuous being who thinks about the meaning of everything that is, not for any particular result, but because he or she is a "thinking, that is, a musing being." If, then, we ask what is the essence of humanity, the answer lies not in some attributes or properties but rather in how people exist.

The basic condition, or state, of humanity (Dasein) is its *being-in-the-world.* To these familiar words *being-in-the-world* Heidegger provides his novel analysis and interpretation by further elucidating the essential nature of Dasein (humanity). He asks us to think of our ordinary daily experiences, which he calls "average everydayness," as the first step in discovering how we become most familiar with the world. To be in the world as Dasein is not the same as one thing being in another thing, as water is in a glass or as clothes are in a closet. Dasein, that is, humanity, is in the world in the sense of "dwelling upon," of "being familiar with," or "I look after something." Here the emphasis is not upon one object related in space to another object but rather upon a mode of understanding. To say, for example, that "she is *in* love" does not refer to her location but rather to her mode of being. Similarly, to say that people are in the world is not only to place them in space but to describe the structure of their existence which makes it possible for them to think meaningfully about the world.

The world is not a collection of things set over against humanity as though humanity is one kind of thing and the contents of the world another kind. Here we discover the reason Heidegger uses the word *Dasein* instead of *humanity,* even though *Dasein* represents Heidegger's new conception of humanity. Instead of viewing people solely as encapsulated in their bodies, the word *Dasein* is used to emphasize their being as a wide "field." This wide-field dimension of people *is* the world. As Heidegger points out, "The world is not a way of characterizing those entities which Dasein essentially is not; it is rather a characteristic of Dasein itself."

To indicate how the world is a characteristic of Dasein, Heidegger describes the unique way we encounter everything in everyday experience: We encounter things as "gear," as what they are for, in short, as utensils. Take, for example, a hammer. Our first encounter with a hammer is how we use it. We use it as a utensil to accomplish some purpose. The more I hammer, the less I am aware of the hammer as an object. There seems to be no distance between me and the hammer. Heidegger distinguishes between something that is "ready-to-hand" (available for its purpose) and "present-at-hand" (simply an object). Each of these ways of "seeing" the hammer is different. When the hammer is working well, we appear to be one with it. We "see" it as part of a project, fulfilling its purpose within a context of various purposes included in the project. If the hammer breaks, we "see" it in a different way, as a thing, an object. What is significant is that the same thing can be seen in two such different ways. The hammer ready-to-hand, available for a purpose, a project, is revealed as an item with a special purpose by a kind of sight which Heidegger calls "circumspection." A tool or utensil is chosen not by inspecting its properties first and then inferring its purpose from those properties. We see its purpose first. This point is fundamental in Heidegger's thought for it means that it is not the *properties* of a thing which determine whether it is a utensil, on the one hand, or an object, on the other; rather, it is Dasein's own *projection* of the context within which any item assumes its unique role that explains our different views of that item. Moreover, an item, such as a hammer, has a purpose only in relation to a project that involves several other purposes. No item possesses any properties which throw light on other purposes in the project; for example, no properties in the hammer indicate that a ladder will also be needed to hammer nails on the roof. Any particular item has meaning only as it is related to other purposes. It is this network of relations of purposes which is disclosed prior to our encounter with things as utensils and which gives us the understanding of items as being utensils; it is the essence of Dasein that it projects this network or context of purposes, and this is what it means to say that Dasein is the world. There can be different worlds even composed of the same things because of the different ways individuals project "their" world. We speak of "a woman's world" or compare the different worlds projected by our different moods.

Dasein, Heidegger's broad designation of human existence, is where the "world" takes place. Dasein possesses a threefold structure which makes possible the projection of the world. One structure is *understanding:* This is Dasein's projecting of the context of purposes and their interrelationships within which any particular thing derives its meaning. A second structure is Dasein's *mood:* Our mood has a bearing upon how we will encounter our environment; in a despairing or joyful mood our projects will open up as either despairing or joyful—despairing or joyful are not mere attitudes but describe our manner of existence and the way the world exists for us. The third structure is *discourse:* Only something that can be formulated in speech can be understood and become subject to our moods. Together these three structures in their interrelationship represent the essential structure of Dasein's existence.

If we ask again what it means for a human being to be, we must recall everything that has been said above about Dasein. In addition Heidegger emphasizes the element of time in human existence. We know time, he says, because we know we are going to die. Our existence is therefore temporal. We attempt to deny our temporality, to evade the inevitability of our limited existence. As Dasein, each of us is situated here and now in the present facing future possibilities. Of our many moods, our fundamental mood, says Heidegger, is the mood of anxiety. Anxiety arises out of our awareness of the precarious nature of our Being. Not only are we "thrown into the world" without asking to be there, but we must constantly become our true selves by making appropriate decisions. Along the way, we experience a "fallenness," a loss of our "authentic" character. Our authentic existence requires that we recognize and affirm our own unique selves with our responsibility for our every action. A person's drift into an inauthentic existence is subtle but in every case it involves a tendency to escape from one's self by finding refuge in a public self, in an impersonal identity, the impersonal "one" in contrast to the concrete "I." The inauthentic person behaves as "one" is expected to instead of as "I" ought to. He reads and judges music, art, and literature as "one" is expected to; in public he suppresses any urge to be unique, to excel. He levels himself downward toward an averageness and behaves like the average "everyman." In this way, it is the "one" who is responsible for what happens to him since the "one" has taken over his decisions; there is no "one" in particular, certainly not the "I," who is answerable for anything. But a person cannot indefinitely avoid confronting his or her true self. Anxiety intrudes. For Heidegger, anxiety is not simply a psychological state; it is rather a mode of a person's being. Nor is anxiety similar to fear. Fear has an object, a snake or an enemy against which it is possible to defend oneself. But anxiety refers to nothing, precisely to *nothing*. Anxiety reveals the presence of "nothingness" in our being. There is no way to alter the presence of nothingness in the center of our being, the inevitability that we shall die. When we affirm our authentic self, when we see transparently what and who we are, we discover that in our inauthentic existence we have been trying to do the impossible, namely, to hide the fact of our limitations and our temporality.

SARTRE AND MERLEAU-PONTY

Jean-Paul Sartre

Born in 1905, Jean-Paul Sartre was the son of Jean-Batiste, a naval officer, and Anne-Marie Schweitzer, a first cousin of the theologian and jungle doctor. Sartre was educated at the École Normale Supérieure in Paris, exhibiting at an early age his precocious gift for literary expression. While at the École Normale, he was attracted to philosophy by Henri Bergson, whose *Essai sur les données immédiates de la conscience* left him "bowled over" and with the feeling

Jean-Paul Sartre *(The Granger Collection)*

that "philosophy is absolutely terrific, you can learn the truth through it." He spent the year 1934–35 at the Institut Français in Berlin, where he studied Husserl's phenomenology. Sartre wrote his *Transcendental Ego* (1936) in Germany while at the Institut, and, as he says, "I wrote it actually under the direct influence of Husserl." It was in Berlin also that he worked on his novel *Nausea,* which he considered his best work even at the end of his career. In that novel, Sartre deals with the pathological feeling one has upon experiencing through intuition the accidental and absurd nature of existence, the feeling that human existence is "contingent" and without explicit purpose. Because he could not find words adequate to describe this philosophical insight to the reader, "I had to garb it in a more romantic form, turn it into an adventure." During World War II, Sartre was active in the French Resistance movement and became a German prisoner of war. While in the prisoner-of-war camp, he read Heidegger and "three times a week I explained to my priest friends Heidegger's philosophy." The notes he took on Heidegger at this time influenced Sartre very strongly and were, he says, "full of observations which later found their way into *Being and Nothingness.*" For a brief period, he taught at the lycée at Havre, the lycée Henri IV, and the lycée Cordorcet, afterward resigning to devote himself exclusively to his writings, which ultimately numbered over thirty volumes. As a sequel to *Being and Nothingness* (1943), Sartre wrote another major work entitled *Critique of Dialectical Reason* (1960). His last book was the three-volume work on Flaubert (*The Idiot of the Family,* 1971–72). Although Sartre was deeply influenced by Marxism and continued to be a political activist, he was never a member of the Communist party. While some commentators sought to moralize about Marxism, they were not very successful, says Sartre, "because it was pretty hard to find much in Marxism to moralize about." His own criticism of Marxism was that it provided no explicit role for morality and freedom. Nor should one consider, says Sartre, "that morality is a simple superstructure, but rather that it exists at the very level of what is called infrastructure." Because of his commitment as an activist, he resisted personal acclaim, and when he was awarded the Nobel Prize in Literature in 1964, he refused to accept it on the grounds that he did not want to be "transformed into an institution."

While still a student at the elite École Normale Supérieure he met a fellow student, Simone de Beauvoir, with whom he enjoyed a lifelong companionship. This was no ordinary relationship. Both were brilliant students. Although she was of immense assistance to Sartre in his prolific literary work, Beauvoir herself achieved great fame as a writer. Sartre never published anything before Beauvoir had a chance to read it critically and to approve it. While Sartre was honored by the Nobel Prize Committee, Beauvoir similarly had moved to first place among women of letters. At the time of Sartre's death, she was considered France's most celebrated living writer. Her novel *The Mandarins* won the Prix Goncourt, while her book *The Second Sex,* in which she wrote the often quoted words "one is not born a woman but becomes one," gave her recognition as a well-known feminist. Her literary works gave her money, fame,

Simone de Beauvoir *(Pierre Boulat/Life Magazine/Time Warner, Inc.)*

and independence. Although Sartre and Simone de Beauvoir never married during their fifty-one years together, theirs was a profound relationship of loyalty and love. There were, however, complications along the way. In one of her memoirs, Beauvoir says "I was vexed with Sartre for having created the situation with Olga." This event became the theme of Beauvoir's first novel, *She Came to Stay,* a couple's intimate secret about the fictional character's relation with another woman, making Beauvoir say about her own situation, "From now on we will be a trio instead of a couple." Sartre had said earlier that Beauvoir was his "privileged," but not his only, female companion. Sartre had once said philosophically that "one can always be free"; Beauvoir asked, "What is the freedom of the women in a harem?" They were a rare couple—she was strikingly beautiful and tall while Sartre was ugly and a full head shorter. Together their fame reached around the world.

Sartre lived simply and with few possessions, finding fulfillment in political involvement and travel and needing only a small apartment on the left bank in Paris. In declining health and virtually blind, Sartre died on April 15, 1980, at the age of seventy-four.

Existentialism Sartre's name has become identified with existentialism primarily because he took the more technical writings of the contemporary German philosophers (especially Heidegger, who had probed into the meaning of Being through the deep recesses of humanity's anxious and restless soul) and expressed their findings with great lucidity and popular appeal. What had appeared first in the heavy language of philosophy now came forth from Sartre's pen in the open and captivating style of novels and short stories. As a philosopher, Sartre was himself capable of writing about existentialism in the most exacting and complex style, which one finds in his massive major book *Being and Nothingness* (*L'Être et le Neant*), 1943. But his best-known work is his lecture *Existentialism Is a Humanism* (*L'Existentialisme est un humanisme*), published in 1946, a work which has become famous because of its brilliance and despite Sartre's later desire to define existentialism in somewhat different terms.

Sartre's version of existentialism is the product of a special mixture of at least three contemporary modes of thought, stemming from Marx, Husserl, and Heidegger. What these three strands of thought had in common for Sartre was their concern about people's active role in forging their own destiny. Marx had expressed his passion for action when he wrote that "hitherto philosophers had merely understood the world; the point, however, is to change it." Husserl also focused his new brand of philosophy, which he called *phenomenology,* on the individual, saying that "true philosophy should seek its foundation exclusively in man and, more specifically, in the essence of his concrete worldly existence." And Heidegger, in his great work *Being and Time* (*Sein und Zeit*), which relies somewhat upon Kierkegaard and Husserl, wrote that our basic understanding of the large question of Being is achieved best through the existential analysis of the *person.* Heidegger's analysis strongly shaped Sartre's thought, but whereas Heidegger was concerned chiefly with *Being,* and with the *existence* of the *person* only as a means for understanding Being, Sartre became preoccupied almost solely with the existence of the individual. Accordingly, Sartre's classical formulation of the basic principle of existentialism, namely, that *existence precedes essence,* is a reversal not only of Heidegger's intentions but of traditional metaphysics, which ever since Plato's time has said that essence precedes existence.

Existence Precedes Essence

What does it mean to say that existence precedes essence, and how does this formula bear upon our understanding of human nature? Sartre argues that we cannot explain the nature of humanity in the same way that we describe an article of manufacture. When we consider, for example, a paper knife, we know that it has been made by someone who had in mind a conception of it, including what it would be used for and how it would be made. Thus, even before it is made, the paper knife is already conceived of as having a definite purpose and as being the product of a definite process. If by the *essence* of the paper knife we mean the procedure by which it was made and the purposes for which it was produced, the paper knife's essence can be said to precede its existence. To look upon a paper knife is to understand exactly what its useful purpose is. When we think about people's nature, we tend to describe them also as the product of a maker, of a creator, of God. We think of God most of the time, says Sartre, as a "supernal artisan," implying that when God creates, He knows precisely what He is creating. This would mean that in the mind of God the conception of humanity is comparable to the conception of the paper knife in the mind of the artisan. Each individual, in this view, is the fulfillment or realization of a definite conception, which resides in God's understanding.

Although it is true that some of the philosophers of the eighteenth century, including Diderot, Voltaire, and Kant, were either atheists or else suppressed the idea of God, they nevertheless retained the notion, distinctive of the theist, that people possess a "human nature," a nature that is found in every person. Each person, they said, is a particular example of the universal conception of Humanity. Whatever the level of development of the particular group of people, whether they be primitive natives, people in the state of nature, or cultured bourgeois, they all have the same fundamental qualities and are therefore all contained in the same definition or conception of Humanity. In short, they all possess the same essence, and their essence precedes their concrete or historic existence, which they confront in experience.

Sartre turned all this around by taking atheism seriously. He believed that if there is no God, there is no *given* human nature precisely because there is no God to have a conception of it. Human nature cannot be defined in advance because it is not completely thought out in advance. People as such merely exist and only later become their essential selves. To say that existence precedes essence means, says Sartre, that people first of all exist, confront themselves, emerge in the world, and define themselves afterwards. At first, a person simply is. Whether it follows that a person does not have a basic and given nature simply because there is no God who stands in relation to him or her the way the artisan stands in relation to the knife is questionable. But what Sartre wants particularly to argue is that people are simply that which they make of themselves.

One's first reaction to this formulation of the first principle of Sartre's existentialism is that it is highly subjective, that people can presumably set out to make of themselves anything they wish. Sartre's chief point here is that a person has a greater dignity than a stone or a table. What gives a person dignity is possession of a subjective life, meaning that a person is something which moves itself toward a future and is conscious that it is doing so. Sartre wants to call attention to two different modes of being, which he calls *being-in-itself* (*l'en-soi*) and *being-for-itself* (*le pour-soi*). Applying this distinction to humanity, one can say that a person shares both of these two modes of being, the *en-soi* indicating that he or she *is* (the way a stone is) and the *pour-soi* indicating that he or she is a *conscious subject* (which therefore differentiates him or her from a stone). To be a conscious subject is to stand constantly before a future. The most important consequence of placing existence before essence in human nature is not only that people create themselves but that people's responsibility for their existence rests squarely upon each person. A stone cannot be responsible. And if people's essential nature were already given and fixed, they could not be responsible for what they are.

Individual Responsibility

What began in Sartre's analysis as an amoral subjectivism now turns out to be an ethics of strict accountability based upon individual responsibility. If, that is, people are what they make of themselves, they have no one to blame for what they are except themselves. Moreover, when people *choose* in the process of making themselves, they choose not only for themselves but for all people. They are therefore responsible not only for their own individuality but, says Sartre, they are responsible for all people. This last point seems to contradict the line of reasoning that Sartre has so far been developing, for to say that before one can choose a way of action one must ask what would happen if everyone else acted so, is to assume a general human essence which makes *my* mode of action relevant to *all* people. Sartre does in fact say that even though we create our own values and thereby create ourselves, we nevertheless create at the same time an image of our human nature as we believe it ought to be. When we choose this or that way of acting, we affirm the value of what we have chosen, and nothing can be better for any one of us unless it is better for all. This all sounds very much like Kant's categorical imperative. But Sartre does not wish to invoke any universal law to guide a person's choice. He is calling attention to one of the clearest experiences of human beings, namely, that all people must choose, must make decisions, and although they have no authoritative guide, they must still choose and at the same time ask whether they would be willing for others to choose the same action. We cannot escape at times the disturbing thought that we would not want others to act as we do. To say that others will not so act is a case of *self-deception.* The act of choice, then, is one that all people must accomplish with a deep sense of *anguish,* for in this act people are responsible not only for themselves but also for each other. Those who evade their responsibility through *self-deception* will not, says Sartre, be at ease in their conscience.

Atheism and Humanity's Abandonment

Although Sartre's moral language sounds at times very much like traditional moral discourse, his intention is to carry out the rigorous implications of atheism. Sartre accepts Nietzsche's announcement that "God is dead" and takes seriously Dostoevsky's notion that "if God did not exist, everything would be permitted." In a Godless world, a person's psychological condition is one of *abandonment,* a word Sartre takes from Heidegger. Abandonment means for Sartre that with the dismissal of God there also disappears every possibility of finding values in some sort of intelligible heaven. Again, there cannot now be

any "good" prior to my choice since there is no infinite or perfect consciousness to think it. People's sense of abandonment is a curious consequence of
the fact that everything is indeed permitted, and as a consequence people are
forlorn, for they cannot find anything on which they can rely either within or
outside themselves. People are without any excuse. Their existence precedes
their essence. Apart from their existence there is nothingness. There is only
the present. In his *Nausea,* Sartre writes that the true nature of the present
was revealed as what exists, that what is not present does not exist. Things are
entirely what they appear to be, and apart from them there is nothing. To say
there is nothing besides the existing individual means for Sartre that there is no
God, no objective system of values, no built-in essence, and, most important
of all, *no determinism.* An individual, says Sartre, is free; a person is freedom.
In a classic phrase, he says that people are *condemned* to be free. Condemned
because they find themselves thrown into the world, yet free because as soon
as they are conscious of themselves, they are responsible for everything they
do. Sartre rejects the notion that human beings are swept up by a torrent of
passion and that such a passion could be regarded as an excuse for their actions. He rejected the Freudian analysis of human behavior because it appeared
to him that it provided an excuse in the form of psychological determinism.
People are responsible even for their passions, because even their feelings are
formed by their deeds. Freedom is appalling (Kierkegaard had similarly spoken of the *dizziness* of freedom) precisely because it means that there is nothing forcing me from behind, so to speak, to behave in any given way, nor is
there a precise pattern luring me into the future. I am the only thing that exists.
We are all free, says Sartre, therefore we must choose, that is, *invent,* because
no rule of general morality can show us what we ought to do. There are no
guidelines guaranteed to us in this world.

There is an element of despair in human existence, which comes, says
Sartre, from the realization that we are limited to what is within the scope of
our own wills. We cannot expect more from our existence than the finite prob-
abilities it possesses. Here Sartre believes that he is touching the genuine theme
of personal existence by emphasizing people's finitude and their relation to nothingness. "Nothingness," he says, "lies coiled in the heart of being, like a worm."
Heidegger located the cause of human anxiety in people's awareness of their
finitude when, for example, one confronts death—not death in general but *one's
own* death. It is not only people who face nothingness, says Heidegger, but all
Being has this relation to nothingness. Human finitude is therefore not simply
a matter of temporary ignorance or some shortcoming or even error. Finitude
is the very structure of the human mind, and words such as *guilt, loneliness,*
and *despair* describe the consequences of human finitude. The ultimate principle of Being, says Heidegger, is *will.* Sartre concurs by saying that only in
action is there any reality. Humanity is only a sum of actions and purposes;
besides people's actual daily life they are nothing. If people are cowards, they
made themselves cowards. It is not the result of a cowardly heart or lungs or
cerebrum, or because of their physiological organism; they are cowards because they made themselves into cowards by their actions.

Although there is no prior essence in all people, no human *nature,* there is nevertheless, says Sartre, a universal human *condition.* He rejects a narrow individual subjectivism as the standard of truth. Rather, to discover oneself in the act of conscious thought is to discover the condition of all people. We are in a world of *intersubjectivity.* This is the kind of world in which an individual must live, choose, and decide. For this reason, no purpose chosen by any individual is ever wholly foreign to another individual. This does not mean that every purpose defines a person forever but only that all people may be striving against the same limitations in the same way. For this reason, Sartre would not agree that it does not matter what we do or how we choose. People are always obliged to act in a *situation,* that is, in relation to other persons, and consequently their actions cannot, must not, be capricious, since they must take responsibility for all their actions. Moreover, to say that people must make their essence, invent their values, does not mean that one cannot *judge* human actions. It is still possible to say that one's action was based on either error or upon self-deception, for any person who hides behind the excuse of his or her passions, or by espousing some doctrine of determinism, indulges in self-deception. To invent values, says Sartre, means only that there is no meaning or sense in life prior to acts of will. Life cannot be anything until it is lived, but each individual must make sense of it. The value of life is nothing else but the sense each person fashions into it. To argue that we are the victims of fate, of mysterious forces within us, of some grand passion, of heredity, is to be guilty of bad faith (*mauvaise foi*) or self-deception, of *inauthenticity.* A woman who consents to go out with a particular man knows very well, says Sartre, what the man's cherished intentions are, and she knows that sooner or later she will have to make a decision. She does not want to admit the urgency of the matter, preferring rather to interpret all his actions as discreet and respectful. She is, says Sartre, in self-deception; her actions are inauthentic. All human beings are guilty, on principle, of similar inauthenticity, of bad faith, of playing roles, of trying to disguise their actual personality behind a facade. The conclusion of Sartre's existentialism is, therefore, that if people express their genuine humanity in all their behavior, they will never deceive themselves, and honesty will then become not their ideal but rather their very being.

The Human Reality   Underlying Sartre's popular formulation of existentialism is his technical analysis of existence. In one respect, human nature is no different from any other kind of existing reality. People are, just the same way anything else *is,* as simply *being there.* Unlike other things, however, people possess consciousness. For this reason, they are related to the world of things and people in a variety of ways. At one level, people are conscious of "the world," which is everything that is beyond or other than themselves and which therefore transcends them. At this level, the world is experienced simply as a solid, massive, undifferentiated, single something that is not yet separated into individual things.

Sartre describes this mode of consciousness in *Nausea* where the character Roquentin is sitting on a park bench. He looks at all the things before him in the park and all at once he *sees* everything differently, everything as a single thing—"Suddenly existence had unveiled itself." Words had vanished, and the points of reference which people use to give meaning to things also vanished. What Roquentin saw was existence as "the very paste of things": "The root [of the tree], the park gates, the bench, the sparse grass, all that had vanished: the diversity of things, their individuality, were only an appearance, a veneer. This veneer had melted, leaving soft, monstrous masses, all in disorder—naked." Only later, when a person reflects, does the world become our familiar one. But, says Sartre, "The world of explanations and reasons is not the world of existence." At the level of Roquentin's experience, the world is the unity of all the objects of consciousness.

Sartre agrees that all consciousness is consciousness of *something*, which means that there is no consciousness without affirming the existence of an object which exists beyond, that is, transcends, itself. As we have seen, the object of consciousness can be "the world" as simply "being there." But in addition to the world as a single solid mass, we speak of specific objects like trees, benches, and tables. Whenever we identify a specific object, we do this by saying what it is not—we differentiate a thing from its background. A chair appears as a chair because human beings give it that meaning by blacking out the background. What we call a chair is fashioned or drawn out of the solid context of the world by the activity of consciousness. The world of things appears as an intelligible system of separate and interrelated things only to consciousness. Without consciousness, the world simply is, it is *being-in-itself (l'en soi)*, and as such it is without meaning. Consciousness constitutes the meaning of things in the world, though it does not constitute their being.

Contingency, Necessity, and Freedom

When he views the world as being-in-itself, as simply being there, Sartre says that "the essential point is contingency. I mean that by definition existence is not necessity. To exist is simply to be there." Contingency means that when something exists, it does so by chance and not because it necessarily follows from something else: "Existences appear...but you cannot deduce them." The world we experience is "uncreated, without reason for being, without any relation to another being; being-in-itself is gratuitous for all eternity." The meaning anything will have in the world will depend, says Sartre, upon the choices people make. Even a table will have alternative meanings depending upon what a particular person chooses to use it for, to serve dinner or to write a letter. A mountain valley will mean one thing to a farmer and something else to a camper. Here, consciousness shifts a person from simply being there, being-in-itself, to *being-for-itself (le pour-soi)*, where consciousness dramatically differentiates the objects of the world from the conscious self as subject.

The activity of consciousness is at this point two-fold. First, consciousness defines specific things in the world and invests them with meaning. Secondly, consciousness transcends, that is, puts a distance between, itself and objects and, in that way, attains freedom from those objects. Because the conscious self has this freedom from the things in the world, it is within the power of consciousness to confer different or alternative meanings on things. The activity of consciousness is what is usually called "choice." People choose to undertake this project or that project, and the meaning of things in the world will depend to a considerable extent upon what project people choose. If they choose to be a farmer, the mountains, the valley, and the impending storm will have special meanings for them, whereas if they choose to be a camper in that valley, the surroundings and the storm will present different meanings. Humanity, as humanity, at first simply *is;* people's existence is primary and precedes what they are to become. What they become will depend upon how their consciousness deals with the world—a world which they view from a distance. From this distance, in this position of freedom from things and persons, people make a choice regarding how they will relate themselves to them. It follows, also, that because people have this freedom from the world, the world does not, cannot, *mechanically and totally* affect people's consciousness and their choices. There is no way for people to alter the fact that they transcend the world, are able to view it, so to speak, from above, and must therefore constantly make choices, take sides, undertake projects. In short, people are condemned to be free. By their free choices, people make themselves—not that they create themselves out of nothing but rather by a series of choices and decisions they convert their existence into the essence of their final self. People possess this freedom to create themselves within some limitations, such as the conditions of their birth and the circumstances of each particular situation. Nevertheless, Sartre says that people's attempts to make excuses for their behavior by attributing their actions to external or underlying causes are self-deception and in bad faith. This strong emphasis on human freedom as worked out in *Being and Nothingness* (1943) was softened by Sartre in the sequel to that book, his *Critique of Dialectical Reason* (1960).

Sartre's Existentialism versus Marx's Materialism

Although Sartre believed that Marxism is the philosophy of our time, he was aware of a striking contradiction between his existentialism and Marxist dialectical materialism. Indeed, one reason why Sartre never became a member of the Communist party is, he says, because "I would have had to turn my back on *Being and Nothingness,*" in which he had placed such a strong emphasis on human freedom. By contrast, Marxist dialectical materialism emphasized that all the structures and organizations of society and the behavior and thinking of human beings are determined by antecedent events. In this view, freedom of choice is an illusion and a person is simply a vehicle through which the forces of history realize themselves. Whereas Sartre had argued that it is a person's consciousness that "makes history" and confers meaning upon the world, Marxism holds that history is a process which produces the material foundations of social and economic structures, a process which therefore contains within itself the conditions and the reasons for its own development. Rather than conferring meaning upon the world, the mind, says the Marxist, discovers this meaning within the historical context as a matter of scientific knowledge.

In his earlier writings, Sartre focused primarily on the individual and freedom. For this reason, he never would accept Freud's theory of the unconscious, which Sartre saw as an irrational and mechanical causation of human behavior. Later, as in his *Critique of Dialectical Reason,* he focused more specifically upon the historical and social context in which people find themselves and which has an effect on their behavior. He thought that Marx had succeeded more than anyone else in describing how social and economic structures develop and how they bear upon human decisions. Sartre accepted increasingly the limitations upon human choice—the limitations of birth, status in society, and family background. Earlier, he sought to describe how an individuals are capable of deceiving themselves by making excuses for their behavior, as if they were not free to have behaved otherwise, a form of self-deception Sartre labeled as bad faith. He never did depart from this emphasis upon the freedom of the individual. But he did adjust his thinking under the influence of Marxism by facing the fact of people's social existence, their relationship to other persons, especially as a member of a group—as, for example, a labor union. Acknowledging the influence of group structures on human behavior and consciousness, resulting particularly in labor's sense of alienation, Sartre revised his optimistic view of human freedom to some extent. Recalling that he had written earlier (1945) that "no matter what the situation might be, one is always free" (giving as an example that "a worker is always free to join a union or not, as he is free to choose the kind of battle he wants to join, or not"), Sartre says this "all strikes me as absurd today" (1972). And he admits, "There is no question that there is some basic change in [my] concept of freedom." In his lengthy work on Flaubert, he concludes that although Flaubert was free to become uniquely Flaubert, his family background and his status in society meant that "he did not have all that many possibilities of becoming something else...he had the possibility of becoming a mediocre doctor...and the possibility of being Flaubert." This means, says Sartre, that social conditioning exists every minute of our lives. Nevertheless, he concludes that "I am still faithful to the notion of freedom." It is true, he says, that "you become what you are in the context of what others have made of you"; nevertheless, within these limitations a person is still free and responsible. This is Sartre's way of reconciling the fact that historical conditions affect human behavior with his intuitive certainty that human beings are also capable of shaping history. In doing this, Sartre sought to overcome with his existentialism what he considered the major flaw of Marxist philosophy, namely, its failure to recognize the individual as a "real person."

MERLEAU-PONTY

While Sartre became famous throughout the world for his philosophical writings, both in technical books and in the more popular forms of novels, plays, lectures, and biographies, there was another philosopher, his contemporary Maurice Merleau-Ponty about whom it was said that he was "the virtually unchallenged teacher of an entire generation" of French philosophy students. Merleau-Ponty, born in 1908, was a fellow student of Sartre's at the prestigious École Normale Supérieure in the class one year behind Sartre. They were not close friends because Sartre was, even then, an atheist while Merleau-Ponty was a Catholic, a "tala," or a person who goes to Mass.

Simone de Beauvoir said to Sartre during an interview, "The years at the École Normale were among the happiest years of your life." Sartre: "Yes, I was perfectly happy...." Beauvoir: "So, at École Normale you found men's company very agreeable." Sartre: "Yes, but I did have relations with women .... There were quite a lot." Beauvoir: "You were standoffish with people you did not like. Merleau-Ponty, for example. You were on very bad terms with him, weren't you?" Sartre: "Yes, but even so I once protected him from some men who wanted to beat him up." Beauvoir: "You were singing obscene songs; and being pious, he wanted to stop you?" Sartre: "He went out. Some fellows ran after him—there were two of them—and they were going to beat him up because they were furious. So I went out, too. I had a sort of liking for Merleau-Ponty.... [I said] Leave him alone, and let him go. So they didn't do anything; they went off."

From these early days at École Normale, the lives and careers of Sartre and Merleau-Ponty would unfold as a stormy relationship during which they would be alternately friends and enemies. What brought them together was the fact that they both became philosophers. They were both influenced by many of the same thinkers, including Descartes, Heidegger, and Husserl, among others. But they would not agree at all points on what these earlier thinkers meant to say. Their different interpretations influenced the unique character of their own creative philosophical writings.

In addition to their days at École Normale, they each saw active duty in World War II, shared many friends in common, had Marxist sympathies, made a commitment to phenomenology, and, especially, expressed a lively concern about political matters. Although during the 1930s Sartre was absorbed in pure philosophical reflection without becoming involved in political activity, following his release from prison camp after the fall of France, he became a vigorous political activist. With the help of Merleau-Ponty, Sartre organized a resistance network, in the winter of 1941, called "Socialism and Liberty." Their goal was to bring into being a form of political society based upon a harmony between a socialist economy and freedom for the individual. Together, Sartre and Merleau-Ponty, in a collaboration which lasted from 1945 to 1952, founded *Les Temps modernes,* a journal aimed at political commentary. The principal editors of this journal were Sartre, Simone de Beauvoir, and Merleau-Ponty.

Around 1952, while Sartre was moving toward closer ties with the communists, Merleau-Ponty left the editorship of *Les Temps Moderne* and accepted a chair of philosophy at the College de France. A few years later, Merleau-Ponty wrote a book, *Adventures of the Dialectic,* in which he included a chapter analyzing in detail Sartre's relationship with communism. The chapter, "Sartre and Ultrabolshevism," ended with this critical sentence: "One cannot at the same time be both a free writer and a communist." Actually, both Sartre and Merleau-Ponty ultimately became disenchanted with communism. As we saw earlier (page 517), Sartre never became a member of the Communist party because it would have forced him to give up his strongly held position that a human being is "free" and therefore responsible for his own behavior. Marxism teaches that both individual and collective history are products of a materialistic determinism.

In 1950, two years before he left *Les Temps modernes*, Merleau-Ponty wrote an editorial denouncing the labor camps in the U.S.S.R. in which he said: "If there are ten million concentration camp inmates while at the other end of the Soviet hierarchy salaries and standard of living are fifteen to twenty times higher than those of the free workers—then... the whole system swerves and changes meaning; and in spite of the nationalization of the means of production, and even though private exploitation of man by man and unemployment are impossible in the U.S.S.R., we wonder what reasons we still have to speak of socialism in relation to it." These labor camps, Merleau-Ponty said, are "still more criminal because they betray the revolution."

That Merleau-Ponty should become so caught up in political thought and action raises the question of what there was about his philosophy of existentialism and phenomenology that focused his thought upon politics. Traditional philosophy was considered abstract and theoretical and could be most successfully pursued by withdrawing from the world of action and the distractions of specific people, events, and geographical locations. Merleau-Ponty was educated in an environment of and by teachers deeply imbued in just such a mode of philosophy. At the École Normale Supérieure, the philosophy curriculum was steeped in the great philosophical tradition, which meant that doing philosophy followed along the lines of thought set out by Descartes. His teacher, Leon Brunschvicg, says Merleau-Ponty, "passed on to us the idealist heritage.... This philosophy consisted largely in reflexive effort... [which] sought to grasp external perception or scientific constructions as a result of mental activity." It was Descartes who emphasized the primacy of rational consciousness in the development of knowledge. Later, Merleau-Ponty would abandon this traditional view of the primacy of rational consciousness in favor of the primacy of perception, a shift that reflected the radical alteration in French philosophy between 1925 and 1945.

Descartes described the primacy of rationality in his famous example of how we know that a substance is a piece of wax. When we first observe the wax it has a certain color, a pleasant fragrance, a special shape and hardness. But if we bring the wax near a flame, it retains none of these visible characteristics. When it melts, its shape is altered, it loses its fragrance, it becomes soft and no longer makes a noise when it is dropped. How do we know that it is the same wax we originally observed? The "real" wax is not seen by the eyes. We can only conceive of the true wax through the action of our minds,

Maurice Merleau-Ponty *(French Embassy Press and Information Division, New York)*

through intelligence. From this example, Descartes drew the conclusion that our rational consciousness, our mind, is what makes it possible for us to know what something really is.

Traditional rationalism, as developed by Descartes, assumed that the human mind is compatible with the way things in the universe really are. In its simple form, this tradition says that there is a human mind, and beyond the mind there are objects. The mind is capable of grasping what really *is,* for what *is* is what is *known.* To be sure, the scientist emphasizes the approach of empiricism, that is, the observation of events and things. But strictly speaking, observation at most tells us *that* something is but not *what* or *why* it is. Kant repaired this deficiency of the empirical scientific approach to knowledge by saying that the mind brings organizing principles to our experience of things. These principles, or categories, which describe how knowledge is possible, consist of such notions as cause and effect and time and space. These categories exist prior to the act of understanding and are indeed what makes knowledge possible. They organize or give form to experiences in order to make them intelligible. This, then, is a way of looking at the world with *reason* and not with the *senses* only. Moreover, this tradition of rationalism emphasizes the difference between the phenomena of the perceived world and the underlying reality of the things which we never perceive. It is the mind, what Descartes described as something different from the body and defined as "a thing that thinks," which has the capacity to represent true reality as if the mind is a mirror reflecting what exists in nature.

This tradition of rationalism and idealism was emphasized in the philosophy courses Merleau-Ponty studied at the École Normale from 1926 to 1930, making him at that time a thoroughgoing rationalist. But already in 1929 he came under the influence of Gustave Rodrigues, director of the Lycée Janson-de-Sailly where Merleau-Ponty was fulfilling his student teaching assignment. Merleau-Ponty, the young Catholic, found Rodrigues, an atheist, to have an "extraordinary character," leading Merleau-Ponty to say that "an atheist resembles other men." He would eventually, in 1936, depart from Catholicism as he worked through his version of phenomenology.

Theories of Truth and Political Philosophy

From Rodrigues, Merleau-Ponty became aware of a problem concerning the connection between traditional rationalism and political philosophy. Specifically, since intellectual certainty is located in the mind of the subject, the individual, how can one mind know another mind, or another person's inner reflections? Can it be assumed that a rational description of the good society or its underlying definition of justice is truly applicable to all people? Moreover, if traditional thought is purely intellectual, that is, the product of reflections upon the relationship of various ideas to each other, how can such thought adequately explain how people can or should actually live together? There is also the serious problem of assuming that a rational system of thought leads not only to *a* truth but presumably to *absolute* truth. If this is the case, should not this truth be accepted by everyone? And if this true design for the good society is not accepted, is it not necessary to impose this truth by force? Ironically, the cause of violence could lie in a system of thought that declares that rational thought can lead to absolute truth. Merleau-Ponty was keenly aware of this possibility when he referred to Hegel's statement that "terror was Kant put into practice." The people who brought on the revolution of '93 in France "ended with pure authority because they believed that they were the bearers of the truth, that this truth...is directly menaced by the freedom of others." Merleau-Ponty concludes that "the revolution of '93 is terror because it is abstract and attempts to pass immediately from principles to the forced application of these principles."

Merleau-Ponty's original political orientation while at the École Normale was toward political conservatism. The rationalist tradition which he inherited emphasized the primacy of the citizen's duties to the existing social system. This view implied that the backbone of French civilization required the continued existence of its traditional institutions, including the church and local authorities. In a speech in 1932 at the Lycée Beauvais to the departing graduating class, he described the "essence" of France as respect for human dignity and a dedication to clear and easily communicated ideas. He warned the students of certain developing revolutionary movements, saying, "Let us be inclined to understand other peoples and let our intelligence be flexible and benevolent. But let it be without illusion, and let us . . . oppose with a decided 'no' any violent attempt to drag us toward what one calls a 'new age,' toward an absurd and inhuman economy, toward unawareness and impulse."

It would not be long before Merleau-Ponty himself would be exposed to, and even attracted by, the changing modes of philosophy following World War II. The French began to focus upon the early writings of Marx. For some, the feeling in the late 1930s was, as one writer said, that "all fundamental truth had, for us, been suspended." In the ferment of ideas, a new emphasis was placed upon aspects of Hegel's philosophy. Heidegger and Husserl became influential. Sartre, who had studied in Berlin and had discovered for himself the works of Husserl and Heidegger, brought their works back to Paris and made it available to Merleau-Ponty. In addition, Merleau-Ponty was greatly influenced by the new advocates of Gestalt Theory. This was a theory of psychology that emerged in the 1920s and offered a new conception of perception. It said that our perceptual experience, the events of our mental life, possess form, structure, sense, meaning, and value, all simultaneously. None of these attributes were considered by the prevailing theory, which focused simply upon each specific, independent element in the thick mosaic of total perception, thereby limiting the texture of knowledge. The consequence of these developments in philosophy was that Merleau-Ponty was inspired to embark upon a new way of thinking about knowledge, about the relation of the mind to meaning, about the primacy of perception.

The Primacy of Perception

Merleau-Ponty explains that our knowledge is the product of our body's perception of the world. There can be no knowledge without the activity of our body. Our bodies are the means by which we have access to everything that exists. Our body's perception of the world is immediate, that is, there is at first no interval or space between our conscious perception, on the one hand, and the object of our perception on the other. Here Merleau-Ponty's reliance upon Gestalt Theory is significant because it helps him to explain that the primacy of perception is focused not upon discrete individual objects but rather upon a field or a structure of reality which only later is separated into individual entities. Moreover, what is immediately given to us through perception is the basic material upon which our thought is grounded.

Merleau-Ponty says, "I have tried, first of all, to re-establish the roots of the mind in its body and in its world." Our body, he says, "is not in space like things; it inhabits or haunts space. It applies itself to space like a hand to an instrument." Similarly, the mind does not at first exist by itself as a blank, without any content, as implied in Descartes' description of the mind as simply "a thing that thinks." Descartes emphasized this nature of the *cogito,* the "I," when he said that "I am therefore only a thinking thing, that is to say, a mind, an understanding or reason. . . . I am, then, a real thing, and really existent. What thing? I have said it, a thinking thing."

But Merleau-Ponty insisted that there can be no consciousness without the consciousness of *something*. The *cogito* is always accompanied by a *cogitatum*. He insists that Descartes was wrong in isolating the self as a "mind" existing without any reference to the world. Descartes was wrong, says Merleau-Ponty, because he failed to see that the body was the vehicle through which we have a world and the means by which we are able to have communication with it. The *"true cogito,"* says Merleau-Ponty, is not simply the awareness that I am because I think; instead, the true *cogito* "must reveal me in a situation... as being-in-the-world... as through and through compounded of relations with the world." This is the experience everyone has, namely, a relation with the world before any reflection takes place. It is what makes reflection possible. Whereas Descartes spoke of "clear and distinct ideas" as the ultimate criterion of knowledge, Merleau-Ponty insists that the mind is "incarnate," that is, encounters the world in a bodily way. In accounting for the function of perception, Merleau-Ponty says that "the perceiving organism seems to show us a Cartesian mixture of soul with body." In this relation of the conscious self to the world, the act of perception does not produce absolute knowledge similar to the rational ideas of Descartes. Still, says Merleau-Ponty, "There is [in perception] no destruction of the absolute or of rationality here, only of the absolute and the rationality separated from experience." Therefore, "by the words, the 'primacy of perception,' we mean that the experience of perception is our presence at the moment when things, truths, values are constituted for us.... It is not a question of reducing human knowledge to sensation, but of assisting at the birth of this knowledge, to make it as sensible as the sensible, to recover the consciousness of rationality."

The Relativity of Knowledge

Merleau-Ponty says that "in the final analysis every perception takes place within a certain horizon and ultimately in the 'world.' " This follows from the fact that perception results from a person's bodily presence in the world. A bodily presence already means that as a subject, a person is situated in the world at a certain time and with a unique perspective. The ideas we ultimately have reflect this partial view and our experience in time so that "the ideas to which we recur are valid for only a period of our lives." The thing we perceive is not a complete thing or ideal unity possessed by the intellect, like a geometrical notion: "It is rather a totality open to a horizon of an indefinite number of perspectival views." This means further that "the things which I see are things for me only under the condition that they always recede beyond their immediate given aspects." For example, we never see all sides of a cube or a lamp or any other thing. Similarly, other observers will see things from *their* perspective. Moreover, my perceptions occur during the ticking away of time, even though I am not aware of this sequence of the segments of time. At this point, Merleau-Ponty asks, "Can I seriously say that I will always hold the ideas I do at present—and mean it? Do I not know that in six months, in a year, even if I use more or less the same formulas to express my thoughts, they will have changed their meaning slightly? Do I not know that there is a life of ideas, as there is a meaning of everything I experience, and that every one of my most convincing thoughts will need additions and then will be, not destroyed, but at least integrated into a new unity? This is," he concludes, "the only conception of knowledge that is scientific and not mythological." It means, moreover, that "the idea of going straight to the essence of things is an inconsistent idea if one thinks about it." The most we can get from our perception of the world is "a route, an experience which gradually clarifies itself, which gradually rectifies itself and proceeds by dialogue with itself and others."

The Self and Others

A dialogue with "others" assumes that everyone can in some way share a similar experience of the world. But can Merleau-Ponty's theory, which concentrates on each subject's internal experience of the world, explain how two people can have a coherent conversation? Perceptions are relative to each person as a result of their unique perspectives, since "our body...is our *point of view of the world.*"

Merleau-Ponty tries to solve this problem by using the concept of an "a priori of the species." As members of a single species, all human beings perceive certain forms in a like manner. He says that "as Gestalttheorie has shown there are for me preferred forms that are also preferred for all other persons." I will, of course, "never know how you see red and you will never know how I see it." But our first reaction to this separation of our consciousnesses is to "believe in an undivided being between us."

As I perceive another person, "I find myself in relation with another 'myself,' who is, in principle, open to the same truths as I am." Even though there are two of us looking at the world, it is not the case that because of our different perspectives, there are "two numerically distinct worlds." There is, says Merleau-Ponty, a demand that "what I see be seen by [you] also."

Perception and Politics

It would appear that Merleau-Ponty's account of the relativity of perceptual knowledge would not be well suited to deal with the problems of political, social, and economic order. After all, these subjects call for the formulation of "ends" and "purposes," for the definition of such concepts as "justice" and "freedom," and for the hope of realizing in the future certain fundamental human values. But to say that there are specific values or certain institutions which are required if there is to be a satisfactory fulfillment of human beings appears to mark a return to earlier modes of philosophy, as in Plato's utopian and Kant's rationalistic accounts of human nature. This would contradict the existential notion that there are no essential, timeless values, that there is no essential human nature to be fully realized, that people must create their own values.

Still, it is clear that Merleau-Ponty was deeply immersed in political philosophy, and our only concern here is to ask how he was able to move from his notion of the primacy of perception to political thought.

Merleau-Ponty asserts that "things" are not all we encounter through perception. Values are just as specifically perceived and have the same status as other aspects of the world. Values are significant, says Merleau-Ponty, "because they are apprehended with a certainty which, from the phenomenological viewpoint, is a final argument." In addition, perception provides us with the important element of *meaning*. This is particularly significant when perception encounters the actual ways people live among each other. From these actual living and working arrangements, says Merleau-Ponty, we can discover certain background meanings which reveal the change and movement of specific groups of people. These changes are not simply facts but reveal the direction of history. It is for this reason that Merleau-Ponty was attracted to communism, for here was a system and theory that could be observed concretely as the bearer of meaning located in the aspirations of the whole class of workers.

Merleau-Ponty was especially concerned to reject abstract theories of politics, justice, and morality. His objection to these theories was that they invariably claimed to be based upon "timeless" notions of the human good, while in fact they were simply reflections of the present circumstances of a particular culture. Imposing so-called universal values in the form of rules of morality or a system of government upon people who had themselves not participated in creating them he considered not a blessing but the heavy hand of oppression. Invariably, the so-called universal values turned out to be to the advantage of special groups. These were further reasons why Merleau-Ponty found in Marxism a congenial mode of thought. Marxism, while abstract up to a point, was nevertheless embodied in an actual system, the communism of the then U.S.S.R. Instead of abstract theories, then, Merleau-Ponty looked to the only sure source of political knowledge, namely, the primacy of perception. Here he felt that he had discovered, not the universality of an idea but the universality of the proletariat, which is the bearer of the meaning of history.

Both Sartre and Merleau-Ponty were drawn to communism after World War II for similar reasons. It represented the chief alternative to the status quo, and the turbulent events of the time called for a new philosophical basis for political action which they felt existentialism and phenomenology could provide. But they did not always agree with Marxism nor with each other's views of Marxism. Their prolonged and heated disagreements ultimately led in 1952 to the termination of their friendship and affected their views on communism. As Sartre wrote in 1961, "Each of us was conditioned, but in opposite directions. Our slowly accumulated disgust made the one [Merleau-Ponty] discover, in an instant, the horror of Stalinism, and the other [Sartre] that of his own [bourgeois] class."

Merleau-Ponty held that it is possible to perceive in actual society the developing consciousness of a special class, the workers, the proletariat. He saw a relationship here between the individual, the institutions of society, a scale of values, and reality. Most important of all, he thought he perceived that the developing consciousness of this class was the bearer of a rather specific meaning, a meaning that was growing steadily stronger and was shaping the direction of history. At the center of this overall perception was the urge on the part of this class to resolve the contradictions of the workers' conditions, to organize a humane appropriation of nature, and "as a universal class... to transcend national and social conflicts as well as the struggle between man and man." This was the heart of the communist promise which Merleau-Ponty originally thought was corroborated by his own perceptions. But he was willing to admit that if the proletariat could not overcome the strong structure of capitalism, if it could not eliminate violence, and if it could not bring about humane relationships among people, then both the ideas of Marx and the evidences of present perceptions would have been refuted. "It would mean," says Merleau-Ponty, "that there is no history—if history means the advent of humanity and the mutual recognition of men as men."

With his philosophical work still far from complete, and while at the height of his creative powers, Merleau-Ponty died on May 4, 1961, at the age of fifty-three.

Glossary
Key Concepts

Aesthetics   The branch of philosophy concerned with the analysis of concepts such as beauty or beautiful as standards for judging works of art.

Agnostic   One who neither believes nor disbelieves that God exists since there is no conclusive evidence either way.

Analytic   An analytic sentence is necessarily true because the predicate is already in the subject, e.g., "all dogs are animals" where the word *dogs* already contains the concept "animal."

A posteriori   After experience (versus *a priori,* before experience).

Appearance   How something presents itself to our senses as compared with its true reality. The oar appears bent in the water, but it really is not bent.

A priori   Before or independent of experience, hence, *a priori* knowledge is what we can know without experiencing it, e.g., "every event has a cause" even though we have not experienced every event.

Autonomy   Independence from external authority; in Kant, freedom of the will to make its own law or rule of conduct in contrast with *heteronomy* (being subject to someone else's rules).

Becoming   The world of becoming is the world in which everything in our daily experience, persons and things, comes into being and passes away.

Being   Considered the ultimate reality. For Plato, the realm of the eternal Forms.

Categorical imperative   According to Kant, the absolute moral law understood as a duty by any rational creature, to be compared with *hypothetical imperatives,* which permit exceptions.

Categories   Term used by Aristotle and Kant, meaning the concepts the human mind brings to knowing, e.g., cause and effect, space and time.

Causality   The relation of cause and effect, in which one event necessarily follows another.

Cause   Something that has the power to produce a change, motion, or action in another thing; this change *(effect)* can be explained in terms of the behavior of the cause.

Change   The alteration of anything, the rearrangement of something's parts, the coming into being of something that did not exist before, and the decline and dissolution of something.

Cogitatum   The content of what is thought; hence, to think *(cogito)* is to think something *(cogitatum).*

Cogito   Literally means in Latin "I think." Used by Descartes to describe the "self" as "a thinking thing."

Cognition   In the broadest sense, knowledge, or the act of knowing.

Cognitive meaning   A statement has cognitive meaning if (a) it asserts something that is true simply because the words used necessarily and always require the statement to be true (as in mathematics) or (b) it asserts something that can be judged as true or false by verifying it in experience.

Contingent   An event that is not necessary, i.e., it may or may not be, depending upon other events which also may or may not be.

Cosmological argument   A "proof" for the existence of God based upon the idea that there had to be a first cause for the existence of the universe.

Deduction   A process of reasoning by which the mind relates the truth of one proposition to the truth of another by inferring that the truth of the second proposition is involved in and therefore derived from the first (*see* **Induction**).

Determinism   The theory that every fact, or even the universe, is determined or caused by previous facts or events; human behavior and the events of history follow strict laws of causation or necessary connection. Accordingly, in this view, human beings do not possess freedom of the will or the power to originate independent or genuine choices.

Dialectic   As in dialogue (Socrates) or debate over opposites (Hegel) and clash of material forces (Marx) producing dynamic change.

   Or, a process of reasoning based upon the analysis of opposing propositions. Socrates used the dialectic method of teaching by distinguishing between opinion and knowledge. Hegel and Marx developed dialectic conceptions of history in which for Hegel, opposing ideas were the key, while for Marx history was explained as the conflict of material forces.

Dogmatism   The act of making a positive assertion without demonstration by either rational argument or experience.

Dualism   A theory which holds that there are two independent and irreducible substances, such as mind and body, the intelligible world of ideas and the visible world of things, and the forces of good and evil.

Empiricism   The theory that experience is the source of all knowledge, which thereby denies that human beings possess inborn knowledge or that they can derive knowledge through the exercise of reason alone.

Epistemology   The branch of philosophy which studies the nature, origin, scope, and validity of knowledge.

Essence   The chief characteristic, quality, or necessary function which makes a thing what it uniquely is.

Ethics   (1) A set of rules for human behavior; (2) a study of judgments of value, of good and evil, right and wrong, desirable and undesirable; and (3) theories of obligation or duty or why we "ought" to behave in certain ways. (Greek, *ethicos;* Latin, *moralis*)

Existentialism   As defined by Sartre, *existence* precedes *essence,* i.e., people have no given identity until they have made specific decisions and have chosen their work and have thereby defined themselves.

A mode of philosophy which focuses on the existing individual person; instead of searching for truth in distant universal concepts, existentialism is concerned with the authentic concerns of concrete existing individuals as they face choices and decisions in daily life.

Extension   In Descartes, the character of physical things as having dimension in space and time.

Finitude   Having definable limits.

Form   Plato's notion of eternal and independent reality, e.g., *Triangle* or *Man,* which makes possible particular things like the shape of this piece of pie or this person, Mary.

Gestalt theory   The theory of perception that our perceptual experience consists of a full range of characteristics—form, structure, sense, meaning, and value—all simultaneously.

Idealism   The view that mind is the ultimate reality in the world. Idealism is, accordingly, opposed to *materialism,* which views material things as the basic reality from which mind emerges and to which mind is reducible.

Illusion   An erroneous impression (e.g., an optical illusion) or a false belief growing out of a deep wish (Freud).

Impression   The same as *sensation,* or the "sense-data" received by us through our senses (Hume).

Indeterminism   The theory that in some cases the will makes decisions or choices independent of prior physiological or psychological causes *(free will).*

Induction   Proceeding from the observation of some particular facts to a generalization (or conclusion) concerning all such facts *(see* **Deduction***).*

Innate Ideas   Certain things that we are born able to know without requiring proof from experience.

Instrumental   Description of something that is a means for achieving something else (Aristotle), versus *intrinsic,* which describes an act, event, or thing existing for its own sake.

Instrumentalism   John Dewey's theory of how thought functions by emphasizing its practical function in determining future consequences; thought is therefore viewed as instrumental in producing consequences.

Intrinsic   Term used to describe an act, event, or thing which exists for its own sake, versus *instrumental,* which describes an act or event that is a means to some other end.

Intuition   Direct and immediate knowledge, or the immediate apprehension by the self of itself, of the truth of certain propositions, of the external world, and of values, without the prior need for the ability to define a term, to justify a conclusion, or to build upon inferences.

Logical positivism   The view that statements are meaningful only if they can be verified either directly or indirectly in experience. Logical positivism seeks to analyze all claims to knowledge, all assertions of science and everyday life; only assertions have meaning which are verified by empirical facts or are connected logically with such facts and therefore verifiable.

Man (*as used throughout this book*)   A human being, or the human creature regarded abstractly and without regard to gender; hence, the human race, or humanity.

Materialism   The view that matter constitutes the basis of all that exists in the universe. Hence combinations of matter and material forces account for every aspect of reality, including the nature of thought, the process of historical and economic events, and the standard of values based upon sensuous bodily pleasures and the abundance of things; the notion of the primacy of spirit or mind and rational purpose in nature is rejected.

Metaphysics   The branch of philosophy concerned with the question of the ultimate nature of reality. Unlike the sciences, which focus on various aspects of nature, metaphysics goes beyond particular things to inquire about more general questions, such as what lies beyond nature, how things come into being, what it means for something to be, and whether there is a realm of being which is not subject to change and which is therefore the basis of certainty in knowledge.

Monism   The view that there is only one substance in the universe.

Naturalistic fallacy   Consists of trying to define a nonnatural object *(good)* in terms of a natural object *(pleasure* or *self-realization)* [G. E. Moore].

Noumenal world   The real world as opposed to the world of appearance. The noumenal world, says Kant, cannot be known.

Ontology   From Greek *ontos,* "being" and *logos,* "science"; hence, the study of being. Ontological "proof" for God's existence based upon the idea of God as the highest Being.

Participation   The internal relation between different levels of being, e.g., between things in our world and the realm of the Forms in Plato, or the relation between Eternal Law (God's Reason) and Natural Law (human reason); hence, Natural Law is man's reason participating in God's Reason.

Perception   The discovery, by the senses, of knowledge about the world; the apprehension of everyday objects, for example, trees, through sense impressions. For Merleau-Ponty, perception is described as the bodily presence of the self in the world and the perception of the world from the bodily self's perspective.

Phenomenal world   The world of appearance versus the world beyond our knowledge (Kant).

Phenomenology   According to Husserl, *phenomenology* means that in accounting for knowledge we should not go beyond the only evidence or data available, namely, the data available to consciousness and the data derived from appearances—from phenomena. Husserl sees virtually no distinction between a knowing mind, on the one hand, and the object of knowledge on the other, between consciousness and the phenomenon. (See section on Husserl.)

Pluralism   The view that there are more than one *(monism)* or two *(dualism)* ultimate and separate substances making up the world.

Positivism   John Stuart Mill defined *positivism* as follows: "We [positivists] have no knowledge of anything but Phenomena, and our knowledge of phenomena is relative, not absolute. We know not the essence, not the real mode of production, of any fact, but only its relations to other facts in the way of succession or of similitude. These relations are constant; that is, always the same in the same circumstances."

Postulate: A practical or moral principle which cannot be proved, such as the existence of God, the freedom of the will, or immortality which, says Kant, must be believed to make possible our moral duty.

Pragmatism   According to William James, pragmatism is a method of solving various types of problems, such as "Does God exist?" or "Is man's will free?" by looking at the practical consequences of accepting this or that answer. James says, "The pragmatic method tries to interpret each notion (or theory) by tracing its respective practical consequences. . . . If no practical differences whatever can be traced . . . they mean practically the same thing," and that ends the argument. As a theory of truth, James says that an idea is true if it works in daily life.

Prime mover: While every event has a cause, the Prime Mover (in Aristotle, God) is the first cause of everything and does not, itself, require a cause; otherwise there would be a constant backward search, an "infinite regress" for the beginning of things.

Probable   Might happen; the middle term between (a) definitely, (b) probably, and (c) definitely will not. I.e., not enough evidence for (a) or (c).

Rationalism   The philosophical view that emphasizes the ability of human reason to grasp fundamental truths about the world without the aid of sense impressions.

Relativism   The view that there is no absolute knowledge, that truth is different for each individual, social group, or historic period and is therefore relative to the circumstances of the knowing subject.

Scholasticism   The method of learning in the medieval cathedral schools by which a combination of philosophy and theology was taught by emphasizing logical or deductive form, and basing thinking and its conclusions upon the sayings or writings of key figures of the past whose tradition was viewed as authoritative.

Sense-data   The impressions we receive through our senses.

Skepticism   The doubt that any knowledge achieved so far is absolute and therefore we must continue to seek after more refined and reliable versions of truth; or, the doubt whether it is ever possible to attain perfect certainty of knowledge.

Solipsism   The theory that the self alone (*solus,* "alone"; *ipse,* "self") is the source of all knowledge of existence, a view that sometimes leads to the conclusion that the self is the only reality.

Sophists   Itinerant teachers in fifth-century Athens who especially prepared young men for political careers, who hence emphasized rhetoric and the ability to persuade audiences and win debates, and who were less concerned with pursuing truth.

Sovereign   A person or state independent of any other authority or jurisdiction.

Substance   A separate and distinct thing; that which underlies phenomena; the essence of a thing which underlies the other qualities of a thing.

Syllogism   A form of reasoning. *Example:* All men are mortal (major premise); Socrates is a man (minor premise); therefore, Socrates is mortal (conclusion).

Synthetic   As compared with an analytic sentence (in which the subject contains the predicate), a synthetic sentence adds an idea to the subject which the subject does not already contain, e.g., "a dog will help catch foxes," but that is not true of all dogs.

Teleology   *Telos* is the Greek word for "purpose"; hence *teleology* is the study of purpose in human nature and in the events of history. In ethical theory (teleological ethics), an action is considered good if it helps to fulfill the purposes of human nature.

Utilitarianism   In this view, an action is considered good or right if its consequence is the greatest happiness *(pleasure)* of the greatest number. In that case, the action is useful *(utilitarian)* in producing as much good or more good than any alternative behavior.

Verification   Demonstrating or proving something to be true either by means of evidence or by formal rules of reasoning.

A Selected
Bibliography

GENERAL HISTORIES OF PHILOSOPHY

Boas, George: *The Dominant Themes of Modern Philosophy,* The Ronald Press Company, New York, 1957.

Burnet, John: *Greek Philosophy: Thales to Plato,* St. Martin's Press, Inc., New York, 1962.

Copleston, Frederick: *History of Philosophy,* Doubleday & Company, Inc., Garden City, N.Y., 1961–1974, nine vols.

Höffding, Harald: *History of Modern Philosophy,* Dover Publications, Inc., New York, 1924, two vols.

Jones, W. T.: *A History of Western Philosophy,* Harcourt, Brace, & World, Inc., New York, 1962.

Leff, Gordon: *Medieval Thought from St. Augustine to Ockham,* Penguin Books, Inc., Baltimore, 1962.

Schneider, H. W.: *A History of American Philosophy,* Columbia University Press, New York, 1963.

Sorley, W. R.: *History of British Philosophy to 1900,* Cambridge University Press, New York, 1964.

Warnock, Geoffrey: *English Philosophy since 1900,* Oxford University Press, Fair Lawn, N.J., 1958.

Windelband, Wilhelm: *History of Ancient Philosophy,* Dover Publications, Inc., New York, 1956.

————: *History of Philosophy,* Harper & Row, Publishers, Incorporated, New York, 1958, two vols.

Zeller, Eduard: *Outlines of the History of Greek Philosophy,* The World Publishing Company, Cleveland, 1955.

CHAPTERS 1 AND 2

Original Writings:

Kirk, G. S., and J. E. Raven: *The Presocratic Philosophers,* Cambridge University Press, New York, 1960.

Nahm, Milton C.: *Selections from Early Greek Philosophy,* Appleton-Century-Crofts, Inc., New York, 1947.

Critical Studies:

Burnet, John: *Early Greek Philosophy,* The World Publishing Company, Cleveland, 1958.

Cornford, F. M.: *Before and after Socrates,* Cambridge University Press, New York, 1932.

————: *From Religion to Philosophy,* Harper & Row, Publishers, Incorporated, New York, 1957.

Guthrie, W. K. C.: *History of Greek Philosophy,* Cambridge University Press, New York, 1962.

Rogers, A. K.: *The Socratic Problem,* Yale University Press, New Haven, Conn., 1933.

Santas, G. X.: *Socrates: Philosophy in Plato's Early Dialogues,* Routledge & Kegan Paul, Ltd., London, 1979.

Taylor, A. E.: *Socrates,* Doubleday & Company, Inc., Garden City, N.Y., 1959.

Vlastos, Gregory: *The Philosophy of Socrates,* Anchor Books, Garden City, N.Y., 1971.

CHAPTER 3

Original Writings:

Plato: *Great Dialogues of Plato,* New American Library of World Literature, Inc., New York, 1956.

————: *Last Days of Socrates* (*Euthyphro, Apology, Crito, Phaedo*), Penguin Books, Inc., Baltimore, 1959.

————: *The Republic of Plato,* ed. by F. M. Cornford, Oxford University Press, Fair Lawn, N.J., 1945.

————: *Selections,* Charles Scribner's Sons, New York, 1927.

Critical Studies:

Brumbaugh, R.: *Plato for the Modern Age,* Crowell-Collier Press, New York, 1962.

Cornford, F. M.: *Before and after Socrates,* Cambridge University Press, New York, 1932.

————: *Plato and Parmenides,* The Liberal Arts Press, Inc., New York, 1957.

————: *Plato's Cosmology,* The Liberal Arts Press, Inc., New York, 1957.

————: *Plato's Theory of Knowledge,* The Liberal Arts Press, Inc., New York, 1957.

Crombie, I.: *Plato, the Midwife's Apprentice,* Routledge & Kegan Paul, Ltd., London, 1964.

Demos, Raphael: *The Philosophy of Plato,* Charles Scribner's Sons, New York, 1939.

Field, G. C.: *Plato and His Contemporaries,* Methuen & Co., Ltd., London, 1948.

Gosling, J. C. B.: *Plato,* Routledge & Kegan Paul, Ltd., London, 1973.

Koyrë, Alexandre: *Discovering Plato,* Columbia University Press, New York, 1960.

Livingstone, Sir Richard: *Plato and Modern Education,* The Macmillan Company, New York, 1944.

Nettleship, R. L.: *Lectures on the Republic of Plato,* St. Martin's Press, Inc., New York, 1962.

Ritter, Constantin: *The Essence of Plato's Philosophy,* Dial Press, Inc., New York, 1933.

Ross, W. D.: *Plato's Theory of Ideas,* Oxford University Press, Fair Lawn, N.J., 1951.

Shorey, Paul: *What Plato Said,* The University of Chicago Press, Chicago, 1933.

Taylor, A. E.: *Plato: The Man and His Work,* The World Publishing Company, Cleveland, 1956.

Vlastos, G.: *Plato's Universe,* University of Washington Press, Seattle, 1975.

CHAPTER 4

Original Writings:

Aristotle: *Selections,* Charles Scribner's Sons, New York, 1957.

McKeon, Richard P.: *An Introduction to Aristotle,* Random House, Inc., New York, 1947.

Critical Studies:

Allan, D. F.: *The Philosophy of Aristotle,* 2d ed., Oxford University Press, Fair Lawn, N.J., 1970.

Jaeger, Werner: *Aristotle,* Oxford University Press, Fair Lawn, N.J., 1948.

Mure, G. R. G.: *Aristotle,* Oxford University Press, Fair Lawn, N.J., 1964.

Randall, J. H., Jr.: *Aristotle,* Columbia University Press, New York, 1960.

Ross, W. D.: *Aristotle,* Barnes & Noble, Inc., New York, 1955.

Taylor, A. E.: *Aristotle,* Dover Publications, Inc., New York, 1955.

Veatch, H. B.: *Aristotle, A Contemporary Appreciation,* Indiana University Press, Bloomington, 1974.

CHAPTER 5

Original Writings:

Aurelius, Marcus: *Meditations,* Penguin Books, Inc., Baltimore, 1964.

Epictetus: *Enchiridion,* Henry Regnery Company, Chicago, 1956.

Essential Works of Stoicism (*To Himself* by Marcus Aurelius, *The Manual* by Epictetus, *On Tranquility* by Seneca, *Life of Zeno* by Diogenes Laertius), Bantam Books, Inc., New York, 1965.

Etheridge, Sanford G. (trans.): Sextus Empiricus, in P. P. Hallie (ed.), *Scepticism, Man and God,* Wesleyan University Press, Middletown, Conn., 1964.

Oates, W. J. (ed.): *Stoic and Epicurean Philosophers,* Random House, Inc., New York, 1940.

Plotinus: *The Philosophy of Plotinus,* Appleton-Century-Crofts, Inc., New York, 1950.

Critical Studies:

Bailey, Cyril: *The Greek Atomists and Epicurus,* Russell & Russell, Inc., New York, 1964.

Bevan, E. R.: *Stoics and Sceptics,* Barnes & Noble, Inc., New York, 1959.

Graeser, A.: *Plotinus and the Stoics,* E. J. Brill, NV Leiden, Netherlands, 1972.

Hallie, P. P. (ed.): *Scepticism, Man and God,* Wesleyan University Press, Middletown, Conn., 1964.

Inge, W. R.: *The Philosophy of Plotinus,* Longmans, Green & Co., Ltd., London, 1929.

Long, A. A.: *Hellenistic Philosophy, Stoics, Epicureans, Sceptics,* Charles Scribner's Sons, New York, 1974.

Masson, John: *Lucretius, Epicurean and Poet,* E. P. Dutton & Co., New York, 1907–1909.

Mates, Benson: *Stoic Logic,* University of California Press, Berkeley, 1961.

Rist, J. M.: *Stoic Philosophy,* Cambridge University Press, London, 1969.

Taylor, A. E.: *Epicurus,* Constable & Co., Ltd., London, 1911.

Whittaker, Thomas: *The Neo-Platonists,* Georg Olms Verlagsbuchhandlung, Hildesheim, Germany, 1961.

Zeller, Eduard: *The Stoics, Epicureans and Sceptics,* Russell & Russell, Inc., New York, 1962.

CHAPTER 6

Original Writings:

Augustine: *The City of God,* Doubleday & Company, Inc., Garden City, N.Y., 1958.

———: *Concerning the Teacher* and *On the Immortality of the Soul,* Appleton-Century-Crofts, Inc., New York, 1938.

———: *Confessions,* Penguin Books, Inc., Baltimore, 1961.

———: *Enchiridion on Faith, Hope and Love,* Henry Regnery Company, Chicago, 1961.

Fremantle, Anne (ed.): *Age of Belief: The Medieval Philosophers,* New American Library of World Literature, Inc., New York, 1955.

McKeon, Richard (ed.): *Medieval Philosophers,* Charles Scribner's Sons, New York, 1959, two vols.

Oates, Whitney J. (ed.): *Basic Writings of St. Augustine,* Random House, Inc., New York, 1948, two vols.

Przywara, E.: *An Augustine Synthesis,* Harper & Row, Publishers, Incorporated, New York, 1958.

Critical Studies:

Bourke, V. J.: *Augustine's Quest of Wisdom,* The Bruce Publishing Company, Milwaukee, 1945.

Cochrane, C. N.: *Christianity and Classical Culture,* Oxford University Press, Fair Lawn, N.J., 1944.

D'Arcy, M. C.: *St. Augustine,* Meridian Books, Inc., New York, 1957.

Gilson, E.: *The Christian Philosophy of St. Augustine,* Random House, Inc., New York, 1960.

Meagher, R. E.: *An Introduction to Augustine,* New York University Press, New York, 1978.

TeSelle, E.: *Augustine the Theologian,* Herder & Herder, Inc., 1970.

CHAPTERS 7 AND 8

Original Writings:

Anselm: *Anselm's Basic Writings,* The Open Court Publishing Company, La Salle, Ill., 1962.

Boethius: *Consolation of Philosophy,* Frederick Ungar Publishing Co., New York, 1957.

Fremantle, Anne (ed.): *Age of Belief: The Medieval Philosophers,* New American Library of World Literature, Inc., New York, 1955.

Hyman, A., and J. J. Walsh: *Philosophy in the Middle Ages: the Christian, Islamic, and Jewish Traditions,* Hackett Publishing Co., 1973.

McKeon, Richard (ed.): *Medieval Philosophers,* Charles Scribner's Sons, New York, 1959, two vols.

Maimonides, Moses: *Guide of the Perplexed,* The University of Chicago Press, Chicago, 1963.

Critical Studies:

Bett, Henry: *Johannes Scotus Erigena,* Russell & Russell, Inc., New York, 1964.

Carré, M. H.: *Realists and Nominalists,* Oxford University Press, Fair Lawn, N.J., 1946.

Church, R. W.: *Saint Anselm,* Macmillan & Co., Ltd., London, 1937.

Rand, E. K.: *Founders of the Middle Ages,* Harvard University Press, Cambridge, Mass., 1941.

Sikes, J. G.: *Peter Abailard,* The University Press, Cambridge, 1932.

CHAPTER 9

Original Writings:

Aquinas: *Concerning Being and Essence,* Appleton-Century-Crofts, Inc., New York, 1937.

————: *Philosophical Texts,* Oxford University Press, Fair Lawn, N.J., 1960.

————: *Treatise on Happiness,* Prentice-Hall, Inc., Englewood Cliffs, N.J., 1964.

Blakney, R. B. (ed.): *Meister Eckhart: A Modern Translation,* Harper & Row, Publishers, Incorporated, New York, 1941.

Duns Scotus: *Philosophical Writings,* The Liberal Arts Press, Inc., New York, 1964.

Fremantle, Anne (ed.): *Age of Belief: The Medieval Philosophers,* New American Library of World Literature, Inc., New York, 1955.

McKeon, Richard (ed.): *Medieval Philosophers,* Charles Scribner's Sons, New York, 1959, two vols.

Ockham: *Philosophical Writings,* The Liberal Arts Press, Inc., New York, 1964.

Pegis, Anton C. (ed.): *Basic Writings of St. Thomas Aquinas,* Random House, Inc., New York, 1944, two vols.

Critical Studies:

Chesterton, G. K.: *St. Thomas Aquinas,* Doubleday & Company, Inc., Garden City, N.Y., 1936.

Copleston, Frederick: *Aquinas,* Penguin Books, Inc., Baltimore, 1955.

D'Arcy, M. C.: *Thomas Aquinas,* The Newman Press, Westminster, Md., 1953.

Gilson, E.: *The Philosophy of St. Thomas Aquinas,* Cambridge University Press, New York, 1937.

Harris, C. R. S.: *Duns Scotus,* Clarendon Press, Oxford, 1927.

Kenny, A.: *Aquinas,* Hill and Wang, Inc., New York, 1980.

Maritain, J.: *St. Thomas Aquinas,* The World Publishing Company, Cleveland, 1958.

CHAPTER 10

Critical Studies:

Bouwsma, W. J.: *The Culture of Renaissance Humanism,* American Historical Association, Washington, 1973.

Burtt, E. A.: *The Metaphysical Foundations of Modern Physical Science,* Harcourt, Brace & Company, Inc., New York, 1925.

Butterfield, H.: *Origins of Modern Science,* Collier Books, a division of Crowell-Collier Publishing Co., New York, 1962.

Cassirer, Ernst: *The Individual and the Cosmos in Renaissance Thought,* Harper & Row, Publishers, Incorporated, New York, 1964.

———, **Paul O. Kristeller, and J. H. Randall (eds.):** *The Renaissance Philosophy of Man,* The University of Chicago Press, Chicago, 1955.

Davies, S.: *Renaissance Views of Man,* Barnes & Noble, New York, 1979.

Kristeller, Paul O.: *Renaissance Concept of Man and Other Essays,* Harper & Row, Publishers, Incorporated, New York, 1972.

———: *Renaissance Thought: The Classic, Scholastic, and Humanist Strains,* Harper & Row, Publishers, Incorporated, New York, 1961.

Pater, Walter: *The Renaissance,* The World Publishing Company, Cleveland, 1961.

Symonds, J. A.: *The Renaissance in Italy,* John Murray (Publishers), Ltd., London, 1937, six vols.

Taylor, Henry Osborn: *Philosophy of Science in the Renaissance,* Collier Books, a division of Crowell-Collier Publishing Co., New York, 1962.

CHAPTER 11

Original Writings:

Bacon, Francis: *New Organon,* The Liberal Arts Press, Inc., New York, 1960.

————: *Advancement of Learning and New Atlantis,* Oxford University Press, Fair Lawn, N.J., 1938.

Hampshire, Stuart (ed.): *Age of Reason: The 17th Century Philosophers,* New American Library of World Literature, Inc., New York, 1956.

Hobbes, Thomas: *Body, Man and Citizen,* Collier Books, a division of Crowell-Collier Publishing Co., New York, 1962.

————: *De Cive* or *The Citizen,* Appleton-Century-Crofts, Inc., New York, 1949.

————: *Leviathan,* The Liberal Arts Press, Inc., New York, 1958.

————: *Selections,* Charles Scribner's Sons, New York, 1930.

Critical Studies:

Anderson, F. H.: *The Philosophy of Francis Bacon,* The University of Chicago Press, Chicago, 1948.

Peters, Richard: *Hobbes,* Penguin Books, Middlesex, 1956.

Raphael, D. D.: *Hobbes, Morals, and Politics,* Allen & Unwin, Inc., London, 1977.

Stephen, Leslie: *Hobbes,* University of Michigan Press, Ann Arbor, 1961.

Stephens, J.: *Francis Bacon and the Style of Science,* University of Chicago Press, 1975.

Strauss, Leo: *Political Philosophy of Hobbes,* University of Chicago Press, 1963.

Warrender, H.: *The Political Philosophy of Hobbes,* Oxford University Press, New York, 1957.

CHAPTER 12

Original Writings:

Berlin, Isaiah (ed.): *Age of Enlightenment: The 18th Century Philosophers,* New American Library of World Literature, Inc., New York, 1956.

Descartes, René: *Philosophical Works of Descartes,* Dover Publications, Inc., New York, 1931, two vols.

————: *Selected Philosophical Writings,* (trans.) John Cottingham, Robert Stoothoff, Dugald Murdoch, Cambridge University Press, Cambridge, England, 1988.

Hampshire, Stuart (ed.): *Age of Reason: The 17th Century Philosophers,* New American Library of World Literature, Inc., New York, 1956.

Leibniz, G. W.: *Selections,* Charles Scribner's Sons, New York, 1959.

————: *Philosophical Papers and Letters,* (ed.) Leroy E. Loemker, D. Reidel, Dordrecht, 1970.

————: *The Rationalists: Descartes, Spinoza, and Leibniz,* Dolphin Books, Doubleday & Company, Inc., Garden City, N.Y., 1962.

Spinoza, Baruch: *Chief Works,* Dover Publications, Inc., New York, 1962, two vols.

————: *Selections,* Charles Scribner's Sons, New York, 1958.

Critical Studies:

Frankfurt, H.: *Demons, Dreamers and Madmen: The Defense of Reason in Descartes's Meditations,* The Bobbs-Merrill Company, Inc., 1970.

Grene, M.: *Spinoza, A Collection of Critical Essays,* Anchor Books, Doubleday & Company, Inc., Garden City, N.Y., 1973.

Hampshire, S.: *Spinoza,* Penguin Books, Inc., Baltimore, 1962.

Joachim, H. H.: *A Study of the Ethics of Spinoza,* Russell & Russell, Pubs., New York, 1964.

Joseph, H. W. B.: *Lectures on the Philosophy of Leibniz,* Oxford University Press, Fair Lawn, N.J., 1949.

Kashap, S. P.: *Studies in Spinoza,* University of California Press, Berkeley, 1972.

Kenny, A.: *Descartes: A Study of His Philosophy,* Random House, Inc., New York, 1968.

McRae, R.: *Leibniz: Perception, Apperception, and Thought,* University of Toronto Press, 1976.

Maritain, J.: *The Dream of Descartes,* Philosophical Library, Inc., New York, 1944.

Parkinson, G. H.: *Leibniz on Human Freedom,* F. Steiner, Wiesbaden, 1970.

Roth, Leon: *Spinoza, Descartes, and Maimonides,* Russell & Russell, Inc., New York, 1963.

Russell, Bertrand: *A Critical Exposition of the Philosophy of Leibniz,* The University Press, Cambridge, 1900.

Smith, Norman Kemp: *New Studies in the Philosophy of Descartes,* Russell & Russell, Inc., New York, 1963.

Williams, B.: *Descartes: The Project of a Pure Inquiry,* Humanities Press, Atlantic Highlands, N.J., 1978.

CHAPTER 13

Original Writings:

Berkeley, George: *Principles of Human Knowledge* and *Three Dialogues between Hylas and Philonous,* The World Publishing Company, Cleveland, 1963.

————: *Selections,* Charles Scribner's Sons, New York, 1929.

————: *Works of Vision,* The Liberal Arts Press, Inc., New York, 1963.

Berlin, Isaiah (ed.): *Age of Enlightenment: The 18th Century Philosophers,* New American Library of World Literature, Inc., New York, 1956.

————: *The Empiricists: John Locke, George Berkeley, David Hume,* Dolphin Books, Doubleday & Company, Inc., Garden City, N.Y., 1961.

Hume, David: *Dialogues Concerning Natural Religion,* The Liberal Arts Press, Inc., New York, 1962.

————: *An Enquiry Concerning Human Understanding,* The Liberal Arts Press, Inc., New York, 1955.

————: *Hume's Moral and Political Philosophy,* Hafner Publishing Company, Inc., New York, 1948.

————: *Selections,* Charles Scribner's Sons, New York, 1927.

Locke, John: *Essay Concerning Human Understanding,* Dover Publications, Inc., New York, 1894, two vols.

————: *Selections,* Charles Scribner's Sons, New York, 1959.

————: *Treatise of Civil Government* and *A Letter Concerning Toleration,* Appleton-Century-Crofts, Inc., New York, 1959.

Critical Studies:

Aaron, R. I.: *John Locke,* Oxford University Press, Fair Lawn, N.J., 1955.

Ayer, A. J.: *Hume,* Hill and Wang, Inc., New York, 1980.

Bennett, J. F.: *Locke, Berkeley, Hume: Central Themes,* Clarendon Press, Oxford, England, 1971.

Chappell, V. C. (ed.): *Hume, A Collection of Critical Essays,* University of Notre Dame Press, Notre Dame, Ind., 1968.

Church, R. W.: *Hume's Theory of the Understanding,* George Allen & Unwin, Ltd., London, 1935.

Gibson, James: *John Locke,* Oxford University Press, Fair Lawn, N.J., 1933.

Hendel, Charles W.: *Studies in the Philosophy of David Hume,* The Liberal Arts Press, Inc., New York, 1963.

Laird, John: *Hume's Philosophy of Human Nature,* Methuen & Co., Ltd., London, 1932.

Pitcher, G.: *Berkeley,* Routledge & Kegan Paul, Ltd., Boston, 1977.

Smith, Norman Kemp: *The Philosophy of David Hume,* Macmillan & Co., Ltd., London, 1941.

Stephen, Leslie: *History of English Thought in the 18th Century,* Harcourt, Brace & World, Inc., New York, 1902, two vols.

Tipton, I. C.: *Locke on Human Understanding,* Oxford University Press, New York, 1977.

Warnock, G. J.: *Berkeley,* Penguin Books, Inc., Baltimore, 1953.

CHAPTER 14

Original Writings:

Rousseau, Jean-Jacques: *On the Social Contract,* (ed.) R. D. Masters, (trans.) J. R. Masters, St. Martin's Press, Inc., New York, 1978.

————: *Political Writings,* (ed.) C. E. Vaughan, Basil Blackwell, & Mott, Ltd., Oxford, England, 1962.

————: *Social Contract, Including Discourses,* E. P. Dutton & Co., Inc., New York, 1976.

————: *Emile,* Everyman's Library, E. P. Dutton & Co., Inc., New York, 1955.

Critical Studies:

Broome, J. H.: *Rousseau: A Study of His Thought,* Barnes & Noble, Inc., New York, 1963.

Einaudi, M.: *The Early Rousseau,* Cornell University Press, Ithaca, N.Y., 1967.

Green, F. C.: *Jean-Jacques Rousseau: A Critical Study of His Life and Writings,* Cambridge University Press, 1955.

Grimsley, R.: *The Philosophy of Rousseau,* Oxford University Press, Fair Lawn, N.J., 1973.

Roche, K. F.: *Rousseau, Stoic and Romantic,* Methuen & Co., Ltd., London, 1974.

Wolfson, Harry Austryn: *Philosophy of Spinoza,* The World Publishing Company, Cleveland, 1958.

Wright, E. H.: *The Meaning of Rousseau,* Russell & Russell, Inc., New York, 1963.

CHAPTER 15

Original Writings:

Kant, Immanuel: *Critique of Practical Reason,* The Liberal Arts Press, Inc., New York, 1956.
———: *Critique of Pure Reason,* St. Martin's Press, Inc., New York, 1965.
———: *Groundwork of the Metaphysics of Morals,* Harper & Row, Publishers, Incorporated, New York, 1964.
———: *Lectures on Ethics,* Harper & Row, Publishers, Incorporated, New York, 1963.
———: *Metaphysical Elements of Justice,* The Liberal Arts Press, Inc., New York, 1963.
———: *Perpetual Peace,* The Liberal Arts Press, Inc., New York, 1957.
———: *Prolegomena to Any Future Metaphysics,* The Liberal Arts Press, Inc., New York, 1950.
———: *Religion within Limits or Reason Alone,* Harper & Row, Publishers, Incorporated, New York, 1960.
———: *Selections,* Charles Scribner's Sons, New York, 1929.

Critical Studies:

Aune, B.: *Kant's Theory of Morals,* Princeton University Press, Princeton, N.J., 1979.
Beck, Lewis White: *Commentary on Kant's Critique of Practical Reason,* The University of Chicago Press, 1964.
Broad, O. D.: *Kant: An Introduction,* Cambridge University Press, 1978.
Cassirer, H. W.: *A Commentary on Kant's Critique of Judgment,* Methuen & Co., Ltd., London, 1938.
Ewing, A. C.: *Short Commentary on Kant's "Critique of Pure Reason,"* University of Chicago Press, 1987.
Hendel, C. W. (ed.): *The Philosophy of Kant and Our Modern World,* The Liberal Arts Press, Inc., New York, 1957.
Koerner, S.: *Kant,* Penguin Books, Inc., Baltimore, 1955.
Paton, H. J.: *Kant's Metaphysics of Experience,* The Macmillan Company, New York, 1951.
———: *The Categorical Imperative,* The University of Chicago Press, 1948.
Smith, Norman Kemp: *A Commentary to Kant's Critique of Pure Reason,* Macmillan & Co., Ltd., London, 1930.
Strawson, P. F.: *The Bounds of Sense: An Essay on Kant's Critique of Pure Reason,* Methuen & Co., Ltd., London, 1975.
Weldon, T. D.: *Introduction to Kant's Critique of Pure Reason,* Oxford University Press, Fair Lawn, N.J., 1945.

CHAPTER 16

Original Writings:

Aiken, Henry D. (ed.): *Age of Ideology: The 19th Century Philosophers,* New American Library of World Literature, Inc., New York, 1957.

Hegel, G. W. F.: *Encyclopedia of Philosophy,* Wisdom Library Paperbacks, Philosophical Library, Inc., New York, 1959.

———: *Lectures on the Philosophy of History,* Dover Publications, Inc., New York, 1956.

———: *Reason in History,* The Liberal Arts Press, Inc., New York, 1953.

———: *Selections,* Charles Scribner's Sons, New York, 1929.

———: *The Phenomenology of Spirit,* (trans.) A. V. Miller, Clarendon Press, Oxford, 1977.

Critical Studies:

Cunningham, G. W.: *Thought and Reality in Hegel's System,* Longmans, Green & Co., Inc., New York, 1910.

Findlay, J. N.: *Hegel: A Re-examination,* Collier Books, a division of Crowell-Collier Publishing Co., New York, 1962.

Lukacs, G.: *Young Hegel,* (trans.) Rodney Livingstone, The M.I.T. Press, Cambridge, Mass., 1976.

Marcuse, Herbert: *Reason and Revolution: Hegel and the Rise of Social Theory,* Beacon Press, Boston, 1960.

Mure, G. R. G.: *A Study of Hegel's Logic,* Oxford University Press, Fair Lawn, N.J., 1950.

Reyburn, H. A.: *The Ethical Theory of Hegel,* Clarendon Press, Oxford, England, 1921.

Stace, W. T.: *The Philosophy of Hegel,* Dover Publications, Inc., New York, 1923.

Taylor, C.: *Hegel,* Cambridge University Press, New York, 1975.

———: *Hegel and Modern Society,* Cambridge University Press, New York, 1979.

CHAPTER 17

Original Writings:

Schopenhauer, Arthur, *Essays and Aphorisms,* (ed. and trans.) R. J. Hollingdale, Penguin Books, Middlesex, England, 1970.

———: *The Fourfold Root of the Principle of Sufficient Reason,* George Bell and Sons, London, 1903.

———: *On the Freedom of the Will,* (ed. and trans.) Konstantin Kolenda, Basil Blackwell, Oxford, England, 1985.

———: *World As Will and Idea,* (trans.) R. B. Haldane and J. Kemp, Routledge & Kegan Paul, Ltd., London, 1948.

———: *Religion: A Dialogue, and Other Essays,* (trans.) T. Bailey Saunders, Greenwood Press, Westport, Conn., 1973.

———: *The Philosophy of Schopenhauer,* (ed. and trans.) Irwin Edman, Modern Library, New York, 1928.

Critical Studies:

Copleston, Frederick: *Arthur Schopenhauer, Philosopher of Pessimism,* Barnes and Noble Books, New York, 1975.

Magee, Bryan: *The Philosophy of Schopenhauer,* Clarendon Press, Oxford, 1983.
Wallace, William: *Life of Arthur Schopenhauer,* Walter Scott Publishing Co., Ltd., London, 1970.
Zimmern, Helen: *Schopenhauer, His Life and Philosophy,* George Allen & Unwin Ltd., London, 1932.

CHAPTER 18

Original Writings:

Aiken, Henry D. (ed.): *Age of Ideology: The 19th Century Philosophers,* New American Library of World Literature, Inc., New York, 1957.

Critical Studies:

Lévy-Bruhl, L.: *The Philosophy of Auguste Comte,* G. P. Putnam's Sons, New York, 1903.
Lewes, G. H.: *Comte's Philosophy of the Sciences,* G. Bell & Sons, Ltd., London, 1904.
Mill, John Stuart: *Auguste Comte and Positivism,* Ann Arbor Paperbacks, University of Michigan Press, 1961.
Thompson, K.: *Auguste Comte,* John Wiley & Sons, Inc., New York, 1975.

CHAPTER 19

Original Writings:

Aiken, Henry D. (ed.): *Age of Ideology: The 19th Century Philosophers,* New American Library of World Literature, Inc., New York, 1957.
Bentham, Jeremy: *Introduction to the Principles of Morals and Legislation,* Hafner Publishing Company, Inc., New York, 1948.
Mill, John Stuart: *Autobiography,* The Liberal Arts Press, Inc., New York, 1958.
————: *Six Great Humanistic Essays of John Stuart Mill,* Washington Square Press, Pocket Books, Inc., New York, 1963.
————: *The Utilitarians: Jeremy Bentham and John Stuart Mill,* Dolphin Books, Doubleday & Company, Inc., Garden City, N.Y., 1961.

Critical Studies:

Albee, Ernest: *History of English Utilitarianism,* Collier Books, a division of Crowell-Collier Publishing Co., New York, 1962.
Baumgardt, David: *Bentham and the Ethics of Today,* Princeton University Press, Princeton, N.J., 1952.
Berlin, I.: *Four Essays on Liberty,* Oxford University Press, Fair Lawn, N.J., 1970.
Dicey, A. V.: *Law and Public Opinion in England,* Macmillan & Co., Ltd., London, 1914.
Halevy, E.: *The Growth of Philosophical Radicalism,* Faber & Faber, Ltd., London, 1949.

Ogden, C. K.: *Bentham's Theory of Fictions,* Littlefield, Adams & Company, Paterson, N.J., 1959.

Plamenatz, John: *The English Utilitarians,* Basil Blackwell & Mott, Ltd., Oxford, 1949.

Stephens, Leslie: *The English Utilitarians,* The London School of Economics and Political Science, London, 1950, two vols.

CHAPTER 20

Original Writings:

Dewey, John: *A Common Faith,* Yale University Press, New Haven, Conn., 1960.

————: *Essays in Experimental Logic,* Dover Publications, Inc., New York, 1916.

————: *Experience and Nature,* Dover Publications, Inc., New York, 1929.

————: *On Experience, Nature and Freedom,* The Liberal Arts Press, Inc., New York, 1960.

————: *Philosophy of Education,* Littlefield, Adams & Company, Paterson, N.J., 1956.

————: *Quest for Certainty,* Capricorn Books, G. P. Putnam's Sons, New York, 1960.

————: *Reconstruction in Philosophy,* Beacon Press, Boston, 1957.

————: *Theory of Moral Life,* Holt, Rinehart and Winston, Inc., New York, 1960.

James, William: *Essays in Pragmatism,* Hafner Publishing Company, Inc., New York, 1948.

————: *Essays on Faith and Morals,* The World Publishing Company, Cleveland, 1962.

————: *Varieties of Religious Experience,* New American Library of World Literature, Inc., New York, 1958.

————: *The Will to Believe* and *Human Immortality,* Dover Publications, Inc., New York, 1956.

Konvitz, Milton R., and Gail Kennedy (eds.): *American Pragmatists,* The World Publishing Company, Cleveland, 1960.

Peirce, C. S.: *Essays in the Philosophy of Science,* The Liberal Arts Press, Inc., New York, 1957.

————: *Philosophical Writings,* Dover Publications, Inc., New York, 1940.

White, Morton (ed.): *Age of Analysis: 20th Century Philosophers,* New American Library of World Literature, Inc., New York, 1955.

Critical Studies:

Bentley, John E.: *American Philosophy,* Littlefield, Adams & Company, Paterson, N.J., 1963.

Brennan, Bernard: *Ethics of William James,* College and University Press, New Haven, Conn., 1962.

Cahn, S. M. (ed.): *New Studies in the Philosophy of John Dewey,* University Press of New England, Hanover, N.H., 1977.

Kaplan, Abraham: *The New World of Philosophy,* Random House, Inc., New York, 1964.

Perry, R. B.: *In the Spirit of William James,* Indiana University Press, Bloomington, 1958.

Scheffler, I.: *Four Pragmatists: A Critical Introduction to Peirce, James, Mead, and Dewey,* Routledge & Kegan Paul, London, 1974.

Smith, John E.: *The Spirit of American Philosophy,* Oxford University Press, Fair Lawn, N.J., 1963.

CHAPTER 21

Original Writings:

Feuer, Lewis (ed.): *Basic Writings on Politics and Philosophy: Karl Marx and Friedrich Engels,* Doubleday & Company, Inc., Garden City, N.Y., 1959.

Marx, Karl: *Economic and Philosophic Manuscripts of 1844,* International Publishers Company, Inc., New York, 1964.

————: *Living Thoughts of Karl Marx,* Longmans, Green & Company, New York, 1939.

————: *Poverty of Philosophy,* International Publishers Company, Inc., New York, 1964.

Selsam, Howard, and Harry Martel (eds.): *A Reader in Marxist Philosophy,* International Publishers Company, Inc., New York, 1963.

Stalin, Joseph: *Dialectical and Historical Materialism,* International Publishers Company, Inc., New York, 1940.

Critical Studies:

Axelos, K.: *Alienation, Praxis, and Technē in the Thought of Karl Marx,* University of Texas Press, Austin, 1976.

Berlin, Isaiah: *Karl Marx: His Life and Environment,* 4th ed., Oxford University Press, New York, 1978.

Cornforth, Maurice: *Introduction to Dialectical Materialism,* vol. I, *Materialism and Dialectical Method,* International Publishers Company, Inc., New York, 1953.

————: *Introduction to Dialectical Materialism,* vol. II, *Historical Materialism,* International Publishers Company, Inc., New York, 1954.

————: *Introduction to Dialectical Materialism,* vol. III, *Theory of Knowledge,* International Publishers Company, Inc., New York, 1955.

Guest, David: *Lectures on Marxist Philosophy,* International Publishers Company, Inc., New York, 1963.

Hoeven, J. v. d.: *Karl Marx: The Roots of His Thought,* Van Gorcum, 1976.

Hook, Sidney: *Towards the Understanding of Karl Marx,* The John Day Company, Inc., New York, 1933.

Lichtheim, George, *Marxism: An Historical and Critical Study,* Frederick A. Praeger, Inc., New York, 1961.

McLellan, D.: *Karl Marx,* The Viking Press, Inc., New York, 1975.

Olsen, R. E.: *Karl Marx,* Twayne Publishers, Inc., Boston, 1978.

Tucker, R. C.: *Philosophy and Myth in Karl Marx,* Cambridge University Press, New York, 1961.

Wetter, Gustav: *Dialectical Materialism,* Frederick A. Praeger, Inc., New York, 1959.

CHAPTER 22

Original Writings:

Nietzsche, Friedrich: *The Birth of Tragedy and the Genealogy of Morals,* Doubleday & Company, Inc., Garden City, N.Y., 1956.

————: *Beyond Good and Evil,* Henry Regnery Company, Chicago, 1959.

————: *Joyful Wisdom,* Frederick Ungar Publishing Co., New York, 1960.

————: *Philosophy in the Tragic Age of the Greeks,* Henry Regnery Company, Chicago, 1962.

————: *The Portable Nietzsche,* Viking Press, Inc., New York, 1954.

————: *Thus Spoke Zarathustra,* Penguin Books, Inc., Baltimore, 1961.

————: *Unpublished Letters,* Philosophical Library, Inc., New York, 1962.

————: *The Use and Abuse of History,* The Liberal Arts Press, Inc., New York, 1957.

Critical Studies:

Alderman, H.: *Nietzsche's Gift,* Ohio University Press, Athens, 1977.

Copleston, F.: *Friedrich Nietzsche, Philosopher of Culture,* Barnes & Noble, Inc., New York, 1975.

Heidegger, M.: *Nietzsche, vol. 1: The Will to Power as Art,* Harper & Row, Publishers, Incorporated, 1979.

Hollingdale, R. J.: *Nietzsche,* Routledge & Kegan Paul, London, 1973.

Jaspers, K.: *Nietzsche: An Introduction to the Understanding of His Philosophical Activity,* University of Arizona Press, Tucson, 1965.

Kaufmann, W.: *Nietzsche, Philosopher, Psychologist, Anti-Christ,* 3d ed., Princeton University Press, Princeton, N.J., 1968.

Love, Frederick R.: *The Young Nietzsche and the Wagnerian Experience,* University of North Carolina Press, Chapel Hill, 1963.

Morgan, G. A., Jr.: *What Nietzsche Means,* Harvard University Press, Cambridge, Mass., 1941.

Nehamas, Alexander: *Nietzsche: Life As Literature,* Harvard University Press, Cambridge, Mass., 1985.

Stern, J. P.: *A Study of Nietzsche,* Cambridge University Press, 1977.

CHAPTER 23

Original Writings:

Bergson, Henri: *Creative Mind,* Philosophical Library, Inc., New York, 1956.

————: *Introduction to Metaphysics,* The Liberal Arts Press, Inc., New York, 1949.

————: *Selections from Bergson,* Appleton-Century-Crofts, Inc., New York, 1949.

————: *Time and Free Will,* Harper & Row, Publishers, Incorporated, New York, 1960.

————: *The Two Sources of Morality and Religion,* Doubleday & Company, Inc., Garden City, N.Y., 1954.

Northrop, F. S. C., and Mason W. Gross (eds.): *A. N. Whitehead: An Anthology,* The Macmillan Company, New York, 1961.

White, Morton (ed.): *Age of Analysis: 20th Century Philosophers,* New American Library of World Literature, Inc., New York, 1955.

Whitehead, A. N.: *Adventures of Ideas,* New American Library of World Literature, Inc., New York, 1955.

————: *Aims of Education,* New American Library of World Literature, Inc., New York, 1949.

————: *The Function of Reason,* Beacon Press, Boston, 1958.

————: *Modes of Thought,* Capricorn Books, G. P. Putnam's Sons, New York, 1959.

————: *Process and Reality,* Harper & Row, Publishers, Incorporated, New York, 1960.

————: *Religion in the Making,* The World Publishing Company, Cleveland, 1960.

————: *Science and the Modern World,* New American Library of World Literature, Inc., New York, 1949.

————: *Whitehead's Interpretation of Science,* Representative Selections, The Liberal Arts Press, Inc., New York, 1961.

Critical Studies:

Alexander, I. W.: *Bergson: Philosopher of Reflection,* Bowes & Bowes, Ltd., London, 1957.

Bright, Laurence: *Whitehead's Philosophy of Physics,* Sheed & Ward, Inc., New York, 1960.

Christian, W. A.: *An Interpretation of Whitehead's Metaphysics,* Yale University Press, New Haven, Conn., 1959.

Johnson, A. H.: *Whitehead's Philosophy of Civilization,* Dover Publications, Inc., New York, 1962.

————: *Whitehead's Theory of Reality,* Dover Publications, Inc., New York, 1952.

Kline, George (ed.): *A. N. Whitehead: Essays on His Philosophy,* Prentice-Hall, Inc., Englewood Cliffs, N.J., 1963.

Leclerc, Ivor: *Whitehead's Metaphysics,* The Macmillan Company, New York, 1958.

Mays, W.: *Philosophy of Whitehead,* Collier Books, a division of Crowell-Collier Publishing Co., New York, 1962.

————: *Whitehead's Philosophy of Science and Metaphysics, and Introduction to His Thought,* Martinus Nijhoff, The Hague, Netherlands, 1977.

Sherburne, D. W.: *Whiteheadian Aesthetic,* Yale University Press, New Haven, Conn., 1961.

CHAPTER 24

Original Writings:

Austin, J. L.: *Sense and Sensibilia,* Oxford University Press, Fair Lawn, N.J., 1962.

————: *How to Do Things with Words,* Oxford University Press, New York, 1965.

————: *Philosophical Papers,* 2d ed., Clarendon Press, Oxford, 1970.

Ayer, A. J.: *The Foundations of Empirical Knowledge,* St. Martin's Press, Inc., New York, 1962.

————: *Language, Truth and Logic,* Dover Publications, Inc., New York, 1946.

————: *Philosophical Essays,* St. Martin's Press, Inc., New York, 1963.

————: *The Problem of Knowledge,* Penguin Books, Inc., Baltimore, 1963.

————: *Logical Positivism,* The Free Press of Glencoe, New York, 1958.

Blanshard, B.: *Reason and Analysis.,* Allen and Unwin, London, 1962.

Carnap, R.: *The Logical Structure of the World,* University of California Press, Berkeley, 1967.

————: *Logical Syntax and Language,* Harcourt, Brace & World, Inc., New York, 1937.

————: *Philosophy and Logical Syntax,* Kegan Paul, London, 1935.

————: *The Unity of Science,* Kegan Paul, London, 1934.

Cavell, S.: *Claim of Reason: Wittgenstein, Skepticism, Morality, and Tragedy,* Oxford University Press, 1979.

Hampshire, S.: *Thought and Action,* Chatto and Windus, London, 1959.

Hare, R. M.: *Language of Morals,* Oxford University Press, Fair Lawn, N.J., 1952.

Marsh, R. C. (ed.): *Logic and Knowledge,* The Macmillan Company, New York, 1956.

Moore, G. E.: *Philosophical Papers,* Collier Books, a division of Crowell-Collier Publishing Co., New York, 1962.

————: *Philosophical Studies,* Littlefield, Adams & Company, Paterson, N.J., 1951.

————: *Some Main Problems of Philosophy,* Collier Books, a division of Crowell-Collier Publishing Co., New York, 1962.

Quine, W. V.: *From a Logical Point of View,* Harvard University Press, Cambridge, Mass., 1953.

————: *Word and Object,* The M. I. T. Press, Cambridge, Mass., 1960.

———— **and Ullian, J. S.:** *The Web of Belief,* Random House, Inc., New York, 1970.

Rorty, R.: *Linguistic Turn,* The University of Chicago Press, Chicago, 1988.

————:*Consequences of Pragmatism,* University of Minnesota Press, Minneapolis, 1982.

————:*Contingency, Irony, and Solidarity,* Cambridge University Press, New York, 1989.

————: *Philosophy and the Mirror of Nature,* Princeton University Press, Princeton, N.J., 1979.

Russell, Bertrand: *Analysis of Matter,* Dover Publications, Inc., New York, 1954.

————: *Human Knowledge,* Simon and Schuster, Inc., New York, 1962.

————: *Inquiry into Meaning and Truth,* Penguin Books, Inc., Baltimore, 1963.

————: *Mysticism and Logic,* Doubleday & Company, Inc., Garden City, N.Y., 1957.

————: *Our Knowledge of the External World,* New American Library of World Literature, Inc., New York, 1960.

————: *The Problems of Philosophy,* Oxford University Press, Fair Lawn, N.J., 1912.

————: *Sceptical Essays,* Barnes & Noble, Inc., New York, 1961.

————: *Scientific Outlook,* W. W. Norton & Company, Inc., New York, 1962.

Ryle, Gilbert: *The Concept of Mind,* Barnes & Noble, Inc., New York, 1950.

————: *Dilemmas,* Cambridge University Press, New York, 1960.

Schlick, Moritz: *The Problems of Ethics,* Dover Publications, Inc., New York, 1939.

Searle, John R.: *Minds, Brains, and Science,* Harvard University Press, Cambridge, Mass., 1984.

Strawson, P. F.: *Individuals: An Essay in Descriptive Metaphysics,* Doubleday & Company, Inc., Garden City, N.Y., 1963.

Toulmin, Stephen: *The Uses of Argument,* Cambridge University Press, New York, 1964.

Urmson, J. O.: *Philosophical Analysis,* Oxford University Press, 1956.

Vesey, G. (ed.): *Understanding Wittgenstein,* Cornell University Press, Ithaca, N.Y., 1974.

Warnock, G. J.: *English Philosophy Since 1900,* Oxford University Press, Fair Lawn, N.J., 1958.

White, Morton (ed.): *Age of Analysis: 20th Century Philosophers,* New American Library of World Literature, Inc., New York, 1955.

Wisdom, John: *Other Minds,* Basil Blackwell & Mott, Ltd., Oxford, 1952.

Wittgenstein, L.: *Tractatus Logico-Philosophicus,* Humanities Press, New York, 1961.

————: *On Certainty,* Basil Blackwell & Mott, Ltd., Oxford, 1967.

————: *Philosophical Investigations,* Basil Blackwell & Mott, Ltd., Oxford, 1968.

Critical Studies:

Ayer, A. J. (ed.): *Logical Positivism,* The Free Press of Glencoe, New York, 1958.

Caton, Charles E.: *Philosophy and Ordinary Language,* The University of Illinois Press, Urbana, 1963.

Copleston, Frederick: *Contemporary Philosophy,* The Newman Press, Westminster, Md., 1963.

Kaplan, Abraham: *The New World of Philosophy,* Random House, Inc., New York, 1961.

Kenny, A.: *Wittgenstein,* Harvard University Press, Cambridge, Mass., 1974.

Malcolm, Norman, with G. H. von Wright: *Ludwig Wittgenstein: A Memoir,* Oxford University Press, Fair Lawn, N.J., 1958.

Pears, D. F.: *Ludwig Wittgenstein,* The Viking Press, Inc., New York, 1970.

Pitcher, George: *The Philosophy of Wittgenstein,* Prentice-Hall, Inc., Englewood Cliffs, N.J., 1964.

Pole, David: *Later Philosophy of Wittgenstein,* Oxford University Press, Fair Lawn, N.J., 1958.

Schilpp, Paul A. (ed.): *Philosophy of Bertrand Russell,* Harper & Row, Publishers, Incorporated, New York, 1963, two vols.

Searle, J. R. (ed.): *The Philosophy of Language,* Oxford University Press, London, 1971.

CHAPTER 25

Original Writings:

Camus, Albert: *The Rebel,* Random House, Inc., New York, 1954.

Heidegger, M.: *Being and Time,* SCM Press, London, 1962.

———: *Basic Writings,* Harper & Row, Publishers, Incorporated, New York, 1977.

———: *Poetry, Language, Thought,* (trans.) A. Hofstadter, Harper & Row, Publishers, Incorporated, New York, 1971.

Husserl, E.: *The Paris Lectures,* Martinus Nijhoff, The Hague, Netherlands, 1964.

———: "Philosophy and the Crisis of European Man," in Quentin Lauer, *Phenomenology, Its Genesis and Prospect,* Harper and Row, Publishers, Incorporated, New York, 1965.

———: "The Crisis of the European Sciences and Transcendental Phenomenology," in Quentin Lauer, *Phenomenology, Its Genesis and Prospect,* Harper and Row, Publishers, Incorporated, New York, 1965.

———: *Phenomenology and the Crisis of Philosophy,* Harper & Row, Publishers, Incorporated, New York, 1965.

———: *Ideas: A General Introduction to Pure Phenomenology,* The Macmillan Company, New York, 1937.

Jaspers, Karl: *Man in the Modern Age,* Doubleday & Company, Inc., Garden City, N.Y., 1957.

———: *Philosophy and the World,* Henry Regnery Company, Chicago, 1963.

———: *Reason and Existenz,* Noonday Books, Farrar, Straus & Cudahy, Inc., New York, 1957.

———: *Truth and Symbol,* College and University Press, New Haven, Conn., 1962.

Kaufmann, Walter (ed.): *Existentialism,* The World Publishing Company, Cleveland, 1956.

Kern, Edith (ed.): *Sartre,* Prentice-Hall, Inc., Englewood Cliffs, N.J., 1963.

Kierkegaard, Søren: *Either/Or,* Doubleday & Company, Inc., Garden City, N.Y., 1959, two vols.

————: *Fear and Trembling: The Sickness unto Death,* Doubleday & Company, Inc., Garden City, N.Y., 1954.

————: *Philosophical Fragments,* Princeton University Press, Princeton, N.J., 1962.

————: *Selections from the Writings of Kierkegaard,* Doubleday & Company, Inc., Garden City, N.Y., 1960.

Marcel, Gabriel: *Creative Fidelity,* Noonday Books, Farrar, Straus & Cudahy, Inc., New York, 1964.

————: *Homo Viator,* Harper & Row, Publishers, Incorporated, New York, 1962.

————: *Man Against Mass Society,* Henry Regnery Company, Chicago, 1962.

————: *Mystery of Being,* Henry Regnery Company, Chicago, 1960, two vols.

————: *Philosophy of Existentialism,* The Citadel Press, New York, 1961.

Merleau-Ponty, Maurice: *The Phenomenology of Perception,* (trans.) Colon Smith, Routledge & Kegan Paul, Ltd., London, 1962.

————: *Primacy of Perception,* (ed.) James M. Edie, (trans.) William Cobb, Northwestern University Press, Evanston, Ill., 1964.

————: *Visible and the Invisible,* (trans.) Alphonso Lingis, Northwestern University Press, Evanston, Ill., 1968.

Sartre, Jean-Paul: *Existentialism and Human Emotions,* Philosophical Library, Inc., New York, 1947.

————: *Being and Nothingness,* Philosophical Library, Inc., New York, 1956.

————: *The Critique of Dialectical Reason,* NLB, London, 1976.

————: *Sartre By Himself,* Urizen Books, Incorporated, New York, 1978.

Critical Studies:

Beauvoir, Simone de: *Adieux: A Farewell to Sartre,* (trans.) Patrick O'Brian, Pantheon Books, New York, 1984.

Biemel, W.: *Martin Heidegger: An Illustrated Study,* Harcourt Brace Jovanovich, Inc., New York, 1976.

Blackham, H. J.: *Six Existentialist Thinkers,* Harper & Row, Publishers, Incorporated, New York, 1959.

Cohen-Solal, Annie: *Sartre: A Life,* (trans.) Annapaoloa Cancogni, Pantheon Books, New York, 1987.

Copleston, Frederick: *Contemporary Philosophy,* The Newman Press, Westminster, Md., 1963.

Flynn, Thomas R.: *Sartre and Marxist Existentialism,* The University of Chicago Press, Chicago, 1984.

Grene, Marjorie: *Introduction to Existentialism,* The University of Chicago Press, Chicago, 1984.

————: *Sartre,* New Viewpoints, New York, 1973.

Heinemann, F. H.: *Existentialism and the Modern Predicament,* Harper & Row, Publishers, Incorporated, New York, 1958.

Kaufmann, Walter: *From Shakespeare to Existentialism,* Doubleday & Company, Inc., Garden City, N.Y., 1960.

Kockelmans, J. L.: *Phenomenology: The Philosophy of Edmund Husserl and Its Interpretation,* Doubleday and Company, Inc., Garden City, N.Y., 1967.

Langan, Thomas: *The Meaning of Heidegger,* Columbia University Press, New York, 1959.

Lowrie, Walter: *Kierkegaard: A Life,* Harper & Row, Publishers, Incorporated, New York, 1962, two vols.

Mehta, J. L.: *Martin Heidegger: The Way and the Vision,* University of Hawaii Press, Honolulu, 1976.

Molina, Fernando: *Existentialism as Philosophy,* Prentice-Hall, Inc., Englewood Cliffs, N.J., 1962.

Murdoch, Iris: *Sartre,* Yale University Press, New Haven, Conn., 1953.

Olson, Robert G.: *Introduction to Existentialism,* Dover Publications, Inc., New York, 1962.

Pietersma, Henry (ed.): *Merleau-Ponty: Critical Essays,* University Press of America, 1990.

Schmidt, James: *Maurice Merleau-Ponty: Between Phenomenology and Structuralism,* St. Martin's Press, Inc., New York, 1985.

Wahl, Jean: *A Short History of Existentialism,* Philosophical Library, Inc., New York, 1962.

Whiteside, Kerry H.: *Merleau-Ponty and the Foundation of an Existential Politics,* Princeton University Press, Princeton, N.J., 1988.

Wild, John: *The Challenge of Existentialism,* Indiana University Press, Bloomington, 1955.

Index